BY ALL MEANS AVAILABLE

BY ALL MEANS AVAILABLE

AVAILABLE

MEMOIRS OF A LIFE IN INTELLIGENCE,
SPECIAL OPERATIONS, AND STRATEGY

Michael G. Vickers

 ALFRED A. KNOPF, NEW YORK, 2023

THIS IS A BORZOI BOOK
PUBLISHED BY ALFRED A. KNOPF

www.aaknopf.com

Knopf, Borzoi Books, and the colophon
are registered trademarks of Penguin Random House LLC.

Library of Congress Cataloging-in-Publication Data
Names: Vickers, Michael G., author.
Title: By all means available : memoirs of a life in intelligence, special
operations, and strategy / Michael G. Vickers.
Description: New York : Alfred A. Knopf, 2023.
Identifiers: LCCN 2022037618 (print) | LCCN 2022037619 (ebook) |
ISBN 9781101947708 (hardcover) | ISBN 9781101947715 (ebook)
Subjects: LCSH: Vickers, Michael G. | United States. Department of Defense—Officials
and employees—Biography. | United States. Central Intelligence Agency—Biography. |
Afghanistan—History—Soviet occupation, 1979–1989—Personal narratives, American. | War on
Terrorism, 2001–2009—Personal narratives, American. | United States. Army. Special Forces—
Biography. | Terrorism—Prevention—United States—History. | Special operations (Military
science)—United States—History. | National security—United States—History. | Strategy.
Classification: LCC UA23 .V4374 2023 (print) | LCC UA23 (ebook) |
DDC 355.00973—dc23/eng/20230112
LC record available at https://lccn.loc.gov/2022037618
LC ebook record available at https://lccn.loc.gov/2022037619

Jacket photograph (beret) by Greg Mathieson/Mai/Getty Images
Jacket design by Linda Huang

Manufactured in the United States of America

First Edition

To Gust L. Avrakotos (1938–2005)
and
Bertram F. Dunn (1930–2018)

Cold Warriors par Excellence

All men dream: but not equally. Those who dream by night in the dusty recesses of their mind wake to find that it was vanity: but the dreamers of the day are dangerous men, for they may act their dreams with open eyes, to make it possible.

—T. E. LAWRENCE

CONTENTS

BY ALL MEANS AVAILABLE

PROLOGUE

SAME HILL, NEW WAR

As I stepped off the Russian-made Mi-17 helicopter the Pakistani Army had used to fly our small group to the Afghanistan-Pakistan border region, I was immediately transported back in time. Twenty-four years earlier, as the CIA's program officer and chief strategist for the Afghanistan Covert Action Program, I had climbed this same scrub-covered foothill. Then, as now, I was dressed in standard intelligence officer garb: a button-down shirt, khakis, and sunglasses. As I looked around, I recalled the faces of the fighters, the smell of gunpowder, the shouts of *"Allahu Akbar"* as gunners hit their targets.

In March 1985, I was visiting a camp that Pakistan's Inter-Services Intelligence (ISI) had constructed near Warsak in Pakistan's North-West Frontier Province (these days renamed as Khyber Pakhtunkhwa) to train the mujahedin, Afghanistan's "holy warriors." The CIA had just received President Reagan's approval for a new strategy that aimed to drive the Soviets out of Afghanistan. I had been a "general" in a secret war, the largest and most successful covert action operation in CIA's history. It turned out to be the decisive battle of the Cold War, and it had helped bring an end to the Soviet Empire. It had been the job of a lifetime.

Much had changed in the region and the world in the intervening twenty-four years. To begin with, a quarter century ago, we were training the Afghan resistance to shoot-down Russian helicopters like the one I had just flown in on. And with our help, the mujahedin had gotten very good at it. Now a new war had emerged out of the old one. Several mujahedin commanders CIA had supported during the 1980s held senior positions in the new Afghan government. Others had joined the Taliban and made common cause with al-Qa'ida, and we were doing our utmost to kill or capture them. Usama Bin Ladin was hiding somewhere in northern Pakistan, though where, exactly, we still didn't know. The vast majority of al-Qa'ida's remaining senior leadership and operatives were plotting attacks against the U.S. home-land, Afghanistan, and Pakistan from their new safe haven in Paki-stan's Federally Administered Tribal Areas, another place familiar to me from the 1980s. But unlike Bin Ladin, whose trail had gone cold after December 2001, we knew where many of al-Qa'ida's other senior leaders and operatives were, and we were taking appropriate action to kill or capture them. And we were working around the clock to find Bin Ladin.

In July 2008, the United States had begun an intense air campaign against al-Qa'ida and its safe haven providers in the Afghanistan-Pakistan border region that was showing promising results. As assis-tant secretary of defense for special operations, low-intensity conflict, and interdependent capabilities and then as undersecretary of defense for intelligence, I had a major role in designing and overseeing the drone war—an operation revolutionary in its precision and strategic effectiveness.

In March 2009, Jim Clapper, my predecessor as undersecretary of defense for intelligence, and I visited the same site at Warsak, but with a very different purpose.[1] We were there to review plans for a new facility we were constructing—the first of four we planned to build in Pakistan's border region—to train Pakistan's Frontier Corps. Led by Tariq Khan, a charismatic Pakistani general, the Frontier Corps was a fifty-eight-thousand-man-strong force that consisted of soldiers from the tribal areas. We hoped to transform it into a key instrument against Pakistan's growing extremist threat, but we would not realize our aims.

With a Pakistan Army colonel seconded to the Frontier Corps, a major from ISI, and Colonel Kurt Sonntag, the commander of our Special Forces in Pakistan, at our side, Jim and I were briefed on con-struction plans and the proposed training curriculum. As our small group made its way up the same hill I had climbed nearly a quarter century earlier toward the briefing site, the major from ISI whispered in a conspiratorial tone and with a smile on his face, "Mr. Vickers knows this place."

I was impressed. ISI had a long memory.

After the contractors responsible for building the site had finished their briefing, the Pakistani colonel gave us a guided tour of the proposed camp. As we started down the path, the colonel took my hand and held it in his, as is custom in that part of the world. After we departed, I reflected on how the most significant periods of my career, spanning a quarter century and two great wars, had been tied up with Afghanistan and Pakistan. A lot of trouble from such a remote place.

"Same hill, new war," I said to myself.

BY ALL MEANS AVAILABLE

As someone who has spent a lifetime keeping the nation's secrets, writing my memoirs didn't come easily for me. I wrote this book for three main reasons.

The first is my duty to history. I played a central role in a world-changing event, the secret war that defeated the Red Army in Afghanistan. As former senior CIA analyst Bruce Riedel argues in the introduction to his outstanding *What We Won: America's Secret War in Afghanistan, 1979–89,* the CIA's defeat of the Red Army in Afghanistan was "a pivotal event in modern history," one that set off a rapid chain of world-changing events: the end of the Cold War and near-constant threat of global nuclear annihilation, the fall of the Berlin Wall and reunification of Germany, and the collapse of the Soviet Empire.[2]

In 1984, when I became the program officer and chief strategist for America's secret war, no one thought that anything like that was remotely possible. During the decisive years of 1984 to 1986, I was responsible for developing the war-winning strategy that led to the Red Army's defeat. Former senior CIA officers, journalists, and historians have described various aspects of CIA's support for the Afghan resistance, but no one has written a detailed, firsthand account of how our strategy was developed and why it succeeded in driving the Soviets out.

Later in my career I had a central role in our war with al-Qa'ida, most notably in our campaign to disrupt, dismantle, and defeat core al-Qa'ida and its senior leadership in the Afghanistan-Pakistan border region, and in the operation that killed Usama Bin Ladin. I am the only operator and operational strategist whose career ranged from the Afghanistan Covert Action Program in the 1980s to our war with al-Qa'ida during the first decade and a half of this century.

Additionally, I directly participated in or oversaw many other important operations over the course of my career, ranging from the invasion of Grenada, counterterrorism operations on five continents, the war in Afghanistan after 9/11, counter-proliferation operations to stop Iran from acquiring nuclear weapons, counter-narcotics operations in Mexico, paramilitary operations in support of Syria's moderate opposition during that country's civil war, and support for Ukraine in its fight against Russian-backed forces in the Donbas. Some of these operations were successful; others were not. During my eight-year tenure as a top national security policy maker, I also played a central role in shaping our nation's intelligence capabilities and our special operations forces and strengthened our air, naval, space, and cyber deterrents against China and Russia.

My career spanned four distinct national security eras: the Cold War, the brief period of American primacy during the 1990s, our wars with the global jihadists after 9/11, and our current era of great power competition with China and Russia. The year 2019 marked the fortieth anniversary of the Soviet invasion of Afghanistan and the thirtieth anniversary of the Soviets' withdrawal; 2021 marked the twentieth anniversary of the 9/11 attacks, the tenth anniversary of the operation that killed Usama Bin Ladin, and the year America decided to accept defeat in Afghanistan. It is time to tell the full story of these and other historic events from my perspective.

My second reason for writing this book is my duty to the American people. I believe it is essential for the sound functioning of our democracy that Americans possess at least some understanding of intelligence, special operations, and strategy if they are to provide their full and willing support for the U.S. government's operations on their behalf. As a former senior national security and intelligence official, I feel a great responsibility to tell my fellow Americans what I can about the critically important work our intelligence professionals, special operators, and defense and national security strategists have done and are doing today.

My final reason is my duty to future special operators, intelligence professionals, and national security strategists. Successful strategies are far more art than they are science, and war-winning strategies are unfortunately much rarer than we would wish. I feel an obligation to our country's future operators and strategists to pass on what I have learned.

I am increasingly concerned about the future of American power and our ability to win our wars, both cold and hot. Our country faces a more challenging national security environment today than it has at any time since the height of the Cold War, and our adversaries believe we are a declining power whose eventual defeat is inevitable. We are in a new cold war with a rising China and a revanchist Russia where victory will likely go to the side that prevails in economic and technological competition, information influence operations, covert action, and proxy war. Like our Cold War with the Soviet Empire, the New Cold War will be a clash of systems. Direct conflict with China and Russia, moreover, cannot be ruled out. Revolutionary advances in automation, artificial intelligence, quantum computing, and biotechnology will transform both wealth and power in the decades ahead. China's economy will likely surpass ours in size sometime in the next decade, and our leadership in artificial intelligence, quantum computing, and other emerging technologies is by no means assured. Meanwhile, information operations, both covert and overt, by Russia, China, and other malign actors, and our own internal divisions are undermining our national will and unity. America is more divided than at any time since the Civil War, and the effectiveness and durability of democracy itself are being called into question. Russia's 2022 invasion of Ukraine has placed the future of Europe and the world order on the table. It is essential that America and the West defeat Russian aggression and win the New Cold War against China and Russia. The world will be a much better place if we do.

———

The book is organized into five parts, following a chronological path for the first half, and a thematic one in the second. During the first decade and a half of my career, I was an operator and operational strategist in the Special Forces and CIA. During the subsequent two and a half decades, I was a defense and national security strategist, a national security policy maker, and a senior intelligence official. The book follows this progression.

The book's title comes from a National Security Council review of the Afghanistan Covert Action Program during the first months of 1985 that led President Reagan to significantly escalate our secret war and seek to drive the Soviets out of Afghanistan "by all means available." We didn't always employ all means available or even the right ways and means over the course of my career, but sometimes we did. I try to show where we did and where we didn't, why we did or didn't, and what difference it made.

My aim was to write an analytical memoir.[3] I have endeavored to provide sufficient historical context for the events in which I participated, to show how intelligence, special operations, strategy, and warfare evolved during my more than four decades of service, and how policy battles in Washington often decided the outcome of our operations and wars as much as our actions in the field did. I served under six presidents, four Republican and two Democratic, and served as a senior national security official in both Republican and Democratic administrations. I hope all readers will conclude that this book is written without any hint of partisanship. I hope the general reader will gain significant insight into the secret worlds of intelligence, special operations, and strategy, and come away with a better understanding of the importance of individuals in driving world-changing events and how the world of today came to be. I hope readers who are very familiar with or even participated in the events described in this book will learn something new about how these operations were actually conducted, and what the strengths and weaknesses of the various alternatives available to us were.

PART I

PREPARATION

1

GREEN BERET

DR. DERIGGI

It was a teacher at Hollywood High School who changed my life. I was sitting at a table in the school library in February 1971, where I was supposed to be researching a paper for my international relations class—one of the few I found interesting. My teacher, Dr. Anthony DeRiggi, was a World War II veteran with strong views about U.S. foreign policy. A proponent of the "realist school" of international relations, DeRiggi was an admirer of President Nixon and a staunch supporter of the Vietnam War. I didn't agree with him about Nixon and I had mixed feelings about the Vietnam War, but I liked his general approach to international relations, which emphasized the importance of power and the pursuit of national interests.

I was either reading or more likely daydreaming about baseball or football when he walked over to my table and slipped a copy of that day's *New York Times* in front of me. He pointed to an article and said, "You might be interested in this."

The New York Times had just published a major story on the CIA's covert operations in Laos and its base at Long Tieng. The agency was employing a secret army of Hmong tribesmen in a large-scale paramilitary operation against the North Vietnamese Army along the Ho Chi Minh Trail.[1] To this day, I don't know why Dr. DeRiggi thought I'd be interested in that article, but I was. I imagined myself leading secret armies in far-off lands and winning against impossible odds. I imagined myself doing things that only a James Bond could do. And, for the first time, at the age of seventeen, I thought seriously about becoming a CIA officer.

There wasn't much about me at that point, though, that suggested I was destined for a life in intelligence and special operations. For starters, I was born with strabismus, or "crossed eyes," and amblyopia, which caused my brain to process images from only one eye at a time, precluding my ability to see in three dimensions. My right eye was also turned significantly inward, which, needless to say, didn't escape the notice of other children. Five surgeries between ages one and nineteen improved my appearance but could not give me 3-D vision. Fortunately, my brain found other ways to judge depth and distance. I was also blessed with excellent eyesight—better than twenty-twenty in my left eye and twenty-twenty in my right.

I didn't come from a military or CIA family. My father had served in the Army Air Corps during World War II and had earned a Silver Star and Purple Heart while flying with the Eighth Air Force as a B-17 bombardier and gunner over France and Germany in 1943.[2] My grandparents were all immigrants, three of whom spoke only limited English. "Vecchiarelli" became "Vickers" a few years after my Italian grandparents, who hailed from a mountain town east of Rome, passed through Ellis Island. My mother's parents had come from eastern Slovakia, her father finding work in Chicago's steel mills. Los Angeles in those days was a magnet for immigrants, including refugees who had fled from Hungary and Cuba, so I had a lot of exposure to foreign cultures growing up. Most of my childhood friends were recent immigrants, and this sparked some interest on my part in world affairs.

Our family watched the evening news once or twice a week, and we talked a bit about the evils of Soviet Communism and America's difficulties in Vietnam. But we focused on international events mostly when we felt our own lives were threatened. During the October 1962 Cuban missile crisis, when it looked as if we were on the verge of nuclear war, my father stocked our shallow and very porous basement with a few canned goods and a radio, and we practiced taking shelter there a few times. Truth be told, I didn't think it would do us much good. If nuclear war came, I was convinced our chances of survival were slim to none.

I did show some taste for adventure. As a kid, I often went hiking in the Hollywood Hills, the big white Hollywood sign a frequent destination, and when I was older, my friends and I hiked and camped in the higher mountains beyond Los Angeles. We'd also drive out to the desert to shoot our .22-caliber rifles at Coke bottles and tin cans. But I was never a Boy Scout, let alone an Eagle Scout, and had never gone hunting or fishing. And to top it off, I was a superb underachiever academically, graduating from high school with a C-plus average. When I applied myself, as I did my senior year in Dr. DeRiggi's international relations class, I did very well. But those successes were few and far between.

My dream growing up was to be a professional baseball or football player. I had a strong arm and was a pretty good quarterback, pitcher, and outfielder. I was also a good hitter, as long as I got a fastball to hit. After high school, I enrolled at a local community college—Los Angeles Pierce—the first in my family to attend college. I had a shot at the starting quarterback position my second year, but a temporary shoulder injury put an end to that. I tried my hand at baseball one last time, with similarly unsuccessful results. It was time to listen to Dr. DeRiggi.

SPECIAL FORCES SELECTION

At the beginning of my final semester at Pierce, I came up with what seemed to me like a plausible plan. I figured my best route into the CIA was to first become a Green Beret. A college degree was required to become a CIA officer, but I didn't want to wait the two or more additional years that would take. The Special Forces seemed as close to CIA, or at least my image of CIA, as one could get, and I could become a Green Beret now. I'd have adventure and get guerrilla warfare training and more foreign-language instruction. (I had already taken a year of Russian at Pierce.) All of this, I reasoned, would make me attractive to the agency. Somehow, I'd also find time to finish my degree in international relations. I planned to go from chronic underachiever to multitasking man of action in the blink of an eye. To my nineteen-year-old brain, it seemed like a straightforward path to a glorious future. The hard part would be doing it.

I read everything I could get my hands on about the CIA and Special Forces and attended a lecture at Pierce on intelligence by a former deputy director for intelligence at the CIA, Ray Cline. A Harvard PhD, Cline was far more cloak than dagger, but his talk was still interesting. I didn't expect the CIA to talk about its secret operational side in public.

I soon went to see an Army recruiter in Van Nuys. I told him I wanted to be a Green Beret and took the Army's required battery of aptitude tests, but he kept encouraging me to enlist in the infantry, get some experience, go to Ranger School, and then try for Special Forces on my second enlistment. My odds of making it would be better that way, he said. He might have been right, but I didn't want to wait. So I walked out the door and went in search of another recruiter.

When I walked into the Army recruiting office in Hollywood, the staff sergeant who greeted me was an affable Greek American named Jim Maniatis—a Green Beret and eight-year Special Forces and Vietnam veteran with silver jump wings, a scuba badge, and a host of medals adorning his khaki uniform. I had found my guy. And it wouldn't be the last time a Greek American would have a profound impact on my career.

He invited me to his cubicle and told me about Special Forces training, his service as a Green Beret in Germany and Vietnam, and what I would need to do to qualify for direct enlistment into SF. I was more than qualified intellectually, having received a perfect 160 out of 160 on the Army's IQ test—way above the 110 needed to become an officer or a Green Beret—and was in great shape. Not surprisingly, though, when I took my physical, the armed forces' examining physician initially disqualified me because of my strabismus. I was devastated. I had already received a very high score on the Special Forces Selection Battery, which is where most candidates for Special Forces fail to make the cut—the reason for those lines in Barry Sadler's "Ballad of the Green Berets," "One hundred men will test today / But only three win the Green Beret." I couldn't believe my strabismus would disqualify me, particularly given my near-perfect vision and proven ability in sports to judge distance well. Fortunately, my crusty examining physician agreed to give me a second look. He administered some additional tests, and once convinced that I indeed had the ability to perceive depth, he grudgingly passed me. I will remain forever grateful to him.

My experience taking the Special Forces Selection Battery convinced me I had made the right career choice.[3] The battery was administered at the central Army recruiting station in downtown Los Angeles, and on the day I took it, I was the only candidate. I took that as a sign that I was joining an elite group.

The SFSB consisted of three timed parts and took several hours to complete. Its origins lay in the selection process for the World War II predecessor of Special Forces and CIA, the Office of Strategic Services, or OSS. The administrator told me to sit down at a table in a large, empty room and handed me the first booklet. It was a psychological aptitude test, consisting of more than a hundred true-false and multiple-choice questions that were designed to assess one's aptitude for unconventional warfare and other Special Forces missions. Did I take risks as a kid and climb trees? Do others see me as a leader? Could I empathize with people with different backgrounds and from foreign cultures? Was I able to master new skills quickly? Was I good at improvising? Did I want to volunteer for dangerous missions? Was I willing to jump out of airplanes? It wasn't too difficult to see what they were after. You bet, I thought. And it had the virtue of being true.

The second section tested my attention to detail and my ability to orient myself and determine location. I was shown photographs of farm scenes, urban areas, and terrain shots. The perspective would shift, and I had to decide from which direction a new photo was taken, or what was missing from or added to a previous photo. Looking at shadows and other clues in the photos was key. It was advanced spatial reasoning with an operational bent.

The third section was by far the most difficult, but the one I liked the most. It was a series of operational scenarios—eighty-eight in all—that required me to make critical decisions within ten seconds. I was given a thick booklet, and the administrator hit play on a reel-to-reel tape recorder sitting on the table in front of me. A male voice described the situation for each problem and let loose with a barrage of tactical details. No pauses or replays were allowed. Ten seconds to rank four to six courses of action from best to worst. I don't know if the TV show had inspired the test or the test had inspired the TV show, but the tape-recorded voice and the tactical situations seemed right out of *Mission: Impossible.* The only thing missing was "Good morning, Mr. Phelps."

It was a stressful and intellectually difficult test, one of the most challenging I'd ever taken. I understood why most candidates failed the SFSB. One of the scenarios particularly got my attention:

> Your Special Forces team has infiltrated Red China. Your team has acquired information about Chinese nuclear weapons and missile delivery systems that is vital to the national security of the United States. Your team's mission has been compromised. You are trapped in a cave and surrounded by a superior force of Chinese troops that has already engaged your team. Most of your team's members have either been killed or are badly wounded. You are among the few who remain combat capable. What do you do?

I quickly concluded that the best course of action was to transmit the critical information we had acquired. My fictional team's chances of fighting its way out and escaping seemed to be near zero, but we could accomplish our mission before we were overrun if we could transmit the information we had been sent in to collect. I found myself wondering (focusing admittedly on the extraordinary nature of the mission rather than on its grave risks), was this what being a Green Beret was really like? If so, sign me up!

When I told my parents I had passed selection and was going to enlist, they were alarmed. They were worried I wouldn't make it through the training, or worse, that I would get killed in combat. I assured them I'd be fine and signed a contract for the three-year, Special Forces direct enlistment option. And as I advanced in my career, I told them less and less about what I was actually doing.

SPECIAL FORCES QUALIFICATION

I reported into Special Forces Training Group for the Special Forces Qualification, or "Q," Course near midnight in December 1973 with a sense of excitement and foreboding. My classmates and I generally knew what was coming, but knowing a bit and experiencing it fully are two very different things.

Before attending the Q Course, I'd had to complete Army basic training, advanced individual training, and the airborne, or basic parachutist, course. Toward the end of my basic training at Fort Ord, California, I'd been encouraged to apply either for Officer Candidate School or West Point. I declined both.

The Special Forces direct enlistment option—today it's called the 18-Xray program—attracts high-quality talent into the service, individuals who otherwise might not enlist in the Regular Army, and my class was no exception. Most of my forty or so classmates were already well into their twenties when they enlisted, so I was on the younger side. We had several college graduates among our ranks, and nearly all of us had the test scores and college credits to qualify for officer training. Several were also accomplished athletes, and all were very fit. We were from all across the United States, and our psychological screening had ensured that we were an unconventional lot. All had joined or reenlisted in the Army with the sole purpose of becoming a Green Beret, attracted by the Special Forces mystique of being the most elite fighting force in the world. It was a bit like showing up at an Ivy League college and discovering that all your classmates were at the top of their high school class too.

The Green Berets, it should be noted, make up only a part of America's special operations forces. When I attended SFQC, the U.S. special operations community also included Army Rangers, Navy SEALs, and Air Force Special Operators. Since then, specialized counterterrorism forces, special operations intelligence units, special operations aviation units, and Marine Corps special operations forces have been added to the mix. The CIA has its own special operations capabilities.

There's a division of labor within the community. Navy SEALs specialize in direct action and special reconnaissance. Rangers focus on direct action and airfield seizure. For the Green Berets, it's unconventional warfare—working with a resistance force behind enemy lines. And that's what SFQC was designed to train us to do.

During the 1970s, SFQC was sixteen weeks long (with the exception of the medic track, which took some seventy-five weeks to complete) and was divided into three phases.[4] SFQC's purpose was to determine if a candidate has what it takes to be a Green Beret, to train him in one of four basic SF specialties—weapons, engineer/demolitions, communications, and medical—and to train him in unconventional warfare and other special operations. Attrition rates ranged from 20 to 50 percent. Some soldiers couldn't meet the physical demands of the training; others failed to achieve the technical and tactical proficiency required. Some decided it just wasn't for them.

The four basic SF specialties taught in SFQC constitute the core of a twelve-man, Special Forces Operational Detachment Alpha, or SFODA, Special Forces' primary operational arm. An SFODA has two soldiers in each specialty. (Having two of each provides operational resiliency and enables "split team" operations.) An SFODA is commanded by a captain, and until the 1980s it had a first lieutenant as an executive officer (subsequently replaced by a warrant officer). It also has an operations or "team" sergeant (the senior enlisted man on a team) and an intelligence sergeant. (Operations and intelligence are advanced specialties that SF operators are trained in later in their careers.) All ten enlisted on an SFODA hold the rank of sergeant or above. Weapons was the only specialty available to me when I went through the Q Course. As my career progressed, I would be very glad it was.

As I began the course, I was more than a bit worried whether I would measure up. Such worries, I quickly learned, were an unstated but common feeling among my classmates. The Q Course is designed to not just train you but test you. Can you keep up with the arduous physical training? Can you master the requisite basic skills like land navigation? Can you apply in the field what you learn in the classroom? And can you do it all on minimal sleep? But as the course progresses, the fear that you might not make it gradually subsides. The emphasis also shifts from testing to training.

Phase I, held fifty miles from Fort Bragg at Camp Mackall, was where most of the testing occurred. It was four very long weeks of physical training, obstacle courses, land navigation, survival training, small boat training, river crossing techniques, Special Forces tactics (raids, ambushes, and reconnaissance patrols), leadership, and methods of instruction (how to teach SF skills to a resistance force). This phase was essentially a compressed version of the Army's Ranger Course and was designed to weed out those who lacked the physical fitness, mental toughness, and resourcefulness to be a Green Beret.

Greater and greater amounts of physical and mental stress were placed on us as Phase I progressed. We subsisted on long-range patrol rations (dehydrated, "backpack" meals) and C rations—two or three a day during the classroom phase and one a day in the field—about nine hundred calories in the latter case. On Sundays, if we weren't in the field, we received our only hot meal of the week in our mess hall. We subsisted on two to four hours of sleep a night during the classroom phase, and much less during the field phase. We took cold showers and slept in unheated tents in Army sleeping bags. We had two hours of guard duty each night, interrupting what little sleep we did get, so staying awake in class was definitely a challenge. If we were caught dozing, we were required to sit on a metal bar swing in the back of our classroom. I was "invited" to try it out once myself, though from the look of my scribbled notes, I dozed off during lectures multiple times.

Under the watchful command of Sergeant First Class Smith, whom we affectionately called "Gator Grin," we began our day at 4:30 a.m. with 90 to 120 minutes of exercises and a long run, the most painful of which was a four-mile run with a fifty-pound rucksack and an M16 rifle. It hurt like hell after the first hundred meters. We climbed lots of ropes and did lots of push-ups, pull-ups, and sit-ups. The rest of our day combined instruction with more physical exertion, long marches with heavy rucksacks, swimming in cold creeks, and land navigation exercises. It was like two-a-day football practices, only much worse.

I performed quite well during the "classroom" portion of the course. I excelled at land navigation and quickly mastered, intellectually at least, SF tactics. And I more than held my own on the long runs, rucksack marches, strength training, and obstacle courses. Applying what I'd learned about SF tactics in the field would be more of a struggle, and as the course reached its climax, my reserves were almost completely depleted.

The final field exercise of Phase I was ten days long, and it was where the physical demands of the course and mental stress were at their maximum. Every night we'd conduct a forced march to get to our target before the beginning of morning nautical twilight (first light before dawn), and then conduct a raid or ambush. During the day we conducted additional operations—ambushing an enemy supply column or reconnoitering a target—all designed to keep us constantly busy. It was a struggle to stay awake during mission planning, particularly late at night when we were huddled in a patrol base for an hour or so.

I learned that exhaustion and freezing weather can play funny tricks on the mind. By the end of the exercise, most of my classmates and I were barely functioning. Most were just going through the motions, reluctant to take on difficult assignments. We found what morale boosts we could to keep going. One freezing night, my patrol buddy, a Native American named Michael Wilson, suggested we combine the little pouches of rice we had been given for dinner with some cream substitute and sugar packets we had squirreled away. That was all we had to eat that night, but our concoction was delicious, and for years afterward we swore it was the best rice pudding either of us had ever tasted.

On one graded exercise, I performed so poorly that there was a chance I'd have to repeat the course or, worse yet, flunk out. I had my raid force assault an enemy strongpoint across an open area, losing the element of surprise. If it had been a real operation, we would have suffered heavy casualties. What I should have done was move my force stealthily through and out of a freezing creek to attack our enemy from an unexpected direction. I didn't consider that option, because my teammates and I were cold, miserable, and dead tired. None of them suggested it either. Needless to say, I flunked that patrol and received a real tongue-lashing from the instructor. It still haunts me to this day.

I learned, however, that failure can be a better teacher than success. I had drawn an unusually difficult patrol, but you're expected to accomplish the mission, no matter what the hardship and obstacles in your path. Fortunately, in training you're usually given additional chances to succeed. I did well enough on a subsequent ambush patrol and other graded exercises and made it through Phase I, though hardly with distinction. I learned a valuable lesson and got much better at field tactics as SFQC and my career progressed.

———

Phase II of SFQC was devoted to specialty training. During the 1970s, weapons, engineer/demolitions, and communications were all eight weeks long, so classmates pursuing those specialties were reunited for

Phase III. (Medics, given their much lengthier training, went through Phase III with a later class.)

The Weapons Course is generally considered the easiest of the four specialties to master, but for me it was the most difficult one I could have been assigned. It's an understatement to say I'm not mechanically inclined. I scored only average on the Army's mechanical aptitude battery, a score my father considered generous, given his frustrations in the garage with me over the years. And sure enough, it took me longer than anyone else in the class to master the detailed disassembly and assembly of complex weapons. I excelled in the weapons planning and tactics portions of the course, however, and the deep understanding I gained of weapons and their combat employment would have a far greater impact on my future career than I could have imagined.

We trained on more than seventy U.S., Western, and Soviet bloc weapons, ranging from small arms to crew-served heavy weapons, including machine guns, anti-tank weapons, mortars, artillery, and man-portable surface-to-air missiles. U.S.-backed insurgents might be equipped with any of these, so we had to master them all. We had to memorize the weapons' technical characteristics, learn to fieldstrip and do higher level, detailed repair on them, and master their combat use. The weapons we trained on ranged from nineteenth-century bolt-action rifles to the most modern. The rationale for training on weapons nearly a century old was that they were in plentiful supply in areas of the world where we might have to conduct guerrilla warfare. Shooting these nineteenth-century bolt-action rifles made me feel as if I'd been transported back to the trench warfare of World War I, but years later, when I encountered these weapons on the battlefield, I was glad I knew how to employ them. Most of all, I really liked the extensive training we received on Soviet bloc weapons. These were the weapons I figured I'd see the most of down the line, and I found Soviet-designed weapons easy to master and very rugged and reliable.

I also enjoyed the training we received on crew-served weapons— weapons that require two or more soldiers to operate—from mortars and artillery to machine guns and then state-of-the-art anti-tank weapons such as the U.S. tube-launched, optically tracked, wire-guided-missile system (or TOW, which would be employed four decades later by the Syrian opposition against the Assad regime). I mastered the calculations that enable indirect fire to be quickly and precisely fired on target and how to prepare detailed fire plans for coordinated direct and indirect fire. We also received training on the U.S.-made Redeye and other shoulder-fired, man-portable surface-to-air missile systems, or MANPADS for short, though we were allowed to practice only on the simulator in our training, because the missiles were too expensive to fire more than once or twice a year. MANPADS would also loom large in my future.

Toward the end of the course, we were given training in advanced marksmanship (sniper training) and counter-ambush techniques (known as immediate action drills). We would walk down "jungle" lanes and have to react after we were ambushed. These live-fire exercises really honed an SF trainee's combat skills. We were also given advanced training in how to prepare our own ambushes.

I wasn't the top student in the Weapons Course by any means, but I performed increasingly well as the course progressed, particularly in the areas of indirect fire planning (mortars and artillery) and small unit tactics. Learning by doing and not being dead tired really improved my tactical competence. I was certified in a core SF specialty, and assuming I made it through Phase III, I could serve as a weapons sergeant on a Special Forces Operational Detachment.

———

"Get out of the way, he's going to fall," one instructor whispered to the others in the group. I was more than forty feet up a tree and didn't have a good way of getting down. Toward the end of the Weapons Course, I made my sixth parachute jump, my first since the five I had made in the Airborne Course four months earlier. Seconds after I'd leaped out of the C-130 turboprop and my parachute had opened, I found myself being blown by high winds off the drop zone and over a heavily wooded area of tall trees. Not good. I turned my parachute to face into the wind to slow my ground speed, just as I'd been taught, but to no avail. The winds were too strong.

After descending several hundred feet and with only a few hundred to go, I realized I had absolutely no chance of steering my parachute back to the fast-receding open space in the distance where I was supposed to land. I thought I'd better turn my chute around so I could at least see where I was going, and then turn back into the wind to slow my speed before landing. It turned out to be a good decision because a second after I could see where I was going, I crashed into a thick horizontal branch.

The branch stretched from the top of one of the tallest pines in the area, about eighty feet high. I hit it hard, at my midsection. My parachute was still inflated, and it continued to be pushed forward by the wind. The risers and parachute lines that connected my harness to my chute became entangled in the tree, and that, thankfully, slowed and then stopped my forward momentum.

When you land in a tree, you're supposed to get out of your harness, pull your reserve chute, and, as if it were Rapunzel's hair, shimmy down to the ground while hoping that the main chute and harness remain attached to the tree. There is only one problem with this guidance: it only works for trees that are about twenty feet tall, not eighty, like the one I was stuck in. I was going to have to get down the old-fashioned way. So I got out of my harness and climbed down several branches, when three instructors and one fellow student arrived at the base of my very tall tree.

The senior instructor stared up at me and asked if I could climb down farther. I replied, "Yes, Sergeant," and climbed down a few more branches until the tree ran out of them. I was still some forty feet above the ground. The tree's trunk was far too wide to slide down. It was clear I'd fall if I tried. I paused and wondered what to do next. Who makes trees like this?

After a brief huddle, the senior instructor asked if I thought I could jump to a nearby tree. It was about forty-five feet tall and had a much narrower trunk that I could slide down. But it was also about six feet away. The instructor didn't sound confident that jumping was all that great a plan, but it seemed like my only option. I positioned myself for the leap, and that was the cue for one of the instructors to warn the rest of the group to get out of the way. Fortunately, I didn't hear him.

One, two, three . . . and six feet later I made the jump, the tree held firm, and I slid down, surviving with only a few scrapes from its thin branches and trunk along the way. The instructors breathed a sigh of relief, gave me a pat on the back, and sent me to the truck waiting on the drop zone for a ride back to the barracks.

I received more than a few "I can't believe you did that" comments from my classmates that evening. The classmate who'd been at the base of the tree told me about the instructor's warning to the group as I was about to jump. It added to the tale, but I'm glad I heard it after I'd made the leap.

With the Weapons Course completed, Phase III was the only thing standing between me and a green beret. Phase III's focus was unconventional warfare—the support of a foreign insurgency or resistance movement against a nation-state or an occupying power through the use of guerrilla warfare, subversion, sabotage, and evasion and escape. It consisted of two weeks of classroom training, followed by a two-week, final comprehensive field exercise. The course brought together all of the skills we'd been honing over the past several months.

During the classroom portion, we were taught how to make initial contact with a (hopefully) psychologically prepared resistance movement and establish rapport with a guerrilla chief; how to infiltrate behind enemy lines and establish guerrilla base camps in remote areas; how to train and lead a guerrilla force in increasingly complex tactical operations and keep it supplied; how to direct an underground and an auxiliary (the guerrillas' clandestine intelligence and support networks); how to perform a target analysis and conduct subversion and sabotage; how to run clandestine escape and evasion nets to return downed U.S. pilots to friendly territory; and how to plan protracted unconventional warfare campaigns that employed the full range of guerrilla warfare tactics—raids, ambushes, mines and booby traps, and sniping and indirect fires. It was a comprehensive introduction to unconventional warfare, and I loved every minute of it. I particularly liked the training we received in intelligence operations—how to arrange clandestine meetings and handle agents and how to collect all the intelligence an SF detachment needs to infiltrate and operate behind enemy lines. I was finally performing at the top of my class.

Phase III concluded with Robin Sage, the Q Course's comprehensive, unconventional warfare field problem in North Carolina's Uwharrie National Forest. The exercise is named after a legendary Office of Strategic Services veteran and former Special Forces colonel, Jerry "Robin" Sage, the basis for Steve McQueen's character in *The Great Escape*.

The exercise began with the isolation of our team—standard operating procedure in Special Forces operations. We thoroughly studied our operational area and made detailed plans for our unconventional warfare campaign. After we completed our plans, we "briefbacked" our instructors on them. A briefback ensures senior commanders that an SF detachment is ready to deploy. A team can be grilled on its plans for hours, and if commanders conclude a team's not ready, it is sent back to isolation or another team is given the mission. After our briefback, we infiltrated our operational area by night parachute jump.

For two weeks, we waged unconventional warfare in the mythical country of Pineland. We had soldiers from the 82nd Airborne as our "G" (guerrilla) force. We trained them on weapons and demolitions and in guerrilla warfare tactics at our base camp. We led them on combat operations against our enemy, who, as it turned out, consisted of more soldiers from the 82nd. We traversed Uwharrie several times, moving from one base camp to another, conducting operations.

As my detachment's intelligence sergeant, I organized the underground, the clandestine part of the resistance, and set up spy networks in local towns to keep us informed about our enemy's plans and movements. I also led our "G" force on a successful ambush of an enemy supply column and participated in several other combat operations that were led by my teammates. I took a downed pilot's fingerprints using lipstick, transmitted his prints to our headquarters, and after verifying that he was who he said he was, arranged for his clandestine exfiltration out of Pineland via the escape and evasion net I had set up. I also organized aerial resupply drops of food, weapons, and ammunition for our forces. After two weeks of operations in exercise time (simulating a few years in "real" time), Pineland was liberated. The final phase of my initial SF training was over.

At our May graduation, we had a green-beret-donning ceremony in front of the statue of a Special Forces soldier—"Bronze Bruce," as he is affectionately known. I wore a green unit flash on my green beret, signifying that I was assigned to the 10th Special Forces Group, then one of only three Special Forces Groups in the active Army. The 10th Group's area of operations was the Soviet bloc and Western Europe. I couldn't have been happier.

I still had a lot to learn; the "Qualification" in SFQC meant just that: I was a qualified SF soldier, but only minimally so. I would require more advanced training, I would need to achieve fluency in an operationally important foreign language, and I would need to gain experience in actual operations and combat. But I was a Green Beret.

SPECIAL FORCES OPERATOR AND COMMANDER

PREPARING FOR WORLD WAR III

I reported into the 10th Special Forces Group at Fort Devens, Massachusetts, in June 1974 and hit the ground running, or more accurately, swimming. Elements from the Group's 2nd Battalion, to which I had just been assigned, had traveled to the Massachusetts shore to conduct waterborne operations training, including long-distance surface or "scout" swimming, a method of clandestine infiltration pioneered by Danish frogmen. Swimmers are inserted by boat at night into the water beyond the visual and radar horizon, out to twelve miles or more. Scout swimming doesn't require as much training as scuba, and thus more SF operators can acquire the skill. It was one of several techniques we could use in the event of war to clandestinely infiltrate teams from the Baltic Sea into Eastern Europe and the Soviet Union.

During real scout swimmer missions, operators use a watertight dry suit in cold waters to keep warm. My team had been conducting this training without dry suits, or even wet suits, for two weeks. The Atlantic was freezing, and I found myself using muscles I didn't know I had to complete the multi-hour night swims. We'd swim on our backs, propelled by fins, to maintain a low silhouette in the water. As we approached the shore, we'd don balaclavas (stretchy, breathable face masks) over our heads to further reduce our visual signature. We learned how to emerge from the water and stealthily move across beaches. We practiced high-speed cast (rolling off a fast patrol craft) and recovery (getting pulled from the water by a rubber lasso and flipped into a speeding boat).

As a final exercise, we conducted a night reconnaissance and sabotage operation in Boston Harbor. More afraid of toxins than we were of sharks, we evaded the Harbor Police, who were out looking for us, and managed to swim in, attach our magnetic mines to ships at anchor, and swim out undetected. Thus began my postgraduate training and education in special operations. It would span more than four years.

———

Activated in 1952, the 10th Special Forces Group was the first formation of its kind. Like the CIA, the Special Forces had evolved from World War II's Office of Strategic Services, and the 10th Group's first commander was Colonel Aaron Bank, an OSS veteran who had parachuted into Nazi-occupied France as a member of a "Jedburgh" team to organize and fight with the French resistance. Later in the war, Bank also organized an unsuccessful operation to capture Adolf Hitler.

Special Forces came of age during the Kennedy administration and the Vietnam War. It was President Kennedy who authorized Special Forces soldiers to wear the green beret, calling it a badge of courage and mark of distinction. Vietnam is one of three "signature" conflicts in which Special Forces played a lead role. The others are El Salvador in the 1980s and Afghanistan in 2001.

In the wake of the Vietnam War, the Special Forces had been reduced to three active groups—the 10th, 5th, and 7th—down from seven in the 1960s. Training funds for live-fire weapons and demolitions training were very limited, and we fired our weapons far less often than needed to maintain our readiness. There was a "never again" mindset in the Army when it came to counterinsurgency and irregular warfare. Generals Creighton Abrams (the Army's chief of staff) and Bill DePuy (the Army's training and doctrine commander), reoriented the service to the "big war" with the Soviets on the central front in Germany. There were very compelling reasons to have done so, but the Army would later pay a high price for its neglect of counterinsurgency doctrine and capabilities.

Nevertheless, the 10th Group was full of exceptional talent, and it was a great place to learn from the experiences of others. Most of the

Group's officers and senior NCOs had served in Vietnam, some for several years. Many, including some of my teammates, had conducted very high-risk reconnaissance and direct action missions into Laos and North Vietnam; some had been on the Son Tay raid, which had attempted to rescue American POWs being held in North Vietnam; and several others had trained and led large irregular forces in the remote areas of Vietnam or had worked for the CIA in Vietnam and Laos.

Given its primary mission to liberate Soviet-occupied territory in the event of war, the 10th Group attracted a large number of Eastern European émigrés, drawn to the U.S. military by the Lodge Act's promise of U.S. citizenship after five years of service. There were native Balts, Czechs, Hungarians, Poles, Russians, Ukrainians, Georgians, Yugoslavs, and East Germans across the Group. Most spoke several languages. All had served in Vietnam, but their consuming passion was liberating their former homelands from tyranny. They were the embodiment of the Special Forces motto, *De oppresso liber* (From oppression we shall liberate them), and they were my first exposure to freedom fighters.[1]

From the émigrés, I learned a store of practical knowledge about their respective homelands, the strict population control measures the Communists employed, and how we might wage unconventional warfare in the Soviet bloc if called upon to do so. I learned from one of the Ukrainian émigrés how the Soviet secret police had infiltrated the Ukrainian resistance in the years after World War II and captured resistance fighters by setting up fake (Soviet-controlled) drop zones. I learned from one of the Hungarians how he'd managed to escape across a border manned by guards, dogs, and barbed wire and thought about how I'd do it.

During the 1970s, the Group had three battalions, each consisting of two hundred–plus special operators. Two battalions were stationed at Fort Devens, and one was forward in Germany. We had two primary missions in the Group: to organize "stay behind" resistance forces in the event the Red Army overran Western Europe, and to conduct unconventional warfare and other special operations in Soviet bloc territory. Those assigned to units with the stay-behind mission studied Norwegian, Danish, German, or French; those assigned the Soviet bloc mission studied Russian and other Eastern European languages.

I was thrilled when I learned that I was being assigned to a team with a Soviet bloc mission. I wanted to be on offense.

I was assigned to B Company, 2nd Battalion as a weapons sergeant on Operational Detachment A (ODA) 225. ODA 225's primary mission in the event of war with the Soviet Union was to infiltrate into northeastern Hungary and wage guerrilla war in Soviet-occupied territory. Our assigned operational area, near the Hungarian cities of Miskolc and Debrecen, was just across the border from where my Slovak grandmother hailed.

To prepare for our wartime mission, we conducted detailed studies of our area of operations, examining the populace, enemy forces, terrain, and so on. It would, of course, have been ideal to go undercover to Hungary, but that was prohibited; there was too great a risk we'd be compromised, so we planned from afar. Using maps and photos, we selected potential drop zones for infiltration and resupply and identified areas for base camps. We memorized Soviet and Eastern European equipment so we could report back intelligence, and we trained on all manner of Soviet bloc weapons. We also trained to operate newly developed targeting beacons so the Air Force's FB-III fighter-bombers could drop their bombs against key targets with greater precision.

Our wartime mission was fraught with perhaps insurmountable challenges, however. We all recognized that there was a high probability that if we were sent in, we weren't likely to make it out alive. We weren't at all confident that we'd have a resistance to work with. It had been crushed by the Soviets in 1956, and there were no signs it had reconstituted. The CIA was supposed to have arranged clandestine contacts for us, but its officers were busy doing more important intelligence and operational tasks. We were told not to count on them. Air Force planners had also warned that the odds of successfully dropping us into Hungary were fifty-fifty at best, given Soviet air defenses. And even if we made it to our operational area, the KGB and Hungarian secret police (AVH) would be looking for us soon after we parachuted in.

When I wasn't engaged in physically demanding training or learning from my teammates, I had my nose buried in books. During my free time, I read Army Field Manuals, special operations studies from the Vietnam War, military and intelligence histories, memoirs and biographies of great commanders and CIA officers, spy novels—really anything I thought would make me a better SF soldier. I read and reread T. E. Lawrence, Mao Zedong, and other works on guerrilla warfare. I was a frequent visitor to the base and military occupational specialty libraries. During one such visit, I had a brief conversation with a young female librarian who was signing out the field manuals I had requested. She was just out of college and asked if women could serve in the Special Forces, adding that she spoke French and Spanish. I told her that they couldn't, but she might consider applying to the CIA. Her name was Gina Haspel, and she would go on to become the agency's director. (Special Forces is now open to women.)

I took to heart the theory that a good leader should derive his (or her) power not from his position or ability to mete out punishment or provide rewards but rather from his expertise and by being the one his followers would select to lead them if they could choose. Leadership based on "expert" and "referent" power became my mantra as I advanced in the Special Forces and one of the key principles I would apply throughout my career.

Noting my studiousness, my SF teammates regularly teased me that I was destined to become a future chief of staff of the Army who would lead the "big push" to Moscow when it came time for war with the Soviet Union. Buoyed by the affirmation, I started to think that maybe an Army career might be for me, and it began to dawn on me that the Army might be thinking so, too, after I was selected as the 10th Special Forces Group Soldier of the Year in 1974.

In November 1975, I almost got my first combat experience. That summer, we welcomed a new battalion commander, Lieutenant Colonel Paris Davis, a fast-rising African American who'd received a Silver Star with SF in Vietnam. I had read the account of Davis's Vietnam heroism in a recently published official history of SF in the war.[2] During a battle in Binh Dinh Province in July 1965, Davis had nearly single-handedly saved his four-man SF team and the company of South Vietnamese soldiers they were advising from certain destruction. Despite being wounded three times, Davis rescued his wounded teammates—including the legendary SF and later CIA operative Billy Waugh, who would go on to capture the infamous terrorist Carlos the

Jackal during the 1990s—and killed nearly thirty of the enemy, some with his pistol and in hand-to-hand combat. Despite being ordered to do so, he refused to leave the battlefield until he had gotten all of the Americans out. It seemed abundantly clear to me that Davis deserved the Medal of Honor for his actions. I was pleased to hear that he finally received it in 2023. He was inspiring, to say the least.

Following Cuba's intervention in the Angolan Civil War that November, Davis was told to place our battalion on alert for possible deployment to the country. Angola was as far away from the Soviet bloc as I could imagine, and we hadn't prepared for such a contingency at all. We made some very rudimentary plans on how we would link up with and support Angola's non-Communist insurgent groups who were battling the Cubans and local Communist forces, but spent most of what little time we had preparing our weapons and other equipment. We would be going in cold. The risk that we would be captured or killed was not insignificant.

I was both excited at the prospect of going into combat and shocked that we'd be going in so unprepared. Later in my career I would learn that this is just part of a special operator's life. You must be able to deal with the unexpected as well as the expected. That's part of what makes special operators special.

After a few days, the alert was called off and we stood down. A U.S. military intervention in Angola, even a small, low-visibility one, just wasn't in the cards so soon after the Vietnam War. Colonel Davis used the alert as a teaching moment, telling us how close our battalion had come to going to war and that we needed to be prepared for any contingency, even if it wasn't World War III. My Vietnam War–experienced teammates shrugged it off—just another day at the office for them. I thought about the what-might-have-beens. The reality of what it meant to be a Green Beret had hit home.

It turned out that when it came to getting wounded, I wouldn't have to wait for combat. During the summer of 1976, I was sent to West Point to teach hand-to-hand combat to second-year cadets. I was demonstrating how to defend yourself against a knife attack when my Green Beret opponent accidentally stabbed me in the thigh with his eight-inch Randall attack survival knife. I had successfully blocked his thrust to my midsection, but when I moved forward to shift the momentum, disarm him, and throw him to the ground, my left leg met his knife.

Despite the pool of blood forming an ever-larger circle on my camouflage pants, I managed to complete the demonstration, which included finishing a second fight by delivering a whirling, roundhouse kick with my wounded leg to my six-foot-four opponent's chest. Adrenaline, I learned, can keep you in the fight for a while. After I walked off the stage and our medics saw the big gash in my leg, they rushed me to the hospital. The eight-inch blade fortunately had just missed my femoral artery. But that was the end of my hand-to-hand combat demonstrations for the rest of the summer.

TRAINING, AND MORE TRAINING

For some Green Berets, graduation from SFQC is an end. After they're assigned to an SF unit, most of their subsequent training is unit based. For me, SFQC was just a beginning. When I wasn't preparing for World War III and other contingencies or training others, I attended several more courses to further develop my skills as a special operator. During my two and a half years with the 10th Group, I'm pretty certain I received more training than any other soldier in the unit. The pace was frenetic, but by the time I left for my next assignment with SF in Europe, I was a far more capable operator. I completed the Ranger Course, which added to my tactical proficiency, an advanced mountain climbing and mountain warfare course with the German Army, formal training in engineering and conventional, improvised, and atomic demolitions, and training in urban unconventional warfare and clandestine operations. In all, I would spend nearly half of my ten years in the Army and Special Forces in formal training. Each course added to my special operations and unconventional warfare skills, and most of them provided foundational knowledge for what was to come down the road.

The Ranger Course was first. It was essentially a repeat of Phase I of SFQC—hand-to-hand combat, obstacle courses, land navigation, raids, ambushes and recon patrols, mountain climbing, small boat operations, jungle training, and survival training—but it was twice the length, more than fifty-eight nonstop days. The course is one of the most demanding the Army has to offer, and only half of those who began the course with me completed it.

At the beginning of the course, I received another signal that the Army might be thinking I had the potential for greater things when the senior tactical officer selected me to be our class's company commander, even though I had been in the Army only a little over eighteen months at that point and there were captains, an SF command sergeant major, and many others far senior to me in my class. Perhaps as a result, I was given some of the most complex operations to lead—a large raid, a night movement in the mountains, and an eighteen-hour infiltration that combined a helicopter insertion with a small boat movement and night patrol through the Florida swamps. I performed much better in tactical leadership roles than I had in SFQC, though still not in every case. A legendary SF noncommissioned officer named "Moose" Monroe dinged me on my night patrol in the mountains. He was a notoriously hard grader, but it stung nonetheless. But repetition is often the mother of learning, and by the end of the course, my tactical proficiency had improved substantially. More important, my confidence in my combat leadership ability also went way up. The course also took its physical toll. By the time I received my Ranger tab, I had lost twenty pounds, and after binge eating at every IHOP, Taco Bell, and Baskin-Robbins I could find on my drive back to Massachusetts from Georgia, I arrived at Fort Devens looking pregnant, which, needless to say, drew more than a few laughs from my fellow Green Berets.

As soon as I returned to Fort Devens, I was notified that I had been selected to attend the German Army's advanced mountain warfare course. The course was conducted in German, and since I knew only a few phrases, I paid extra close attention when things like knots and climbing techniques were being demonstrated. Major Blaufus, our lead instructor, drove this point home, recounting how, as he began an eighty-foot fall that had broken his back while abseiling (rappelling) a few years earlier, he could picture in his mind precisely how his incorrectly tied knot had come undone.

Over six weeks we climbed every major peak in the Bavarian and Austrian Alps, and by the end I was a pretty accomplished climber. As a result, I became a climbing instructor after I returned to Fort Devens and served on a mountain team during my brief tour with the 10th Group's 1st Battalion in Germany. I had also learned about mountain warfare tactics, which would come in handy down the road. I enjoyed the physical and mental challenges of technical climbing—how to ascend a vertical face, relying on only small purchases for your hands and feet, and how to select the route as a lead climber. It was just you and the mountain, and a different kind of adrenaline rush compared with close-quarter battle and free-fall parachuting.

Six months later, I was sent to master a second core Special Forces specialty: engineer/demolitions. The engineer portion of the course taught us how to design and construct base camps for our defense and other structures that might endear a local populace to us. We learned how to design and build roads, bridges, and buildings. It was a crash course in civil engineering. My dad, who'd built houses and apartments himself, just shook his head when I told him about my newly acquired construction skills. "I could have taught you all that," he said with a sigh. During the demolitions portion of the course, we learned how to analyze targets, how to calculate and emplace charges, how to fashion improvised explosives out of commercially available materials, and how to plan and conduct sabotage operations. Like the weapons course, the demolitions training would prepare me for what was to come after I joined the CIA.

(A "misfire" during our training on improvised explosives drove home the point about the care that must be taken when working with these chemicals. Our instructor was demonstrating an improvised explosive that is volatile to moisture. As he was mixing it in a bowl in front of our class, it detonated, releasing a heat wave that blew past us. Fortunately, the instructor had blocked most of the blast with his hand and no one was seriously injured.)

A few weeks after I completed the SF Engineer/Demolitions Course, I was sent to West Berlin for clandestine operations and urban unconventional warfare training with our Special Forces detachment in the city. Since the mid-1950s, Special Forces had maintained a small undercover unit there for stay-behind operations in the event of war.[3] The urban unconventional warfare training required me to grow my hair long and wear civilian clothes. I learned how to operate undercover in the city and how to conduct sabotage operations against Soviet forces in the event of war. In our final exercise, our twelve-man team was divided into several operational cells, and we managed to evade detection by the Berlin police, who were tasked with looking for us. I was responsible for devising our clandestine communications plan and was also tasked with doing the target analysis and preparing the explosive charges for the late-night demolition raid we conducted on a major industrial facility. Our targets were huge gantry cranes towering over Berlin's largest docks. We approached our target in "SWAT" vans we had clandestinely rented and were on and off the target in fifteen minutes, with most of the time consumed by having to climb the massive cranes to emplace our charges. This training, too, would have its own operational echoes for me down the road.

The final training I received before being reassigned to the 10th Group's 1st Battalion in Europe was the most unusual: the Special Atomic Demolition Munition Course. The SADM (pronounced "Say-dem") was a small nuclear weapon, a "backpack nuke." As with all nuclear weapons, its initial use could only be authorized by the president. The SADM provided a four-star theater commander with a very low-yield nuclear weapon that could—in theory—be used to break up an enemy's offensive by blocking the movement of follow-on forces. Targets for SADM missions included bridges, dams, tunnels, and mountain passes that were too difficult to destroy with conventional explosives.

Selected personnel from the Special Forces and the Navy SEALs were trained on the device, and each of the three battalions in the 10th Group had a four-man SADM team. Most wartime Special Forces missions were high risk, but many Green Berets viewed SADM missions as far riskier still; they were in the "no return" category. And, as with all nuclear weapons, two-man control of the SADM had to be maintained at all times, and the codes needed to arm the weapon would only be transmitted just prior to employment. "Positive control" had to be maintained over the device, meaning that even after the nuke was emplaced, a team had to remain in close visual range of it. While we hoped that this wouldn't result in the team's vaporization, there's no way you can be close enough to watch it without getting a heavy dose of heat, blast, and radiation.

The device had a timer that provided a delay of up to twenty-four hours, though more than a few SF operators believed that the moment the timer was activated on a real device, the bomb would detonate. Conspiracy theories aside, some three decades after my SADM training, I met with engineers from Sandia National Laboratories (Albuquerque, New Mexico) for a briefing on Pakistan's nuclear weapons.

Aware of my prior operational history with the device, they began their briefing by showing me a slide of the SADM and commented, "You know, we never really got that timer to work properly."

As with any assignment involving nuclear weapons, those selected for SADM training and duty had to be enrolled in the Personal Reliability Program—a security, medical, and psychological evaluation that ensures that only the most trustworthy personnel have access to these weapons. The Saturday morning before my course started, I heard a knock on my barracks room door, and when I opened it, there was Colonel Davis, the officer who almost led me into combat in Angola. And there I was, in my underwear. He gave me a look over, shook his head, and told me to get dressed so he could interview me for the battalion's nuclear weapons program.

The training was fascinating. I learned about the physics of nuclear fission, how the device was constructed, and how to carefully—and I mean carefully—arm it. We also were taught how to rig it for a parachute drop and parachute with it, using both static line techniques and military free fall.

I had joined the elite of the elite. Several decades later, when I was a senior policy maker overseeing U.S. nuclear strategy, I was glad that I'd had some operational exposure to the nuclear world. But this was one area of expertise I never wanted to use. In 1986—three years before the Cold War ended—all SADMs were retired from the U.S. inventory.[4]

EUROPEAN INTERLUDE

In June 1976, I reenlisted in the Special Forces for an assignment with the 10th Group's 1st Battalion (its forward unit) in Bad Tölz, Germany, with Czech-language training at the Defense Language Institute in Monterey, California, prior to my assignment there. I had been given a choice of Russian, Polish, Hungarian, Serbo-Croatian, and German, but chose Czech, since it was the only Slavic language that came with an assignment to the 10th Group's 1st Battalion at Bad Tölz. I was also offered an assignment to Det A—the undercover unit in Berlin that I'd trained with—but preferred to gain fluency in another Slavic language rather than learn German. In any event, I thought that having a second operationally useful language to go with my college Russian would make me even more attractive down the road to a certain three-letter agency. During my yearlong language course, I mastered an extensive military vocabulary, and by the end of it I was able to give an hour-long, detailed Special Forces operations order in Czech.

In January 1978, I reported to Special Forces headquarters at Bad Tölz and was assigned to Operational Detachment A-2, a mountain warfare team. ODA 2's wartime mission was to conduct special operations and follow-on unconventional warfare in Czechoslovakia. One of my teammates was a native Czech, so I had lots of opportunities to further improve my language skills.

After signing in, I was immediately sent on a winter warfare exercise in the Alps. Despite my nearly three years in the 10th Special Forces Group, I had somehow missed ski training each winter, and had never been on the slopes growing up in Los Angeles, so I was given some rudimentary instruction before we deployed. It was completely inadequate to the task. I had been assigned to a team of top skiers, and once we had made our way to the top of one of the highest peaks in the Alps, they schussed and slalomed down the hill, abandoning me at the top. I quickly realized that I wouldn't get down the steep slope using the basic techniques I'd been taught, so after pondering my situation for a moment, I took my poncho out of my ruck, folded it into a small square so I could sit on it, inserted my skis vertically in the slots behind my rucksack pockets, and zigzagged down the hill on my rear end, passing some of the fallen schussers as I did. Not the most elegant approach, but it got me down safely.

Through this and subsequent exercises, I gained the confidence of my team and was promoted to staff sergeant that April. My superiors saw me as my team's foremost tactical expert, so they revised our wartime standing operating procedures to put me in charge of all tactical movements, despite my junior rank and lack of combat experience. Also that April, Major Jim "Ranger" Roach, my company commander, encouraged me to apply for Officer Candidate School. (Roach would go on to command the 7th Special Forces Group.) Normally, a soldier had to complete two years of service in Europe before he was eligible to apply for OCS, but my chain of command up through the commanding general, U.S. Army Europe, approved a waiver so I could apply after only three months on station. I was accepted and given a report date of late August. I liked being an SF operator, but becoming an SF officer was the pathway to leading operations at a more complex level. I saw it as my next step on the path to becoming a CIA officer while I completed my college degree.

But there were some more James Bond skills I needed to learn first. With OCS looming, I was sent to counterterrorist close-quarter battle training with the British Special Air Service in Hereford, England. It was my first exposure to counterterrorism tactics and operations, and it provided the foundation for several subsequent counterterrorism assignments. Some of our instructors had served undercover against the IRA, one had climbed Mount Everest, and others had advised tribal elements and put down rebellions in Oman. They were hard, talented, and serious men, and I did my best to emulate them.

The training was first-rate, and I became an expert with a Browning Hi-Power pistol and a Heckler & Koch MP5 submachine gun. We started off with the basics, with plenty of range time. As we progressed, we learned four- and five-man room-clearing techniques and how to shoot with precision in close quarters. My favorite part of the room-clearing training was diving headfirst through a window and coming up shooting. I later told a senior Army special operations officer about this training, and he replied, "That's just show-off stuff—we just blow the wall down." I still thought it was cool.

We learned how to select a dominant position in a large room while engaged in a clandestine meeting, and how to conceal a handgun under a magazine or newspaper to get the drop on potential adversaries in a pub or restaurant, a technique I am sure came in handy for SAS operators in Northern Ireland. We learned how to quickly exit a car if ambushed and return suppressive fire. During one such drill, a special operator from Denmark, increasingly bothered by the hot brass that was hitting him in the neck as it was ejected from the handgun of the operator on his left, turned his head and fired several rounds into the "bonnet" ("hood" in American English) of the sedan we had just exited. Our SAS instructors grimaced but shrugged it off. It was, of course, an Aston Martin.

Training accidents aside, it was a great experience. Counterterrorism was becoming a new mission for U.S. special operations forces, and I was at the forefront. It was also my introduction to the SAS. More broadly, the extensive training I had received during my first five years in the Army had developed me into a full-performance SF operator. I felt more than ready for what came next.

SPECIAL FORCES OFFICER

I reported into Fort Benning, Georgia, for Officer Candidate School in late August 1978. During the ninth week of our course, we went through the branch selection and assignment process. We were given a choice of branches—Infantry, Armor, Artillery, Military Intelligence, and so on. I went Infantry, since its skill set was closest to Special Forces. Our assignment officer at Infantry Branch, Captain John Maher, pulled aside three of us who had prior SF or Ranger Battalion experience and told us that he had three Special Forces assignments he needed to fill. We could have them if we wanted. He added that with our prior experience we didn't need to be infantry platoon leaders—the normal first assignment for an infantry officer—we could go straight into infantry company command after we'd been promoted to captain.

I couldn't believe my good fortune. Officers couldn't normally serve in SF until they were at least first lieutenants. I'd already decided that I would apply to CIA before the end of my obligatory service as an officer, so I made plans to finish my bachelor's degree in the four and a half years I still owed the Army. In CIA, I'd get the chance to do battle with our enemies in peacetime, and I'd be in charge of my own operations. I knew that an SF assignment would be a lot more exciting than a tour in the infantry would. One of the assignments was with the 10th Group at Fort Devens, another with the 5th Group at Fort Bragg, and the third with the 3rd Battalion, 7th Special Forces Group in Panama. The last one came with Spanish-language training and the Military Free-Fall Parachutist Course. I was given first choice, since I was at the top of my class. After mulling over the possibilities, I chose 7th Group; learning another foreign language and becoming a free-fall parachutist were too good to pass up. Plus, the Sandinistas had taken over Nicaragua, and it seemed as if Central America might be heading toward a region-wide insurgency. Following the sound of guns is almost always a good idea for an SF—or CIA—operator.

After OCS, I completed the fourteen-week Infantry Officer Basic Course, where I acquired a few new tactical skills like maneuvering tanks and attack helicopters with infantry and supporting artillery fires. My course adviser wrote that I had an "uncanny ability to visualize the battlefield." I certainly had matured as a tactical leader by that point. IOBC was followed by the twenty-eight-week Spanish Language Course at the Defense Language Institute in Monterey—my second time there in two years.

The Special Forces Officer Course is designed to prepare officers to become detachment commanders, the leader of a twelve-man Special Forces "A" Team. As a graduate of the enlisted Q Course, I could have opted out of SFOC, but I felt the additional training I'd get as an officer would be valuable. The officer course provided more in-depth instruction in unconventional warfare and clandestine operations, and I thrived on it. Most of my classmates were infantry officers, with five to twelve years of experience. A few were combat veterans. Most were my age or a bit older; I was nearly twenty-seven when I graduated. A few were foreign officers. One went on to become the vice chief of the Indian Army; another is currently the Indonesian minister of defense. Our primary instructors were SF majors and senior captains, several of whom had had combat experience.

One special feature of SFOC I particularly liked was the research paper on some aspect of special warfare that each officer had to write and present. I wrote mine on urban unconventional warfare, drawing on my Berlin experience and a few Rand studies on the theory and practice of guerrilla warfare in cities. I examined what skills and tradecraft Special Forces would need to be able to wage unconventional warfare in the cities of Eastern Europe. I argued that there would need to be an already established underground to receive, hide, and support special operators. Operators would need to have adequate cover to escape the notice of informants and authorities, real fluency in the language and culture, and advanced training in surveillance detection and clandestine communications to be able to operate successfully. One could get "lost" in the noise and anonymity of a big city, but base areas would need to be selected with care. This would put a premium on detailed intelligence and peacetime preparation. The scope and scale of operations would depend on the size and reach of the underground. It was an opportunity to think deeply about an operational problem where there was no doctrine to guide us. Although I didn't know it at the time, it also helped prepare me for operations in Afghanistan's cities and for irregular warfare in the twenty-first century.

I graduated first in my class of fifty-eight and was declared the distinguished honor graduate—the only time, I was told, a second lieutenant had done so. My performance was in stark contrast with my experience in SFQC, where I struggled to apply in the field what I had learned in the classroom and had had challenges mastering the technical aspects of weapons maintenance. After my five years as an SF operator and extensive post-SFQC training, SF tactics and technical proficiency in a wide range of SF skills were now second nature to me. As a result, I knew more about SF operations than the captains and majors in my course, who, though senior to me in rank, were new to SF, and my performance reflected that. I admittedly had an unfair advantage, but creating that advantage had been my plan, and that strategy would pay even greater dividends down the road.

The Military Free-Fall Parachutist Course, or HALO, as it's more popularly known, was a different kind of challenge. HALO stands for "high altitude, low opening," one of the techniques employed by military free-fall parachutists. In HALO, a jumper exits an aircraft between twenty-five thousand and thirty thousand feet—at night, while breathing oxygen, and with full combat equipment—and free-falls to around twenty-five hundred feet before opening his parachute. Free-falling twenty-five thousand feet takes only a few minutes.[5] Military free-fall operations are conducted when the risk of detection from low-level, static line jumps is too high.

Military free-fall students these days receive extensive training in wind tunnels, learning how to get stable and maneuver in the air before they leap out of an airplane. In my day, we simply practiced the proper body positions lying on tables for a day or two and then went up to 12,500 feet and jumped out. Learning by doing, as they say. HALO students start by jumping "Hollywood"—without weapons and equipment strapped to their bodies—and then add these after they learn to get stable. Oxygen bottles and pre-breathing oxygen on the ground get added as jumps increase in altitude. I got stable on my first jump, so I was handed a forty-pound, sandbag-filled rucksack to jump with on my second. I took one look at the rucksack the instructor handed me and protested. It hadn't been packed properly, with most of the sand bulging out on one side of the ruck. I knew this would make it very difficult to control in flight, but didn't appreciate the extent of it. The instructor—an SF NCO—assured me it would be fine. I didn't believe him, but not wanting to make an issue of it, I went ahead and jumped with it. Big mistake. I should have had another instructor who had more sense look at it. I suspect my instructor was trying to have a little fun with a second lieutenant that day.

As soon as I exited the plane, I went into a violent spin. It took me several thousand feet to get stable, and when I finally did, I was on my back. Something told me I shouldn't continue to fall this way, so I arched my back as hard as I could and, after a few tries, managed to turn over. I then had to twist my upper body as hard as I could in the opposite direction to stop the violent spin the lopsided rucksack was causing. I finally got stable, oriented myself to where I was falling, and completed the jump. After I landed safely, I took the rucksack home that night and repacked it myself.

Enough can go wrong during free fall without taking foolish risks; even today, with much better and safer training and equipment, very experienced special operators still lose their lives or get badly injured during free-fall jumps. What my instructor had done was reckless, even criminal. We were both lucky I survived. Fortunately, my subsequent free-falls during and after the course were much less eventful.

COUNTERTERRORISM COMMAND

In June 1980, I reported into the 3rd Battalion, 7th Special Forces Group at Fort Gulick, Panama, and was given command of ODA 14, the sniper team in Charlie Company. For the previous two years, Charlie Company had been assigned a counterterrorism mission, so it had been organized into assault, sniper, and clandestine intelligence troops. The Communist insurgency in El Salvador was growing rapidly, and in the summer of 1980 we received an alert that our embassy in San Salvador might be attacked. Fifty-two American hostages were being held captive in Iran, and we didn't want a second embassy taken over. Our ambassador accordingly requested assistance from the U.S.

Southern Command (in charge of operations in Latin America), and I was selected to lead a team of snipers and clandestine operators to reinforce security at the embassy. I was still a second lieutenant at the time.

Unlike the combat alert for action in Angola I had been involved in five years earlier, I felt completely prepared for this mission. Several years of special operations and leadership training had done their trick. I was confident in my ability to employ my snipers and the clandestine operators. We loaded our weapons, ammunition, night vision devices, and other equipment and boarded a C-130 for San Salvador. While en route, however, the immediate threat to our embassy subsided, and our ambassador called off the mission. It was quite a letdown, for both my team and me.

Five months later, I had another false start. A new special mission unit was forming up and preparing for what we were told was a very important operation. The unit's recruiters wouldn't provide the full details, but it was pretty clear it was a second Iran hostage rescue attempt.[6] If there was a second rescue operation, I wanted to be part of it. The recruiters were particularly interested in my free-fall skills, the close-quarter battle training I'd had with the British SAS, and the clandestine operations training I had with Det A in Berlin. They also asked me if I had training in evasive driving, which I had. I successfully screened for the mission—the only officer to do so— but Lieutenant Colonel Gene Russell, my battalion commander, told the recruiting team leader that he would soon be giving me a special counterterrorism command and couldn't spare me.

At first, I was disappointed, but as it turned out, the American hostages being held in Tehran were released six weeks later (on the day President Reagan was inaugurated), so planning for a second rescue attempt stopped, though the new special mission unit was still established. And as luck would have it, my new counterterrorism command in 3/7 would prove even more eventful than service in the new special mission unit would have.

I had now been in the Special Forces for eight years. I had received extensive training, but I hadn't deployed on any real operations or engaged in combat. But it was also clear from my near misses in Angola, El Salvador, and Iran that my work as Special Forces operator and commander was increasingly tied to world affairs. My next five years would be completely different, nearly nonstop operations and some close combat. My string of false starts had come to an end.

In early 1981, even though I was a newly promoted first lieutenant in a battalion full of senior captains, Colonel Russell made good on his word. I was given command of the clandestine operators, Special Forces Operational Detachments A 16 and A 18, which had been merged together for a special counterterrorism intelligence mission. It was a troop command, which would normally be filled by a major or senior captain.[7] I would command this twenty-two-man unit until I left the Army for CIA in 1983. It was the first of several big jumps in operational responsibility I would have in my career.

The unit's members, all Special Forces operators, wore civilian clothes and were allowed to grow their hair long. They were trained in advanced photography, architectural drawing, and report writing. A few were trained in clandestine audio techniques and satellite communications systems. All were equipped with Walther PPK handguns—just like James Bond.

After the Iran hostage crisis, there was growing concern within the U.S. government that terrorists might take over U.S. embassies in other high-threat areas. My aborted mission to El Salvador was just one example. Several additional embassies in Latin America were also at high risk. My unit's mission was to collect the basic but detailed intelligence that a rescue force would require, should one of our embassies be overrun. Should there be a hostage incident, an element from my unit would deploy on scene to collect additional intelligence and advise the U.S. ambassador on military options. Our collection missions were overseen by a special division within U.S. Southern Command's Intelligence Directorate and coordinated with the Department of State and the CIA. I worked closely with the State Department's Diplomatic Security Service and its network of regional security officers to collect the necessary intelligence. Crisis deployments, those in response to a terrorist incident, were overseen by SOUTHCOM's Special Operations Division.

Over the duration of my command, I led collection missions to El Salvador, Nicaragua, Honduras, Guatemala, Costa Rica, Colombia,

Venezuela, Ecuador, Peru, Argentina, Bolivia, and Suriname, with multiple deployments to the most high-threat posts. We would map ingress and egress routes, select helicopter landing zones, sniper positions, and assault positions, obtain blueprints, take detailed photos of the exterior and interior of our diplomatic compounds, and describe in detail exterior lighting and all locks and doors. It was painstaking work. In every country I deployed to, I would brief the ambassador and CIA chief of station on my unit's mission and capabilities and how we would respond if there was a crisis.

My unit received high-level attention from our leaders in Washington. Bill Casey, the director of central intelligence and director of the CIA, stopped by while on a trip to the region for a briefing on my unit and on 3/7's training and advisory missions in Central America, as did the Army's chief of staff, General Edward "Shy" Meyer. No visit is more important to an Army unit than one by the chief. We'd prepared extensively for Meyer's visit, and my boss, Colonel Russell, was confident that the chief would be far more interested in 3/7's training and advisory missions in El Salvador than he would be in our clandestine counterterrorism operations. He accordingly cut my briefing slides to the bare minimum to allow more time for the other presenters. I protested, but to no avail.

No plan survives contact, as they say. General Meyer strode briskly into the 3/7 conference room and barked, "Tell me how you support counterterrorism operations." Not missing a beat, Colonel Russell quickly called an audible, looked at me, and matter-of-factly said, "Mike, tell the chief."

Early in my command, I had paid a call on Major General Dick Scholtes, the commander of the new Joint Special Operations Command at Pope Air Force Base in North Carolina, to discuss just that. JSOC had been established in the aftermath of the disastrous Iran rescue mission to ensure that U.S. special operators could execute these kinds of missions far more effectively, and Meyer had played a key role in getting JSOC established. I briefed Meyer on my unit's counterterrorism mission and how we would support JSOC. The chief went away happy. Colonel Russell joked with me afterward that he had been right: I didn't need the slides after all. During the visit of another Army general officer to 3/7, Colonel Russell was asked to describe what actions he takes when he gets alerted to a terrorism incident in the middle of the night. He replied, "I call Mike Vickers and go back to sleep." He was a great supporter and mentor, and we remain friends to this day.

I received one of those calls in late April 1982. A Cuban-backed Honduran terrorist group, the Lorenzo Zelaya Revolutionary Popular Forces, had hijacked an airliner in Tegucigalpa, Honduras. There were as many as forty-eight hostages on board, including several American citizens.

I selected two of my teammates to accompany me on the mission, and we were immediately flown by helicopter over to SOUTHCOM headquarters. Once there, I helped Bob Nelson, a Navy SEAL assigned to the Special Operations Division, draft the "Options Cable" to our ambassador in Tegucigalpa to authorize my team's deployment. Two hours later, I was on the SOUTHCOM commander's plane headed for Tegucigalpa. On board with me were my two teammates, Sid Vest and Pete Peterson, both fluent in Spanish and experts in very low-light, long-distance optical and photographic surveillance. Sid was also our clandestine technical operations specialist, and Pete had been on the ODA that had assisted the Bolivians in tracking down Che Guevara.

After we landed, I headed straight to the embassy to confer with our ambassador, John Negroponte. An Army special operations unit deployed to Tegucigalpa a few hours later, and CIA sent an Incident Response Team from its Counterterrorism Group. While I was at the embassy, Pete and Sid had headed to Tegucigalpa airport to begin setting up surveillance. I soon joined them, and several hours later we were augmented by the Army special operators who had deployed from the United States and had prepared an assault plan. I then returned to the embassy with Colonel Rod Paschall, the commander of the Army special operations unit, for a briefing for Ambassador Negroponte on assault contingencies. I had gotten to know Paschall during a Fort Bragg visit the previous year and thought very highly of him. He'd served with SF in Vietnam and had later commanded an SF battalion.

The Honduran high command soon informed us, however, that any assault would have to be conducted by Honduran forces. Colonel Paschall and his men reviewed the Honduran plans and judged them to pose unacceptable risks to the safety of the hostages. There would not be a deliberate assault of the plane, by the United States or Honduras. It was a lesson I would internalize: when a host nation has its own citizens at risk, the United States will usually be kept at arm's length or limited to an advise-and-assist role. But it is also usually the case that host nations lack the capability for precision assault. The Army special operators developed an emergency assault plan in case the terrorists started killing the hostages, and Colonel Paschall positioned his forces accordingly. For the remainder of the crisis, I was at the airport, managing the flow of intelligence, overseeing technical collection operations, and providing regular situation reports via SATCOM to the Joint Staff's director of operations in Washington and to SOUTHCOM in Panama. To help us monitor what the terrorists were saying, the National Security Agency sent one of its top engineers to Tegucigalpa from NSA headquarters. The Vatican's representative to Honduras, the papal nuncio, served as our negotiating intermediary.

Even with the deliberate assault option taken off the table, it was still a hostage crisis and it had plenty of tense moments. The four terrorists had a bomb on board that included dynamite sticks made with nitroglycerin. The dynamite was sweating under the hot temperatures inside the plane, which made it unstable and a mortal risk to the hostages. Worried about their own safety, the terrorists notified the papal nuncio about their predicament, and he in turn notified us. After conferring with our bomb disposal experts, we hastily procured kitty litter at a grocery store in Tegucigalpa and provided it, along with instructions, to the terrorists on board the plane. It was a field expedient, but it worked. The kitty litter stabilized the bomb.

The terrorists agreed to release eighteen hostages two days into the crisis in exchange for food and water and the opportunity to publicly convey their demands. We continued to collect additional intelligence about what was going on inside the plane. The following night, ten of the remaining hostages managed to escape by diving out of smashed windows and an emergency door while the terrorists slept. The terrorists fired a few shots, but thankfully no one was killed. Some of the hostages, though, sustained injuries from broken glass and their fall. Brian Ross, chief investigative correspondent for ABC News at the time, was among those who escaped. Three decades later, at a national security forum in Aspen, Colorado, Ross publicly thanked me and the other special operators for coming to his rescue. After seventy-two hours, the terrorists agreed to release their remaining hostages in return for safe passage to Cuba. I had been awake for all but three of those hours.

After the hijacking was over, the SOUTHCOM commander sent his plane to bring Pete, Sid, and me back to Panama. The operation, the first of its kind, was considered a model deployment of our nation's evolving counterterrorism capabilities. Our national counterterrorism posture was mostly reactive in those days, responding to, rather than trying to preempt, terrorist incidents, but we had done well, and my small team had played a supporting but important role. I fell asleep during dinner that evening at the Fort Gulick Officers' Club. I was even more exhausted after this mission than I had been in SFQC or Ranger School. While I had succeeded by running on adrenaline, I learned another valuable lesson about the importance of forcing some rest during a crisis. Colonel Paschall had taken several naps, but I had taken only one. It was pure luck that I hadn't become impaired and ineffective at a critical moment.

———————

To capture the lessons learned from the Honduran terrorist hijacking (and a subsequent terrorist incident in San Pedro Sula four months later to which I also deployed—this one with 109 hostages, including 3 Honduran government ministers), SOUTHCOM hosted a high-level conference on Contadora Island off the coast of Panama in early 1983. All the major participants and decision makers were there, with U.S. ambassadors attending from all over Latin America. I briefed the group on my team's role in the incidents, which the SOUTHCOM staff called "Vickers Deployment One" and "Vickers Deployment Two." It was an overstatement of my role, but a flattering one nonetheless. After all these years, I was at the center of events.

I loved the counterterrorism mission, not just because I was part of the special operations elite, but because it seemed black and white morally. We were trying to rescue innocent civilians whose lives had been placed at great risk by bad people. Unlike insurgents or soldiers who usually observed the law of war, terrorists showed no such restraint. This view would stay with me as counterterrorism became even more important in the coming decades.

I had a similar moral view about unconventional warfare—guerrilla warfare, subversion, sabotage, and evasion and escape—one that would only get strengthened as I progressed through my career and got to practice unconventional warfare for real. While guerrilla warfare has an undeniable exotic, romantic appeal, what attracted me to it was more than that. I was proud to stand with the oppressed. Freeing people from tyranny is a noble calling.

In March 1983, in what turned out to be my final operational responsibility as an SF officer, I was detailed to SOUTHCOM headquarters to develop plans for unconventional warfare in Nicaragua. By then, Central America had become engulfed in a region-wide conflict. The Sandinistas were supporting Communist insurgencies in El Salvador and Honduras, and an insurgency was developing in Nicaragua to oppose the Sandinista regime. I had read intelligence reports with interest about the formation of the Nicaraguan Democratic Force under Adolfo Calero in Honduras and the Southern Front under Edén Pastora in Costa Rica—who, collectively, would come to be known as the contras. Their rise was unconventional warfare in practice. I helped craft a plan to deploy and employ two battalions of Special Forces in Nicaragua, should President Reagan decide to intervene militarily there. Reagan, however, opted to keep the conflict covert— that is, conducted under the covert action authorities of the CIA. It was another lesson I would internalize about the important policy differences between covert and overt operations. CIA was our nation's primary "peacetime" paramilitary force; SF was our "wartime" unconventional warfare force. The techniques employed were similar, but the policy circumstances under which these operations were authorized and conducted were very different.

When I joined the Special Forces, I thought I'd serve for only three years. I ended up staying for ten. I loved my time as a Green Beret. I had risen to the rank of captain, had been given a great deal of responsibility, and liked the challenge of dealing with national security problems for which there was no textbook solution. I was not the best at every Special Forces skill, but I was pretty good at most of them and I excelled in more than a few. I also learned a lot about leadership and influence, both up and down the chain of command.

I had focused during my first five years on preparing to wage unconventional warfare against the Soviet Empire in Eastern Europe. I learned a lot about unconventional warfare strategy and tactics, and the Soviet bloc military and security forces I expected to face. I mastered U.S. and foreign weapons and demolitions techniques and became proficient in mountain warfare. Then, during my last five years, I concentrated on counterterrorism operations and intelligence. Although I didn't realize it at the time, the two missions I had focused on during those ten years—unconventional warfare and counterterrorism—would become a major part of my career from then on. I would soon apply what I had learned on a much larger stage.

GOING TO WAR WITH CIA

"YOU DON'T LOOK LIKE A GREEN BERET"

In December 1982, at twenty-nine, I formally applied to the CIA's Career Training Program. It was the most prestigious way to join CIA—the agency's "West Point." The other way was as a direct hire. The CT Program was mostly for officers bound for the Directorate of Operations, CIA's espionage and covert action arm, the part of the agency I was applying to.[1]

Prospective operations officers had the longest program: the ten-week Career Trainee Orientation Course, the five-month Operations Course, and the three-month Special Operations Training Course, in addition to two or three three-month "interim" assignments in different DO offices.[2] All told, it took a minimum of fifteen months for an operations officer to complete the training. Before an officer was sent to the field, he or she might also receive one to two years of language training and more advanced tradecraft training if they were being sent to Moscow or other hostile operating environments.

A career in the CIA's Clandestine Service appealed to me for several reasons. First, I liked the individual autonomy and responsibility CIA gave its officers. This, I would soon learn, applied not just to espionage but even to large-scale covert action programs. An individual could move history. During my ten years in the Special Forces, I had served in the most elite part of the Army, and CIA's Clandestine Service seemed like the elite of the elite. Second, CIA was in large measure our nation's primary instrument in the Cold War. While I had dreamed of leading large army formations in decisive battle, the big war might never come. The Cold War was a war in the shadows. Finally, I thought I'd be given greater responsibilities at an earlier age in CIA than I would in the Army. I wouldn't be disappointed.

After completing the lengthy application process, in late January 1983 I was invited to Washington for a week of testing and interviews. I took the agency's Professional Applicant Test Battery, a several-hour exam that tested a candidate's IQ, knowledge of world affairs, ability to learn a foreign language, and ability to write well under time pressure. For the last part, we were asked to write an essay on an assigned topic—mine was the United Nations—within thirty minutes. This test supposedly measured one's ability to write an intelligence report under deadline. The all-day battery of tests was a draining experience, but the CT staff told me I'd excelled, particularly in knowledge of world affairs and aptitude for foreign languages. I was also grilled about my willingness and ability to recruit and handle foreign spies. Did I have what it takes to engage in espionage? Could I persuade someone to betray his country and spy for the United States? The Career Training Program officer interviewing me almost snarled as he asked these questions. I couldn't tell whether he found the subject itself unpleasant or whether it was just his way of trying to convey the mental toughness an operations officer must have if he is to succeed in this line of work. In any event, I passed muster and moved on to the next phase.

I then had to complete a psychological aptitude test, which was very similar to the one I had taken a decade earlier as part of the Special Forces Selection Battery. One question, drawing on the agency's OSS heritage and Cold War experience, asked if I'd be willing to parachute out of an airplane. Hell, yeah, I thought, since I'd already made nearly a hundred jumps by then. Another asked whether I preferred going out to a party or staying at home and reading a book. I actually liked both, but I knew the correct answer for an operations officer was going out and engaging with people.

Over several decades, the agency had developed psychological profiles for successful operations officers and analysts. Operations officers, also called case officers, recruit and handle spies and, when directed, conduct covert action to influence events abroad while concealing the fact that the United States is behind those events; agents are the foreign spies and covert action assets they recruit and handle. Operations officers must possess high "emotional intelligence"—the ability to read people and assess their motivation—and they need to have excellent persuasion skills. Above all, they have to have a high degree of self-confidence—how else could you get someone to risk their life by stealing secrets for you? They must be able to perform in rapidly changing, unanticipated, and unstructured situations, have a high tolerance for ambiguity, and be very good at thinking on their feet. They need to be meticulous in their attention to detail and employ sound "tradecraft," because an agent's life may well depend on it. The agency assesses whether a candidate has what it takes for operational work through five means: the PATB, psychological assessment, multiple interviews with experienced operations officers, on-the-job training on a headquarters desk, and performance in the Operations Course. The real test, of course, is how well an officer performs in the field.

After I completed the tests, I had an interview with an assessment psychologist, who told me that I had an ideal profile to be an operations officer. The one minor flag she noted was that "being liked" seemed important to me. She advised that I should guard against it, because it could be an exploitable vulnerability. As we were concluding the interview, she said offhandedly, "You know, you don't look like a Green Beret. I would have guessed that you were an insurance salesman." I suppose I could have been offended. I was clearly very fit. My owlish glasses must be throwing her off. I wondered for a moment whether I should show her how many push-ups I could do. But I just laughed and assured her that I'd indeed been a very successful SF operator and commander for ten years. And then I added, "This is the CIA. Aren't we supposed to look like something other than what we are?" She smiled and nodded in agreement.

I then had two interviews with senior agency operations officers: the first, with the chief of Ground Branch, the agency's primary paramilitary unit, focused on my SF experience and fluency in Spanish. The second, with a native-born Czech who was a deputy chief in the Soviet and East European Division, the group that handled spies behind the Iron Curtain and oversaw worldwide recruitment operations against Soviet and Eastern European targets, focused on my Russian and Czech and my desire to serve in Moscow and elsewhere in the Soviet bloc. I felt as if I was being recruited rather than assessed.

Both described the virtues of the work they were doing and why their part of the agency would be a good fit for me. It seemed as though I was already in.

A month later, I was invited back to take the medical, psychiatric, and polygraph exams. I was also given language proficiency tests in Czech and Spanish and scored well on both, though higher in Spanish, since I hadn't had much opportunity to use my Czech since I left Special Forces Europe. I was told I would be brought into the agency as a senior GS-11, the highest grade possible for a career trainee. It was about a $10,000 pay cut from what I'd been making as a captain in the Special Forces, but I knew I'd make it up once I was assigned overseas and got promoted. In May 1983, I received a formal offer of employment and was invited to join the Career Training Program beginning June 27. Application to acceptance took just under six months.

While I was going through the process, I finally completed my BA in international relations via the University of Alabama's External Degree Program—twelve years after I had begun my studies at Pierce College. In all, I'd received credits from ten different colleges and universities—taking courses wherever I was assigned. It was certainly a nontraditional path to a college degree, but across all those schools I'd put together my own curriculum—graduate courses in political and social revolutions, international terrorism, and problems of Communism, in addition to advanced undergraduate courses in American foreign and national security policy, international relations theory and geopolitics—all aimed at becoming a CIA operations officer. The final requirement before I received my BA was an honors thesis in my field of study. Not surprisingly, I wrote mine on U.S. intelligence policy. Intelligence was becoming a new field of academic study, and as part of my thesis I examined the state of clandestine collection, analysis, counterintelligence, and covert action. I argued that in the decade ahead the United States would need to revitalize and make much greater use of the CIA's capabilities, particularly its ability to covertly influence events abroad. And that's what I hoped I was heading to CIA to do.

I continued to read voraciously, and the memoirs of former CIA officers were at the top of my list. I devoured Bill Colby's *Honorable Men: My Life in the CIA,* Ted Shackley's *Third Option,* and Douglas Blaufarb's *Counterinsurgency Era.* I was also very intrigued by William

Hood's *Mole,* the story of the first Soviet spy handled by CIA, and Dave Phillips's *Night Watch,* about his career in Latin America Division. I'd spent a decade developing my skills as a special operator, and I was trying to get as much of a head start as I could on the new challenges I'd face in CIA.

CAREER TRAINEE

My classmates in the CT Program ranged in age from their early twenties to their early thirties. At thirty, I was on the older side and had a lot more operational experience, which made me stand out. A few classmates were internal transfers who'd already been with the agency for a few years. Most of my classmates were graduates of top schools, and several had master's degrees. A number had fluency in a foreign language, including Chinese and Russian, and a few spoke several. A couple of classmates had grown up overseas, and most had had significant foreign travel or experience studying and living abroad. One had tried out for the Green Bay Packers. A few had prior military service, though I was the only one with a special operations background. Forty percent of my classmates were women; CIA was ahead of its time in the 1980s in seeking out the best talent regardless of gender. Racial diversity was another matter. There, CIA struggled, though it has done much better in recent decades in recruiting people of color. Like my former Special Forces colleagues, my CT classmates were a highly motivated group, having made it through a rigorous selection process just to get in the door. We bonded easily and our esprit de corps was high. The overwhelming majority ended up staying with CIA for a career—the agency's attrition rate is only around 5 percent—though a few left for the foreign service and other pursuits, either during training or after completing one or two assignments.

The Career Trainee Orientation Course introduced CTs to agency organization and the missions and capabilities of its various components. Senior officers from the Directorate of Operations, CIA's Clandestine Service, would tell us stories about important recruitments they had made, ranging from penetrations of the Soviet Foreign Ministry to the Palestine Liberation Organization. Martha "Marti" Peterson (now Marti Shogi), a Directorate of Operations case officer who had served in Moscow, briefed us on the Alexander Ogorodnik, or TRIGON, case. Peterson had successfully handled Ogorodnik, a CIA spy in the Soviet Foreign Ministry who had provided outstanding reporting on Soviet diplomacy and other topics before he was finally caught by the KGB.[3] She described how Ogorodnik had committed suicide with a concealed, agency-provided poison while in detention before the KGB could execute him, driving home the point that espionage is a life-and-death business. The CIA officer who recruited Ogorodnik while he was posted abroad also spoke to our class. From that case and another one we were told about on the recruitment of a PLO official, we learned that a deep personal bond between a case officer and a prospective agent (a "developmental," in CIA parlance) could be a powerful recruiting tool.

We were taught how to prepare the reports an operations officer must complete after meeting with an agent, covering both operational issues and the intelligence obtained. One of our reports officer instructors told our class as she was introducing herself that she had served in Laos during the agency's large paramilitary operation there during the 1960s and early 1970s and that "she'd seen war and she'd seen peace" in her overseas assignments with the agency and "she liked war much better." Her not so tongue-in-cheek remark reminded me of the *New York Times* article Dr. DeRiggi put in front of me that got me interested in the agency. I liked her instantly.

We learned about covert action, including some of the agency's more subtle successes, like providing dissidents in the Soviet Union with miniature copies of Aleksandr Solzhenitsyn's *Gulag Archipelago* and other banned works through a clandestine pipeline.[4] It was impressive and noble work.

Senior officers from the Directorate of Intelligence (now Analysis) told us about the President's Daily Brief and National Intelligence Estimates, major issue papers that looked out three to five years. We learned that the PDB contains the most sensitive and important intelligence the CIA and the U.S. intelligence community has. Senior Directorate of Science and Technology officers told us about key satellite programs (including how a young CIA officer, William Kampiles, had betrayed the CIA and provided the operating manual for the National Reconnaissance Office's most modern imaging satellite to the Soviets), signals intelligence collection, and technical support for CIA operations. We were also given some exposure to the work of CIA's imagery analysts and the instruments they use to reveal things of intelligence interest in 3-D. With my strabismus and amblyopia, I quickly discovered I couldn't see what my non-impaired classmates could, so it was clear that a career processing imagery wasn't in the cards for me. No loss. Officers from CIA's Directorate of Administration (today, the Directorate of Support) covered agency communications, logistics, and medical support. CIA was a worldwide enterprise with a logistics capability that would make FedEx blush.

Career trainees served two or three "interim assignments" as part of their training program. Mine turned out to be anything but typical. When I was asked where I'd like to serve for my first one, I said, "Latin America Division." There was a covert war under way in Central America, and having just completed three years of special operations service there, I wanted to be part of it. I expected to be assigned to the division's Central American Task Force, which was overseeing the war. I was shocked—to put it mildly—when CIA's career training staff informed me that I had been requested by name to serve in LA Division's Caribbean Branch. There must be some mistake, I thought, the Caribbean is where people go on vacation.

Things cleared up as soon as I met with Bill Rooney, the Caribbean Branch chief. The reason I'd been requested by name, Bill told me, was due to one country, Suriname, and my background in Special Forces. The branch's area of operations, as its name implied, included the Caribbean, except for Cuba. (Within LA Division, there was a separate Cuban Operations Group to manage Cuban operations worldwide.) It also included the three Guyanas: British, Dutch (now Suriname), and French. The Caribbean Branch had a large station in Miami that provided "circuit riders" to cover the region, and stations in several Caribbean and a few South American capitals.

A rising star in the Clandestine Service, Bill had served several tours in Latin America and had a great reputation as a recruiter of "hard targets," Soviets, Eastern Europeans, and so on. He had just completed a tour as a chief of station in Central America, where I had briefly met him on one of the counterterrorism intelligence collection missions I had led. It was a demanding assignment, and he appreciated that we had his back. I felt fortunate that he was my first operational boss in the agency. I knew I'd learn a lot, and I wasn't disappointed. Bill would go on to distinguish himself as the CIA's chief in Berlin during the final years of the Cold War and would rise to become chief of the Military and Special Programs Division (later known as the Special Activities Division, and more recently as the Special Activities Center) and then as chief of Latin America Division. He was a key mentor. We became friends and stayed in touch until he passed away in December 2020.

The day I reported into the branch, Bill passed me a satellite photo of a prison in Paramaribo, the capital of Suriname. CIA had an asset who was being held there, and Bill wanted my help in getting him out. The asset was fortunate in some ways to be in prison. Dési Bouterse, Suriname's authoritarian leader, had seized power in a military coup in 1980, and in December 1982 he'd ordered his forces to round up fifteen members of the political opposition and had them summarily executed. I told Bill that I was already quite familiar with the situation in Suriname. The previous December, while still a Special Forces officer, I had been tasked with leading an Emergency Evacuation Assistance Element that had five helicopters assigned to it to evacuate our embassy personnel from Paramaribo, where the political situation had grown very tense. We established a satellite communications link with our embassy in Paramaribo and developed a rescue plan, which we planned to stage out of French Guyana. As we were about to deploy, however, the situation stabilized and our mission was canceled.

Bill asked for my thoughts on how I would pull off a jailbreak. We had an officer, he quickly added, who would be meeting in a few days with a group of smugglers who had access to the area where the prison was located. This is why I joined the CIA, I thought to myself.

My first response was to ask if the smugglers could get access to prison staff and bribe one of them. In that case, there were likely several ways we could arrange an escape, though we'd need more tactical intelligence about prison routines, times during which there were fewer staff, which areas our asset had access to, and so on. Bill told me he was looking for my thoughts on more "direct" options.

The prison was a fairly primitive wooden structure, without an extended guarded perimeter, so a breaching operation was feasible.

The prison was also located close to the coast, so a maritime exfiltration of the asset should be doable. The problem would be getting the asset out of the prison before forces loyal to Bouterse could respond. For that, we would need more intelligence about security forces within the prison, and the speed and capability with which any reaction forces could respond. We obtained that in short order. Surinamese forces were only lightly armed and not very capable.

The most surefire ways to free the asset had already been rejected. The Reagan administration had appealed to the Dutch to intervene militarily in their former colony, but the Dutch supported only noninterventionist actions. CIA had proposed a covert action program using Surinamese exiles and third-country nationals with special operations experience to overthrow Bouterse, but the Reagan administration abandoned the effort after the congressional Intelligence Committees vehemently objected to the proposed "finding," seeing it as another Bay of Pigs in the making. All covert action programs since the later 1970s have required that the president "find" in writing that the proposed operation is necessary to protect our national security interests and report his finding within hours to the congressional Intelligence Committees. The committees then have to authorize the funding for it. Secretary of State George Shultz was also not enamored with the idea.[5]

I told Bill we would need to know a lot more about the smugglers and their capability to pull off such an operation. They would almost certainly require significant training if the operation was to have any chance of success. We could arrange some training, Bill informed me, but time was of the essence. I provided Bill with some questions our officer could ask the smugglers when he met with them to start exploring the feasibility of an operation. Bill said we should meet again as soon as our officer reported back.

Bill, our officer, and I met several times over the next few weeks, including once with the leader of the smuggling network. As I feared, the smugglers did not have the ability to carry out the operation without the benefit of substantial training. I quickly developed a plan to train our smuggler team at one of our clandestine facilities and started working on what we'd need to have in place in Suriname to have a reasonable chance of success, but it was clear that it would be some time before we would be ready to break our asset out of jail. In the end, the agency would conclude that a rescue operation just wasn't feasible. Our asset, fortunately, was eventually freed. Meanwhile, a crisis occurred in another Caribbean country that took me away from my jailbreak planning.

CIA POINT MAN IN GRENADA

Sunday, October 23, 1983, was cold and rainy in Washington as I boarded a CIA aircraft to fly to Bridgetown, Barbados. Bill had called me at my apartment a few hours earlier and told me to come into the office right away and to pack for two weeks. I was being operationally deployed. He didn't tell me where, but I knew it would somehow involve Grenada. Though it was still a closely guarded secret, a U.S. military operation was set to begin there in two days. I stuffed my suitcase with clothes and quickly drove to CIA headquarters.

After I arrived, Bill told me that he, I, and a communicator would go in with the initial invasion force, more specifically with a Special Operations Task Force that would constitute the operation's main effort. We would establish a CIA station and conduct some critical early operations—providing intelligence support to the military during its takedown of the Communist Grenadan government and establishing a clandestine reporting and covert influence network on the island. We would pre-stage in Barbados, where we would be issued all of our necessary weapons and gear. I had been in the CIA just under four months at the time. I wouldn't begin the Operations Course, completion of which was required to "certify" me for CIA operations, until February 1984. It didn't matter. I was going to war with CIA.

––––––––

Located more than fifteen hundred miles south of Florida, with a territory only thirteen miles long and ten miles wide and a population of around 100,000, Grenada hadn't been on my radar screen. Four and a half years earlier, Maurice Bishop, a pro-Cuban Marxist-Leninist and the leader of the New Jewel Movement (New Joint Effort for Welfare, Education, and Liberation), had seized power in a bloodless coup. Within a month, Cuban weapons and advisers began arriving on the island. By September 1979, nearly four hundred Cuban troops had arrived to train a Grenadan three-thousand-man special force. That December, Cuba began a $50 million project using several hundred military engineers to construct a nine-thousand-foot runway at Point Salines, capable of accommodating the largest military aircraft. In January 1980, Grenada had been the only Latin American country other than Cuba to vote against the UN resolution condemning the Soviet invasion of Afghanistan.

The growing Cuban presence on the island got the attention of the Carter White House right from the start. In May 1979, President Carter's national security adviser, Zbigniew Brzezinski, sent the DCI, Stansfield Turner, a memo outlining the president's concern and suggested a covert effort to counter Cuban influence. CIA responded with a draft presidential finding that would authorize a covert effort to support resistance to the Marxist regime on Grenada and a return to democracy. Carter signed the finding on July 3. The Senate Intelligence Committee strongly objected, arguing that the covert program was inconsistent with the administration's position on nonintervention, and informed the president that they couldn't support the effort.[6] Covert action had fallen out of favor since the end of the Vietnam War and wouldn't be revived as a key policy instrument until the Soviets invaded Afghanistan. As a result, the Grenada problem would fester until President Reagan's military intervention four years later.

The presence of Cuban military advisers and the ongoing construction of the large airport at Point Salines increasingly concerned the Reagan administration. Recent satellite imagery had noted the Cubans were constructing military-style revetments and fuel storage facilities, and the large airfield when completed could pose a threat to American interests in the region. Still, some in the Reagan administration thought that Bishop might be co-opted, and in May 1983 the administration tried to woo him away from the Soviet Union and Cuba, to no avail. Perhaps fearful that Bishop was about to break with the revolution, on October 13 Bernard Coard, Grenada's deputy prime minister and the leader of a more radical faction in the Communist government, had Bishop placed under house arrest. On October 19, Grenada's Army chief and an ally of Coard's, Hudson Austin, had Bishop and his supporters executed by firing squad. Radio Free Grenada, headed by Coard's wife, Phyllis, then announced the formation of the Revolutionary Military Council, headed by Austin. Approximately six hundred Americans were attending medical school in Grenada, and the State Department's leadership grew increasingly concerned for their safety.

With the situation on the island rapidly deteriorating, CIA established the Grenada Task Force on October 19 to more closely monitor the fast-breaking events. When I reported in for work on the morning of October 20, I was immediately tasked with assembling the latest intelligence, preparing talking points, and putting together a Grenada briefing book for CIA's senior leadership. Vice Admiral John Poindexter, the deputy national security adviser, convened the Crisis Preplanning Group. Later that evening, Vice President Bush convened the Special Situation Group, the highest-level crisis management group in the Reagan administration. I worked nonstop all day and very late into the night, providing regular updates to the CIA's deputy director, John McMahon, and Dewey Clarridge, the chief of the DO's Latin America Division.

Our intelligence on Grenada was limited; there was no American embassy or CIA station on the island. The Soviets and Cubans both had large embassies. Other Soviet bloc nations and the Libyans were present there as well. To rectify this somewhat, Clarridge had Linda Flohr, a CIA officer stationed in Barbados, travel to Grenada with the State Department's consular team that was headed there to check on the well-being of the American medical students. Flohr provided important reporting over the weekend on the airfield at Point Salines and the heavy machine gun emplacements around the southern portion of the island.[7]

Back in Washington, the situation grew even more intense. On October 21, the Organization of Eastern Caribbean States formally requested U.S. intervention. The night before, the Special Situation Group chaired by Vice President Bush had also recommended military intervention.

On Saturday morning, October 22, the National Security Planning Group, the U.S. government's top national security decision-making body, chaired by President Reagan, was convened via teleconference to consider the OECS request and SSG recommendation. Bill Casey was on travel in Europe, so Deputy Director McMahon attended for CIA. To support him, I worked through the night on Friday and remained at CIA until mid-afternoon on Saturday.

The invasion of Grenada would be the largest military operation since the Vietnam War, and Secretary of Defense Caspar Weinberger and the Joint Chiefs were initially less than enthusiastic about it. On Saturday morning, however, President Reagan, on travel in Georgia with Secretary of State George Shultz and National Security Adviser Bud McFarlane, approved a military operation to rescue the American students and to restore democracy to Grenada.[8] Cautioned by his political advisers that the operation could have negative implications for his reelection chances, Reagan replied, "My reelection and national security issues are very divisible. We go."[9]

While the principal motivation for the operation was the safety of American students, the chaotic situation also presented a strategic opportunity to deal Cuba a blow and put Grenada back on a better course. The invasion was set for the predawn hours of October 25. Two days earlier, the president had redirected a naval task force bound for the Middle East to the Caribbean. Word of this unfortunately soon leaked, and Castro began preparing for the defense of Grenada. On October 22, he sent one of his top commanders, Colonel Pedro Tortolo Comas, to the island. The Cubans primarily prepared for a "Bay of Pigs" invasion across the beach, but also placed bulldozers on the runway at Point Salines to block any air landing there. The Cubans also advised Austin that Grenada would need to keep the American students as hostages when the Marines came across the beach, so the Grenadan government rejected a last-minute request by the United States to allow the American students to leave via a cruise ship that had been diverted for that purpose.

The U.S. invasion had been planned in three days. General Jack Vessey, the chairman of the Joint Chiefs of Staff, had a large and direct role in shaping the operational design of the invasion. The operation was conceived as a coup de main, a single strike to take down the Grenadan government. A Special Operations Task Force would assault the southern portion of the island, while a Marine Corps Task Force would assault the north. The Special Operations Task Force would be reinforced and relieved in the south by the 82nd Airborne Division following initial operations. The overall commander for the operation was Vice Admiral Joseph Metcalf, commander of the Navy's Second Fleet. Then Major General Norman Schwarzkopf was assigned as the overall ground operations adviser (and later, deputy commander) to Admiral Metcalf.[10]

———

I had gone home Saturday afternoon expecting to work a night shift beginning late Sunday afternoon, but Bill's call on Sunday morning changed all that. As soon as I arrived at CIA headquarters and Bill told me where he and I were going, I thought all the suits I had packed weren't going to do me much good. I was being sent in with the invasion force. Fortunately, I had packed a few casual clothes.

Before we left for the airport, we received our operational guidance via secure call from Dewey Clarridge and Jim Glerum, the chief of the International Activities Division, CIA's covert action arm. Joining us was Dick B., a paramilitary operations officer assigned to CIA's Special Operations Group. Dick, who had served in the 10th Special Forces Group before he joined the agency, had conducted a clandestine reconnaissance of Grenada six months earlier, identifying beach landing sites and other areas of potential operational interest. He had also worked for Bill on the aborted Suriname covert action.

Our call with Clarridge and Glerum was largely a last-minute "signals check." Both were experienced operations officers. Clarridge had served in Nepal, India, Turkey, and Italy and had headed up Arab Operations during a previous assignment at CIA headquarters. Glerum had overseen paramilitary operations in Indonesia and Laos and had served in Hong Kong and other locales in the Far East. Our plan was still very much a work in progress, and both knew that they'd have to rely on our operational judgment as the situation evolved.

Joining us for the plane ride down to Barbados was Andy P., the chief of the Covert Media Group within the International Activities Division, and a senior State Department officer. Part of our plan involved identifying candidates for the interim government that would govern Grenada until elections could be held. I'd read about covert political action—the CIA's support for Christian Democrats in Italy during the 1948 election, for example—but reading about it and being involved in it are two different things. It was pretty heady stuff.

On Monday, October 24, at our station in Bridgetown, I was issued a Browning Hi-Power 9 mm pistol and $15,000 in East Caribbean currency, which I could use to pay assets that we hoped to reactivate once on the island. I had been a special operator for more than a decade, and I felt as ready as I could be for what would follow.

Grenada's armed forces consisted of about three hundred active soldiers, called the People's Revolutionary Army, supplemented by another thousand or so partially trained militia, about thirteen hundred troops in all. Eight Soviet BTR-60 armored personnel carriers and two BRDM-2 scout cars, all armed with heavy 14.5 mm machine guns, constituted the PRA's main strike force. The main threat to the U.S. intervention force was the seven hundred–plus Cuban "construction workers" who were organized into military units. The Cubans also had Soviet ZU-23 (23 mm) anti-aircraft guns positioned around Point Salines airfield and other key facilities in the south, along with several 12.7 mm heavy machine guns. We expected the Cubans to put up a tough fight.

CIA's immediate tasks in the operation were threefold: to help pave the way for military intervention; to obtain a formal request for intervention from Governor-General Sir Paul Scoon (who was being held under house arrest); and to rescue an asset of ours who was being held in Richmond Hill Prison. We would go in with the Special Operations Task Force, the main effort for the operation. We didn't plan to have a CIA officer accompany the Marines, who had a supporting role in the operation. After the initial assault was completed, we would set up a CIA station and conduct additional intelligence missions as circumstances dictated.

The Special Operations Task Force included Navy SEALs, an Army special operations unit, Rangers, and special operations aviation elements. Bill would accompany a SEAL assault force to free Governor-General Scoon and obtain his formal request for intervention. Scoon had passed on his request informally a few days earlier to a State Department consular officer, but the administration rightly wanted something more formal. I would accompany the Army's two Ranger Battalions and the lead elements of the 82nd Airborne Division in their seizure of Point Salines airfield, where we planned to establish our CIA station. A few miles away, an Army special operations unit would assault Richmond Hill Prison in St. George's, where our asset and a number of other political prisoners were being held, while another SEAL element would conduct an assault to seize Radio Free Grenada.

The night before the invasion Dick B. was supposed to go in with an asset of ours who owned property in Grenada on a specially equipped CIA helicopter with a forward-looking infrared radar. The plan was to occupy an overwatch position located on the asset's property that overlooked the airfield. The asset, however, got cold feet at the last minute, and Dick's mission had to be aborted. It was frustrating, to say the least, but wasn't central to our plan.

To provide additional tactical intelligence before the invasion, four-man teams of Navy SEALs were dropped by parachute on October 24 into the water off Point Salines on Grenada's southwest side and off Pearls airfield on the island's northeast side. The team inserted off Pearls accomplished its mission, reporting that the beach conditions did not favor an amphibious landing. Accordingly, the Marines changed their plan to assault "over the beach" via helicopters. Tragedy, however, struck the SEAL Teams inserted off Point Salines. Parachuting into the water in darkness and encountering unexpectedly rough seas, one four-man team vanished without a trace.

The original plan was for the Special Operations Task Force to assault under the cover of darkness in the early morning of October 25. The jump-off time was delayed by an hour and a half, however, to conduct additional reconnaissance of Point Salines and then due to a mechanical problem with one of the transport aircraft and the late arrival of the assault helicopters. Launching the operation in daylight caused additional U.S. casualties and initial mission failures.

The Ranger assault on Point Salines had called for air-dropping one company, with the remaining elements of the two battalions air landing after the runway had been cleared. After receiving additional intelligence during the flight that the Cubans had placed more obstacles on the runway, Lieutenant Colonel Wes Taylor, the 1st Battalion commander, ordered his entire battalion to rig en route for airdrop. To minimize the time his soldiers would be exposed to anti-aircraft fire, Taylor also lowered the drop altitude to five hundred feet.

Both turned out to be very good decisions. No Rangers were killed or wounded due to anti-aircraft fire. Hot-wiring a bulldozer and using it to clear obstacles strewn on the runway and assault Cuban positions, the Rangers, aided by Air Force and Navy air support, swiftly attacked and overwhelmed the Cuban defenders. Within two hours the airfield had been secured. By 9:00 a.m., the Rangers had rescued 138 American medical students at the True Blue campus adjacent to the airfield, and by noon all of the high ground around the airfield had been secured. A bit later, they forced the surrender of 150 Cubans at a military camp at Calliste, north of the airfield, bringing the total Cubans captured to more than 400.

The SEALs and Army special operators fared much worse. The shift from a night to a daylight assault cost both units the element of surprise. As SEALs fast-roped into Governor-General Scoon's residence, they came under withering fire, and only a portion of the assault force made it inside. The helicopter carrying Bill and Captain Robert Gormly, the SEAL Team commander, had been badly shot up and had to fly off and abort the mission. Despite suffering several wounded personnel, the SEALs, aided by air strikes, successfully held off repeated assaults by Grenadan forces. They were rescued by a Marine force the next day. Governor-General Scoon survived unharmed and signed the formal request for U.S. intervention.

The assault on Richmond Hill Prison was even less successful. Arriving at their objective in daylight, the Army special operations assault force lost the element of surprise, just as the SEALs assaulting the governor-general's residence had, and after receiving heavy fire from 12.7 mm machine guns, the mission was aborted. All six helicopters in the flight had been badly shot up. One Black Hawk pilot had been killed by gunfire, and twenty-two special operators had been wounded, some critically. That ended the Army special operations unit's operations on the island. The assault on Radio Free Grenada was initially successful, but a Grenadan counterattack with armored vehicles forced the SEAL unit that had taken it to retreat and swim out to sea where a U.S. destroyer recovered them. Our most elite units were being repelled, but what couldn't be achieved with precise special operations raids was quickly made up for with overwhelming force, as the Rangers, Marines, and 82nd Airborne secured their initial objectives and advanced across the island.

As soon as the initial wave of Rangers had secured the airfield at Point Salines, I air landed with the follow-on force and linked up with Bill, who'd flown in with our communicator on a helicopter from the USS *Guam* a few minutes earlier. I went into Grenada with my handgun, a bag of operational cash to pay assets, and quite literally the shirt on my back—an olive-green Ralph Lauren polo, linen pants, and loafers, having packed completely inappropriately for a combat mission I didn't know I was going on. No one can say that we don't go to war in style at CIA! Our travel bags with our remaining clothes were supposed to follow on a subsequent flight, but somehow our bags got misplaced at the military airport in Barbados and didn't show up until the operation was almost over. My stylish outfit got riper as the days passed. Fortunately, Admiral Metcalf, the operation's commander, arranged to get us Navy dungarees when we met with him and the senior State Department representative about a week into the operation after combat was largely over. What I lost in style, I made up in cleanliness and utility.

Immediately after I landed, I scrounged several AK-47 assault rifles, magazines, and 7.62 mm ammunition that had been captured from the Cubans from former colleagues in the 2nd Ranger Battalion, along with three parachutes for us to sleep in. The CIA had armed us with handguns, but I wanted weapons with more firepower, just in case. The Rangers were happy to let us have all the AKs we wanted, and I took several of them for station defense, but they wanted their parachutes back as soon as we acquired more suitable bedding. We hot-wired a large Cuban construction truck abandoned on the airfield, and it became our initial means of transport until the CIA's Office of Logistics purchased and flew in a Suzuki jeep for us. We took over the Jamaican ambassador's residence overlooking the airfield and began setting up the CIA station.

The lead elements of two brigades of the 82nd Airborne Division also air landed on the afternoon of the twenty-fifth, along with the division headquarters. After the special operators redeployed to their home bases, the 82nd became our most important military partner. As the lead elements of the 82nd joined the Rangers on the airfield perimeter, they found themselves under attack by a Grenadan column of BTR-60s. They successfully repelled the attack, but it caused Major General Edward Trobaugh, the 82nd commander, to accelerate the flow of infantry battalions to ensure he had overwhelming combat power. And overwhelm Grenada's remaining defenses it did, an early example for me of using all means available.

Around 1:00 p.m. on October 26, the second day of the operation, Bill and I were informed that an 82nd company had discovered a major arms storage facility north of the airfield. We ran to the division tactical operations center and told General Trobaugh that we wanted to see the site. Trobaugh's operations officer warned us that there was still fighting going on in the area. Duly warned, we jumped in a jeep with a major from Trobaugh's staff and drove to Frequente, the site of the captured arms and ammunition.

As Bill and I arrived at Frequente, the troops from C Company, 2nd Battalion, 325th Infantry had just deployed in a defensive position around the site. They were clearly on edge. We examined the warehouses, surrounded by barbed wire and a chain-link fence, that the troops had just captured. Inside were large quantities of Soviet- and Cuban-supplied small arms and military equipment, enough, it turned out, to outfit six infantry battalions, far in excess of Grenada's military needs.

A few minutes after we exited the warehouse, a firefight broke out, and Bill and I hit the dirt, as Cuban rounds whizzed by. Cuban forces had ambushed the battalion's reconnaissance platoon, and a sustained engagement with machine guns, mortars, and small arms erupted. The major who accompanied us, his face down in the dirt, looked at me and said, "This is it, the Big C, combat." I said, "Yep." Bill and I had brought only our Browning Hi-Power handguns with us to the site, so I told Bill to stay put and keep his head down while I got some better weapons for us. I low crawled and then sprinted back into the warehouse to grab a couple of AK-47s and canvas chest packs containing magazines of AK ammunition and then ran, dived, and crawled back to rejoin the company's defensive position. I told the sergeant on my left, the squad leader in charge of this portion of Charlie Company's perimeter, that I was CIA and a former Special Forces officer. He asked me what he should do. I told him to just keep returning fire and encouraging his men. After ten minutes or so, the battle was over. The Cubans broke contact and fled, leaving four dead behind. Bill and I returned to the station and reported what we'd seen to CIA headquarters.

Earlier that morning, Bill and I had visited the Cuban ambassador's residence, which had been abandoned by the Cubans at the outset of the invasion. U.S. soldiers had trashed the residence and had written scatological graffiti on the walls, expressing disgust at the ambassador's wife, an American from Chicago named Gail Reed. Reed had illegally traveled to Cuba as early as 1970 as a member of the Venceremos Brigade, American students sympathetic to the Cuban revolution who went there to harvest sugarcane. She became radicalized further and had married Julian Torres Rizo, a Cuban diplomat, in 1978. The couple was posted to Grenada a year later. To say the least, she was not a favorite among American troops engaged in combat with her adopted comrades.

Good intelligence remained in short supply during the first several days of the operation. After rescuing the American students at the True Blue campus on the twenty-fifth, the Rangers learned that there was another campus farther north at Grand Anse. On the twenty-sixth, the 2nd Ranger Battalion, transported in Marine helicopters, assaulted the Grand Anse campus, overcame the Grenadan defenders, and rescued 233 additional students. The Rangers then learned that a large contingent of Americans resided near Lance aux Epines, east of Point Salines. On the twenty-eighth, the fourth day of the operation, the final group of students was rescued, bringing the total to 581.

On October 27, we received a cable from CIA headquarters informing us that the United States had intelligence that Libya's mercurial leader, Muammar Qaddafi, had instructed his ambassador in Grenada to take American hostages. CIA had additional intelligence that confirmed that a Libyan intelligence operative was assigned to its embassy in St. George's, and Dewey Clarridge had instructed us to find the operative and bring him into American custody.

The commander of the Special Operations Task Force had left behind an eight-man military liaison element in the station that included several SEAL operatives, so we briefed them on the intelligence and asked the Army lieutenant colonel in charge if a few of them could accompany us on the mission. He relayed our request to his command's headquarters in North Carolina but was told to stand down; they were to conduct no more operations. Undeterred, Bill told me to get my AK. We'd go find and capture the Libyan operative by ourselves. Seeing me grab my AK and head out of the station, a SEAL operative said, "Man, you guys have balls." I nodded and hoped that we weren't thinking with them. We'll just have to make do with what we have, I assured myself. Bill certainly didn't lack for confidence.

Bill asked a case officer and former Marine to join us, and off we went into St. George's in the new Suzuki jeep the Office of Logistics had flown in for us the day before. After some effort, we found the Libyan embassy, a two-story structure with reinforced steel doors, and asked to speak with the ambassador about an urgent matter. He appeared on the second-floor balcony and invited us to come in.

"We need to talk to you outside, Mr. Ambassador," Bill shouted.

"No, you come inside," the ambassador responded.

Acutely aware of the intelligence that had sent us there, the craziness of Muammar Qaddafi, and fearing that we could become hostages ourselves, we went back and forth with the ambassador a few times, trying to persuade him to come outside. After it was clear the ambassador wasn't going to budge, Bill made the decision for the two of us to go in. He instructed the case officer and former Marine who had accompanied us to wait down the street about fifty yards with our AK-47s and jeep while we went in with only our Browning Hi-Power handguns for protection. Our backup registered a brief protest against the idea, believing that we'd taken leave of our senses, but complied with Bill's instructions. I chambered a round and took the safety off of my weapon.

After we exchanged the briefest of pleasantries, Bill asked the ambassador about the whereabouts of his intelligence officer colleague. The ambassador said he hadn't seen him in three days and thought he might be at the Soviet embassy. Now, why would he be there? we asked. The ambassador said he didn't know. I added that we had concerns that someone might get the crazy idea to take hostages and that we wanted him to know that if that were to occur, there were eight thousand U.S. troops on the island who would resolve the matter with all necessary force. To make sure he got the message and in case anything should go wrong, I kept my hand on my sidearm, which was tucked into my front trousers and very visible to the ambassador— diplomacy, CIA style. We told him to call us immediately if the intelligence officer returned. We then left to rejoin our very relieved colleague standing watch down the street. We later confirmed that the Libyan operative had indeed beat feet to the Soviet embassy. At least no American hostages were taken.

Combat operations were largely over by the twenty-eighth. On the twenty-ninth, the Marines captured Bernard Coard, and Hudson Austin was captured by the 82nd Airborne. Both were initially sentenced to death for the murder of Maurice Bishop and other Grenadan citizens, but their sentences were later commuted to life in prison. They were released from prison in 2007 and 2008, respectively.

The last bit of operational drama was the evacuation of the Soviet embassy. Armed Cuban troops had sought refuge there, and we did not want them to leave with their weapons, since they would be evacuated on U.S. Navy aircraft. Among the troops was Castro's commander, Colonel Tortolo. It was said that the only injury he had sustained during the operation was a hurt thumb from ringing the Soviet embassy's doorbell so hard. Sure enough, the Soviets tried to smuggle out large quantities of weapons in crates marked "Foreign Ministry, Moscow, USSR," but were caught in the act.

Our new station in Grenada grew rapidly during the operation. Beginning on the twenty-sixth, CIA officers flowed in and the station soon surpassed fifty personnel. Many were Spanish-speaking case officers from across Latin America, sent to Grenada to assist with the interrogation of Cuban detainees, which became our principal focus as combat operations wound down. Significant intelligence was obtained about Cuban operations, and opportunities to collect more down the road were fully exploited. One of my early tasks was to set up the defense of the station, brief incoming personnel on the situation, and provide them with familiarization training on the use of the Soviet small arms I had obtained. Given my close relationship with Bill and participation in major operations, several mid-level CIA officers who had flown in assumed I was the deputy chief of station and asked where I had previously served. They were surprised when I told them I had been with CIA for all of four months.

The press had been excluded from the operation for the first three days. When they were finally let in, a few foreign opinion leaders who were covert influence assets of ours were among them. Bill asked me to meet with them to go over the press themes we wanted them to emphasize in their countries, and to arrange for them to see the conditions political prisoners had been subjected to under the Marxist government. Covert influence operations were new to me, but I took on the task with alacrity. As I looked for our asset in the press gaggle, I overheard some major network broadcast reporters, all decked out in their finest, discussing the nightlife they longed to get back to in Barbados. It was a bit surreal after several days of combat, but after I made contact with our asset and found a discreet place for us to chat, I refocused on the themes we wanted him to emphasize.

A couple days later, Dewey Clarridge visited the station to see how his troops were doing. Linda Flohr, the case officer who had been inserted into Grenada before the invasion, joined us, and we had a good time filling Dewey in on what had transpired over the past several days. After the operation, Dewey's jeep could be seen in the headquarters parking lot sporting a new bumper sticker: "Nicaragua's Next."

Two weeks into the operation, and with combat operations over, we received a cable from CIA headquarters directing me to return to Washington. CIA's career training staff hadn't been informed that I'd been sent on a combat operation before I had completed my operational training, and needless to say, it caused them some heart palpitations. Truth be told, that's one of the things I loved about CIA: its flexibility and its focus on doing whatever it takes to get the job done. I turned over my firearm and what was left of the operational funds I received before the invasion to Bill and hitched a ride on a military transport to Barbados, where I dumped my dungarees in a trash can in the men's room at the airport, changed into a white guayabera and dress slacks, and bought an airline ticket home with my American Express card. I kept the Polo shirt and linen pants as keepsakes.

I felt as if I had just participated in something momentous. Going to war with CIA was pretty cool. I brought a Cuban soldier's belt home and gave it to Colonel Russell, my former Special Forces battalion commander, who had given me the special counterterrorism command. He knew better than to ask for too many details about how I'd obtained it.

———

Grenada was the first rollback of Soviet and Cuban power by the United States in the Third World. Far more significant setbacks would soon follow for the Communists. The invasion also showed that the United States had begun to recover from the "Vietnam syndrome"— the American public's perceived aversion to overseas military intervention.

The invasion had been a humiliation and foreign policy disaster for Castro. The Cubans had suffered twenty-five killed and 59 wounded. Ambassador Torres was stripped of his rank and imprisoned without the benefit of trial for his failure to detect the coup against Bishop. Colonel Tortolo was brought before a secret tribunal that reduced him in rank to private for his inability to mount an effective defense and was shipped off to Angola, where he died in 1986. The Grenadans had forty-five killed and 358 wounded.

From a U.S. perspective, the invasion was successful—but costly. The U.S. military lost nineteen killed in action and had another 116 wounded. Thirteen of the killed in action were special operators. While the invasion's conceptual design as a special-operations-intensive coup de main had been innovative, its execution had been badly flawed. Problems with planning, joint doctrine, intelligence, command and control, communications, and logistics abounded. As a result, a number of major congressionally imposed reforms followed in the operation's wake: the 1986 Goldwater-Nichols Act, which strengthened the role of the JCS chairman and the unified combatant commanders and made the military more joint in structure; and the 1987 Nunn-Cohen reforms, which established the U.S. Special Operations Command.

For CIA, the impact was far more modest, a few already very successful careers propelled forward even more. For me, though, it was a big leap forward, one that would be followed by far greater leaps in responsibility in the coming years. A year after the operation, I received an award for heroism for my role in it. The Career Training Program staff dined out on my experience for a couple of years after the operation, telling trainees that they, too, might be sent into dangerous situations as I had been. And in the Caribbean Branch, Bill's secretary had welcomed us back to the office with a poster of *The Magnificent Seven* that had our faces superimposed on the actors'.

The Grenada operation remains a great example of the rapid action and improvisation that is a hallmark of the agency. We made much of it up as we went along. I learned how CIA could go to war alongside the U.S. military and integrate its operations with the military's special operations forces, foreshadowing what CIA would do two decades later in Afghanistan and Iraq. I learned how to establish a station from the ground up in a very austere environment and saw firsthand the amazing responsiveness and reach of CIA's logistics enterprise. I learned a few things about clandestine intelligence collection and covert action: how to build and reconstitute intelligence networks from nothing; that it's important not to focus solely on the immediate collection task at hand but to look for any opportunities to gain new intelligence and sow doubt in an adversary about his operations; and how political action and covert influence operations can contribute to mission success. All in all, not a bad couple weeks' work for a brand-new CIA officer who had yet to complete training.

My next assignment would provide far more sobering lessons.

4

COUNTERTERRORISM OPERATIONS, OPERATIONAL CERTIFICATION

WELCOME TO THE MIDDLE EAST

On October 23, 1983, the very day I had flown to Barbados to stage for the Grenada operation, a massive truck bomb exploded at the Marine barracks at Beirut International Airport, killing 241 American servicemen. A nineteen-ton yellow Mercedes-Benz truck crashed through the five-foot barrier of concertina wire protecting the building, passed through an open gate between two sentry posts, and smashed into the lobby of the building. The Marine sentries guarding the entrance were not allowed to have their weapons loaded and didn't get off a shot. In the bed of the truck was pentaerythritol tetranitrate, or PETN, a high explosive we would later learn had been supplied by Iran, along with canisters of compressed butane. The bomb rested on concrete and a slab of marble to direct the blast upward. The improvised fuel-air explosive bomb detonated with a force of twenty-one thousand pounds of TNT, collapsing the four-story building that housed the 24th Marine Amphibious Unit. It was the single deadliest day for the U.S. Marine Corps since the Battle of Iwo Jima. The driver of the truck was an Iranian national. Minutes later, a similar truck bomb, about half the size of the one that had struck the Marine compound, was detonated by remote control at the French military barracks six kilometers away, killing 58 paratroopers. It was France's worst military loss since the Algerian War.

Six months earlier, a black GMC pickup carrying two thousand pounds of explosives had crashed into the American embassy, killing sixty-three, including seventeen Americans and eight CIA officers. Among the dead were CIA's top Middle East analyst, Bob Ames, the agency's chief of station in Beirut, Ken Haas, and his deputy, Jim Lewis. CIA's intelligence capabilities in Beirut had suffered a crippling blow. A shadowy, pro-Iranian group called the Islamic Jihad Organization (IJO) claimed credit for all three bombings. A new era of mass-casualty terrorism had been born.

––––––––––

After my return from Grenada on November 10, I was informed by CIA's Career Training Staff that I was being given another directed assignment. The Near East and South Asia Division was forming a Counterterrorism Task Force to respond to the Beirut bombings, and I had been requested by name to serve on it. I hadn't thought about serving in NE Division; with my Russian and Czech, I had requested an assignment to Soviet and East European Division, but was pleased that I had been asked for by name for another special assignment, and needless to say, I wanted to do everything I could to bring justice to those responsible for these attacks. I was told to report to Sam Wyman, the chief of Arab-Israeli Operations in NE Division. Wyman was one of the agency's premier Arabists, having served multiple tours in the Middle East, most recently as chief of station. He had spoken to our Career Trainee Orientation Course and could reasonably pass for Sean Connery.

I joined the NE Task Force and got right to work. I had led tactical counterterrorism intelligence operations in the Special Forces; now I would learn how the CIA approached CT intelligence and operations. Our first assignment was to try to attribute responsibility for the Marine barracks bombing. The principal threat stream seemed to run through Ali Akbar Mohtashamipur, the Iranian ambassador to Syria, to Ahmad Kan'ani, the commander of the Islamic Revolutionary Guard Corps Brigade located at Sheikh Abdullah barracks in Ba'albek in Lebanon's Beka'a Valley. A late September message we had intercepted from the Iranian Ministry of Intelligence and Security in Tehran to Mohtashamipur in Damascus instructed Kan'ani to contact Hussein Musawi, leader of the newly formed Shi'ite militia

Islamic Amal, and order him "to take a spectacular action against the United States Marines." Unfortunately, the intelligence wasn't passed by the director of naval intelligence to the Marines until October 25, two days after the bombing. U.S. intelligence had provided a general warning of the impending attack a month before the bombing, but excessive compartmentalization had prevented its dissemination. Had that sensitive reporting been shared in a timely manner, 241 American servicemen might not have lost their lives.

We believed that IJO was a cover name for Islamic Amal, a radical breakaway faction from Amal, the Shi'ite political party led by Nabih Berri. The group had been formed by Iran in the summer of 1982 in response to the Israeli invasion of Lebanon. The Israelis had gone into Lebanon to eject one enemy, the Palestine Liberation Organization, and in the process they created another. IJO would soon become known as Hezbollah, the Party of God. Mohtashamipur had played a key role in creating Hezbollah.[1] The group's spiritual adviser was Ayatollah Mohammed Hussein Fadlallah.

Hussein Musawi and Islamic Amal had seized Sheikh Abdullah barracks from the Lebanese gendarmerie in November 1982, and immediately turned it over to Iran's Islamic Revolutionary Guard Corps, which moved in with fifteen hundred troops. We had imagery that showed that the truck used in the Marine barracks bombing had been prepared at the IRGC camp. We had additional intelligence reporting asserting that Sheikh Fadlallah had blessed the driver.

The Iranians and their Islamic Amal/Hezbollah proxies were waging a covert war in Lebanon, not just against the Israelis, but also against the United States and the multinational force. Their principal instruments were suicide bombings and kidnappings. David Dodge, the acting president of the American University of Beirut, was the first American kidnapped. On July 19, 1982, Dodge was abducted on the AUB campus by Islamic Amal and then trucked to Damascus, where a waiting Iran Air flight transported him to Tehran. Dodge spent a year in prison in Iran before Syria, Iran's only ally in the region, pressured the Iranians to release him. Iran's first foray into kidnapping Americans had been too overt; future victims of Hezbollah would be held in secret prisons in Lebanon.

Evidence tying Iran and Islamic Amal/Hezbollah to the bombings was fairly strong from the outset, but there was clandestine reporting that pointed to Syrian intelligence as well. The Iranian embassy in Damascus had transferred $50,000 to finance the operation, a Syrian intelligence lieutenant colonel had been involved in its planning, and Sheikh Fadlallah had been in Damascus three days before the bombing to discuss attack plans.[2] Our task force developed a list of potential targets for counterterrorism action, but most of them, such as Sheikh Fadlallah's residence, were high-rise buildings in heavily populated areas, and thus not suitable for a strike. (In March 1985, Lebanese intelligence attempted to kill Fadlallah with a car bomb parked outside his building, killing eighty and wounding two hundred more. CIA was not involved. Fadlallah died of old age in 2010.) I went over the targets with Bill Buckley, our new chief of station, and worked with Beirut Station case officers to target the Islamic Amal network. I admired Buckley. In addition to service as a Green Beret, he had been a founder of CIA's Counterterrorism Group and had served as a paramilitary operations officer in Laos. He was a brave and thoroughly decent man who brought renewed energy to Beirut Station.

Recruiting and handling assets who had access to our targets and who could meet with us in divided Beirut was a major challenge. This was my first experience with denied-area CT operations—acquiring intelligence from assets in the most hostile of operational environments. We had one asset, a young Shi'ite from South Beirut, who was able to provide clandestine photography of several important targets. His reporting helped us identify potential targets and assess how well they were guarded and whether there was reasonable access to them. Most of the targets were located deep in Hezbollah territory. I still hadn't been to the CIA's Operations Course, but between Suriname, Grenada, and Lebanon, I was getting a pretty good look at the ins and outs of espionage.

Ultimately, the most suitable target for a CT strike was Sheikh Abdullah barracks, so that is where we focused most of our immediate energy. President Reagan was prepared to authorize a strike, but Secretary Weinberger and some of the Joint Chiefs were opposed, citing insufficient evidence of Iranian complicity, and the attack was never carried out. French warplanes did attack the barracks in mid-November, but their bombs missed their targets. On December 4, two U.S. aircraft carriers, *Kennedy* and *Independence*, launched a twenty-eight-plane strike package against Syrian air defenses near the facility, but managed to destroy only a couple of gun positions and a radar. Two planes were shot down and a third was damaged. One pilot was killed, and another, Lieutenant Robert Goodman, was captured. He remained in a Syrian prison until Jesse Jackson negotiated his release a month later. CIA's role in these strikes was limited to providing supporting intelligence.

Sam Wyman had also tasked me with developing a plan to employ U.S. Special Forces under CIA authorities to target Syrian forces in Lebanon. I came up with a design that looked very similar to the plan we had developed for Nicaragua several months earlier: a Special Forces battalion and SEAL task force, working with Lebanese forces, supported by air, artillery, and naval gunfire. But the disastrous U.S. air strike against Syrian air defenses put an end to that planning.

Three and a half months after the Marine barracks bombing, facing strong opposition in Congress, President Reagan ended the U.S. military presence in Lebanon. The U.S. military and intelligence posture in Lebanon had been too weak to make a difference. It was a good decision on President Reagan's part, just as putting the Marines in there under untenable conditions had been a bad decision. Hezbollah had killed more Americans than any other terrorist group, and they had gotten away with it.

I left the Special Counterterrorism Task Force in early February 1984 to finally attend the Operations Course. I was sickened to learn a few months later that Bill Buckley had been kidnapped by Hezbollah. He was tortured and had every bone in his body broken. He died in captivity in June 1985. His remains were dumped on the side of the road near Beirut Airport in 1991 and repatriated to the United States. He rests today in Arlington National Cemetery. He is an American hero.

In 1986, a Near Eastern intelligence service provided CIA with the identity of Buckley's captor: Imad Mughniyeh. Born in the southern suburbs of Beirut to a poor Shi'a family, Mughniyeh had originally been recruited into the PLO's intelligence unit, Force 17. After the PLO was expelled from Beirut in 1982, Mughniyeh was recruited into Islamic Amal/Hezbollah by the IRGC. He was only twenty years old at the time. In addition to kidnapping and torturing Bill Buckley to death, Mughniyeh was implicated in the Marine barracks bombing, the bombing of the U.S. embassy annex in 1984, the hijacking of TWA

Flight 847, the murder of the U.S. Navy diver Robert Stethem in 1985, the kidnapping of dozens of Westerners in Lebanon during the 1980s, the 1992 bombing of the Israeli embassy in Buenos Aires, the 1994 bombing of a Jewish cultural center in Argentina, and the bombing of Khobar Towers in 1996 in Saudi Arabia that killed nineteen American servicemen—though Khobar Towers was likely the work of Saudi Hezbollah, not Lebanese Hezbollah. He had one of the longest rap sheets of any terrorist in history and had made a lot of enemies.

The challenge for his many enemies was finding him in a place where something could be done about it. With sanctuary in Iran since the mid-1980s, Mughniyeh was largely out of reach—until he wasn't. On February 12, 2008, he died in a precision strike that targeted and killed only him. After he attended a reception celebrating the twenty-ninth anniversary of the Iranian Revolution in Damascus that evening, a bomb that had been placed in his Mitsubishi Pajero exploded as he sat down in the driver's seat, blowing him across the road, severing his arms and legs from his body.[3] As an assistant secretary of defense, I traveled to Lebanon shortly after Mughniyeh's death. While driving from the airport through Hezbollah territory in South Beirut on the way to our new embassy, I saw scores of posters with pictures of him along the highway commemorating his "martyred" death. Images of Bill Buckley flashed through my mind. "Bill, your tormentor is no more."

Grenada and Lebanon were the only two military interventions with U.S. boots on the ground during the Reagan administration. Whereas Grenada had been an exhilarating experience for me, Lebanon was a searing one. It was a counterterrorism campaign the United States clearly lost, with tragic consequences. I had played a minimal role, and there was nothing I could have done that would have changed the outcome, but there's no escaping the fact that I felt as if CIA had failed and that I had failed too. Decades later, I would reflect back on this experience as we sought to penetrate al-Qa'ida's leadership and target it for action and counter Iranian aggression.

A major lesson that came out of our Lebanon experience was the need to relocate and harden our embassies to make them much less vulnerable to attack. Within CIA, we developed new operational trade-craft more appropriate for hostile counterterrorism environments—including arming case officers, providing them with armed escorts, and teaching evasive driving techniques to officers bound for these areas. There were strategic lessons as well. We learned, or should have learned, that it's critical to fully think through what you're getting into before you go in, especially in the Middle East, and not cede the advantage to our enemies or pick unnecessary fights. But if you must go in, go in on the offense and with what it takes to win. We had been engaged in peacekeeping and limited intelligence and military operations while our enemies were engaged in a ruthless terrorism campaign. Hezbollah, Iran, and Syria had escalation dominance. We were the hunted rather than the hunter, a position that's never good to be in in counterterrorism operations. They were lessons I would take to heart.

THE "FARM"

I spent February through August 1984 attending CIA's Operations Course and Special Operations Training Course at the "Farm," CIA's primary clandestine training facility. An operations officer had to be "certified" in the Ops Course to receive a field assignment, but the training was honestly more than a bit anticlimactic after the operational experiences I'd already had.

The course was heavily hands-on, with graded exercises in all aspects of the agent recruitment cycle, agent handling, operational reporting, intelligence reporting, surveillance detection, and technical operations. It was a very intense experience, with students subsisting during the workweek on a few hours' sleep a night.

The first eight weeks were devoted to instruction in operational tradecraft, and it was pretty basic fare. What makes a foreigner want to spy for CIA? Money, ideology, compromise, and ego, or "MICE." During our instruction on agent handling, we were taught to ask the most important questions up front, such as whether an agent (a Soviet agent, in this case) was aware of any plans for a nuclear attack on the United States. We were also taught to ensure up front that arrangements for the next meeting were in place before we got very far into our current one.

During surveillance detection training, we were taught how to unobtrusively detect surveillance and convince the hostile service that we were of no operational interest. The highlight of this portion of the course was having a large surveillance team show us how rough surveillance could get when they had reason to believe an operational act was taking place or when they just wanted to intimidate a suspected foreign intelligence officer. I was finishing an operational "run" on one exercise when I was surrounded by a swarm of vehicles, stopped, yanked out of my car, braced up against the wall, and interrogated as to what I had been doing. It all happened with lightning speed. My cover story more or less held up, and after a few minutes of being roughed up and having my vehicle searched, I was released.

We had a week of "personal communications" training—how to conduct car meetings, picking up and dropping off an agent so as not to be detected by surveillance—and a week of "impersonal communications" training: learning how to operate in the "gap," where surveillance can't observe what you're doing; how to select, emplace, and recover "dead drops"; and how to conduct "car tosses," throwing a concealment device containing agent instructions out of a car window for later retrieval by one's agent after maneuvering your vehicle into a position where surveillance can't observe the toss.

During our technical operations training, we were instructed in the use of disguises, clandestine photography, secret writing, concealment devices, and covert communications. I was given a brown wig, a fake mustache, and some old clothes. My classmates applauded how much my disguise had changed my appearance, but added that it made me look like a drug dealer. We also received training in "audio" operations—how to bug a room.

At night, students could be found at the "Student Recreation Building," otherwise known as the bar. Once a week, senior officers from the Directorate of Operations would visit to tell us about their divisions, and stay the night to chat up interested students at the SRB. During two such presentations, Marsh Niner, the deputy chief of Latin America Division, and Chuck Cogan, the chief of Near East and South Asia Division, both singled me out for praise for the operations I'd already participated in before I attended the Ops Course. That impressed my classmates, but no doubt made my instructors all the more determined to test my mettle.

Toward the end of the course, we had to make a "hard target" recruitment of a hostile intelligence officer. It wasn't yet the final exam, but it was one of the culminating exercises of the program. I drew Kathy, one of CIA's senior female case officers. She was a tough target, playing the role of an "I've seen it all" intelligence officer from a fictional hostile service that for all intents and purposes was the KGB. Our meeting was without pretenses from the start: I knew who she was and she knew who I was—cat and mouse, but it wasn't clear who was the cat. She exuded an air of superiority as an intelligence professional and seemed to draw power from the "older woman, younger man" character of our relationship. I tried appealing to her ego, without success. She hadn't been compromised in any way that I could tell, and was devoid of any ideology. I had serious doubts whether my carefully crafted pitch would succeed.

Finally, she hinted that what she needed was money. She desired a more comfortable retirement than the one she would have if she didn't work for CIA, and wanted to ensure she'd have the top-quality health care as she aged that only the West could provide. In that, she found me and the agency useful. I told her she could have what she wanted, but only after working in place for us for a few years and providing us with intelligence we couldn't get from any other source. She countered that she wanted out now—a common response from hostile intelligence officers after they make the decision to defect. I showed her what she'd get if she defected now versus what she'd receive if she worked in place for us for a few years. That seemed to give her pause. I realized that she was carefully sizing me up professionally, so I worked on convincing her that we could meet with her securely in her capital and clandestinely exfiltrate her when the time came. She finally agreed to work in place. Through the recruitment process, I learned why "hard" targets are called hard, but also concluded that many assets essentially recruit themselves, with help, of course, from CIA. We then got down to business—professionally, collaboratively, and transactionally—and delved into the denied-area tradecraft we would need to employ to keep her safe while she stole our adversary's secrets.

The course concluded with a weeklong, final problem in a major U.S. city where all our newly acquired tradecraft skills would be put to the test. We were given a couple of days to select operational sites and then had to conduct a series of operational acts and meetings. I had selected a good dead drop site under a church pew—admittedly one that did not have worldwide applicability—and received a good grade on that exercise. I miscalculated a bit in my recruitment meeting, however. My target was a Soviet military intelligence officer, and I tried to bond with him, as one professional military officer to another. He launched into a tirade about how much he hated the military. I thought, Oh, s——, but I soon recovered and told him how I could help him defeat them. The motive for Kathy had been money. For this guy, it was hatred of his system.

I passed the final problem and was certified as a CIA operations officer, along with 80 percent of my classmates. I found the Operations Course challenging in some ways—the sheer workload, for example—but insufficiently rigorous and realistic in others. It seemed too disconnected from the real world and didn't provide instruction in the advanced tradecraft needed for operations in hostile operational environments. The Ops Course was also devoid of any training in covert action planning and operations and lacked advanced training in counterintelligence and out-of-embassy operations.

I had gone through the motions, doing enough to pass, but not giving it my best, and my course evaluation reflected my uneven performance. Unusually, however, the course instructors recommended that I be assigned as a chief of station—a command position—for my first tour. I was the only one of my classmates to receive this recommendation, and, needless to say, was pleased by it, but I quickly put it out of mind. I had another course to complete before I'd find out what I'd be doing after graduation.

That course was the twelve-week Special Operations Training Course, or SOTC. The SOTC was designed to provide general operations officers with training in paramilitary operations, because the agency was engaged in a lot of paramilitary covert action during the 1980s supporting anti-Communist insurgencies or countering Communist ones around the world. The course was like old home week for me. It was a lot more fun than the Ops Course had been, with weapons and demolitions training, guerrilla warfare field exercises, and parachute jumps, even if a bit redundant.[4]

The part that wasn't fun was the survival, escape, resistance, and evasion training, during which we were captured, placed in cells, and subjected to what today would be called "enhanced interrogation techniques" for three days, deprived of sleep and forced to remain in stress positions for long periods of time, listen to loud music, and relieve ourselves in "honey buckets" placed in our cells. It was my third time through such "training," and it doesn't get any better with repetition. The SERE module was dropped soon after our class after it received a critical evaluation from CIA psychologists.

HOME BASING AND A NEW PATH

Following completion of the SOTC and graduation from the Career Training Program, operations officers usually receive their field assignments after they are "home based" in one of the DO's area divisions.[5] A home base division is where an officer would usually spend the preponderance of his or her career, with the division's leadership overseeing their professional progression. Most of my classmates were home based in the "area" (regional) divisions—Soviet and Eastern Europe, Near East, Latin America, and so on—and received language training before heading overseas. A few who were bound for hostile environments in Moscow, Beijing, and so forth—so-called sticks-and-bricks operators—also received training in the special tradecraft needed to operate under 24/7 surveillance.

I was selected for a different path. Jim Glerum, the chief of CIA's International Activities Division, told me that the CIA was creating a new career track for operations officers who would provide the agency's future covert action leadership. It would be the fast lane to the most senior ranks, he said, and I would be the first test case. International Activities Division was responsible for managing CIA's covert action infrastructure and conducting political, psychological, and paramilitary operations (overseen today by IAD's successor, the Special Activities Center). IAD also oversaw counterterrorism and counter-narcotics operations, which, today, are separate centers within the agency. Officers pursuing this new path, Glerum told me, would alternate between assignments in the field and in CIA headquarters, where they would manage large covert action programs and the agency's global missions, particularly counterterrorism. That sounded fine to me.[6] I was offered an assignment in El Salvador, where Marsh

Niner was now chief of station and a war was raging, and another one in CIA's Counterterrorism Group. I told Glerum that even though I was a general operations officer, I wanted to spend the next few years conducting paramilitary operations. The agency was at war with the Soviets and their proxies in several regions, and I wanted to be part of it. There would be plenty of time down the road for tours as a traditional case officer and assignments as a chief of station. I wanted to follow the sound of guns. That's where I thought I could make my biggest contribution to the agency. He granted me my wish and assigned me to Ground Branch, the agency's primary special operations arm. And within a few weeks, I would be running the biggest secret war of all.

PART II

WAR WITH THE RED ARMY

5

THE GREAT COMMISSION

THE JOB OF A LIFETIME

In September 1984, two weeks after I reported into Ground Branch, I was told that Gust Avrakotos, CIA's chief of South Asia Operations and its Afghanistan Task Force, wanted to see me. A first-generation Greek American, Gust was a twenty-two-year veteran of the CIA's Clandestine Service and a tough, street-smart officer whose gruff demeanor concealed a shrewd operational mind. He had served for more than a decade in Greece under some very dangerous conditions. Countering Soviet subversion in Greece and Turkey had been a feature of the Cold War from its inception, and Gust was in the thick of it. He also provided critical intelligence on Greece's internal affairs, warning in early 1967, for example, that a group of colonels was about to overthrow Greece's democratically elected government. After CIA's station chief in Athens was assassinated in December 1975 by the Greek terrorist group 17 November, Gust became a marked man. Greece's *Communist Morning Daily* vilified him as a CIA snake, and he quickly found himself being targeted by both 17 November and the KGB. Through the use of careful tradecraft, he managed to survive his tour and then spent three years as the chief of a CIA office in the United States, where he further distinguished himself.

Gust became the chief of covert action in the Near East and South Asia Division in 1982. In 1983, he became acting chief of South Asia Operations, and in the summer of 1984 he became chief. NE Division in those days had responsibility for CIA operations from Morocco to Bangladesh. Sam Wyman, whom I had served under during my special Lebanon counterterrorism assignment, was chief of Arab-Israeli Operations, which covered Morocco to Iraq and the Arabian Peninsula. Gust had responsibility for Iran, Afghanistan, Pakistan, India, Sri Lanka, Nepal, and Bangladesh. By far, the most important of his responsibilities, though, was his role as chief of the Afghanistan Task Force, which brought together Soviet and Near Eastern analysts, paramilitary operations officers, covert influence specialists, demolitions and sabotage experts, logisticians, covert finance specialists, and communications and medical specialists from across the agency. The Soviet-Afghan War had been raging for nearly five years by the summer of 1984, and the Afghan resistance, or mujahedin, had fought the Soviets to a stalemate. CIA had been covertly supporting the Afghan resistance since the Soviets invaded in December 1979, and the program's base budget had just been increased by a factor of more than four from $120 million to $500 million for the fiscal year that began on October 1, 1984.

With this huge increase in program funding, the Soviet-Afghan War would soon enter a far more intense phase. Gust became convinced he needed a full-time program officer, Soviet weapons expert, and guerrilla warfare strategist to oversee the secret war. The new position would combine two jobs into one: Afghanistan Covert Action Program officer, currently performed by a senior operations officer and Soviet specialist, and chief of paramilitary operations, which for the past three years had been performed by a Marine Corps colonel on detail to CIA. I had been told by CIA's paramilitary operations leadership that I was being considered for the new position, and I really wanted it.

As I walked into Gust's outer office on the C corridor of the sixth floor in CIA headquarters, the first to greet me was a mannequin of a Soviet soldier wearing a gas mask, holding an AK-47 assault rifle, and outfitted in full combat gear. The mannequin reminded everyone that the Soviet-Afghan War was being fought with few restraints. A February 1982 Special National Intelligence Estimate concluded that the Soviets had used lethal chemical weapons on mujahedin positions and Afghan villages on more than forty occasions since the December 1979 invasion, causing more than three thousand deaths.[1] The mannequin was also a reminder that the CIA's Near East and South Asia Division was engaged in a covert war against America's main enemy, the Soviet Union. As Gust's predecessor, John McGaffin, had grimly put it, an unstated purpose of the covert program was to "kill Russians."

Gust and his senior deputies grilled me for nearly an hour about Soviet weapons and guerrilla warfare strategy. The chief of Pakistan-Afghanistan-Bangladesh Branch, Larry, began by asking if I knew a lot about Soviet weapons. "Yes, sir, I do," I replied, summarizing my Special Forces training while at the same time hoping that the job would involve a lot more than weapons expertise. I then pivoted to offer my views on the program's overall direction. I told Gust that while the program should be commended for fighting the Soviets to a stalemate, much more could and should be done. With the large increase in resources the CIA had just received, the mujahedin might actually have a chance at winning, though this still remained a low probability outcome. The assessment among CIA analysts was that the resistance couldn't win. The mujahedin could, for sure, make the Soviets pay a high price for their occupation, but that was it. By disagreeing with the analysts, I had gone out on a limb in my answer, but I felt it in my gut. With the unprecedented infusion of resources, it seemed that the strategic possibilities had expanded substantially. We shouldn't just do more of the same, I added. We should use these new resources to try to change the course of the war. Gust smiled and nodded.

After that exchange, Gust told me I had the job, and asked if I could start immediately. I assured him I could and told him that I had the full support of my leadership in Ground Branch, the Special Operations Group, and International Activities Division. Gust, it turned out, already knew all that. After reviewing my file, he had made a by-name request for me and had selected me over several far more senior candidates. The hour-long interview was just confirmation.

I felt as though I had just been handed a great commission to wage a secret war against the Red Army in Afghanistan and to directly confront Soviet power. As a young Special Forces soldier, I had dreamed of waging unconventional warfare against the Soviets to liberate Eastern Europe or to defeat a Soviet invasion of China, but I never imagined that my great war of liberation might occur in Afghanistan instead. After spending a decade in the Special Forces preparing for a war that never came and another two years in the CIA fighting Soviet and Iranian proxies and preparing for the intelligence battles of the

Cold War, I was being offered the opportunity to direct the covert action of a generation.

READING IN

The first thing a CIA operations officer does when he begins a new assignment is to "read in." For a CIA case officer, reading in involves reviewing in detail the "cases" he or she has been assigned and the "201" or personnel files of the agents that will be turned over to him or her. The review includes operations and intelligence cables that detail when, where, and how the agents were recruited, what motivated them to spy for the United States, how they are communicated with, met, and paid, what tradecraft training they have received, what intelligence they have produced, and any counterintelligence issues associated with the case. Reading in also includes a review of targets for recruitment, including "developmentals" that are well along the path.

For a CIA chief of station, reading in involves reviewing the station's operating directive, or OD, which provides the missions the station has been assigned. An incoming chief of station also reviews the files of the assets the station handles and how well they are meeting the objectives of the OD. He or she also reviews the liaison relationships the station has with foreign intelligence and security services and all covert action programs, if any, that are conducted by the station. For a covert action program officer, reading in involves reviewing the program's authorities, budget, operations, and success to date in achieving its objectives.

Given the scale, scope, and strategic importance of the Afghanistan Covert Action Program, I spent the better part of my first two months as program officer conducting a detailed review of the program's history and assessing the situation. The Soviet-Afghan War had been going on for almost five years by then, and I had a lot of catching up to do.

I had to get up to speed with Afghanistan's history, geography, people, and culture, so one of the first things I did was to I immerse myself in Louis Dupree's magisterial study, *Afghanistan.* My only connection to the country up to that point was an Afghan Army captain who'd been a Ranger classmate of mine in 1975. He was not the most cheerful fellow, nor a particularly good teammate. From Dupree, I received a much better introduction to the Afghans. I learned that Pashtuns belong to tribes (and confederations of tribes) and *khels* (clans), whereas Tajiks, Afghanistan's second-largest ethnic group, identify with the valley they are from. Most of the resistance consisted of Pashtuns and Tajiks, though Uzbeks, Hazaras, Turkmen, and Nuristanis were fighting the Soviets and Communist Afghan government as well. I learned about the differences between the Durrani, or southern, Pashtuns, who had ruled Afghanistan for most of the past three centuries, and the Ghilzai, or eastern, Pashtuns, who provided much of the resistance's leadership.

I learned about the Pashtunwali, the code of the Pashtuns, of *badal* (blood revenge), *ghayrat* (defense of property and honor), *tureh* (bravery), *nanawati* (the obligation to fight to the death for a person who has sought refuge from a Pashtun), and *melmastia* (the obligation of hospitality). It was a tough code for a tough people whose ideal archetype was the warrior-poet, brave in battle and articulate on any subject in the *jirga* (tribal meeting).

On his deathbed, Abdur Rahman Khan, one of the last emirs of Afghanistan, warned his countrymen to "never trust the Russians." Afghanistan's history was marked by near-constant rebellions against central authority. Guerrilla warfare came naturally. One of Afghanistan's greatest poets, Khushal Khan Khattak, instructed his seventeenth-century Khattak tribesmen to resist Moghul invaders as follows:

The Qazaki "guerrilla" method of warfare is more effective than a pitched battle. There are two prerequisites for this kind of warfare: good horses (mobility) and good archers (fire power). These two can help a small force defeat a large enemy. When you fight a smaller enemy detachment, you should decisively attack with surprise. But if the enemy receives reinforcement and you encounter a stronger enemy force, avoid decisive engagement and swiftly withdraw only to hit back where the enemy is vulnerable. By this you gain sustainability and the ability to fight a long war of attrition. A war of attrition eventually frustrates the enemy, no matter how strong he may be and that gives the chance of victory to a small force fighting against an invading army.

Mao couldn't have said it better himself. These days we would substitute rockets and other weapons for arrows, but the principles were the same.

I met with CIA's Afghanistan analysts in the Office of Near East and South Asia Analysis (NESA) for hours on end to review how the Afghan Communist Party had come to power, how they and Soviets had struggled to impose their will on the Afghan people, and most important, the strengths, weaknesses, and potential of the Afghan resistance. From analysts in the Office of Soviet Analysis (SOVA), I gained a detailed understanding of Soviet military operations and capabilities. From all this I learned that NESA's analysts were far more bullish on the prospects for the Afghan resistance than were SOVA's analysts. Each group of analysts seemed to be "rooting" for their "home team."

I became intimately familiar with the key commanders and organizations who made up the Afghan resistance, their aims and the number of fighters they had under arms, their areas of operation and the operations they had conducted, and their bases and logistical supply lines. I reviewed the weapons, quantities of ammunition, training, and intelligence we provided to the insurgency. I read the presidential findings that provided authorization for the program and reviewed the funding levels Congress and our foreign partner, the Saudis, had provided to date and the program's evolution under Presidents Carter and Reagan. I got briefed on our foreign intelligence sources, which Afghan resistance commanders we had special relationships with, and the key personalities and strengths and weaknesses of the foreign intelligence services who were our partners in the program. To get an appreciation of the situation firsthand, I met with our key foreign partners—the Pakistanis, Chinese, Saudis, Egyptians, and British—and several of our best mujahedin commanders and reporting assets.

I felt as if I had been possessed. With increasing intensity, I thought about how we could shift the balance decisively in favor of the Afghan resistance, and by the end of 1984, I had formed the core ideas of how we might actually win.

COMMUNIST COUP, SOVIET INVASION AND OCCUPATION

Before getting into how we transformed the Afghanistan Covert Action Program and developed what turned out to be a war-winning strategy, I need to review in some detail the situation I inherited when I took command in the late summer of 1984. A look at the key developments between 1978 and 1984 will provide the context and point of departure for the massive change that followed, and will aid in understanding why the attempt to impose Communism on Afghanistan met with such fierce resistance, why the Soviets invaded, and why they struggled to defeat the insurgency.

The origins of the Soviet invasion and occupation and the Afghanistan Covert Action Program can be traced to the Communist coup of April 27, 1978. The People's Democratic Party of Afghanistan (PDPA), the perpetrators of the coup, had been organized by the Soviet KGB in 1965. The coup and its aftermath is a tale of Afghan and Soviet treachery that is hard to top.[2] The coup's leaders had been on the KGB's payroll since the 1950s. The KGB had also penetrated the prime minister's office, government ministries, the Afghan secret police, universities, and commercial businesses. The GRU (Soviet military intelligence) had recruited a number of officers in the Afghan military.[3]

From its inception, Afghanistan's Communist Party had been divided into two hostile factions, which the KGB had unsuccessfully tried to fuse into a united Communist party. The Khalq, or "Masses," led by Nur Mohammed Taraki and Hafizullah Amin, drew its support almost exclusively from rural Pashtuns. They were particularly strong in the Afghan military. The Parcham, or "Flag," faction, led by Babrak Karmal, attracted mostly urban, educated Afghans, principally Dari-speaking Tajiks. Parchamis believed that Communists could achieve power gradually by allying with other progressive groups. The Khalqis vehemently rejected this.

On April 27, 1978, a Khalqi-led force quickly captured the Ministry of Defense. Within twenty-four hours Afghanistan's prime minister and most of his family were executed. Taraki became president and prime minister, and Amin became the first deputy prime minister and foreign minister. The Soviets asserted the "Brezhnev Doctrine," first enunciated a month after the 1968 invasion of Czechoslovakia, insisting that Afghanistan had voluntarily joined the socialist community and that "the clock could not be turned back." Thousands of Soviet and Soviet bloc advisers—party, military, and intelligence—quickly arrived in Afghanistan.

The PDPA rapidly began implementing its radical agenda, alienating almost every segment of Afghan society in the process. A land reform decree limited single-family holdings to fifteen acres; any excess land was seized and given to the landless or to collective farms established by small farmers. A decree on gender equality and marriage was even more radical, and high school textbook chapters on religion were replaced with paeans to Taraki, Lenin, and Stalin. Mullahs, who outnumbered Communist Party members across Afghanistan by more than twenty to one, railed against the PDPA's decrees in their Friday sermons.

The military's Khalqi leadership nearly eliminated the senior ranks of the Afghan Army. Officers who managed to escape execution fled to Pakistan. The regime's extension of military conscription from one to three years further accelerated the exodus of terrorized Afghans to Pakistan. The secret police, armed with lists of "regime enemies," hunted down and executed religious and tribal leaders in Kabul and the provinces. Tens of thousands of Afghans died in the terror, many of them executed after being taken to Pul-e-Charki prison in Kabul's eastern outskirts.

Within two months of the Communist coup, armed uprisings broke out, quickly spreading across the country. The first occurred in Nuristan and Konar in the northeast and in the Hazarajat in the center-west.[4] The revolt then spread to the Pashtun belt, with mujahedin attacks across the eastern provinces, including Paktia, Ghazni, and Nangarhar. The most dramatic uprising against Communist rule occurred in the western city of Herat. On March 17, 1979, the Afghan Army's 17th Army Division mutinied, murdering hundreds of regime officials and Soviet officers and their dependents. Taraki pleaded with his Soviet masters for armed intervention, but the Politburo refused. A week later, PDPA air and armored forces launched a ferocious counterattack against the rebels and civilian population. Afghan dead were in the many thousands, perhaps as high as twenty-five thousand.

Meanwhile, Taraki and Amin were exclusively focused on eliminating each other. During a meeting at the palace on September 14,

Taraki had an ambush waiting for Amin, but it succeeded in killing only his advance team. Hours later, Amin launched his own coup, using members of Taraki's Presidential Guard force secretly aligned with him to arrest Taraki. Despite Soviet pleas to spare his life, on October 8, Taraki was smothered in his bed by Amin's assassins.

Leonid Brezhnev, the Soviet Union's general secretary, was incensed: "What a bastard, Amin, to murder the man with whom he made the revolution." To address the deteriorating situation, the Soviets stepped up their military involvement. Red Army advisers engaged in direct ground combat operations and Soviet pilots conducted air strikes in support of Afghan government forces. The KGB also developed plans to kill Amin, hoping to lull him into a false sense of security by convincing him he had Moscow's full support. The Soviets provided him with a personal physician, a nanny, and a cook, who was actually a KGB illegal (a nonofficial cover officer from the Eighth Direct Action Department) with orders to poison Amin as soon as possible.[5] The Soviets also provided Amin with a 520-man personal security guard, a GRU *spetsnaz* (*spetsialnogo naznacheniya*, or "special purpose troops") battalion, made up of Soviet soldiers from central Asia.

In late October, a KGB officer was sent to Prague, where Babrak Karmal, one of the coup's leaders, had been exiled as ambassador. The KGB officer was there to work with Karmal on forming a new PDPA regime. Karmal would become president, prime minister, and party general secretary once Amin had been eliminated. On December 7, the Soviets secretly flew Karmal and other conspirators to Bagram Air Base to stand by. Across the Amu Darya River in Soviet central Asia, fifty-five thousand Soviet troops were mobilized and a command post was established at Termez in Uzbekistan. At the same time, Soviet airborne and KGB troops were inserted into Bagram Air Base and at Kabul Airport, and a Soviet armored battalion was tasked with securing the road between the Soviet border and Kabul.

As Soviet troops began arriving in force over Christmas 1979, Amin's military chief reported that they were coming in quantities that far exceeded what had been agreed to. Amin responded by saying, "So what, the more they come, the better for us." Amin had been deceived to the end. But it didn't matter. His problems would soon be over. The Soviets', however, were just beginning.

By the time I had become the Afghanistan Covert Action Program officer, the Soviet invasion of Afghanistan was largely only of historical interest within CIA. I included it in my read in mainly to make sure I understood how the Soviets had transitioned from invasion to occupation and what new vulnerabilities occupation had brought. Truth be told, I wanted to know how they did it.

The invasion had been formally approved in a Politburo meeting on December 12.[6] The KGB chairman, Yuri Andropov, was the driving force behind it, arguing in a one-on-one meeting with Brezhnev for the overthrow of Amin with a KGB special operation supported by Red Army units already in Afghanistan. Should his preferred course of action not succeed, Andropov added that the Soviet Union should be prepared to launch a large-scale military intervention to ensure Amin's overthrow. All of this was couched in very vague terms to the ailing Brezhnev. Andropov asserted that Amin had turned to the West, and the CIA might have recruited him when he was a graduate student at Columbia in the 1960s. Andropov also asserted that the CIA was trying to create a "New Ottoman Empire" in central Asia and that U.S. troops had already arrived in Afghanistan. None of this was even remotely true.

Up to this point, the Soviets had been reluctant to intervene directly in Afghanistan, but the deteriorating situation, the failure of lesser options, and Marxist ideology ultimately forced their hand. Soviet leaders had embraced a doctrine that once a state went Communist, it had to remain that way, lest it violate the Marxist view of history. The Soviets had intervened in Hungary and Czechoslovakia for this reason and now felt compelled to intervene in Afghanistan.

Two days before the December 12 Politburo meeting, Minister of Defense Dmitry Ustinov had instructed the Soviet chief of the General Staff, Marshal Nikolai Ogarkov, to finalize plans for an invasion with seventy-five thousand to eighty thousand troops, to be led by the recently reactivated 40th Army. The concept of operations was to invade along two ground approaches and one air corridor. Soviet forces would quickly seize all the important population centers and conduct a coup de main to seize the government.

Late in the evening on December 24 Washington time, U.S. intelligence began reporting a massive airlift by Soviet military transport aircraft. Two days earlier, Vice Admiral Bobby Inman, the director of the National Security Agency, had warned that the Soviets would intervene in a major way within seventy-two hours. By Christmas Day it had become clear that waves of Soviet military aircraft were surging into Afghanistan. The airlift continued at a high level until the evening of December 27, totaling some three hundred flights in all. On December 28, U.S. intelligence confirmed that two Soviet motorized rifle divisions had also moved into Afghanistan, using all-weather roads and the 11,200-foot-high Salang Tunnel that had been built by the Soviets fifteen years earlier to seize the population centers.[7] By the morning of December 28, the fighting in Kabul was largely over. The Soviets had taken control of the capital with a force of eight thousand special operators and paratroopers.

A seven-hundred-man GRU/KGB task force was given the mission to seize Taj Beg Palace and kill Amin. Two KGB *spetsnaz* units, *Zenit* and *Grom,* under the command of KGB Colonel Grigory Boyarinov from the KGB's *Alfa* counterterrorist force, conducted the interior assault. Hours before the operation was initiated on the evening of December 27, Amin's KGB cook finally managed to successfully poison him, but the prime minister was revived prior to the assault by an unwitting Soviet physician. The KGB's assassination plots against Amin seemed more like Inspector Clouseau than James Bond, but what they lacked in sophistication they made up in ruthlessness.[8] Soviet *spetsnaz* troops killed the prime minister as soon as they reached him. The whole operation took less than forty-five minutes. Approximately one hundred Soviet special operators—nearly 15 percent of the total force—died in the operation. Colonel Boyarinov was mistakenly shot by his own troops as he exited the palace. Recalling my close-quarter battle training with the British Special Air Service, I thought, Not the most precise of raids, to say the least.

The Soviet invasion caught U.S. policy makers by surprise, and President Carter was not happy about it. Right up to the invasion, the CIA's view was that the Soviets wouldn't go in. As the former director of central intelligence Robert Gates would later write, "CIA's Soviet analysts just couldn't believe that the Soviets actually would invade.... They saw all the reasons why it would be foolish for the Soviets to do so...[and] thought that the Soviet leaders thought as they did."[9] The same error was made by U.S. officials before Saddam Hussein invaded Kuwait in 1990, and, reportedly, by some senior officials in the Biden White House in the summer and fall of 2021 before Russia's February 2022 invasion of Ukraine. Each of these moves was telegraphed in advance. The moral of the story is that when dictators tell you what they're going to do, believe them.

———————

After I reviewed how the Soviets got into Afghanistan, a much larger part of my read in was focused on studying their strategy and military operations between 1980 and 1984. Soviet leaders had hoped for a quick victory and a rapid withdrawal of their combat forces. Their experience in Hungary in 1956 (where Andropov had been ambassador) and Czechoslovakia in 1968 gave them confidence that their model of invading with overwhelming force and changing the government to one more to their liking could be applied to Afghanistan. But Afghanistan was not Hungary or Czechoslovakia. The Soviets had invaded much smaller Hungary and Czechoslovakia with five times the forces and had met far less resistance. As the United States would learn a few decades later, toppling a regime is a lot easier than defeating an insurgency.

Soviet planners had assumed that the Afghan Army would carry the brunt of combat with the resistance, with the 40th Army playing a supporting role. Soviet leaders in Kabul quickly realized, however, that these plans had depended on a crucial, faulty assumption. In early 1980, Marshal Sergei Sokolov, the head of Soviet forces in Afghanistan, confided to Leonid Bogdanov, the KGB chief in Kabul, "You know what I'm afraid of? The Afghan Army is going to melt away and leave us face-to-face with the guerrillas."[10]

That's exactly what happened. A massive popular demonstration shook Kabul on February 21. After dark, a continuous, thunderous roar of *"Allahu Akbar"* rang from the throats of some 400,000 Kabulis—men, women, and children—standing on rooftops or in the streets. Shopkeepers and workers joined in a general strike. Soviet helicopters and regime troops attacked at dawn, leaving hundreds of civilians dead and many more wounded. Another five thousand were imprisoned and later executed. Marshal Sokolov declared martial law the next day.

During the first three months of the Soviet occupation of Afghanistan, entire Afghan Army divisions mutinied in Kandahar, Jalalabad, and Konar. By June 1980 the strength of the Afghan Army had declined by about 75 percent, from eighty thousand to twenty thousand. What was left of Afghanistan's Army, moreover, became more and more penetrated by the Afghan resistance, providing valuable warning to the mujahedin and clandestinely enabling their special operations in Kabul.

Soviet brutality fueled a general uprising in the countryside. Rural tribal and religious leaders proclaimed jihad against the Soviet-backed government. Between February and June, two Soviet battalions were destroyed in mujahedin ambushes. Soviet forces moved in heavy columns along major roads without flank security and were thus very vulnerable to ambush by numerically inferior resistance forces. The Red Army had been trained to fight large tank battles on Europe's plains, not counterguerrilla warfare in Afghanistan's rugged mountains. The Red Army had lost only a few hundred troops—mostly special operators in the raid on Taj Beg Palace—during the invasion. But as a result of counterinsurgency operations in 1980, they lost ten to fifteen times that number.

Once it became clear to the Soviets that their plan to transition security responsibilities to the Communist Afghan government wasn't viable, they shifted to a strategy of depopulation. The Soviet view seemed to be "no men, no resistance." Large areas of the Afghan countryside became free-fire zones. Soviet aircraft, artillery, and tanks leveled villages, and the 40th Army seeded the countryside with millions of mines and destroyed crops. The cumulative effect, in addition to civilian casualties that would reach into the hundreds of thousands, was to send millions of Afghan refugees fleeing across the border into Pakistan and Iran. But the resistance only grew.

Meanwhile, the KGB installed Mohammad Najib, a Pashtun from Paktia Province and a member of the Parchami wing of the PDPA, as the new chief of the intelligence service and secret police, now known as KHAD (*Khedamati Ittlaati-e Dawlet*). KGB officers of Uzbek, Tajik, and Turkmen origin were transferred to Kabul to work as KHAD operatives. The service would grow to several hundred thousand personnel and would become Afghanistan's most powerful security organization. The KGB hoped that what the Red Army's depopulation couldn't achieve could be made up by spies, prisons, and torture. It didn't work either.

In 1982, the Soviets again shifted strategy, combining airmobile operations with large-scale ground sweeps in an attempt to encircle resistance strongholds and block insurgents from escaping. The Soviets had realized early on that air mobility was essential to the conduct of counterinsurgency operations, and as the war dragged on, they increased the number of helicopters they had in Afghanistan severalfold. The Mi-24 "Hind" attack helicopter, nicknamed the Crocodile by Soviet troops, became the signature weapon of the war on the Soviet side.[11] This strategy also failed, however. The insurgents were still able to withdraw out of the numerous side valleys that bisected Afghanistan's major valleys before Soviet airmobile units could trap them.

The 40th Army's strength grew from 80,000 in 1980 to 105,000 by 1982.[12] Only about 10,000 to 20,000 troops, however, were available for offensive combat operations at any given time. The rest were needed to secure vital sites and lines of communication. About 80 percent of Soviet forces, moreover, were inexperienced conscripts and reservists.

In 1983, the Soviets shifted operational strategy yet again, doubling down on their air war and depopulation campaign, while still conducting heliborne operations and ground sweeps. By the end of 1983, Soviet killed in action had surpassed ten thousand.[13] At least three times that many had been wounded in combat. Heroin and disease were ravaging the 40th Army even more. Afghan government casualties, moreover, were five times the Soviet level. In terms of equipment, the Soviets and Afghan government had lost more than five hundred aircraft in combat by the beginning of 1984 and thousands of tanks and other military vehicles.

Perhaps most emblematic of the failures of Soviet counterinsurgency strategy was their seven major offensive operations in the strategic Panjshir Valley between 1980 and 1984. Located a hundred kilometers northeast of Kabul, the Panjshir is a "dagger" pointed at Bagram Air Base and Kabul and was the base of Ahmad Shah Massoud, the famed Afghan guerrilla leader. Massoud had learned from his intelligence sources of Soviet preparations for the 1984 offensive, so he moved to preempt it, ambushing a fuel convoy along the Salang Highway in March, which led to a severe fuel shortage in Kabul. During the offensive, the Soviets employed "hammer and anvil" tactics, using heliborne forces as the anvil, or blocking force, and mechanized forces advancing up the valley as the hammer, but they couldn't bring Massoud's forces to decisive battle, and the Soviets withdrew in late June after suffering five hundred dead. Resistance dead totaled only two hundred.[14]

After completing my review of Soviet strategy and operations, I was reassured. After nearly five years of conflict, the war was a stalemate. The Soviets suffered from poor strategy and tactics, insufficient forces, and a lack of intelligence. They had thoroughly penetrated the Afghan government, but knew little about the resistance, and certainly not enough about it to take effective action. Ironically, the longer the Soviets stayed in Afghanistan, the less they seemed to know.

With the forces they had in country, the Soviets could more or less secure the key population centers, though by no means entirely, and they could keep the major lines of communication open for the majority of the time, though not without incurring significant casualties. They could clear an insurgent base area temporarily, but couldn't hold it for more than a few weeks at a time. The insurgents would engage, inflict casualties on the Soviets, withdraw with most of their force intact, and return after the Soviets had left. Any Soviet gain was illusory, and the impact on the Red Army's morale was substantial.

I concluded the Soviets would need at least five times the forces they had in Afghanistan to have a chance at winning, and even with that large an increase, without a change in strategy and tactics and substantially better intelligence, they still wouldn't be able to defeat the resistance. To make matters worse, they had about as poor an ally as one could have in the Communist Afghan government. The Soviets were in a worse predicament in Afghanistan than the United States had been in Vietnam. I looked forward to making it far worse for them.

THE AFGHAN INSURGENCY

Afghanistan is a predominantly Sunni Muslim country, and so the resistance was predominantly Sunni Muslim as well. There were seven major Sunni political parties that made up the resistance, and I quickly got up to speed on their relative fighting strengths and philosophical differences. Four of the parties were Islamist, and three were traditionalist. The Islamist groups wanted an Islamist government; the traditionalist groups favored a return to monarchy and more secular rule. The Islamists differed among themselves as well, with some more fundamentalist and others less so. The Islamist groups did most, but not all, of the fighting and received most of the external support as a result. CIA mostly concentrated on the top three, but dealt with commanders in all seven groups. The key was who could produce results.

The first of the Islamist groups was Gulbuddin Hekmatyar's Hezb-e-Islami (Islamic Party). It was the favorite group of the Pakistanis and the largest recipient of external assistance, but also the most controversial of the seven groups. Gulbuddin's forces regularly fought against other mujahedin groups, particularly Massoud's, ambushing the Tajik commander's resupply caravans during the Soviet offensive in 1984, as just one example. His forces were strongest in the east and north and in Helmand in the southwest. He led a fairly large group of fighters, but had only a few strong commanders from CIA's perspective.

The second major party was Jamiat-e-Islami (Islamic Society), led by Burhanuddin Rabbani, a Tajik from Badakhshan in Afghanistan's far northeast. Jamiat was also Islamist in orientation, but more moderate than the other Islamist groups. It was a Dari-speaking, Tajik-dominated group, though it also included Pashtuns. Jamiat had the strongest regional commanders with the widest geographic reach due to the non-tribal structure of Tajik society. It was active throughout Afghanistan's north and west.

The third major group was Yunis Khalis's Hezb-e-Islami, or Hezb-e-Islami Khalis. Maulvi Mohammad Yunis Khalis was a Pashtun (Khogiani tribe) from Nangarhar. His forces would frequently cooperate with Jamiat. His party was strongest in the eastern provinces. Jamiat's and Khalis's groups were the strongest in my estimation, and, accordingly, they received the most attention from us.

The fourth Islamist group was Etihad-e-Islami (Islamic Alliance), led by Abdul Rasul Sayyaf. Sayyaf's group, the most Wahhabist of the four Islamist parties, was the favorite of the Saudis. He was accordingly well financed. His forces were strongest in the east and in Kabul.

The three traditionalist parties were the Mahaz-e-Milli-e-Islami (National Islamic Front), Jebh-e-Nejat-e-Milli (National Liberation Front), and Harakat-e-Inquilab-e-Islami (Islamic Revolutionary Movement). The National Islamic Front was the largest of the three. It was headed by Pir (saint or elder) Sayed Gailani, a Sufi Muslim of the Qadria sect. The NIF was derisively called the "Gucci muj" because of its leaders' fondness for things Western, but the group had some good fighters and commanders. They had strength in the east and south. The second traditionalist group was the National Liberation Front led by Sibghatullah Mojaddedi. Mojaddedi's group was also strongest in the east and south. The third traditionalist group, the Islamic Revolutionary Movement, was headed by Mohammed Nabi Mohammedi, a Maulvi from Logar. Because it was village based, its leaders were often local mullahs. It was strongest in the southwest and east.

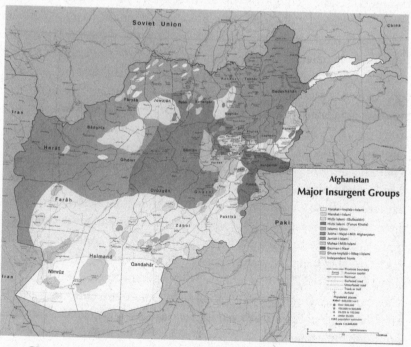

CIA map of major Afghan insurgent groups and their operational areas, 1985

The most important part of my review of the Afghan resistance was not the political parties but the major resistance commanders fighting the war. By 1984, there were around three hundred commanders across the Afghan resistance who commanded forces ranging from the few hundreds to the tens of thousands. Of these, there were six to whom I paid special attention. They all commanded significant forces, were the most effective in fighting the Soviets, and had wide geographic reach and access to critical targets, and through direct contact by one means or another we could influence their operations. Two of the commanders were from Jamiat, two were from Khalis's party, and two were members of Gailani's National Liberation Front. As a group, these six commanders gave us reach across Afghanistan and into Kabul. Four of the six were still in their twenties and thirties. I personally met with several of them while visiting mujahedin training camps in Pakistan.

Ahmad Shah Massoud, a Panjshiri Tajik and Jamiat commander, was the most important of the six. Known as the "Lion of the Panjshir"—"Panjshir" means "five lions" in Dari—Massoud was the most visible symbol of the anti-Communist resistance and an excellent strategist and tactician. He had studied military affairs at a Pakistani-intelligence-run training school for two years during the late 1970s. He had carefully read the guerrilla warfare writings of Mao Zedong and others and tried to adapt them to Afghanistan. In May 1979, with a few dozen followers and only twenty-six years old at the time, he infiltrated into Afghanistan to begin establishing his insurgent front, first in Nuristan and then in the Panjshir Valley. He had a gift for using intelligence and deception to lure the Soviets into ambushes where his firepower could be concentrated, and was equally skilled at conducting large-scale raids. His forces posed a continuous threat to Bagram Air Base and the Salang Highway, the vital logistics artery for the Soviets, and had reach throughout several provinces in Afghanistan's north. His brother Ahmad Zia served as his representative in Pakistan, and I met with him several times, though, unfortunately, never with Ahmad Shah, who never left Afghanistan.

Ismail Khan, another Tajik and the Jamiat commander in western Afghanistan, had been a captain in the Afghan National Army before joining the resistance. Born in Shindand in Herat Province and in his late thirties in 1984, Khan had led the mutiny of the Herat garrison in March 1979. He became Jamiat's western region commander, with reach across several provinces.

Abdul Haq, an Ahmadzai Pashtun from Nangarhar, was the Kabul Front commander for Yunis Khalis. He had started out in the resistance with Jalaluddin Haqqani in Paktia, but soon opened his own front. Haq had a very good intelligence network among the Khalqis, and this enabled him to conduct operations in and near Kabul. He was a good planner and an excellent tactician. His Kabul Front numbered around a thousand mujahedin. Haq was still in his twenties when I met with him in early 1985.

Jalaluddin Haqqani, a Pashtun member of the Zadran tribe and another Khalis commander, was in his mid-forties when I met him. From his base in Miram Shah in North Waziristan, Haqqani organized an effective insurgent network in Khost, Paktia, and Paktika Provinces. His forces had reach into Nangarhar and Logar as well. With ISI assistance, beginning in 1981, Haqqani constructed a large base in a deep canyon at Zhawar, just inside Afghanistan. It had a hospital, a machine shop, and numerous reinforced caves for weapons and ammunition storage.

Amin Wardak, a Pashtun and a member of the Wardak tribe, conducted operations in and near Kabul for Gailani's National Islamic Front. Later in the war, he shifted his allegiance to Yunis Khalis. He was in his early thirties when I met him. He was most effective in his native Wardak Province and in Kabul Province, but his operational reach extended into Ghazni as well.[15] Like Massoud, he was very effective at civic action, establishing health clinics and schools for the local population, and was close friends with Abdul Haq.

Haji Latif, or "Haji Baba" as he was more affectionately known, was in his seventies by the 1980s. Earlier in his life, he had been the leader of a Kandahar "mafia" gang that demanded money from wealthy businessmen and landowners for "protection." He had also spent twenty-one years in prison on a murder charge. The National Islamic Front had the most fighters in the Kandahar area, and Haji Latif was their most effective commander. Although a secondary theater, Kandahar saw some of the most intense fighting of the war. Haji was a pragmatic royalist and supported the king's return. The monarchy had been good for his racketeering business. Like Massoud, Haji Baba never left Afghanistan. I regret that I never got to meet him.

Due in no small part to the successes of these commanders, the insurgency had grown from around 50,000 in 1980 to around 150,000 full-time or mostly full-time fighters by 1984.[16] Anywhere from a fifth to a third of this force would be engaged in operations on a given day during the fighting season. Another 150,000 to 300,000 or so were armed villagers who provided support to the resistance.

Unfortunately, the Afghan resistance was equipped with mostly small arms—a mix of bolt-action rifles and a smaller number of modern assault rifles, machine guns, and anti-tank grenade launchers—which limited its combat effectiveness. Resistance tactics of necessity emphasized raids and ambushes by small detachments—thirty- to one-hundred-man groups. The mujahedin had an abundance of supply routes through the mountain passes from Pakistan into Afghanistan, some three hundred in all, the so-called Jihad Trail, making it impossible for the Soviets to seal the border.

Over the first nearly five years of war, the resistance had gained more and more control of the countryside. Up to 75 percent of Afghanistan was now under tacit insurgent control. CIA's analysts didn't think the insurgents could win, but the resistance had thus far fought the Soviets to a draw, and we were about to increase their capabilities dramatically.

THE SECRET WAR

I had to get up to speed on the Afghanistan Covert Action Program—America's secret war—right from the start. I could take a bit of time to get smart on Soviet and resistance operations and personalities, but I needed to know how our program worked from day one.

The general objective of covert action programs is to influence events abroad in a way that protects and advances U.S. national interests while concealing the U.S. hand. Covert action programs are thus compartmented, with access to them strictly limited. The Afghanistan Covert Action Program was no different. It was a "proscribed and limited," or PL, program in CIA terms. Some aspects of it were even more tightly controlled in RH, or restricted handling, channels.

On December 28, 1979, just three days after the Soviet invasion of Afghanistan had begun, President Carter signed a covert action finding authorizing the CIA to provide lethal support—weapons, ammunition, other war matériel, training, and intelligence—to the Afghan resistance. The first CIA-supplied arms were in mujahedin hands by January 10.[17]

Zbigniew Brzezinski, Carter's national security adviser, had played a pivotal role. He argued that whatever Moscow's motives for the invasion had been, its ambitions might grow now that they were in Afghanistan, leading to a Soviet presence at the edge of the Persian Gulf. To stop the Soviets, it was essential to provide "more money as well as arms shipments to the rebels in concert with Islamic countries."[18] The lethal finding signed by Carter on December 28 came on the heels of two nonlethal findings he had signed on July 3. The two nonlethal findings had authorized the provision of political and psychological warfare support, both within and from outside Afghanistan, and worldwide support to build opposition to the Soviet invasion. They also authorized CIA to provide communications support to the Afghan resistance, along with cash payments. The nonlethal findings were initially funded at only $500,000, however.[19]

President Carter made the major strategic decisions to contest the Soviet occupation of Afghanistan: to arm the mujahedin, to use Pakistan as a base for the covert action operation, and to enlist Saudi Arabia's help in funding the secret war. President Reagan would make additional strategic decisions that would win the war.

Repairing the U.S. relationship with Pakistan was critical. A 1977 coup had brought General Mohammad Zia ul-Haq to power, and his decision to order the execution of his predecessor had severely strained relations with the United States. Pakistan's pursuit of nuclear weapons—with Chinese assistance—made any rapprochement even more challenging. To add fuel to the fire, in November 1979 a large mob, incited by false claims by the Iranian government that the United States was behind the seizure of the Grand Mosque in Mecca, Islam's holiest site, stormed the U.S. embassy in Islamabad, killing a Marine security guard and causing embassy personnel to seek refuge in a secure vault. By the time the Pakistani Army arrived four hours later, the air supply in the vault had run dangerously low and the embassy was a charred ruin. I would be reminded of that dreadful incident on the many visits I made there over the next three decades.

The initial goal of our Afghanistan program was to increase the cost of the Soviet occupation, not end it, to bleed the 40th Army, not defeat it. This remained U.S. policy through 1984. Initial funding for the lethal covert action program was $10 million, but it would be increased to $50 million within nine months. It leveled off between 1981 and 1984 at $60 million per annum. Saudi Arabia's kings, Khalid and then Fahd, had agreed to match the U.S. contribution dollar for dollar, so the total program funding was $120 million annually through September 1983. A special $40 million supplemental appropriation, pushed through largely by Texas Congressman Charlie Wilson, a member of the House Appropriations Defense Subcommittee, increased the U.S. contribution to $100 million for fiscal year 1984, bringing total funding for that year to $160 million. (The Saudis weren't asked to match Wilson's supplemental.) Wilson had earmarked $17 million of his supplemental for the purchase of ten Swiss-made Oerlikon 20 mm anti-aircraft cannons and ammunition in hopes that it could be the answer to the Hind threat. This earmark caused considerable angst within CIA for a host of reasons. CIA officials believed the Oerlikon was too heavy, expensive, and complex for the Afghan resistance. (Each cannon, which weighed twelve hundred pounds and took a team of mules to transport, cost $165,000—twenty times the cost of a Chinese 14.5 mm heavy machine gun. Each round of ammunition cost $42—twenty times the cost of a 14.5 mm round.) CIA also didn't like Congress meddling in its affairs.[20]

At CIA headquarters, the covert action program was overseen during the first five years of the war by Chuck Cogan, the chief of the Near East and South Asia Division, and managed day-to-day by John McGaffin, who was Cogan's chief of South Asia Operations. Both were experienced operations officers who had served several tours in the Near East. In the field, the program was overseen by the CIA's chief of station in Islamabad and Islamabad Station's chief of paramilitary operations. There was a small station in Kabul, but it was focused solely on intelligence collection. From 1981 to 1984, CIA's chief in Islamabad was Howard Hart, who had served in Iran during the Iranian Revolution.[21] Hart had done a masterful job rebuilding the CIA's (and the U.S. government's) relationship with Pakistan. Hart's main Pakistani interlocutor was Lieutenant General Akhtar Abdur Rahman Khan, the director general of Inter-Services Intelligence. Hart won

Akhtar's trust and friendship, without which the Afghanistan Covert Action Program would have been far less effective.

The key to solidifying the early relationship with ISI and President Zia had been to give the Pakistanis near-total control over the weapons mix and its distribution to the Afghan resistance during the first five years of the program. Zia had established early that he alone would decide how much strategic risk he would take. He wanted our help, but on his terms. His aim, as he frequently said, was to "keep the pot boiling in Afghanistan, but not have it boil over." This arrangement had served us well for the first five years of the war, but by late 1984 it was clear to me that it had become an impediment to major change. Zia had to retain the final say, because Pakistan was taking most of the strategic risk in the secret war, but I would have to find a way to shift strategic control of the program to CIA if we were to expand our aims and efforts in Afghanistan.[22]

CIA's relationship with the Saudis centered on three people: the king; Prince Turki al-Faisal al-Saud, the head of the kingdom's General Intelligence Directorate, or GID; and Prince Bandar Bin Sultan, the Saudi ambassador to the United States.[23] CIA officers would regularly brief the Saudi leadership on program results, but the Saudis weren't involved in program decisions. They would simply wire transfer their matching funds on a quarterly basis into our Swiss bank accounts (though often only after significant delays and only after receiving personal appeals from CIA's director). As a result, the program adopted a policy of spending the entire U.S. contribution during the first half of a year, hoping that the Saudi matching funds would arrive in time to sustain operations at the agreed-upon level.[24] They did, but not without some periodic arm-twisting.

Other major allies in the secret war were Egypt, China, and the U.K. China and Egypt were our two principal sources of weapons and ammunition, and the U.K. played an important intelligence role.

Finally, the program enjoyed strong bipartisan support in Congress. During the summer of 1984, Congressman Wilson put the program on a new course. On top of the $40 million supplemental appropriation he had added to the program's budget the previous year, he'd increased it more than fourfold to $250 million ($500 million with the matching Saudi contribution) for the fiscal year that began on October 1, 1984. It might not have been "Charlie Wilson's War," but he was sure helping to escalate it. "Good Time Charlie," as he was known, financially transformed our covert war—against the wishes of the program's leadership at the time.[25] CIA had requested only a 10 percent increase in funding for FY 1985, to $66 million, $132 million with the Saudi match, but Charlie prevailed. I would have a lot more to work with than my predecessors had.

After completing my review of the program's first four-plus years, I had come to the same conclusion as former CIA director Robert Gates would later: U.S. support for the Afghan resistance from 1979 to 1984, while successful, had been limited. This was partly the result of the initial cautious approach of CIA's Clandestine Service; partly because President Zia was reluctant to challenge the Soviets too aggressively; partly because of a U.S. desire to keep the program covert and deniable; and partly because some in the U.S. government were apprehensive that a larger program would provoke the Soviets into a massive reinforcement and result in a terrible slaughter of the Afghan resistance.[26] But all that was about to change: our covert war was about to be escalated dramatically, and I was one of those most bent on doing it. From the beginning of my read in, I started thinking about how I would change program strategy—and with it the war.

6

DEVELOPING A WAR-WINNING STRATEGY

ONLY IN CIA

In 2006, three years after the book *Charlie Wilson's War* had come out and the movie by the same name was in production, I was asked to give a talk with Charlie about our secret war to drive the Soviets out of Afghanistan during the 1980s.[1] The event, held at a large private home in Vail, brought together NFL Hall of Famers, top entrepreneurs and leaders of unusual businesses (one of whom supplied research stations in Antarctica), a petroleum geologist, and a dinosaur paleontologist, in addition to Charlie and me. Also attending was Lieutenant General Harold "Hal" Moore (U.S. Army, retired), the subject of the book *We Were Soldiers Once . . . and Young* and the movie based on it, which told the story of the first major battle between U.S. combat forces and the North Vietnamese Army during the Vietnam War. Soon after my arrival, I introduced myself to General Moore, who, by then, was well into his eighties and sitting by himself near a fireplace in one of the chalet's many sitting areas.

"You're the fellow who wrote his own orders," Moore said, after hearing my name.

"Yes, I suppose I am," I mumbled.

Moore paused, smiled, and said, "I'm glad you did."

I hadn't thought of my experience as the Afghanistan Covert Action Program officer in quite that way, but General Moore had pretty much nailed it. To be sure, what I had done to transform the program and put in place the strategy that would win the Soviet-Afghan War had been fully blessed by my superiors within CIA, by the Reagan administration, and by Congress. But it is equally true that I took the initiative and developed and implemented this strategy with minimal direction. I had been an operations officer for only a few years and was still in my early thirties. In less than a year, I had gone from participating in operations to directing a secret war on an unimaginable scale. Only in CIA could this happen.

TRANSFORMING THE AFGHANISTAN COVERT ACTION PROGRAM

As part of my read in, I identified several problems I needed to fix right away. But I didn't want to just fix problems. I wanted to change the direction of the war. To accomplish this, I developed four operational aims: to significantly shift the air balance in the insurgents' favor; to enable the resistance to conduct more complex operations; to enable it to significantly increase its operational tempo, that is, its frequency of operations; and to enable it to take the fight into the urban areas, particularly into Kabul.

Insurgencies are won through strategies of attrition, death by a thousand cuts, eventually causing an occupying power to withdraw or a regime to collapse. With the huge increase in funding that Charlie Wilson had provided, I believed we could dramatically increase the scale, scope, and sophistication of the Afghan resistance and in doing so, dramatically increase Soviet losses. If we could force the Red Army to withdraw, the collapse of the Communist Afghan regime would be inevitable. To achieve these operational and strategic aims, we would need to make major changes to the weapons mix to make the insurgency far more lethal. We would need to provide the resistance with some advanced Western weapons, which almost certainly would be seen by the Soviets as a major escalation of the war. We would need to dramatically increase the quantity and quality of training and intelligence we provided and force greater unity of effort among the political parties that constituted the Afghan resistance. And we would also need to intensify our covert influence operations inside and outside Afghanistan to build and sustain support for the resistance.

Our covert influence operations consisted of four mutually reinforcing lines of effort. We distributed cassette tapes and other propaganda materials inside through our covert logistics pipelines. Jointly with the Pakistanis, we used mobile radio platforms to beam our messages into the border provinces. A Radio Free Afghanistan that we sponsored transmitted programs in support of the resistance daily across Afghanistan. Internationally, we conducted a large, worldwide covert media program to ensure that the brutality of the Soviet occupation and the heroic resistance to it remained in the news.

Accomplishing these tasks, I knew, would depend on my ability to get CIA, the Reagan administration, Congress, and our foreign partners to support a far more aggressive and ambitious strategy. We had to "win the war" in Washington and in the capitals of our key foreign partners to win it on the battlefield. Within CIA, there were concerns that the program had already grown too large. John McMahon, CIA's deputy director, was particularly concerned that CIA would be left holding the bag if Congress turned against the secret war. Other senior leaders in CIA outside the Near East and South Asia Division, including the then chief of Ground Branch, CIA's paramilitary operations arm, were concerned about the ability of the Afghan resistance to "absorb" the large increase in covert support Congressman Wilson had forced on the agency, fearing that the resistance was already stretched to the maximum. There were growing concerns in Congress that also had to be addressed. Some believed that the program suffered from large-scale corruption, that the Pakistanis were diverting CIA-supplied weapons and ammunition for their own use, and that the CIA wasn't doing enough to help the resistance win. Others expressed concerns that the Soviets would inevitably defeat the resistance and that we were fighting to the "last Afghan." Winning the war would require a lot more resources—far above the huge increase in funding CIA had just received. We'd have to get the White House and Congress on board for another large increase in program funding. Finally, we had significant challenges to overcome with our key foreign partners. Getting the Saudis to provide their matching funds on time was one, and getting the Egyptians to provide better quality control in their supply of weapons and ammunition was another. But by far the biggest challenge I would face was how to establish greater U.S. strategic control over the direction of the program, which had largely been ceded to the Pakistanis.

How my CIA colleagues and I were able to transform the program and put in place a war-winning strategy is the subject of this and the next chapter. How that strategy succeeded in driving the Soviets out of Afghanistan is described in the subsequent two chapters.

————

The most pressing need, as I began to formulate my transformation strategy, was for anti-aircraft weapons that could neutralize the Soviets' Mi-24 Hind attack helicopter. That was the problem that caused Charlie Wilson to provide additional funds to the program in the first place. The Hind's armor plating made it impervious to the 12.7 mm machine guns the resistance employed, and it was devastating resistance columns. The mujahedin referred to the Hind as *Shaitan Arba*, "Satan's chariot."

Only twenty or so man-portable surface-to-air missile systems had been provided to the resistance, and most of these were malfunctioning. All of them, moreover, had been procured through a less-than-reliable covert supply channel. To reduce the air threat to insurgent operations and impose much greater losses on the Soviets, the resistance would need many more of these man-portable air defense systems, or MANPADS. Shifting the air balance, I knew, would be key to shifting the overall military balance in Afghanistan.

The current weapons mix strongly favored small arms, and it limited insurgent operations and effectiveness. To enable more complex and lethal insurgent operations, the resistance would need more heavy weapons and more sophisticated training and actionable intelligence. There was a great need for indirect fire capabilities with greater range—mobile rocket launchers, for example. This would enable the resistance to continually harass Soviet positions and inflict additional casualties on the Soviets at little cost. The resistance also lacked sniper rifles. The use of snipers is a key tactic in guerrilla warfare. They harass the enemy, achieve psychological effects disproportionate to the battlefield losses they inflict, and enable precision kills of key enemy personnel.

The resistance needed more and better anti-tank weapons to ambush Soviet armored convoys more effectively. It needed demolitions kits for sabotage, and man-portable mine-clearing systems to get access to targets that the Soviets had protected with minefields. It also needed more secure means of communication. The Soviets were successfully exploiting the insurgents' use of insecure devices to target them.

To increase operational tempo, I had to solve what we in CIA called the "ammunition crisis." CIA program leaders and their Pakistani counterparts had focused during the first five years of the war on getting as many weapons as they could into the hands of the resistance. "A gun for every Afghan," was how General Akhtar, the head of Pakistan's Inter-Services Intelligence, had described it. The supply of ammunition, though, had not kept pace with the cumulative supply of weapons, even allowing for wastage and battlefield losses. Ammunition supply directly influences combat intensity and tempo—how hard and how often a force is able to fight. As a result, CIA officials realized in early 1984 that even at a low level of combat activity, the ammunition requirements for the cumulative available weapons supply would consume the program's entire budget, originally expected to be only $132 million in the coming fiscal year. Fortunately, the budget slack that Wilson's large increase in funding provided allowed me to bring cumulative weapons and ammunition supply into better balance.

Another problem was training. The insurgents weren't receiving enough of it, and not enough of them were being trained—only about two thousand per year. The program would need to increase its throughput dramatically and increase the range provided, from training on advanced weapons like MANPADS, to larger-scale combined arms operations for resistance commanders.

The resistance also needed to strengthen its ability to take the fight into the major cities. Rockets, demolitions, special operations training, and good intelligence would help them do so. Finally, the resistance suffered from disunity among the resistance political parties and an unwillingness to combine forces from different groups on the battlefield. Even more concerning, some groups—Hekmatyar's in particular—fought with other mujahedin groups almost as frequently as they did with the Soviets.

What may look at first glance like a series of actions designed merely to remedy the program's shortfalls was anything but. Fixing them would require a major change in strategy and another huge increase in resources. The major tasks that constituted my transformation strategy, moreover, were highly interdependent. The provision of heavier weapons and tens of thousands of tons of additional ammunition would require dramatic improvements to the logistical system; the employment of more sophisticated weapons would require specialized training; the shift to new tactics and more complex operations would require additional training, better intelligence, more operational advisers, and greater collaboration among insurgent groups. Accomplishing a few of these tasks would have been difficult enough. Accomplishing them all in less than a year was a massive challenge, but it turned out to be a war winner.

Fortunately, I had the wind at my back—four winds, to be specific. The first was of course the dramatic increase in program funding that Congressman Wilson had just provided. As former DCI Robert Gates notes in his memoirs, 1984 marked a major turning point in U.S. covert support for the Afghan resistance and it was largely because of Charlie Wilson. Our secret war had already been escalated. My challenge was to make maximum use of the opportunity Wilson had provided.

The second involved changes in the program's chain of command. During the summer of 1984, a new team had taken over leadership of the program. At CIA headquarters, in addition to Gust and me, Bert Dunn had taken over as chief of the Near East and South Asia Division, and Clair George had become the new deputy director for operations. In Islamabad, Bill Piekney had just arrived as our new chief of station.

Bert was the perfect man to be chief, NE. He had been a founding member of the U.S. Army Special Forces in the early 1950s. After joining the CIA, he mastered Pashto and spent several years in Pakistan, where he had been instrumental in establishing Pakistan's special forces, the Special Service Group, and had supported U-2 flights over the Soviet Union from Peshawar. Bert knew the Afghanistan-Pakistan border region like his native West Virginia. He later served in Vietnam and as chief of station in Kabul. He had worked with the Tibetan resistance and had held several important field commands where he had helped wage the global Cold War. Both Bert and Gust had worked previously for Clair George and had Clair's trust.

Moreover, Bill Casey was hell-bent on doing everything he could to deal a fatal blow to the Soviet Empire and saw increasing opportunity to do so in Afghanistan. There were few layers between me and Director Casey, which facilitated transformational decision making. The program also had a very lean organizational structure, with fewer than twenty personnel working on it full time, but with another hundred or so providing significant support of one kind or another. The stars could not have been more aligned from my perspective.

The third advantage I had going in was good intelligence from multiple sources—overhead imagery, signals intercepts, captured Soviet matériel, and agents we sent into Afghanistan.[2] This all-source intelligence informed program decisions in several areas. We had a number of Soviet assets reporting to us on a range of issues, including on Afghanistan, and several high-level Soviet defections in 1985—the so-called year of the spy—provided additional valuable intelligence. (That special source of intelligence would unfortunately soon dry up when CIA officer Aldrich Ames began selling our secrets to the Soviets, resulting in the execution of several of our most valuable assets.)[3]

To monitor combat operations, we relied on satellite imagery and communications intercepts. Soviet and Communist Afghan human sources of ours provided additional reporting on the conflict. Detailed reporting on the status of insurgent groups was provided by two dozen third-country nationals who would travel into Afghanistan on our behalf for weeks at a time. I was amazed at the bravery of these third-country nationals, many of whom were from Europe. It was a silent but important contribution to the Soviet-Afghan War.

A key part of our human source reporting on the Afghan resistance came from our closest liaison partner, the British Secret Intelligence Service. The SIS had a special relationship with Ahmad Shah Massoud, the resistance's most effective commander. Small teams of retired operators from the British special forces would infiltrate Afghanistan, link up with Massoud in the Panjshir Valley, and report on the status of his forces. This added to the reporting we received from the other third-country nationals. Retired British special operators would also provide training, specialized equipment, such as secure communications devices, and operational advice to Massoud.[4]

During a visit to London soon after I assumed my program officer duties, I met with one of the retired British SF operators who had just returned from the Panjshir. He went by "Awk" and had spent three weeks inside Afghanistan with Massoud. We instantly hit it off, special operator to special operator, and talked well into the night about the status of Massoud's forces, their morale, mix of weaponry, supply of ammunition, training, recent operations, and so on. But what made the biggest impression on me was his description of his encounters with Soviet forces. Awk told me how Massoud's fighters and he had been able to pass undetected within feet of a Soviet perimeter. "I don't think they want to detect us," he said, showing evident disdain for the poor conscript troops who manned the Red Army's observation posts. Soviet soldiers mostly hunkered down and were literally afraid of ghosts, or *dukhy*, as they called the mujahedin. They also called them *dushman* (bandits).

The fourth and most important wind I had at my back was the Afghan resistance itself. Its prospects were much better than many within CIA believed. Several factors contribute to an insurgency's prospects for success, and the Afghan resistance had all of them going for it. Insurgents need a cause to justify and sustain their movement. Islam and Afghanistan's tradition of resisting foreign invaders provided the necessary cause. An armed resistance movement needs guerrillas, those willing to take up arms against the regime and/or occupying power and endure the hardships of protracted conflict. Afghanistan's martial tradition, its predominantly rural population, and the size of its population provided an ample supply of fighters. Insurgency critically depends on popular support. The resistance enjoyed broad support among the Afghan population across ethnic groups. It could operate freely across most of the countryside and receive logistics support and intelligence from rural villagers. It also enjoyed substantial clandestine support in the cities and in Afghan government ministries. Insurgents need remote and difficult terrain for secure internal base areas and to achieve the element of surprise in operations. The mountains of Afghanistan were perfect guerrilla warfare country. Insurgents benefit immensely from an external sanctuary that can provide a secure base of strategic resupply and command and control. Pakistan provided this. Finally, resistance movements have a much better chance at winning when they have an external sponsor. The Afghan resistance had the United States, Pakistan, Saudi Arabia, China, Egypt, the U.K., and many other nations on its side. The Red

Army, to be sure, was a formidable adversary, an army that had never lost a war. But it had never faced an insurgency with as favorable conditions as the Afghan resistance.

THE WEAPONS MIX AND RESISTANCE FORCE STRUCTURE

It's time to delve deeper into the elements of my transformation strategy. What we in CIA referred to as the "weapons mix" was the core of the Afghanistan Covert Action Program. The weapons mix specified what types of ordnance (weapons and ammunition) and in what quantities the program provided, and it consumed the vast majority of the program's budget. Set in consultation with Pakistan's Inter-Services Intelligence each year, the weapons mix determined how much combat power the resistance could generate.

We divided it into three broad categories, reflecting their intent from a program perspective: anti-personnel, anti-armor, and anti-air. In the first category were rifles, light machine guns, mortars, rocket launchers, and anti-personnel mines; in the second were anti-tank rocket-propelled grenade launchers, recoilless rifles, and anti-tank mines; and in the third were heavy machine guns and surface-to-air missile systems. Demolition kits, medical kits, and radios were additional, ancillary categories. Ammunition associated with a particular weapon or weapon system was included in each respective category. For each weapon or weapon system, we would show the cumulative total that had been provided since the program's inception. After allowing for wastage and battlefield losses, this gave us a sense of the weapons stock in insurgent hands that had to be supplied with ammunition.

When I joined the program, there was no "end state" or goal within CIA as to what weapons mix and resistance force structure the program should be aiming toward. Similarly, there were no models for how to equip a large insurgent force. I had hoped there might be some left over from the CIA's experience in Laos, but there weren't. I quickly discovered that there also weren't any models for resistance force structure in the Army's unconventional warfare manuals, and certainly nothing for an insurgency on the scale of the Afghan resistance. During my early years in the Special Forces, I had been trained to organize, train, equip, and lead in combat a resistance force of five hundred to fifteen hundred fighters. But that amounted to less than 1 percent of the fighters the Afghan resistance had under arms. The lack of a force-planning objective had led to significant imbalances across the program, which limited insurgent effectiveness. There were too many small arms and not enough anti-tank, indirect fire, and anti-air weapons. There was also a great imbalance between the cumulative weapons we had supplied and the ammunition required to effectively employ them.

Using data on our cumulative weapons supply and current year procurement plans, a small desk calculator, and yellow notepads, I created a model force structure and force employment plan for the Afghan resistance during my first two months on the job. I notionally organized the resistance into two categories: a full-time guerrilla force of 150,000 to 200,000 that CIA's analysts believed constituted total insurgent strength, and an auxiliary force of 300,000. The auxiliary, per unconventional warfare doctrine, supports a guerrilla force by providing security, intelligence, transportation, logistics, and so on, but it's not a direct combat force. In Afghanistan terms, I thought of it also as a part-time militia.

The program had already supplied 300,000 Lee-Enfield bolt-action rifles with five-round magazines, and this was the perfect weapon for the part-time and supporting fighters that made up the auxiliary. It also seemed like the right quantity, so I stopped procuring these rifles and focused on providing ammunition for those already in the field. To do this, we engaged the Pakistan Ordnance Factories to produce .303-caliber ammunition for the program.

Knowing the decentralized structure of the Afghan resistance and the varying numbers of fighters that individual resistance commanders controlled—which ranged from 300 to 15,000—I designed my model weapons mix for the guerrilla forces, or main combat groups, from the bottom up. Guerrilla force units fight primarily at the platoon (30- to 50-man groups) and company (150- to 200-man groups) levels and rarely exceed battalion or regimental size (800 to 2,000 fighters).

Armies have long been organized on a triangular structure, and guerrilla armies follow this general rule. Three rifle squads make up a rifle platoon, three rifle platoons plus a weapons platoon make up a rifle company, and so forth. This allows for a maneuver or assault force, a fire support force, and a security force. I believed that an insurgent rifle squad should have nine to eleven fighters and be equipped with AK-47 assault rifles, an RPG-7 rocket-propelled grenade launcher (a more recent vintage Soviet anti-tank weapon than the RPG-2), and a light machine gun, the RPD or the newer RPK. To reach proper balance, we would need to procure additional AK-47s, RPG-7s, and RPK light machine guns, but based on my calculation and budget projections, I expected to reach my force goal at the squad level within two years.

The platoon level (30 to 50 fighters) is the basic insurgent fighting group. In addition to its three rifle squads and a command element, I believed that a resistance platoon should be equipped with two PK general-purpose machine guns. The PK has a greater maximum effective range than the RPD and RPK, out to six hundred meters or more, and packs a bigger punch with its 7.62 x 54 mm ammunition. I set a goal of supplying two PKs for every 30 insurgent fighters. Given projected funding and my other priorities, I assessed that it would take three years to realize my force structure goals at the platoon level.

An insurgent or guerrilla force company (150 to 200 fighters) would have three rifle platoons, plus a weapons platoon. I determined that a weapons platoon should have a three-gun section of 82 mm mortars for indirect fire support, a three-gun section of 12.7 mm DShK heavy machine guns for air defense and heavy direct fire support, and a three-gun section of 82 mm recoilless rifles for anti-armor operations. It should also have three two-man sniper teams equipped with Soviet SVD sniper rifles. More than enough 12.7 mm machine guns had already been supplied to reach my goal, but there was a significant shortfall of the other weapons, particularly the SVD sniper rifles, whose procurement I was just about to initiate. These weapons would enable a resistance company-sized force to conduct complex ambushes and raids and harass enemy strongpoints. Based on my calculations under various budget scenarios, it would likely take three years to reach my force structure goals at the company level.

Three companies would make up a guerrilla battalion, and three battalions would make up a regiment. The battalion and regiment, as defenders of insurgent base areas and providers of longer-range fires, should have additional heavy machine guns (Chinese 14.5 mm ZPU-1s) and single-barrel (Egyptian 122 mm) and multibarrel (Chinese Type 63, twelve-barrel, 107 mm) rocket launchers. These heavy weapons would also enable more complex offensive operations than a resistance company-sized force could currently conduct. Very few of these weapons had been provided to date. I set my force structure goal at one 14.5 mm machine gun per 90 AK-47s and one rocket launcher per 270 AK-47s. I thought that I could reach my goals in this area in two years.

To shift the air balance in the insurgents' favor, I wanted to increase the number of surface-to-air missiles by up to two orders of magnitude, from twenty to two thousand. My initial goal was to reach twelve hundred. I would typically purchase three missiles for every launcher, but the number could be as many as six depending on the particular system. The number of missiles and launchers would be determined as much by the available budget as by combat requirements, but two thousand missiles would give me several hundred engagements per year, assuming two to four missiles expended per engagement.[5] That would dramatically increase the number of Soviet aircraft shot down.

More than sixty thousand mines had been supplied, so I stopped procuring these, but I started the procurement of man-portable, mine-clearing line charges so the insurgents could attack infrastructure targets protected by minefields. I also significantly expanded the number of demolition kits we provided.

A tougher challenge was determining the optimal ammunition supply for the cumulative weapons stock. The supply of ammunition determines operational tempo. Again, there were no manuals to guide me. This is where my primitive hand calculator really got a workout. Starting with an insurgent force of 150,000, I assumed that no more than one-third, or 50,000, would be engaged in combat at a time. The rest would be in operational or strategic base areas recovering, being trained, and/or getting resupplied. I assumed that an engaged force would conduct an operation or engage in battle at most every three days, or ten days a month. I used a smaller factor, one-third of a month's supply during the fighting season, to determine ammunition requirements for the four winter months of combat. This tempo would enable thousands of operations across Afghanistan each month. It would give the Soviets fits.

I assumed that of the cumulative weapons stock that had been supplied, only 80 percent would be available. The rest would be lost in combat or damaged beyond repair. I then established "basic combat loads"—the amount of ammunition needed for a "typical" operation—for each weapon or weapon system. An insurgent rifleman equipped with an AK-47 should go into combat with at least three magazines, or ninety rounds of ammunition. A machine gun crew should have at least two hundred to six hundred rounds. A mortar crew should be able to fire at least four to eight rounds in an engagement, or twelve to twenty-four rounds for a three-gun section. Similarly, a multibarrel rocket launcher crew might fire twelve to twenty-four rockets, depending on the operation. An anti-tank gunner should be able to fire two to three rockets. A sniper would often fire only one or a few rounds, but should have the capacity to fire at least ten. I would then factor in the prices we paid to our suppliers for each item. During the mid-1980s, an AK-47 cost us $165. The AK's 7.62 x 39 mm ammunition cost fifteen cents a round. A surface-to-air missile would cost from $20,000 to $60,000, depending on the system.

Armed with my force structure goals, the likely rate of ammunition consumption at the desired operational tempo, and the cost of each weapon and round of ammunition or rocket or missile, I would perform a series of repetitive calculations until I arrived at what I thought was the optimal weapons mix for that year's program budget. That became the program plan and the basis for the Afghanistan Covert Action Program's procurement of ordnance for the remainder of the war.

As I was putting the program's new weapons mix in place, I ran into Howard Hart, our former chief in Islamabad, in the hall at CIA headquarters. Hart had been in charge of the war from 1981 to 1984 and was now running a very compartmented collection program for CIA. We had had little interaction since his return from Pakistan a few months earlier.

"Why have you stopped buying 12.7 machine guns?" Hart asked.

"Because we have enough of them," I responded, "and we need to buy other weapons that are in much shorter supply." I explained how we were planning to buy surface-to-air missiles, multibarrel rocket launchers, and other arms and ammunition in much greater quantities to increase the resistance's combat power. I started to tell him about the model insurgent force structure I had developed, but decided it wasn't necessary.

Hart nodded and added, "It's a wonderful weapon," referring to the 12.7 mm DShK heavy machine gun.

"It is indeed," I replied.

The torch had passed.

———

We were always looking for ways to improve the weapons mix. During my second month in the job, Gust and I traveled to Cairo to join up with Charlie Wilson to see what the Egyptians could provide in terms of additional air defense weaponry for the Afghan resistance. Charlie wanted us to look at an Egyptian knockoff of the Soviet SA-7 man-portable air defense system, called the Sakr-Eye. I was interested in procuring hundreds more SA-7s for the program but wasn't interested in the Sakr-Eye. It suffered from poor quality control and was too expensive. I planned to get my SA-7s from another source—China.

The Egyptians also wanted to sell us a very heavy anti-aircraft gun. They arranged a demonstration to show us how the Soviet ZU-23-2, a twin-barreled 23 mm anti-aircraft gun that weighed a ton and couldn't be disassembled, could be employed by the mujahedin in the mountains of Afghanistan. On top of a small hill overlooking Cairo, Gust, Charlie, a few CIA colleagues, and I sat on plastic armchairs under colorful umbrellas enjoying a takeout box of Kentucky Fried Chicken provided by the Egyptians as a team of mules and a squad of Egyptian soldiers tried to pull the gun up the hill's dirt switchback road. An Oxford-educated, three-star Egyptian general was our host and narrator for the demonstration.

The demo did not go as planned. "Cajoled" by the Egyptian soldiers, the mules tried to pull the gun up the hill, only to stop in protest after taking one or two steps. The soldiers tried to coax the lead mules by pulling on their harnesses, all to no avail. To preserve what minimal progress had been made, one soldier tried putting a rock behind the hooves of the rear mule. At that point, the demonstration was called off.

Charlie turned to Gust and me and joked, "This is the damnedest CIA operation I've ever seen."

Needless to say, we didn't buy that anti-aircraft gun, but we did buy a new weapon I liked, a 122 mm single-barrel rocket launcher used by

Egypt's special forces. It had a range of eleven kilometers and would be perfect for the mujahedin. We placed orders for twenty initially, with more to follow. We also purchased $40 million of traditional program ordnance during our visit, so the Egyptians came away happy. Egypt's defense minister, Field Marshal Muhammad Abu Ghazala, hosted us with an elaborate dinner, with belly dancers and sword swallowers for entertainment. What a way to fight a secret war, I thought.

The best part of the trip, however, was the bond that I forged with Charlie Wilson. I explained where we were going with the weapons mix and program strategy and why we wanted to focus our covert supply from Egypt on some weapons and not others. Our Oerlikon experience had made us concerned that we would be forced to buy more weapons we didn't want. But it turned out not to be the case. From that trip to Cairo on, Charlie gave us a free hand to determine the weapons mix and all other program decisions. He got us the money and let us do our work.

—————

I started adding Soviet SVD sniper rifles into the program's weapons mix in early 1985. But before I did, I had to get the approval of CIA's deputy director, John McMahon. McMahon had a great antenna for anything that might get the agency in political trouble, and the provision of sniper rifles looked like a good candidate to do just that. I was summoned to his office, where I was grilled about our need for the weapons and how we would explain their inclusion in our program briefings to Congress. The CIA was still reeling from the publication a year earlier of a so-called assassination manual that had been provided to the contras.[6] I explained that the SVD was just another tool in the insurgents' arsenal and that we would treat them as one of several line items in our anti-personnel weapons mix. Nothing special, just a rifle with greater range. He ultimately approved, though less than enthusiastically.

One of our paramilitary operations officers then had the idea of converting a 14.5 mm heavy machine gun into a long-range sniper rifle, and a gunsmith on contract to the agency had developed a plan to do it. It involved adding a stock, firing mechanism, magazine, ten-power scope, and bipod to the gun's receiver and barrel. The gun would have a range well in excess of a mile, and its round would be useful against a range of targets. It would cost us $6,500 a copy. I agreed to fund a prototype, which quickly became known as the "buffalo" gun. My paramilitary operations colleagues and I test-fired the weapon at a covert CIA facility. The protype was primitive looking and had quite a recoil, but I concluded it could fill an important niche in the resistance's capabilities, allowing the insurgents to engage the Soviets from much greater range.

When I returned to CIA headquarters, I briefed McMahon on the experimental weapon, the test results we had achieved, and how the program might use it. I recommended that we adopt it in limited quantities. He made it clear that the gun was to be listed in our program documents as an "anti-material" weapon—to be used against fuel tanks, thin-skinned vehicles, and so on—and not as an anti-personnel weapon. But once again, he supported our introduction of another sniper weapon. We purchased seventy weapons and began deploying them into Afghanistan in January 1986.

TRAINING, OPERATIONAL SUPPORT, AND RESISTANCE UNITY

In December 1984, I wrote a long operational cable outlining our new strategy, which Bert Dunn had blessed as the way forward for the program. I highlighted our new goals for the weapons mix and the significant emphasis we would need to place going forward on the "software" of the insurgency, its training, intelligence, operational advice, and command and control. I called for a major increase in the quality and quantity of training provided to the resistance.

For the first several years of the program, there had been only two camps in Pakistan for resistance training, each with a capacity of two hundred trainees at a time. The annual throughput was limited to around two thousand, and the training was rudimentary. In 1985, with Inter-Services Intelligence's support, we increased our annual throughput by an order of magnitude to twenty thousand annually, a level we sustained until the Soviets withdrew. The number of training camps increased from two to seven, and the camps were much larger. ISI's Afghan Bureau, led by Brigadier Mohammad Yousaf, was in charge of the training and provided several hundred instructors, detailed to ISI from the Pakistan Army.[7]

An expanded range of courses were now offered, from specialized weapons, demolitions, and communications training, to training in the planning and conduct of combined arms operations for company- and higher-level commanders. Additional specialized training would be added for the Oerlikon 20 mm cannon and the Blowpipe and Stinger surface-to-air missile systems. Paramilitary operations officers from CIA's Ground Branch would train Pakistani instructors on the specialized weapons, and the Pakistanis would then train the mujahedin. Nick, Steve, George, and Serge were our main trainers, and they did a fantastic job. Nick was a Marine Corps officer on detail to CIA. Steve was a former Marine, and George and Serge had served in the Special Forces, Serge with me in the 10th Special Forces Group.

Gust and I visited two of these camps in the Peshawar area in 1985, where we witnessed several of the courses. I came away impressed. The visits also gave me a chance to talk directly to political party leaders, resistance commanders, and insurgent fighters. At the ISI training camp near Warsak, I had watched several live-fire exercises and discussed our increased support for the resistance with mujahedin commanders. Morale was high among the mujahedin, strengthening my resolve to help them win their war.

Afterward, Gust and I met with Gulbuddin Hekmatyar, the mujahedin leader most favored by ISI, but also the problem child of the resistance. We knew he liked to be addressed by the honorific "Engineer," so "Engineer Gulbuddin" it was. As I sat across from him and stared at his black eyes, I recalled how he had regularly ordered his men to ambush fellow resistance fighters from other parties. I thought his eyes were a perfect match for his black heart. On that sunny late winter day in early 1985, he was all sweetness and light, however, telling Gust and me in excellent English how much he appreciated American support and how his sole focus was on driving the Soviets out of Afghanistan. If only it had been true.

During our visit to another ISI camp, I met a young teenage fighter who really wanted to talk with me and began our chat by saying, "America good." With the occasional help of an interpreter, he proceeded to tell me how many Russians he had killed and how his unit conducted ambushes and other operations. He claimed to have shot down two Mi-8 transport helicopters with a 12.7 mm machine gun. I had no way of knowing if it was true, but I liked him, and wished him even greater success in the future.

With our encouragement, ISI also stepped up significantly the operational advice it provided to mujahedin fighting groups in Afghanistan. It sent Pashto-speaking, three-man teams "inside" to act as special forces advisers to the resistance. This increased advisory support also had a big impact on the effectiveness of insurgent operations. I met with a Pakistani major from the Special Service Group who had made several trips into Afghanistan as an operational adviser and was very impressed with his professionalism. We bonded as SF soldier to SF soldier, and he told me he would be honored to accompany me "inside." I told him I would like nothing better than to go in with him, but U.S. government policy unfortunately prohibited CIA officers from doing so; the potential strategic cost if we were captured vastly outweighed any operational benefit. Plus, the Pakistani and U.K. special forces advisers who were acting as our surrogates were doing a bang-up job. He opened up about what a difficult boss Brigadier Yousaf was and how much he longed for his two- to three-year tour with ISI to be over so he could see his family more often.

I also met with two of ISI's top special operations advisers, Colonels "Iman" (true name Sultan Tarar) and Khalid Khawaja. They were serious and dangerous men, whose interests and actions would diverge substantially from America's after the Cold War had ended. But at that moment, we were on the same side.[8] We discussed the war at length—which insurgent groups were most effective, the vulnerabilities of Soviet forces, and what we should do to capitalize on them. We didn't see eye to eye on everything, but we were able to forge an effective partnership—at least for the time being.

———

While we had good intelligence about the war and the Afghan resistance, we hadn't been providing much in the way of timely and actionable intelligence to insurgent commanders. If we were going to improve the overall effectiveness of the resistance, we needed to address that shortfall as well.

During the 1980s, CIA had imagery analysts in the National Photographic Interpretation Center and in the Directorate of Intelligence's Office of Imagery Analysis. NPIC, staffed by both CIA and DOD, was responsible for the initial exploitation (processing and interpretation) of imagery collected by our reconnaissance satellites, while OIA did post-collection analyses and provided support to the Directorate of Operations. OIA had representatives on the Afghanistan Task Force who provided imagery analysis to the program's leadership. In early 1985, we asked our senior OIA officer, Tom, to prepare target folders for ISI and key resistance commanders. We weren't permitted to provide the actual imagery to the resistance—that could reveal the capabilities of our satellites—so OIA prepared "line drawings" from the imagery. This greatly improved the insurgents' operational planning. During training in Pakistan, select groups could rehearse an operation before going into Afghanistan to execute it.

In the communications area, we had two operational problems, one tactical and the other strategic. First, the Soviets were getting increasingly good at geolocating ("direction finding") insurgent tactical communications—typically, handheld walkie-talkies. The mujahedin resisted using good communications security procedures, often transmitting for lengthy periods, which made it easy for Soviet signals intelligence units to locate them and enable Soviet aircraft to strike insurgent concentrations.

Larry, the Office of Communications representative on the Afghanistan Task Force, recommended that we supply key resistance commanders with state-of-the-art, frequency-hopping, tactical radios—advanced communications equipment that hadn't even been fielded to the U.S. military yet. The radio's ability to constantly shift frequencies would make it difficult for Soviet SIGINT elements to lock on long enough to geolocate it. Larry and I visited the manufacturer, and I was quickly sold on the idea. The program placed a large order for the radios, and we had them in insurgent hands within two months. The new radios quickly made a dramatic difference in communications security and survivability for the Afghan resistance.

Our other problem was we had no way of communicating in a timely manner with our best commanders inside Afghanistan. For this, Larry recommended that we provide long-range HF radios with burst transmission capabilities. I was very familiar with these kinds of radios: we used them in the Special Forces to communicate with our operational headquarters, which could be hundreds or even thousands of miles away. Burst transmission—sending the whole message in a few seconds—greatly reduced the probability of interception and geolocation. We provided this long-range communications system to our best commanders in the north, east, south, and west of Afghanistan. In addition to giving us a command-and-control mechanism, the HF radios allowed the insurgents to send regular intelligence and operational reports to us. It didn't work perfectly, to be sure, but it did improve our ability to monitor and influence events on the battlefield in real time.

———

By the fall of 1984, CIA had both political and operational imperatives to seek greater unity at the top of the Afghan resistance. In March 1985, Pakistan, with strong U.S. encouragement, forced the parties into a real alliance, informally dubbed the Peshawar Seven, with leadership rotating among leaders each year. As a practical matter, the only thing the parties could agree on was their common goal of forcing a Soviet withdrawal and toppling the Communist Afghan regime, but the formation of the alliance still helped politically, particularly in sustaining broad international support for the resistance. It also enabled greater intra-party operational collaboration on the battlefield and helped reduce, though by no means eliminated, intra-insurgent conflict. Its biggest contribution to the program, however, was to reduce ISI's logistical burden. Before the seven-party alliance was formed, ISI had supplied several mujahedin commanders directly. Afterward, almost all insurgent resupply was funneled through the parties. This greatly simplified things from a supply perspective.

THE WAR IN WASHINGTON AND PATH TO FULL IMPLEMENTATION

Our secret war wasn't just fought in Afghanistan. There were also battles to be won in Washington—within CIA, with the Department of Defense, at the White House, and in Congress. The most important of these was the White House, and I'll have more to say about its role in supporting our war-winning strategy in the next chapter. But there were also critics within CIA, the Pentagon, and Congress who posed a threat to the program that I had to deal with.

By early 1985, the CIA was supporting several anti-Communist insurgencies through covert action. The largest program by far was CIA's support for the Afghan resistance. The Nicaragua, or "contra," program was the second largest. Alan Fiers, a rising star in CIA's Clandestine Service, had taken over as chief of the Central American Task Force, and the Nicaragua program was his top priority.

Ed Juchniewicz, CIA's associate deputy director for operations, called a meeting in late January to discuss our global covert action strategy. Juchniewicz chaired the Covert Action Planning Group at CIA, the body that oversaw the development of covert action programs. Fiers represented the Central American Task Force at the meeting, and I represented the Afghanistan program. The meeting was ostensibly about how we could share resources and lessons learned, but it quickly turned into a discussion of our covert action strategy and priorities.

Fiers was well aware that the Afghanistan program's budget was several times larger than his. A former offensive lineman for Ohio State, a Marine, and a career NE officer, Fiers had returned to headquarters the previous summer after completing an assignment as chief of a major NE station.

"We can't win in Afghanistan," Fiers asserted. "We should shift resources to Central America. We can win there."

"How?" Juchniewicz asked.

"With a four-corner offense that stretches out their defense," Fiers replied, referring to Sandinista regime forces.

Fiers loved sports metaphors. It seemed sound enough as a guerrilla warfare strategy, but Nicaragua was a sideshow in our struggle with the Soviet Empire. Fiers was far senior to me, so when Juchniewicz asked me what I thought, I did my best to be non-provocative. I wasn't sure yet where Director Casey's priorities were, and I knew there was still apprehension within CIA's senior leadership about the rapid growth of the Afghanistan program. I also knew, however, that Juchniewicz had helped Gust get the chief of South Asia Operations job, which Fiers had wanted, and like most people of Eastern European heritage Juchniewicz passionately hated the Soviets.

"Afghanistan is the only place where we can take the fight directly to our main enemy," I argued. "It should remain CIA's main effort." I also reminded Juchniewicz about an NSC strategic review of the program that was just getting under way. I told him that from what I had seen thus far, after the review was finished, it was quite possible that President Reagan would decide to escalate the war in Afghanistan.

That was enough for Juchniewicz, and the discussion moved on to potential collaboration across programs. That was the last meeting of the CAPG I attended during my tenure. President Reagan's signature on a new National Security Decision Directive would soon settle the covert action priorities debate.

The U.S. military also paid a call on me early in my tenure. Special operations officers from the U.S. Central Command, which had responsibility for the Middle East, visited CIA headquarters and told us that in the event of a Soviet invasion of Iran—CENTCOM's principal planning contingency—they wanted to be able to gain control of the Afghan resistance so they could task it in their war plans. They were good officers, and I understood their rationale, but told them that there was no way CIA's leadership would agree to this. We were fighting the Soviets now. If there were a Soviet invasion of Iran, we'd of course do our best to support CENTCOM's operations, but we would not transfer control of the resistance. They weren't happy, but they understood this was a nonstarter for us.

A few policy civilians in the Office of the Secretary of Defense had a different agenda. They wanted a much larger role in the direction and conduct of the program. They wanted U.S. Special Forces under DOD's control to directly train the mujahedin (not feasible in a covert program) and proposed air-dropping supplies to the resistance using Air Force C-130s—a harebrained idea if there ever was one, because the aircraft would be quickly shot down by Soviet air defenses. An overt role for DOD would also put Pakistan's participation and the program at risk and trigger a direct confrontation with the Soviets. We made it clear that the Afghanistan Covert Action Program was just that, a covert action program, and that it was the exclusive responsibility of CIA. Senior OSD and Joint Staff representatives had a policy voice in the interagency process, but that was it. This DOD request, too, was quickly shelved.

Finally, while the program enjoyed strong bipartisan support in Congress, it also had its critics. Many of them, surprisingly, given that Ronald Reagan was president, were Republicans. Senator Gordon Humphrey of New Hampshire had been a particularly persistent one. Four Republican senators, Orrin Hatch of Utah, Jesse Helms of North Carolina, Chic Hecht of Nevada, and Humphrey, referred to within CIA jokingly as the "4H Club," had taken a special interest in the program. Covert action programs depend critically on congressional support, so we wanted to do whatever we could to win Humphrey and his Senate colleagues over.

In April 1985, I was asked to provide a program briefing and put on a weapons demonstration for Senator Humphrey at the Farm. We flew in weapons from several warehouses. With Bert Dunn in attendance, I briefed Humphrey on the program and its weapons mix. With the assistance of our paramilitary operations officers, Humphrey got to fire most of the program's weapons, save for surface-to-air missiles, mortars, and multibarrel rocket launchers.

Humphrey had a great time, but we hadn't fully won him over. He would remain a frequent critic of the program. By April 1988, after the Soviets had begun withdrawing their combat forces from Afghanistan, he would concede that the CIA had done a great job in more recent years. That was good enough for me.

––––––––––

During my first few months on the job, I had developed a vision for how we could dramatically escalate the war in Afghanistan and had begun implementing that vision to the full extent of the authorities and resources provided to the program up to that point. But I also knew that to fully implement my new strategy, I'd need a lot more resources and decisions by others who were far senior to me. I'd need another doubling of program funding and new weapons, particularly large numbers of advanced surface-to-air missile systems. I would need to wrest strategic control of the program from the Pakistanis to make the changes I knew we needed, and I'd need to get the Chinese, the Saudis, and the British to agree to escalate the war along with us. And I'd of course need support from CIA's leadership, the administration, and Congress for all of it.

The key break would come with a National Security Council–directed review of the program that began in December 1984. While not its intent at the beginning, it produced a strategic inflection point for the program, and I seized on it. In a little over twelve months, our war-winning strategy would be fully in place.

CRITICAL DECISIONS:
MARCH 1985 TO JANUARY 1986

THE PATH TO ESCALATION DOMINANCE

Escalation dominance is a key concept in strategy, and it can be the difference between victory and defeat. When we have it, we win our wars or end them on our terms. When we don't, we lose. We had it in World War II due to our superior mobilization capacity, and we had it at the end of the Korean War when President Eisenhower threatened to use nuclear weapons if the North Koreans did not agree to an armistice. Escalation dominance shows your adversary that he can't win because you can escalate the conflict to levels he can't match. If he persists anyway, his defeat is inevitable.[1] It would prove to be a key component of our strategy during our secret war in Afghanistan during the 1980s, and it would be a key component during our war with al-Qa'ida decades later.

Between March 1985 and January 1986, four critical decisions gave us escalation dominance over the Soviets and enabled my strategy to become a war-winning one. First, President Reagan fundamentally changed our war aims, escalating our objective from making the Soviet occupation of Afghanistan as costly as possible to driving the Soviets out by all means available. Next, we persuaded the leaders of Pakistan, China, Saudi Arabia, and the U.K. to support our major escalation of the war. Then we persuaded CIA's leadership, the president, and Congress to double funding for the program, reaching more than a billion dollars per annum. And finally, President Reagan approved the deployment of the Stinger surface-to-air missile system to Afghanistan, which dramatically shifted the air balance in the insurgents' favor.

Strategy is about ends, ways, and means—establishing attainable ends and employing effective ways with sufficient means to achieve them. I had already begun changing the ways of our covert war strategy with more and different kinds of ordnance, more and better training, and increased operational support. What I still lacked to fully implement my strategy was a change in ends that would make additional means and even more new ways possible. President Reagan's decision to change our war aims provided the necessary catalyst for both. Nineteen eighty-five would turn out to be the decisive year of the war. We and the Soviets would both escalate the war dramatically in 1985, but only we would see our escalation through. By the end of that year, Soviet leaders would start looking for the exit.

NATIONAL SECURITY DECISION DIRECTIVE 166

A crisis often contains a strategic opportunity within it. Such was the case with the National Security Council's review of the Afghanistan Covert Action Program between December 1984 and March 1985.

In late December 1984, Republican Senator Gordon Humphrey from New Hampshire said at a press conference that the Afghan insurgents "remain critically, tragically and scandalously short" of weapons.[2] Humphrey and a few others in Congress were alleging that as much as 90 percent of the weapons and ammunition CIA was procuring for the Afghan resistance was being diverted by the Pakistanis for their own use. It wasn't true, but the White House had to take these congressional concerns seriously.

That same month, the NSC launched a review of the program under Donald Fortier on how to "bound the corruption problem." Fortier, who was battling cancer and would tragically pass away eighteen months later, assigned a member of his staff, Stephen Rosen, to solicit the interagency responses needed for the review. It was conducted under a new top secret security compartment called VEIL the NSC had established to restrict distribution of information about covert action programs. Rosen developed a series of questions about the program, beginning with how large the corruption problem was and how we could "bound it." He also included questions about what our policy goals should be for the program. It was largely what was called a "paper" NSC review, in which agencies submitted their responses on paper to the NSC staff. Within CIA, I was tasked to prepare CIA's response.

I worked on it for the better part of the month and in the process met with Rosen at CIA to brief him in detail on the program and the major changes we were making to it. I explained why we were very confident that the overwhelming majority of program-supplied ordnance was reaching the resistance inside Afghanistan, citing the multiple intelligence sources we had that confirmed this. The program had several problems that needed immediate attention, I explained, but "bounding the corruption problem" wasn't one of them.

The most important part of the review was the questions Rosen had asked about our policy goals and strategic approach. Should we "stay the course" in Afghanistan, or should we change our policy and seek to drive the Soviets out "by all means available"? Those last words jumped out from the page as I read them.

"Yes, that's exactly what we should do," I almost blurted out as I sat at my desk, "and we're already putting in place the strategy to do it."

By the time I had finished working on CIA's response to the NSC, the package was more than one inch thick. It contained not only CIA's response to the NSC's questions but all the intelligence and program data necessary to support our position.

Up to this point, the program's policy goal had been to impose costs on the Soviets for their occupation of Afghanistan, and it had remained unchanged through President Reagan's first term, even after the big increase in funding that Charlie Wilson had provided. President Reagan had signed National Security Decision Directive 75 in January 1983, outlining U.S. strategy toward the Soviet Union, but it had had no effect on the program. On February 6, 1985, President Reagan had announced in his State of the Union address what would become known as the "Reagan Doctrine"—that "we must not break faith with those who are risking their lives on every continent, from Afghanistan to Nicaragua, to defy Soviet-supported aggression"—but this likewise did not alter the program's policy goal.

What did change the program's policy objective was National Security Decision Directive 166, signed by President Reagan on March 27, 1985, "U.S. Policy, Programs, and Strategy in Afghanistan."[3] NSDD 166 explicitly established the removal of Soviet forces from Afghanistan and the restoration of Afghanistan's independent status as the goal of U.S. policy. It also established five "interim" objectives and assigned eight tasks to CIA. The interim objectives and tasks were boilerplate. What truly mattered was the change in our policy goal. As I ran through the eight tasks, I noted that we were already on the path to accomplishing all of them. The most important task was to improve the military effectiveness of the Afghan resistance, and we were intent on dramatically improving it. What we still lacked, though, was the additional funding and advanced weapons we would need to do it.

It is not true, as a 1999 Harvard Kennedy School case study claims, that the Defense Department drove the NSC review and its policy outcome. Some former DOD officials, it appears, were trying to claim more credit for the policy change than warranted. The review was NSC-initiated and NSC-led, and the change in policy that resulted from it had the strong support of CIA and State as well as DOD. If any department or agency shaped the policy outcome of the review, it was CIA. When it came to the Afghanistan Covert Action Program, CIA was a policy maker.

It is also not true that after NSDD 166 was signed, the Afghanistan Covert Action Program became an interagency program under the supervision of a lower-level interagency committee on the NSC, nor did the program "change its management structure" from a presidential finding with oversight by the congressional Intelligence Committees to an NSC program in which all agencies had a part.[4] Again, this is nonsense on multiple levels. Covert action programs with their required presidential findings are always at the direction of the White House and under the oversight of the congressional Intelligence Committees. CIA remained in full control of the program, and made all of the program decisions, save for the subsequent one by President Reagan to introduce the U.S.-made Stinger missile into the conflict. Other U.S. government departments were asked to provide their views on U.S. policy for the secret war in Afghanistan, but they did not materially participate in the Afghanistan Covert Action Program. It was all CIA.

ASKING FOR MORE FUNDING AND ASSERTING STRATEGIC CONTROL

Near the end of the March 1985 trip to Pakistan I had made with Gust, I sent a long cable to CIA headquarters describing what we had accomplished during our visit, referencing the new strategy cable I had sent to the field a few months earlier. I provided additional thoughts on what its implementation would entail. I argued that to expand the weapons mix and provide the ammunition required for more frequent and intense combat operations, the program could use nearly two and a half times the funding it was currently receiving. Based on my calculations, we needed $1.2 billion annually.

After months of calculations, I had gotten comfortable with the necessity for such large sums. That wasn't the case for everyone in CIA, however. Director Casey called Gust's deputy, Larry, on that Saturday morning to express his displeasure with my cable.

Casey let loose. "Why does the program need another huge increase in funding? Wasn't the program budget quadrupled just a few months ago?" Fortunately, Larry, a lawyer as well as a career case officer, didn't flinch. "Vickers knows his stuff," he replied. "He's done the analysis."

Casey grunted and nodded, which we took for tacit acquiescence. The director had been content to keep the Afghanistan program on a path of continuity during President Reagan's first term and had focused most of his attention on the insurgencies and counterinsurgencies in Central America. He had traveled to Pakistan and Saudi Arabia in 1982, but didn't return there until two years later. Until 1985, moreover, Casey believed that the Soviets would eventually "overpower and wear down the rebels."[5]

But Casey had served in the Office of Strategic Services as a young man during World War II and modeled himself after the head of the OSS, General "Wild" Bill Donovan, a portrait of whom hung in Casey's seventh-floor office. And like Donovan, Casey was a risk taker and a man determined to do what he could to weaken and eventually bring down the Soviet Empire. CIA was President Reagan's sword in the global covert war with the Soviet Empire and Bill Casey was its wielder, a man with a mission. Bob Gates put it best:

What truly set Bill Casey apart from his predecessors and his successors as DCI [director of central intelligence], though, was that he had not come to CIA with the purpose of making it better, managing it more effectively, reforming it, or improving the quality of intelligence. What I realized only years later was that Bill Casey came to CIA primarily to wage war against the Soviet Union.[6]

Casey's grunt soon turned into full-throated support. "Can you live with $800 million?" Bert Dunn asked me a month after my return from overseas. "Yes, with that amount we will get major gains in resistance effectiveness," I responded, "but we really could use the full $1.2 billion." Many of the changes I wanted to make, including providing large quantities of surface-to-air missiles, could be accomplished with $800 million. The additional funds would mostly provide further increases in combat intensity. "Okay," Bert said, "draw up two plans: one for $800 million and one for $1.1 billion." I had no idea why he had docked me $100 million, but I was very happy with the guidance.

My new strategy also required shifting strategic control of the program from the field to Washington. I knew this wouldn't be an easy sell with the Pakistanis and it wasn't. The Pakistanis had pretty much gotten their way in terms of what we provided to the resistance and how we provided it during the first five years of the program, and weren't keen on relinquishing control. We butted heads regularly through much of 1985, particularly with Brigadier Mohammad Yousaf, the head of ISI's Afghan Bureau.

Fortunately, Bill Piekney, our chief of station in Islamabad from 1984 to 1986, turned out to be masterful at working that relationship. The CIA's chiefs in Islamabad from 1981 to 1984 and 1986 to 1989, Howard Hart and Milt Bearden, have deservedly received a large share of the credit for the success of the program, but Bill Piekney played his own pivotal role. The Pakistanis would say no to one of our initiatives, and Piekney and his chief of paramilitary operations would keep at them, explaining why CIA headquarters wanted to go in this direction. Piekney's deferral to headquarters' judgment on these strategic issues was critical. Islamabad Station would convey ISI's objections to what we proposed, and we would reply with our counterarguments.

Eventually, we won over General Akhtar, and Brigadier Yousaf was forced to go along. To be sure, President Zia still retained ultimate control over program operations in Pakistan and Afghanistan, but as long as Akhtar was on board, Zia enthusiastically embraced our plans to dramatically escalate the war. Strategic control of the direction of the war and much of its operational execution shifted to CIA head-quarters and its Afghanistan Task Force between 1984 and 1986. I could check off that part of my strategy, but that's not to say CIA and I didn't continue to have major headaches with my Pakistani counterpart. Although a good infantryman, Yousaf was very difficult to work with. He was very critical and mistrusting of CIA, resentful of the West, and domineering and dogmatic in his approach to military matters.

We invited him to Washington during the summer of 1985 to see CIA's sabotage capabilities. The program was now supplying thou-sands of demolition kits for insurgent use, and we wanted to show Yousaf how to use them effectively.[7] CIA's demolitions experts are among the best in the world. We flew him in a small plane to CIA's demolitions training facility with the windows blacked out so as not to reveal the location of the base. He took great umbrage at this, though he was impressed with what he witnessed at the facility. After our discussion about sabotage techniques, we took him to see the Friday evening concert and parade at the Marine barracks at Eighth and I Streets, which he seemed to enjoy, at least somewhat. Earlier that day, I had also arranged to take him to the Army's post exchange store so he could stock up on gear.

We took him to Washington's best Afghan restaurant the next night, but by then his mood had darkened considerably. "Do you know how little money I make, and I'm a general in the Army," Yousaf said, wav-ing his hands to show his disdain for Georgetown's opulence. His mood turned even darker the following evening. Our foreign visitor team had purchased tickets for us to see *Godspell* at Ford's Theatre. When I heard about where we were taking him, I asked our team if we had any alternative. "The guy's a fundamentalist Muslim," I said. "Are we really going to take him to see *Godspell*?" Truth be told, I had no interest in seeing the musical myself. There wasn't an alternative, the staffer who had purchased the tickets informed me. Besides, she said, "the show is full of color and dancing. He'll like it, and won't pay attention to the content." I should have objected more firmly.

Seeing *Godspell* might have been fine for a less devout Muslim visitor to Washington, but it wasn't for Brigadier Yousaf. He sat rigid throughout the whole show. "He must have thought that we were not only trying to recruit him, but convert him as well," Gust said with a chuckle after we dropped Yousaf off at the Four Seasons in Georgetown, where we had put him up. (It didn't escape our notice that he hadn't railed against the opulence of his hotel accommodations.) At the end of the day, Yousaf would do as he was told, however grudgingly, but the dark feelings he harbored toward CIA would grow into a near jihad following his forced retirement from the Pakistani Army in 1987.

THE CHINESE AGREE TO ESCALATE

In early May 1985, Bert Dunn and I went to Beijing to try to persuade the Chinese to match our escalation in Afghanistan with one of their own. The Chinese were already the program's primary supplier of arms, and I wanted them to provide a lot more, qualitatively and quantitatively.

There were four specific things on my list. First, I wanted the Chinese to significantly expand the quantity of arms they provided to keep pace with the program's growing budget. Second, I wanted them to supply heavier weapons, 82 mm mortars and recoilless rifles, 14.5 mm heavy machine guns, and 107 mm multibarrel rocket launchers, to increase the combat power of the Afghan resistance. Third, I wanted them to supply the resistance with large quantities of improved SA-7 surface-to-air missile systems to neutralize the Soviet air threat. Fourth, I wanted them to develop a tungsten carbide round for the 12.7 mm heavy machine gun.[8]

Before I departed, I was told by the national intelligence officer for East Asia that the Chinese would be very unlikely to accede to my requests. The Chinese would follow their ally Pakistan's lead on the war, and the Pakistanis hadn't requested such a dramatic escalation. Plus, while the Chinese were happy to see the Soviets bogged down in Afghanistan, they didn't want their involvement to become too provocative. These were all good points, but I still wanted what I wanted, and China was my best source for meeting each of these requirements.

CIA had forged an intelligence relationship with the Chinese in 1979 to monitor Soviet missile tests from western China, and that relationship had steadily expanded through the first five years of the Soviet-Afghan War. China started supplying arms through the program in 1982 and also provided its own support through training for the mujahedin in China and a limited direct supply of arms.[9] The Chinese had fought a border skirmish with the USSR in 1969 and, deep down, were as anti-Soviet as we were.

The host for our visit to Beijing was Xiong Guangkai, the deputy director of the People's Liberation Army's General Staff Intelligence Department, or 2PLA, as it is known in shorthand. Xiong would go on to become a four-star general and be a major force in Chinese security policy for the next two decades. Bert and I had three days of meetings with the Chinese, which were like nothing I'd experienced before. Accompanying us was Joe DeTrani, a fluent Chinese speaker and a great partner of the program.

I was asked to make a lengthy presentation on our assessment of the situation in Afghanistan and to describe our requests in detail before there would be any Chinese response. Then it was their turn. They provided their assessment of the situation and what they saw as the needs of the Afghan resistance, with no interruption permitted during the lengthy presentation. Not being able to ask any questions during the forty-five-minute monologue was, to say the least, a challenge.

Initially, it seemed we were ships passing in the night. The Chinese argued, as the Pakistanis had, for more small arms. I argued for heavier and more advanced weapons. We debated theories of guerrilla warfare at length and their applicability to the current situation in Afghanistan. I provided detailed lists of what I wanted in terms of types of ordnance and monthly delivery schedules. The Chinese wouldn't commit to anything, other than the 12.7 mm tungsten carbide round. I thought that perhaps they believed it might be a good idea to develop it for their own use.

The most difficult issue was my request for Chinese improved SA-7s. The program had previously procured a very small number of the missiles from another covert source, but several of the missiles had failed to work when they finally made it into Afghanistan. I wanted to supply the Afghan resistance with a lot more of the anti-aircraft missiles, and I wanted a more reliable supply source, so that led me to China and its improved SA-7. I asked the Chinese to provide six hundred missiles and two hundred launchers. I knew this would represent a major escalation of the war for the Chinese, because there was a high probability that the Soviets would capture some of the weapons and trace them back to China. But I also knew that the Chinese wanted to stick it to the Soviets as much as we did.

The night before we departed, the Chinese held a banquet in our honor, Peking duck and all. Our Chinese hosts delighted in offering us all parts, feet included. During the dinner, a server accidentally poured hot tea down Bert's back. Lots of toasts were offered, with *bai-jiu*, a clear Chinese liquor. I said *ganbei* (dry your cup) plenty of times, but surreptitiously switched to water very early.

As we left for the airport without a deal, I consoled myself that at least the Chinese had heard our requests. We would keep trying, just as we had in the face of the other initial noes we had encountered. But waiting for us in a private room at the airport was He Pengfei, a three-star general and the head of the PLA's Armaments Department. The Chinese had agreed to all of our requests, including the six hundred SA-7s, which we would get at nearly half the price we had paid previously. We shared a number of toasts with He, drinking to making life miserable for the Soviets and kicking them out of Afghanistan. As we drank, I remembered my earlier dreams of fighting with the Chinese to repel Soviet aggression. This was close enough. The only disappointment that came from our trip to China had been the improved 12.7 round. The initial test results in China had been positive, but after more detailed tests in the United States we determined that the Chinese round couldn't penetrate the Hind's armor, so we dropped the project. We would have to kill the Hind with other weapons. Another Chinese weapon, the "Red Arrow," a wire-guided anti-tank missile similar to the U.S. TOW, would also prove faulty and would not be bought by the program.

Between the beginning of 1985 and the end of 1988, the Chinese would provide nearly $1.5 billion in arms and ammunition to the Afghan resistance. They would also provide nearly two thousand improved SA-7 missiles. We could not have won our secret war without the Chinese.

WILSON'S $300 MILLION SUPPLEMENTAL

Meanwhile, Charlie Wilson was the gift that kept on giving for the Afghanistan Covert Action Program. In late September, he notified us that $300 million had suddenly become available in the defense budget after an anti-submarine warfare program had been canceled. As a member of the Defense Appropriations Subcommittee, he could reprogram it to CIA. It would be a supplemental appropriation for fiscal year 1985, which would close in a little over a week. It would bring the U.S. funding for the program to $550 million for FY 1985. Wilson's $300 million supplemental would turn out to be the largest single increase in funding in the program's history. We immediately contacted our station in Riyadh to ask if the king would agree to match it. King Fahd quickly agreed. I knew I'd now have at least $800 million for each of the next two years, and possibly $1.1 billion each year if DOD made a similar transfer the next year and the Saudis matched it again. I knew I'd have $1.1 billion to spend right away in any event, more than nine times what we'd had in the base budget just a year earlier, and that our new strategy would be funded through September 1987.

Before the reprogramming could be completed, however, we had to brief the Intelligence and Appropriations Committees of the House and Senate on how we planned to use the funds. Fortunately, I had already completed most of the necessary work. Working through the night with Tim B., the task force's chief logistics officer, and CIA's graphics shop, I prepared detailed, color-coded charts showing the ordnance deliveries that would be provided to the resistance over the next twenty-four months. Bert Dunn and I explained to our congressional overseers that this was the implementation of our new strategy, as directed by NSDD 166. We informed the members that there would be four thousand to eight thousand metric tons of arms and ammunition flowing into Karachi each month, a nearly sevenfold increase in the monthly tonnage from what the program had been providing just a year earlier. There would also be a more than sixty-five-fold increase in the number of surface-to-air missiles to counter the Soviet air threat to the resistance. Congress was fully on board, and we were notified that the reprogramming had been completed on September 28.

Now we had to obligate the funds before the end of the fiscal year, just two days away. Gust and I had planned to travel to Cairo to place another order for ordnance with the Egyptians in October, so we moved up our trip to accommodate the spending deadline. I had a $60 million order for the Egyptians ready to go. I also placed orders for arms and ammunition with the Chinese that were worth more than $240 million.

Even though the first nine Oerlikons (for three three-gun sections, with one spare kept in reserve) had just been deployed into Afghanistan, I also placed a new order using other funds for another twenty-six guns and ammunition, bringing our total to thirty-six, or twelve three-gun sections that we could deploy along the border. I also knew that we would need to strengthen our operational and tactical logistics inside Pakistan and Afghanistan to accommodate the increases in ordnance that were coming, so I sent a cable to Islamabad, requesting that the station contact ISI to obligate $10 million for additional warehouses and trucks. Islamabad Station came back with a positive response within hours. Through the Chinese, Egyptians, and Pakistanis, I had obligated more than $300 million for the program in a single evening.

MEMORANDUM OF NOTIFICATION

A memorandum of notification is required when a covert action program changes significantly in scale or scope. MONs are essentially amendments to presidential findings and are reported by the administration in writing to Congress.[10] With the dramatic increase in program funding, CIA's lawyers had determined that a MON was required. I was the action officer for getting it done.

As with the NSC strategy review, preparation of the supporting package for the MON took considerable time. I had to document where the program had been and where we intended to take it, explaining our rationale for the change in scale and scope to the presidential findings that had authorized the program. I had to detail the program's accomplishments to date, its challenges, and the strategic risk that this expansion entailed. It became another inch-thick package by the time I had finished it.

The most unusual part of the process was a specific tasking from the

NSC that required CIA's deputy director for intelligence, Bob Gates, to certify that the proposed increase in the program's scale and scope would not trigger a wider war with the Soviet Union—an invasion of Pakistan, for example. I explained the requirement to him and added, "They're [referring to the NSC] afraid that we're going to start World War III." He chuckled and told me he had already read the package and was good with it. Before I could say anything more, he signed off on the package and handed it back to me. I quickly left his office before he could change his mind.[11]

STRENGTHENING THE COVERT ARMS PIPELINE

With Wilson's $300 million supplemental and the Saudi match on top of the program's base budget of $500 million, the amount of ordnance delivered to Pakistan now ran upward of 65,000 metric tons annually. Based on our projections, yearly deliveries could even reach 100,000 metric tons by late 1987. ISI was increasingly vocal about how we were overwhelming their logistical system, particularly when ships carrying the program's matériel temporarily stacked up offshore. It was abundantly clear that the program's operational and tactical logistics needed strengthening.

Most ordnance would arrive by ship in Karachi and then be transported by railcars to ISI warehouses in Rawalpindi and Quetta for onward distribution to the resistance parties. Specialized ordnance, like surface-to-air missile systems, would typically be transported by air to Chaklala Air Base in Rawalpindi. We strove to provide ISI with a regular schedule of strategic supply to avoid having ships bunch up at Karachi's port and to keep operational stores full.

ISI would then deliver the supplies to the parties using five- and ten-ton trucks. The parties used a mixture of light trucks, usually Toyotas, and pack animals to transport ordnance into Afghanistan. All of this had to be done covertly to avoid attracting unwanted attention.

There were five main supply routes into Afghanistan, but sixty times that number in sub- or alternative routes. The route at Chitral led into the Panjshir Valley and the other northern provinces. It was closed by snow for several months of the year. The route at Parachinar in Kurram Agency was the most heavily used, because it offered the shortest route through Logar Province to Kabul. The third route was from Miram Shah in North Waziristan Agency, which offered access to Paktia, Logar, and Ghazni Provinces. The fourth route was from Chaman, which provided the most direct access to Kandahar. Farther west in Baluchistan was the fifth route at Girdi Jangal, which provided access into Helmand Province and southwestern Afghanistan.

The four fundamentalist parties received 70 to 75 percent of the ordnance, with Gulbuddin getting the most, followed by Rabbani, Khalis, and Sayyaf. Gailani, Mojaddedi, and Mohammedi divided up the rest.

To shore up the program's operational and tactical logistics, we provided funds to ISI to build additional cargo-handling equipment, railcars, warehouses, and trucks. We provided the resistance parties with funds to procure more warehouses, light trucks, and pack animals. It was a covert version of UPS. I felt as if CIA should have owned stock in Toyota for all the trucks we purchased.

The resistance used a variety of pack animals to transport supplies inside Afghanistan. A mule could carry 250 to 335 pounds, up to 100 pounds more than a central Asian horse could, so, accordingly, we preferred mules for logistical movement in the mountains and four-wheel drive Toyota light trucks for use along the small dirt tracks leading into Afghanistan. Horses, particularly white ones, were a status symbol among mujahedin commanders, so we purchased some of them as well.

Soviet air strikes regularly attrited the insurgents' stock of pack animals, so, as the program grew, our "mule gap" widened. We tried supplying U.S. mules, mostly from Tennessee, to help close the gap, but they consumed more food, carried less, and died more quickly than the local variety. China, for a host of reasons, became our preferred source of supply. We procured ten thousand mules from the Chinese in late 1985 and repeated the purchase a year later.

LIFTING THE VEIL: BLOWPIPE AND STINGER

My number one priority in redesigning the program's weapons mix in the fall and winter of 1984–1985 was to significantly improve the anti-air capabilities of the Afghan resistance, particularly against the Hind helicopter. I had concluded that I wanted to shift SA-7 procurement to China and buy a lot more of the missiles—six hundred initially, with more to follow if they worked well. But I didn't know yet if the Chinese would agree to what would be a major escalation of the war for them. I needed another option.

My paramilitary operations colleagues and I quickly discovered that the British Blowpipe was our only other option. The Blowpipe is a man-portable surface-to-air missile system developed by Short Brothers in the U.K. The system had entered service with British forces in 1975 and had seen combat in the 1982 Falklands War. Unlike other man-portable SAMs that rely on infrared, heat-seeking sensors to home in on their target, such as the Soviet/Chinese SA-7 and the U.S. Redeye and Stinger, the Blowpipe is radio guided.

A key difference is that the heat seekers are "fire and forget" missiles. After a gunner launches a missile, he's done; the missile guides itself to its target—assuming it doesn't lock onto the sun or flares ejected from an aircraft, which can happen to missiles equipped with less sophisticated sensors. The Blowpipe in contrast must be guided all the way to the target by a gunner, using a thumb-controlled joystick to direct the missile's flight. The system consists of the optical sight/control unit, a missile, and a launch tube, which is discarded after the missile is fired. Its missile has a range of 3.5 kilometers.

The Blowpipe has three advantages over an SA-7: it can engage an airborne target head-on and from any angle of attack, whereas the "tail-chasing" SA-7 can only engage a target from the rear (where the heat given off by an aircraft engine's exhaust is at its maximum); the Blowpipe's radio guidance is not susceptible to infrared countermeasures, such as flares; and its warhead has four times the explosive weight of the SA-7 and contains steel fragments, so near misses could still bring down an aircraft. There was also a shape-charge warhead that was capable of penetrating thin armor. The system was most effective against slower-flying aircraft, and its characteristics seemed like a good match for the Hind.

The Blowpipe had two big disadvantages, however. While the ability to engage a target head-on provided more tactical flexibility, having to guide the missile all the way to its target means much greater exposure for the gunner. Controlling the system with the thumb-controlled joystick is also a very difficult skill to master, requiring weeks of training and practice. The system had achieved only a 10 percent kill rate during the 1982 Falklands War (nine Argentine aircraft shot down out of ninety-five launches). Despite its disadvantages, we hoped that with proper training, the Blowpipe would add significantly to the insurgents' anti-air capabilities.

CIA can supply insurgents with weapons from the Soviet bloc, the West, or in rare cases the United States, depending on the level of deniability a covert action program requires. (Soviet bloc weapons were widely available from a number of sources, including China and Egypt, the program's principal ordnance suppliers.) From its inception, the Afghanistan Covert Action Program had been at the most deniable end of that spectrum, relying almost exclusively on Soviet bloc weapons, with the sole exception of the 1900-vintage Lee-Enfield bolt-action rifle, which had been widely distributed around the world for decades. The introduction of the Swiss-made Oerlikon had started to erode this restriction, but only a bit. We knew that introducing a technologically sophisticated Western weapon system such as the Blowpipe would likely be seen by the Soviets as a major escalation of the war. For that, we would need to gain approval of the British, U.S., and Pakistani governments. The U.S. government quickly signed on; it did not require high-level approval, just notification to the White House and Congress. I socialized the idea with the Pakistanis who were not opposed but hardly enthusiastic. Now I had to seek British approval.

Accordingly, in January 1985, I flew to London for discussions with our British Secret Intelligence Service colleagues. My aim was to clandestinely purchase hundreds of Blowpipe missiles and firing units. Our request was staffed up through Her Majesty's Government. In early March, we received word back from Sir Robert Armstrong, the senior civil servant in the British government and the cabinet secretary to Prime Minister Thatcher, that the British weren't ready to supply the Blowpipe to the Afghan rebels. Our SIS colleagues encouraged us to not give up hope, however. Prime Minister Thatcher was a staunch supporter of the mujahedin and took a keen interest in SIS operations in Afghanistan. The senior leadership of SIS, moreover, was very grateful for the financial support CIA provided to them for their Afghanistan operations, and wanted to have an even greater impact on the war.

After NSDD 166 was signed by President Reagan, we made another run at Prime Minister Thatcher. In June, she agreed to supply the Blowpipe. It was an incredibly gutsy decision. The United States had declined thus far to introduce U.S. weapons into the conflict. Prime Minister Thatcher was leading the way in escalating the conflict and lifting the program's veil of deniability a bit while still maintaining its essential covert status. (A tension often exists between the degree of covertness and strategic and operational effectiveness in covert action programs. This was the case in Afghanistan in the 1980s and was also the case in our counterterrorism operations against al-Qa'ida after 9/11. The challenge is finding the right balance for each situation.)

I made several trips to the U.K. during July and August. CIA attorneys accompanied me to provide advice on contract and delivery terms. When I told Short Brothers that I wanted to initially obligate $25 million, with more to follow, the head of SIS's South Asia operations nearly fell out of his chair. We placed an initial order for 120 control units and 720 missiles.[12]

We had many challenges with the Blowpipe system over the next twelve months. Many of the missiles had faulty guidance systems, causing them to fail during testing. We had to ship hundreds of systems back to the manufacturer from Pakistan for repair. Achieving proficiency on the system also proved very difficult for CIA and ISI officers, with most of the initial firings failing to hit the target.

The Pakistanis initially rejected deployment of the system, not because of the escalation risk it posed, but because they wanted to wait until something better came along. I couldn't understand why nothing was preferable to something, particularly if through better training we could improve the performance of the system. The Afghan resistance was getting decimated by Soviet attack helicopters, so I kept at it. Finally, in August 1986, after several successful tests in Pakistan, President Zia and General Akhtar (overruling Yousaf) approved the deployment of the Blowpipe into Afghanistan.

The next and much larger escalation was to add the U.S.-made Stinger surface-to-air missile system into the conflict. The Stinger was a far more advanced system than the Blowpipe or SA-7. Like the SA-7, it is a fire-and-forget weapon, but its infrared sensor is far superior, which dramatically increases the probability of hitting the target. The Stinger's sensor is so good that a gunner could engage a target from any angle of attack, head-on, across his front, or from the rear. It is also much easier to master than the Blowpipe. Thus, the Stinger combined the best features of the SA-7 and Blowpipe. Its only drawback was that it was a U.S. weapon, which made it unsuitable for covert action programs where secrecy and deniability are paramount.

Introduced into U.S. military service in 1981, the Stinger man-portable surface-to-air missile system consists of a missile in a launch tube, a reusable gripstock, and a battery coolant unit. To fire the missile, an operator inserts the BCU into the gripstock and then must fire the missile within forty-five seconds. The missile has a slant range of 5.5 kilometers. The Afghan resistance had requested Stingers as far back as 1983, but the United States and Pakistan were opposed to what would be seen by the Soviets as direct American involvement in the war. During a visit by Senator Sam Nunn to Pakistan in November 1984, President Zia had raised the issue of introducing Stingers into the conflict, and I noted with great interest Islamabad Station's cable that summarized what had transpired during Nunn's meeting with Zia. But Zia soon backtracked and clarified that he wanted Stingers for Pakistan's border defense only. Zia soon received two hundred Stinger missile systems from CIA.

Zia's refusal to provide Stingers to the Afghan resistance was repeated to numerous congressional delegations visiting Pakistan throughout 1985, including one led by Senator Orrin Hatch in June. I again took note.

Fred Iklé, the undersecretary of defense for policy, raised the idea of providing Stingers to the Afghan resistance during a meeting with the Joint Chiefs of Staff in September 1985, but the chiefs were strongly opposed, raising concerns that there was a high risk that the Soviets would capture a weapon and gain access to its technology. The Soviets, however, had already clandestinely acquired the Stinger through a GRU operation in Greece, a crucial bit of information we had learned from one of our Soviet assets.[13] The chiefs also noted that the Army had limited stocks of the weapon, and didn't want the Army's readiness for war negatively impacted. Some at the State Department also raised concerns about escalation risk if the U.S.-made Stinger was introduced into the Soviet-Afghan War. These were reasonable objections.

All that changed in December 1985. Two senior State Department officials, Assistant Secretary of State for Intelligence and Research

Morton Abramowitz and Undersecretary of State for Political Affairs Michael Armacost, persuaded Secretary Shultz to support the introduction of Stingers into the conflict.[14] If one man can claim to have been the catalyst for the decision to provide Stinger missiles to the mujahedin, it was Mort Abramowitz. He convinced Armacost, Armacost won over Shultz, and then Shultz and Casey got Secretary of Defense Weinberger on board.

At a breakfast meeting with John McMahon on December 6, Iklé asked if CIA could use any Stingers. McMahon knew about the change in views at State and said, "Fred, I'll take every Stinger you can send me, but I want them at no cost to CIA." McMahon turned out to be a great rug merchant. CIA got the Stingers at no cost.

As I started making plans for the Stinger's introduction into Afghanistan, I thought back to my training on the Redeye, the predecessor to the Stinger, in the SF Weapons Course more than a decade earlier. I had come a long way since then. Before we could introduce the Stinger into Afghanistan, we would need to train our officers on the system, train ISI's instructors, and then train the mujahedin, just as we had with the SA-7 and Blowpipe. We reviewed the training program for the Stinger at the Army's Air Defense School at Fort Bliss, Texas, and modified it for CIA and mujahedin use. We conferred with General Dynamics, the U.S. manufacturer of the Stinger, about ramping up production quantities, given the Army's low inventories. We tentatively targeted having the first Stingers deployed in Afghanistan by early fall.

President Zia hadn't given his approval yet, however. During a visit by Senator Hatch to Pakistan in January, President Zia confirmed that he would accept the introduction of Stingers. Hatch had been accompanied by Michael Pillsbury, one of Iklé's deputies and a strong advocate himself for introducing the Stinger into the conflict.

A National Security Planning Group meeting on the Stinger was held at the end of January, and Shultz, Casey, and Weinberger all supported the Stinger's introduction. The Joint Chiefs were still opposed, but with Weinberger supportive, it was easier to overrule their objections. General Dynamics' ramp-up of production would ease the military's shortfall concerns.

President Reagan notified Congress in early March of his decision to provide Stingers to the Afghan resistance. The Army initially provided four hundred missiles and twenty-five gripstocks to CIA. We subsequently received an additional twelve hundred missiles and three hundred gripstocks. It was another strategic breakthrough for the program.

By the beginning of 1986, the last major element in my strategy had been put in place. It was even more than I had hoped for. We would introduce not only sophisticated Western weapons into the conflict but U.S. ones as well. The great commission I had received eighteen months earlier had been completed. We had used all means available. And we were about to win our secret war against all odds.

DRIVING THE SOVIETS OUT

CIA'S ASSESSMENT OF THE WAR, MAY 1985

In May 1985, as the new fighting season in Afghanistan was just getting under way, analysts from CIA's Offices of Near Eastern and South Asian Analysis and Soviet Analysis jointly produced an intelligence assessment, "The Soviet Invasion of Afghanistan: Five Years After." It was a major stocktaking of the war to date and a solid piece of work, reflecting the best intelligence available at the time.

The assessment noted that the Soviets were bogged down in a guerrilla war of increasing intensity and that, after five years of war, they had had little success in reducing the insurgency, which continued to grow stronger, or in winning the support of the Afghan people. The Soviets controlled less territory than they had in 1980, and their airfields, garrisons, and lines of communication were increasingly subject to insurgent attack. They had shown little imagination in developing effective counterinsurgency tactics, and poor intelligence was a continuing problem for them.

The analysts noted that while the insurgents had serious problems of their own—few local leaders of quality, rivalries and factionalism that inhibited cooperation and often resulted in bloody fighting, inadequate training, and regular supply shortages—they were likely to show greater aggressiveness as they received better weapons and more training. The Soviets were showing renewed resolve to break the military stalemate and had begun to adopt a more aggressive posture.

They were stepping up efforts to halt insurgent infiltration and make greater use of airpower along the Pakistani and Iranian borders.

Our analysts' bottom line was that the Soviets were unlikely to make real progress in quelling the insurgency in the next two years and were likely to increase their forces only incrementally, perhaps by another five thousand to ten thousand men. They believed that Gorbachev would be preoccupied over the next year or so with consolidating his power as the Soviet Union's new leader and that he had a strong interest in avoiding positions that would make him look weak. He was therefore unlikely to seek sharp revisions in Soviet goals or strategy.[1]

As I read through the assessment, I thought that the 1985 fighting season, which was just getting under way, would be the first major test of my new strategy, though I anticipated even bigger effects in 1986. The Soviets were surging a lot more forces into Afghanistan than our analysts had assumed they would, and Gorbachev was proving to be far more aggressive in Afghanistan than they thought he would be. But we were also embarked on a major surge of our own. Nineteen eighty-five would turn out to be an even bigger test of my strategy than I had anticipated. It would be the decisive year of the war.

GORBACHEV'S STRATEGY FOR VICTORY

Upon becoming general secretary of the Communist Party of the Soviet Union in March 1985, Mikhail Gorbachev, a protégé of deceased KGB Chairman and General Secretary Yuri Andropov, would make one final push for victory in the Soviet-Afghan War. Needless to say, we monitored every aspect of the new Soviet leader's strategy for its impact on the war and to make sure our strategy could still counter his.

Contrary to the expectations of CIA's Soviet analysts, Gorbachev immediately authorized the deployment of an additional 26,000 troops, bringing Soviet totals to more than 125,000, the highest level of the war.[2] The 40th Army now had four divisions, five separate maneuver brigades, four separate maneuver regiments, and six separate battalions, along with an organic air force and combat support arms. The 40th Army, though, still had its forces concentrated in and around the major population centers. As part of this expansion of forces and as the lead element in a new strategy for victory, the Soviet high command had also authorized the deployment of two *spetsnaz* brigades, each made up of four battalions, approximately one-third of all *spetsnaz* in the Soviet armed forces at the time.

Gorbachev transferred his top military commander from the NATO front, General Mikhail Zaitsev, commander of the Group of Soviet Forces in Germany, to command of the Southern Strategic Direction, which had responsibility for the war in Afghanistan, and gave him a year—"two at most"—to win the war. The previous summer General Valentin Varennikov had replaced Marshal Sokolov as the head of the Ministry of Defense Operational Group in Afghanistan, the Soviet Union's senior military officer in country. Both Zaitsev and Varennikov would remain in their positions until the Soviets withdrew in 1989.

The appointment of Zaitsev received a lot of attention in CIA, signaling to our analysts that Gorbachev was serious about winning the war. A veteran of the Battles of Kursk and Berlin, Zaitsev was an accomplished commander of armored forces. He had commanded the Group of Soviet Forces in Germany for five years and was known for encouraging operational initiative among his junior officers. We soon learned, however, that Zaitsev was also a bit of a germaphobe, concerned more about contracting hepatitis and other diseases that were wreaking havoc among the 40th Army's troops than he was about defeating the insurgency. According to one Soviet officer's account of the war, based on classified documents and on his own service in Afghanistan, Zaitsev would cancel visits to field units if his staff learned that the units were operating in disease-ridden areas.[3] A veteran of the Battle of Stalingrad and one of the commanders who captured the Reichstag during the Battle of Berlin, Varennikov would have a much larger influence on the war, overseeing the shift to night fighting with the two *spetsnaz* brigades and leading the major border offensives that sought to disrupt insurgent supply lines. A year later, he would lead the move to "Afghanize" the war. Varennikov was also, along with Minister of Foreign Affairs Eduard Shevardnadze and the KGB chairman, Viktor Chebrikov, one of Gorbachev's closest advisers on Afghanistan. It was Varennikov who was actually my chief adversary.

The Soviets made five adjustments to their operational strategy in 1985. First, consistent with Gorbachev's direction to win the war within one to two years, they focused more on trying to destroy insurgent fighting forces rather than depopulating the countryside (thereby denying the resistance its base of support). Second, they relied more on air assault (heliborne) operations to try to achieve the element of surprise and entrap insurgent fighting groups. Third, they relied more on night raids and interdiction operations by *spetsnaz* against insurgent base camps and supply caravans. Fourth, they doubled down on their goal of closing off insurgent supply lines from Pakistan. And finally, they significantly increased their overt and covert cross-border operations in Pakistan. The Soviet high command assured Gorbachev and the Politburo that these moves would enable victory within two years.

During the 1985 fighting season, the Soviets conducted four major offensives, and we monitored them all closely. Soviet operations had four main purposes: reduce pressure on Kabul; relieve besieged outposts; cut off insurgents from their base of supply; and conduct punitive action following successful insurgent operations. Eastern Afghanistan remained their primary focus.

In their assault on the Maidan Valley south of Kabul in April, the Soviets had used newly developed cluster bombs for the first time. In the Panjshir in June, the Soviets had rapidly responded to Massoud's successful raid on an Afghan Army garrison with heliborne forces in an attempt to rescue prisoners Massoud had captured, but the Soviets succeeded only in killing all the prisoners while Massoud and his forces escaped. (I'll have more to say about Massoud's raid in a bit.) It would be the last offensive the Soviets conducted in the Panjshir Valley during the war.

Also that April, a company from the 22nd *spetsnaz* Brigade had been ambushed in the mountains of eastern Konar Province, with thirty-one Soviet soldiers killed. Seven of the soldiers had killed themselves rather than surrender, because a minor mujahedin commander from Gulbuddin's party had made it a practice to skin Soviet prisoners alive after a successful ambush and leave them booby-trapped to inflict more casualties on Soviet rescue forces. It was a brutal war on both sides.

The second Konar offensive of 1985 kicked off on May 23. By mid-June, a Soviet-Afghan Army column had succeeded in reaching Barikot, but only after taking additional heavy losses. Shortly afterward, the Soviets withdrew to Jalalabad and Kabul, and the resistance resumed its siege against the Barikot garrison. Konar, like the Panjshir, was a graveyard of Soviet offensives throughout the war.

The Soviets conducted an even larger operation—involving some twenty thousand Afghan and Soviet troops—in August and September in Paktia and Khost Provinces. Within CIA, we took a special interest in this operation. The Soviets were employing new air assault tactics aimed at cutting off resistance supply lines into Afghanistan from Pakistan. The operation, moreover, was being launched into the territory of one of our best resistance commanders, Jalaluddin Haqqani. And we had also just deployed our first three-gun section of Oerlikon anti-aircraft cannons into the Ali Khel area.

The main ground column attacked through Logar Province along the Kabul–Gardez Road, the site of frequent mujahedin ambushes, and reached Gardez on August 26. They reached the besieged garrison at Ali Khel and captured our Oerlikon battery. The loss of our Oerlikons so soon after they had been deployed sent a few shock waves through CIA. There were also more than a few concerns within CIA whether the Soviets would keep going and conduct a limited cross-border operation into Pakistan.

The combined Soviet thrust stalled, however, as resistance forces close to the border were resupplied and reinforced with fresh fighters. The Soviets realized they could not get to Khost or the Pakistan border with these ground columns without taking prohibitive losses, so they withdrew their forces back to Gardez on September 10.

The Soviets had more success in 1985 with their special operations forces. *Spetsnaz* were called "black soldiers" by the mujahedin because of the way they darkened their faces for night operations. All in, there were at least ten thousand Soviet SOF in Afghanistan.

The large-scale introduction of *spetsnaz* into Afghanistan and the night operations they conducted initially took the Afghan resistance by surprise—and caused more than a few fluttering hearts within CIA—during the early months of the 1985 fighting season. Throughout the spring and summer of 1985, Soviet *spetsnaz* conducted interdiction, decapitation, and direct action assaults against insurgent supply lines and strongholds all across Afghanistan, with a particular concentration in the eastern provinces bordering Pakistan.

As I watched their deployment and initial operations unfold in the late spring and early summer of 1985, I drew several conclusions. First, it was apparent that the Soviets were switching from a failed large-scale conventional war to a special operations and unconventional war. I knew that Soviet *spetsnaz* would pose a significant new threat to insurgent supply lines and base camps.

But, equally important, I was convinced that the Soviets couldn't win the war with *spetsnaz* raids and ambushes. I believed that the resistance would adapt to the new Soviet tactics and that the *spetsnaz* would be vulnerable to misuse and attrition. They wouldn't have enough force structure to carry the brunt of sustained offensive operations against the resistance, and they would also be operationally handicapped by the same poor intelligence that had plagued Soviet conventional operations. They would be vulnerable to mujahedin standoff attacks on their bases, and their use of helicopters would become increasingly untenable as the air balance shifted.

For the Soviets to defeat the insurgency, they would need to win the war in the countryside. This required tribal engagement, not just raids and ambushes, but the Soviets had so alienated the Afghan population that the prospects for large-scale tribal engagement were very slim.

Sure enough, the Afghan resistance adapted to the new threat, surprising the *spetsnaz* with counter ambushes of their own (anticipating their insertion areas and lying in wait for them). The influx of additional air defense weapons also inflicted heavy losses on the *spetsnaz*.

During one raid on an insurgent base camp in eastern Afghanistan in the late summer, one mujahedin gunner armed with a 12.7 mm machine gun shot down four Soviet transport helicopters as they were approaching his position, killing all on board. NSA's intercepts of Soviet tactical communications vividly revealed the shock the Soviet commander had experienced. The raid was quickly aborted.

The final element of the Soviets' 1985 strategy for victory was the increased use of cross-border operations and terrorism against Pakistan. It might have been a covert war, but the Soviets knew who was behind it. Their aim was to intimidate Pakistan into ceasing support for the Afghan resistance through four means: support for the al-Zulfiqar terrorist group, weapons and other support for Baluch separatists, assassinations and sabotage by the KGB and KHAD (the KGB's Afghan client), and by cross-border air attack.

Al-Zulfiqar was founded by the eldest son of the man President Zia had hanged after deposing him in a coup, Zulfikar Ali Bhutto (also the father of the former prime minister Benazir Bhutto). The group had conducted a major terrorist operation in Pakistan, the 1981 hijacking of a Pakistan International Airlines flight, with support from KHAD and the KGB.

The plane flew to Kabul, where it was welcomed by the Communist Afghan leadership, and a Pakistani diplomat on board was executed. From Kabul, the plane flew to Damascus, where, following the advice of the head of Syrian intelligence, the hijackers threatened to kill the Americans on board unless their demands were met—the release from jail of fifty-four members of Bhutto's Pakistan People's Party. Zia reluctantly agreed. The group received terrorist training (its supporters, in addition to KHAD and the KGB, included the PLO and Libya) and made several unsuccessful attempts to assassinate Zia using surface-to-air missiles.[4]

Assassination and sabotage operations by the KGB and KHAD in Pakistan were a key part of Soviet strategy. The KGB and KHAD attempted to kill the resistance commander Abdul Haq in Peshawar in February 1985, but failed. Beginning in 1982, the KGB's Eighth Department of the First Chief Directorate's Directorate S set up a training camp in Afghanistan to train Afghan agents to conduct sabotage and other operations in Afghan refugee camps in Pakistan. Several of these operations were successful.[5] In 1985, the KGB and KHAD expanded their sabotage operations into Pakistan's settled areas, that is, outside the North-West Frontier Province.

Soviet Air Force fighters and fighter-bombers also routinely penetrated Pakistani airspace, dropping bombs and occasionally engaging in dogfights with the Pakistani Air Force. In addition to cross-border air strikes, the Soviets shot artillery into Pakistan, conducted special operations raids, and engaged in sabotage, occasionally with dramatic effect.

The increased frequency of these cross-border attacks in 1985 caused considerable concern at CIA. The number would triple in 1986 and would be sustained until the Soviets withdrew.[6] Overall, however, Soviet cross-border incursions accomplished little strategically. President Zia held firm in the face of increasing Soviet pressure. Soviet aircraft were shot down on more than one occasion, and Soviet *spetsnaz* suffered major losses when the element of surprise was lost and their exfiltration back into Afghanistan was blocked.

The big threat that loomed over Pakistan, of course, was a Soviet invasion, perhaps in conjunction with India. For the reasons noted above, the Soviets knew they didn't have the forces to do it without increasing their risk in more strategic theaters. We believed that the Soviets would stick with their covert action/limited airpower strategy and that Zia would not buckle in the face of it.

That judgment was central as we escalated the war dramatically between 1985 and 1987 until we had achieved escalation dominance.

HIGHWAY OF DEATH

The imagery from our reconnaissance satellites was stunning. In August 1985, Tom S., the senior imagery analyst assigned to the program, brought me high-resolution photos showing the wreckage of a large Soviet column that had been destroyed along Route 157, the Kabul–Gardez Road. Route 157 had been a frequent ambush target for the mujahedin since the war began, especially at a site near the Marmur Hotel in Logar Province. Most of these operations, however, had been relatively small-scale, typically involving anywhere from fifteen to fifty mujahedin armed primarily with small arms.

The scale of destruction from this ambush was vast, much greater than anything we'd seen before. The kill zone stretched for nearly fifty kilometers, and it was strewn with hundreds of Soviet and Afghan government trucks, armored personnel carriers, and tanks. It was a "highway of death," comparable only, in my mind, to the destruction of Iraqi forces by U.S. airpower as they retreated from Kuwait at the end of the 1990–1991 Persian Gulf War.

In September 1984, Mullah Malang, a commander for Yunis Khalis's party in the Kandahar area, had ambushed a large Soviet and Afghan government column in the Arghandab River valley just west of Kandahar with a force of 250 mujahedin, resulting in the destruction of more than fifty fuel trucks and combat vehicles, but Malang's kill zone had extended only ten kilometers.[7] Most of the smaller-scale ambushes conducted by the mujahedin had kill zones only a kilometer in length.

The road from Shindand Air Base to Kandahar was littered with destroyed vehicles, as were other major lines of communication across Afghanistan. The road leading up the Panjshir Valley showed similar carnage from the several Soviet and Afghan government attempts to seize and occupy it. But the destroyed vehicles that littered the Panjshir and the road between Shindand and Kandahar had been the result of multiple insurgent operations.

The Logar ambush involved large fighting groups of hundreds of men from three different political parties—Hekmatyar's, Yunis Khalis's, and Sayyaf's. The combined forces of the mujahedin had halted the column by destroying the convoy's lead vehicles and preventing the rest of the extended column from escaping.

What the mujahedin had executed in essence was a "heavy weapons ambush," a tactic we had been advocating. Large numbers of RPG-7 anti-tank grenade launchers and recoilless rifles destroyed Soviet and Afghan government combat vehicles and trucks, and what they didn't destroy, the insurgents' mortars and heavy machine guns finished off. Heavy machine guns in turn provided fire support for mujahedin assaulting the kill zone to capture prisoners and supplies.

We learned from signals intelligence that the resistance, with multiple, coordinated SA-7 launches and heavy machine-gun fire, had driven off several Hind attack helicopters that had come to rescue the beleaguered convoy. I told Tom that I had conducted hundreds of ambushes in Ranger, Special Forces, and CIA training, but had never conducted anything remotely approaching the size and sophistication of this one. I simply shook my head in amazement.

It was a clear indication that our strategy was working. This kind of sophisticated combined arms operation would not have been possible without the dramatic increases in the quantity and quality of ordnance we were now providing, nor would it have been possible without the commensurate increases we had made in training, intelligence, battlefield communications, and battlefield logistics (mules and light trucks). The combat integration of heavy weapons—anti-tank recoilless rifles, heavy machine guns, and mortars—coupled with large numbers of surface-to-air missiles made large-scale ambushes like this feasible, provided the mujahedin could retain the element of surprise, a task made easier by the Soviets' failure to ensure route security, and provided they continued to combine forces from different parties from time to time, as we urged them to do.

I drafted a brief memo describing the ambush and, with the approval of Gust and Bert, took it and the photos to show Director Casey. After I was ushered into his office for our brief meeting, I placed the imagery on the director's small conference table and described the ambush to him.

"This shows that the increases we received last year are already having a major impact," I said.

Casey stared at the imagery showing destroyed vehicle after destroyed vehicle and said, "Just imagine what the muj will do to the Sovs next year after all those missiles you've bought show up," referring to the large quantities of SA-7s and Blowpipes we would soon be receiving from the Chinese and the Brits.

"Yes, sir," I replied, "the Russians aren't going to know what hit them."

The director thanked me, and I left. After I had departed, I thought, *And they will really feel the pain if I get the additional funds I've been asking for.*

HITTING THEM EVERYWHERE WITH EVERYTHING

A month later, Tom brought me more stunning imagery, this time from the west rather than the east of Afghanistan. Our imagery showed not an ambush but an act of sabotage, on an equally grand scale.

Using CIA-provided demolition kits, Ismail Khan's Jamiat-e-Islami forces destroyed twenty-one Soviet combat aircraft on the ground at Shindand Air Base. The imagery was as jaw-dropping as the imagery of the ambush along the Kabul–Gardez Road had been. Where there had been twenty-one fighters and fighter-bombers parked on the runway's apron, there were now twenty-one burn marks.

The sabotage at Shindand was further dramatic evidence that our strategy was working. The two operations alone had destroyed hundreds of millions of dollars of Soviet combat equipment and had killed or captured hundreds of personnel. I drafted another cover memo and brought the Shindand photos to show Director Casey.

"Twenty-one aircraft blown up on the ground," Casey said, as I showed him the imagery with its neat rows of burn marks. "Jesus, the base commander must really be in hot water." "No doubt," I responded. The remainder of 1985 brought more reports to the director's office about how the tide was turning in Afghanistan.

Three additional operations further demonstrated the insurgents' increasing ability to conduct larger-scale raids and ambushes during the 1985 fighting season. These operations, combined with thousands of smaller-scale ambushes, raids, and shelling attacks, allowed the resistance to blunt Soviet offensives and new tactics and prevail in what turned out to be the bloodiest and decisive year of the war. For the first time in the five-year war, the Afghan resistance demonstrated the ability to face the Soviets in sustained direct combat.

In June, as noted earlier in the chapter, Massoud's forces conducted a large-scale raid on the Afghan Army garrison at Pechgur, the regime's northernmost position in the Panjshir Valley. The garrison at Pechgur had a 500-man battalion, with ten mortars, four 76 mm guns, two T-55 tanks, and five BTR-60 armored personnel carriers. The garrison was protected by sandbagged bunkers, barbed wire, and mines. Massoud's forces cleared the mines at night and then assaulted the garrison, killing an Afghan Army general and colonel, who happened to be visiting the base, and capturing 450 prisoners, including 5 more colonels. It was a spectacular raid. The Soviets launched a counteroffensive aimed at rescuing 130 of the prisoners moving in one column out of the valley, but it was unsuccessful. All the prisoners died during the operation, and Massoud's forces escaped.

In October, another Jamiat-e-Islami force led by Wazir Gul successfully overran several Afghan government bases and security outposts in a mountain pass along the Kabul–Jalalabad Road (Highway 1). Blowing two key bridges with CIA-provided demolition kits, the insurgents were able to block the road for eight days, enabling them to capture tons of arms and ammunition. Gul employed the program's recently provided 122 mm and 107 mm rocket launchers, along with 82 mm mortars, 82 mm recoilless rifles, RPG-7 rocket-propelled grenade launchers, and 14.5 mm heavy machine guns to gain fire superiority over Afghan forces. Also in October, several mujahedin groups combined to conduct a large-scale ambush of a Soviet/Afghan government convoy in Wardak Province along the Kabul–Ghazni Highway. Employing anti-tank weapons, mortars, and heavy machine guns, over the course of two hours, the mujahedin destroyed seventeen armored vehicles and forty-five GAZ-66 trucks.[8]

The strategy that we put in place between March 1985 and January 1986, moreover, was just beginning to take effect. Combat intensity and operational tempo had significantly increased in 1985, with an average of two hundred combat incidents reported by the Soviets each month during the fighting season. In 1986, the number of combat incidents reported by the Soviets would increase again by more than 60 percent and would more than double by 1987. Our large-scale introduction of heavy weapons, severalfold increase in the ammunition supply, and improved battlefield logistics were having increased effects. Ambushes of Soviet and Afghan government columns were a daily occurrence in multiple areas across the country, as were insurgent raids on isolated outposts. Insurgent raids into urban areas also increased significantly, as did acts of sabotage. Soviet and Afghan government bases were now under near-constant shelling attack. There was nowhere for the Red Army to hide.

Although the most dramatic gains for the Afghan resistance in counter air operations would not be realized until the introduction of the Stinger and other surface-to-air missile systems in large numbers in 1986, the insurgents started to develop effective counters to Soviet air supremacy during the 1985 fighting season with the adoption of the "anti-air ambush" tactics that we had advocated. There were several variants of this tactic. The one used most by the mujahedin was to position multiple heavy machine guns (12.7 mm and 14.5 mm) in canyon walls above an ambush site or base area. When Soviet transport and attack helicopters would swoop in to attack insurgent forces, mujahedin gunners would fire horizontally at the approaching rotor-craft, maximizing their likelihood of downing them.

Small-scale ground ambushes would often be used as bait to lure in Soviet helicopters. As Soviet transport helicopters descended and landed to discharge assault troops, the mujahedin would attack them with direct fire using their RPG-7 anti-tank grenade launchers. They would also mine suspected landing sites to inflict even more casualties. In all, some two hundred helicopters were shot down by the resistance in 1985.

A second tactic, as illustrated by the Shindand Air Base sabotage operation, was to seek to destroy Soviet/Afghan government aircraft on the ground. Two methods were used: sabotage by clandestine resistance supporters inside air bases, using CIA-provided demolitions kits, and/or small teams of specialized resistance fighters who would infiltrate the base at night; and standoff rocket attack.

The Chinese 107 mm multibarrel rocket launcher, which could fire twelve rockets at a time out to a range of nine kilometers, became the principal standoff indirect fire weapon for the resistance after 1984. For attacks against targets with extended defense perimeters, the longer-range and lighter single-barrel 122 mm rocket launcher would be used, or alternatively and frequently the insurgents would launch rockets from makeshift wood stands.

As rockets were launched, mujahedin would frequently shout, "*Mordabad Shuravi*" (death to the Soviets). Several tens of aircraft were destroyed by rocket fire at Soviet air bases around Afghanistan between the fall of 1984 and the fall of 1988. At Bagram Air Base northeast of Kabul, twenty aircraft were destroyed by rocket strikes in late 1984 and early 1985. Similar results were achieved at Kandahar Airfield.

The final anti-ambush tactic was to mass surface-to-air missiles and to employ them in "hunter-killer ambushes" in the vicinity of Soviet airfields. This tactic would be employed with great effectiveness beginning with the introduction of the Stinger and Blowpipe in September 1986.

The highlight of 1985, from a surface-to-air-missile perspective, was the shoot-down, using one of the new Chinese SA-7s, of a Soviet Air Force major general flying a MiG-21 from Kandahar to Shindand Air

Base. The general safely ejected but was captured by the mujahedin, triggering a massive search and rescue operation by the Soviets. We later learned that the insurgents had shot the Soviet officer soon after his capture.

UNCONVENTIONAL WARFARE OR CONVENTIONAL?

Coalition warfare inevitably involves disagreements over strategy and tactics, secret coalitions no less so. The only thing worse than having allies on your side is not having them. Pakistan was the frontline state in the conflict, the one with the most to lose if the war extended into Pakistani territory, and our primary conduit to the mujahedin. Their views on the conduct of the war had to be taken into account. During the 1985 fighting season, we had disagreements with ISI and some mujahedin commanders over strategy and tactics in three areas: how much to prioritize operations in Kabul versus other areas of Afghanistan and what kinds of tactics were appropriate for insurgent operations in and around Kabul; whether it was appropriate for the resistance to conduct conventional offensive operations to seize and hold territory; and whether the insurgents should conduct positional defense of their key base areas.

CIA's view was that the Afghan resistance had the best chance of success if it stayed on the offensive and employed standard guerrilla warfare tactics (raids, ambushes, standoff attacks, mines, booby traps, sniping, and sabotage). CIA and ISI had agreed on a strategy to attack Kabul using three principal methods. First, we sought to interdict supplies of oil and gas, electricity, and war matériel by destroying pipelines and electricity pylons with demolition charges and conducting ambushes of supply convoys along the major highways leading into Kabul. (Brigadier Yousaf also wanted to blow up the Salang Tunnel, which extended for some five kilometers through the Hindu Kush mountain range. He was eventually convinced by CIA demolitions experts and operational planners that it was infeasible.) Second, we sought to target key Soviet and Afghan government officials and headquarters within Kabul using demolitions and small-scale, close-quarter combat. Third, we sought to target key installations with standoff attacks using 107 mm and 122 mm rockets. Standoff rocket attack was our primary tactic to bring the war into Kabul.

In the spring of 1985, however, General Akhtar wanted to conduct an even more dramatic operation inside the city. Akhtar was convinced that Kabul was the key to the war. If Kabul fell, the war would be over. The majority of Pakistani special forces teams sent into Afghanistan were directed against Kabul-area targets employing the three methods we had agreed upon, but Akhtar wanted an operation that would take and hold an area of Kabul for thirty-six hours. ISI proposed using a force of five thousand mujahedin in a joint operation conducted by groups from Hekmatyar's and Sayyaf's parties. This sounded to me like a suicide mission that would accomplish little. Fortunately, the mujahedin commanders assigned to the operation were less than enthusiastic about it. After two months of studying the plan, Akhtar's great Kabul offensive was quietly shelved.[9]

At the beginning of the 1985 fighting season, mujahedin commanders from Khalis's and Gailani's parties proposed a major conventional operation of their own, a daytime, large-scale attack to take the border city of Khost. Attacking and holding Khost was also not an appropriate mission for a guerrilla force, and attacking the city during daylight bordered on madness. Unfortunately, however, the mujahedin, led by Jalaluddin Haqqani, believed in the plan, and so it went forward. It was a fiasco. The mujahedin suffered heavy casualties and had to abort the operation after failing to take a security outpost nine kilometers from Khost.

I hated watching it. As Mao noted, there is a time for a guerrilla force to shift to offensive conventional operations, but it is only after insurgents have achieved battlefield superiority. The Afghan resistance, as rapidly as its capabilities were increasing, was far from achieving that in 1985.

And it only got worse. During the summer of 1985, Brigadier Yousaf made a controversial decision to have the mujahedin mount a conventional defense of the border region. His staff, particularly his special forces officers, had argued that this was tactically unsound and against the principles of guerrilla warfare, and that an attempt to have the insurgents hold ground and fight a conventional battle would lead to defeat and heavy casualties. The Pakistani leadership, however, was concerned about Soviet forces moving into Pakistan and a possible two-front war with the Soviets and India. Afghan insurgent strongpoints, in the Pakistan Army's view, could delay the Soviet advance, cause casualties, and buy time for the Army to mobilize and deploy.

The insurgents could defend their base areas for a limited period of time and could inflict substantial casualties on the Soviets in the process, but they suffered when they tried to defend fixed positions for too long. Defending in place played to Soviet strengths, particularly their ability to mass fires, and not to those of the insurgents.

The wisdom of Yousaf's decision would be tested at Zhawar, a major training, supply, and staging base just four kilometers inside Afghanistan in Paktia Province. ISI had encouraged the establishment of the Zhawar base initially as an insurgent training center to provide a measure of plausible deniability for their covert support of the resistance.

Zhawar had been built using explosives and bulldozers (the latter provided by Usama Bin Ladin) to dig eleven five-hundred-meter-long tunnels into the southeast-facing side of the Sodyaki Ghar Mountain. The base had a hotel (for visiting VIPs such as Afghan party leaders, journalists, wealthy Arabs, U.S. congressmen, and ISI generals), a mosque, arms depots, repair shops, a garage, a medical clinic, a radio room, and a kitchen. It was permanently defended by the five-hundred-man "Zhawar Regiment," whose actual duties were more logistical than combat defense. The base had two captured Soviet tanks and one howitzer and several 107 mm multibarrel rocket launchers and 14.5 mm heavy machine guns in addition to its complement of small arms. Unfortunately, the base's construction had prioritized building and expanding the underground facilities over defensive fighting positions.

A Soviet-Afghan task force took Zhawar at the beginning of the 1986 fighting season. The Soviets had used precision-guided munitions to score direct hits on some of the entrances to the base's cave complex, trapping mujahedin fighters inside and wounding Jalaluddin Haqqani. Subsequent air strikes had fortunately cleared away some of the rubble, allowing the trapped mujahedin to escape, but the battle was essentially over. The combined Soviet-Afghan task force secured the tunnels and destroyed the base. They then withdrew. The Afghan regime celebrated a major victory, though government forces had taken significant casualties. The mujahedin suffered nearly 650 killed and wounded in action. I again watched this unfold in horror.

Desperate to counter Soviet airpower during the battle's final two weeks, Brigadier Yousaf prematurely deployed a Pakistani team armed with the Blowpipe missile system before the team had been adequately trained on the weapon. Faulty missiles had also been discovered in the initial shipment and were being replaced or repaired by Short Brothers, the system's manufacturer. The Pakistani team fired thirteen missiles and all missed. (The Blowpipe would perform better during the fall of 1986 and the 1987 fighting season after the mujahedin had been properly trained on it.)

Yousaf blamed CIA and the British for the disaster, but it was he who had made the poor operational decision to deploy the system before it was ready. It had been a foolish thing to do, and as time wore on, I would learn that this was just the beginning of decisions by Yousaf that would sabotage the program and undermine our alliance with Pakistan. Fortunately, he would be gone from the program before he could do too much damage, though that didn't prevent him from continuing to try to undermine it in retirement.

Yousaf's decision to wage a conventional defense at Zhawar fortunately came under great criticism from General Akhtar, CIA, and the mujahedin. Yousaf acknowledged that the Afghan resistance had been dealt a severe tactical blow, but its overall guerrilla warfare strategy was still intact and succeeding.[10]

Zhawar would be the last of conventional offensive or defensive operations by the resistance until the withdrawal of Soviet combat forces.[11] Then another Pakistani general even worse than Yousaf would make similar blunders.

YEAR OF DECISION AND AFGHANIZATION

Despite these setbacks, 1985 turned out to be the decisive year of the Soviet-Afghan War. There is a myth that the Red Army's defeat became inevitable only after the United States started providing Stinger missiles to the Afghan resistance in September 1986. Soviet records, however, do not support this view.[12] By late 1985, Gorbachev and key Soviet leaders had become convinced that the Soviets couldn't win, at least anytime soon. The Red Army's strategy for victory had failed. The United States had won the battle of surges. Nineteen eighty-five turned out to be the bloodiest year of the war, with more than four thousand Soviet troops killed in action. Beginning in 1986, the Soviets moved to "Afghanize" the conflict—transfer primary security responsibility to the Afghan government—and begin the process of withdrawal.

In October 1985, Gorbachev summoned Babrak Karmal, Afghanistan's ruler, to Moscow and informed him that the Afghan revolution did not have enough popular support and that the Soviets needed to adopt a new approach. He encouraged Karmal to "give up all ideas of socialism, return to Afghan and Islamic values, and share power with the opposition." Gorbachev warned Karmal that Soviet troops would soon leave Afghanistan. According to Karmal's successor, Mohammad Najibullah, Karmal's face turned white when he heard about a pending withdrawal of Soviet troops.[13] In November, at the end of the 1985 fighting season, Gorbachev secured Politburo approval for his strategy of "military and political measures" to "expedite the withdrawal" of Soviet troops while leaving a "friendly" Afghan government in place.

In February 1986, Gorbachev took another major step forward when he went public at the Twenty-Seventh Party Congress, describing Afghanistan as a "bleeding wound." He added, "We should, in the nearest future, withdraw Soviet troops stationed in Afghanistan." Then, in May 1986, Gorbachev removed Babrak Karmal, who vehemently opposed Soviet withdrawal, and replaced him with KHAD Chief Mohammad Najibullah. In July, Gorbachev ordered the withdrawal of six regiments from Afghanistan. The coup de grâce came in November 1986. At the November 13 meeting of the Politburo, Gorbachev got the ultimate Soviet objective changed from a "friendly" to a "neutral" Afghanistan. The Politburo also imposed a deadline for the withdrawal of all Soviet combat troops—in Gorbachev's words, in "one year, at a maximum two years."[14]

It was now only a matter of time.

9

"WE WON"

MILT TAKES COMMAND

Bill Piekney left as CIA's chief in Islamabad in the summer of 1986 and was succeeded by Milt Bearden. Bearden had most recently been the deputy chief of the Soviet and East European Division during the very difficult "year of the spy," when CIA lost nearly all of its Soviet assets. Only years later would CIA learn that we had been betrayed by Aldrich Ames, who was serving in a key counterintelligence position in SE Division at the time. The Soviets had temporarily won the espionage war as a result of Ames's betrayal, but they were badly losing the covert action war, and it was the latter that would prove decisive.

Piekney had played his role well, but with the new strategy fully in place and with the war seeming to be entering its final phase, it was now time to shift control back to the field. Bert Dunn and Gust both believed that Milt, a larger-than-life Texan (by adoption if not birth), was the perfect person to take command. Before his assignment as deputy chief of SE Division, Milt had completed two very successful tours as a chief of station in Africa (in Nigeria and Sudan) and had started his career as a China hand.

As Milt arrived in Islamabad in August 1986, two events within his first six weeks showed him the power of our new strategy and the good fortune it would bring him.

On August 26, the first of these events occurred in Kabul. At 1700 (5:00 p.m.), acid in the brass barrel of a "time pencil" developed by

CIA's Office of Technical Services ate through the thin wire that had restrained a spring-loaded firing plunger, completing an electrical circuit that fired a dozen Chinese-made 107 mm white phosphorus rockets toward their target, the large Soviet ammunition depot at Kharga. The rockets were fired from improvised wooden "launchers" to allow mujahedin from Abdul Haq's group to infiltrate through Soviet and Afghan government security perimeters to within range of their target. The time pencil delay allowed the mujahedin to safely depart from the area well before the rockets went off.

One of the high incendiary rockets struck a warehouse that contained surface-to-air missiles. It ignited the fuel tanks of the SAMs, setting off a series of secondary explosions that spread from storage area to storage area. By the time the explosions were over, more than forty thousand tons of Soviet ammunition had been destroyed. Poor storage procedures had contributed to the scale of the inferno.[1]

The biggest arms depot in Afghanistan had just been blown up by a CIA-backed mujahedin operation. The cost of the attack in matériel terms was around $1,500 (rockets, time pencils, batteries, and firing wire). The cost to the Soviets was estimated at $250 million.

It was a great start to Bearden's tour as chief of station.[2]

A month later, on September 25, the air balance in Afghanistan changed. The event that caused this shift would be an even greater shot in the arm for Bearden and the program.

At 1505 (3:05 p.m.), a group of three dozen fighters, led by Engineer Ghaffar from Hekmatyar's party, were armed with newly provided Stinger surface-to-air missiles and positioned about one and a half kilometers northeast of Jalalabad airfield in eastern Afghanistan, employing the offensive "hunter-killer" ambush tactics we had taught them. We had selected Ghaffar for the mission because he had already proven himself proficient with SA-7s, accounting for two shoot-downs of Soviet aircraft.

As eight Mi-24D Hind attack helicopters approached the airfield after completing a mission, Ghaffar got his team ready and prepared their Stingers for firing. Preparation is fairly simple and consists of three steps: removing the front cover and raising the sight; inserting and activating a battery coolant unit, which allows the system to track its target and identify it as friend or foe; and "uncaging" the missile, which arms the system. Once the BCU is activated, a gunner has forty-five seconds to engage his target.

Ghaffar engaged first, but his missile failed and fell to the ground as it left the tube. The other two shooters, however, scored direct hits on two of the Hinds. Ghaffar quickly reloaded and brought down a third Hind, while another gunner fired at a fourth aircraft and narrowly missed. Three kills during the first Stinger engagement. Soviet flight operations were shut down at Jalalabad air base for a week while the stunned Russians sorted out what to do.[3] High-tech U.S. weapons were now part of the insurgents' arsenal.

Satellite imagery quickly confirmed the Soviets' losses. The mujahedin had also captured the shoot-downs on video, though much of the footage turned out to be of the ground and sky after the video man got too excited and jumped up and down shouting, "*Allahu Akbar.*" Both the satellite photos and the video were immediately taken to Director Casey and then to President Reagan.

When Jack Devine, the new chief of the Afghanistan Task Force, brought the initial satellite imagery to Casey, the director immediately sensed that the Soviets were finished and on the path to defeat.

"This changes it all, doesn't it?" Casey mused.[4]

The video was also shown to key congressmen and senators on the Hill. There were a lot of *Allahu Akbar*s said in Washington in late September 1986.

The endgame years of the Soviet-Afghan War saw several other leadership changes in the Afghanistan Covert Action Program. Bert Dunn received a promotion to associate deputy director for operations. Gust moved on to become chief of operations in Africa Division (and later, deputy chief of the Domestic Collection Division) before retiring from CIA. And I left CIA for Wharton Business School (more on why in the next chapter).[5] It was a complete changing of the guard.

In early 1986, John McMahon retired from CIA and was succeeded as deputy director by Bob Gates.[6] Since 1984, McMahon had been coming under increasing criticism from conservative groups, alleging that he was an obstacle to greater U.S. escalation in Afghanistan.

Though he was not the biggest fan of covert action, not once during my tenure did McMahon object to any of our escalation initiatives. If you could make your case, he would support you.[7]

The biggest change of all, however, occurred at the top. In mid-December 1986, Bill Casey collapsed from a brain tumor and became incapacitated. He died on May 6. Casey had run CIA for six years and had reveled in it. He had been the point man for the Reagan administration's "Third World War" against the Soviet Union and the first DCI to be given cabinet rank. Whichever laws he might or might not have broken during the Iran-contra affair, he was a giant and a visionary, one with flaws, to be sure, but a giant and a visionary nonetheless.[8] It was a tragedy that Casey did not live to see America's victory in Afghanistan and in the Cold War. He had been without doubt the most consequential CIA director in our nation's history, and it had been a privilege to serve under him.

POURING IT ON

The 1986 and 1987 fighting seasons were primarily about holding the Soviets' feet to the fire to make sure they withdrew. Beginning in 1986, they were deescalating and we were still escalating. There were no significant adjustments to CIA's strategy after March 1986. We had escalation dominance.

The Red Army increasingly shifted to defensive operations, though they still conducted a few major offensives in an unsuccessful attempt to disrupt the Afghan resistance's strategic supply lines. The intensity of mujahedin attacks increased significantly through 1986 and 1987 as the strategy we had set in place became fully implemented.

As the 1987 fighting season began, however, CIA's analysts were still skeptical that the mujahedin had achieved a decisive advantage or that the Soviets were really committed to withdrawing their forces. In an interagency intelligence assessment published in February 1987, "The War in Afghanistan: Taking Stock," CIA's analysts had acknowledged that the Afghan resistance had demonstrated dramatically enhanced capabilities in the last half of 1986 by capturing three regime garrisons, and effectively employing anti-air missiles, and that they had raised the costs of the war for the Soviets.[9]

With my brother Alan (left) in front of the house my father built in Hollywood for my grandparents

Not exactly a rock star

ABOVE, LEFT Going to church at age fourteen with my parents and brother Rick

ABOVE, RIGHT Aspiring pro baseball player

LEFT Dr. Anthony DeRiggi, the high school international relations teacher who sparked my initial interest in becoming a CIA officer

Graduation from the Special Forces Qualification
Course, May 1974

Teaching hand-to-hand combat at West Point, 1976

The Special Forces soldier statue ("Bronze Bruce")
at Fort Bragg where SFQC graduates don their
green berets for the first time

Afghanistan Covert Action Program officer, 1984

Gust Avrakotos, CIA's chief of South Asia Operations and chief of the Afghanistan Task Force, 1984–1986

In Cairo, 1984, watching a team of mules struggle in vain to pull a heavy air-defense gun up a hill

est-firing CIA's 14.5 mm sniper rifle ("Buffalo Gun"), 1985

William J. Casey, director of central intelligence, 1981–1987

Charlie Wilson, congressman from Texas, 1973–1996

With Bert Dunn, CIA's chief of the Near East and South Asia Division, 1984–1986, in Beijing, May 1985. We encouraged the Chinese to dramatically increase their support for the Afghan resistance.

General Akhtar Abdur Rahman Khan, the head of Pakistan's Inter-Services Intelligence, 1979–87

LEFT Ahmad Shah Massoud, the most effective commander in the Afghan resistance. Subsequently Afghanistan's minister of defense and leader of the Northern Alliance, he was assassinated by al-Qa'ida just before the 9/11 attacks.

LEFT With Tom Hanks and Amy Adams at the New York premiere of *Charlie Wilson's War*, 2007

BELOW Christopher Denham, the actor who played me in *Charlie Wilson's War*

ABOVE, LEFT Al-Qa'ida emirs Usama Bin Ladin and Ayman al-Zawahiri

ABOVE, RIGHT Discussing Iraq War strategy with President George W. Bush in the Oval Office, May 2006

LEFT The Predator, America's most important weapon in the campaigns to disrupt, dismantle, and defeat al-Qa'ida

With my wife, Melana, as I was being sworn in as undersecretary of defense for intelligence by Secretary of Defense Robert Gates, 2011

Anwar al-Awlaki, external operations planner for al-Qa'ida in the Arabian Peninsula; killed in a Predator strike, September 2011

Meeting with Yemeni special forces in Sana'a, Yemen

Usama Bin Ladin's
compound in
Abbottabad, Pakistan,
viewed from the north

Admiral William McRaven, the commander
of Operation Neptune's Spear

The author in the White House Situation Room with President Obama and the national security principals
in the aftermath of the UBL operation

Briefing President Obama in the White House Situation Room

Mike – Thanks for your counsel these six years. The country is safer because of you. [signature]

BELOW, LEFT Holding a local *shura* at an Afghan Local Police site in the Arghandab River valley

BELOW, RIGHT Visiting a Chinese special forces unit in Beijing, January 2015

Being awarded the National Security Medal by President Obama in the Oval Office with my wife, Melana, and our daughters Alexandra, Natasha, Oksana, and Kalyna; my daughter Sophia unfortunately couldn't attend but was able to make it to my retirement ceremony and the Donovan Award dinner.

A few Soviet analysts even believed the Soviets might be winning. The year prior, Fritz Ermarth, the national intelligence officer for the Soviet Union, suggested that the Soviets had succeeded in choking off insurgent supply routes. They had not. Soviet pressure against insurgent logistics routes had made it a bit more challenging and costly to supply the resistance, but the routes remained open. The amount of weapons and ammunition in fact increased significantly as the fighting season progressed. Ermarth also believed that Gorbachev needed a win in Afghanistan if his domestic reforms were to succeed. Fred Iklé, the undersecretary of defense for policy, also still believed that the Soviets would win in the end.

Through the 1987 fighting season until the Soviet withdrawal, I was kept generally abreast about the success of the strategy I had put in place by my former colleagues, particularly the success the resistance had enjoyed in shooting down Soviet aircraft and the changes this had caused in Soviet air tactics. Although representatives of General Dynamics, the manufacturer of the Stinger, had told us during our procurement discussions with them in early 1986 to expect a kill rate of around 25 percent from the system, the Stinger outperformed that estimate by a factor of as much as three. By September 1987, the Stinger had been credited with nearly 140 kills.[10]

In November 1986, the mujahedin achieved their first two aircraft shoot-downs with the much-maligned British Blowpipe. While it required far greater proficiency to operate, the Blowpipe was credited with twelve confirmed kills and had a much higher success rate than the SA-7. One particularly proficient mujahedin gunner accounted for four shoot-downs by himself. I must admit I took some pleasure in hearing that news. Interviews with General Varennikov and Soviet helicopter pilots after the war, moreover, revealed that they had significant respect for the threat the Blowpipe posed to Soviet air operations.[11]

The SA-7 accounted for some twenty kills in 1986 and 1987. The mujahedin's heavy machine guns, particularly the 14.5 mm, continued to shoot-down scores of Soviet and Afghan government aircraft, and even the Oerlikon was credited with four kills. Overall, the Soviets lost between 150 and 200 aircraft a year in 1986 and 1987.

The impact on Soviet air operations was immediate. Fixed-wing aircraft flew above the Stinger's engagement ceiling (fifteen thousand feet), significantly reducing their combat effectiveness. Helicopters flew low-altitude, nap-of-the-earth routes to reduce their exposure but in the process made themselves more vulnerable to ground fire from heavy machine guns. Mujahedin anti-air operations in 1986 and 1987 hadn't driven Soviet airpower off the battlefield, my former colleagues told me, but they did make it a lot less effective. The air balance had been shifted.

The outsized performance of the Stinger of course had implications for the weapons mix. Once it was clear that the Stinger could be made available in large numbers, there was less need for the other anti-air missile systems. The Blowpipe program was terminated after our initial purchases, and procurement of additional improved SA-7s and Oerlikons was also halted.[12]

During the war's final fifteen months, CIA introduced another Western weapon, a 120 mm mortar that was used to attack a Soviet *spetsnaz* base at Asadabad. The mortar had much greater range than the standard 82 mm mortar we procured from the Chinese and Egyptians. Even more important, it had much greater accuracy due to its integration with the Global Positioning System of satellites, giving it a high probability of a first-round hit.

After being forced to abort mission a few days earlier due to misfires, a combined Pakistani-mujahedin team struck the garrison with round after round, killing more than thirty *spetsnaz* soldiers. Imagery from our reconnaissance satellites showed that many of the camp's buildings and vehicles had been completely destroyed. The GPS-guided mortar had nowhere near the impact on the war that the surface-to-air missiles had, but it added another standoff precision strike tool to the insurgents' arsenal. I was impressed when I heard about its introduction.

Late in the war, the CIA also introduced the French-made Milan anti-tank missile system, which further added to the resistance's capabilities. By the end of 1987, the mujahedin had become equipped with more technologically advanced weapons than any insurgent force in history.

The Soviet General Staff noted the increasing intensity of mujahedin attacks between 1985 and 1987. The General Staff recorded that the Afghan resistance conducted more than 10,000 ambushes during those final three years of serious fighting. They continually mined the major highways—Kabul–Kandahar–Herat, Kabul–Termez, Kabul–Jalalabad, and Kabul–Gardez–Khost—to facilitate the ambush of Soviet and Afghan government columns. There was a 33 percent increase in urban attacks between 1985 and 1987, from 450 to 600. The number of mujahedin raids had nearly doubled, from 2,400 to 4,200. In 1985 and 1986 alone, the mujahedin conducted more than 23,500 shelling attacks.[13] The war had cost the Soviets at least $75 billion in today's dollars. The cost to the United States for the Afghanistan Covert Action Program barely reached $10 billion.

SOVIET WITHDRAWAL AND ITS AFTERMATH

On April 14, 1988, the Soviets signed the Geneva Accords, committing to withdraw all their forces from Afghanistan within nine months. The agreement, which went into effect on May 15, also committed Pakistan and Afghanistan to mutual noninterference in each other's affairs. A private understanding between the United States and the Soviet Union confirmed that as long as the Soviets continued to support the Communist Afghan regime, the United States would continue to support the Afghan resistance. Our covert program had become even more of an open secret. The Soviets withdrew their forces in two phases: 50 percent by August 15, and the remainder by February 15, 1989.

The war had taken quite a toll on the Red Army. According to a Russian General Staff study published after the war, Soviet forces in Afghanistan suffered more than twenty-six thousand war dead, twice the number that had been officially released by the Soviet government.[14] Hepatitis, typhoid, dysentery, malaria, and other infectious diseases had ravaged the 40th Army during its nine-year occupation. More than three-quarters of the 620,000 Soviet soldiers who served in Afghanistan had to spend time in the hospital for disease.[15] Rampant alcohol and drug abuse also took its toll. It was estimated that up to 50 percent of the 40th Army's soldiers were regular drug users.[16]

The damage to the Red Army's reputation was even greater. Opinion back home during the final five years of the Soviet occupation had turned not only against the war, but also against the soldiers who had fought it. Gorbachev's policy of glasnost enabled open criticism of the Red Army's performance. Mothers who had lost their sons were particularly vocal in their criticism. Non-Russian citizens of the USSR were especially critical of the war. Street protests, while small compared with what the United States had experienced during the Vietnam War, had grown steadily. A CIA assessment on domestic fallout within the Soviet Union from the Afghan War noted that there had been fifteen major antiwar demonstrations in the Soviet Union between 1985 and 1988.[17]

The Soviets withdrew the last of their forces, as agreed, on February 15. The 40th Army's commander, Lieutenant General Boris Gromov, was the last Soviet soldier to cross the Termez (Friendship) Bridge. He did so in his BTR armored fighting vehicle.

Milt Bearden sent a two-word cable to Langley that read, "WE WON."[18] CIA director William Webster (Bill Casey's successor) hosted a huge celebration at headquarters.[19] Gust, now retired, sent me a letter that I treasure. It read in part, "No one will ever know how much you did to get that fucking general to walk across that bridge."

In November 1989, the Berlin Wall fell and Eastern Europe was liberated. As I watched these historic events, I thought of the dreams I had had when I was a young Special Forces soldier that I might be called upon to help liberate Eastern Europe. The path to that happy outcome turned out to be far different than I had imagined, but I was proud of what we had done in Afghanistan to contribute to it.

On August 18, 1991, a coup led by the KGB Chairman and old Soviet Afghan hand Vladimir Kryuchkov removed Gorbachev from power. Among the plotters were two of Gorbachev's former commanders in Afghanistan and personal military advisers, Marshal Sergey Akhromeyev and General Varennikov. The coup collapsed on August 21 when Boris Yeltsin climbed on a tank and demanded that the security forces stand down, setting in motion a popular uprising. The KGB and Soviet armed forces then refused to follow the coup plotters' orders. I was amazed at how suddenly the power of the once-mighty Soviet state had collapsed. Soviet republics that hadn't already declared independence from the Soviet Union took advantage of the weakness in Moscow to do so. By the end of December, the Soviet Union itself collapsed.

Following the Soviet Union's demise, all aid to Afghanistan was cut off, fatally weakening the Afghan regime. On April 15, 1992, Najibullah sought refuge in the UN compound in Kabul. Communist rule in Afghanistan was over. It is no small irony that Najibullah's regime outlasted the Soviet Union by nearly four months.

WHAT WE WON, WHY WE WON, WHAT WE MISSED

The Soviet defeat in Afghanistan was not *the* reason the Soviet Empire collapsed, but it certainly contributed to it in a major way. The United States and its allies had won the covert "Third World War"—in Angola, Nicaragua, and elsewhere, but above all, in Afghanistan. There the Red Army suffered the only defeat in its history and, with it, lost its reputation for invincibility. The Soviet-Afghan War was the decisive battle of the Cold War, a conflict that, thank heavens, was fought by proxies and other means short of a direct confrontation and all-out war between the superpowers.

As the U.S. ambassador to Afghanistan between 1973 and 1978, Theodore Eliot Jr., wrote, "When a future historian tackles the question of 'The Decline and Fall of the Russian Empire,' it will be [clear] that the Afghan war was one of the key factors in causing the disintegration of the Soviet Union."[20] Former senior CIA analyst Bruce Riedel was no less effusive, arguing that the U.S. victory in the secret war in Afghanistan was a world historic event that played a major role in bringing an end to one era of history and ushering in another.[21]

What we won was the end of the Soviet Empire and, with it, the end of the Cold War and the liberation of hundreds of millions of people. Why we won requires a more detailed explanation.

First, from a U.S. and Afghanistan Covert Action Program point of view, we showed the Soviets they couldn't win in Afghanistan and then we dramatically increased our support for the Afghanistan resistance to force the Soviets to withdraw. During the first five years of the war, the resistance grew at least three- or fourfold, from 50,000 or so fighters to 150,000 to 200,000, despite intense Soviet political, economic, military, intelligence, and information operations to suppress it. The Soviets could invade Afghanistan and quickly topple the Amin regime, but they could not put down the widening insurgency.

Our 1985 escalation countered the effects of Gorbachev's, convincing him that the Soviets couldn't win. We outmatched the Soviets with the speed, scale, and scope of our escalation, trading off some secrecy for decisiveness. In 1986 and 1987, we stayed the course, despite increasing Soviet retrenchment. The new strategy we put in place between October 1984 and March 1986 dramatically transformed the Afghan resistance's capabilities, most notably in the anti-air area, but also in combined arms operations, standoff attack, combat sustainment, and several other areas. By 1986 onward, the Afghan resistance was the most technologically advanced insurgency the world had ever seen.

What made this transformation possible was our success in shifting strategic control of the program from ISI and the field to CIA headquarters between 1984 and 1986, the unwavering support of the secret international coalition we had assembled to fight the war, and the bipartisan support we enjoyed in Congress. The support we received from Charlie Wilson was critical. The U.S. Department of Defense also provided vital financial and other support from 1985 onward.

President Reagan's decision to stay the course and continue to escalate our covert efforts, despite warming relations and strategic arms control breakthroughs with Gorbachev, was also critical. Reagan could have backed off, but he didn't. The decision by the Bush administration and Congress to continue support for the mujahedin after the Soviets withdrew was also important.

The Afghan resistance had the greatest external support of any movement in history. Deng Xiaoping fully supported the Afghanistan program, as did Prime Minister Thatcher, most notably by her willingness to provide Blowpipe missiles to the mujahedin. The Saudis matched our escalation dollar for dollar.

Pakistan's role, as the frontline state, was critical. Former senior CIA analyst Bruce Riedel has called the Soviet-Afghan conflict "President Zia's War."[22] There is much truth in that. Pakistan bore most if not all of the strategic risk from the secret war, and President Zia not only never blinked but made critical decisions of his own to escalate the conflict in 1985 and 1986.[23] The availability of a sanctuary is another key success factor for a resistance movement, and Pakistan provided that.

The indomitable fighting spirit, toughness, and resilience of the Afghan people, however, was the most important reason why we won. We did not have to create the Afghan resistance. We only had to expand it, transform it, and sustain it. The insurgents enjoyed broad popular support, even among regime elements, another key success factor for a resistance movement. The Afghan people suffered one million dead during the war, one-fifteenth of the population at the time. Another five million were driven into exile by the Soviet scorched-earth campaigns. But Afghans never wavered in their resistance to the Soviet occupation.

From a Soviet point of view, the most important factor was Gorbachev and his view that to save the Soviet Union and posture it for a long-term competition with the West and China, he needed to transform its economy, political system, and individual freedoms and reorient its foreign policy to a less confrontational stance with the West. Even though he was a committed Communist, he knew the Soviet model was hopelessly obsolete. To achieve his economic restructuring and gain access to Western technology, Gorbachev fervently believed he had to end Soviet combat involvement in Afghanistan.

Years later, some of Gorbachev's hard-line critics would allege that he had been an agent of the CIA. He wasn't, and it was a good thing he wasn't. If he had been, as Bob Gates wrote in his memoirs, we wouldn't have had near the ability to direct him to destroy the Soviet Empire as completely as he was able to do all on his own. Indeed, he never intended to go that far. If he had understood the consequences of his actions, he almost certainly would have pursued a different course.[24] (Gorbachev died in August 2022 at the age of ninety-one.)

Had Gorbachev not been general secretary, and had he not been as determined and politically able as he was to end the Soviet-Afghan War, the withdrawal of Soviet forces likely would not have occurred as quickly as it did. A different Soviet leader, to be sure, would still have been trapped in a quagmire of dramatically increasing intensity in Afghanistan and would have been confronted with all of the economic and social problems that had plagued Gorbachev. Indeed, those conditions would have deteriorated during the 1980s under any leader. But a different Soviet leader might have dithered longer about pulling his troops out of Afghanistan.

A second critical factor contributing to the Soviets' failure in Afghanistan was their wildly unrealistic political goal. Afghanistan, with its strong religious makeup, overwhelmingly rural character, tradition of decentralized rule, ethnic tensions and factionalism, and strong hostility to foreign invaders, was not the world's best candidate for subjugation and transformation into a foreign-dominated, centrally directed, secular, cohesive, socialist state. It wasn't just the stage of Afghanistan's economic development that doomed Marxism-Leninism to failure in Afghanistan.

The Red Army, dependent on conscripts and mass firepower, was not designed for the war it found itself in. Soviet *spetsnaz* and airborne troops performed much better, but special operators and elite troops can't win a major war all by themselves. The 40th Army's main failing, however, was its inability to create sufficiently strong indigenous forces.

———

So what did we get wrong? Our Soviet analysts didn't believe the Soviets would invade, that they would escalate their war effort in 1985 as much as they did, or that the Red Army could possibly be defeated by the insurgents. More important, they didn't believe the early signs that Gorbachev was serious about withdrawing Soviet troops from Afghanistan or that he had the political strength to do so. Our Near East and South Asia analysts consistently assessed the state of the war more accurately than their counterparts in the Office of Soviet Analysis. One time when they didn't was when they expected the Communist Afghan regime to rapidly fall following the Soviets' withdrawal. It must be stressed, however, that CIA's analysts provided critical operational and tactical support to the program throughout the war. That mattered far more to the final outcome than a few misjudgments in predictive analysis.

We also missed the strategic significance of the "Afghan Arabs," the volunteers who would provide the foundation for al-Qa'ida, and the ties they were developing with some elements of the resistance (the Haqqanis and Yunis Khalis, in particular). We were rightly dismissive of the foreigners' contribution to the insurgency—they were mostly combat tourists who did little actual fighting—but we failed to penetrate them early enough; Usama Bin Ladin, for example, didn't become a focus of CIA counterterrorism attention until the 1990s. We also did not anticipate how the defeat of one superpower would motivate al-Qa'ida, which was established in the Pakistan border region in 1988, to want to wage a global war against the sole remaining superpower.[25] Disengaging from the region after 1990 enormously compounded our al-Qa'ida problem.

On the operational side, our big errors were not escalating the secret war sooner and not pushing for the introduction of the Stinger sooner. With respect to Western and U.S. weapons, we let covert action theory—the need to hide the hand of the United States—blind us to the reality that covert action doesn't have to be completely covert to be viable. It's the "action" part that matters most. Indeed, the sheer scale and sophistication of the program made it something of an open secret. It was these "open secrets" that made our covert action program unusual in the agency's experience, and far more strategically effective as a result. That said, the program had to be kept at least somewhat covert to succeed.

What did we get wrong after the Soviets withdrew and the war finally ended? The most important thing was our error in believing that Afghanistan had lost its strategic significance after the Red Army had been forced to withdraw and the Soviet Empire had collapsed. As a result, we disengaged from Afghanistan and Pakistan, the latter mandated by the Pressler Amendment, and lost any influence in the two countries, particularly after 1992, when the program ended. The civil war in Afghanistan paved the way for a Pakistani-supported conquest by the Taliban four years later. The Taliban's near conquest of most of Afghanistan, in turn, made possible al-Qa'ida's transformation into a global threat. I will have more to say about these developments in the next several chapters.

My role in the Afghanistan Covert Action Program during its decisive years was the assignment of a lifetime, one that would mark my transition from tactical to strategic and operational leadership. In his assessment of CIA's overall performance during the Cold War in espionage, technical collection, covert action, and analysis, former DCI Robert Gates argues that while CIA had many operational successes, the greatest of them all was the Afghanistan Covert Action Program.

It is hard to quarrel with his judgment.[26]

10

BUILDING NEW INTELLECTUAL CAPITAL

LEAVING CIA

With my strategy now fully in place, I had started thinking about what I might do after the Afghanistan Covert Action Program. So I made an appointment with the Career Management Staff to see what they thought. It is an understatement to say the meeting did not go well. It didn't help that the CMS staff officer struck me as just another cynical bureaucrat in a job far from operations, not exactly in fighting shape, and certainly not a thinker outside the box. He was about as far from my vision of what a CIA operations officer should be as I could imagine.[1] He informed me that I essentially needed to start over. I needed to do some traditional case officer tours in the field to show that I could recruit and handle assets if I wanted to be promoted to higher grades. "The DO has developed 'precepts' for promotion to various grades," he said. He smiled and added, "Your work on the program doesn't fit the precepts for a general operations officer."

I was stunned and angry, but I kept my cool. "I'm currently serving in a job that is at least three grades above my current one. I'm responsible for the most important program in the Directorate of Operations, and I control 60 percent of the DO's budget." "That's why you received accelerated promotion," he acknowledged, "but the precepts are the precepts, and that's all the promotion boards consider." Well, the promotion boards need to be given better guidance, I thought.

One of Gust's deputies, Larry, had asked me several months earlier if I was interested in becoming the chief of base in Peshawar. It was a command position and two grades above my current rank. I was flattered that I'd been asked, but its focus was on collecting foreign intelligence and recruiting and running human sources, not on running the war. It seemed like a big step down from what I was currently doing, so I declined the offer.

Given my broad program responsibilities, I had been declared to several foreign liaison services—the Chinese, the Pakistanis, the Saudis, the Egyptians, and others all knew me by my true name—which would limit my opportunities as a traditional case officer. I was probably known to the Russians as well. Switching to CIA's paramilitary branch didn't seem like a good option either. I loved paramilitary operations, but only the most strategically consequential ones, like Afghanistan. Training liaison services or running smaller programs was not something I aspired to. Plus, in the 1980s, there was no clear path for paramilitary operations officers to rise to the top of the Directorate of Operations. That's why I had become a general operations officer in the first place.

I'd had the adventure of a lifetime for three years. I regularly interacted with the top levels of the CIA and the chiefs and other top officials of several foreign liaison services around the world. I loved what I had done, and I loved CIA, but, perversely, it seemed that I had risen too fast and, more to the point, too unconventionally. It was my first career setback, and it was an odd one: I was being penalized for too much success. I had joined CIA not to begin a new career but to accelerate an existing one. I had succeeded beyond my wildest dreams, but it was clear there were still limits.

I recalled Jim Glerum's plan to fast-track a few covert action officers to the top of the DO. Much had changed, however, in the intervening two years. Glerum's International Activities Division had been broken up, and what was left had lost much of its clout. There was now an independent counterterrorism center within CIA. Political and psychological operations had become its own staff and counternarcotics was about to get its own center. By the time the restructuring was finally complete, the only thing left in what had been IAD was special activities—paramilitary operations and covert influence. That remains the case today.

I had been encouraged by Gust and Bert to switch my home base from IAD to NE Division. I did, but as a consequence I was now even more on the regular case officer track from a career management perspective. Bert and Gust had also recently informed me that they would be moving on to other jobs. Bert told me he wanted me to stay for at least another year to provide strategic continuity for the program. Then I could have any assignment in NE Division I wanted. I briefly thought about working against the Iranian target or serving in an NE station unrelated to the war. But it would essentially mean starting over.

Once I got over my frustration at the inflexibility of the system, I came to several conclusions. I'd had broad exposure to all parts of the agency, its senior leaders, and its global operations. It would not be going too far to say that in some respects I'd gained the equivalent of decades of CIA experience in only a few years. I knew I'd made special and important contributions, but that's what they were, special and outside the norm. Lloyd, a senior program colleague, had asked me on one of our foreign trips together if I could be satisfied with what would almost certainly lie ahead for me. He said that it would very likely be twenty years or more before I would again have responsibilities anything like my current ones. That sank in.

During my visits to CIA stations around the world, I came to realize that what I enjoyed the most about my program job was its global responsibilities and its strategic importance. As I thought about my future within CIA, I concluded that there were not many chief of station jobs that I'd really be interested in. Islamabad—as long as there was an Afghanistan program—would be number one on my list, but the Afghanistan program was coming to an end. Large, strategically consequential, covert action operations like the Afghanistan program would probably come around only once in a generation.

Moscow and Beijing would also have been on my short list, but that was about it. I had been attracted to the idea of working in the most hostile of operating environments, and helping to invent the new operational methods required to succeed there, but that train had almost certainly already left the station for me. I had been too exposed in my Afghan job. Plus, operations in Moscow were largely at a standstill due to the loss of so many of our agents. In any event, I knew that the big chief of station jobs, like the ones above, were, under the best circumstances, at least a decade or more away for me. What was I going to do in the meantime?

So I came to my biggest and most unexpected conclusion: I'd had my great war, just as Bill Casey had had his during World War II with the OSS. It was time to leave CIA.

I still aspired to be director of central intelligence someday, but if I wanted to serve in senior national security positions that were any-where near as consequential as my current responsibilities, I would need to leave CIA and come back into government from the outside. That's what Bill Casey had done, after all.

What I thought I needed next was something that would propel me into a new world, so I applied and was accepted into the Wharton School's MBA program. After I informed my colleagues that I was seriously thinking about leaving CIA, a few advised me to ask Bert to make a special appeal to the DDO for two to three additional pro-motions if I agreed to stay in the program job for a few more years. I would have stayed if that had been possible, but it wasn't. The system didn't work that way. Even if it had, I just couldn't see a path within CIA that would build on my Afghanistan experience and propel me upward into the senior management ranks anywhere nearly as rapidly as I wished. The rapid, unconventional path upward that I wanted just didn't exist.

That CMS officer had probably been right. To continue at the pace I wanted, I would have to become even more unconventional and chart my own way forward. And I had only the vaguest idea what that might look like. To this day, I still don't know if I made the right decision to leave CIA. I was profoundly grateful that I had been given such immense responsibilities at such a young age. I had been blessed to serve in a "golden age" for CIA.

Just before I left, Bert invited me to his office and told me how proud I should be of what I had accomplished. I was very proud. Only in CIA, I knew, would all this have been possible.

THE WHARTON SCHOOL AND JOHNS HOPKINS SAIS

The 1980s were an unusually great time to get an MBA. Investment bankers on Wall Street were making unheard-of sums doing merger and acquisition deals, and I thought, Why not me? At least for a little while.

I had gotten into Wharton's Executive MBA program, designed for mid-career professionals, so my classmates were older and more experienced and already well on their way to career success. I thoroughly enjoyed the program, and it stretched and challenged me in several ways, particularly the advanced math courses, such as operations research and probability and statistics. I took electives in advanced corporate finance, operations management, technology strategy, mergers and acquisitions, and entrepreneurship to make sure I received a comprehensive business education. As part of a multinational strategy course, we went to Japan, where we met with senior government and corporate executives across industries. "Japan as #1" was all the rage then, so it was a stimulating experience.

After graduation, I tried my hand at a couple of high-tech start-ups. One paid off reasonably well, the other, not at all. I knew early on that I didn't want to make a career in the business world, which I viewed solely as a path to acquire some financial security before I returned to government as a senior national security official or, possibly, in elected office. A lesson that I took from my brief start-up experience was that I would be happiest if I built a business around my core expertise and passion—national security. Truth is, I missed that world. It was what I'd been born to do, and I'd ventured too far away from it.

With some of the proceeds I received from my second venture, I applied for and was accepted into Johns Hopkins's School of Advanced International Studies. There, I met Eliot Cohen, the director of the school's Strategic Studies Program, and quickly decided that I wanted to pursue a PhD under him. By early 1995, I had completed all the course work and comprehensive exams for my doctorate. I was able to finance the degree through a very generous fellowship named after Alexander Hamilton, which encouraged public officials of high caliber to pursue graduate studies, and by continuing to do some strategy consulting, both for the private sector and for the Department of Defense.

I benefited immensely from my studies at SAIS, deepening my knowledge of strategic theory, military history, American foreign policy, international economics, and other subjects. I studied Clausewitz,

Thucydides, and Sun Tzu and gained a deep knowledge of military history since the Renaissance. I particularly enjoyed courses I took with the late Al Bernstein, especially one on policy and strategy in republican Rome. I was deeply honored to return to SAIS more than two decades later to give an annual lecture named after Al on lessons from ancient history for twenty-first-century strategists. I also enjoyed the PhD work I'd done in economics, which built on my Wharton degree.

My favorite course—on revolutionary change in warfare—was one of five I had taken with Eliot Cohen, and it became the basis for my PhD dissertation. I became obsessed with the topic, and the result was a thousand-page tome that offered a structural theory to explain the causes of revolutionary military change. I argued that while there was no precise "formula" for revolutionary change in war, advances in military technology, operational concepts, organization, and/or resources available periodically change military capabilities in revolutionary ways that increase the power of the strategic and operational offense, making large-scale conquest far more feasible. Not surprisingly, these periods have profound consequences for the international system, and strategic surprise is endemic. I argued that while there have been only eighteen true military revolutions in history, the frequency of revolutionary change in war has increased significantly during the past two centuries as a result of the industrial and scientific revolutions. With four thousand years of history to cover, my dissertation took almost as long to complete.[2] I finally finished it after I had returned to government in the George W. Bush administration, and even then, only after my wife, in a last-ditch effort to get me to complete it, told me that I'd set a bad example for my daughters if I didn't.

After I completed my course work and PhD exams in international relations, strategic studies, American foreign policy, and international economics, I was asked to fill in for Eliot as acting director of the department for a year while he was on sabbatical. I taught classes on strategy and policy and on my dissertation topic, which helped refine my thinking on the subject. As an added bonus, several former CIA colleagues doing the mid-career program at SAIS took my courses.

CHINA'S RISE AND THE REVOLUTION IN MILITARY AFFAIRS

My seven years of graduate study at Wharton and SAIS furnished me with new analytical tools and a deep appreciation of history and strategic theory that greatly furthered my transition from the world of operations to the world of strategy and policy. While completing my PhD studies, I worked between 1993 and 1995 in the Pentagon's Office of Net Assessment, headed by the legendary Andy Marshall, affectionately called Yoda. Marshall headed ONA from 1973 to 2015. Among his protégés are a former deputy secretary of defense (Bob Work), a secretary of the Air Force (Jim Roche), a counselor at the State Department (Eliot Cohen), and a top Middle East policy maker and negotiator (Dennis Ross).

Marshall had been an intellectual leader during the early Cold War on the strategic implications of nuclear weapons and had conducted groundbreaking work on organizational theory, which had a profound impact on our understanding of the Soviet leadership's decision-making process. During the 1960s and 1970s, his work informed U.S. strategies for long-term competition with the Soviet Union. His work on the Soviet defense burden led CIA to double its estimate of the costs that defense spending imposed on the Soviet economy. It also led to a fundamental rethinking of our long-term competitive position, namely, that time was on our side.

Some of Marshall's net assessments had even been responsible for major shifts in defense strategy, particularly one he oversaw in the late 1970s that changed our approach to undersea warfare and exploited the Soviet military's fears about the vulnerability of its seaborne nuclear deterrent. With the Cold War now over, Marshall thought the next big things on the strategic horizon would be, one, a military revolution (also called the revolution in military affairs) that could profoundly shift power balances in favor of those who exploited it first, and, two, the rise of China as a rival to the United States.[3]

In 1992, I had written a seminar paper for Eliot describing my initial theory of revolutionary change in warfare. I was also taking a course on net assessment at the time from Andy Krepinevich, an adjunct professor at SAIS. A West Point graduate, Harvard PhD, and military assistant to three secretaries of defense and to Andy Marshall, Krepinevich had just completed a preliminary assessment of what he described as a military-technical revolution based on rapidly advancing conventional, precision, long-range strike capabilities, so I told him about the paper I had written. He asked to see it and immediately passed it on to Marshall. Marshall loved it and offered me a job. He would become one of the important mentors in my life.

I agreed with Marshall that the next big challenges for the United States were the rise of China and a prospective military revolution that could significantly alter global power balances. I believed that the most important contribution I could make to U.S. national security now was to help the United States prepare for those two challenges. I thought that I was done with special operations, intelligence, covert action, counterterrorism, and Afghanistan. I also thought Russia had become a fairly benign and severely crippled power that would no longer pose a threat to the United States and might even become a future U.S. ally. I would be right on China and the revolution in military affairs and wrong on everything else.

The first task Marshall gave me was to write a concept paper on what theater warfare might look like in 2020, assuming that both China and the United States had exploited an emerging military revolution to transform their military capabilities. I learned that China's People's Liberation Army had gone to school on the U.S. victory in the 1990–1991 Persian Gulf War. Chinese military strategists concluded that in any future conflict a U.S. adversary should focus on not allowing the American military to build up combat power in the theater. I described this as an "anti-access" strategy, later modified to anti-access/area denial to include naval operations within reach of China's mainland.

I argued that this strategy would be at the core of China's exploitation of a future military revolution. China would be able to asymmetrically hold U.S. forces at risk, and perhaps even deter the United States from responding to aggression in the western Pacific. I also thought that China would eventually present not just a military threat that would require the U.S. military to transform itself but an economic one as well, resulting in the United States' losing the "economic escalation dominance" it enjoyed in the twentieth century when no rival—the Soviet Union, Nazi Germany, or Japan—possessed more than 50 percent of U.S. GDP.

Advances in battlespace awareness, the ability to strike with precision at great range, and continued improvements in stealth and automation would lead to a world in which unmanned systems would dominate. Missiles would play a much larger role in precision air warfare. Even with stealth, power projection using aircraft would have to be conducted from much greater range due to the increasing vulnerability of forward bases to Chinese missile strikes.

Undersea warfare, with its inherent stealth, would dominate future naval power projection. It would be very difficult to insert ground forces into an area that was defended by an adversary with anti-access/area-denial capabilities, so those that were able to be inserted by some form of stealthy delivery means would need to have their combat power augmented as much as possible by robotic, electrically propelled systems.

The capabilities and reach of "finders" would dramatically increase, but some "hiders" would still be able to hide. Information operations that could intensify the "fog of war" would become increasingly important on the future battlefield. Space would become far more important to operations and would become a new domain of conflict. Cyber operations could be used to disarm an adversary without firing a shot, a new form of fire and maneuver. All this I described as a "multidimensional revolution."

Once it had become clear that China's anti-access/area-denial capabilities would be able to hold current U.S. methods of projecting power at increasing risk, there would be a new competition between China's standoff strike (mostly offensive missiles and cyber weapons) and anti-access/area-denial capabilities and new U.S. methods of projecting conventional power based on stealthy long-range surveillance, strike and air mobility aircraft, hypersonic missiles, fast attack and missile-launching submarines, robotic ground systems, and information-spoofing capabilities. There would be important sub-competitions between offensive missiles and missile defenses, stealth and counter-stealth systems, "hiders" and "finders," cyber offense and defense, and space and counter-space systems. At the strategic level of war, there would be a competition between offensive and defensive capabilities in biological warfare. There would also be a peacetime competition between coercion and reassurance.

Missiles would prevail over missile defenses, stealth would prevail over counter-stealth systems, and cyber offense would find success against cyber defenses. The combination of stealthy long-range air-craft, missiles, and submarines would provide the United States with an effective conventional deterrent against China's growing standoff strike and A2/AD capabilities. I turned out to be right in almost all of these areas.

However revolutionary these changes in high-end theater warfare might be, the potential gains from theater war would still likely be stra-tegically constrained by the continued threat posed by nuclear weap-ons. I described this as the "nuclear overhang." Survivable nuclear weapons and delivery systems would allow a belligerent on the losing end of things to limit his strategic losses by threatening escalation. This would be true even for regional powers that possessed a nuclear deterrent. Future powers, moreover, would field new forms of strate-gic strikes, ranging from cyberattack to genetically engineered weap-ons and stealth pathogens. These new bioweapons could be used in the future to target particular ethnic groups or even individuals, to control or alter the behavior of populations, and to wage covert eco-nomic warfare. It was, admittedly, not the most pleasant future vision, but it was one that the United States had to be prepared for.

Marshall liked the paper, "A Concept for Theater Warfare in 2020," and shared it with Admiral Bill Owens, the vice-chairman of the Joint Chiefs of Staff, and other senior leaders in the Pentagon. He encour-aged me to continue to refine the concept, and sponsored a series of war games to further explore its assumptions. These games became known as the "Future Warfare 20XX" series, and they have been going on for nearly three decades now. They had the benefit of exposing up-and-coming military leaders to important future warfare concepts. Among the regular players was a future vice-chairman of the Joint Chiefs of Staff, General Paul Selva.

Three decades on, the research I conducted for Marshall between 1993 and 1995 turned out to be pretty accurate. I will have more to say about these developments in subsequent chapters.

———

After I completed my PhD exams at SAIS, Andy Krepinevich and I co-founded a new think tank and strategic consultancy, the Center for Strategic and Budgetary Assessments. Steve Kosiak, who would later become the associate director for national security and international affairs at OMB during the Obama administration, led the budget side, and I led the strategy side, where I concentrated on future warfare concepts and management strategies to transform the American military for a new era of conflict.

Our primary customer on the strategy side was Andy Marshall. Following the 9/11 attacks, CSBA's strategy portfolio expanded substantially to cover the full range of current and future challenges facing the United States, including the strategies and capabilities needed to prevail in a protracted counterterrorism war and grand strategy for a new national security era.

It was a stimulating place to work. Building on the special operations, intelligence, and covert action base that I had spent the first fifteen years of my career focused on, I had now acquired expertise in grand strategy, operational strategy, long-range precision airpower, space warfare, undersea warfare, information warfare, and nuclear strategy.

My strategic horizons had broadened substantially. They would broaden even further after I got called back into government service.

PART III

WAR WITH AL-QA'IDA

11

NO SANCTUARY

9/11

I was as shocked as most Americans by the 9/11 attacks. I was in my think tank office on Rhode Island Avenue in Washington, D.C., when the first plane slammed into the North Tower of the World Trade Center at 8:46 a.m. I watched in horror as the second plane slammed into the South Tower seventeen minutes later, and then, thirty-four minutes after that, a third plane struck the Pentagon. I had just been at the Pentagon the day before, helping to put the finishing touches on DOD's 2001 Quadrennial Defense Review, the assessment DOD does every four years of its strategy, major investment programs, and force structure. Were my colleagues killed or injured in the attack?

Until this point, the QDR had principally focused on the need to transform the U.S. military for a potential future conflict with China. There hadn't been a word in it about al-Qa'ida or Afghanistan until after the 9/11 attacks, an oversight that would quickly be rectified before the report was released on September 30.[1] Of all the places DOD anticipated it might have to go to war, Afghanistan wasn't among them. The threat from global jihadist terrorism just wasn't on DOD's radar screen.

Amid the chaos and shutdown of mass transit and cell phone networks, it took hours to get home and be reunited with my family. I felt rage at al-Qa'ida, who I knew was almost certainly behind the attacks. I was also furious at myself for underestimating the threat the group posed. This attack was on a far greater scale than the terrorism I had confronted in the 1980s. Four simultaneous airline hijackings with planes used as weapons. More Americans dead than at Pearl Harbor.

How had we let this happen? Were additional attacks coming?

———————

How the 9/11 attacks happened had its origin in 1988. Al-Qa'ida, which means "the base" in Arabic, was formed that year in Peshawar, Pakistan, as the Soviet-Afghan War was coming to an end. Usama Bin Ladin, the new organization's emir, wanted to create a "foundation" for future global jihad. UBL had created a "Services Bureau" (*Maktab al-Khadamat*) in Peshawar during the Soviet-Afghan War to provide foreign fighters who had come to join the jihad with food and housing. Thousands of "Afghan Arabs" had come to Pakistan's border region, but few did much actual fighting in Afghanistan.

I had been aware of the "Afghan Arabs" when I was the Afghanistan Covert Action Program officer, but like my CIA colleagues at the time, I was dismissive of them. And as former senior CIA analyst Bruce Riedel has pointed out, CIA had no role in creating this foreign fighter network.[2] UBL had returned to Saudi Arabia after the Soviet withdrawal but his anti-U.S. views caused him to run afoul of the Saudi government. The Saudis had allowed hundreds of thousands of U.S. troops to stage from Saudi territory during the 1990–1991 Gulf War, which Bin Ladin vehemently denounced. After becoming persona non grata, Bin Ladin moved to Sudan in 1991. He established terrorist training camps there and financed the travel of hundreds of Soviet-Afghan War veterans to receive training at them. A defector from al-Qa'ida informed CIA that UBL was the head of a worldwide terrorist organization and was seeking to acquire material for chemical, biological, radiological, or nuclear weapons. The defector also warned that Bin Ladin wanted to strike the United States on its own soil and believed that America could be defeated even more easily than the Soviets had been.[3]

The United States placed intense pressure on the Sudanese government to expel him, so Bin Ladin fled to Afghanistan on May 19, 1996. CIA created a new special unit at CIA headquarters called Alec Station to report on and disrupt UBL's activities there. By 1997, CIA had learned that UBL wanted to establish a global caliphate and that the United States, AQ's "far enemy," was his prime target. To achieve his caliphate, UBL believed that he had to drive the United States out of the Middle East and then overthrow what he saw as U.S.-supported "apostate" governments in the region, which AQ referred to as the "near enemy." In February 1998, UBL issued a fatwa asserting that all Muslims had a religious duty to "kill Americans and their allies, both civilian and military," worldwide. Under the protection of the Taliban, Bin Ladin significantly increased al-Qa'ida's capabilities between May 1996 and September 11, 2001. Al-Qa'ida built and ran training camps that attracted recruits from all over the world and turned out committed jihadis by the thousands. The group also built a document forgery capability and mechanisms to move money securely.[4]

CIA had issued several warnings to policy makers between 1995 and 2001 on the growing threat posed by al-Qa'ida, but to no avail. National Intelligence Estimates in 1995 and 1997 warned of the threat posed by radical Islamists and their increasing ability to operate in the United States. The NIEs also warned that the most likely targets of a terrorist attack would be symbols of U.S. power, such as the White House, the Capitol, and Wall Street, and that civil aviation was an especially vulnerable and attractive target. A President's Daily Brief article in December 1998 carried the same warning. The alerts continued through the end of the Clinton administration and into the first months of the Bush administration.

During President Clinton's second term, CIA had been given limited covert action authorities to mount a capture operation against Bin Ladin, but the agency lacked the specific intelligence and capability to conduct it. Alec Station had put together a plan in the fall of 1997 to ambush and capture Bin Ladin using members of a tribe in southern Afghanistan CIA had code-named the TRODPINTS. At the time, UBL was staying at al-Qa'ida's heavily guarded Tarnak Farms compound near Kandahar. The plan was to breach the compound's ten-foot walls, find Bin Ladin, who could be staying that night with any of the several wives he had there with him, capture him, roll him up in a rug, and hide him in a cave for a month until an aircraft could be clandestinely flown in to exfiltrate him out of Afghanistan. The operation had little chance of succeeding, and George Tenet, the director of central intelligence, rightly rejected it. A year later, a new plan involving the TRODPINTS was given the green light, but it failed miserably.[5]

After al-Qa'ida struck our embassies in Kenya and Tanzania with suicide bomb attacks that killed 224 people, including 12 Americans, and wounded more than 4,000, the U.S. military conducted a cruise missile strike against one of al-Qa'ida's training camps in eastern Afghanistan. It did nothing to set back al-Qa'ida or deter UBL. By the time the missiles struck the compound, Bin Ladin and the other AQ senior leaders had already departed. It is likely al-Qa'ida's leadership had been warned by someone in Pakistan's national security establishment who had been advised of the strike by a senior U.S. military officer ahead of time.

In 1999, President Clinton authorized CIA to work with Ahmad Shah Massoud's Northern Alliance to collect intelligence on UBL's whereabouts. Massoud had been our best insurgent commander during our secret war to drive the Soviets out of Afghanistan during the 1980s and was leading the resistance to the Taliban takeover of Afghanistan. (President Clinton had not authorized the agency to conduct lethal covert action through Massoud, but it probably wouldn't have accomplished much if he had. Massoud's forces were bottled up in northeastern Afghanistan and had little ability to project power in the Pashtun belt where UBL was hiding.)

CIA's capacity to collect technical intelligence on al-Qa'ida, however, improved dramatically with the advent of an unmanned aerial vehicle known as Predator. During a Predator flight over Afghanistan on September 28, 2000—only three weeks after the aircraft was initially deployed—a tall man in flowing white robes was observed walking around surrounded by a security detail. It was almost certainly UBL. But the Predator had not been armed, so all CIA could do was watch.[6]

In October 2000, al-Qa'ida struck again, blowing a gaping hole in the USS *Cole*, in port at Aden, Yemen, killing seventeen sailors and wounding thirty-seven. It took the intelligence community a couple of months to attribute the attack to core al-Qa'ida. In its final months in office, the Clinton administration did not retaliate for the attack. The Bush administration likewise decided to wait until it had developed a new strategy before it went after al-Qa'ida.

CIA issued another warning in the August 6, 2001, PDB article "Bin

Ladin Determined to Strike in the US." But like the CIA warnings that had preceded it, it contained no actionable information about the time, method, and place of attack. A month later, al-Qa'ida struck.

The 9/11 attacks were not inevitable. While the U.S. intelligence community for the most part lacked the actionable intelligence it needed to take out Bin Ladin and al-Qa'ida's senior leadership before 9/11, an important lesson we would learn about counterterrorism strategy after 9/11 is that action begets intelligence. Counterterrorism action disrupts terrorists' plans and operations, and disruption creates more opportunities to collect intelligence.

With the benefit of hindsight, after 1998 we should have conducted a military and covert action campaign to deny al-Qa'ida's sanctuary in Afghanistan. After 9/11, we would understand the critical importance of denying al-Qa'ida any sanctuary and would shift from a reactive counterterrorism strategy to a proactive one. Not shifting sooner was a policy failure, not an intelligence failure. Additional cruise missile strikes and stealthy B-2 bomber strikes could have been conducted on al-Qa'ida's training camps. Mohammed Atta, the leader of the nineteen hijackers, was trained for the operation at a special al-Qa'ida camp in Afghanistan. A special operations raid could have been conducted against Tarnak Farms while UBL was there. It would have had a much better chance of success than the TRODPINT covert action plan. Making no distinction between al-Qa'ida and its safe haven providers is a prerequisite for decisive CT operations. Taking more aggressive covert action to expand resistance to Taliban rule into the Pashtun heartland, as we did after 9/11, could also have disrupted al-Qa'ida's operations. Another very important lesson on the offensive CT side is that the Predator must be armed to be an effective counterterrorism instrument. Observing in real time is great, but it is much better to be able to also strike in real time.

Given all the warnings about al-Qa'ida's interest in hijacking U.S. airliners, moreover, we should have hardened our cockpit doors much sooner. Building a global counterterrorism network to enable intelligence sharing with and action by our international partners is also important, as is ensuring that there are no legal impediments to our IC agencies and the FBI in working together. As the former secretary of state Condoleezza Rice would later put it, "Al-Qa'ida was at war with us, but we weren't yet at war with them." We would address all these shortcomings after 9/11.

ELIMINATING THE AFGHAN SANCTUARY

The Bush administration moved swiftly after the 9/11 attacks to eliminate al-Qa'ida's sanctuary in Afghanistan, with CIA in the lead. CIA teams had made five trips into northern Afghanistan during the previous two years, renewing ties to Ahmad Shah Massoud, the head of the Northern Alliance, and other leaders opposed to the Taliban.[7] Massoud, unfortunately, was assassinated on September 9 by two al-Qa'ida operatives posing as journalists. The operatives had hidden explosives inside their video camera and had detonated the improvised device soon after they began the interview.[8] The Taliban also executed Abdul Haq, another of my former mujahedin commanders, on October 26. Haq had tried to reenter southern Afghanistan to build up resistance to the Taliban but was captured and killed soon after he crossed the Pakistan-Afghanistan border.

I was shocked when I heard the news about Massoud's assassination. He had been our best commander in the Afghan resistance and an honorable man. Years later, I would visit his tomb in the Panjshir Valley. His death was a severe blow to the Afghan opposition to the Taliban. I was equally sad to hear about the death of Abdul Haq, who had also made important contributions to the Afghan resistance. On September 9, al-Qa'ida's assassination of Massoud looked like a strategic decapitation attack to try to consolidate the Taliban's rule over Afghanistan. Two days later, it was clear it had been far more—a preemptive strike by al-Qa'ida against an expected U.S. invasion of Afghanistan in the aftermath of the 9/11 attacks.

Fortunately, CIA had relationships with other leaders of the Afghan opposition that were robust enough to withstand the loss of Massoud. All had been known to CIA since the 1980s Soviet-Afghan War. CIA would soon have more than a hundred sources and subsources and had relationships with eight tribal networks spread across Afghanistan.[9]

At National Security Council meetings on September 13 and 15, Director of Central Intelligence George Tenet proposed an aggressive covert action plan CIA's Counterterrorism Center had been working on since the final months of the Clinton administration. Called the "Blue Sky" memo, it became the basis for CIA's war plan after 9/11. Working closely with military Special Forces, CIA teams would use speed and agility to defeat the Taliban and al-Qa'ida, Tenet told President Bush. "We will be the insurgents," Tenet said. "Bin Ladin and his followers expect a massive invasion. They are going to get the surprise of their lives." Tenet said he would use the large infusion of funds that was coming CIA's way to strengthen CIA's foreign partners, both inside and outside Afghanistan. He explained that CIA would provide immediate lethal assistance to the Northern Alliance and accelerate its contacts with southern Pashtun leaders. Tenet suggested arming the Predator and using it to kill UBL's key lieutenants.[10] He also raised the possibility of being able to unilaterally detain al-Qa'ida's operatives around the world, which would be crucial in generating additional intelligence. CIA's global network of partners would also be used to go after al-Qa'ida's sources of funding. In short, CIA proposed to strangle al-Qa'ida's safe haven in Afghanistan, seal Afghanistan's borders, go after AQ's senior leadership, shut off AQ's sources of money, and pursue al-Qa'ida terrorists in ninety-two countries around the world.[11] President Bush liked CIA's approach, and on September 17 he approved Tenet's plan and provided the agency with the new authorities it needed to execute an offensive counterterrorism campaign. Congress quickly approved the necessary funding.[12]

It was the beginnings of a global CT strategy, one that we would refine and build upon as the war with al-Qa'ida evolved. After I returned to government in 2007, we would expand the use of the Predator substantially and continue to build our global network of counterterrorism partners. CIA's rendition, detention, and interrogation program would be terminated. I will have more to say about how our counterterrorism operations evolved in the next chapter.

DOD's Central Command under General Tommy Franks had gone to work on developing an unconventional military campaign in line with Tenet's proposal. On September 21, Franks and Major General Dell Dailey, the commander of the Joint Special Operations Command, presented their initial concept: Special Forces teams would accompany CIA to work with the Afghan resistance to the Taliban, beginning in northern Afghanistan. Other special operators would augment the main effort by conducting raids against key strategic targets. Franks and Dailey told the president they could begin the campaign in two weeks. The president liked this plan much better than the initial options DOD had proposed—limited cruise missile and air strikes or a massive conventional force invasion from Pakistan that would take several months to put in place.[13]

A week or so after the attacks, Jim Thomas, a former classmate of mine at Johns Hopkins SAIS who had become a career policy official at DOD, asked if I could come to his office in the Pentagon right away. He had just become the senior civilian assistant to Deputy Secretary of Defense Paul Wolfowitz and was working on DOD's response to the 9/11 attacks. In his office, a Secure Compartmented Information Facility, or SCIF, Jim brought me up to speed on the planning that had occurred within DOD for a war with al-Qa'ida.

After filling me in on DOD planning, Jim asked me what I thought. There were concerns, including at a very high level within DOD, that we were being lured into a trap in Afghanistan and that we should strike Iraq first.[14] I told Jim that this would be the height of strategic insanity. We got hit from Afghanistan, not Iraq. I told him that the unconventional-conventional approach CIA and CENTCOM were advocating was the right one, because it would let us respond immediately and forcefully, but we would need to aggressively employ our heavy airpower to ensure that the resistance could achieve escalation dominance over the Taliban.

Jim then handed me the Joint Staff's strategic guidance to the combatant commands for a global war with al-Qa'ida and its allies. Joint Staff planners had called for the decisive defeat of al-Qa'ida worldwide as the primary objective, but the guidance was mostly boilerplate; there was nothing in it that showed how we would accomplish this objective and over what period of time. We worked at a whiteboard to refine the war's objectives and prioritize them over time. Little did I know, however, the shifts in momentum that would occur in our war with al-Qa'ida and other global jihadists, and how long the war would go on.

Jim thanked me for my help and I left. That two-hour meeting was the extent of my participation in America's immediate response to the 9/11 attacks.

————

The air campaign in Afghanistan began on October 7. It started with B-2 stealth bomber and cruise missile strikes against the Taliban's limited air defenses and other fixed targets. CIA's first team to enter Afghanistan after 9/11 was the Northern Alliance Liaison Team, headed by Gary Schroen, a former chief of station in both Kabul and Islamabad with deep ties to the mujahedin. The team was inserted into the Panjshir Valley from Dushanbe, Tajikistan, on a Russian-made, CIA-owned and modified Mi-17 helicopter on September 26. Included on the team were Schroen's deputy Phil Reilly, a career paramilitary operations officer and former Special Forces soldier, and "Chris," an operations officer who had worked previously in Pakistan on the Taliban/al-Qa'ida target.[15] I would work with both men extensively between 2007 and 2015.

The NALT, code-named Jawbreaker, would primarily support General Fahim Khan, Massoud's successor as the leader of the Northern Alliance, and his subordinate commanders. One of Fahim's key subordinate commanders was General Bismullah Khan, commander of the Kabul front. BK, as he was known, would later become the Afghan Army's chief of staff, and I would work closely with him. I knew about him during the Soviet-Afghan War, but hadn't met him. The NALT's mission was to attack across the Shomali Plain and take Kabul. It was also tasked with cutting the road from Kabul to Kunduz to isolate the Taliban forces there, and then to take Taloqan and Kunduz. It served as CIA's command unit in Afghanistan, overseeing several other teams that CIA deployed.

All of the teams had similar compositions to the NALT, with no more than eight personnel assigned to each. Team "Alpha" would be inserted into the Mazar-e-Sharif area. Team Alpha's mission was to capture Mazar and open the route to the Uzbek border, which would provide an overland supply route for the Northern Alliance. Team "Bravo" would soon be subdivided from Team Alpha. Team "Charlie" would link up with Ismail Khan, my former mujahedin commander, in the west. Its mission was to take Herat and cut the ring road north and south of Herat to prevent Taliban forces from using it. Team "Delta" would be inserted into Bamiyan to work with the Hazaras. Team "Echo," led by "Greg V.," a senior paramilitary operations officer with whom I would work very closely in subsequent years, would support Hamid Karzai's campaign to take the south of Afghanistan and Kandahar.[16] Two more teams would be added later, "Foxtrot" in the south and "Juliet" in the east.[17] Team Foxtrot would support Gul Agha Sherzai, the son of my former mujahedin commander Haji Latif ("Haji Baba"); Team Juliet would help lead the hunt for Bin Ladin in the Tora Bora mountains. It was CIA at its best.

The 5th Special Forces Group, under the command of Colonel John Mulholland, was the principal boots-on-the-ground force for CENTCOM. The first Special Forces teams were inserted into Afghanistan on October 19. More quickly followed. With CIA, and supported by U.S. airpower, Mulholland and the 5th Group invented a new and more powerful form of unconventional warfare.[18] One SF team, ODA 595, even conducted a "cavalry charge" during the operation to take Mazar-e-Sharif.[19]

I had to laugh at the thought of Green Berets on horseback. My wife and I had taken my daughters to a dude ranch in Utah the summer before for a week of horseback riding. Unfortunately, as we were galloping down a trail, the latigo holding my saddle had come loose. I found myself hanging on the side of my horse with my hands still holding the reins, but with only one foot in a stirrup. I quickly realized this wasn't going to end well and prepared myself to do something resembling a parachute landing fall. The horse soon bucked and threw me off. I survived with only a bad headache and a sore shoulder for a few days. After hearing about the SF cavalry charge in Afghanistan, my daughter Natasha told me, "Dad, it's a good thing you're not in Special Forces anymore. You'd have fallen off your horse!"

Also on October 19, the Army's 75th Ranger Regiment conducted a parachute drop near Kandahar. Other Army special operators raided Mullah Omar's house on the outskirts of Kandahar, which, when I visited it a few years later, bore a strong resemblance to Disneyland's "Small World" ride. Omar, unfortunately, had fled to Pakistan by the time our special operators assaulted the target.

For the first month of the war, air strikes against Taliban and al-Qa'ida formations were fairly limited and were conducted primarily by Navy F/A-18 fighters. The Northern Alliance, America's primary ally at the time, refused to move until the United States got serious and conducted more decisive air strikes to break the Taliban's defenses.[20] A Defense Intelligence Agency assessment issued in late October was particularly gloomy. It stated that "Northern Alliance forces are incapable of overcoming Taliban resistance in northern Afghanistan, particularly around the strategic city of Mazar-e-Sharif." It also stated that "Northern Alliance forces will not capture Kabul before winter arrives, nor does the Alliance possess sufficient forces to encircle and isolate the city." DIA further argued that "no viable Pashtun alternative exists to the Taliban."[21]

As I watched from the sidelines, I was frustrated with the slow pace and ineffectiveness of the air campaign. I thought, Why aren't we using our heavy bombers? I had been advocating for a greater emphasis on bombers for several years. Bombers combined long range and endurance with a large payload. During the 1990s, the bomber fleet had received upgrades that enabled it to deliver precision-guided munitions, which was a game changer. Bombers could deliver mass with precision from range, all essential attributes for twenty-first-century air campaigns. On November 1, the air campaign finally became more intense. B-1 and B-52 bombers dropping precision-guided munitions struck six key Taliban positions near Mazar-e-Sharif, killing more than three hundred fighters and a senior Taliban commander. U.S. bombers broke the Taliban's defenses. Bombers would fly only 10 percent of strike sorties during the war but would deliver 75 percent of the bombs dropped.[22] Special Forces teams, with attached joint terminal attack controllers, or JTACs, did the precision targeting for bombing missions. The United States demonstrated even more novel precision strike capabilities when it located and killed al-Qa'ida's military chief, Mohammed Atef, with a combined Predator and Marine F/A-18 strike in Kabul in mid-November, opening up a new era in counterterrorism operations.[23]

Mazar-e-Sharif fell on November 9. On November 12, Ismail Khan took Herat in the west. I followed his campaign in western Afghanistan particularly closely. When I heard how rapidly he had routed Taliban forces, I remarked to a senior Air Force officer, "I told you so. He was one of our best muj commanders." Kabul fell on November 14.

Given my think tank position and background in Special Forces, CIA, and Afghanistan, I was asked periodically to provide analysis on TV. After the fall of Mazar-e-Sharif and Kabul, Chris Matthews of MSNBC asked me in his rapid-fire way when the war would be over. I replied, "Before Christmas." I was right—at least where the opening campaign against al-Qa'ida was concerned.

Hamid Karzai, who would soon become Afghanistan's president, waged a brilliant campaign in the south, from Uruzgan to Kandahar, partnering with CIA's Greg V. throughout. Greg flew in on a helicopter with a Special Forces team on November 4 and 5 to rescue Karzai and his small group of followers after they had been surrounded by Taliban forces at Tarin Kowt, and then went back into Afghanistan with Karzai and the SF team a few days later to continue the fight. Greg provided operational advice to Karzai during his lightning campaign to take the south during the final two weeks of November. At Tarin Kawt in Uruzgan Province, he personally rallied Karzai's troops to hold their positions during a major battle with the Taliban. He also saved Karzai's life by throwing him to the ground and lying on top of him when an errant U.S. bomb struck their position.[24] Not bad for a few weeks' work. Kandahar fell in early December to Gul Agha Sherzai's forces. ("Sherzai" means "son of a lion," and that he was.) I would meet Sherzai eight years later when he was governor of Nangarhar Province.

The routing of the Taliban and al-Qa'ida had been accomplished by 110 CIA officers, 316 Special Forces personnel, and scores of other special operators.[25] Counting the Marines, who were inserted into southern Afghanistan in late November, a few thousand U.S. ground troops, supported by U.S. airpower, had defeated 50,000 Taliban and al-Qa'ida. Tenet was right: it is much better to be the insurgents.

The rapid defeat of the Taliban and al-Qa'ida was like watching all my children—Special Forces, the CIA, and long-range precision airpower—perform spectacularly. It was a great example of employing all means available through the integration of new means. According to one estimate, al-Qa'ida had lost close to 80 percent of its operatives during the campaign, in addition to its top military commander, Mohammed Atef. I was amazed and impressed by how well the war had been conducted. I also wondered more than a few times whether my decision to leave CIA had been the right one.

The initial war in Afghanistan ended on a bitter note, however, with the escape of UBL and other al-Qa'ida leaders and operatives to Pakistan. CIA and SOF sent pursuit teams with Northern Alliance fighters to the Tora Bora (Black Caves) region near the Pakistani border where UBL was holed up, but the mountainous terrain made preventing UBL's escape nearly impossible. Hundreds of al-Qa'ida operatives were killed, but UBL got away. President Bush was furious when he was told that UBL had survived and was still on the loose. "How the hell did you lose him?" he asked his PDB briefer, Michael Morell. "How could he possibly have eluded you?"[26] Little did I know at the time that UBL's fate and mine would become intertwined a decade later.

DISRUPT, DISMANTLE, DEFEAT

THE NEW SANCTUARY IN PAKISTAN

During the first five years of our war with al-Qa'ida, I sat on the side-lines. I was consulted briefly on the initial war plan, and in 2002 I was asked by the deputy secretary of defense to conduct a major study on strategy for the war and how DOD should transform itself to pros-ecute it.[1] In 2005, I was asked by the secretary of defense to conduct a review of our special operations forces, and in 2005–2006 I played a large role in shaping the outcome of the Quadrennial Defense Review, which, among other things, led to a major expansion of our special operations forces. I also closely followed developments in the war with al-Qa'ida and the wars in Afghanistan and Iraq, but that was about it.

Al-Qa'ida had reconstituted in Pakistan's tribal areas after its Afghanistan sanctuary had been eliminated, and by 2006 the threat the group posed to the American homeland was once again severe. Fol-lowing the collapse of the Taliban regime, many of al-Qa'ida's senior leaders fled to "prearranged" safe houses in Pakistan's "settled areas," a Pakistani term for its territory east of the Indus River. Bin Ladin, aided by loyal Afghans, most likely took an indirect route to Pakistan, remaining in Afghanistan near the Pakistani border for several months and evading capture by U.S. forces who didn't know he was there. The United States simply didn't have the intelligence assets or the forces in theater to find him after he escaped from Tora Bora. It was a cost of the otherwise very successful "small-footprint warfare" waged by CIA and SOF, though UBL would likely have escaped even if a much larger force had been on the ground.

The mastermind of the 9/11 attacks, Khalid Sheikh Mohammed (or KSM as he was known), was promoted to al-Qa'ida's chief of operations. He got right to work, planning several additional attacks against the West. He had a hand in Richard Reid's unsuccessful attempt to use a shoe bomb to bring down an American Airlines flight from Paris to Miami, and he oversaw the April 2002 assault that killed nineteen worshippers at a synagogue in Tunisia. He was planning to use operatives recruited in Saudi Arabia to hijack aircraft and crash them into London's Heathrow Airport and had planned a similar attack against skyscrapers in Los Angeles using operatives from Southeast Asia.[2] He sent a team of Pakistanis to smuggle explosives into New York to blow up bridges and other targets, and he had several operations planned in Karachi, including one against the U.S. consulate.[3]

By March 2002, CIA had identified a number of sites in Pakistan that appeared to be al-Qa'ida safe houses. CIA persuaded the Pakistanis to raid thirteen of the sites simultaneously, resulting in the capture of more than two dozen al-Qa'ida members. Among them was Abu Zubaydah, who had been captured in Faisalabad and badly wounded in the operation. After his condition stabilized, he was turned over to CIA. Thus began CIA's secret detention and interrogation program.[4]

For years, CIA had been seeing in intelligence traffic references to "Mukhtar," a senior al-Qa'ida leader who had been heavily involved in a number of AQ's plots. During his interrogation, Abu Zubaydah acknowledged that "Mukhtar" was KSM. CIA found KSM in Rawalpindi through a human source. In March 2003, a joint Pakistani-American team stormed KSM's safe house. He was quickly moved to one of CIA's "black sites," where he was subjected to enhanced interrogation techniques, including waterboarding, the most controversial method. Zubaydah and Abd al-Rahim Nashiri had been water boarded as well. The three of them were the only detainees in CIA custody that were subjected to it.

After he became compliant, KSM provided a treasure trove of information about al-Qa'ida, save for what he knew about UBL's location and the group's means of communicating with him, which he still withheld.[5] KSM's replacement as al-Qa'ida's number three, Abu Faraj al-Libi, was captured in Mardan in 2005.[6] Being the group's number three was not a path to career longevity.

CIA's use of secret detention facilities and enhanced interrogation techniques is, it goes without saying, very controversial and I want to address it up front. I had been subjected to EITs during my Special Forces and CIA training, and it wasn't pleasant. And I knew it was just training. It is important to remember, however, that the use of secret detention and enhanced interrogation techniques was reviewed by the Department of Justice, approved by President Bush, and briefed to the congressional leadership.[7] It is also important to remember the fear of additional attacks by al-Qa'ida that existed in the months following the 9/11 attacks.

EITs contributed significantly to CIA's understanding of al-Qa'ida's structure, plans, and operations after the 9/11 attacks and provided important intelligence in the hunt for Usama Bin Ladin; if they hadn't, there wouldn't be much of a debate about their use. Whether we could have collected the same intelligence without their use during the early days of the war with al-Qa'ida is unknowable but unlikely. But the strategic cost to America of these practices was too high, and their use was a violation of the Geneva Conventions to which the United States is a signatory. A key principle for covert action programs is to never do anything in secret that you can't defend if made public. EITs and secret detention were not in keeping with this principle.

In 2006, the number of EITs authorized was significantly reduced by the Bush administration, and CIA's secret detention program was ended. Detainees in CIA custody were transferred to the military facility at Guantánamo Bay, Cuba, where several remain today. Upon his inauguration in 2009, President Obama rescinded the authorities for the use of any EITs, limiting interrogation techniques to those contained in the Army Field Manual.

———

After having its senior leader ranks reduced considerably from U.S. and Pakistani operations in the settled areas, al-Qa'ida relocated again, this time to Pakistan's Federally Administered Tribal Areas, or FATA.[8] Al-Qa'ida first moved into South Waziristan, and later to North Waziristan and other agencies in the FATA. AQ's leaders assumed, correctly, that they would be harder to locate and target there. From 2005 to 2008, the threat from al-Qa'ida grew substantially.

The FATA, described by one Pakistani journalist as "the most dangerous place on earth," is very remote and extremely mountainous.[9] As its name implies, it is also very tribal, and territories are fiercely

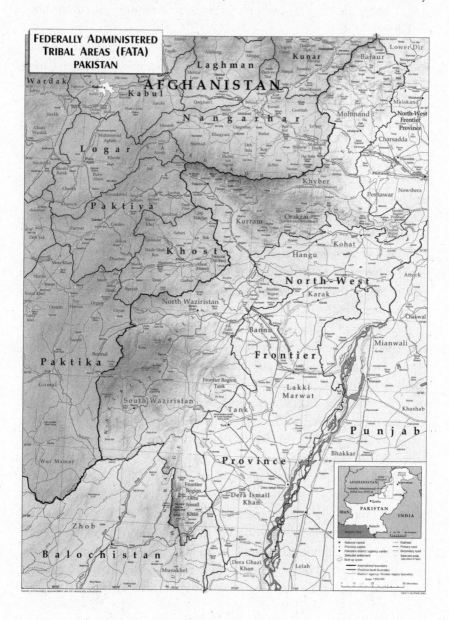

defended. The Mehsuds rule in part of South Waziristan, the Wazirs in another. In North Waziristan, the Daurs and Utmanzai Wazirs are dominant.

North and South Waziristan became al-Qa'ida's primary safe havens in the FATA. The group also had a strong presence in Bajaur Agency in the northern FATA. The FATA is not very large, about the size of Maryland, but if one counts the sides of mountains, it's the size of Texas.

During our covert war against the Soviets in Afghanistan, I had spent time in the FATA, principally in North Waziristan's capital, Miram Shah, and in Parachinar in Kurram Agency. A few years after 9/11, it became "no-go terrain" for Americans unless they were jihadists who had been vetted by al-Qa'ida or the Pakistan Taliban. Al-Qa'ida had renewed its former ties with the Haqqanis, now headed by Jalaluddin's son, Sirajuddin, and developed new ties with the Pakistan Taliban, headed by Baitullah Mehsud. UBL and other al-Qa'ida leaders had gone into Afghanistan with the Haqqanis during the 1980s, and UBL had helped the Haqqanis construct their base at Zhawar. AQ also developed ties with the Commander Nazir Group in South Waziristan.[10] To deepen these ties, the children of al-Qa'ida leaders married into prominent local militant families. All three militant groups provided safe haven to AQ, and all, accordingly, would become targets for U.S. counterterrorism operations.

By 2005, al-Qa'ida had recovered sufficiently to conduct sophisticated operations in the West. By mid-2006, the group had grown strong enough to possibly pull off additional 9/11-scale attacks against the U.S. homeland.[11] On July 7, 2005, al-Qa'ida struck in London, detonating in quick succession improvised explosive devices on three underground trains and then detonating a fourth on a double-decker bus at Tavistock Square. More than fifty-two U.K. residents were killed in the blasts, and more than seven hundred were injured. The four explosions quickly became known as the U.K.'s "7/7" attacks.

That al-Qa'ida had recovered its global strike capabilities was beyond doubt when CIA learned in August 2006 that a team of al-Qa'ida operatives was plotting to blow up ten to fifteen airliners flying between London and the United States. Al-Qa'ida's plan was to smuggle different components of homemade liquid explosives (concentrated hydrogen peroxide and other chemicals, mixed with Tang as an accelerant) on board in innocuous bottles. If successful, the plot would have been worse than 9/11 in terms of casualties, and the economic impact would have been devastating. Only terrific intelligence and law enforcement work in multiple countries had stopped the plot, which had been orchestrated by a British citizen of Pakistani descent named Rashid Rauf. MI5 and Scotland Yard rolled up the twenty-five plotters.[12]

In Pakistan, the new Inter-Services Intelligence chief, General Ashfaq Kayani, passed intelligence to CIA that Rauf would be leaving the FATA to visit Bahawalpur. At CIA's urging, ISI arrested Rauf, but in late 2007, he mysteriously "escaped" from a high-security prison when his guards let him go to a local mosque for prayers. He was killed in a U.S. drone strike in the Afghanistan-Pakistan border region in 2008.[13]

With an increasingly violent insurgency in the FATA, particularly in the Mehsud tribal areas of South Waziristan where the Pakistani Army had been forced to send in troops to try to put down the rebellion, President Pervez Musharraf decided he needed a new strategy. He directed Kayani to negotiate a peace accord in North Waziristan. The accord's terms could not have been more favorable to al-Qa'ida. The Pakistani government agreed to cease all air and ground operations in the area and release all captured militants. It agreed that tribal militias would man all checkpoints. Foreigners, meaning al-Qa'ida and other jihadists, would be allowed to "live peacefully" in North Waziristan if they weren't able to leave Pakistan.

The mood in CIA's Counterterrorism Center in 2006 was one of frustration that the threat had been allowed to reconstitute. "We're going to get hit again" was a frequent refrain. These warnings were strongly reemphasized in a 2007 National Intelligence Estimate. It concluded that al-Qa'ida's senior leaders in Pakistan were planning high-impact, mass-casualty attacks on the U.S. homeland. Al-Qa'ida's safe haven in the FATA, where its senior leaders felt secure, and the group's development of capable operational planners were key factors in AQ's resurgence.[14] I was back in government when the 2007 NIE was published, and it was a clear call to action.

As al-Qa'ida reconstituted, the United States began new CT operations in the Afghanistan-Pakistan border region. The United States conducted a handful of drone strikes against local militants and some al-Qa'ida leaders between 2004 and 2008. In June 2004, Nek Mohammed, a senior Pakistani Taliban commander with ties to al-Qa'ida, was killed.[15] In early December 2005, the United States successfully removed a key al-Qa'ida senior leader, Hamza Rabia, from the battlefield.[16]

The limited number of strikes, however, was nowhere near enough pressure to keep pace with, let alone get ahead of, the rapidly growing threat. By mid-2007, it was clear that our approach of occasional CT operations against al-Qa'ida's leadership was not working and that we had to get a lot more aggressive.[17]

MEETINGS WITH PRESIDENT BUSH, MAY–JUNE 2006

During May and June 2006, I had two meetings with President Bush on Iraq war strategy. The first, in late May, was in the Oval Office. The war was going badly, and the president wanted some outside advice as he searched for a better strategy. Two distinguished retired four-star generals, Wayne Downing and Barry McCaffrey, attended with me. I had worked closely with Downing the year before on a special operations study for Secretary of Defense Donald Rumsfeld, and I had the highest regard for both him and General McCaffrey. I walked the short distance from my think tank office to the White House, carrying a memo I had written for the president. I tried not to dwell too much on whom the memo was for, or where I was delivering it.

My memo, "Transitioning to an Indirect Approach in Iraq," was very frank.[18] I recommended that we shift to a smaller footprint and more "indirect" approach in Iraq over the next two years and transition primary security responsibility to Iraqi forces. Our large-scale occupation of Iraq—a "direct" approach—was inflaming the insurgency. We could win that way, given enough forces and time, but only at a high cost in blood and treasure. I told the president it was imperative that our strategy have bipartisan support in order to be sustained by the next administration. We could lose the war here at home before we won it in Iraq.

The president asked a lot of thoughtful questions of the three of us during our hour together. He asked me to clarify exactly what I meant by an "indirect approach." I said that it meant working by, with, and through the local forces, something our Special Forces excelled at, as we had seen in Afghanistan. He told me he was particularly taken with what I had said about the need to have a politically sustainable strategy for the war after he left office. Downing and McCaffrey told the president that they agreed with my recommendations. McCaffrey also provided his observations from his recent trips to Iraq.

The president then surprised me by asking me to stay afterward. He told me he had just finished reading *Charlie Wilson's War* and asked me if the book was accurate. I told him that it mostly was, because a number of senior CIA officers had been authorized to speak with the author on background. He then asked a few questions about how we had won against seemingly impossible odds. From his command of the facts and questions, it was clear that the president had closely read the book. I offered my views of the strategy and critical decisions that led to our victory, and then the president asked me the hardest question of all: "Why did you leave CIA?'"

"To this day I'm not sure I made the right decision," I responded, flustered by his question. "I loved CIA, but I came to the realization that I'd risen too fast and too unconventionally for the bureaucracy to handle. I thought I wouldn't be given anything nearly as exciting and important to do for another decade or more." I felt sheepish as I said it, since we were now engaged in wars I hadn't foreseen—wars where my expertise would have been very useful. The president just nodded and, thankfully, let me off the hook. We chatted a bit more about Afghanistan in the 1980s and the war in Iraq from 2003 to 2006. The president thanked me for coming and closed by repeating the point I had made regarding the imperative of politically transitioning the war to the next administration.

As I walked back to my office, I felt confident about the advice I had given President Bush about Iraq. But his question about why I left CIA really unnerved me. I felt like I wasn't where I needed to be.

Two weeks later, the president's NSC staff asked me to attend a follow-up meeting with the president and his war cabinet at Camp David.[19] Joining me this time were Eliot Cohen, professor of strategic studies at SAIS and my PhD adviser; Fred Kagan, a military historian and scholar at the American Enterprise Institute; and Bob Kaplan, a former journalist and author of several books on the global security environment. All were friends of mine and men whose views I respected. Kagan argued for an additional surge of forces in Iraq to quell the insurgency and the emerging civil war. Cohen focused mainly on the need for the president to find his "war general." I repeated my views about the need to transition to an indirect approach and a strategy that could be politically sustainable after the president left office.[20] The president and his team asked plenty of questions, but no decisions about Iraq strategy were made. The meeting had been purely informational, to present the president with a range of views. A few days later, the next shoe dropped.

RETURN TO GOVERNMENT SERVICE

Eric Edelman, DOD's undersecretary of defense for policy, asked me to come to his office to talk about the Camp David meeting. As soon as I walked in, he told me that the president had called Rumsfeld a couple of times already and told him that he needed to find a senior position for me in DOD.

A career foreign service officer with a PhD in history from Yale who had been U.S. ambassador to Turkey before becoming USD(P), Edelman said he was contemplating a major reorganization of OSD Policy. He wanted to create a new position that would be called the assistant secretary of defense for special operations, low-intensity conflict, and interdependent capabilities. ASD SO/LIC had been created by Congress in 1987 as the senior civilian official overseeing special operations forces, essentially a "service secretary-lite" position. With the addition of the "interdependent capabilities" portfolio, Edelman now wanted to broaden the position's remit dramatically.

ASD SO/LIC&IC would combine all of DOD's core operational capabilities—its strategic forces (nuclear, missile defense, space, cyber, and information operations), conventional force transformation (how the Air Force, Army, Navy, and Marine Corps should posture themselves for future war), and oversight of SOF. Edelman pulled a book I had recently co-authored, *The Revolution in War,* off his bookshelf and told me that I was the only person he knew who had the background and experience for this job. To sweeten the pot further, he told me I would have oversight of counterterrorism strategy and operations and be the policy lead in DOD for covert action conducted by CIA. I would be the principal at Deputies Committee meetings of the NSC on these issues. He asked if I would at least consider the position. I told him I certainly would, but I needed to talk with my wife first.

I had declined several positions in DOD over the previous several years, but this one really grabbed my interest. The job would combine all of my skills and interests—what I had done in the 1970s and 1980s in Special Forces and the CIA, along with what I had done during the 1990s and the first decade of the twenty-first century on an emerging military revolution and the rise of China. After talking it over with my wife and assuring her that she and our daughters would still see me once in a while, I accepted. I really wanted to get back in the fight. We were at war with al-Qa'ida, and I wanted to help us win it.

Senator John Warner introduced me at my confirmation hearing before the Senate Armed Services Committee, recalling many of Charlie Wilson's exploits. After my hearing, I was unanimously confirmed. Several former CIA colleagues, Milt Bearden and Bill Rooney among them, attended my swearing-in ceremony at the Pentagon. Secretary Gates, who had replaced Rumsfeld in December 2006, presided. He said some very nice things about how we had worked together on Afghanistan during the 1980s and how it had been my strategy that had won the war. He then joked that since he had one daughter and I had five, he was confident I had the "low-intensity conflict" part of my job down pat.

As I assumed my new position, I was blessed to have some outstanding colleagues. Foremost among them was Todd Lowery, who had worked for me at my think tank fresh out of his master's program at the University of Chicago before going on to serve in OSD Strategy, where he worked on China issues. He would become my closest adviser and remain at my side for the next eight years. Subsequently, he would go on to serve in very senior positions in the U.S. intelligence community.

During my four years as an assistant secretary of defense, I spent most of my time on operations, mainly on the war with al-Qa'ida and the war in Afghanistan, but also on the war in Iraq, on counterproliferation operations to prevent Iran from getting a nuclear weapon, on the counterinsurgency war in Colombia, and on counternarcotics operations in Mexico. I traveled to war zones and other areas of conflict for about ten to fourteen days out of each month. When in Washington, I mainly attended Deputies Committee meetings at the White House or had meetings with Secretary Gates and DOD's senior leadership at the Pentagon. I also participated in major reviews of our strategy for the war with al-Qa'ida and the war in Afghanistan. I regularly briefed Secretary Gates on proposed operations to get his approval. I visited CIA at least once every week or two to be briefed on their operations, analysis, and development programs across the global scope of my portfolio. Periodically, I would also be called to testify before Congress, mostly on operations, but also on capabilities.

(Noting the "interdependent capabilities" part of my portfolio, some described my new job as "secretary of everything." I replied that I was just secretary of all the important stuff. Admiral Eric Olson, the commander of U.S. Special Operations Command from 2007 to 2011, initially worried that my non-SOF responsibilities might take away from my oversight of SOF, and described my job as "SOF and lots of other stuff." I liked his description better.)

I spent much less time on the capabilities part of my job because we had accomplished most of what I believed was needed during the 2006 Quadrennial Defense Review.[21] The QDR directed the largest expansion of our special operations forces in our nation's history, it initiated a next-generation stealth bomber program, and it directed a significant expansion of our submarine fleet.[22] I had spent a decade and a half thinking about and advising DOD's senior leadership on the challenges a rising China and revolutionary change in warfare would pose for U.S. strategy, and despite my heavy engagement in current operations and policy I still saw China as our greatest long-term threat. Strengthening our conventional deterrent against China was critical, and I took that part of my job very seriously.

One area where I did spend a fair amount of time on force structure and capabilities after I became ASD SO/LIC&IC was the expansion of our Predator and Reaper fleet of unmanned, armed reconnaissance aircraft. Predators and Reapers were our primary operational instruments in our war with al-Qa'ida, and the intelligence and precision fires they provided were critical to our special operations missions in Afghanistan and Iraq as well. I sought to increase the size of the fleet as rapidly as possible, develop new, far more capable sensors and weapons for the aircraft, and get as much of the fleet as I could assigned to our strategic counterterrorism mission against al-Qa'ida in areas of operations outside war zones.

I also helped oversee the establishment of our new Cyber Command and the development of new space capabilities. Because the latter remains highly classified, I can't say more than that. Every year, I also had mandatory refresher training on our nuclear weapons plans and capabilities, flying around in our "doomsday" aircraft and going through strike procedures. Traveling to conflict areas overseas, advising on counterterrorism and other operations, attending NSC meetings, or making decisions about capabilities and force structure made up a typical day in my life as an assistant secretary of defense. It was a great job, but perhaps with a portfolio only suited for me, as some critics of the office contended. In any event, the position reverted back to SO/LIC after I left.

DEVELOPING A WAR-WINNING COUNTERTERRORISM STRATEGY

Coming up with a new strategy to defeat al-Qa'ida and eliminate its sanctuary in Pakistan's Federally Administered Tribal Areas became job one for me as soon as I assumed my duties in the Pentagon. Al-Qa'ida had affiliates in Iraq, Yemen, Somalia, and North Africa, but by far the most serious threat to the U.S. homeland emanated from the group's safe haven in the FATA. Our counterterrorism strategy against core al-Qa'ida, which relied almost exclusively on Pakistani intelligence and military operations, supplemented by the occasional drone strike, had clearly failed. With the threat the group posed once again at a 9/11 level, President Bush had had enough. In the early fall of 2007, he asked CIA and DOD to come up with a more effective strategy.[23]

Within two weeks of being sworn in, I traveled to Pakistan and Afghanistan with Admiral Eric Olson to get a firsthand look at the situation. Our joint trip also provided the opportunity to forge a close bond with my key partner in the oversight of SOF. The first SEAL to command our four-star Special Operations Command, or SOCOM, Eric was a special operator's special operator, a quiet professional who got the job done. He had been awarded a Silver Star for his actions leading a rescue convoy during the Battle of Mogadishu, better known as Black Hawk Down, in October 1993, and had commanded at every level from SEAL platoon to the Naval Special Warfare Command.

Before I departed on my trip, Eric Edelman told me that he had just had a conversation with National Security Adviser Steve Hadley about the rapidly growing threat from al-Qa'ida and its allies in the Afghanistan-Pakistan border region. Hadley wondered why we couldn't do to al-Qa'ida what we had done to the Soviets during the 1980s, referring to my previous role as program officer for CIA's support for the Afghan resistance, and asked Eric for my thoughts. I replied that we might be able to do some similar things, to use insurgents to increase pressure on al-Qa'ida's safe haven, but the situations were very different. We didn't want to destabilize Pakistan any more than it already was. We'd be more effective, I added, if we expanded our Predator strikes and coupled them with special operations raids. We needed to significantly change the ways of our strategy and increase the means at our disposal. Al-Qa'ida, with its FATA sanctuary, had achieved escalation dominance over us. We needed to reverse that before we were hit again. We needed to disrupt their operations, deny them their FATA sanctuary, and dismantle and defeat the group. Eric told me that Secretary Gates wanted me to work with CIA to develop a plan for the NSC to take to President Bush. I was thus assigned as the DOD lead for developing the new strategy with CIA's Counterterrorism Center.[24] It was the second time in my career I had been asked to develop a strategy to change the direction of a war.

There were several options that weren't feasible. We weren't going to invade Pakistan, and the Pakistanis weren't going to cooperate with us enough militarily to jointly dislodge al-Qa'ida's safe haven. What we needed was an industrial-scale covert war strategy that we could largely conduct on our own, with only general Pakistani buy-in required. Once again, we needed to wrest strategic control of a program from the Pakistanis if we were to achieve our objectives. It was back to the future for me.

The United States had proposed to strike al-Qa'ida high-value targets (HVTs) more than a dozen times in 2007, with no success. Either our targets had moved before approval to strike had been granted by the Pakistanis, or our strike nomination had been disapproved by the Pakistanis outright. We were "Oh for Oh-Seven" (zero successful AQ HVT strikes in 2007), as Mike Hayden, CIA's director, regularly put it.[25] We had the intelligence to successfully target al-Qa'ida's senior leaders. The Pakistanis and our policy of ceding control to them were the problem. It reminded me of the challenge I had in persuading the Pakistanis to cede strategic control of the Afghanistan Covert Action Program to CIA between 1984 and 1986.

We came up with a new plan that would combine far more intense and essentially unilateral Predator strikes with cross-border special operations raids to take away al-Qa'ida's safe haven in the FATA. Our aim was to eliminate al-Qa'ida's senior leaders, key operators, and safe haven providers faster than they could be replaced. By doing so, we hoped to shut down core AQ's operations and to dismantle and eventually defeat the group. We added two smaller covert lines of operation to further increase pressure on AQ's safe haven. These remain classified, however, and can't be discussed here. We would also continue to conduct joint capture operations with the Pakistanis as al-Qa'ida leaders tried to flee the FATA. Our new strategy would substantially change the "ways" of our counterterrorism operations in the Afghanistan-Pakistan border region, and implementing it would require substantially more means, primarily Predator orbits. It would shift the strategic initiative back to us, and, in time, it would eliminate al-Qa'ida's sanctuary in the FATA.

By early 2008, we presented our plan to a small group of the NSC's Deputies Committee headed by Ambassador Jim Jeffrey, President Bush's deputy national security adviser. There was unanimous support among the Deputies Small Group for our new strategy.[26] Several of the NSC's principals strongly advocated for the new strategy we had developed, with Mike Hayden the most vocal proponent. Hayden had become director in 2006, succeeding Porter Goss, whose difficult tenure had left CIA with a serious morale problem. A great leader and a very effective communicator, Mike, like George Tenet, deserves to go down as one of CIA's "reform" directors. The only NSC principal who didn't initially agree with our new CT strategy was Admiral Mike Mullen, our new JCS chairman. Mullen was working very hard to build a relationship of trust with General Kayani, Pakistan's chief of Army Staff, and wanted that to be our priority in dealing with Pakistan. A more aggressive unilateral CT campaign in the Afghanistan-Pakistan border region could have very serious implications for our relationship with the Pakistani military. Mullen sent his strategic plans and policy director, Lieutenant General Phil Breedlove (later to become our NATO commander), to see me. Breedlove brought a copy of a highly classified CT strategy memo I had just written for Secretary Gates after one of my trips to Pakistan, and said, "You know, the chairman and you aren't on the same page." I responded that I knew we weren't but al-Qa'ida posed an imminent threat to the U.S. homeland that had to be addressed. I added that while I fully supported Admiral Mullen's efforts to forge a close relationship with Kayani, we needed to dramatically change our counterterrorism strategy if we wanted to prevent another 9/11 attack. By the time we were ready to present our new strategy to President Bush, Admiral Mullen was fully on board. From then on, he and I would be on the same side on most issues.

As we got ready to present our new counterterrorism strategy to President Bush in early 2008, however, Pakistan became convulsed in a political crisis. President Musharraf faced rapidly growing opposition to his continued rule, and the resulting political turmoil caused us to put our new strategy largely on hold for a few months. Musharraf had already survived several assassination attempts by Pakistani extremist groups for his decision to align Pakistan with the United States and for his moderate views on Islam, but this was different. Both the populace and the Army, the real source of power in Pakistan, had turned against him. The growing threat from Islamic militants based in the FATA only added to Musharraf's troubles.[27]

I had met with Musharraf a few times and liked him. His special forces background made rapport between us easy. When we told him we would need to get more aggressive in the FATA, he supported the idea. Referring to the increasingly violent insurgency in the Afghanistan-Pakistan border region, but also to our proposed new campaign, Musharraf opined that "Men die violently in the FATA every day." The implication was that a few more—or a lot more— wouldn't matter. It was increasingly clear, however, that his rule was coming to an end. In 2007, Pakistan's generals forced Musharraf to resign as chief of Army Staff, with Kayani succeeding him. In August 2008, he was forced to resign the presidency and then forced into exile that November.[28]

As the political situation in Pakistan began to stabilize, we met more frequently as deputies to refine our presentation to President

Bush. I was selected by Steve Hadley and Secretary Gates to present the overall strategy. Mike Hayden would brief the CIA portion, and Lieutenant General Marty Dempsey, our acting CENTCOM commander, would cover the DOD part. (Marty would go on to become Army chief of staff and then chairman of the Joint Chiefs, succeeding Mullen.) Anne Patterson, our outstanding ambassador to Pakistan, would brief for the State Department, outlining a new FATA Development Program we were proposing to provide assistance to the Pakistani government's beleaguered political agents in the border region.

On August 4, 2008, we presented the plan to President Bush for his approval. Secretary Gates, Admiral Mullen, Director of National Intelligence Mike McConnell, and Mike Hayden joined our small group in the White House Situation Room. General Dempsey also joined, as did Vice Admiral Bill McRaven, the JSOC commander, by secure video teleconference. President Bush was at Camp David with Vice President Cheney, Secretary Rice, and Steve Hadley, so they joined the decision briefing by secure video teleconference as well.[29]

I was a bit nervous, given the audience and my lead role in the briefing. I provided a summary of the overall strategy and its new ways and expanded means. With new ways and expanded means, we intended to achieve escalation dominance over al-Qa'ida, much as we (CIA) had done against the Red Army in Afghanistan during the 1980s.

In going over our proposed lines of operations, I noted that inside war zones, special operations raids were our primary counterterrorism instrument. Outside war zones—where al-Qa'ida was principally located after being forced to flee Afghanistan—the Predator would be our principal strike instrument. The other lines of operations would reinforce Predator's effects.

The Predator is a remotely piloted, armed reconnaissance aircraft that is ideally suited for counterterrorism operations. It's both a hunter and a killer and by far our best CT platform to reach into the ungoverned areas where ground forces can't go or sustain a presence. The Predator has a crew of two (a pilot and a sensor operator) and is equipped with a high-definition, full-motion video camera, a laser designator, signals intelligence pods, and missiles and bombs, depending on the aircraft model. It can loiter over a target, assuming its launch and recovery site is reasonably close by, for more than twenty hours. Predator A (also known as the MQ-1) can carry two laser-guided Hellfire missiles. Predator B (also known as the MQ-9 Reaper), with eight times the payload, can carry a mix of Hellfire missiles and five-hundred-pound laser-guided bombs. Predator C (also known as the Avenger) is a jet-powered aircraft that can carry a thousand-pound bomb. By 2011, we had all three variants in the field. The Air Force crews who flew the missions were great innovators in developing the tactics, techniques, and procedures we needed to make optimum use of the aircraft, and I visited with them regularly at their base in Nevada.

I had persuaded Secretary Gates to approve additional Predator orbits (24/7 coverage of a target area, which requires two to three aircraft and several pilots and sensor operators to sustain) for the strategic counterterrorism mission against al-Qa'ida. With the wars in Iraq and Afghanistan, Predator orbits were in high demand and short supply. When I began my duties as ASD SO/LIC&IC on August 3, 2007, the strategic CT mission against al-Qa'ida in the Afghanistan-Pakistan border region had only three Predator orbits. By the summer of 2008, we had increased that to eight.

Our campaign strategy and plan for substantially increased Predator strikes in the Afghanistan-Pakistan border region depended not just on additional capacity but on several critical policy changes as well. The first was shifting to essentially unilateral operations, providing concurrent notification to the Pakistanis but not asking for their approval.[30] The Pakistanis would still have to grant general access to a portion of their airspace, however. The second policy change, one that would turn out to be the real game changer, was to expand Predator operations to include what has been described as "signature strikes"— strikes designed to disrupt known al-Qa'ida locations and activities even when the specific identities of the al-Qa'ida members or safe haven providers observed at the sites were not known.[31] We still were required to confirm, however, that the targets were AQ or militant combatants. Signature strikes would turn out to be nearly as precise a targeting method as so-called personality strikes, except in rare cases where the group size was very large or there was someone hidden inside a structure that we couldn't see. Signature strikes were responsible for taking some 60 percent of al-Qa'ida HVTs off the battlefield—AQ leaders we wouldn't have been able to strike otherwise—without sacrificing the "near certainty" requirement that strikes are conducted only against targeted enemy combatants. The third policy change was to expand the number of al-Qa'ida senior leader targets severalfold and add al-Qa'ida's safe haven providers—the Haqqanis, the Pakistan Taliban, the Commander Nazir Group—to the list of authorized targets. For a target to be added to or remain on the list, we had to provide recent intelligence that showed that the individual or group posed a "continuing and imminent" threat to the United States.

It is not enough, as some advocate, to just eliminate a terrorist group's leadership. To dismantle and defeat a global jihadist group you have to also take out its operational planners and its facilitators, trainers, and safe haven providers. To do this, we needed the authority to conduct an unrelenting barrage of signature strikes against the whole set of targets that made AQ's operations possible. The decision to strike, except in rare circumstances, was left to the operational arms. And then you have to prevent the group from reconstituting by eliminating its safe haven. If the group has affiliates in multiple countries around the world, you need to dismantle each of them using the same general approach, though the ways may differ from theater to theater. Core al-Qa'ida was the group's center of gravity. Its sanctuary in the FATA was where the renewed threats to the American homeland were emanating from. We needed to concentrate our resources on dismantling and defeating core al-Qa'ida and its safe haven providers first. Then we could turn our attention to the group's affiliates.

We planned to supplement our Predator strikes with special operations raids. Borrowing a concept that then–Lieutenant General Stan McChrystal and his Special Operations Task Force had pioneered in the wars in Iraq and Afghanistan called "Find, Fix, Finish, Exploit, and Analyze," or F3EA, our plan was to conduct frequent special operations raids to further disrupt al-Qa'ida and generate valuable intelligence. F3EA is essentially a continuous targeting cycle. Intelligence is used to "find" and precisely geolocate a target and then "fix" it in place, that is, maintain custody of the target through the finish phase. The target can then be "finished" by air strike or raid. Capturing a terrorist is always preferred to killing him, but capture operations aren't always feasible. The most important parts of the cycle, those that turn individual operations into a series of operations and a series of operations into a campaign, are the exploit and analyze phases. Intelligence collected from raids, both human and technical, can be quickly exploited and lead to follow-on operations before the targets are warned and able to relocate, dramatically increasing the strategic effects of a single operation.[32] We wanted to do to al-Qa'ida in Pakistan what we were doing to al-Qa'ida in Iraq.

We knew we couldn't conduct raids in Pakistan with anywhere near the frequency we did in war zones—as many as ten to twenty in a single night—but two a week, coupled with an intense Predator air campaign, would be enough, in our judgment, to undermine al-Qa'ida's confidence in its safe haven and defeat the group. We also recognized that there would likely be tensions between striking as soon as feasible with Predator and waiting for a raid that might collect valuable intelligence, but we would decide that as situations presented themselves.

Continuing to work with ISI to capture fleeing al-Qa'ida members would also be important. It would allow us to contain al-Qa'ida in our FATA kill zone.

President Bush approved our new strategy without a lot of questions. Our briefing had been thoroughly staffed by Jim Jeffrey during the month prior, with the president receiving regular updates on its progress. After the president approved the necessary new authorities, they were transmitted to CIA and DOD, and we commenced our campaign.

It was a very bold decision by President Bush, as bold as his decision to send additional forces to Iraq during the 2007 surge and President Obama's decision to send a SEAL assault force to Abbottabad in May 2011 to kill Usama Bin Ladin. The major change to our CT strategy that President Bush approved is, in my mind, comparable to what President Reagan had done in March 1985 when he directed CIA to drive the Soviets out of Afghanistan by all means available. President Reagan, moreover, had made his bold decision at the beginning of his second term. President Bush made his decision to fundamentally change our CT strategy during the last six months of his administration, a period when presidents usually don't do anything too bold, lest they tie the hands of their successor.

Hadley, Hayden, and I were tasked with briefing the leaders of Congress and the chairs and ranking members of the Intelligence, Armed Services, and Foreign Relations Committees. The formal briefings had to be delayed several weeks because of the August recess and the classification of the material. (The White House had given a heads-up to key members of Congress via secure phone very soon after the new strategy had been approved.) As it turned out, we briefed the House leadership right in the middle of their tense and critical negotiations on the 2008 financial crisis. I was surprised at the attention they gave us. I was even more surprised by Speaker Nancy Pelosi's reaction when we briefed her on the plan, "What took you so long?" she asked us. Bipartisanship is always stronger behind closed doors. In my experience, that's where our leaders are at their most impressive.

DISMANTLING CORE AL-QA'IDA

The shift to unilateral Predator strikes had actually been rolled out gradually during the first seven months of 2008 as al-Qa'ida HVTs were found and fixed. In late January 2008, al-Qa'ida's operational chief for Afghanistan and Pakistan, Abu Layth al-Libi, was killed in a Predator strike. Abu Layth, a leader in the Libyan Islamic Fighting Group before joining al-Qa'ida, had been responsible for a bombing attack on Bagram Air Base in Afghanistan a year earlier while Vice President Cheney had been visiting. He was a top ground commander and trainer for al-Qa'ida and a deputy to Zawahiri.[33] This was followed a few months later by another unilateral strike on another al-Qa'ida senior, Sulayman al-Jaza'iri, an Algerian who was involved in planning attacks against the United States. In the summer of 2008, another senior al-Qa'ida leader was killed, Abu Khabab al-Masri, an Egyptian who was the chief of AQ's weapons of mass destruction program.[34]

During the final five months of 2008, the United States conducted nearly thirty unilateral Predator strikes in the Afghanistan-Pakistan border region, more in five months than we had in the previous four years combined. Eight al-Qa'ida HVTs were taken off the battlefield in 2008, "Eight for Oh-Eight," as Mike Hayden would say.[35] Among them were Khalid Habib, a senior paramilitary trainer and commander of al-Qa'ida's "shadow army" in northwest Pakistan and Afghanistan, and Abu Ubaydah al-Tunisi, another al-Qa'ida military commander.[36] The loss of its senior leadership in rapid succession shocked al-Qa'ida. One operative told another, "The brothers are evaporating."

Events outside the Afghanistan-Pakistan border region confirmed the wisdom of the new policy. On September 20, 2008, al-Qa'ida set off a bomb at the Marriott hotel in Islamabad, killing more than fifty and wounding another three hundred. The following two years also saw two attempted attacks on the U.S. homeland—both targeting New York City—emanating from the Afghanistan-Pakistan border region.[37] It could have been far worse had we not escalated the war when we did.

Our new strategy's other lines of operation did not have anywhere near the success of our Predator strikes and joint capture operations. On September 3, 2008, we conducted our first special operations raid of the new campaign. The target was a militant staging area just across the border in South Waziristan. Our intent was to select as non-provocative a target as possible for the first operation. The raid was successful, but it was too much to bear for the Pakistanis who viewed it as a violation of their sovereignty.[38] Kayani, who had been briefed by senior U.S. military leaders before the new campaign began, told us we had undermined his position as Army chief. Predator strikes were acceptable; cross-border raids were not. Accordingly, after some deliberation at the NSC, we decided to suspend the unilateral raid line of operations. There would be no F3EA in the Pakistan border region.[39] It was a real blow. A steady stream of raids would have put intense pressure on al-Qa'ida and its safe haven providers, produced valuable intelligence, and quite possibly enabled us to dismantle core al-Qa'ida in the Afghanistan-Pakistan border region even sooner.

Our two classified lines of operations failed to produce significant results. One failed entirely, and the other, after enjoying some initial success, also proved ineffective. Our foreign aid program in the FATA also fizzled out over time under militant pressure. After 2010, when the Pakistanis drastically curtailed joint capture operations, we would largely be down to Predator strikes alone.

When I joined the Bush administration, I thought I'd be in government for only two years. In December 2008, however, I was asked, along with Secretary Gates and Undersecretary of Defense for Intelligence Jim Clapper, to stay on in the Obama administration. I was deeply honored, because it is a very rare thing to serve at a senior political level in both Republican and Democratic administrations. I was also very grateful, because I had a lot of unfinished business I wanted to get done, foremost among which was the dismantlement and defeat of al-Qa'ida. There would be a lot more continuity between the last two years of President Bush's administration and the first term of the Obama administration than most Americans realized.

Given my broad operational portfolio, I was asked by Secretary Gates to prepare DOD's transition briefing for President Obama on our most sensitive policies and operations, from nuclear weapons targeting strategy and missile defense procedures in the event of an attack on the United States, to our most sensitive operations overseas that would be under way at inauguration. Different parts of the Joint Staff brought me briefs in their areas. Assembling all the sensitive briefs in one book was considered "radioactive," so I had to maintain personal custody of it. I briefed Secretary Gates and Admiral Mullen on it, who then briefed the president-elect just before his inauguration. Once that was done, I got right back to work on my core task of disrupting and dismantling al-Qa'ida.

———

In 2009, our strike tempo slowed, but the program successfully transitioned to the Obama administration. On August 5, 2009, Baitullah Mehsud, the leader of the Pakistan Taliban, was killed. Kayani and the rest of Pakistan's leadership were very pleased. Baitullah's successor, Hakimullah Mehsud, was badly wounded in a strike five months later and killed in 2013.[40] Hakimullah's injury and death had special meaning for CIA. Five days before the strike that injured him, Hakimullah had been seen in a video with Humam al-Balawi, a Jordanian doctor and militant who had detonated a suicide bomb at our base in Khost, Afghanistan, killing seven CIA officers and a Jordanian intelligence officer. CIA had hoped that Balawi would lead us to Ayman al-Zawahiri, al-Qa'ida's number two. The Jordanian provided evidence that he had indeed met with Zawahiri and had provided medical treatment to him. That sent CIA's interest sky-high. CTC wanted to meet with him face-to-face, and the only place to do it was Khost. He turned out to be the Pakistan Taliban's agent, however, and not ours.[41] While visiting our base at Khost a few months after the attack, I paused in each spot where our officers had died. It is hallowed ground.

Several senior al-Qa'ida leaders, Abu Ubaydah al-Masri and Usama al-Kini among them, were also taken off the battlefield by Predator strikes in 2009. Abu Ubaydah had played a central role in the July 2005 London bombings. Usama al-Kini was integral to the 1998 embassy bombings and the 2008 attack on the Marriott in Islamabad.[42] Also taken off the battlefield in 2009 was Sa'ad Bin Ladin, one of UBL's sons, who had been released by the Iranians a few months earlier; Tohor Yuldashev, the leader of the Islamic Movement of Uzbekistan; and Abdullah Said, who had replaced Khalid Habib as the commander of al-Qa'ida's shadow army.[43]

––––––––––

During the summer of 2009, President Obama's counterterrorism and homeland security adviser, John Brennan, convened the Deputies Small Group on counterterrorism to develop an "accelerated defeat plan" to further exploit the success we were having against al-Qa'ida and its allies in the Afghanistan-Pakistan border region. I led the effort for DOD. During a discussion about what defeat would look like, I proposed that we separate defeat into two phases: operational defeat and strategic defeat. Operationally defeating core al-Qa'ida would come first. It would be achieved when the group had no operational capability left in the Afghanistan-Pakistan border region. Strategic defeat would occur only when AQ was no longer able to physically reconstitute and al-Qa'ida's ideology had been rejected. The same pattern would follow against al-Qa'ida's affiliates around the world. When both the core and AQ's affiliates had been strategically defeated, our war with al-Qa'ida would be over. We were a long way from that end state.

During a major NSC review of our strategy and force commitment in Afghanistan, President Obama narrowed our primary mission to "disrupting, dismantling, and defeating" al-Qa'ida in the Afghanistan-Pakistan border region and preventing al-Qa'ida from regaining a safe haven in Afghanistan. It was great presidential guidance. Dismantlement became synonymous with operational defeat.

It became clear that as part of our accelerated defeat plan, we would need additional Predator orbits. I advocated for six more and Secretary Gates approved, bringing the total dedicated to the strategic counterterrorism mission to fourteen. We were fighting an increasingly dangerous insurgency in Afghanistan, and still had a large troop presence in Iraq, but core al-Qa'ida was in Pakistan. That had to be the main CT effort as far as I was concerned, and the Predator had become our main and most effective CT instrument. By the summer of 2011, the strategic counterterrorism mission in Pakistan and Yemen would have twenty-two orbits, more than a third of the sixty-five orbits we had increased our fleet to after five years of buildup and intense surging of crews.[44]

In May 2010, we took another al-Qa'ida senior leader off the battlefield in the Afghanistan-Pakistan border region, Sheikh Sayid al-Masri, the group's chief financial officer.[45] Qari Hussein, the chief suicide bomb trainer for the Pakistan Taliban, was also killed in 2010. Joint capture operations with ISI continued to produce very good results until the semi-rupture of U.S.-Pakistan relations following our raid on UBL's compound in Abbottabad in May 2011. Several HVTs were also captured trying to flee the border region.

Between 2008 and 2015, the United States conducted some 350 Predator strikes in the Afghanistan-Pakistan border region, a third of them in 2010 alone.[46] Core al-Qa'ida's back was broken in 2010, with strikes during the last half of the year coming every two days on average. By the end of that year, Ayman al-Zawahiri, al-Qa'ida's number two, ordered al-Qa'ida to go to ground in the hopes of outlasting the onslaught. We unfortunately couldn't use "all means available" due to Pakistani sensitivities about their sovereignty and restrictions on U.S. support, but the means we did have we used to the fullest extent possible, and the results were dramatic. By the end of 2010, we had achieved escalation dominance over al-Qa'ida.

With core al-Qa'ida closer than ever to operational defeat following the intense Predator barrage of 2010 and the death of UBL in May 2011, which I will cover in a subsequent chapter, we then developed a core al-Qa'ida "finish plan" focused on taking out the remaining HVTs. In 2011, Ilyas Kashmiri, a veteran of Pakistan's special forces and a key al-Qa'ida operational planner who had been plotting attacks against the U.S. homeland, was killed, as was al-Qa'ida's new second-in-command after the death of Bin Ladin, Atiyah Abd al-Rahman.

A senior leader of the Haqqani Network, Jan Baz Zadran, was also killed. In 2012, Atiyah's replacement, Abu Yahya al-Libi, was killed along with Hassan Gul, a Pakistani who had been KSM's deputy. In 2004, Gul had been captured while on a mission from the Pakistan border region to Iraq and placed in CIA detention for two and a half years. The intelligence we obtained from him turned out to be very important in the hunt for Usama Bin Ladin. In 2006, he was transferred to a Pakistani prison, but was released a year later. He quickly returned to al-Qa'ida.[47]

Also taken off the battlefield in 2012 were Badruddin Haqqani, a top deputy to and brother of the Haqqani Network's leader, Sirajuddin Haqqani, and Badr Mansur, a senior al-Qa'ida commander. In 2013, Abd al-Rahman al-Sharqi, a Bahraini, was killed, along with several other al-Qa'ida military commanders and trainers and the group's intelligence chief. Several al-Qa'ida safe haven providers were also killed, including Commander Nazir, Wali Ur Rehman, and Mullah Sangin. In 2014, 2015, and 2016, several more AQ senior leaders were killed, including Sufiyan al-Maghrebi, Mansur al-Harbi, Abu Khalil al-Sudani, and Faruq al-Qatani. Qatani, based in northeast Afghanistan, had been involved in several plots against the U.S. homeland. He had been viewed as a potential future leader for all of al-Qa'ida.[48]

In all, more than 50 al-Qa'ida senior leaders and other HVTs were taken off the battlefield with Predator strikes between 2008 and 2015. More than 2,500 al-Qa'ida and militant operatives were killed with a collateral damage rate that is extremely low. In a 2016 report on U.S. counterterrorism strikes outside areas of active hostilities (meaning outside Afghanistan and Iraq), the Office of the Director of National Intelligence confirmed that 473 strikes had been taken in areas outside war zones (principally in Pakistan, but also in Yemen) between January 20, 2009, and December 31, 2015, resulting in 2,372–2,581 combatant deaths and 64–116 noncombatant deaths.[49] Most of the civilian casualties, it must be emphasized, came from a few errant strikes that targeted large groups.

To be sure, there has been considerable controversy about the accuracy of U.S. drone strikes, but critics frequently conflate strikes in war zones with those outside them. The latter are held to a much higher standard—near certainty that the target has been correctly identified and near certainty of zero collateral damage—than are strikes in war zones, where the standard is only reasonable certainty. Critics also conflate strikes by other aircraft, which are far more numerous but unfortunately less precise, with strikes by drones. Every precaution is taken to avoid civilian casualties, including the requirement to "shift cold"—diverting a strike to a safe, uninhabited area at the last minute if noncombatants are observed.

That's not to say that Predator strikes are collateral-free—they're not—but the Predator campaign against AQ is hands down the most precise air campaign in the history of warfare, made possible by the great professionalism of the Air Force crews flying the missions and the officers of the CIA, NSA, and National Geospatial-Intelligence Agency (NGA) who provided the exquisite intelligence.[50] Intelligence for Predator operations comes from human sources, technical collection, and the "unblinking eye" of the Predator, and is fused to reach the near-certainty standard required.[51] Predator strikes were our primary and often only weapon outside war zones and have been a tremendous source of asymmetric advantage and escalation dominance for the United States in our war with al-Qa'ida. They are what has kept America safe.

By the time I retired from federal service in 2015, core al-Qa'ida had largely been operationally defeated. CIA women, the so-called sisterhood of CTC, made particularly important contributions to our long war against al-Qa'ida in both operations and analysis—no small irony given al-Qa'ida's dismissive view of their gender. I wish I could say more about who there are and what they've done to keep America safe. They are unsung heroines.

Continued HVT strikes from 2016 to 2019, including one that killed UBL's son Hamza, have brought the group even closer to the precipice. In August 2020, al-Qa'ida's number two, Abu Muhammad al-Masri, one of the masterminds of the 1998 embassy bombings, was killed in a vehicle ambush on the streets of Tehran. Finally, on July 31, 2022, a U.S. Predator strike killed al-Qa'ida's leader, Ayman al-Zawahiri, as he sat in the early morning hours on the balcony of a Taliban-provided guesthouse in Kabul. With Zawahiri's death, core al-Qa'ida in Afghanistan and Pakistan had largely been dismantled.

But in the coming years, that dismantlement may be placed at risk by our withdrawal from Afghanistan, the Biden administration's adoption of very restrictive drone strike policies, and al-Qa'ida's ability to reconstitute itself. Some of al-Qa'ida's main safe haven providers, most notably Siraj Haqqani, are now occupying key positions in the Taliban government, which will create a lot more operational space and possibilities for the group. America's self-inflicted defeat in Afghanistan has greatly emboldened the global jihadist movement. As a result, more global jihadists will likely head to Afghanistan, much as they did during the late 1990s, and Afghanistan could once again become jihad central. Several hundred al-Qa'ida operatives were freed from Afghan government detention as part of President Trump's "peace" deal with the Taliban, and it is hard to believe they haven't returned to the battlefield. Potential successors to Zawahiri are in Iran and Afghanistan, most notably Saif al-Adel, a former Egyptian army special forces officer whose ties to al-Qa'ida date back to pre-9/11 Afghanistan.

Over time, our ability to collect intelligence will be degraded and our Predator operations will be less effective flying from "over the horizon."[52] The Biden administration's new counterterrorism policy, announced on background to the media in early October 2022, will make matters worse still, with its elimination of signature strikes and its extremely tight restrictions on strikes outside of warzones. Outside of warzones is where al-Qa'ida predominantly operates. The administration professes confidence that the reduced means it will have available will be enough to prevent a resurgence of the threat al-Qa'ida could pose to the American homeland and our interests abroad. Let's hope its confidence is justified. But given al-Qaida's ability to reconstitute after being ejected from Afghanistan in 2001, I wouldn't bet on it.

THE WAR BEYOND THE CORE

THE AL-QA'IDA NETWORK

Until the U.S. invasion of Iraq, al-Qa'ida was a single global terrorist enterprise, with operatives in several countries. One of the group's major successes since the 9/11 attacks has been its ability to extend its global reach through affiliates. In April 2004, al-Qa'ida in Iraq, core al-Qa'ida's first affiliate, was formed under the leadership of Abu Musab al-Zarqawi. In 2006, al-Qa'ida in Yemen was stood up. In early 2007, al-Qa'ida in the Lands of the Islamic Maghreb (North Africa) was established. In 2009, al-Qa'ida in Yemen merged with al-Qa'ida's members in Saudi Arabia to become al-Qa'ida in the Arabian Peninsula, or AQAP. In 2011, Jabhat al-Nusra was formed and became al-Qa'ida in Syria. In February 2012, a merger between Somalia's al-Shabaab and core al-Qa'ida was announced. Finally, in September 2014, al-Qa'ida's emir, Ayman al-Zawahiri, announced the formation of al-Qa'ida in the Indian Subcontinent.

Most of the affiliates—al-Qa'ida in Iraq, AQIM in North Africa, al-Shabaab in Somalia, and the newest affiliate, al-Qa'ida in the Indian Subcontinent—focused on targets limited to their regions. A few— al-Qa'ida in the Arabian Peninsula and al-Qa'ida in Syria—plotted against the U.S. homeland while also engaging in local attacks. Eventually, these two groups became a greater threat to the American homeland than core al-Qa'ida, particularly after the latter had been largely dismantled.

Selected Locations Where Al-Qa'ida and Its Affiliates Operate
○ Number of terrorists, estimated

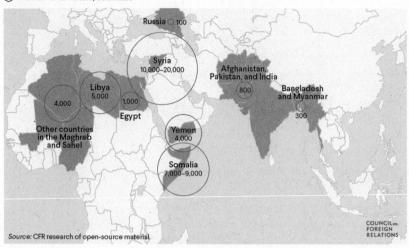

Source: CFR research of open-source material.

COUNCIL on
FOREIGN
RELATIONS

There were strong communications links between core al-Qa'ida and AQAP in Yemen and al-Qa'ida in Syria, and in the latter's case the movement of key leaders as well. There were also strong links and movement of personnel between al-Shabaab and AQAP. There were links between core al-Qa'ida and al-Qa'ida in Iraq, though its leader, Abu Musab al-Zarqawi, often refused to follow the core's orders. (I will have more to say about AQI and its successor, the Islamic State, in a few chapters.) Al-Qa'ida in the Indian Subcontinent and core al-Qa'ida were largely colocated in the Afghanistan-Pakistan border region, and that proximity enabled them to exchange personnel and collaborate on operations. AQIM also took direction from core al-Qa'ida.

Al-Qa'ida's affiliates thus greatly extended the group's global reach. Its most dangerous affiliate, AQAP, successfully conducted attacks in Europe (the attack on *Charlie Hebdo*, the French weekly) and the United States (shootings at Fort Hood, Texas, and Pensacola National Air Station in Florida) and attempted several others.

Accordingly, in addition to my work on core al-Qa'ida, I spent considerable time on our strategy and operations to defeat al-Qa'ida's affiliates, particularly its most dangerous ones, al-Qa'ida in the Arabian Peninsula and al-Qa'ida in Syria. Between 2008 and 2015, I helped design and oversaw several campaigns and operations to disrupt, dismantle, and defeat al-Qa'ida's other affiliates. I traveled regularly to

Yemen, Somalia, Jordan, Turkey, and North Africa to get a firsthand look at and advise on our operations. "It takes a network to defeat a network," as we say in the counterterrorism business, and we developed a global posture to do just that, arraying ourselves to conduct CT operations in five theaters: Afghanistan-Pakistan, Yemen-Somalia, Syria-Iraq, North Africa, and global jihad, the latter a euphemism for the rest of the world.

AL-QA'IDA IN THE ARABIAN PENINSULA

Our war with al-Qa'ida in Yemen began soon after 9/11. Intelligence gathered from the initial takedowns of al-Qa'ida's senior leaders and operational planners around the world suggested some troubling connections to individuals in the United States, particularly in the Buffalo area. Following an FBI counterterrorism investigation, six Yemeni Americans who had received training at an al-Qa'ida camp in Afghanistan were arrested in September 2002. Dubbed the Lackawanna Six, all pleaded guilty to terrorism-related charges and were sentenced to up to ten years in prison.[1]

In November 2002, the United States conducted its first Predator strike in Yemen, targeting Salim al-Harethi, a major player in the attack on the USS *Cole*. A year earlier, Yemen's president, Ali Abdullah Saleh, had traveled to Washington to request U.S. counterterrorism support in Yemen, fearing that it could become another Afghanistan. UBL's father hailed from Yemen, and the Yemeni government had welcomed back its citizens who had gone to fight in the anti-Soviet jihad and allowed them to establish training camps in the country. Saleh understood that if an attack on the United States was linked back to Yemen's ungoverned spaces, the consequences could be devastating.

Yemeni special forces had tried to capture al-Harethi, without success. At that point, Saleh turned to the United States. Harethi had been found and fixed while traveling in a car with five others in Marib Governorate, east of Sana'a, the capital of Yemen. His car was struck with a single Hellfire missile. A U.S. citizen, Kamal Derwish, was among the passengers. The United States had not been aware of his presence when it conducted the strike.[2]

Yemen had much bigger problems beyond its inability to capture al-Qa'ida leaders in special forces raids and assert government control over its territory. Yemen's government couldn't keep al-Qa'ida members it had managed to arrest in prison. In the southern port city of Aden in February 2003, ten al-Qa'ida operatives escaped from the intelligence service's local headquarters. Among them was Jamal al-Badawi, who had also been involved in the *Cole* attack. Badawi was recaptured, only to escape from prison again, this time from a detention facility in Sana'a in February 2006. Joining him in the 2006 prison break along with twenty other AQ operatives was Nasir al-Wahishi, UBL's former bodyguard and the soon-to-be leader of AQAP, and Qassim al-Rimi, the group's military commander. In June 2011, in the southern city of Mukalla, some sixty al-Qa'ida operatives would escape from prison.

Other global jihadists were simply released. In April 2003, Saleh released 146 militants with suspected ties to al-Qa'ida. Yemeni citizens made up 8 percent of the foreign fighters in Iraq, according to captured al-Qa'ida in Iraq records.[3] Not surprisingly, by 2008, the threat emanating from Yemen had grown substantially. I participated in deputies' meetings in the summer and fall that year to consider a strike against a senior al-Qa'ida leader in northern Yemen, but in the end we didn't execute it. The intelligence wasn't precise enough, the plan was too complicated (dropping a U.S.-supplied bomb out of a Yemeni aircraft), and the risk of collateral damage was too high. We did not have Predators flying over Yemen in 2008.

In September 2008, I traveled to Sana'a to confer with U.S. and Yemeni officials about the growing threat from al-Qa'ida. I met with President Saleh, his defense minister, and the head of the National Security Bureau, our main counterterrorism partner. Saleh had had a meeting with a U.S. journalist just before I met with him in which he had revealed some sensitive matters that he shouldn't have. When we met, Saleh was clearly agitated and asked me if the United States could do something to muzzle the journalist. I told him that we didn't do things like that in the United States.

I visited Yemen's special forces, which were pretty good, but they could operate only in the big cities: Sana'a, Aden, and Mukalla. I was most impressed with the all-women surveillance squad I met with. As I was leaving Sana'a, the U.S. embassy was attacked by suspected al-Qa'ida operatives. The attackers drove up to the main gate, breached the outer barrier with an explosive device hidden in their vehicle, and began firing small arms and rocket-propelled grenades. Fortunately, the Marine Security Guards and the embassy's local security force were able to fend them off before the attackers could penetrate too deeply into the compound. Ten Yemenis were killed, six policemen and four civilians. Qassim al-Rimi had planned the attack.

It was clear we needed to substantially step up our operations against AQAP. As the threat from the group grew worse, I made multiple trips to Yemen between 2009 and 2013. During the first year of the Obama administration, my DoD colleagues and I proposed greater military engagement—special forces advisers and air strikes—to combat the threat from AQAP. The new policy was established in a memo from President Obama's first national security adviser, retired Marine Corps General Jim Jones, to Secretary Gates. It spelled out what U.S. advisers could and couldn't do, basically limiting our participation to actions short of the objective.

On November 5, 2009, Nidal Malik Hasan, a U.S. Army major, leaped atop a desk in a medical screening facility at Fort Hood, Texas, shouted, *"Allahu Akbar,"* and then began firing on those inside. Thirteen people died in the attack and more than thirty others were wounded. Hasan had been in email contact with Anwar al-Awlaki, an American-born cleric and a senior leader in AQAP. Awlaki had counseled three of the 9/11 hijackers from his mosque in Northern Virginia and was now radicalizing and recruiting Western Muslims online from Yemen.[4]

AQAP's next plot against the U.S. homeland—intended to cause far more deaths—came on Christmas. A young Nigerian man, Umar Farouk Abdulmutallab, boarded Northwest Airlines Flight 253 in Amsterdam, bound for Detroit. Abdulmutallab had been trained in explosives in Yemen and had met with Awlaki. As the plane started its descent, he tried to set off plastic explosives hidden in his underwear. The explosives fortunately didn't detonate, but Abdulmutallab had managed to set his underwear on fire. Other passengers, noticing what was happening, overwhelmed him with physical force.

It had been a near miss. The bomb design had been sound, and hundreds would have been killed if it had been detonated. After the attack, John Brennan produced a report that found considerable fault at the National Counterterrorism Center, specifically in its management of terrorism databases.[5] There were derogatory reports about Abdulmutallab in them, but they were overlooked.

In June 2009, AQAP also tried to assassinate Muhammad Bin Nayef, a Saudi prince whom everyone in the U.S. government referred to as "MBN." MBN was the head of Saudi Arabia's internal intelligence service, the Mabahith, and the son of the interior minister and a nephew of the king. MBN had been the target of several previous assassination attempts by al-Qa'ida: a car bomb had been detonated outside his office, and a missile had been fired at his plane.[6] MBN had been critical to Saudi Arabia's success in suppressing al-Qa'ida in the kingdom, and I would meet with him several times between 2009 and 2015. One of UBL's highest priorities was to incite a revolution in Saudi Arabia and overthrow the monarchy.[7]

As part of his strategy to defeat the extremism in the kingdom, MBN had established a novel and very effective program to deprogram extremists and integrate them back into normal society. One of Saudi Arabia's most wanted enemies, Abdullah al-Asiri, sent word from Yemen that he was prepared to turn himself in and renounce violence. MBN agreed to meet with him. As they sat shoulder to shoulder on pillows on the floor, Asiri detonated a bomb that had been hidden underneath his clothes. Fortunately, most of the charge had been directed downward. Asiri was blown to bits, but incredibly MBN survived with only minor injuries. Asiri's older brother, Ibrahim, had built the bomb, as well as the underwear bomb that Abdulmutallab had tried to detonate.[8] Ibrahim would quickly become the world's most dangerous bomb maker.

The United States conducted five strikes in Yemen in 2009 and 2010, mostly using cruise missiles and conventional aircraft. An errant strike in Wadi Abida in Marib, an al-Qa'ida stronghold, killed the deputy governor in May 2010. Saleh asked for a suspension of strikes and the United States complied. Meanwhile, AQAP grew stronger. In late October 2010, AQAP smuggled two bombs inside printer cartridges on cargo aircraft bound for Chicago.[9] The packages had been addressed to two Jewish organizations. Good intelligence fortunately allowed us to disrupt the plot.

The "Arab Spring" revolution hit Yemen in early 2011 and was a boon to AQAP, increasing its ranks more than twofold and expanding its territory significantly. AQAP was strongest in the so-called al-Qa'ida crescent, which ranged from al-Jawf in the north to Abiyan in the south. The group also had an enduring presence in Hadramawt and other governorates.

We knew we would have to get back in the strike business and in a much more effective way. I persuaded Secretary Gates in his final months as secretary of defense to transfer six additional Predator orbits to the strategic counterterrorism mission, with these orbits to be used against AQAP in Yemen.

Gates had made a very difficult decision. Several of DOD's top military commanders, Admiral Mullen and General Petraeus among them, were opposed. We were in the midst of a major surge of forces in Afghanistan, and every spare Predator orbit was needed there to support our troops.

Soon after Leon Panetta replaced Gates as defense secretary, I asked him to approve the transfer of two additional orbits, which he promptly did. In four years, I had increased the number of Predator orbits dedicated to the strategic counterterrorism mission against al-Qa'ida more than sevenfold, from three to twenty-two.

The growth in Predator orbits dedicated to the strategic CT mission was similar in some respects to the dramatic increase in ordnance I had put in place between 1984 and 1987 for the Afghan resistance. A large increase in means available was required to win our secret war in Afghanistan during the 1980s, and an equally large increase—though of a different kind—was required to defeat core al-Qa'ida and its affiliates. Defeating a global, transnational movement like al-Qa'ida, as I observed in the previous chapter, is different from defeating a state adversary. Operationally dismantling the groups is necessary but not sufficient. You also have to defeat their ideology and prevent their reconstitution. That requires a lot more than Predator strikes. But a relentless barrage of Predator strikes is the necessary first step in dismantling and defeating a group like AQAP that poses a significant threat to the American homeland.

Beginning in June 2011, we had a much better counterterrorism partner to work with in the acting president and later president, Abd Rabbu Mansur Hadi. We received quick approval from Hadi to resume air strikes and began a new program advising Yemeni special forces on capture missions in Sana'a and Aden. (Saleh, as I will discuss later, was forced from power but remained in Yemen, undermining the new government whenever the opportunity arose.)

On Friday, September 30, 2011, we killed Anwar al-Awlaki, whom we had located the previous Sunday. We had been trying to find him for months, with no success. Deputy CIA Director Michael Morell and I were both just entering our respective church services, his in Georgetown and mine in upper Northwest Washington, D.C., when we had to step outside to take secure calls and redirect Predators from tactical missions in Yemen to the Awlaki target.

Michael and I became close friends as well as colleagues. We frequently traveled overseas together and supported each other in Deputies Committee meetings. As Morell describes it, John Brennan, he, and I were probably more focused on al-Qa'ida between 2010 and 2013 than anyone else at the senior levels of the U.S. government.[10]

Another friend, Admiral Sandy Winnefeld, the vice-chairman of the Joint Chiefs, joined us on the call. Awlaki had been hiding in a safe house in al-Jawf Governorate. When he got in a vehicle to move, we were on him and destroyed his vehicle with Hellfire missiles.[11]

Because Awlaki was a U.S. citizen, his placement on the target list required a special review by the Department of Justice's Office of Legal Counsel, in addition to approval by President Obama.[12] The OLC concluded that killing Awlaki, a senior leader of al-Qa'ida who was directly involved in plots against the United States, was justified by the U.S. government's public authority and other statutes. The attorney general had to also determine that OLC's review had provided Awlaki with due process as required by the U.S. Constitution. Killed along with Awlaki was another U.S. citizen, Samir Khan. Khan had not been a target of the attack.[13]

Admiral Mullen, our JCS chairman from 2007 to 2011, retired from the Navy the same day as Awlaki was killed. I had told him at a meeting in the White House Situation Room three days earlier that we would kill Awlaki before he retired. He told me he'd buy me a beer if we did. He still hasn't paid up.

———

As our intelligence on AQAP got better and better, we were able to conduct more aggressive CT operations. In 2012, we conducted nearly fifty Predator strikes. It was the high-water mark of our campaign against AQAP, which lost much of the territory it had gained in 2011 as a result.

Unlike in Pakistan, the White House initially restricted us to "personality" strikes in Yemen, which limited the operational tempo we could achieve. Morell and I argued in deputies meetings for signature strikes, and eventually we were successful in getting a limited form of them approved.

Signature strikes, as I noted in the previous chapter, were responsible for taking more than 60 percent of high-value targets off the battlefield in our primary counterterrorism theater, the Afghanistan-Pakistan border region. In Yemen, with an equally dangerous adversary, we opted for a more surgical approach. We would rely on a "scalpel" to go after AQAP's senior leadership and external operations capability rather than its whole range of operational planners was how John Brennan put it. What we needed as the threat grew worse was not a scalpel but a sword. The National Counterterrorism Center, not surprisingly, assessed that because of the more constrained permissions we had in the campaign against AQAP, we were not on course to achieve our strategic objective of dismantling and defeating the group by 2016. We could disrupt AQAP and gradually attrit its capabilities, but that was about it. I argued strongly against this more constrained approach, believing that the CT strategy we were using against core AQ was the right one, but unfortunately I did not prevail.

That said, we did have our successes. In 2012, we took Fahd al-Quso, a key plotter in the *Cole* attack, off the battlefield. The men we were most looking for, however, were Nasir al-Wahishi, AQAP's emir and the newly designated successor to Ayman al-Zawahiri as al-Qa'ida's leader; Qassim al-Rimi, AQAP's military commander; and especially Ibrahim al-Asiri, AQAP's master bomb maker.

Asiri had caused great concern in 2012 when he developed a nonmetallic bomb that could be smuggled undetected onto commercial airliners. Fortunately, his suicide bomber was arrested before he could board a flight to the United States.[14] We were also targeting a laparoscopic surgeon who was helping Asiri place bombs inside people. We got the surgeon in 2012. It would take several years more before Wahishi, Asiri, and Rimi were killed.

In May 2013, President Obama gave a speech at the National Defense University to outline a major shift in our counterterrorism strategy. It was a tightly reasoned and eloquent speech, and I was deeply moved as I listened to it. The president emphasized that our war with al-Qa'ida was just and that our strategy with some major exceptions had been effective and wise. He rightly noted that he had significantly stepped up the pace of our counterterrorism operations and that core al-Qa'ida was now on the path to defeat. He also rightly noted that most of al-Qa'ida's affiliates, with the exception of AQAP, were focused on operations in the countries and regions where they were based. Thus, they did not pose a direct threat to the U.S. homeland in the way that core al-Qa'ida had or AQAP still did. He warned against the danger of perpetual war and said that it was coming time to shift our strategy from our heavy reliance on unilateral drone strikes to reliance on counterterrorism partnerships as our primary CT instrument.

I thought he had been right on the mark until this last point. He had declared victory too soon.

The administration had come under increasingly strong criticism for its reliance on drone strikes, both from the right and from the left. The right argued that it was preferable to capture terrorists with boots on the ground. True, but not often possible. The left questioned the legality and morality of our use of drones. There was also a wide discrepancy between what those outside the government assessed regarding the number of civilian casualties resulting from drone strikes and our internal assessments. It didn't matter, as I noted in the previous chapter, that we had the facts on our side. How we knew those facts was secret, and we couldn't share that.[15] As a result, it became much harder to get drone strikes approved by the White House. The president's NDU speech became Presidential Policy Guidance.

We conducted no Predator strikes in Yemen during the first half of 2013. A few months after the NDU speech, however, AQAP marshaled significant forces under the leadership of one of its top military commanders, Shaki al-Badani, and posed a grave threat to our embassy in Sana'a. Morell and I argued strenuously in the deputies meetings for Predator strikes, in particular signature Predator strikes, because that's what the crisis situation demanded.

Morell said that the threat to our embassy in Sana'a was the most serious terrorist threat the United States had faced since al-Qa'ida tried to bring down several airliners over the Atlantic Ocean in 2006. After some debate among deputies and principals, the president approved an intense barrage of ten strikes in two weeks. That defeated the pending attack.[16] Quantity has a quality all its own.

During the remainder of 2013 and in the years that followed, we made continual if gradual progress in taking AQAP's leadership and external operations planners off the battlefield. In 2013, we killed AQAP's deputy emir, Sa'id al-Shihri, who, after being released from detention at Guantánamo, had returned to terrorism. In November 2014, we got Shaki al-Badani, the leader of the embassy plot. In 2015, we got AQAP's emir and heir apparent to Ayman al-Zawahiri, Nasir al-Wahishi. In 2016, another senior AQAP military commander was taken off the battlefield, Jalal al-Bala'idi. In October 2017, the master bomb maker Ibrahim al-Asiri was finally killed, and in January 2020 Qassim al-Rimi was at last eliminated. Later in 2020, AQAP's new emir, Khalid Batarfi, was captured in al-Mahrah Governorate.

Between 2011 and 2015, the United States had conducted more than one hundred Predator strikes in Yemen against AQAP. Our operational tempo wasn't as intense as it had been against core al-Qa'ida—we conducted more strikes in the Afghanistan-Pakistan border region in 2010 than we had in five years in Yemen—but it had been enough to prevent a major terrorist attack on the United States. It was a long march—too long—to operational defeat. With pressure on the group likely to recede as a result of the Biden administration's restrictive counterterrorism policies, AQAP will almost certainly be back.

AL-QA'IDA IN SYRIA

Syria became a new front for al-Qa'ida in 2011 with the beginning of Sunni insurgency against Bashar al-Assad's regime. Ayman al-Zawahiri, al-Qaida's leader after the death of UBL, believed that Syria would become al-Qa'ida's new main theater, as the center of the global jihad movement shifted from Pakistan and Afghanistan to the Arab world. He sent Abu Khayr al-Masri, one of his top lieutenants and a co-founder of al-Qa'ida, to Syria, along with several other al-Qa'ida operatives. A global jihadist rival, the Islamic State, would also see its ranks greatly strengthened as a result of the Syrian civil war and would establish the headquarters of its caliphate there. (More on the rise of ISIS in a subsequent chapter.) Accordingly, between 2011 and 2015, I paid a lot of attention to the global jihadist threat in and emanating out of Syria. The threat emanating from there soon competed with the threat emanating from Yemen as the world's most dangerous one.

In August 2011, Jabhat al-Nusra, the al-Qa'ida affiliate in Syria, was established under the leadership of Abu Mohammad al-Jawlani. The group initially focused on conducting terrorist attacks against the Syrian regime and was responsible for most suicide bombings in Syria during the first two years of Syria's civil war. Al-Nusra quickly developed global ambitions, however, and worked on plots against the United States. Jawlani broke with al-Qa'ida in 2017, merged al-Nusra with several Syrian opposition groups, and renamed his group Hay'at Tahrir al-Sham (Organization for the Liberation of the Levant), focusing his efforts on the ongoing civil war in Syria rather than on global jihadism. The group still retains its Salafi-jihadist ideology, however.

Al-Nusra had a group of external plotters who became known as the Khorasan Group. Khorasan, which means "Land of the Sun," refers to a historical region that encompassed northeastern Iran, southern Turkmenistan, and northern Afghanistan. It was established as a region by the Sasanian dynasty, the last Iranian Empire before the rise of Islam. Its significance to global jihadists stems from a Hadith that states that "black banners will come out of Khorasan" in the end times. The defeat of the Red Army in Afghanistan was seen as a sign that the end times were drawing near. ISIS was clearly confused about what forces were at work in Afghanistan during the 1980s.

The term "Khorasan" among Syrian extremists, however, referred to al-Qa'ida operatives who had come from Pakistan and Afghanistan. The leader of the group was Muhsin al-Fadhli, a Kuwaiti national and veteran al-Qa'ida operative who had begun his jihadi career by fighting the Russians in Chechnya. Sanafi al-Nasr was Fadhli's deputy, and David Drugeon, a Frenchman, was its chief bomb maker. By the summer of 2013, the Khorasan Group had a number of plots under way against the U.S. homeland and other Western targets, some of which appeared to employ sophisticated bomb-making technology similar to what Ibrahim al-Asiri had developed.

We debated what to do about the Khorasan threat for a year in the Deputies Committee before taking action. On September 23, 2014, the United States conducted a large air and missile strike on suspected Khorasan facilities. We didn't get the key leaders and operatives we were hoping to, however. We had waited too long before taking action.

Over time, however, we had more success. Muhsin al-Fadhli was subsequently killed, along with David Drugeon, in a drone strike in July 2015. Fadhli's deputy, Sanafi al-Nasr, was killed three months later. In February 2017, Abu Khayr al-Masri, one of al-Qa'ida's long-standing senior leaders and Zawahiri's designated successor after the death of Nasir al-Wahishi, was killed in his car by a special weapon that had been launched from a Predator. Syria remains a dangerous place, however. Assad's brutal, sectarian civil war is still a rallying point for Sunni extremists, and parts of the country remain ungoverned space where jihadists can freely operate. I will have more to say about the Syrian civil war and its strategic implications in a later chapter.

AL-SHABAAB

Al-Shabaab was mostly a regional threat, so it received far less of my attention than AQAP and al-Qa'ida in Syria, but I did oversee several raids and other operations against the group. I also oversaw a few operations against Somali pirates who had taken Americans hostage. And as was the case with our other war zones, I traveled to Somalia to get a firsthand look at our efforts there.

Al-Shabaab, or the "Youth," had come to power in southern Somalia in 2006 following an invasion by Ethiopia. Several of the group's senior leaders had ties to al-Qa'ida long before al-Shabaab became an official AQ affiliate. We believed the group was sheltering some senior AQ operatives, including those who had been involved in the 1998 embassy bombings in Kenya and Tanzania.[17] In late April 2008, our Special Operations Task Force found al-Shabaab's leader, Aden Ayrow, in Dusa Mareb, Somalia, and took him out with a cruise missile strike.[18]

In April 2009, I gained Secretary Gates's approval for and oversaw the rescue of Richard Phillips, the captain of the U.S.-flagged merchant ship the *Maersk Alabama,* which had been hijacked by Somali pirates. After boarding and seizing the ship, the pirates had taken Captain Phillips off the ship in one of the *Maersk Alabama's* lifeboats. A group of SEALs were deployed via a parachute jump into the water and onto the USS *Bainbridge,* a guided-missile destroyer. Two other ships joined the task force, the USS *Boxer,* a large-deck amphibious ship, and the USS *Halyburton,* a frigate. A much larger group of SEALs, along with four high-speed assault craft, then parachuted into the water and came aboard the *Boxer.* A key aim was to prevent the pirates from making shore with Phillips.

The SEAL task force was under the command of Captain Scott Moore, a world-class mountain climber who had nearly summited Mount Everest and an excellent tactical operator. Moore had deployed a fifteen-man SEAL troop onto the *Bainbridge* with three of his best snipers.

Four pirates were on the lifeboat with Phillips. After they had run low on gas, food, and water, the pirates agreed to negotiate, and the lead pirate came aboard the *Bainbridge.* All the pirates wanted was money, and they thought Maersk would pay the ransom. Our lead negotiator convinced the lead pirate that it would be best to hook up a towline to their lifeboat. The pirate inexplicably agreed, which allowed the task force to make the pirates seasick and then pull them inside the wake to reduce the boat's rolling motion, thereby enabling a better chance at simultaneous sniper kills. The three snipers locked on and took out the three remaining pirates. It was masterful shooting.[19]

That September, I gained approval for and oversaw another SEAL operation in Somalia, this one a helicopter ambush. The target was Saleh Nabhan, a senior al-Qa'ida operative who was number three on the FBI's most wanted list. Nabhan had been involved in the planning and execution of the 1998 embassy bombings in Kenya and Tanzania. He had also orchestrated the suicide bombing attack on the Paradise Hotel in Mombasa in 2002 and had attempted to shoot down an Israeli

THE WAR BEYOND THE CORE **257**

charter plane. He was a difficult target to find, because he never used a phone or computer, relying on human couriers to communicate, and changed locations every twenty-four hours. Our Special Operations Task Force had struck a compound that Nabhan was believed to be hiding in with cruise missiles in early 2008, but our missiles struck the wrong part of the compound and he survived.[20]

We found Nabhan again twenty months later through a human source. We learned that he traveled periodically from the Somali town of Barawe to Marka. More important, we learned that he would be making another trip in a few days in a blue four-door sedan. We also learned that Nabhan's courier did use a phone.

We knew we would have only about fifteen minutes to target Nabhan while he was outside a high-collateral-damage area. Our concept was to use two MH-6, "Little Bird," assault helicopters with a pair of SEAL snipers on each skid, two AH-6 attack helicopters, and a newly developed, very small precision-guided munition that could be launched from a small airplane. The air-launched weapon, called the Griffin, would be the primary strike option, with the AH-6s' mini guns as a backup. The Little Birds and SEALs would be pre-positioned on a destroyer offshore, ready to launch when Nabhan moved. The aircraft carrying the Griffin would take off from a clandestine base in a neighboring country.

The task force had already done several of these vehicle interdiction missions successfully in Iraq. I had high confidence in the mission and told Secretary Gates and the Deputies Committee so. I thought the Little Birds were the best option, but the NSC's principals feared another "Black Hawk Down" incident and preferred to use the Griffin.

A Predator was orbiting over Nabhan's compound, providing real-time intelligence, as he departed Barawe. Once he was on the coastal road, the Little Birds launched. At the last minute, cloud cover had made the Griffin option infeasible. The SEAL task force commander, Captain Pete Van Hooser, requested permission from Vice Admiral Bill McRaven, McChrystal's successor, to shift to guns. McRaven gave his approval. As the helos crossed the beach, the sedan's driver spotted them and sped up. Shots were fired at the approaching helos. The AH-6s responded with a heavy volume of fire. The driver and all passengers were killed immediately. The assault helicopters landed on the road, and the SEALs recovered the bodies for identification. Photos were immediately sent to the FBI. An hour later, the task force received confirmation: Saleh Nabhan, and three known accomplices.[21]

In June 2011, Harun Fazul, al-Qa'ida's senior military commander in East Africa, was killed by local forces. In January 2012, I oversaw another successful hostage rescue to free Jessica Buchanan, an American aid worker, and her Danish colleague, who were being held by pirates. I watched in real time as the SEALs parachuted into the target area via military free fall and then rescued Buchanan and her colleague in the middle of the night. The operation was executed flawlessly.

———

In 2012, I made my first trip to Somalia. Our principal CT instrument in Somalia during most of my tenure was not Predator strikes or special operations raids but forces provided by the African Union, primarily Ugandans and Burundians. Part of the reason for this was that all of our Predators were in other theaters, principally Afghanistan and Pakistan and Yemen. We did what we could with what we had in Somalia.

AU forces had just ejected al-Shabaab from Mogadishu, with the assistance of a small group of SEALs, and I was eager to visit our troops and get a firsthand look at the situation. I was the first senior American official to do so, though not without having to win a battle in Washington first. The State Department's assistant secretary for African affairs, Ambassador Johnnie Carson, was concerned that my visit could "militarize" our policy in Somalia. I told Ambassador Carson that it was al-Shabaab that was militarizing the situation in Somalia, and Secretary Clinton and the White House approved my travel.

I flew in low over the water on a small special operations aircraft to arrive at the position the United States had established at Mogadishu's airport. The Ugandan operational commander, a graduate of the U.S. Army's Command and General Staff College at Fort Leavenworth, had performed brilliantly, as had the SEALs. The Ugandan brigadier general had used snipers, artillery, and maneuver effectively to push al-Shabaab out. I was very proud of what he and our small group of SEALs had accomplished. CIA also had established a small presence there and was assisting the Somali National Intelligence Service. It was a different approach to CT, but it worked for the most part in the limited strategic theater of Somalia.

In 2014, the leader of al-Shabaab, Mukhtar Abu al-Zubair, better known as Godane, was killed in a drone strike, as was Talil Abdishakur, the head of the group's assassination unit. In 2015, two members of al-Shabaab's external operations cadre, Yusuf Dheeq and Aden Garaar, were also killed in a drone strike. Garaar had been the mastermind behind the Westgate Shopping Mall massacre in Nairobi in 2013.

By 2015, the situation had improved considerably in Somalia, but al-Shabaab still posed a threat, both within country and in neighboring Kenya.[22] Somalia for us had been an economy of force operation, and unfortunately what we got in return was economy of results. President Biden's recent decision to redeploy hundreds of U.S. special operators back into Somalia, reversing President Trump's unwise decision to pull them all out, is a step in the right direction.

AL-QA'IDA IN THE ISLAMIC MAGHREB

From 2012 onward, I also started paying more attention to al-Qa'ida's affiliate in North Africa, al-Qa'ida in the Islamic Maghreb (AQIM). Even more so than in Somalia, our CT efforts in North Africa were an economy of force operation, working mostly through our host nation and international partners.

Prior to 2012, AQIM had primarily focused on kidnapping Westerners for ransom, a strategy that had netted tens of millions of dollars for the group. Under its leader, Abdelmalek Droukdel, AQIM had conducted a series of car and cell phone bombings in Algiers in 2007 and 2008. Core al-Qa'ida hailed the attacks as the beginning of its jihad in the Maghreb.

The threat from AQIM and its local allies got much worse in 2012, when the group seized control of the northern half of Mali and was threatening to advance on Bamako, Mali's capital. The takeover started as a Tuareg rebellion, fueled by arms and returning mercenaries from Libya after the fall of Muammar Qaddafi. While part of the Tuareg insurgency was secular, another part was Salafist, Ansar al Din. A second Salafist group also emerged, the Movement for Unity and Jihad in West Africa, better known by its French acronym, MUJAO. Both Salafist groups were aligned with AQIM.

By early April, separatist and Salafist forces had taken all the major cities in the north, Kidal, Gao, and Timbuktu, and were imposing a harsh form of Sharia law on the populace. On January 9, 2013, the jihadists crossed the Niger River and advanced on Bamako.

At that point, the French president, François Hollande, decided to intervene militarily. French special forces stationed in nearby Burkina Faso were in action within hours, temporarily halting the Salafist advance. The special operators were reinforced by French air strikes from Chad, targeting jihadist positions. French conventional forces were flown in, increasing their boots on the ground by a factor of ten, to twenty-five hundred. The first two weeks of French operations saved Mali from falling into the hands of al-Qa'ida and its allies.

The French intervention force would grow to forty-five hundred, supplemented by a Chadian force of twenty-five hundred and troops from other African nations. They would fight a war of speed and rapid engagements over long distances, stretching French logistical capacity to the maximum. France's operational commander was Brigadier General Grégoire de Saint-Quentin, a veteran of France's First Special Forces Army Group. I would confer with him several times in Mali in 2013. Our main role was in providing intelligence, surveillance, and reconnaissance, or ISR, support to French operations. We established a joint intelligence cell in Paris and provided direct support in the field.

The French retook Timbuktu and then Gao, with their paratroopers and special forces leading the way. Gao was particularly important, because the only road north to Kidal ran from there. French special forces seized the airport at Kidal and an airfield at Tessalit. From there, they began operations in the Ifoghas Mountains, an AQIM stronghold. French and Chadian forces killed close to four hundred jihadists and seized 130 tons of weapons and ammunition. Among those killed was the AQIM senior military commander Abu Zeid. Only eight French soldiers were killed in the operation.

As a result of the Mali crisis, I made several trips to the Maghreb and Sahel between 2012 and 2014, meeting with defense and intelligence leaders in Algeria, Morocco, Libya, Mauritania, Mali, and Niger. I was amazed by the strategic leverage we gained from the small numbers of special operators and CIA personnel working in the Sahel. I was also impressed with the CT capabilities of the Mauritanians, though I didn't care much for the camel's milk they offered me.

I was in regular contact with Hollande's military adviser, General Benoît Puga, another special forces veteran whom I had known for years. Many of France's senior special forces officers had family ties of some sort to former French colonies in Africa and, more important, they had a deep understanding of the area of operation. As in Israel, service in the French special forces was a ticket to high military command or to the top of its intelligence services.

AQIM was down but not out, however. In December 2012, another AQIM military commander, Mokhtar Belmokhtar, seized the In Amenas gas plant in eastern Algeria, taking a number of hostages. He was the target of U.S. and French air strikes but is believed to have survived. In 2015, AQIM attacked a hotel in Bamako and killed nineteen people. In 2016, the group conducted a similar operation in Ouagadougou, killing twenty-eight. AQIM's leader, Abdelmalek Droukdel, was killed in northern Mali by French special forces in June 2020. French President Emmanuel Macron recently ended France's CT operations in North Africa, so this may not be the last we've heard from AQIM.

AL-QA'IDA IN THE INDIAN SUBCONTINENT

Al-Qa'ida in the Indian Subcontinent, which conducts operations in Afghanistan, Pakistan, India, and Bangladesh, is the only franchise that core al-Qa'ida has started from scratch. Established in 2014, AQIS has suffered considerable losses since its inception. Most of the founding members and key operatives of AQIS had long-standing ties to other militant groups in the Afghanistan-Pakistan border region, so I paid some attention to them. My role against the group, however, was largely limited to overseeing drone strikes between 2014 and 2015 against some of its key members.

A member of AQIS's Shura Council, Imran Ali Siddiqi, was killed in a U.S. drone strike in October 2014, a month after the group was formed. Ustad Ahmad Farooq, the group's deputy emir, and Qari Imran, a member of the group's Shura Council and the group's lead bomb maker, were killed in U.S. drone strikes in 2015 in South and North Waziristan, respectively. Also in 2015, a massive AQIS-run training camp was discovered and struck by U.S. airpower in the Shorabak district of Kandahar Province.

Omar Khattab, AQIS's chief of operations, was killed in Afghanistan in 2017. The leader of its India Wing, Muhammad Asif, was arrested in December 2015. The leader of its Bangladesh Wing, Tariq Sohel, was killed in 2017. Asim Umar, an Indian national, former commander in the Tehrik-e-Taliban Pakistan (Pakistan Taliban), and the group's first emir, was killed in a raid by Afghan security forces in Helmand Province in 2019.

AQIS has managed to mount a few attacks—one on a Pakistan Navy shipyard in Karachi and another, an attempted hijacking of a Pakistani frigate. The group also assassinated a Pakistan Army brigadier in the Punjab, all in 2014. The group has also conducted a few successful operations in Bangladesh. It is down but not out.

SAFER, BUT NOT YET SAFE

As a result of U.S. counterterrorism operations, Americans were a lot safer from the global jihadist threat when I left senior government service in 2015 than when I began it in 2007. The new strategy we put in place in 2008 has been very successful, dismantling core al-Qa'ida in the Afghanistan-Pakistan border region, and then largely dismantling al-Qa'ida's most dangerous affiliates. Our long war with al-Qa'ida and its allies has been the most aggressive and far-reaching counterterrorism effort in history. We have been very successful at killing or capturing al-Qa'ida's senior leaders and key planners and operatives, and have been somewhat successful in eliminating the group's many safe havens. But the underlying conditions that gave rise to global jihadist terrorism remain largely intact. If we maintain a robust intelligence collection posture and constant pressure on the group and its affiliates, we can keep the threat posed by al-Qa'ida down to manageable levels. We will regret it if we don't.

14

HVT 1

ABBOTTABAD COMPOUND 1

At the end of an NSC Deputies Committee meeting in October 2010, Michael Morell, CIA's deputy director, asked General Hoss Cartwright, the vice-chairman of the Joint Chiefs of Staff, and me if we could stay after so he could brief us on an important development. The meeting would take about forty-five minutes. We rearranged our schedules and followed Michael to the NSC's Intelligence Programs Office in the Eisenhower Executive Office Building just across West Executive Avenue from the White House. As we took our seats, Morell got right to the point. "We think we have found Usama Bin Ladin," he said, as he passed slide decks to Cartwright and me. If you're a national security professional, it's moments like these you live for.

Morell told us that Director Panetta had just briefed Secretary Gates and Admiral Mullen, the JCS chairman. Outside a very small group within CIA, Morell emphasized that in addition to the four of us only President Obama, Vice President Biden, Tom Donilon (the president's national security adviser), Denis McDonough (Tom's deputy), John Brennan, and Jim Clapper had been briefed on this. It was the most tightly guarded secret in the U.S. government.

CIA's Counterterrorism Center had been on the hunt for UBL, known as "High Value Target Number One," or "HVT1," since he escaped from the Tora Bora mountains in eastern Afghanistan in

December 2001. There had been some reporting that Bin Ladin had been in Afghanistan's Konar Province in mid-2002, but after that the trail had gone cold.[1]

After 2003, CTC believed that UBL was hiding somewhere in northern Pakistan, but the ellipse of where he could be was very large, stretching from the border region to well into the settled areas. Between 2003 and 2009, there had been several "Elvis" sightings of UBL. During my first trip as a new assistant secretary to Pakistan and Afghanistan in August 2007, I watched the Special Operations Task Force led by Lieutenant General Stan McChrystal spin into action when intelligence reporting indicated that UBL had returned to the Tora Bora region. Intelligence, surveillance, and reconnaissance aircraft soaked the area. Rangers and SEALs were inserted by helicopters to strike the initial targets. B-2 bomber sorties were launched but then recalled when the intelligence was shown to be erroneous. There had been a gathering of insurgents in the Tora Bora mountains, but UBL was not among them.[2]

CIA had pursued a three-pronged strategy in the hunt for Bin Ladin.[3] There was an extensive effort devoted to learning about and locating UBL's many family members in hopes that one of them would lead us to him. Our best chance in this line of effort came when one of UBL's sons, Sa'ad, was released from detention in Iran and relocated to Pakistan. CIA tracked him into the border region, but there was no indication that he had joined up with his father. Sa'ad was later killed in a Predator strike.[4] Finding UBL through his extended family never bore fruit, though the intelligence obtained in this effort would help CIA understand who was likely with UBL in Abbottabad Compound 1 and who wasn't. The second prong of CIA's find strategy was to analyze UBL's public statements for any clues they might contain. Periodically, he would issue audio statements, and on rare occasions he would release a video. Agency analysts would scrutinize these videos for technical details and background images, looking for anything that might point to a general location for UBL. CIA also tried to reverse engineer how the messages had gotten from UBL to the media outlets that broadcast them to see if that could narrow the search area. This approach failed to produce results as well.[5] The third approach focused on how UBL communicated with his immediate subordinates. And that was the one that ultimately led us to Bin Ladin.

CIA had concluded that UBL communicated only by courier. Starting in 2002, the agency had learned from detainees in its custody the *kunya* (nom de guerre) of a person who served as a courier for messages to and from Bin Ladin, Abu Ahmed al-Kuwaiti. CIA had heard the name before from other detainees, but only in the context that this individual had been with UBL at Tora Bora.

Two detainees were particularly important: Ammar al-Baluchi and Hassan Gul. Both had been subjected to enhanced interrogation techniques while in CIA custody, and both had provided vital insights into Abu Ahmed's role. Ammar was the first detainee to reveal that Abu Ahmed served as a courier for messages to and from Bin Ladin. Gul, before undergoing enhanced interrogation techniques, speculated that Abu Ahmed could be one of three people with UBL, and further speculated that Abu Ahmed might have handled Bin Ladin's needs, including sending messages to UBL's gatekeeper, Abu Faraj al-Libi. After undergoing EITs, Gul got more specific, revealing that Abu Ahmed had passed a letter from Bin Ladin to Abu Faraj in late 2003 and that Abu Ahmed had "disappeared" from Karachi, Pakistan, in 2002.[6]

Even after undergoing waterboarding, the most severe and controversial of EITs, Khalid Sheikh Mohammed denied that Abu Ahmed was Bin Ladin's courier, and claimed that Abu Ahmed had left al-Qa'ida in 2002. Ammar and Gul confirmed for CIA that KSM had been lying when he said this. Ammar stated that KSM had told him that Abu Ahmed continued to deliver letters from Bin Ladin after 2002, a point that Gul corroborated.[7]

Waterboarding was at the extreme outer edge of EITs, but it hadn't worked on KSM, at least not where UBL was concerned. Fortunately, KSM confirmed Abu Ahmed's key role after he returned to his cell by warning other prisoners that they should not mention anything about "the courier."[8]

The denial of the courier's existence by Abu Faraj al-Libi also caught CIA's attention. Abu Faraj, al-Qa'ida's number three, had been captured in Mardan, Pakistan, in 2005. Even after undergoing EITs, he denied knowing Abu Ahmed. Both KSM and Abu Faraj had given CIA information extremely damaging to al-Qa'ida, yet they were refusing to give up this secret. CIA's interest in finding who Abu Ahmed was, and where he was located, was now sky-high.

In 2007, a source provided CIA with Abu Ahmed's true name, Ibrahim Saeed Ahmed.[9] He was indeed a Kuwaiti, hence his *kunya* al-Kuwaiti, but was a Pakistani Pashtun by ethnicity. Other information from detainees further rounded out the picture. Abu Yasir al-Jaza'iri told CIA interrogators that Abu Ahmed mixed "Pakistani words" with Arabic. Ahmad Ghailani told CIA that Abu Ahmed's first child was a daughter born around 2002, which would match what CIA would later learn from other sources about individuals living at the Abbottabad compound.

Khallad Bin Attash told CIA interrogators that after UBL had fled Afghanistan, he would not meet face-to-face with al-Qa'ida members. He had few bodyguards and relied on a small group of individuals native to the area to carry messages and handle daily chores. UBL would not leave the house and did not relocate frequently. All this would later match the circumstances CIA observed at Abbottabad Compound 1. During their CIA interrogations, KSM and another detainee, Sharif al-Masri, had also speculated that Bin Ladin's youngest wife, Amal, was probably located with UBL. Sharif had also told CIA that he had passed letters to Abu Faraj for UBL and one of his wives, Siham, suggesting that UBL and Siham might be colocated as well.[10]

It took another two years to learn Abu Ahmed's general location, which was in Pakistan. Abu Ahmed practiced extraordinary operational security. He would power up and use his cell phone only when he was tens of miles away from UBL's Abbottabad compound, and when he used the phone, it was only for very brief calls. We learned that Abu Ahmed periodically traveled to a certain city in Pakistan, but we had no idea yet where he had come from.[11]

In the summer of 2009, I got very excited when I read an intelligence report that we had briefly geolocated Abu Ahmed's phone. We unfortunately lost him as soon as his brief call had ended, but how close we had come stayed with me. It would be another year before we found him again, but this time it would be for good. The big breakthrough came not from human sources but from technical collection, though the former played an important supporting role. The specific sources and methods we used remain highly classified, so I can provide only a general description here. CIA geolocated Abu Ahmed on one of his trips and then followed him back to the Abbottabad compound on August 27, 2010. The final phase of the operation to locate Abu Ahmed was a team effort, with NSA and NGA making critical contributions. That would continue to be the case as we learned more about Abu Ahmed and Abbottabad Compound 1.

————————

As Morell started to brief General Cartwright and me on the intelligence that led CIA to AC1 and what CIA knew about the compound, I recalled an intelligence report earlier that year that had really caught my attention. Umar Patek, a senior jihadist from Indonesia, had been captured in Abbottabad by the Pakistanis. As I read it, I thought to myself, *Now, what was he doing there?*

CIA maintained a detailed database of several thousand compounds in the Afghanistan-Pakistan border region. AC1 was deep within Pakistan's settled area, however. A well-to-do mountain town of about 200,000 that is only thirty-five miles north of the capital, Islamabad, Abbottabad is home to a Pakistani nuclear missile site in addition to its military academy (Pakistan's West Point).[12] Due to its generally cooler climate, Abbottabad is where many of Pakistan's elite spend their summers, and it is a year-round home for many retired Pakistani military and intelligence officers. Ironically, Admiral Olson and I had visited the Pakistan Army's military academy at Abbottabad in October 2008 to observe a graduation ceremony for Pakistan's Frontier Corps, a force our Special Forces had just started training. We were less than a mile and a half from AC1. I later joked with Eric that had we known that UBL was so close by, we could have captured him ourselves.

As General Cartwright and I went through the slides Morell had handed us and peered at satellite photos of the compound, AC1 became more interesting with each turn of the page. Abu Ahmed, or Ibrahim, lived there with his brother, Abrar, and with their wives and children. But oddly, even though property records showed they were the owners, they lived in a small guesthouse on the compound. Ibrahim and his brother had paid cash for the property, which was valued at $1 million and had been built in 2005. They had no visible sources of income. CIA learned that the two brothers were living in Abbottabad under aliases and that their wives were lying to their own extended families about where they lived.

The main structure was by far the largest in the neighborhood—eight times the size of the next largest. Another family lived in the main house. The compound contained a garage and an animal pen in addition to its main house and guesthouses and was surrounded by twelve- to eighteen-foot walls. There was no internet connection to or landline telephone in the compound. Even more strange, the main house had a third-floor balcony that had a seven-foot wall surrounding it, obstructing all views. As Director Panetta commented when he first saw the photos, "Who puts a wall that high around a balcony? Isn't the whole purpose of a terrace to see out?" The compound's occupants burned their trash, and none of the multiple children living there attended school or went outside to play. The adults occupying the main house never left either.

We caught a few glimpses of a very tall man walking around inside the compound, taking laps around a mostly covered garden, like a prisoner in a yard. CIA dubbed him the Pacer. I watched the imagery multiple times. It certainly looked as if it could be him. CIA had asked the National Geospatial-Intelligence Agency's experts to try to determine the Pacer's height by analyzing shadows, since UBL was six feet four inches. The answer, unfortunately, came back that the Pacer was somewhere between five and seven feet tall. As Director Leon Panetta put it, "He's somewhere between Danny DeVito and Arnold Schwarzenegger."

In November, we obtained additional critical information that Abu Ahmed was still working with his former colleagues. To CIA, me, and others on the hunt, that meant Bin Ladin.[13] It was a very strong if still circumstantial case. No direct intelligence tied Bin Ladin to AC1, but every indicator suggested that he was likely there. CTC's analysts had done an extraordinary job. Admiral Bill McRaven, who would command the operation that killed Bin Ladin, would later call it the greatest intelligence operation in U.S. history. During our covert action program to drive the Soviets out of Afghanistan in the 1980s, CIA's analysts had played an important but not a central role. During our campaigns against core al-Qa'ida and its affiliates and our operation to find, fix, and finish Usama Bin Ladin, they were absolutely central. There would be no operations without them.

Panetta pressed CTC hard for additional intelligence. The director was driving CTC crazy.[14] The Counterterrorism Center's Pakistan-Afghanistan Department was tasked to come up with a list of options for additional intelligence collection. No idea, no matter how seemingly outlandish, was to be ruled out in the quest to collect intelligence to confirm the identities of those at AC1. CTC produced a list of thirty-eight options, many of them indeed crazy. Some carried a high risk of tipping our hand. They ranged from throwing a stink bomb in the compound and photographing the occupants as they exited, to broadcasting over a loudspeaker that Allah wanted the occupants to leave. If CTC could get everyone out of the compound, they perhaps could get a listening device inside.[15] Other ideas involved tapping into the sewage pipes to conduct DNA testing on the outflow, or placing surveillance cameras in the few trees surrounding the compound. Abu Ahmed and his brother must have had the same idea as CTC; they were soon seen outside the compound chopping down the trees.[16] Most of these ideas for additional collection unfortunately came to naught. A few paid off, however.

FINISH OPTIONS

After Morell's briefing, the UBL operation became nearly all consuming for me. I received constant updates from CIA between October and December. During the summer of 2009, Director Panetta had placed two senior CIA officers in charge of the hunt for UBL. Once CIA believed it had found him in Abbottabad, the two were in charge of generating further intelligence. "Gary" (not his true name) was the chief of CTC's Pakistan-Afghanistan Department. He was a career NE operations officer, and a very talented and aggressive one. "Sam" (again, not his true name) was CIA's chief al-Qa'ida analyst. Sam had encyclopedic knowledge of al-Qa'ida and great operational judgment as well.[17] We had worked together on al-Qa'ida for years (and, subsequently, on several other issues as well), and both became good friends.

In late December, Morell asked me to come to CIA to begin developing "finish" options—how we would capture or kill UBL. During a short break for Christmas, I couldn't wait to get back to work. All I could think about was how we would finish off the man responsible for 9/11. It was hard keeping my secret focus hidden from my family, but I had to and I did. Through the first few weeks of the New Year, I worked with operators from CTC and SAD, CIA's Special Activities Division (today, the Special Activities Center), on finish options. Our small planning group came up with five initial options: three unilateral and two bilateral with the Pakistanis. We analyzed the strengths and weaknesses of each. Our first option was an air strike using B-2 stealth bombers. The air strike would flatten the compound, but would also cause a lot of collateral damage, killing the nearly twenty women and children inside and some neighbors as well. We also wouldn't likely know for sure if we got Bin Ladin, and wouldn't be able to collect intelligence from the site that could lead to follow-on operations. But it had the virtue of being the simplest of the five options to execute.

Our second and third options were unilateral raids that would be conducted by Bill McRaven's Special Operations Task Force. In one scenario, our special operators would fly directly to the target in helicopters. Another option would have our special operators clandestinely infiltrating into Pakistan over time, assembling, and then driving to the target area. The helicopter option was the least complicated, but things could still go wrong. All of us remembered the failed operation to rescue American hostages held in Iran in 1980 and the "Black Hawk Down" incident in Somalia in 1993. The clandestine infiltration option, however, seemed the riskiest, because the full force we needed might not make it into Pakistan.

Our fourth and fifth options were joint ones (more accurately, "combined" ones) with the Pakistanis, and they were also variants on a theme. In one, we'd tell the Pakistanis about AC1 and place a small team of CIA and SOF advisers with their top special operations unit to plan a deliberate assault. A second option was to notify the Pakistanis just a few hours before the operation and have them provide the security force while U.S. forces conducted the raid. Both carried the risk that the Pakistanis would balk or, worse, tip off the occupants of AC1. Given all the strange behavior at AC1 and how close it was to some of Pakistan's most sensitive sites, how could ISI not know who was living there?[18]

Our five options, not surprisingly, reflected the range of experience I had acquired across my career, from special operations raids and CIA paramilitary operations to B-2 bomber strikes and working with the Pakistanis. We presented the options to Director Panetta and Morell. They liked what they saw. Morell told me it was time to bring in Admiral McRaven for a briefing at CIA. Michael added that President Obama had asked Director Panetta on January 24 to bring the military into the discussion.[19]

McRaven had been in command of the Joint Special Operations Command for nearly three years by then. He was an inspirational leader and a great special operator, and I had tremendous confidence in him. He was also a thinker, having written a book on special operations theory while a student at the Naval Postgraduate School. Just before he assumed command of JSOC in 2008, I had taken him aside and filled him in on our plan to defeat core al-Qa'ida and its safe haven providers in the Afghanistan-Pakistan border region. I told him he was the perfect man for the job. Bill and I had worked closely together on a range of operations between 2008 and 2011, the raid line of operations in Pakistan, a cross-border raid into Syria, raids and hostage rescues in Somalia, and countless operations in Afghanistan.

I called Bill in Afghanistan in late January and told him that we needed him to come to CIA to be briefed on some extremely compartmented intelligence we had acquired. When he arrived in Washington, I explained to Bill in general terms why we had asked him to fly here on such short notice and how closely the intelligence was being held. We went to CIA together in early February.

Morell, "Sam," and "Gary" briefed Bill on the intelligence on AC1. Bill was very impressed, to say the least. "Great work," he told Morell. Bill told the analysts that the depth and detail of the intelligence on AC1 was unlike anything he had seen before. When Director Panetta asked him after the briefing if his Special Operations Task Force could successfully raid AC1, Bill said he thought so, but would need to study the problem further before giving a firm answer. Bill and I had a similar discussion with Secretary Gates and Admiral Mullen after we returned to the Pentagon that afternoon.[20]

The operation to bring justice to Usama Bin Ladin would consume nearly all of my time for the next three months. It was a period unlike any other in my life.

15

NEPTUNE'S SPEAR

"WE'RE GOING TO DO IT"

Our meeting with President Obama on March 14, 2011, is one I'll never forget, the first of five we'd have with the president on the Usama Bin Ladin operation. We briefed him on the intelligence case that led us to believe we had found Usama Bin Ladin at Abbottabad Compound 1 and the five finish options we had developed. The president listened to the briefs, which took the better part of an hour, and then said, "If we do this operation, we're going to do it without Pakistan, and we're going to do it sooner rather than later."[1] I couldn't believe what I had just heard: we were very likely going to bring justice to Usama Bin Ladin. I had gone to the meeting expecting the president not to show his cards at that point. But he did. "We're actually going to do it," I said to myself. It was electrifying.

INITIAL OPERATIONAL PLANNING AND WHITE HOUSE MEETINGS

Extremely restricted small groups of NSC deputies and principals began meeting on the Bin Ladin operation in mid-February and continued through the weekend of May 1. We had five NSC meetings with President Obama: the one on March 14, one in late March, one in mid-April, and two in late April. I attended all of them—the small group deputies and principals meetings, and the meetings with the president.

Tom Donilon chaired the principals meetings, and John Brennan chaired the deputies. The main items of the agenda were the strength of the intelligence that Bin Ladin was at AC1, the finish options we had developed, and the implications for U.S.-Pakistan relations if we conducted a unilateral operation. Options and recommendations were thoroughly vetted by deputies before going to principals, and by principals before going to the president.[2]

The security was extraordinary: on the official White House calendar they were listed as "Mickey Mouse" meetings. Each time we met, the security cameras in the White House Situation Room were turned off.[3] As one of only four DOD personnel read in initially, I just told my staff that I had to attend meetings at the White House and did not require any prep materials. They knew not to ask questions.

In late February, we asked Bill McRaven to come back to CIA to discuss finish options. The National Geospatial-Intelligence Agency had built a model of the compound, which was laid out on the table before Bill. We would use the model at several White House briefings as well. CIA also had had the foresight to construct a full-sized mock-up of AC1 at one of CIA's clandestine facilities in the United States. When "Gary" and the SAD officers asked me in early January what I thought about the idea and the expenditure of funds, I said, "Great idea, let's do it." With the quick approval of CIA's leadership, they did. Bill was impressed.

We reviewed the five options, with a particular focus on options two and three, the unilateral special operations raids. A key question was could our helicopters fly to AC1 without being detected or, worse, shot down by Pakistan's air defenses? For that, Bill said we needed to do some detailed air planning. Bill asked if he could assign two of his senior air planners to our small operational planning group. Morell approved that on the spot. Bill also asked if one of his best planners, a SEAL captain, could join our planning group. Morell said "yes, of course" to that, too.[4] Those three, plus Bill, would be all that would be read into the operation from the Special Operations Task Force for several more weeks.

CTC and SAD had added a unilateral, CIA-only "snatch and grab" option that would be conducted by a small team of agency paramilitary operations officers. Having chased UBL for a decade and found him at AC1, they wanted to be the ones to bring justice to Bin Ladin. Director Panetta, Michael Morell, and John Bennett, CIA's deputy director for operations, however, thought this was beyond SAD's capabilities. SAD's Ground Branch officers usually operated with partner forces, not as a unit by themselves. CIA's leadership was adamant that if the president decided to approve a raid, McRaven's task force should be the force to carry it out. Some senior operations officers within CTC wanted the operation to be conducted bilaterally with the Pakistanis. The president would rule out that option.

Bill was asked to attend a Deputies Committee meeting in preparation for our first (mid-March) meeting with the president. Bill offered his preliminary views on how the task force might conduct a raid on AC1. In Bill's eyes, even though AC1 was located very deep in Pakistani territory, it was just another compound. The task force raided compounds like AC1 every night in Afghanistan. The biggest challenge was how to get the assault force to AC1 without being detected. Bill had initially considered inserting the assault force via a free-fall parachute jump and approaching the target on foot. I told him I thought it was too risky. The aircraft at that altitude would be seen on radar by the Pakistanis, and additional things could go wrong after the jumpers landed. His planners agreed with me, and Bill dropped the free-fall option.

The gradual, clandestine infiltration option also seemed too risky. A "Trojan horse" commercial truck filled with armed operators might get stopped and discovered en route. The Pakistanis had recently been denying visas to special operators assisting the Pakistan Army and any individuals they knew or suspected of being CIA officers. Clandestine infiltration by visa could take too long to execute. That option, too, got dropped, leaving a helicopter insertion as our sole remaining unilateral raid option. It was our most certain means of achieving the "relative superiority," to borrow a concept from Bill's book, that was essential for mission success. Sometimes the simplest option is also the best option.[5]

Based on our experience in Afghanistan, we knew that our helicopters would likely be heard a couple of minutes out from the target. Our preference was usually to land several kilometers from the target and patrol to it, a technique called "offset infil." That didn't seem like a good approach for AC1, however. As we looked at the target, we became convinced that we could still achieve tactical surprise with a direct "on the X" approach without incurring unacceptable risk to our force.

Bill had initially favored using MH-47s for the insertion. The MH-47 is SOCOM's long-range, heavy helicopter, but it is big and noisy and has a large radar cross section. I was concerned that MH-47s would be at high risk of being detected well before they got to the target, and reminded Bill of some experimental, specially configured helicopters we had. They could very likely get to the target undetected.[6] The main question was whether they had the lift capacity to carry the number of special operators we would need for the mission from the Afghanistan border to AC1 in Abbottabad—a distance of 162 miles.

Three years earlier, I had persuaded SOCOM's leadership not to kill the experimental helicopter program, and I'd maintained a special interest in it. I didn't have the Bin Ladin operation in mind at the time, of course, but thought there were plenty of scenarios where we might need to infiltrate a SOF team into a denied area without being detected. Bill became convinced that the specially configured helicopters could carry the requisite number of troops and fly unrefueled to AC1 from the Afghan border. They could also get there undetected.

Over the next two months, I worked very closely with Bill and his team to further develop and refine the raid concept of operations. After the operation, Bill would say that my ability to explain the operational concept to the deputies and principals and convey why I had high confidence in it had been critical in obtaining the president's and NSC principals' approval. Morell would say that my skill at explaining the intelligence case to DOD's leaders had also been vital. As usual, I was straddling both the intelligence and the special operations worlds. Months later, Morell would also comment that I was the only one in the NSC's deputies and principals meetings who really understood both the intelligence and the special operations parts of the Bin Ladin operation.[7] I don't know if either of those statements was true, but I felt as if I were made for this moment. The only other times I'd felt that way were when I was developing and implementing our strategies to drive the Soviets out of Afghanistan and to disrupt, dismantle, and defeat core al-Qa'ida in the Afghanistan-Pakistan border region.

———

Initially, the president and most of the principals had favored the B-2 bomber option, because it was the least risky from an operational point of view.[8] At the March 14 NSC meeting, the president told us to bring him a detailed concept of operation for the B-2 strike option in two weeks. General Cartwright read in one action officer on the Joint Staff to facilitate air planning, an Army major known by his nickname, Scotty, and he became my action officer for the B-2 strike option. We tasked a couple of planners from the 509th Bomb Wing at Whiteman Air Force Base in Missouri to develop a strike package. The planners came back with a strike package involving three B-2s, one for backup and two for the mission. Each bomber would drop sixteen two-thousand-pound bombs, a total of sixty-four thousand pounds of ordnance. Everyone in AC1 would be killed, as would neighbors who lived close by. Others farther away would have their windows shattered from the explosions. The rationale for using so much ordnance stemmed from uncertainty whether AC1 had a tunnel network constructed underneath it to facilitate UBL's escape if necessary. When the plan was presented to the president and NSC principals in late March, the B-2 option was dropped.[9]

At our March 14 meeting, the president also told us to continue to develop the raid option. At that meeting, Bill showed photos of the specially configured helicopters whose use he was now seriously contemplating. He told the president that it was certainly possible these special helicopters could fly to the target undetected but he wasn't certain about their carrying capacity. He explained that he would need at least twenty men, probably a few more, to carry out the mission at an acceptable risk. He pointed out that a lot of factors go into determining the lift capacity of a helicopter, ranging from fuel, temperature, altitude, and time on target. A small change in temperature or time on target could have significant effects, requiring a forward refueling, which would add to the mission's risk. Bill promised to come back with answers on March 29.

At the March 29 meeting, Bill briefed his more fleshed-out concept for a special operations raid, which he had gone over with me before the meeting. The assault force would move, when directed, from the United States to Afghanistan, its launch point for the raid. The force would consist of twenty-four SEAL operators, a CIA officer, two specially modified Black Hawk helicopters, and a military working dog.

Operators from the first helo would fast-rope into the center of the compound (sliding down their thick ropes like firemen), clear the guest quarters, breach the bottom door of the main house, and clear from the ground floor up. The second helo would lift one element onto the roof of the living quarters so they could get to UBL, who was believed to be living on the top floor, as soon as possible and then, after he had been taken out, would clear the structure from the top down. The second helo would also drop off a security element outside the compound to prevent anyone from escaping and provide early warning and security for the assault force against anyone who might approach the compound. Bill added that it was about ninety minutes of flight time to and from the target. He planned to have his force on the ground at AC1 for no more than thirty minutes.

The president asked, "Can you do the mission, Bill?" Bill replied, "Sir, I don't know yet. Before I can tell you with any assurance, I need to identify the assault force, do more planning and conduct several rehearsals." "How much time do you need?" the president asked. "Sir, three weeks," McRaven replied. "Okay," the president said, "get back to me in three weeks."[10]

After the B-2 option was taken off the table, General Cartwright proposed a new air option: striking the Pacer with a small precision-guided bomb dropped from an unmanned aircraft.[11] It was more surgical, but had a low probability of success. The odds of killing UBL with this particular unmanned aerial vehicle and weapon were not great, and we had no precedent for this kind of operation. The warhead was very small, and if the munition missed by just a bit, UBL would likely survive. The munition's aim point would depend on where we thought UBL would be when the munition hit. It was GPS guided and thus less accurate. (Laser-guided weapons are more accurate, because the weapon can be guided all the way to the target, provided there aren't any obstructions that block the laser.) If we missed, or only injured UBL, he would almost certainly leave the compound, and we would likely lose the best chance we had in nearly ten years to bring justice to him. Plus, for a variety of reasons, we might not have the aircraft overhead when the Pacer went outside for exercise, which happened infrequently and irregularly as far as we knew. Even if successful, moreover, we wouldn't be able to confirm that we had killed UBL.

I had been open to the B-2 strike initially, particularly if the raid option was rejected as too risky. But now I was completely in the raid camp. CIA was also vehemently opposed to Cartwright's drone strike plan.[12]

ASSAULT FORCE SELECTION AND MISSION REHEARSALS

As Bill's air and ground planners were refining their operational concept for the raid, CIA's experts briefed them on Pakistani air defenses and radars. NGA's imagery analysts answered questions about the heights and thickness of the walls and outdoor lighting, critical information an assault force needs to know. CTC's analysts briefed on the number, gender, age, and identity of the people living at AC1 and where they were likely to be found inside the compound. CTC's analysts turned out to be 100 percent right on this, a remarkable piece of intelligence work. Other CIA analysts provided briefings on the location, capabilities, and likely reaction time of Pakistani police and military forces in the area. It was outstanding work by our intelligence professionals.

It was now time to select and assemble the assault force. Bill told me he had two candidates he was considering to be the ground force commander for the raid. I knew and thought very highly of both. One was an Army special operator, the other a SEAL. For a variety of reasons, Bill thought the SEAL was the better choice, and I agreed. Both were outstanding special operators and leaders, but the SEAL had more experience in the Pakistan-Afghanistan theater.

The assault force was made up of senior enlisted SEALs, all with extensive combat experience and handpicked by the SEAL ground force commander. The aviation crews were similarly experienced and handpicked. They were asked to come to a secret facility in North Carolina during the first week of April without being told what they were being summoned for. The operators initially thought they were headed to Libya for a counter-proliferation mission to recover weapons of mass destruction. The United States and NATO had gone to war in Libya a few weeks earlier after Qaddafi had moved to massacre protesters who had risen up in eastern Libya in response to the Arab Spring.

After signing nondisclosure agreements, the operators were told by a senior CIA analyst in the facility's conference room that we believed we had found Usama Bin Ladin. As soon as UBL's name was mentioned, there was silence in the room. After the briefing was over, Bill stood up and told his assault force, "Gentlemen, the President has asked us to develop a raid option to capture or kill Bin Ladin. We have a little more than two weeks to test and rehearse the plan and determine if it's executable. The CIA has built a mock-up of the compound just a mile from this conference room. You have two days to work through the movements on target. After that, we will move to another location out west to do full dress rehearsals of the entire mission profile."[13]

I had flown down in a CIA plane for the briefing and rehearsals, along with Admiral Olson and several senior CIA officers. We watched as the SEALs did a dozen or so ground movements and the helicopter pilots flew multiple approaches on the compound. Bill and the SEAL assault force commented that the agency had done a masterful job in constructing the mock-up. Every key observable feature of AC_1 had been accounted for. Owing to the short amount of time CIA had to construct the simulated compound, which was made up of stacked shipping containers and fabricated wooden stairs and surrounded by a chain-link fence, we couldn't replicate the thick concrete walls that protected AC_1. We also didn't know what the inside living quarters looked like and how the rooms were laid out.

The full-dress rehearsals were conducted at an Air Force base in a remote area out west. While our earlier rehearsals had focused on actions on the objective, the rehearsals out west would run through the full mission profile of the operation. Bill tested how he would command and control the operation from the mission launch and recovery site in Afghanistan. His staff developed plans for every contingency they could think of—what if the force was detected en route, a helicopter had mechanical problems, UBL was not there, and so on. The pilots of the special helicopters flew a number of practice missions against radars that simulated what we would find in Pakistan, and the results were encouraging: the helicopters could likely get to the target undetected. The SEALs rehearsed their ground tactical plan on another mock-up that had been rapidly constructed to simulate AC1 to the greatest extent possible.

While out west, Bill learned from his 160th Special Operations Aviation Regiment commander, Colonel J. T. Thompson, that they would need a forward air refueling point, or FARP, to refuel the specially configured helos to ensure that they could make it back to Afghanistan with fuel to spare. The need for a FARP meant that an additional helo, an MH-47, would have to fly to a remote area some distance from AC1 to pre-position a large fuel bladder where the special Black Hawks could refuel on the way home.

As the task force completed its week of full-dress rehearsals out west, I joined Admiral Mullen on his plane, accompanied by Admiral Olson and several senior CIA officers, to watch the final rehearsal. Admiral Mullen asked how much time the assault force would have on target before Pakistani security forces arrived. About thirty minutes, a SEAL master chief answered.

"Our biggest concern," the SEAL explained, "is the locals who will hear the helicopters, and come over to see what's going on." He pointed to the CIA officer, a Pakistani American fluent in Urdu and Dari, and said that if that occurred, "he would tell the crowd that this was a Pakistani military exercise and to go back to their homes."[14] I looked at the officer and thought, I hope he's persuasive.

I spent time on my own talking with the SEAL operators to make sure they felt ready. They did. After the rehearsal, we flew directly back to Washington, arriving early the next morning. We had been gone about fourteen hours.

REFINING THE PLAN

During one of our principals meetings in preparation for our next meeting with the president on April 19, Tom Donilon asked me to stay after. Tom told me that, given my background, "the president is really going to want to know your views on the raid." I just said, "Sure, sir, no problem," but he repeated it again, so I thought I'd better say a bit more. Tom is famous for his great attention to detail and his ability to keep at things until he's satisfied with the answer. I told him I was confident that we could do this, "very confident," and I would be happy to tell the president that. Over the previous two and a half years, Tom had come to value my opinion on operational matters, ranging from covert action to special operations. He told me at first that he had been skeptical of me as a Bush administration "holdover," but he had changed his mind after he had seen what I could contribute to President Obama's national security team.

On April 19, Bill presented his plan to the president and told him the mission was executable. "What happens if the Pakistanis surround the compound while the SEALs are still inside?" the president asked. Bill answered that we didn't want to get into a firefight with the Pakistanis. The president understood, but then told Bill to come up with a plan to "fight your way out."

Secretary Gates added that, given the high level of anti-Americanism in Pakistan, it could take months to get our force released if it were detained by the Pakistanis. He said he also was concerned that ISI was aware that UBL was located at AC1 and that there might be rings of security around the compound that we didn't know about. He reminded the president about the cross-border raid we had conducted in September 2008. It was supposed to be a quick and clean in and out, but it had turned into a serious firefight. The Pakistani reaction had been so hostile that we had not undertaken another mission like that since. Gates told the president that perhaps his experience dating back to the failed Iranian rescue mission had made him too cautious.[15]

Bill promptly added a powerful quick reaction force. The QRF would fly in on two MH-47s and laager only a few minutes away from AC1.[16] The addition of the QRF would triple the size of the force, with roughly one-third going on the target and two-thirds being held in reserve. As an extra precaution, Bill also added a "Gorilla Package" of fighters and radar-jamming aircraft in Afghanistan to deal with any Pakistani air threat that might arise.[17]

At the end of the meeting, the president approved the movement of the force forward to Afghanistan while making it clear that he had not decided to go ahead with the mission yet.[18] It was another big step along the way to mission approval and execution. Bill's deputy, Tony Thomas, traveled with the assault force to make sure everything was ready to go. Bill would follow shortly.

Who would have authority for conducting the raid, if approved, was never really in question. We debated for a bit the pros and cons of Title 10, DOD's authority, which would allow us to bring back detainees, and Title 50, CIA's authority, which would provide greater deniability if, for example, UBL wasn't there but our force made it in and out without incident. Deputies, principals, and the president all concluded that conducting the raid under CIA's authorities was the best option. That meant that DOD would "detail" its forces to CIA for the mission, a process that I oversaw. Bill would report to Director Panetta and Panetta to the president.[19]

In late April, I read in DOD's general counsel, Jeh Johnson, so he could review the paperwork "Scotty" had prepared for me detailing the force to CIA. As Jeh entered my office and I closed the door, I told him, "I am about to brief you on the biggest secret in Washington."[20] I gave Jeh a briefing about the intelligence and the two finish options—the raid and the drone strike—that the president might approve. I then reviewed the forces that would be detailed to CIA and asked him to sign the paperwork. He was the only person other than Scotty and Secretary Gates within DOD to see it. Jeh also worked with CIA and White House lawyers on the legal aspects of the raid.

ASSESSING PROBABILITIES

Well into late April, the intelligence about and possible operation against AC1 remained highly compartmented. Secretary Clinton wasn't read in until March. Mike Leiter, the director of the National Counterterrorism Center, was told about it only two weeks before the raid. The attorney general, FBI director, and secretary of homeland security learned about it a day or two before the operation, as did the president's strategic communications adviser, Ben Rhodes.[21] General Jim Mattis, our CENTCOM commander, and General Dave Petraeus, our commander in Afghanistan, were fully read in when McRaven deployed forward.[22]

During the multiple meetings of the small group of NSC deputies and principals in March and April, we debated the strength of the intelligence case and whether and how to strike AC1. Vice President Biden and Secretary Gates were the primary skeptics. Gates was worried that the Pakistanis could shut down our supply lines to Afghanistan that ran through or overflew Pakistani territory. Some 50 percent of the fuel and 55 percent of our cargo came via this route, with the remainder transiting Russia and central Asia. Gates was also concerned that the intelligence case was circumstantial and that we didn't have a single piece of hard evidence that UBL was at AC1. CTC's top al-Qa'ida analyst said he was 80 percent confident that UBL was there, but Gates knew these estimates were based on little more than gut instinct.

While Gates would eventually support the raid, the vice president would remain opposed. I never really understood why. In March and December 2009 he had opposed both of President Obama's surges of forces in Afghanistan, and in March 2011 he had opposed U.S. military intervention in Libya. Perhaps his earlier support, as Senate Foreign Relations Committee chairman, for the U.S. invasion of Iraq had soured him on the use of force. In any event, I'll have more to say about Vice President Biden's (now, of course, President Biden) views on Afghanistan in the next chapter.

After Mike Leiter had been read in, he proposed that the National Counterterrorism Center conduct a "Red Team" assessment of the intelligence. Leiter briefed the president and the rest of us on his team's conclusions in late April. One of his analysts thought there was a 60 percent chance Bin Ladin was at AC1, two assessed it at 50 percent, and a fourth at 40 percent. NCTC's assessment had largely been overcome by events, however, and discussion of it lasted for only one White House meeting. CIA's lead analyst on the hunt for UBL said she was 95 percent certain that UBL was there. "Sam," CIA's chief al-Qa'ida analyst, put it at 80 percent. The two of them had the most expertise with the target, and I trusted their judgment the most.

During one deputies meeting when we were again reviewing the intelligence case, we were asked for our individual assessments of the probability that UBL was there. I put it at 80 to 85 percent. At a subsequent meeting, the president asked Morell why intelligence analysts were seemingly "all over the place" on the likelihood that UBL was at AC1. Morell told the president that one's experience influenced one's judgment. Our CTC analysts, who were immersed in our very successful operations against al-Qa'ida, would justifiably have higher confidence, around 80 percent. Morell said his views had been shaped by the Iraq WMD experience, and therefore he was only at 60 percent. Then he added that the intelligence case for Iraq WMD had been stronger than the AC1 case.

For a few seconds, you could have heard a pin drop in the White House Situation Room. I thought, Oh, crap. Fortunately, the president followed up by asking Michael if he would still do the raid even though he assessed the chance that UBL was there at only 60 percent. Morell said yes, he would definitely go forward with the raid.[23] He added that if we had a human source who told us that Bin Ladin was there, he still wouldn't be 100 percent certain. Human sources are sometimes wrong.

A few hours earlier, in a meeting at CIA, a very senior officer in the Directorate of Operations told Director Panetta that he was also at 60 percent but had come to a different conclusion. He recommended against going forward with the raid until we had confirmation that Bin Ladin was there. He proposed a last-ditch collection operation to try to get confirmation of UBL's presence. Unfortunately, it didn't work.[24]

DECIDING TO GO

We had a few loose ends to tie up before the final NSC meeting with the president on April 28. One concerned how to bury UBL. A number of options were considered before all were rejected save one. We assessed that the Saudis would not want his body returned to the kingdom. Any burial on land, moreover, risked that the site would be discovered and become an inspiration for jihadists. Burial at sea became the best option. We developed a plan to fly UBL's body from Afghanistan out to our aircraft carrier in the Arabian Sea, the USS *Carl Vinson*, conduct last rites according to Islamic tradition, and commit his body to the sea.

The meeting on April 28 was a decision meeting, though the president would defer his decision until the next morning. Each principal was asked for his or her recommendation. Choice one was to go ahead with the raid in the next few days while we had zero illumination, the perfect condition for a raid, and before it would get too hot in Pakistan, affecting the lift capacity and range of the specially configured helicopters. Choice two was to recommend a drone strike, which would mean waiting until we had a targeting opportunity against the Pacer. Choice three was to do nothing until we had direct intelligence that confirmed that UBL was there.

The deputies had been strongly in favor of the raid, with Michèle Flournoy, Michael Morell, Bill Burns, the deputy secretary of state, and me all voting in favor. Only General Cartwright was opposed, advocating instead for the drone option. Denis McDonough and John Brennan didn't vote, although we knew they were both in favor of the raid.

At the NSC meeting with the president, Director Panetta, Secretary Clinton, Admiral Mullen, and Director Clapper all voted in favor of the raid. Panetta gave a powerful speech in which he said, "If the average American knew what we knew, he'd say go. That's what we should do, too."

Secretary Gates supported the drone option. Cartwright, who had already expressed his strong support for the drone option at the deputies meeting, was asked by the president to provide it again at the NSC meeting. Vice President Biden strongly argued that we should wait for better intelligence. Tom Donilon didn't vote, although we knew that he, too, favored the raid. The president thanked everyone and said he would decide in the morning after sleeping on it.

Early the next morning I called Michèle Flournoy and told her that we needed to see Secretary Gates and persuade him to change his mind and support the raid. We got in to see him right away, and he listened attentively as we made our case. I began by telling him that after I got home that evening, I pulled out his memoir from his CIA days and noted how important he felt it was to tell one's boss privately when you think he or she is wrong. Gates had been the executive assistant to former DCI Stansfield Turner and CIA's deputy director under Bill Casey. I told him that's what we had come here to do. I said that my confidence in the intelligence was high, even though there was no direct evidence confirming that UBL was there. I told him that I had very high confidence that we could successfully conduct the raid. Michèle made similar points. Gates thanked us and said he'd think about what we had to say. Less than an hour later, his chief of staff, Robert Rangel, called me and said that the secretary had changed his mind and had called Tom Donilon to tell him he supported the raid.[25] My admiration for Gates, already sky-high, went up even further.

President Obama approved the raid that morning. Tom Donilon passed the information to Director Panetta, who in turn passed the information to Admiral McRaven. The raid was set for Saturday night, April 30.[26] The president could easily have gone with one of the air strike options or elected to conduct a joint operation with the Pakistanis. He could also have decided to wait until we had intelligence that confirmed UBL was at AC1. But he had chosen none of these. He had taken the harder path, and it was a gutsy decision, just as President Reagan's had been in March 1985 to dramatically expand our covert war aims in Afghanistan, and as President Bush's had been to dramatically expand our ways and means to disrupt and defeat core al-Qa'ida in the Afghanistan-Pakistan border region in August 2008. I was proud to serve under him.

THE RAID AND ITS AFTERMATH

Upon arrival at his headquarters at Bagram Air Base, Bill was advised that there was some low-lying fog along our planned infiltration route on Saturday. Nothing that would present a major problem for the helos, but there was no need to take a chance. The weather forecast looked great for Sunday, so Bill postponed the mission one day. It was now set for Sunday, May 1.[27]

Bill then flew to our base in Jalalabad, which would serve as the launch and recovery site for the operation and Bill's mission headquarters. With Bill in the small Joint Operations Center on the SEAL compound were Captain Pete Van Hooser, the SEAL Team commander, who would oversee the tactical execution of the mission, and Colonel J. T. Thompson, who would oversee the helo portion.[28] CIA officers were there as well, including the lead analyst on the hunt for UBL and the chief of station, "Chris."[29]

I was at the White House all day on Saturday for final deputies and principals meetings to review our plans for the immediate period after the mission. That morning, *The Washington Post* had run a front-page story on me, so I received considerable teasing from my colleagues, including Bill Daley, the president's chief of staff.[30] Michael Morell was particularly cutting, saying, "There I am having a nice, early breakfast with my wife and kids before coming in here and what does my wife put in front of me, a picture and front-page article on you. So of course she asks me, 'How come they're not writing about *you?*'"

That evening, the president and a number of senior Obama administration officials, me included, were scheduled to attend the annual White House Correspondents' Dinner. No one wanted to go, given what was about to transpire, but it would look odd if we canceled at the last minute, so we went. Morell and I were the guests of Reuters; Director Panetta sat at *Time's* table.

A number of celebrities, including Donald Trump, were there. President Obama used the occasion to trumpet the release of his birth certificate and to witheringly mock Trump, who had waged a shameful campaign that questioned whether the president had been born in America. Everyone laughed except Trump. I don't think there was a person in the room that evening who thought we were laughing at the expense of the next president of the United States—save one, perhaps. All I could think about, though, was the operation we were going to do the next day. I couldn't wait for the dinner to be over so I could get back to work.

Sunday morning I went into the office to reread a few papers pertaining to the raid and our post-operation plans before heading to the White House for more deputies and principals meetings. As I was leaving the building, I decided to stop at the Pentagon's 9/11 Memorial for a few moments of silent reflection. The memorial has 184 illuminated benches honoring the 184 victims who died on American Airlines Flight 77 and in the Pentagon. The benches are engraved with each victim's name and arranged in order from youngest to oldest. I sat on one of the benches and collected my thoughts. This is for you, I thought, all of you.

After our morning meetings at the White House, Director Panetta, Michael Morell, and I left for CIA headquarters, where the operation would be monitored in real time. Joining us in the director's wood-paneled conference room on the seventh floor were the senior CIA leaders who had overseen the operation. Also there were Admiral Eric Olson and Tish Long, the NGA director. General Keith Alexander, our NSA director, was on secure video teleconference from NSA headquarters at Fort Meade, Maryland. Bill was on the line from Jalalabad. One of Bill's deputies, the Air Force brigadier general Brad Webb, was in a small room across from the main White House Situation Room conference room with a secure laptop so the principals who had remained at the White House could receive updates on the operation from there.[31] General Cartwright monitored the operation from a secure room at the Pentagon.

————————

At exactly 2300 (11:00 p.m.) local time, the two specially configured Black Hawk helicopters carrying the assault force lifted off from Jalalabad. Bill reported as each phase line was crossed on the ninety-minute flight to Abbottabad, and Pakistani air defenses did not detect the infiltration. Trailing thirty minutes behind due to their much higher radar signature were the two MH-47s, carrying the QRF and the fuel bladder that would be needed at the FARP.[32] Bill selected the code name for the mission, Operation Neptune's Spear, in honor of the SEALs who would be conducting it.

As the pilot of the first helo maneuvered into fast-rope position between the three-story living quarters and the eighteen-foot-high wall that bordered the southern fence line, the helicopter wobbled and pitched upward. The pilot was struggling to maintain lift due to the higher-than-expected temperature and a vortex that had been created between the walls and the main structure. The plan to fast-rope into the courtyard between the main residence and the small guesthouse was quickly aborted, and the pilot forced the helo's nose down and landed it into the open animal pen. It was a hard landing. There were gasps, particularly among the principals watching the operation on Webb's small laptop in the White House Situation Room.

I thought for a moment that the helo had taken fire. We had snipers and door gunners positioned on the right side of the aircraft for just this contingency. It also flashed through my mind that maybe Secretary Gates had been right after all in warning about the things that could go wrong in a helicopter raid. I was relieved when I saw the SEALs exit the damaged aircraft and proceed to the inner compound, executing an alternate plan we had rehearsed.

Bill was cool as a cucumber. He informed Director Panetta, "Sir, as you can see, we have a helo down. The SEALs are continuing on with the mission. I will keep you posted."

There was also a quick change of plans made on the spot by the

Operation Neptune's Spear

1. Two specially configured Black Hawk helicopters fly the SEAL assault force from Jalalabad, Afghanistan, to Bin Ladin's compound in Abbottabad, Pakistan.

2. Two Chinook helicopters with a quick reaction force and a fuel bladder onboard fly to a forward area refueling point in Pakistan.

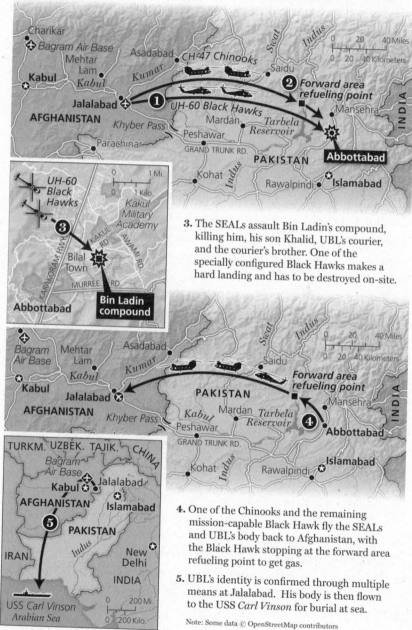

3. The SEALs assault Bin Ladin's compound, killing him, his son Khalid, UBL's courier, and the courier's brother. One of the specially configured Black Hawks makes a hard landing and has to be destroyed on-site.

4. One of the Chinooks and the remaining mission-capable Black Hawk fly the SEALs and UBL's body back to Afghanistan, with the Black Hawk stopping at the forward area refueling point to get gas.

5. UBL's identity is confirmed through multiple means at Jalalabad. His body is then flown to the USS *Carl Vinson* for burial at sea.

Note: Some data © OpenStreetMap contributors

crew and SEALs in the second helo. Instead of dropping off the security element and then inserting assaulters on the roof of the main living quarters, all SEALs, the CIA officer, and our working dog, Cairo, disembarked on the ground. McRaven and Thompson also quickly adjusted plan to use one of the MH-47s as an exfil bird. It was an amazing adaptation on the fly, one made possible by the extensive planning we had done and the combat experience of the operators.

I thought, Okay, all that's left is to find UBL and shoot him. Let's hope he's there. Flowing in two directions, the first SEAL element approached the guesthouse, and a small burst of gunfire lit up the screen. Moments later, the SEALs reported, "One EKIA" (enemy killed in action). At the same time, multiple explosions flashed as the other SEAL element blew down the hardened steel doors protecting the outer and inner cordons of Bin Ladin's home. We couldn't see what was going on inside the main building after the SEALs entered, but we quickly received audio reports of two more EKIA, one on the first floor and one on the stairwell leading to the second floor. Both brothers, Ibrahim and Abrar, were now dead, along with UBL's son Khalid.

CIA's lead analyst had told the SEALs before they took off from Jalalabad that if they found Khalid, UBL's twenty-three-year-old son, "Usama's on the next floor." She nailed it. The SEAL point man had tricked Khalid into poking his head out by saying in Arabic and Urdu, "Khalid, come here." It was the last sound Khalid heard.[33]

A two-man element of SEALs had nearly reached the third floor of the main residence when a shadowy figure emerged. The lead SEAL fired at him, but his shots impacted high. The two SEALs stormed up the stairs and into the room. Two young girls stood at the entrance. Nearly certain that the girls were wearing suicide vests, the lead SEAL threw himself on the young women, shielding his partner from the blast. It was an incredibly heroic action. The second SEAL, Senior Chief Petty Officer Rob O'Neill, entered the room and came face-to-face with UBL, who had grabbed one of his wives and appeared to be using her to partially shield his body. O'Neill fired two rounds at him, aiming over the woman's shoulder. Both struck UBL in the head. As UBL crumpled to the ground, O'Neill fired one more shot into UBL's head for good measure. UBL was dead before he hit the ground.[34] There was an AK-47 and a Makarov pistol nearby, but al-Qa'ida's leader hadn't been able to reach them in time. He had been found and killed within ten minutes of the assault force arriving at AC1.

UBL, Khalid, Ibrahim, and Abrar had all been killed. Abrar's wife, Bushra, had also been accidentally killed when she lunged in front of her husband. UBL's youngest wife, Amal, the woman Bin Ladin had been using to partially shield himself, had been slightly wounded in the calf by the first SEAL to reach the third floor.

An Arabic-speaking SEAL gently questioned two of UBL's young daughters, asking who the man dead on the floor was. They lied at first, but one soon admitted, "That's him, Sheikh Usama."[35]

About five minutes after O'Neill had killed UBL, Bill received the words he had been waiting for from the ground force commander: "For God and Country, Geronimo, Geronimo, Geronimo," the code word that indicated UBL was dead. He passed that on to Director Panetta and the rest of us at CIA headquarters. There were smiles all around, though we knew we still had to get the assault force safely back to Afghanistan.

As the SEALs were clearing the compound, a crowd had gathered to see what was going on. As planned, the CIA officer told them that it was a Pakistani military exercise and to return to their homes. It worked.

After killing UBL and securing the compound, the SEALs spent the remainder of time gathering as much intelligence as they could, what we call "sensitive site exploitation," or SSE. They found several computers, whose hard drives could contain information essential to follow-on missions, on the second floor. The SEALs and helo pilots were also rigging the damaged Black Hawk for destruction. Other SEALs were moving the women and children to a safe area. After thirty-eight minutes on target, the SEALs exfiled on the one remaining Black Hawk and the MH-47. UBL's body had been loaded onto the Black Hawk. A sample of his DNA was extracted and carried on the MH-47 as a backup. As they took off, the SEALs detonated the explosive charges, mostly destroying the damaged Black Hawk.

We soon received reports that the Pakistanis were trying to scramble their F-16s, so the mood at CIA and the White House Situation Room was tense until the remaining Black Hawk and the two MH-47s landed in Jalalabad. I was glad we had added the "Gorilla Package" to the mission. The FARP was about a thirty-minute flight from Abbottabad. Refueling the Black Hawk added another nineteen minutes to the return trip. By 0330 local time, all of the force had safely landed back at Jalalabad.

Bill and the CIA officers went to the airstrip to welcome the assault force home and to examine UBL's body. As they looked at the body, the two CIA officers told Bill that it was UBL. They compared a photo taken by the SEALs after UBL had been shot with another photo CIA had. The photos seemed to confirm that it was UBL. Remembering that Bin Ladin was well over six feet tall, Bill asked a tall SEAL to lie down next to UBL on the ground. UBL, whom we knew to be six feet four, was two inches taller than the six-foot-two SEAL. "It's definitely him," CIA's chief of station said.

Director Panetta, Michael Morell, and I then rushed downtown to the White House to meet with the president and the other principals. Bill told the president that while we couldn't be certain that we had killed UBL until the DNA tests were complete, all the physical features matched. Bill apologized for destroying a $60 million helicopter. The president said, "Put it on my tab." When Bill told the president how he had determined UBL's height, the president said, "Bill, let me get this straight, you can afford to blow up a $60 million helicopter, but you can't afford a tape measure." President Obama later presented a commemorative plaque to Bill with a tape measure attached to it.

Early that evening, CIA's technical experts reported that based on facial recognition measurements and analysis, they were 95 percent certain it was UBL.[36] President Obama had wanted to wait until the next day when we would have DNA confirmation to tell the nation that we had killed Bin Ladin, but events in Pakistan had forced our hand. The president's speechwriters prepared a speech, and the president addressed the American people at 11:30 p.m. eastern time.

As word was passed to the networks that the president would be addressing the nation shortly, the chyrons on CNN and other networks reported it and speculated that Qaddafi had been killed. Literally seconds after the notifications were made to key members of Congress, the chyrons changed, and they were now reporting that it was Bin Ladin who had been killed. We were now allowed to call our spouses at home, so I called Melana and told her to turn on the TV. "I can't say anything more," I told her, "just turn on the TV." I also told her that I still had work to do and wouldn't be home for several more hours.

Admiral Mullen called General Kayani in Pakistan to tell him that we had killed Bin Ladin. Kayani was somewhat taken aback by the news, particularly when Mullen told him that UBL had been living in the Abbottabad compound for more than five years. As we were meeting in the White House, Bin Ladin's body was being flown on a Marine MV-22 Osprey from Afghanistan out to the USS *Carl Vinson,* where he would receive a proper Islamic burial at sea. His body was wrapped in a white shroud, final prayers were said in Arabic, and then he was placed inside a thick black bag along with three hundred pounds of heavy chains and dropped into the sea. Our lead CIA analyst had accompanied the body out to the *Carl Vinson.* Those of us who knew her joked that she dived in after him to make sure he didn't come back up. She was not the easiest CIA officer to manage, but she is a genuine American hero.

Around 12:30 a.m., a few of us were asked to do a brief backgrounder for the press on the operation. Tom Donilon covered the presidential decision-making process, Michael Morell described the intelligence that had led us to AC1, and I provided a brief summary of the military operation, saying little more than our force had flown to Abbottabad in a helicopter, raided the compound where UBL was hiding, killed him, and returned home. There were no American casualties.

I finally left the White House a little after 2:00 a.m. to return to CIA headquarters with Director Panetta and Morell, because I had left my car there. As we walked outside the White House, we heard loud chants from college students who had gathered outside the White House grounds, "U.S.A., U.S.A., U.S.A.," and then, "CIA, CIA, CIA." I thought to myself, I bet I'll never hear that again.

———

I visited the SEALs who had conducted the mission a week after the raid. A week later, my wife, Melana, and I were invited to the British embassy for a reception with Prince (now King) Charles. The chief of staff of the Air Force and my good friend General Norty Schwartz told the prince that I had played a major role in the operation to kill Bin

Ladin. Prince Charles looked at me and then at Melana and said to her, "And you, my dear, didn't know a damned thing about it." Melana and I both laughed at the true but awkward royal humor. In July, I presided with General Petraeus, CIA's new director, and Admiral McRaven at an awards ceremony in the CIA auditorium for the CIA officers who had participated in the operation.

After UBL's death and the intense counterterrorism campaign we had conducted since 2008, core al-Qa'ida was now closer to strategic defeat than ever. Our war with al-Qa'ida was far from over, however. In the aftermath of the raid, I worked with CTC's officers on plans to "finish" core al-Qa'ida. We had brought the group close to operational defeat but had not yet ensured its strategic defeat—defeating its ideology, preventing its reconstitution, and dismantling and defeating all of its affiliates.

Our intelligence community would exploit and analyze the intelligence the SEALs had gathered at ACI. There was nothing actionable that enabled immediate follow-on operations, but we did learn a lot about UBL as a leader and the problems he perceived with the global jihadist movement. UBL was far more of a hands-on manager of his organization than many analysts had believed, issuing instructions regularly to his deputies, Atiyah Abd al-Rahman and Abu Yahya al-Libi, about personnel assignments, promotions, and so forth. He was frustrated by the repeated killing of Muslims by al-Qa'ida's affiliates and allies. He lectured Hakimullah Mehsud, the leader of the Pakistan Taliban, that this was un-Islamic and hurting the global jihadi cause. He exhorted Nasir al-Wahishi, the emir of AQAP, to focus on attacking the United States and not on establishing an Islamic state in Yemen. He exhorted the Taliban and other jihadi groups to continue to fight U.S. forces in Afghanistan, believing that the war was weakening the United States. He saw the Arab Spring as a strategic opportunity, the "most formidable event in the modern history of Muslims," and encouraged al-Qa'ida's media strategists to devise campaigns to incite further rebellion.[37]

The extensive experience we had accumulated in counterterrorism operations, the priority and resources given to CTC and Admiral McRaven's task force, the relentless hunt for Bin Ladin after 9/11, and some new capabilities—the drones that provided surveillance over

AC1 and the specially configured helos that flew the assault force there undetected—all greatly contributed to mission success.

On September 11, 2011, we had a ceremony at the Pentagon 9/11 Memorial to commemorate the tenth anniversary of the 9/11 attacks. President Obama and our new secretary of defense, Leon Panetta, spoke. We were seated not far from the benches honoring the 184 victims who had lost their lives in the attack.

As I listened to the president and Secretary Panetta, I looked up at the clear blue sky and saw one commercial airliner after another leaving Reagan National Airport every ten seconds or so. It was a good feeling. America had largely healed from its wound. And justice had been served.

16

AF-PAK

RETURN TO AFGHANISTAN

Our war with al-Qa'ida wasn't the only thing on my plate when I assumed my duties as assistant secretary of defense for special operations, low-intensity conflict, and interdependent capabilities in 2007. There were two big wars in Iraq and Afghanistan that also commanded my attention, so we must go back in time a bit to pick up this part of the story. The situation in Iraq was dire, and the surge of forces that President Bush had ordered to turn the war around was just getting under way. Meanwhile, the situation in Afghanistan was getting worse with each passing year. In neighboring Pakistan, a virulent insurgency posed a threat to that country's stability and, potentially, to the security of its nuclear weapons. Turning the situation around in Iraq was Secretary Gates's top priority during my first year as ASD SO/LIC&IC, but it was Afghanistan and Pakistan that received most of my attention. Not only was the insurgency growing in both countries, but the renewed threat that al-Qa'ida posed to the American homeland was emanating from Pakistan's tribal areas along the Afghan border. Our bases in Afghanistan and our relationship with Pakistan were of critical importance to the success of our operations against al-Qa'ida, and the Taliban and Pakistani militant groups were allied with and provided safe haven to al-Qa'ida, so preventing the former from returning to power and the latter from seizing power was a necessary part of our strategy.

I traveled to Afghanistan and Pakistan in August 2007 only a few weeks after being sworn in as assistant secretary to assess the deteriorating situation there and to start putting together a strategy to eliminate al-Qa'ida's FATA sanctuary. As I landed in Kabul and looked at the mountains ringing it, I thought, It's good to be home. My engagement with Afghanistan had begun almost a quarter of a century earlier, and I had a deep attachment to the place. The Afghans had known nothing but war for nearly three decades, and there was no sign that would end anytime soon. Still, I thought Afghanistan and the United States had been given a second chance to make things right, and I was hopeful that we could do so.

During my week on the ground, I met with our military commander, General Dan McNeill, our ambassador, Bill Wood, and the CIA's station chief, "Jim." I met with our special operators and traveled to CIA and SOF bases in the Afghanistan-Pakistan border region. I particularly enjoyed my meetings in Kabul Station and would be a regular there between mid-2007 and late 2014. It would soon become CIA's largest station in the world. One of the things I enjoyed most was a visit to the station's "Talibar" on the first floor. On its walls were various inscriptions by CIA officers who had served in Afghanistan and memorabilia from the war. I even got a Talibar coffee mug.

On the Afghan side, I met with two old friends who had been resistance commanders for us during the 1980s. One was now Afghanistan's defense minister, Abdul Rahim Wardak, and the other its Army chief, General Bismullah Khan Mohammadi. Wardak is a Pashtun and had been a commander for Gailani's party during the Soviet-Afghan War. Bismullah, or BK, as we called him, is a Panjshiri who served under Ahmad Shah Massoud. When Wardak and I met, he told me about the expanding insurgency and what he thought he needed to defeat it—mostly aircraft, tanks, and artillery. As a gift, I brought him a copy of *Charlie Wilson's War,* which partially chronicled our exploits during the 1980s. As he perused the book, he smiled and said in a soft voice, "Mike, you and I like being insurgents much better than we like being counterinsurgents." So true. It was also clear that the pressure of his new responsibilities was taking a toll on him.

I also made a new friend, Amrullah Saleh, a Tajik and the head of

Afghanistan's intelligence service, the National Directorate of Security, or NDS. Only thirty-five, he was whip smart and very mistrusting of Pakistan—with good reason, I might add. Saleh also had more than his share of challenges working for Afghanistan's president, Hamid Karzai, but it was Saleh who was usually right. I came to believe that NDS would be the most important security institution in Afghanistan over the long run.

I met with Admiral Bob Harward, a Navy SEAL who was one of Stan McChrystal's deputies, and Captain Scott Moore, who had taken command of one of our SEAL Teams and would later command the operation to rescue Captain Phillips in the waters off Somalia. I was briefed on the operations McChrystal's task force had been conducting in Afghanistan and its close partnership with CIA. During my visit, I also inspected some of the clandestine commercial vehicles Admiral McRaven would consider using for the Bin Ladin raid four years later. The SEALs, Rangers, Special Forces, and CIA were fighting the war almost single-handedly.

With CIA's chief of station, Jim, I traveled to Asadabad in Konar Province one night to get an up-close look at the border region. It brought back many memories of our days fighting the Soviets there. With its beautiful, rugged terrain, Konar is in some ways the Colorado of Afghanistan. It was also by far the most dangerous place for U.S. forces in the country.

A few days later, I met with Colonel Ed Reeder, the commander of the 7th Special Forces Group, one of my old units, and the Special Forces' Combined Joint Special Operations Task Force in Afghanistan. Ed is a great warrior and as hard as woodpecker lips. He would become a good friend. Ed's CJSOTF had had a fabulous six-month rotation, and Ed was one of America's best Afghan hands. He had about the best Rolodex in Afghanistan and knew everyone. He was on his third or fourth command tour there when I visited his headquarters. He would serve several more after he was promoted to general. Ed briefed me on the Afghan Commando program that he had just stood up. I also met with Ed's subordinate task force in Kandahar, which was doing most of the fighting for CJSOTF-Afghanistan.

I came back very impressed with what our intelligence professionals and special operators were doing, but worried about the deteriorating security environment. I reported my findings to Secretary

Gates. The security environment would get much worse in 2008. Our "good war" was about to turn bad.[1]

HOW THE GOOD WAR TURNED BAD

I had metaphorically "returned" to Afghanistan. The Taliban had returned for real and in force. The first to recover were the Haqqanis in Miram Shah, their former base of support during the Soviet-Afghan War. Known as the Haqqani Shabaka (Haqqani Network), the group was immediately embraced by the Pakistanis and began operations against the U.S. and Western presence in Afghanistan in 2002. The Haqqanis were supplemented by al-Qa'ida commanders and fighters, Pakistani militants, and other volunteers, but initially they had little more than a thousand fighters under their command.[2]

The top leaders of the Taliban in the south were slower to reconstitute their organization, because they were concerned that the Pakistanis would arrest them and turn them over to the Americans. Pakistan's president and chief of Army Staff, General Pervez Musharraf, had sided with the United States during its 2001 invasion of Afghanistan and had helped the United States capture al-Qa'ida leaders and operatives in 2002 and 2003. The Pakistanis had welcomed the Taliban back after the regime had been overthrown but hadn't yet provided support to the group. By early 2003, however, the Pakistanis relaxed the restrictions that had been placed on the activities of the Taliban's leadership in Quetta in southwestern Pakistan. In February, Mullah Mohammed Omar, the leader of the Taliban, called on all Afghans to wage a holy war against American forces. He accused American forces of atrocities against Muslims and warned that anyone who collaborated with the United States would be killed.[3] On March 14, 2003, Omar and a few other former senior Taliban leaders established the Rahbari Shura (Leadership Council), better known as the Quetta Shura. Its establishment marked the beginnings of a centrally led insurgency in southern Afghanistan.[4]

A major turning point for the insurgency came in 2005.[5] The Taliban's fighting strength swelled from ten thousand to fifteen thousand.[6] Pakistan ended all restrictions on the Taliban and increased its support for the group substantially. Funding for the Taliban from wealthy private citizens in the Arabian Peninsula had also increased, and the group was generating additional revenue from the share of the opium trade it commandeered and the taxes (*zakat* and *ushr*) it imposed on the Afghan population.[7] From all sources, the Taliban's annual budget had grown to at least $200 million between 2003 and 2008.

The insurgency accelerated considerably in 2006 as the Taliban gained strength due to increased Pakistani and other foreign support, the Taliban's ability to extort revenue from the drug trade and confiscatory taxes, the growing unpopularity of the Karzai regime in the Pashtun belt, and corruption and abuse by Afghan government authorities. Tribal rivalries were also effectively exploited by the Taliban, with tribes who had been marginalized and excluded from their share of the spoils particularly attractive targets. Rivalry with the Achakzais pushed some Noorzais toward the Taliban. Marginalized subtribes within the Alokozai and Alizai also supported the insurgency. The number of Taliban attacks tripled in just a year.[8]

Consumed by the war in Iraq, the U.S. military turned over much of the mission in Afghanistan to NATO in 2006. Local militias were disbanded across Afghanistan, leaving a security vacuum that the Taliban fully exploited. Afghan security forces were nationalized and centralized, and constrained by limited funding, which compounded the problem. A completely inappropriate security and governance model was being imposed on Afghanistan by its international backers, with predictably poor results. It reflected an Afghanistan as the United States and its allies wished it would be, not the country it actually was.

The heaviest fighting was primarily confined to the south through 2007.[9] U.S. special operations forces, supported by airpower, waged the war, with major contributions from our Canadian, British, and Dutch allies. The Taliban made numerous military errors, periodically massing their combat groups where they could easily be destroyed by U.S. air strikes. As a consequence, Taliban combat groups suffered attrition as high as 20 percent a year.[10] But the insurgency was resilient if nothing else. It replaced its combat losses and continued to grow. The Pakistan sanctuary was a critical factor in the Taliban's resiliency.

Now under the command of Jalaluddin's son, Sirajuddin, the Haqqanis became a much more potent force from 2008 onward. They became the shock troops of the insurgency and the group responsible for most of the attacks inside Kabul. I knew them well from my

Afghanistan Covert Action Program days and took note of the increase in the sophistication and scale of their attacks. They had clearly improved their ability to conduct combined arms attacks between 2007 and 2008. The size of their combat groups had grown from ten to twenty (called *zerbati*, or "Fast Teams") to a hundred (called *delayez*, "Groups of 100"). I strongly believed that the Haqqanis' increase in tactical sophistication and scale was a direct result of the support they received from ISI.[11]

In July 2008, the Haqqanis conducted a suicide bombing attack against the Indian embassy in Kabul, killing fifty-four and wounding scores more. The attack was tied directly back to Miram Shah in real time. A year later, in October 2009, they attacked the Indian embassy again with a suicide bomb, killing seventeen and wounding dozens more. On September 10, 2011, the Haqqanis detonated a truck bomb at a NATO base south of Kabul, killing five American soldiers and wounding more than six dozen. It could have been far worse. Three days later, they attacked the American embassy and the International Security Assistance Force, or ISAF, headquarters with mortars and assault rifles, killing sixteen—five Afghan policemen and eleven civilians, including six children. Two weeks after the embassy attack, Burhanuddin Rabbani, the seventy-one-year-old leader of the Jamiat-e-Islami party and the head of Afghanistan's High Peace Commission, was killed by a suicide bomber who had hid a bomb inside his turban.

Just before he retired at the end of September 2011, Admiral Mullen, chairman of the Joint Chiefs, told the Senate Armed Services Committee that the Haqqanis planned and conducted the truck bomb attack, as well as the assault on our embassy, with ISI support. He added that the Haqqani Network acts as a "veritable arm of ISI." There was little reason to doubt the chairman's assertions.

THE SEARCH FOR A NEW STRATEGY

In November 2006, the NSC completed a strategic review of the deteriorating situation in Afghanistan. The NSC's plan called for more funds for Afghanistan; a reenergized effort to improve governance and security; more schools, roads, and electricity; a new push to undermine the booming drug economy; and more American troops. More troops, however, weren't really available. The pending surge in Iraq would consume what was left of our strategic reserve. The war in Iraq was the priority for President Bush. He had bet his presidency on it. As Admiral Mike Mullen, our JCS chairman, would repeatedly testify to Congress, "In Iraq, we do what we must. In Afghanistan, we do what we can."[12]

During the fall of 2008, President Bush concluded that the war in Afghanistan was not going well. He directed an NSC-led review of the war, led by his "war czar," Doug Lute.[13] Doug was a three-star Army general who had been detailed to the White House to help the NSC oversee the wars. In reality, he was senior NSC staff more than a "czar," but he could call meetings of senior interagency officials and had the president's confidence. He would be asked to stay on during the Obama administration, retire from the Army, and eventually become our ambassador to NATO. I was assigned to Doug's review for DOD. It was the first of three that I'd participate in during the next twelve months.

In late September, I met with Secretary Gates and other senior DOD officials to develop the department's views on the deteriorating situation in Afghanistan and what could be done about it. The intelligence community was in the final stages of completing a National Intelligence Estimate that would describe the situation in Afghanistan in very bleak terms. CENTCOM had advised us, moreover, that the twenty thousand troops that General David McKiernan had requested wouldn't be available until October 2009. We reviewed a number of options: dramatically accelerating and increasing the size of the Afghan security forces, particularly the Afghan Army; engaging the tribes to bolster local defenses in rural areas; bolstering local governance; repositioning some of our forces from the east to the south; and planning for a larger and longer-term commitment of U.S. forces.[14] We hoped these steps would deal with the deteriorating situation inside Afghanistan. As long as we continued to train and advise Afghan security forces and use our big advantage in airpower, the Taliban couldn't win. But neither were we on a path toward victory. The war was a stalemate, and our position was getting weaker with each fighting season.

As I've noted, Afghanistan's problems extended to Pakistan as well. Indeed, the sanctuary and support that Pakistan provided to the Taliban was our most intractable challenge. Since the summer, we had been taking bold action to deny sanctuary to al-Qa'ida in the Afghanistan-Pakistan border region. Those same actions over time would also render the Haqqanis' safe haven less secure, but we didn't have the permissions and airspace clearance from the Pakistanis that we would need to get at the Quetta Shura and its sanctuary in the south. We also, frankly, didn't have the actionable intelligence we would require, though I was confident we could generate that if we could solve the other problems. Even if we did acquire the necessary intelligence, Quetta was a large, densely populated city, and not the place for a sustained air campaign, even the most precise one. Whether we liked it or not, we were largely dependent on the Pakistanis for operations in Quetta, and they were denying that the Quetta Shura even existed.

Lute's review recommended a comprehensive counterinsurgency effort in Afghanistan, including more troops and civilian advisers. It also recommended closer cooperation with the Pakistanis to go after extremists who were beyond our reach.[15] In December, President Bush was prepared to approve McKiernan's request for an additional twenty thousand troops, but the incoming Obama team asked that he hold off.

Within days of taking office, the president asked Bruce Riedel, a former senior CIA analyst and NSC official during the Clinton administration, to lead a sixty-day review of our Afghanistan strategy. Independently, given the need to make a decision on additional troops as soon as possible if they were to arrive before the 2009 fighting season was over, there were also deputies and principals meetings on Afghanistan strategy during the first weeks of the Obama administration. McKiernan's request had been shaved to seventeen thousand by the Deputies Committee based on how many troops could actually get to Afghanistan before the fall of 2009. On February 13, the president chaired an NSC meeting to discuss the request for additional troops. All but Vice President Biden and Deputy Secretary of State Jim Steinberg supported the request for seventeen thousand troops. On February 17, the president approved the additional troops.[16]

Riedel's strategic review considered four options for the way forward in Afghanistan: reducing our commitment to a pure counterterrorism mission, referred to as "mowing the grass"; "counterterrorism plus," which added training for Afghan security forces and renewed support for regional warlords to stabilize the countryside; limited counterinsurgency; and fully resourced counterinsurgency, which meant adding more troops beyond what McKiernan had requested. The options built on one another. I participated in Riedel's review as well.

Riedel argued that only "a fully resourced counterinsurgency campaign would enable us to regain the initiative and defend our vital interests." He argued for more effective governance in Afghanistan and for further expansion of Afghan security forces. Riedel also recommended that we continue to disrupt terrorist networks in Afghanistan, where there were very few, and in Pakistan, where there were many. He argued that we should pressure Pakistan to end its support for the Taliban, and do more to eliminate the sanctuary al-Qa'ida maintained in the border region, enhance civilian control of the military in Pakistan, and work to reduce mistrust and enmity between Pakistan and India.

All were laudable goals, but most, beyond eliminating al-Qa'ida's sanctuary in the border region and building up Afghan security forces, were beyond our reach. All of the NSC principals concurred with Riedel's report with the exception of Vice President Biden, who argued that the war was politically unsustainable at home. After Riedel's review, President Obama approved an additional four thousand trainers for Afghanistan, bringing the total troop increase under Obama to twenty-one thousand. The new presidentially approved force level for Afghanistan was now sixty-eight thousand, more than double what it had been just a year earlier.[17]

Riedel's biggest contribution, in my view, had been to recognize the centrality of Pakistan. He argued that in many respects Afghanistan and Pakistan should be viewed as one theater of operations. "Af-Pak" became the shorthand for this strategic insight. Unfortunately, Pakistan's support for the Taliban was a problem that we just couldn't solve.

Even more important, on March 27, the president clarified our mission in Afghanistan and Pakistan. The United States' goal was to "disrupt, dismantle, and defeat Al Qaeda and its safe havens in Pakistan, and to prevent their return to Pakistan and Afghanistan."[18] Fully resourced counterinsurgency was just one of several possible means to accomplish the president's objective and only a partial means at that. Al-Qa'ida was in Pakistan, and to deal with the threat it posed, we needed a counterterrorism strategy. The shift to a counterinsurgency strategy was widely credited with our remarkable turnaround in Iraq, though, as I'll discuss later, the causes of that turnaround were different from what many believed. There was, not surprisingly, a desire to apply the same methods to the war in Afghanistan, and to hopefully achieve the same results.

In early February 2009, Michèle Flournoy, our new undersecretary of defense for policy, wanted to get a look at Afghanistan firsthand, so I accompanied her on a trip there to show her around. Michèle combined a strong knowledge of strategy and military capabilities with excellent policy judgment and great leadership. She quickly became one of Secretary Gates's most trusted advisers. We met with the Afghan leadership, including President Karzai and Minister of Defense Wardak, General McKiernan, the commanders of our special operations forces in country, the generals in charge of Regional Commands East and South, Ambassador Karl Eikenberry, who had commanded in Afghanistan as a three-star in 2005–2007, and the CIA station. I also took her to see our first village defense site and a school for young girls in Wardak Province. She quickly concluded that we were working at cross-purposes in Afghanistan and that things needed to change.

After our trip to Afghanistan and the completion of Riedel's review, Michèle and I became increasingly convinced that General McKiernan was not the right commander in Afghanistan at this critical juncture. McKiernan was an outstanding officer, but his career had been in the heavy conventional forces.

Changing generals had been the right thing for President Bush to do in Iraq, and it looked as if the time had come to do the same thing in Afghanistan. Once again, the Iraq war and the successful surge in 2007 had cast a long shadow over the war in Afghanistan. Michèle and I conveyed our thoughts to Secretary Gates, recommending that Stan McChrystal replace McKiernan. Admiral Mullen and General Petraeus, now the commander of CENTCOM, had reached the same conclusion. Gates concurred. In addition to McChrystal, Gates selected his senior military assistant, Dave Rodriguez, one of the best operational generals in the Army, to head the new International Security Assistance Force Joint Command under Stan.[19]

Stan and Rod departed for Afghanistan, and Stan, following the guidance he had received from Secretary Gates, began his own sixty-day strategic review of the war, to include whether our projected force level of sixty-eight thousand troops was adequate. Stan briefed his assessment, strategy, and force structure recommendations to Secretary Gates, Admiral Mullen, and other senior DOD leaders at an air base in Belgium on August 2. He told the secretary that the situation in Afghanistan was much worse than he had expected, particularly in the south. He proposed an "inkblot" counterinsurgency strategy, focused on eighty key districts, which represented about 20 percent of Afghanistan's total. The fundamental intent of Stan's strategy was to protect the Afghan population, focusing on the key population centers, and win their trust. ISAF's priority would shift from eastern Afghanistan, closer to al-Qa'ida's safe havens in Pakistan and where the Haqqanis operated, to southern Afghanistan, the stronghold of the Taliban. Most of the combat between 2003 and 2008 had occurred in the south. Most U.S. forces, however, were in the east. Stan hoped that greater cooperation with Pakistan could induce the Pakistanis to eliminate the Taliban's sanctuaries in Pakistan. Secretary Gates was very skeptical about this aspect of Stan's strategy, but thought it couldn't hurt to give it a try. I was skeptical as well.

Force, particularly airpower, would be used far more discriminately. Counterterrorism operations would continue to take Taliban commanders off the battlefield. Stan said he thought the next twelve months would be decisive: we needed to significantly shift momentum in the conflict from the Taliban to ISAF and the Afghan government, or "we risked mission failure." Stan added that "if we didn't seize the initiative and reverse insurgent momentum within the next 12 months, defeating the Taliban insurgency might no longer be possible."[20] Stan believed that Afghan security forces needed to be substantially increased, from our current goal of roughly 220,000, to 400,000. Stan's goal was to turn over primary security responsibility to the Afghans within three years. An Afghan force of this size would be required after ISAF drew down. Stan's team had derived these numbers by using a counterinsurgency rule of thumb of 20 security force personnel for each 1,000 of the population. As Stan would admit, this calculation was just a rough guide. Counterinsurgency was more art than science. And in what would create shock and anger in the White House, Stan concluded that he needed forty thousand additional U.S. troops—forty thousand beyond the twenty-one thousand President Obama had just approved only months before.

Secretary Gates was shocked when he first heard that Stan wanted forty thousand more troops. He was still concerned that we were in danger of being seen as occupiers as our footprint grew larger and larger, and he knew that Stan's request would get a cold reception at the White House. He was right.

Secretary Gates gradually embraced Stan's request, however. A leak of Stan's report, widely suspected to have come from Stan's staff itself, to Bob Woodward and *The Washington Post* only three days after Gates had forwarded it to the White House, set off a political firestorm, greatly complicating Gates's task of winning the president's approval. President Obama and his top advisers felt as if they were being jammed by the military and feared that they were being forced into an open-ended commitment. The president decided to conduct a thorough National Security Council review of Stan's strategy and request for additional forces.

On September 13, the president chaired the first of nine very long meetings he held on Af-Pak strategy. The meetings focused on four broad areas. The first was the nature of the threat, focusing on the relationships among the Taliban, al-Qa'ida, and other extremist groups in the Afghanistan-Pakistan border region—whether it was necessary to defeat the Taliban in order to defeat al-Qa'ida, whether al-Qa'ida would once again be given sanctuary in Afghanistan if the Taliban regained power there, and, finally, if a more stable Afghanistan would change Pakistan's strategic calculus and cause the Pakistanis to stop backing the Taliban. The second major issue was which strategy, "fully resourced counterinsurgency" or "counterterrorism plus," would be most effective in achieving the goals the president had established on March 27. The third issue was about indicators of strategic success or failure: specifically, what would inform us that it was time to change course. The fourth issue was our relationship with Pakistan. "If Pakistan is so critical to the success of our strategy," Vice President Biden rightly asked, "why are we spending thirty times more in Afghanistan than we are in Pakistan?" The review was focused on the right issues, but its outcome was pretty much foreordained.

During a secure Sunday phone call among Secretary Gates, Admiral Mullen, Michèle Flournoy, and me, Gates provided his thoughts on the operational goals we should set for our strategy and asked me to incorporate them into a strategy paper I had been working on. Gates believed that while the core goals the president had articulated in March remained valid and should be reaffirmed, we needed to narrow our mission to what was achievable in Afghanistan. We could not realistically expect to eliminate the Taliban; they were part of Afghanistan's political and social fabric. We could realistically work to reverse their military momentum, deny them the ability to hold or control major population centers, and pressure them along the Pakistani border. We should strive to reduce their level of activity back to 2004 or so. (Keeping the Taliban there, we would soon discover, would be the hard part.) I was scribbling furiously as Gates spoke, but managed to get it all down.

In early 2009, in a hearing before the Senate Armed Services Committee, Gates had been explicit about what he thought was achievable in Afghanistan and what wasn't. "If we set out to create in Afghanistan a central Asian Valhalla," he said, "we will lose. We need to keep our objectives realistic and limited, or we will set ourselves up for failure." The key question, Gates would regularly remind us, was, what was "Afghan good enough"?

Gates believed that while al-Qa'ida was now under great pressure in the Afghanistan-Pakistan border region and highly dependent on other extremist groups for sustainment, the success of those other groups—the Taliban above all—would greatly strengthen al-Qa'ida's message to the Muslim world that the global jihadists were on the side of God and on the winning side of history. Pakistan and Afghanistan were the epicenter of global jihad, the place where Muslims had already defeated one superpower and from which they had inflicted great losses on another. I fully concurred with Gates's views.

There was too much universality in counterinsurgency thinking. Each situation was different. We could employ similar strategies, but the differences in the situation would in the end be determinate. The key difference between Iraq and Afghanistan was the sanctuary the insurgents enjoyed in Pakistan. Until we solved that problem, the best we could do was to strengthen Afghanistan, take the Taliban down several levels, and prevent them from winning.

The strategy paper I wrote described what I believed should be the three operational pillars of our new strategy. Based on what had worked in Iraq, and adapting counterinsurgency strategy to the Afghan environment, I proposed a combination of conventional force operations to secure the major population centers and protect lines of communication, an intensive campaign of special operations raids to keep constant pressure on the Taliban and take their commanders off the battlefield, and a new program of Special Forces–led tribal engagement to increasingly deny rural villages to the Taliban. I described this as the "new triad" of counterinsurgency operations.

Another component of the strategy would be to reintegrate lower-level Taliban fighters who wanted to stop fighting. Reconciliation with Taliban leaders might eventually follow, but only after they had been convinced that they couldn't win by outlasting us. Given Pakistan's support for the Taliban and the Quetta Shura, and the growing insurgency in Pakistan—a nuclear power—U.S. engagement with Pakistan remained a must, however frustrating that might be.

The new counterterrorism strategy we were conducting against al-Qa'ida and its safe haven providers in the Afghanistan-Pakistan border region was a central part of our Afghanistan strategy, I wrote. Though it required a vastly smaller claim on our resources, it was our main effort, not the war in Afghanistan.

Gates, Mullen, and Flournoy all liked the paper. I sent it to Dave Petraeus and Stan McChrystal for their comments, and they liked it too. Petraeus asked me to put even more emphasis on the reintegration part of the strategy, which I did, though I was skeptical that we would have much success in that area anytime soon. My paper implicitly became the basis for our operational strategy in Afghanistan until our drawdown of forces.

Three force options were settled upon for principals and the president to consider: twenty thousand additional troops—ten thousand for counterterrorism and ten thousand for training and advising Afghan security forces; Stan's recommendation for forty thousand more troops; and an alternative option Secretary Gates had personally developed, thirty thousand additional U.S. troops, with an additional five to seven thousand to be provided by our NATO allies. The first, which became known as the "Hoss" option—after General Cartwright independently provided it to the White House, causing great concern among Admiral Mullen, General Petraeus, and General McChrystal that our vice-chairman was "freelancing"—was aligned with the counterterrorism-plus strategy.

What I didn't get, however, was Hoss's call for two additional heavy conventional brigades to support the counterterrorism mission. It made no operational sense. All conventional forces would do if given this mission was kick up dust. I called it the "Mad Max" strategy, after the Mel Gibson movies that featured road warriors battling in an apocalyptic future. If we were going to go all-in on counterterrorism, we would need additional intelligence assets and special operations forces.[21]

The argument against the counterterrorism-plus strategy was twofold. First, it was what we were essentially doing now against the Taliban in Afghanistan and it wasn't working in Afghanistan. (Against al-Qa'ida and its safe haven providers in Pakistan, our CT strategy was working spectacularly.) Even with additional resources—twenty thousand more troops—it wasn't clear that a CT strategy could ever defeat the Taliban. We could do a lot better than we were doing—by going all in on tribal engagement, for example, and conducting more raids, but we'd be "mowing the grass" in Afghanistan for a long time. Second, President Karzai was growing increasingly frustrated with our CT approach to the war and our reliance on airpower.

Vice President Biden, Tom Donilon, John Brennan, and General Cartwright all favored the CT-plus strategy. The vice president also made it clear during our NSC discussions that he favored withdrawal from Afghanistan sooner rather than later, saying several times that the American people had lost support for the war. That wasn't on the table, but it did preview what was to come a decade later.

Pakistan was where our only vital interests in the Af-Pak theater—eliminating al-Qa'ida's sanctuary in the FATA and ensuring that Pakistan's nuclear weapons didn't fall into the wrong hands—were threatened. We needed Afghanistan as a base to conduct counterterrorism and counterproliferation operations in the Afghanistan-

Pakistan theater, but that didn't mean we should overinvest in Afghanistan. A look at our vital interests in Af-Pak also implied that a narrow mission was the right answer in Afghanistan.

Secretary Gates's and Stan's options were aligned with the fully resourced counterinsurgency (COIN) strategy, albeit with the mission now narrowed considerably by Gates. The argument against the COIN approach was that it wasn't clear that it could defeat the Taliban either, and it would cost tens of billions more in treasure and, more important, in the blood of American soldiers. Secretary Gates, Secretary Clinton, Admiral Mullen, General Petraeus, and General McChrystal all supported the COIN strategy.

While I fully supported Secretary Gates, I was honestly torn between the two strategies. I thought the CT-plus strategy was better aligned with the president's goals in Afghanistan and Pakistan. Al-Qa'ida was in Pakistan, after all, not in Afghanistan, and I wasn't convinced that a fully resourced COIN would work as fast as it had in Iraq, largely due to the Pakistan sanctuary that the Taliban enjoyed, but also because Afghanistan was far more rural and mountainous than Iraq—the perfect environment for an insurgency.

The COIN versus CT-plus debate, moreover, had been somewhat of a false choice. CT would remain central to our strategy in Afghanistan. Similarly, if the president had opted for the CT-plus strategy, we would have still been doing a lot of COIN. The president had not been well served. The real choices were about our strategy's relationship to the goals the president had set, and what force levels could accomplish them and, more important, over what time frame.

That said, I came down squarely in the fully resourced COIN camp. Secretary Gates, who had many of the same reservations as I did, had gotten there, and so did I. I had a very high regard for Stan, Rod, and Dave Petraeus, and they all strongly supported COIN over CT-plus. That was enough for me. It wasn't COIN versus CT; it was COIN plus CT. My primary focus, moreover, was on the CT campaign against core al-Qa'ida in the Afghanistan-Pakistan border region. As long as that remained our top priority, I was fine with trying a COIN strategy in Afghanistan.

But I also felt that we needed to try a different approach, particularly to go all in on tribal engagement, to deny the Taliban access to Afghanistan's villages. Tribal engagement had worked in Iraq, turning the tribes against the al-Qa'ida-led insurgency. It had worked for the Najibullah regime after the Soviets withdrew. It could work for us. It was organic to Afghanistan's tradition of decentralized power. We needed to change the ways of our strategy, not just the means—surging more U.S. conventional and special operations forces and building up the regular Afghan security forces. Adopting this new approach, however, would be a huge challenge. President Karzai and much of the Afghan leadership opposed decentralization of power. Several U.S. policy makers and many in Congress feared a return of the warlords as well. But in the end, tribal engagement was adopted. I will have more to say about this in the next chapter.

President Obama approved Secretary Gates's 30,000 troops recommendation on November 29. U.S. force levels would rise to 100,000 with the surge. The president emphasized in a one on one with Secretary Gates two days earlier, however, that "Stan needed to grasp that there has been a shift in mission" to the narrower objectives Gates had proposed. The president also imposed an eighteen-month time restriction on the surge of forces. Withdrawal of the surge forces was to begin not later than July 2011.[22] As we drew down our forces after 2011, the 2009 "great strategy debate" looked increasingly irrelevant to the outcome in Afghanistan.[23]

DEALING WITH A "FRENEMY"

In January 2010, just as the U.S. force surge was getting under way in Afghanistan, Generals Kayani and Ahmad Pasha—the heads of the Army and ISI, respectively, and the real power in Pakistan—started trying to exploit President Karzai's growing alienation from the United States.[24] "The U.S. is on its way out," Pasha told Karzai in Kabul. "It is time to make peace with the Taliban and Pakistan." Pasha had been making the same argument publicly in Pakistan, telling a journalist that President Obama's surge in Afghanistan would inevitably fail. Though he denied that ISI was supporting the Taliban and Haqqanis, he told Karzai that only Pakistan could deliver them as part of a political solution to the war.

Kayani reinforced Pasha's message when Karzai flew to Islamabad in March to follow up. "If there is to be peace, it has to come through

Pakistan," Kayani told the Afghan president. "The support of ISI is essential to any workable solution of the war. We can turn off the insurgency." In return, Pakistan would expect Karzai "to end the Indian presence in Afghanistan," Kayani said. Kayani also offered to train Afghan Army officers in Pakistan.

What a bunch of duplicitous shits, I thought, as I read the intelligence. I also knew, however, that the only thing worse than living with Pakistan is living without it.

———————

During the spring of 2010, under the rubric of a "strategic dialogue," we invited Kayani to Washington to try to persuade him to abandon Pakistan's support for the Taliban. There were high hopes for the dialogue within the top echelons of the Obama administration, but it ended up producing nothing of substance. I participated for DOD.

In an effort to find common ground, I traveled to Pakistan several times a year between 2007 and 2013 to meet one-on-one with Kayani. He was a very intelligent man, a military strategist who had studied at our Command and General Staff College during the late 1980s and had written a study on the Afghan resistance to the Soviet occupation of Afghanistan. (He was also a chain-smoker. I thought I would develop lung cancer from all the secondhand smoke I inhaled during my many meetings with him.) He could be very candid, but also very deceitful. His soft way of speaking and the way he would mumble also made him hard to understand.

During our meetings, I emphasized that our two countries' interests had been much more closely aligned during the 1980s, and we had accomplished great things as a result. We could do the same to prevent al-Qa'ida and its allies from destabilizing Afghanistan and Pakistan if only we could get over the trust deficit that had arisen between our two countries since the 1990s and work more closely together. Eventually, I gave up. We'd share assessments about the situation in Afghanistan, but that was about it. He was always very pleasant, but wouldn't budge an inch from what he saw as Pakistan's core interests and constraints.

———————

During a visit to Pakistan at the beginning of 2010 by General Jim Jones, President Obama's national security adviser, Kayani had handed Jones a 106-page document that sought to explain Pakistan's views on the war against al-Qa'ida and its extremist allies. It quickly became known as "Kayani 1.0." Kayani presented a PowerPoint version of the paper at Blair House, the guest home across the street from the White House, where the strategic dialogue was being held.

Kayani's paper was basically a recitation of Pakistan's contributions to the fight against extremism and a plea for our understanding that the Pakistanis weren't playing a double game. Kayani argued that the number of Pakistani soldiers and paramilitaries deployed to the FATA had more than tripled between 2001 and 2009, from 40,000 to 140,000. Kayani called this a "silent surge," a reference to his reluctance to share these figures with the Pakistani public. He noted that more than 2,300 Pakistani soldiers had been killed in the fighting, with another 6,800 wounded. This was all true.

But it was also true that Pakistani security forces had tried to establish security in the FATA without any lasting success. They had suffered significant losses and settled on a general strategy of trying to encourage militants to fight in Afghanistan rather than in Pakistan. They also had close ties to groups like the Haqqanis, whose operations they didn't want to disrupt. The Haqqanis were not only killing Americans in Afghanistan; they were providing safe haven to al-Qa'ida in Pakistan. Kayani hadn't mentioned any of that.[25]

In July, ten weeks after Faisal Shahzad, the son of a Pakistani Air vice-marshal, had tried to blow up Times Square in New York with a car bomb and the Pakistan Taliban had released a video of Shahzad training with them, claiming how easy it is to attack and defeat the United States, Kayani gave us another hundred-page paper, which became known as "Kayani 2.0." The gist of it was this: "You Americans are just focused on the military and counterterrorism. You are running up against how far our relationship will go in these fields." He called for large American investment in Pakistan's economy, energy supplies, and water supplies. (It had not escaped my notice in recent meetings with Kayani in Pakistan that he was intensely concerned about the threat he believed India posed to Pakistan's water supply.)

In a letter to Admiral Mullen a few weeks later, Kayani complained about the threats senior American officials had been making publicly and privately for years that any act of terror in the United States or against American interests that had links to Pakistan would lead to direct military action by the United States against Pakistan. He warned that these threats were pushing the Pakistani Army to the wall. He implied that in the event of an attack on Pakistan his forces would abandon all restraint in backing the Taliban against American troops in Afghanistan. He also said that he would not give in to American pressure to conduct an offensive in North Waziristan (the stronghold of the Haqqanis and al-Qa'ida). "The fallout would destabilize Pakistan," he asserted.[26]

This confirmed something I had long suspected: Pakistan used the Haqqanis as a strategic instrument, but it feared them as well. It was riding a tiger with its support for militancy. Kayani concluded by saying that "if the Pakistani people were let down again by the United States, their alienation would be complete and perhaps last forever." It was not a happy marriage.

In October, Kayani returned to Washington for yet another round of strategic dialogue. This one was hosted at the State Department, and I again attended for DOD. During a meeting at the White House, Kayani handed President Obama an updated and much shorter paper (ten to fifteen pages), which we called "Kayani 3.0." The essence of Kayani's argument was this: "You can't win your war [in Afghanistan]. They beat the Russians, they beat the British, they are beating you." He asked if the United States and Pakistan could talk honestly about what would follow America's defeat. Kayani's growing list of grievances with the United States were palpable. He said that Pakistan had transitioned from America's "most sanctioned ally" to its "most bullied ally." He continued to deny that Pakistan supported the Haqqani Network or the Quetta Shura.[27] But by then I had become numb to Kayani and Pasha's lies.

After the Bin Ladin raid, Pasha told Pakistan's Parliament that Pakistan's relationship with the United States had "gone bad." Kayani and Pasha began thinking about how to reinvigorate Pakistan's relationship with China to reduce their dependence on us.

We tried everything we could to improve our relations with Pakistan, to no avail. During a meeting Secretary Gates and I had with Kayani in January 2010, Gates told him, "We don't want your nuclear weapons. We have plenty of our own." The United States by this time had come to accept Pakistan as a nuclear power and was mainly concerned with the security of Pakistan's arsenal, fearing a nuclear warhead could fall into terrorists' hands. Gates also assured Kayani that we did not covet "a single inch" of Pakistani territory.[28] "Noted, let's move on," Kayani's body language implied.

As Secretary Gates wrote in his memoirs, we continued to ask the same things from the Pakistanis year after year—capture senior Taliban and al-Qa'ida leaders, grant the United States permission to take direct action against Taliban and al-Qa'ida targets in Pakistan, dismantle insurgent and terrorist camps, shut down the Taliban headquarters in Quetta, Miram Shah, and Peshawar, and conduct joint operations with U.S. forces, with America providing special operations advisers and intelligence, surveillance, and reconnaissance—without hardly any success.[29]

Pakistan's military leaders viewed India as an existential threat and wanted strategic depth and a friendly government in Afghanistan, even at the expense of its relations with the United States. In their view, Afghanistan offered vast territory that their Army could retreat into in the event of war with India and a large population base that could be mobilized for Pakistan's defense. Our "frenemy" would continue to support the Taliban until America was defeated.

SURGE, DRAWDOWN, TRANSITION, DEFEAT

THE EIGHTEEN-MONTH SURGE

After our surge operations in Afghanistan got under way in February 2010, I made several trips there to get a firsthand look at them. As the surge progressed, there were not unreasonable grounds for optimism that we might actually turn the war around. The surge began in Helmand Province, and Major General Nick Carter (U.K.) led the operation. The first objective was Marjah, a town about the same geographic size as Washington, D.C., but with a fifth of the population. Carter's aim was to rapidly project overwhelming power, while limiting the employment of fires, in order to reduce damage to the area and minimize civilian casualties. This raised the risk to our force, but it is a choice that is often necessary in counterinsurgency warfare where the real battle is for the support of the population. Carter also planned to introduce as many government services as possible, described as "government in a box," to build legitimacy with the local populace. Raids by Bill McRaven's Special Operations Task Force and allied special operations forces against Taliban commanders in the area had already begun before the main operation, a critical element of our new approach to counterinsurgency, one that was essential to degrading insurgent strength and undermining insurgents' confidence.

By nightfall on February 13, U.S. Marines and Afghan soldiers had established positions in the center of Marjah. The Marines, who were a large part of the first of President Obama's two surges of forces, were surprised by how tactically proficient the Taliban fighters were. Clearing the town was slow, dangerous work. Two weeks later, however, the governor of Helmand, the commander of Afghanistan's 205th Corps, and Carter were raising the Afghan government flag in the town center.[1]

At the same time as the Marjah operation was being launched, we had another big success against the Taliban in Pakistan. The group's number two commander, Mullah Abdul Ghani Baradar, had been captured by ISI in Quetta. Intelligence provided by the United States had led the Pakistanis to him. At first, the ISI team didn't know whom they had caught. When they discovered who it was, there was a big "oh, shit" uttered. Soon, however, ISI found it had good reason to detain Baradar, because he had apparently decided to move to reconcile with the Karzai government without consulting his Pakistani sponsors. He was detained for several years before being allowed to return to Taliban senior leadership.[2]

Kandahar was the next target. The key node was Kandahar City itself, but the aim of the operation was to expand contiguous areas of security in the south, known as Greater Kandahar or Zabulistan, a subregion formed by the provinces of Helmand, Kandahar, Uruzgan, and Zabul. "Kandahar" is a derivation of "Iskander," the Afghan name for Alexander the Great, who supposedly founded the city in the fourth century BCE.

As in Marjah, before conventional operations around Kandahar could begin, our special operators had to conduct shaping operations. Unlike Marjah, Kandahar City did not have to be taken. It was already in ISAF and Afghan government control, more or less. Kandaharis had painful memories of the destruction the Soviets had visited on the city during the Soviet-Afghan War and feared a reprise by ISAF. Karzai flew down and assured the elders that there wouldn't be an "operation" in Kandahar City. Karzai's brother Ahmed Wali was the power broker in Kandahar, which helped the Afghan president get his message across.[3] But like the "belts" al-Qa'ida in Iraq had used around Baghdad to stage operations into the city, the challenge in Kandahar was in its outlying areas—Panjwayi, Zhari, Arghandab, and Shah Wali Kot. Clearing Kandahar's "belts" was an infantryman's war, much like the hedgerow fighting in Normandy in World War II.

"Hamkari" (or cooperation) as the operation around Kandahar was called, kicked off in the summer of 2010. Security checkpoints were established on the major roads leading into and out of the city. The Arghandab, a center of IED production and staging area for the Taliban, was next. It would see some of the bloodiest fighting of the war, with an Army Stryker Brigade in the lead. Operations in Zhari and Panjwayi followed.

By late fall, insurgent violence had dropped dramatically in the Kandahar area. I flew down for a visit and walked the streets of Panjwayi, with Green Berets and Afghan National Civil Order Police in tow. The bazaars were bustling. The operations in Helmand and Kandahar had taken longer than we'd hoped, and the governance part of the plan, particularly in Helmand, had not been fully realized, but overall the surge was working in the south. Like al-Qa'ida in the Afghanistan-Pakistan border region, the Taliban started hunkering down in hopes of waiting us out.[4]

————————

Unfortunately, just as the surge had gotten under way, my good friend Stan McChrystal was relieved of command by President Obama in June 2010, after members of his staff made disparaging comments to a *Rolling Stone* reporter about the Obama administration and, in particular, about Vice President Biden. Though unaware of the comments his staff had made, Stan took full responsibility.[5] Stan is one of the greatest special operators and leaders of this generation, and had been destined for even greater responsibilities before the incident, but President Obama had to remove him. Civilian control of the military is essential in our system of government.

I was sitting with Dave Petraeus at a CIA-DOD counterterrorism conference reviewing our strategy for the war with al-Qa'ida when we first heard the news about the *Rolling Stone* article.[6] We both felt as if we had been punched in the gut. With the surge just getting under way, it was a terrible time to lose our commander. The president asked Dave, at the time our CENTCOM commander, to take command, and Dave, being the good soldier that he is, accepted on the spot, and was succeeded as CENTCOM commander by General Jim Mattis.[7]

Dave picked up where Stan had left off in the summer of 2010. Dave brought with him an updated version of the "Anaconda" slide he had used to explain his strategy during the surge in Iraq. The slide showed seven coordinated activities that he believed would, over time, squeeze the life out of the Taliban insurgency.

The first was what he called "kinetic" operations: raids by special operations forces (both U.S. and Afghan), conventional force operations (both U.S. and Afghan) to clear and hold key areas, and operations by the Afghan Local Police. Dave expanded both the number of raids and the size of the ALP. The second area was called "politics," by which Dave meant better governance, but also reintegration of and reconciliation with the Taliban. Dave also placed his anticorruption efforts under politics.[8] The third area was called "intelligence"—more ISR assets and biometric capabilities.[9] (For some reason, Dave also included counter-narcotics operations under "intelligence.") The fourth area was called "detainee operations." Afghanistan's prisons were a haven and recruiting ground for Taliban, and Dave aimed to fix that. The fifth area, which Dave called "non-kinetics," included economic development, education, and rule of law. The sixth area was "international," building and sustaining the ISAF coalition and engaging Pakistan. The seventh and final activity was "information." Dave's intent here was to have his strategic communications get out in front of and dominate the Taliban's.

Dave's strategy represented a tweaking rather than a wholesale revision of Stan's strategy. Stan had been a bit too cautious in the tactical restraints he had imposed on operations, so Dave relaxed them a bit. One involved restrictions Stan had placed on the use of close air support. The other concerned rules of engagement for ground combat. The overall effect on the battlefield of both changes was positive.

Stan had expanded the number of strike forces in country fourfold, and Dave and Bill McRaven, the task force's commander, made good use of the additional capacity. During Dave's first ninety days in command, nearly three thousand raids were conducted. Nearly three hundred insurgent leaders were killed, along with a thousand insurgent fighters. Another two thousand insurgents were captured. As a strike force arrived on target, "callouts" were increasingly used by the operators to capture insurgents without having to fire a shot. It was an important innovation, one that helped sustain our raid campaign.

Our special operations raid campaign was very precise and discriminate in its application of force, and it minimized harm to noncombatants. Nevertheless, our raids did result in occasional tragedy. During a raid in Konar in October 2010, Linda Norgrove, a British aid worker who had been kidnapped by the insurgents, was accidentally killed by a grenade thrown by a SEAL operator. To make matters worse, it took some effort by Bill McRaven and our other commanders to get the truth as to what exactly had gone wrong on that mission. We finally got to the bottom of it when Admiral Olson had then Major General Joe Votel conduct an independent inquiry.

After the surge, CIA's district assessments showed a marked improvement in the areas under government control and a reduction of those under Taliban control.[10] We had not quite pushed the Taliban back to 2004 levels of violence, but we did push them back several years, to 2006 or thereabouts. The gains wouldn't last, however. After we drew down our forces, the situation would return to where it had been before the surge and get worse from there. A relatively short-duration surge had worked in Iraq—until al-Qa'ida in Iraq transformed itself into ISIS and came back several years later, that is—but it didn't prove as durable in Afghanistan. The Taliban, though beaten down by the surge, never left. (As I will explain in the next chapter, AQI reconstituted in Syria after being largely defeated in Iraq. Strategic depth works for terrorist groups, too.) We would have to accept the fact that Afghanistan would be a much longer war. The Taliban could be prevented from taking over with a small footprint of ground forces backed by U.S. airpower, but they couldn't be defeated in anything like the time constraints President Obama had placed on the surge. And we had our "frenemy" Pakistan to thank for that.

AFGHAN LOCAL POLICE

One of the greatest successes of the surge of forces in Afghanistan was a new program: Afghan Local Police and Village Stability Operations (ALP/VSO). As I noted in the previous chapter, I had been advocating for tribal engagement in Afghanistan since early 2008. The ALP/VSO program would have a bigger impact on the Taliban than most of our other efforts, and it should have been started a decade earlier. Unfortunately, it couldn't be sustained after U.S. forces drew down between 2012 and 2015.

In February 2009, I had visited a pilot program our Special Forces were conducting called the Afghan Public Protection Program in Wardak Province. An SF team had engaged a local tribe and had vetted, trained, equipped, and organized some of its members into a local defense force in an area where the Taliban operated freely.[11] I talked at length with the Special Forces operators and local tribal chiefs, and both believed that village defense was an important innovation. I came away impressed and wanted to expand the program. For that, however, I needed to get the buy-in of not just our four-star commander in Afghanistan but President Karzai and the senior Afghan leadership and some senior officials in the Obama administration as well.

Several months later, a highly decorated Special Forces major, Jim Gant, self-published a forty-five-page monograph called *One Tribe at a Time* that caught the attention of both Admiral Olson and me. Gant believed that engaging tribes, particularly the Pashtun tribes from whom the Taliban drew the vast majority of their recruits, was the key to success in Afghanistan. Eric and I became seized with the idea and set out to get the political support required. Gant became known as the "Lawrence of Afghanistan," recalling T. E. Lawrence's exploits with the Arab tribes during World War I. Gant would deploy to Konar, where he helped pioneer our early tribal engagement efforts there. He, unfortunately, also apparently suffered from post-traumatic stress syndrome from his years in combat and would later get into trouble with his commanders for inappropriate behavior. He was reprimanded and forced to leave the Army.[12] His personal failures notwithstanding, Gant had made an important contribution to our counterinsurgency strategy in Afghanistan with his tribal engagement efforts, and had given much in the service of his country.

Also in early 2009, we had created a new command in Afghanistan to strengthen the influence of our Special Forces commander, the Combined Forces Special Operations Component Command-Afghanistan. It had CJSOTF-A as its tactical element. CFSOCC-A was led by a brigadier general and had its own staff. My friend Ed Reeder became its first commander. Ed was a big supporter of village defense, as was Colonel Don Bolduc, the new CJSOTF-A commander. I detailed a bright member of my staff, Seth Jones, a University of Chicago PhD, to Ed to further develop the concept. Ed and Seth refined the concept and rebranded it as the Community Defense Initiative.

Stan McChrystal obtained Karzai's tentative approval in July, and the program was launched. By the time Reeder completed his tour in 2010, there were seven CDI sites established across Afghanistan. We joked that it was like Neighborhood Watch in the United States—but with AK-47s.

Karzai hadn't really bought in, however, which severely constrained the program.[13] He feared a return to warlords and militias that would be outside his control.[14] Some in the Obama administration were also opposed, particularly Ambassador Richard Holbrooke, our special representative for Afghanistan and Pakistan. Our ambassador in Afghanistan, Karl Eikenberry, was also not supportive.[15] During the period when Eikenberry had been our commander in Afghanistan between 2005 and 2007, he had ordered the demobilization of militias that SF had been using for local defense. It was not a wise decision.

Another friend, Austin Scott Miller, replaced Reeder in March 2010. Miller was a distinguished Army special operator who had won a Bronze Star for his actions during the Battle of Mogadishu in 1993. He had commanded an elite special operation unit under McChrystal in Iraq from 2005 to 2007. He would go on to four-star rank and command all of our forces in Afghanistan during the Trump and Biden administrations. Before he left for Afghanistan, I told Miller about the power of the Community Defense Initiative, and he fully embraced it.

Under Miller and Bolduc, we rebranded CDI again into the Afghan Local Police and Village Stability Operations. Petraeus quickly embraced Afghan local defense and tribal engagement as a potential "game changer" in the war. It goes without saying that I thought he was right. We made a few adjustments to the program to help Dave win Karzai's full support. The ALP wouldn't have arrest powers, but they could detain suspected militants. Most important for Karzai, the ALP would be under the Ministry of Interior, led by Mohammad Hanif Atmar, and would report to the district commander of the Afghan National Police in the district where an ALP element was located.[16] To further reduce the risk that the ALP would give rise to powerful, independent militias, there would be no more than three hundred troops in any one district. The ALP would be paid $120 a month, along with a food voucher of $65 a month. That was enough to buy the loyalty of village men, and they wouldn't have to join the Afghan Army and get sent to another part of Afghanistan away from their families to protect their villages from the Taliban. The program was supposed to sunset after five years, but I thought we could deal with that when the time came. We set our initial goal for a force of thirty thousand. If Afghanistan's past was any guide, we could use several times that number.

A key measure of control and effectiveness was that each ALP site had special operators mentoring and living with the tribal force in their village until an ALP element had proven its ability to stand on its own. The ALP program would consume nearly all the Green Berets, SEALs, and Marine special operators we had available. At Petraeus's direction, conventional force soldiers from the 82nd Airborne Division were also assigned to CFSOCC-A to augment our ALP deployments. The same procedures were applied to all ALP sites: careful vetting of candidates by the NDS, Afghanistan's intelligence service, and training, equipping, organizing, and advising by our special operators.

As an ALP force matured, our special operators would shift to overwatch, visiting the sites regularly but not remaining at them full-time. Our special operators would eventually be replaced by Afghan special forces, who had been stood up by Reeder to supplement the Afghan commandos. Improvements in local security would be tied to development assistance, the village stability part of the rebranding and reconceptualizing of the program. Within ten days, Dave had won over Karzai, who signed a formal decree establishing the program on August 16, 2010.

The ALP quickly expanded to ten thousand and then to more than twenty-two thousand by 2013. Given the success the program had shown, in late 2012 Afghanistan's deputy interior minister had raised the force ceiling to forty-five thousand and extended the program to 2025. By early 2013, the ALP was in 104 of Afghanistan's districts, nearly a quarter of the total.

Training and advising the ALP wasn't unconventional warfare in the purest sense of the term, but it was definitely an unconventional approach, one that got our Special Forces back to doing its core mission. While the program had its share of growing pains and problems, the rapid expansion of the ALP between 2010 and 2013 contributed significantly to weakening the Taliban in Afghanistan's rural areas. Since the ALP was drawn from the local people who knew their area, they could tell who the strangers were. Before the ALP arrived, the Taliban had been able to operate in these rural areas without hindrance.[17]

Nearly three-quarters of Afghans consistently told pollsters that they supported the ALP in their area, a much higher percentage than those who expressed support for the government in Kabul. A Rand study showed a significant reduction in the number of violent attacks within a five-kilometer radius within five to twelve months of an ALP site being established. Economic activity around the site also picked up, with an average of one new market or bazaar opening within fifteen months. The ALP also had a much lower incidence of bribe taking than the Afghan National Police. In February 2013, the United Nations Assistance Mission in Afghanistan found that the majority of communities in Afghanistan that had an ALP presence had reported an improvement in their security environment.[18]

In several areas of Afghanistan, the ALP had truly been the game changer that Petraeus and I predicted. Intelligence reporting showed that the Taliban's leadership was clearly threatened by it. An Afghan elder who lived in Quetta and knew many of the Taliban's senior leaders reported that insurgent fighters were more scared of the ALP than of NATO forces and all their firepower. "Forty-two countries have come here with all their high-tech equipment, but the Taliban are not as scared of their technology as they are of the local police."[19]

In Kandahar, the results were particularly striking. By early 2013, more than two thousand villagers were under arms, with another twelve hundred on the way. In Zhari, a traditional Taliban stronghold to the west of Kandahar, the ALP had prevented the insurgents from regaining a foothold there. In the Arghandab, just to the northeast of Kandahar and another longtime Taliban stronghold, Karimullah Naqib, a local leader, had used his ALP force to eject the Taliban. Soon afterward, I visited Karimullah and his men and sat down for a local *shura* with them. As we sat on the ground, we reminisced about the old days fighting the Soviets and discussed how we would soon do the same to the Taliban. Karimullah said to me through an interpreter, "We kicked the Soviets' ass, and now we'll do the same to the Taliban." I roared.

Even though the ALP became a primary target for Taliban attacks, they held their own, successfully defending their posts nearly 90 percent of the time. Their attrition rate, due to death or desertion, was only 2 percent—way below the level of attrition the rest of Afghanistan's security forces were experiencing. On my frequent trips to Afghanistan between 2009 and 2014, I always made it a point to visit at least one, and sometimes more than one, ALP site. I visited sites in Konar, Nangarhar, Paktia, Paktika, Ghazni, Kandahar, Helmand, and Faryab, among others. In Konar, I had another *shura* and shared an evening meal with the local ALP leaders. The main course was some kind of small fried animal, though to this day I'm not sure what it was. Thankfully, there wasn't much light in the room.

In July 2012, we merged all of our special operations forces—the Task Force, CFSOCC-A and ISAF SOF, which commanded allied SOF—into one command, NATO Special Operations Component Command-Afghanistan and U.S. Special Operations Joint Task Force-Afghanistan. Major General Tony Thomas was selected as its first commander. Ed Reeder would follow Tony two years later. By early 2013, with the drawdown of U.S. forces well under way and the transfer of security responsibility from NATO to the Afghan government coming soon, Tony wanted to accelerate the ALP program even faster before handing it completely over to the Afghans.[20] Tony knew he and his special operators were running out of time.

In late 2012, spontaneous uprisings against Taliban forces occurred in Ghazni, Nuristan, Wardak, Ghor, Faryab, and Logar, which showed the promise—though admittedly on a smaller scale and more local in effect—of another "Anbar Awakening," the revolt of the tribes in western Iraq that had so damaged al-Qa'ida's affiliate there. The Afghan government was slow to respond to the uprisings, however, and failed to seize the moment.

Our investment in the twenty-thousand-plus ALP between 2010 and 2013 had paid huge dividends, and it was our most cost-effective counterinsurgency instrument in the war. It was deeply unfortunate that we hadn't begun the program in 2002. If we had, there might not have been a Taliban insurgency of any significance.

DRAWDOWN AND TRANSITION

We began the drawdown of the surge in July 2011, and tragedy struck a month later. The shoot-down of a CH-47D Chinook helicopter by the

Taliban in the Tangi Valley of Wardak Province on August 6, 2011, was the largest loss of American lives in a single battle during our long war in Afghanistan. Thirty Americans died, along with seven Afghan commandos, an interpreter, and a military working dog. It was the worst loss in the history of Naval Special Warfare and in the history of U.S. Special Operations Command. Among the thirty Americans who lost their lives were seventeen SEALs. Fifteen of them were from the same team, though from a different squadron, as the group that had killed Usama Bin Ladin. Also killed were five NSW support personnel, three Air Force special operators, and five aircrew.

A platoon of forty-seven Army Rangers had set off in two helicopters a few hours earlier to kill or capture Qari Tahir, a local Taliban commander. As the Rangers approached their objective, an airborne reconnaissance platform providing overwatch for the mission observed two groups of Taliban fighters leaving Tahir's compound. The Rangers called for fire support, and one of the insurgent groups was engaged and eliminated by Apache attack helicopters. The second group of Taliban took up defensive positions, with Tahir believed to be among them. The Ranger commander decided to call in his reserve. When the helicopter carrying the SEAL reserve force was one minute from touchdown, rocket-propelled grenades struck the Chinook and brought it down. Everyone on board died in the crash.[21] Two days later, an air strike killed Tahir and the RPG gunner. It was small consolation.

During the past four years, I had grown very close to the operators in that SEAL Team. I had visited them several times during their deployments to Afghanistan and knew their commanders and senior enlisted operators very well. A former member of my staff had later become the commander of the unit. I had just spent a couple months working with the unit on the Bin Ladin raid. I greatly admired the operators' combat skills, ingenuity, and dedication to mission. As with the seven CIA officers who had been killed by a suicide bomber at Khost some seventeen months earlier, it was like losing family.

On August 10, I accompanied Secretary Panetta to Dover Air Force Base in Delaware to offer our condolences to the families and loved ones of our fallen heroes. We joined President Obama, who spent hours with the families, reassuring them that their loved ones had died in a noble cause, defending their country. We then stood at attention in a large hangar as each flag-draped transfer case was carried from the aircraft into waiting hearses. The silence was interrupted only by soft sobbing.

Dave Petraeus was nominated by President Obama to become CIA director in the summer of 2011. He was succeeded by three of our best war fighters: John Allen, Joe Dunford, and John "JC" Campbell. Two additional Afghan hands, John "Mick" Nicholson and Austin Scott Miller, would follow them in the Trump and Biden administrations. We sent our best to Afghanistan, but we still hadn't won. We had achieved President Obama's goal of disrupting, dismantling, and largely defeating core al-Qa'ida in Pakistan, and until we completely withdrew our forces in 2021, we had prevented the Taliban from overthrowing the Afghan government and had successfully transitioned security responsibility to the Afghan government.

Between 2007 and late 2014, I made multiple trips to Afghanistan to help oversee our strategy there. I met regularly with Afghanistan's presidents, Hamid Karzai and Ashraf Ghani, its ministers of defense and Army chiefs and the heads of its national intelligence service. Two other old friends, Rahmatullah Nabil and Asadullah Khalid, would succeed my friend Amrullah Saleh as the head of NDS. Asadullah would also become Afghanistan's minister of defense.

I also met regularly with former resistance commanders of ours, like Abdul Rahim Wardak, Bismullah Khan, and Ismail Khan. It was a point of continuity for me between the covert war in the 1980s and our overt war since 9/11. During a visit to Herat, Ismail Khan's son arranged for me to visit the "mujahedin" museum his father had built to commemorate the Afghan resistance's victory over the Soviets. It was very well done and brought back many memories.

I visited our "line" of CT bases that ran along the Afghanistan-Pakistan border in the east, from Barikot to Skhin. I visited Spin Boldak, just across the border from the Pakistani city of Chaman, where the Taliban had many of their IED factories. I traveled to Kandahar and Helmand in the south, Herat and Shindand in the west, and Mazar-e-Sharif in the north. There was hardly a place in Afghanistan

I hadn't visited, some many times. In late 2014, only a few months away from my retirement from federal service, I made my final trip. My thirty-year adventure in Afghanistan had come to an end.

Mullah Omar died of tuberculosis on April 23, 2013. The Taliban kept his death a secret for two years. One of my regrets is that we weren't able to bring him to justice before he died. Mullah Mansur succeeded Omar as the leader of the Quetta Shura, having essentially run it as Omar's deputy for the previous five years. He was killed in May 2016 in a U.S. strike after he crossed from Iran into Pakistan. Mawlawi Hibatullah Akhundzada succeeded Mansur. And none other than Sirajuddin Haqqani was made Akhundzada's deputy.

The United States withdrew ten thousand troops in the summer of 2011, followed by another twenty-three thousand the following summer. That brought U.S. force levels back to the pre-surge number of sixty-eight thousand. In June 2013, ISAF transferred full security responsibility across Afghanistan to the Afghan government. U.S. forces drew down further to fifty-two thousand in November 2013, and then to thirty-four thousand in February 2014. At the end of December 2014, U.S. combat operations in Afghanistan came to an end, and a new mission of training, advising, and assisting Afghan forces and conducting limited counterterrorism operations was established.

When President Obama left office, U.S. forces had drawn down to eighty-four hundred. I had successfully argued in multiple White House meetings that we needed to keep a force of at least seven thousand in Afghanistan to protect our counterterrorism interests, along with bases at Bagram, Jalalabad, Kandahar, and Camp Dwyer in Helmand Province, and that's what President Obama in the end decided to do.

DEFEAT

President Trump reluctantly agreed to a doubling of the U.S. presence in Afghanistan early in his administration but soon grew tired of the war and sought to end it. In February 2020, as part of a "peace" deal with the Taliban to end the war, the Trump administration agreed to withdraw all U.S. forces by May 2021. Our ally, the Afghan government, was not a party to this agreement. To make matters worse, the Trump administration also agreed to the release of five thousand Taliban and al-Qa'ida prisoners, who quickly returned to the battlefield. As Trump's former national security adviser H. R. McMaster accurately put it, it wasn't a "peace deal"; it was a surrender agreement. In April 2021, President Biden announced that all U.S. troops would be out of Afghanistan by September 11, 2021, the twentieth anniversary of the 9/11 attacks, fulfilling his campaign pledge to end what he called our "forever war." U.S. forces completed their withdrawal in August. By the time they did, the Taliban had already taken over Afghanistan.

Presidents Trump and Biden turned a stalemate that protected U.S. interests into a defeat that has placed our interests in jeopardy. It was, in my view, a major and completely unnecessary strategic blunder.

Some assert that the war was lost long ago and that all Presidents Trump and Biden did was recognize reality. But the war hadn't been lost. Presidents Trump and Biden lost the war. Trump and his supporters argue that it was President Biden who lost the war, claiming that if Trump had been reelected, he would not have withdrawn U.S. forces if the Taliban hadn't complied with the terms of the agreement, which they haven't. But this strains credulity. President Trump had already drawn our forces down to twenty-five hundred, an untenable number, and sought to withdraw all U.S. forces five days before leaving office, an action that was fortunately halted by General Mark Milley, the chairman of the Joint Chiefs, and Robert O'Brien, Trump's national security adviser. The Biden administration has argued that the deal the Trump administration signed with the Taliban and the low level of forces Trump left in Afghanistan gave them no choice but to withdraw. This, too, strains credulity. An increase of a few thousand troops would have returned U.S. presence to a sustainable level that would have prevented a Taliban takeover.

The United States made plenty of mistakes, to be sure, during the twenty-year war. We succumbed to "mission creep" in our nation-building efforts, and should have done only what was necessary to protect our core counterterrorism interests after we overthrew the Taliban in 2001. We started too late to build Afghan security forces, and we built the wrong kinds of forces. We should have built more forces with ties to local areas like the ALP, and with less dependence on U.S. air and logistical support. And we should have transitioned to Afghan-led operations long before 2015.

As the special inspector general for Afghanistan recently concluded, the Afghans only gave up the fight after it became clear we were abandoning them.[22] The rapid collapse of the Afghan government was a policy failure far more than it was an intelligence failure.[23] Even with the Taliban's sanctuary in Pakistan, it remained demonstrably within our means to the very end to prevent the Taliban from winning and al-Qa'ida from returning. The strategic paradox of the Afghan war is that while we couldn't win with 150,000 U.S. and coalition troops in country, we couldn't lose with only seven to eight thousand as long as we had the escalation dominance that U.S. airpower provided.

With our withdrawal and the Taliban takeover, al-Qa'ida has been significantly strengthened. AQ's safe haven providers now control the country. The Taliban's victory has greatly emboldened global jihadists. And Afghanistan, in time, could once again become jihad central. As CIA Director Bill Burns has testified, our ability to collect critical intelligence will be significantly hampered. We will no longer have a local partner we can leverage for counterterrorism operations. And our Predator operations will become less effective flying from "over the horizon."

The strategic consequences of our defeat, moreover, could extend well beyond counterterrorism. Our withdrawal has placed at greater risk our other vital interest in the region: ensuring that any instability in Pakistan doesn't lead to terrorists' getting their hands on that country's nuclear weapons. We were much better able to look after our counter-proliferation interests in Pakistan with bases in Afghanistan. (U.S. bases in Afghanistan also contributed to our deterrent against China.) Our defeat will embolden China and other adversaries and could lead them to conclude that the United States is weak and unwilling to defend its interests. It is hard to see how our ignominious retreat didn't lead Putin to think he wouldn't get much of a U.S. response if he invaded Ukraine. (Fortunately, he miscalculated, but at Ukraine's and the free world's expense. I will have more to say about the U.S. response to Putin's invasion of Ukraine in a few chapters.) There is no other way to say it: withdrawing from Afghanistan was a major strategic blunder.

18

IRAQ: HIDDEN SURGE TO ISIS

INVASION, INSURGENCY, CIVIL WAR

It is a bit of an irony that while my meetings with President Bush on Iraq war strategy had been the catalyst for my coming back into government, I ended up playing a far lesser role in our wars in Iraq than I did in our war with al-Qa'ida and the war in Afghanistan. A few months before the invasion of Iraq, I had been asked by Paul Wolfowitz, the deputy secretary of defense, to meet with General Pete Pace, then the vice-chairman of the Joint Chiefs of Staff. Pace referenced my experience with the Afghan resistance in the 1980s and asked if I'd be interested in doing something similar in Iraq. Pace told me I would work with the Kurdish Peshmerga (those who face death), the Kurdish national militia. I told Pace, "Great, I like the Kurds. They're good fighters." I also recalled that the United States had broken faith with the Kurds in the 1990s when we abandoned them after encouraging them to rise up against Saddam and covertly supporting them—until we didn't.[1] This would be a way to make amends.[2]

I asked if the Peshmerga would be the main effort in northern Iraq. I knew the Turks had refused to grant us access to their territory for an invasion from the north. I could imagine an unconventional warfare campaign supported by U.S. airpower, just as we'd done in Afghanistan in 2001. Pace told me that U.S. conventional forces would have the lead, advancing from the south. What he wanted me to do was to train and organize a three-thousand-man unit of Peshmerga to conduct mop-up operations after the invasion. My disappointment was palpable. I told Pace that I wasn't the guy for that job. He thanked me for considering it, and soon found a more appropriate candidate.

After I returned to government service, I traveled to Iraq regularly to help oversee our strategy there. I contributed to the success of our special operations campaign by pushing for the rapid procurement of additional Predator armed ISR aircraft and oversaw a cross-border raid to kill a key al-Qa'ida facilitator in Syria. I had a regular engagement with General Talib Shaghati al-Kenani, the head of Iraq's counterterrorism forces, and participated in the initial policy discussions at the White House on the war with ISIS. But mostly I monitored rather than helped shape our Iraq wars. That doesn't mean I don't have views on how our wars in Iraq were conducted.

Looking at our plans to overthrow the Iraqi regime in late 2002 and early 2003, I thought that our forces would have a fairly easy time destroying Saddam's army and taking Baghdad. We had done something similar in 1991, and our capabilities for conventional war had advanced substantially since then. I also didn't think that we'd have too much trouble establishing a new government and stabilizing the country afterward. I had been right on the invasion—Saddam was overthrown in four weeks—but wrong on how things would go afterward.

I didn't consider the possibility of what a boon it would be to al-Qa'ida if we were to get bogged down in a protracted war in Iraq. Al-Qa'ida had been easily defeated in Afghanistan in late 2001, and several of its senior leaders and fighters were being captured in Pakistan in 2002 and early 2003. I had also forgotten the lessons about sectarian conflict that had been seared into my brain from my experience in Lebanon during the early 1980s. Iraq's civil war would remind me of Lebanon's. The Middle East is not a place for high hopes.

Some very poor U.S. decisions—to disband the Iraqi Army and purge the government of all Baathists—of course greatly contributed to the mess in Iraq, and these decisions weren't evident beforehand, but I should have thought harder about what could follow in the invasion's aftermath.[3] I had perhaps focused too much on conventional warfare since the 1990s.

It goes without saying, moreover, that the invasion of Iraq had been based on poor intelligence.[4] In 2002, well before the war, I had seen a DIA report from a clandestine source who claimed that Saddam possessed a mobile biological weapons production capability. It was very detailed, and on its own it seemed credible. It turned out to be a complete fabrication.[5] After the invasion, we would learn that Saddam had concealed the fact, even from his top generals, that he no longer had an active WMD program. Saddam felt it was important that Iraq be seen as having WMD for deterrence purposes, to deter Iran and the United States from invading Iraq. It was a fatal error in judgment.

In the latter half of 2006, the situation in Iraq looked bleak. Sectarian conflict between Sunni and Shi'a sharply intensified. Al-Qa'ida in Iraq was killing twenty-five hundred Iraqi civilians a month with its suicide bombings and other attacks. In mid-August, Colonel Pete Devlin, the Marines' senior intelligence officer in theater, wrote an intelligence assessment that all but conceded defeat in al-Anbar Province. A January 2007 National Intelligence Estimate made abundantly clear how bad the situation had gotten in Iraq, and helped convince President Bush that he needed to change strategy.[6]

The biggest revelation I would have after entering government, though, was that things weren't nearly as bleak in Iraq in late 2006 as they seemed. It was a good lesson in how hard it can be to measure progress in an unconventional war. The tribes in Anbar were revolting against al-Qa'ida's brutality. Our Special Operations Task Force was engaged in a fight to the death with al-Qa'ida and had battered the group more than most people realized. There was also an intelligence revolution about to take place in Iraq that would greatly accelerate the U.S. counterterrorism campaign.

THE HIDDEN SURGE

On January 10, 2007, President Bush told the American people that he was adopting a new strategy to "change the course of the war in Iraq." The president approved a surge of forces of nearly thirty thousand troops—five Army brigades and two Marine battalions, plus enablers. Secretary Gates told the president he would need to expand the Army by sixty-five thousand soldiers and the Marine Corps by twenty-seven thousand Marines to sustain the surge.[7] The president was betting his presidency and legacy on the new strategy. It was a bold decision.

I made my first visit to Iraq in early October 2007. On the U.S. side, I met with General Petraeus; Ambassador Ryan Crocker; Kevin, the CIA's chief of station and a former classmate of mine in the CIA's Career Training Program; Lieutenant General Ray Odierno, the commander of the Multi-National Corps in Iraq and the chief operational architect of surge operations; and Lieutenant General Stan McChrystal, the commander of the Special Operations Task Force. I also met with Brigadier General John "JC" Campbell, the assistant commander of the Army's 1st Cavalry Division, which had responsibility for operations in Baghdad; and Colonel Ken Tovo, the commander of the Combined Joint Special Operations Task Force–Arabian Peninsula and the 10th Special Forces Group, my former unit.

Petraeus and Crocker had just testified before Congress on the success of the surge, but parts of Baghdad and other areas in Iraq were still very dangerous. I spent most of my time in Baghdad but also traveled to Balad to see McChrystal and his task force and to Tikrit, Saddam's hometown, to see Ken Tovo and CJSOTF-AP. It was a good first trip.

Tovo's 2nd Battalion, in which I had served, had its headquarters in one of Saddam's palaces. It was commanded by then Lieutenant Colonel Sean Swindell, who would later serve as my military assistant after I became the undersecretary of defense for intelligence, and would rise to two-star rank. His battalion's area of operations was Baghdad, and it went after Shi'a extremist targets. My old battalion was doing a bang-up job under Sean, an operational commander who "got after things," but all I could think about when I visited my old unit was that I never got to live in a palace when I was in the 2nd Battalion.

The 10th Group had also done a great job in the area of tactical HUMINT, or human intelligence. Its "advanced special operations"–trained operatives had recruited several sources who produced actionable intelligence for the Group's operations. I had seen the same thing with Ed Reeder's 7th Group in Afghanistan. I was proud of what my old units were doing.

On the Iraqi side, I met with Mohammed Shahwani, the head of the Iraqi National Intelligence Service; Lieutenant General Talib Shaghati al-Kenani, the commander of Iraq's new Counter Terrorism

Bureau (later changed to the Counter Terrorism Service); and Major General Fadhil Jalil al-Barwari, the commander of Iraq's special operations forces, which had been placed under Kenani's new command. I saw demonstrations by several Iraqi CT units, including the Iraqi Counter Terrorism Force under Fadhil, and the Special Tactics Unit, under Shahwani. The STU conducted far fewer CT operations than the task force and CJSOTF-AP, but it was very surgical. My old CIA classmate Kevin told me that the STU had to fire their weapons on only 5 percent of their missions. The vast majority of the time, they were able to capture their target without firing a shot.[8]

At General Casey's direction, in 2006, McChrystal had created a new subordinate task force to go after Shi'a extremists, specifically the Iranian-backed "Special Groups."[9] Another subordinate task force of McChrystal's would continue to dismantle al-Qa'ida in Iraq and other Sunni extremist groups. The two operational task forces were firing on all cylinders, conducting more than ten raids a night, a result of a very improved intelligence picture from a variety of new sources. McChrystal's task force, CJSOTF-AP, and conventional force operations in Sadr City, Basra, and other Shi'ite areas of Iraq would be critically important to the continued success of the surge.

I came away very impressed by what our commanders in Iraq had accomplished to bring down the violence there. The team of Petraeus, Odierno, and McChrystal had been operationally brilliant. In Baghdad, I visited the troops from the 1st Cavalry Division, who were manning joint security stations with Iraqi forces. A key aspect of Petraeus's strategy was to get U.S. conventional forces off their big bases and out "with the people." The strategy worked. A darker factor also contributed to the surge's success in Baghdad, though—ethnic cleansing and separation. It had occurred voluntarily and involuntarily as a result of the horrible sectarian violence in 2006 and early 2007, and it and the joint security stations separating neighborhoods helped bring down the violence. Then Brigadier General JC Campbell, the commander really responsible for day-to-day operations in Baghdad, had done a great job. He would rise to four-star rank and later command all our forces in Afghanistan.

As I reflected on my trip, and prepared a report for Secretary Gates, I realized that as impressive as the surge was, there had been a "hidden surge" that had been responsible for bringing down most of the violence in Iraq. It had three components: the special operations campaign that had battered al-Qa'ida in Iraq and killed its leader, Abu Musab al-Zarqawi; new signals intelligence capabilities that made our special operations and conventional operations far more effective; and the "Awakening" by Sunni tribes, which began in al-Anbar Province in September 2006, months before the surge.

––––––

Stan McChrystal completely transformed his Special Operations Task Force between 2003 and 2006, and the task force's counterterrorism campaign played a key role in turning the tide in Iraq. He transformed a command of superb "shooters" into an intelligence-driven network. Stan recognized the central importance of intelligence to sustained counterterrorism operations, and the need to have a wide range of intelligence capabilities to enable rapid action and follow-on operations. He built up his ISR fleet and understood how important the "unblinking eye" of the Predator was to his operations. He expanded his forward interrogation capabilities and professionalized his detainee operations and facilities. He established Joint Interagency Task Forces to bring representatives of national intelligence agencies into his command, and he ordered the installation of high bandwidth secure communications networks so he could get the increasing volume of intelligence rapidly to where it was needed. He also established daily operations and intelligence briefs to synchronize operations across the force.

On the strategy side, Stan understood several important principles of modern counterterrorism operations. The first was the need to target an organization's mid-level leadership. It was network-on-network warfare, and we needed to take apart the enemy's network, not just his command-and-control nodes. Decapitation strategies targeting only the senior leadership weren't enough. The network's leaders would be replaced. Terrorist groups such as al-Qa'ida depended on their capabilities, not just on their leaders. Second, achieving a high operational tempo was key to defeating al-Qa'ida. Terrorist and insurgent groups succeeded by controlling tempo, speeding it up when feasible and slowing it down when necessary for survival. By expanding our operational tempo, we could seize the initiative in speed of operations and force the groups to react to us. He understood that to sustain a high operational tempo, his task force would need to get much larger, so he added more strike forces. Third, he knew that great precision was required in operations so as to not create more supporters for al-Qa'ida.[10] We would apply intelligence-driven operations and this same general approach to strategy in our Predator campaigns against core al-Qa'ida in the Afghanistan-Pakistan border region.

In December 2003, Stan's task force captured Saddam Hussein near Tikrit.[11] In June 2006, it killed Abu Musab al-Zarqawi, the leader of al-Qa'ida in Iraq.[12] In April 2004, Stan's task force was conducting ten raids per month. Within two years, the task force's operational tempo had increased by a factor of thirty. The task force's precision targeting prepared the way for the Second Battle of Fallujah, and it helped reduce the foreign fighter flow coming into Iraq from the west. It took out more and more of AQI's second-tier and lower operational leaders so that by 2008 the decline in quality was noticeable. As a result of the task force's contributions, McChrystal was given an increasingly central voice in overall war strategy.

Operational intelligence in Iraq had improved substantially by 2007. Detainee operations and exploitation of media captured on special operations raids was one source. CIA clandestine reporting was another. The increased availability of Predator and other airborne ISR support was another major factor in the improvement in the intelligence picture available to our war fighters. But the revolutionary change in actionable intelligence came from signals intelligence—specifically, from an innovation the National Security Agency had made called the "Real Time Regional Gateway," or RT/RG for short.

Immediately after the 9/11 attacks, in addition to seeking and receiving new authorities for collecting SIGINT, NSA began research and development programs to try to keep ahead of the dramatic increases in the volume and velocity of the global communications system. An early effort, called Trailblazer, which had as its aim the goal of bringing massive amounts of global communications intercepts back to NSA headquarters, proved technologically infeasible.[13] NSA's researchers then pursued a different technical approach that would lead to RT/RG. The driving force behind this innovation was Lieutenant General Keith Alexander, NSA's director.

RT/RG enabled massive SIGINT collected regionally to be

accessed by forward-deployed NSA officers in real time. It was a "complete change in how [NSA] provided signals intelligence support to the war fighter," Deputy Director Rick Ledgett would note after RT/RG was declassified.[14] It would alert American soldiers to IED attacks and enable U.S. forces to dramatically improve their targeting of insurgents. The program harnessed big data in a way that could be immediately used on the battlefield, employing special software to draw connections and put information in graphical displays so operators and analysts could immediately act upon it.

One of the U.S. senior military commanders in Iraq told NSA that RT/RG had been responsible for taking more than four thousand insurgents off the battlefield during the surge. RT/RG was expanded to Afghanistan a few years later, a development I pushed after I had seen what the system had done in Iraq. An exhibit on RT/RG was put on display at NSA's National Cryptologic Museum in May 2017.

More than any other factor, however, the tribal rebellion in Anbar against al-Qa'ida that began in September 2006 turned the war around. The rebellion was the product of some great work by CIA, the State Department, and the military, and it was embraced by General Petraeus as soon as he assumed command. The surge of forces and the task force's relentless special operations campaign against AQI served as catalysts to further extend and sustain the rebellion across Sunni-populated areas in Iraq. I don't think the surge would have been as great a success, however, if the "Anbar Awakening," as it came to be known, had not occurred. It was the decisive blow to the Sunni insurgency.

CIA had been engaging tribal leaders in Anbar for several years and had developed very good intelligence on the changing power positions of the local sheikhs. Senior State Department officers, particularly Robert Ford, also played an important role in our engagement efforts. The operational aim of tribal engagement was threefold: to separate Sunni insurgents like the 1920s Brigade from al-Qa'ida in Iraq; to provide jobs for unemployed Sunni youth (the United States and al-Qa'ida were competing over largely the same manpower pool); and to bring "rejectionist" Sunni political leaders in from the cold and into the political mainstream.

In addition to very good intelligence on changing tribal power balances, the use of sound clandestine tradecraft was critical to early engagement efforts. Enhanced physical protection for tribal leaders through the provision of armored vehicles and body armor was also important.

Tribal engagement efforts didn't succeed at first. This was because the tribes had been alienated by the loss of Arab Sunni influence after the fall of Saddam's regime, and had joined the insurgency to try to redress their change in fortune. What caused the tribes to turn was three things. First, AQI had waged a brutal campaign to keep the tribes in check and impose its harsh views on the populace and by the summer of 2006, the group had way overplayed its hand. Second, Sunni leaders had concluded that violence against the government wasn't achieving their political and economic goals. Third, Sunni tribal leaders came to believe that they could be protected by U.S. forces if they switched sides. The task force had waged an intense, sustained campaign against AQI in Anbar, and by the summer of 2006 it had battered the group substantially. As tribal leaders indicated they were ready to come over, CIA turned them over to local U.S. military leaders for protection and security assistance.

On September 9, 2006, Sheikh Abdul Sattar al-Risha al-Rishawi, the thirty-five-year-old head of a minor tribe located on the outskirts of Ramadi, Anbar's capital, met with fifty other sheikhs to form the Sahwa al-Anbar (Awakening of Anbar). Sahwa called for the Iraqi Army to return to Anbar and for tribal sons to join the police and military. The group declared war on al-Qa'ida, who had cut off the tribes' smuggling routes from Jordan, their main source of income. The Awakening's leaders demanded that "the respect that was due to tribal sheikhs be shown." Sahwa also affirmed that the tribes considered U.S. forces friendly, and they forbade any attacks against them. And finally, they asked to join the political system in Iraq.

Sattar's move gave then Colonel Sean MacFarland, the 1st Brigade commander of the 1st Armored Division based in Ramadi, the opening he was looking for, and he went all in. Sattar and other tribal leaders began offering up hundreds of their tribesmen to join the police force. MacFarland responded by training, arming, equipping, and later, with Petraeus's approval, paying them. The police were soon apprehending or killing hundreds of al-Qa'ida members and uncovering the group's weapons caches.

AQI fought back by assassinating some of the tribal leaders and conducting suicide bombing attacks against the new police stations, but they couldn't stop the rebellion. U.S. forces continued to pummel AQI, reinforcing the success of the tribes. By early 2007, every tribe in the Ramadi area had joined the Awakening. Insurgent attacks were down 70 percent. Ramadi had gone from the most dangerous city in Iraq to the safest nearly overnight.[15]

The Marine Expeditionary Force under Brigadier General John Allen quickly got on board and supported the uprising. Allen worked the leaders of the major tribes, and by the summer of 2007 most of al-Anbar Province had been reclaimed from the insurgents. The Awakening spread beyond Anbar and morphed into the Sons of Iraq movement, or *Abnaa al-Iraq*. Many SOI were former insurgents who had decided to cast their lot with the Americans and the Iraqi government to fight their al-Qa'ida tormentors. The Awakening soon reached the Sunni neighborhoods of Baghdad. Eventually, 100,000 SOI were put on the U.S. payroll at $300 per month before the program was turned over to the Iraqi government in late 2008. Al-Qa'ida in Iraq was running out of places to hide and get new recruits. Tragically, though, the hero of the Awakening, Sheikh Sattar, was killed in a roadside bomb in September 2007, a year after he launched his rebellion.[16] The revolt he sparked, however, continued.

THE RISE AND FALL OF ISIS

I made several more trips to Iraq during 2008. During one, I was asked by Rear Admiral Ed Winters, the senior U.S. adviser to Iraq's new Counter Terrorism Bureau and a highly decorated Navy SEAL, to tell General Kenani that Shi'a extremists needed to be on his target list and not just Sunnis. Prime Minister Nouri al-Maliki had placed the CT Bureau directly under him, and there were fears that it would become a sectarian Praetorian Guard for Maliki. A task force raid in Basra a year earlier that accidentally captured Qais Khazali, the head of one of the Iranian-backed Special Groups who had been placed on a no-target list by Iraq's government, had created political tension between the United States and Maliki. It had only been resolved when

Dave Petraeus showed Maliki a document that had been captured on the raid, revealing that Maliki was being undercut by Khazali.[17] Kenani turned out to be a professional and an Iraqi patriot. He would become one of our best partners in Iraq for the war against AQI and Shi'a extremists and later for the war with ISIS.

During another trip in late March 2008, Admiral Olson and I were having dinner with Dave Petraeus when we heard that Maliki had independently ordered his forces to take Basra in Iraq's south. The Iraqi operation was called Charge of the Knights. Basra was a hotbed of Shi'a militancy, and Petraeus feared the worst—an Iraqi defeat that would set back much of the progress he'd made. Dave quickly dispatched our friend Ed Winters to Basra to serve as his liaison to Maliki during the battle. Ed was joined by Marine Major General George Flynn. The United States provided fires and logistical support to the Iraqis and the British-commanded Multinational Division that was based nearby. Soon, the battle was over. The Shi'a militants had been routed. Winters and Flynn played major roles in turning the tide of the battle, but it had been a close-run thing.[18]

By late 2008, the number of AQI attacks had been dramatically reduced. The number of Iraqis who were being killed monthly by AQI was down by 80 percent.[19] Shi'a extremist leader Muqtada al-Sadr, moreover, was forced in 2008 to stand down his militia and flee to Iran.

After Zarqawi's death, Abu Ayyub al-Masri, an Egyptian, became AQI's new leader. To put an Iraqi face on the group, AQI's nominal head was Abu Umar al-Baghdadi. On October 15, 2006, Abu Ayyub and Abu Umar changed the group's name to the Islamic State of Iraq to further enhance AQI's local brand and differentiate the group from the excesses of the Zarqawi period. IS was still AQI, despite its name change.

AQI continued its steep decline under Abu Ayyub. By the summer of 2010, the group had lost 90 percent of its fighting strength, and what was left had largely been pushed into the wadis of the western Iraqi desert. Global jihadists were despondent, convinced that AQI had lost the war in Iraq. Even Abu Ayyub's Yemeni wife was giving him a hard time. "Where is this Islamic State of Iraq that you're talking about? We're living in the desert."[20] In April 2010, Abu Ayyub and Abu Umar were killed in their desert hideout just south of Tikrit by U.S. and

Iraqi special operations forces. Just as with Bin Ladin, identifying and following the leaders' couriers had led our special operators to Abu Ayyub's and Abu Umar's hideout. Our special operations commander in Iraq, Brigadier General Darsie Rogers, had done a magnificent job.

U.S. forces withdrew from Iraq at the end of 2011. After 2011, the vacuum created by the withdrawal, the civil war in Syria, Maliki's sectarian, "winner take all" politics, IS's covert campaign to intimidate and win over Sunni tribes in Iraq, and U.S. inaction all contributed to the rise of the Islamic State. We watched this occur, but did nothing until IS invaded Iraq in June 2014, seizing much of the Sunni north before being halted short of Baghdad by U.S. airpower and Shi'a militias.

Abu Bakr al-Baghdadi replaced Abu Ayyub as the leader of the Islamic State.[21] Just before he assumed command, his fellow jihadists had circulated a strategic plan outlining the steps that they believed would lead to the group's recovery. IS planners took solace in the return of the Taliban, noting that they had recovered after having been initially defeated in Afghanistan. The planners anticipated an American withdrawal from Iraq. That would be their moment, they believed, to strike. In the interim, IS should focus their attacks on Iraqi security forces, since the Americans were leaving, concentrating, in particular, on the Iraqi units most capable of fighting the jihadists. The IS planners knew that to be successful, they would have to co-opt the Sunni tribes who had abandoned them in the Awakening. They acknowledged that the Awakening had been a deathblow to the group. What they hadn't anticipated was the strategic opportunity the Syrian civil war would present beginning in 2011.

Abu Bakr left Iraq for Syria in 2011. IS/AQI already had a jihadist network in place there; some 85 to 90 percent of foreign fighters who had joined AQI in Iraq had come through Syria with the support of the Syrian regime. As Syrians began peacefully protesting their government as part of the Arab Spring in early 2011, Bashar al-Assad, Syria's autocratic leader, released a large number of jihadists from his prisons to foster greater violence among the protesters, which he hoped would provide international justification for a crackdown.

It was a huge gift to IS and other extremists and a major strategic blunder by Assad, because the released jihadists would accelerate the armed insurgency that almost led to his downfall.

Abu Bakr al-Baghdadi initially joined forces with al-Qa'ida's affiliate in Syria, Jabhat al-Nusra, led by Abu Mohammad al-Jawlani. Baghdadi and Jawlani, however, had very different visions for the global jihadist movement in Syria. Jawlani's al-Qa'ida-affiliated group sought to embed itself in the Syrian opposition to overthrow the Assad regime while also using their sanctuary in Syria to plot attacks against the "far enemy," the United States. Baghdadi wanted to establish an Islamic State in the hinterland between Syria and Iraq. Baghdadi and his followers also had a far more apocalyptic vision for the global jihadist movement, believing that the "end times" were nigh, and that Dabiq, a small town in Syria near Aleppo, would be the site of a battle where Muslims under a black flag would finally defeat the West.

The two soon had a falling-out. On April 9, 2013, Baghdadi publicly asserted that Nusra was a branch of the Islamic State and would be absorbed into a new entity he would lead, the Islamic State of Iraq and al-Sham (the Levant), or ISIS. Jawlani responded by declaring Nusra's independence from ISIS and pledged allegiance to Ayman al-Zawahiri and al-Qa'ida. Zawahiri directed Baghdadi to renounce his claim on Syria and return to Iraq. Baghdadi refused, publicly rejecting Zawahiri's directive. On February 2, 2014, Zawahiri publicly kicked ISIS out of al-Qa'ida.[22] Al-Qa'ida now had a rival for the leadership of the global jihadist movement.

More than forty thousand foreign fighters, coming from nearly a hundred countries, flowed into Syria to join ISIS—more than had joined the jihad in Iraq between 2003 and 2011. Baghdadi further strengthened ISIS's ranks by incorporating former Iraqi intelligence and military personnel who had fled to Syria. The former Baathists represented a third of ISIS's leadership. ISIS's top military commander, Haji Bakr, was a former Iraqi Army intelligence colonel.

Within Iraq, Baghdadi ran a sophisticated assassination campaign against tribal leaders who had supported the Awakening. In July 2012, Baghdadi announced a "Breaking the Walls" campaign, a series of bombings and assassinations, combined with prison raids to free ISIS/AQI prisoners, and attacks on government installations. By mid-2013, violence in Iraq had spiked to its highest level since 2007. Within Syria,

ISIS fought against Syrian opposition forces as much as it did against the Assad regime. In 2013, ISIS had captured Raqqa, which became the capital of ISIS's caliphate, and swaths of other territory in Syria, including the oil fields near Deir ez-Zour, from which they sold oil on the black market to fund the group's operations.

Maliki, meanwhile, wasted no time in seeking to dominate Iraq and rid it of his Sunni rivals. The day after the last American soldier left Iraq, Maliki issued an arrest warrant for his Sunni vice president, Tariq al-Hashemi, on terrorism charges. He later sentenced Hashemi to death in absentia after Hashemi had fled to Turkey. The incident intensified Sunni distrust of the Maliki government and led to demands for Sunni autonomy. Maliki also disarmed the Sons of Iraq. And in December 2012, government forces raided the home of the finance minister, Rafi al-Issawi. Issawi had fled to Anbar, but ten of his bodyguards who were there were arrested on terrorism charges. Issawi was a Sunni hero from the powerful Albu Issa tribe in Fallujah, and Maliki's move against him triggered massive demonstrations in Fallujah, Ramadi, Samarra, Kirkuk, and Mosul. Tribal leaders in Anbar backed the protests.

In retribution, Maliki removed some Anbari leaders from positions of power and reduced Anbar's police force by 20 percent, further facilitating ISIS's return to Iraq. In April 2013, Iraqi forces fired on protesters in Hawja in northern Iraq, killing or wounding 120 civilians. Outraged Sunnis in the north started attacking government forces. In Anbar, tribal militias were organized to defend the province against the Iraqi Army.[23] Maliki had snatched defeat from the jaws of victory. It was a stark reminder that, as Clausewitz had observed, war is subservient to politics. What we had won at very high cost militarily in Iraq had been lost politically.

The U.S. intelligence community increasingly warned about Iraq's deteriorating security environment between the end of 2011 and mid-2014, but the Obama administration was content to monitor events in Iraq and do little else. There was no appetite to reinsert a small contingent of special operators back into Iraq. To be fair, Maliki wouldn't have approved it if we had wanted to. I tried to get more ISR overflights over the Sunni areas of Iraq, but most of our assets were still deployed in our strategic counterterrorism campaign against al-Qa'ida and its affiliates or in Afghanistan. There were no Predators left to spare. We were able to fly a few Global Hawk missions over Iraq once or twice a month, but they flew too high and too infrequently to be of any operational use. They simply weren't designed for the CT mission.

We were monitoring events in Syria much more closely because of the terrorist threat to the U.S. homeland that was emanating from there and because of our policy to seek the removal of Assad from power. I traveled to Iraq in early 2014 to assess the situation, but came away very discouraged. Our embassy was mostly tied up with facilitating foreign military sales to Iraq. We were treating Iraq as a "normal" country, and it was fast becoming anything but.

There was shock in Washington when ISIS invaded Iraq in June 2014 and its forces advanced halfway to Baghdad. Iraqi security forces, in which we had invested $25 billion between 2003 and 2011, collapsed without hardly engaging ISIS. It was a major intelligence failure, and President Obama was none too pleased.[24] Security forces are a reflection of the society from which they come, and Iraq suffered from increasing political dysfunction and sectarian polarization. ISIS didn't have superior forces in any quantitative or qualitative sense. Iraqi security forces had simply lost the will to stand and fight for a regime they no longer believed in. At the height of its power, ISIS controlled one-third of Syrian territory and 40 percent of Iraq's.

ISIS's takeover of major areas of Iraq, however, was also a policy failure, and the invasion finally galvanized the Obama administration into action. U.S. airpower and mobilized Shi'ite forces were employed to halt ISIS well short of Baghdad, and Maliki was forced from power. U.S. military trainers were then deployed back into Iraq to begin rebuilding Iraqi security forces. Al-Qa'ida in Syria's external operations group, the part responsible for plotting attacks in the West, was struck a little over a month after U.S. air operations had begun in Iraq. I had participated in numerous Deputies Committee meetings at the White House on the growing al-Qa'ida threat in Syria and was pleased that we had taken the strike. I only wished that we had followed it up with more. ISIS's forces in Syria weren't struck until a year later.[25]

Operations to destroy ISIS's caliphate in Iraq and later in Syria began at a very measured pace. I wondered why we were using airpower so ineffectually. It reminded me of Afghanistan in 2001, before we started using our bombers to break the cohesion of the Taliban and enable the opposition to advance through their forward positions.

Our special operators in Iraq were restricted to training missions and were not allowed to accompany Iraqi forces into combat. This further constrained our combat effectiveness. When I retired from government at the end of April 2015, we were still training Iraqi forces and conducting limited air strikes against ISIS positions in Iraq. We clearly weren't using all means available, even in what was rightly intended to be a small-footprint war.

Eventually, under General Joe Votel, we developed a better strategy, using airpower and U.S. special operations advisers to dislodge ISIS, first in Mosul and later in Raqqa. The Iraqi Counter Terrorism Service was central to our campaign against ISIS in Iraq. The Kurdish-dominated Syrian Democratic Forces were central to the success of our campaign in Syria.[26]

In December 2015, Iraqi forces took back Ramadi. By the end of 2017, ISIS had lost 95 percent of its territory, including Mosul in Iraq and Raqqa, its capital in Syria. ISIS's last stronghold in Syria, Baghouz, fell in March 2019.[27] U.S. counterterrorism forces, aided by exceptional intelligence, killed Abu Bakr al-Baghdadi in Syria's Idlib Province on October 26, 2019.

It had taken less than two months to defeat the Taliban in late 2001. It took five years to defeat ISIS. ISIS was essentially the Taliban and al-Qa'ida rolled into one. The longer a war goes on, the higher the casualties that result from it. The "Taliban" part of ISIS—its need to hold territory—was its Achilles' heel. It made them easy to defeat. We had become way too timid in the way we conducted special operations and proxy war and employed U.S. airpower. In the end we won, but it took way too long, with the consequence that the U.S. homeland and Europe were vulnerable to ISIS attacks longer than they should have been.

Our experience in Iraq is flush with lessons, good and bad, but I will offer only a few of them here. Most apply to Afghanistan as well. The first is knowing what kind of war you're getting into—a lesson that dates back to Thucydides. Invading a country is generally a lot easier than pacifying it afterward. In a sectarian conflict, moreover, you can easily become everyone's enemy. Keeping the main thing the main thing is a core principle of strategy and is a second lesson. After 9/11, we should have remained focused on preventing another large-scale attack on the American homeland. A third lesson is the importance of good intelligence. While it is unrealistic to expect perfection, intelligence officers have a duty to be clear about what they know, what they don't know, and how confident they are about what they know. A high level of confidence can only be given if it is based on very reliable reporting and multiple sources. Intelligence is also an increasingly critical enabler of combat operations. The Predator, SIGINT collection from RT/RG, and clandestine HUMINT made a world of difference, but they took time to develop. Fourth, special operations raids and tribal engagement are central components of many modern counterinsurgency campaigns. As a result of U.S. conventional overmatch, insurgency has become very similar in tactics to terrorism and must be countered accordingly. Locals are usually far better at defending their territory than outside forces, and it is strategically wise to place the burden on them. Local security forces, moreover, are your ticket out. We need to get a lot better at building appropriate and reliable ones. Fifth, it is critical to deny your adversary any sanctuary if at all possible. ISIS wouldn't have been able to invade Iraq if we had dealt with them in Syria. Sixth, short wars are better than long wars. Be in it to win it, sooner rather than later. Finally, you're not done until you're done. With our complete withdrawal from Iraq after 2011, we had enabled AQI/ISIS's return. And with our withdrawal from Afghanistan in 2021, we enabled the Taliban and al-Qa'ida's return. We shouldn't have to fight the same war again.

PART IV

FIGHTING ON MULTIPLE FRONTS

COUNTER PROLIFERATION, COUNTER NARCO-INSURGENCY

DELAYING IRAN FROM GETTING THE BOMB

Our war with al-Qa'ida and the wars in Afghanistan and Iraq occupied a lot of my time between 2007 and 2015, but by no means all of it. We were engaged on multiple fronts against a wide range of adversaries, and I was engaged in all of them one way or the other. I worked with our Colombian and Mexican partners in their campaigns against Marxist insurgents and drug cartels, I participated in operations to delay North Korea's development of ballistic missiles, I helped oversee our program to support the moderate opposition in Syria, and I assisted the Ukrainians in their efforts to counter Russian aggression in eastern Ukraine. But of all these operations on multiple fronts, stopping or at least delaying the Iranians from getting the bomb was the most important.

Counter proliferation of weapons of mass destruction was a critical mission for the U.S. government during the Bush and Obama administrations, second only in importance to counterterrorism. As former CIA director Mike Hayden put it, there was CT (counterterrorism), CP (counter proliferation), and ROW (the rest of the world).[1] Our objective was to prevent the acquisition, use, and international transfer of nuclear, chemical, biological, and radiological weapons and their associated delivery systems. If we couldn't prevent a state from acquiring nuclear weapons, we sought to delay it from acquiring them for as long as possible through a variety of means. If a state of concern already possessed weapons of mass destruction and the means to deliver them, our objective was to prevent further acquisition, the use of these weapons, and their international transfer to other states. Iran's pursuit of a nuclear weapons capability was at the top of our CP priorities. Approximately 80 to 85 percent of our efforts in this area was aimed at preventing Iran from getting the bomb.

A usable fission weapon (an "atomic" bomb) requires three things: fissile material, a proven weapons design, and a warhead that can be detonated reliably, miniaturized sufficiently to fit on a delivery system, and survive reentry if delivered by a ballistic missile.[2] And by 2007, Iran had made substantial progress in each of these areas. In November 2007, the U.S. intelligence community produced a National Intelligence Estimate on Iran's nuclear intentions and capabilities.[3] We had learned from clandestine intelligence sources that Iran had suspended its nuclear weapons program in 2003 following the U.S. invasion of Iraq.[4] As I read the NIE, I thought at least we've bought some time.

But how much was uncertain. The U.S. invasion of Iraq had unnerved the Iranians, but they seemed to have recovered and were regularly sponsoring attacks by Shi'a militant groups against U.S. forces in Iraq. As the NIE warned, Iran's leaders wanted to keep their nuclear options open. Persuading Iran's leadership to forgo eventual development would be difficult, given the many linkages between nuclear weapons and Iran's national security objectives. The NIE noted that Iran had resumed uranium enrichment in 2006 and had made significant progress in 2007 in installing centrifuges at its declared uranium enrichment production facility at Natanz. A growing body of intelligence indicated that Iran was pursuing covert enrichment in facilities other than Natanz. Finally, the IC assessed that the earliest Iran would have enough fissile material for a bomb was late 2009. Most likely, however, Iran wouldn't possess enough highly enriched uranium until the 2010–2015 time frame.

Iran's nuclear weapons complex consisted of several different facilities and activities, most of which were concealed by the Iranians. Weapons design was under Mohsen Fakhrizadeh and other Iranian scientists. Components necessary for nuclear weapons were produced by several Iranian companies or sourced internationally. Kalaye Electric Company in Tehran was just one of several companies that provided the components necessary for nuclear weapons design and production. In addition to Iran's declared uranium enrichment facility at Natanz, we discovered that there was an underground covert enrichment facility at Fordow, near the holy city of Qom. Iran also announced in 2010 that it had begun enriching uranium to 20 percent at Natanz, which the Iranians claimed was necessary for a research reactor in Tehran.

Uranium enrichment proceeds through three phases. First, uranium is enriched to 3 or 4 percent, then to 20 percent, and finally to 85 to 90 percent, the level needed for weapons-grade material. The hard part is getting to 20 percent; after that, it is pretty clear sailing. Because of the peculiar physics involved, achieving 20 percent enriched uranium constitutes most of the effort required to get to 85 to 90 percent.

The covert facility at Fordow was particularly troubling. Built in secret on an Islamic Revolutionary Guards Corps base under a granite mountain, it could accommodate about three thousand centrifuges, just enough for a modest weapons effort.[5] The facility at Natanz could accommodate several times that number. Were there other covert facilities in Iran that we didn't know about? my colleagues and I wondered. The lights were blinking red.

For those of us on the operational side, it was a call to action. After the NIE was published, I met with CIA's clandestine operators and analysts to go over the key reporting and to gain a deeper understanding of Iran's nuclear weapons complex. There was still plenty of uncertainty about how far and how fast Iran would go in pursuing a nuclear weapons capability.

During the final two years of his administration, President Bush grew frustrated at the two stark choices he had been given to prevent Iran from developing nuclear weapons. We could bomb Iran or accept that it would inevitably become a nuclear power. The first course of action risked a war and, even if successful, would likely set the Iranian nuclear program back only a couple years at most. A military strike on Iran's nuclear facilities, moreover, would almost certainly make its leadership even more determined to acquire nuclear weapons. If, on the other hand, we acquiesced to Iran becoming a nuclear-armed state, our nuclear arsenal would likely deter it from launching its weapons against the United States in almost all scenarios, but it would also embolden Iran's leaders to become far more aggressive in their use of proxies to further destabilize the Middle East, confident that their possession of nuclear weapons would deter us from using military force to overthrow the regime.

President Bush wanted more options—a "third option," between military force and traditional diplomacy. He recognized that the most we could do with our counter-proliferation efforts was to buy time for sanctions and other pressure to bring Iran to the negotiating table. President Obama would pursue a very similar strategy. My colleagues in the IC and I set out to give both presidents the options they had requested.

Our primary counter-proliferation options were aimed at making it as hard as possible for the Iranians to produce fissile material and develop a nuclear warhead and ballistic missiles. This could conceivably be accomplished through overt or covert means, through unilateral operations or in operations with key partners that could be direct or indirect, virtual or physical, and kinetic or non-kinetic. We could impose further sanctions, squeeze Iran's supply chain, and "name and shame" Iranian scientists working on the program.[6] CIA's Counter Proliferation Center (now called the Weapons and Counter Proliferation Mission Center) was the agency's lead for operations against WMD and missile targets worldwide, and I worked closely with Shaun, Jon S., and other leaders of that center in generating a range of options for the president.

We of course also had the option of using military force—an air strike or a special operations raid. Secretary Gates strongly opposed an air strike, which would require a number of strikes against large, dispersed, and in some cases very hardened targets. "A military attack on Iran's nuclear program," I heard him warn frequently, "will guarantee that the Iranians will develop nuclear weapons."[7] A special operations raid would be even more problematic. Our force could get trapped in Iran, and a raid would cause far less disruption to Iran's program. Not surprisingly, Gates's view was almost universally accepted within the U.S. national security establishment.

A second broad option was to focus on the Iranian regime. There were two possible approaches in this area: trying to change the Iranian regime's behavior or trying to change the regime itself. Iran had many fault lines. The clerical regime was not popular, particularly among the urban, educated, and reasonably affluent segments of the population. Food shortages and Iran's international isolation added to the discontent. Iran also had substantial minorities. The Azeris, about 25 percent of the population, composed a significant part of the *bazaari* merchant class. The Kurds, about 10 percent of Iran's population, had long wanted a homeland of their own. The corruption that was pervasive among Iran's elites, particularly within the Islamic Revolutionary Guard Corps, or IRGC, was another exploitable issue.

To provide greater focus on the Iranian target, Mike Hayden established a separate Iran Operations Division in 2007. Its first chief, Norm, was a former classmate of mine in CIA's Career Training Program. Norm was a veteran Clandestine Service officer with experience throughout the Middle East. He described the threat from Iran as "lethal, strategic, and urgent."[8] I met with Norm, his successors, Tom R. and Jonathan, and other IOD officers regularly between 2007 and 2015.

In 2009, an opportunity presented itself when Iran's "Green Movement" filled the streets of Tehran with three million protesters, after the Iranian government announced that the hard-liner Mahmoud Ahmadinejad had won the presidential election. Signs in English pleaded for external assistance. The Iranian regime cracked down and cracked heads, unleashing the million-man Basij resistance force, the regime's militia and street thugs, on the protesters. The United States could help keep the opposition alive, but it couldn't help it prevail short of overt military action.

Israel was a key partner of ours on Iran, and between 2008 and 2015, I met regularly with Israeli senior intelligence and military officials. Foremost among them were Meir Dagan and Tamir Pardo, the heads of Mossad, Israel's secret intelligence service. I respected and liked both men. Our meetings were always very candid and operationally focused.[9] During the early 1970s, Dagan had commanded Sayeret Rimon, an undercover special operations unit whose mission was to combat the increasing violence in the Palestinian territories. He had held several other commands in the Israel Defense Forces before retiring as a major general and becoming Mossad's director in 2002. Throughout his long career, Dagan was known for not being reluctant to take lethal action against Israel's enemies, but he thought that bombing Iran to set back its nuclear program would be strategic folly. After he retired from Mossad, he clashed with Israeli prime minister Benjamin Netanyahu repeatedly on this issue. (Dagan died of cancer in 2016.)

Pardo had participated as an officer in Sayeret Matkal, Israel's premier counterterrorism unit, in the 1976 rescue of Israeli hostages at Entebbe, Uganda. He was a career Mossad officer who rose to become its deputy director for operations before succeeding Dagan as Mossad's director in 2011. Pardo and I would talk about where the United States and Israel were in our Iran strategy. Tamir liked to use a metaphor of a building with many floors when discussing our options. We agreed that we weren't close to the top floor—the highest level of intensity short of war—but we had moved up several floors in recent years. As the years went by and the Middle East was plunged deeper and deeper into chaos, Tamir and I noted that every time we saw each other, it seemed the world had gotten worse.

I also regularly met with Amos Yadlin, Aviv Kochavi, and Herzi Halevi, the heads of Israeli Defense Intelligence, or IDI; Nadav Zafrir, the head of Israel's SIGINT National Unit, or ISNU, the equivalent of our NSA; and Yuval Diskin, the head of Shin Bet, Israel's Internal Security Service, and his successors. Yadlin, Kochavi, Halevi, and Nadav were Israeli military heroes. Yadlin had flown in Israel's 1981 air strike that destroyed Iraq's nuclear reactor at Osirak. Kochavi, a rising star in the Israel Defense Forces, had come up through the paratroops and became the IDF's chief of staff in 2019. Halevi was a special operator like me who had previously commanded Sayeret Matkal. In addition to being a cyber expert, Nadav had a background in special operations and was the youngest general in the IDF at the time.

ISNU was particularly impressive in what it was able to collect. Because of Israel's universal military service, it was able to attract Israel's best and brightest into its ranks before they went off to college and started high-tech companies. Part of me wished that we could find a way to do something like that in the United States. Our IC attracted top talent, to be sure, but not to the same degree that Israel did with its national service.

The U.S. intelligence community rarely disagreed with the Israelis regarding the facts on the ground in Iran. But we did disagree about Iran's intentions: Was Iran's leadership determined to acquire a nuclear weapon, as the Israelis believed, or did it simply want to have the option to acquire nuclear weapons and to get as close as possible, as we believed? Given the existential threat Israel faced, it was not surprising that their intelligence professionals were more pessimistic than we were on this question.

The IDF consistently requested special equipment from the United States that could facilitate an air strike or a special operations raid on Fordow and other nuclear sites in Iran. Presidents Bush and Obama deflected Israel's requests, wanting to keep counter-proliferation efforts against Iran short of an overt strike. A second core objective of our counter-proliferation strategy was to prevent an Israeli attack on Iran.

There was good reason for this concern. In June 2008, the Israelis conducted a military exercise that appeared to be a rehearsal for a strike. One hundred Israeli F-15s and F-16s took off from Israel and flew over the eastern Mediterranean to Greece and back. The exercise included the use of combat search and rescue helicopters, necessary if a plane gets shot down or a pilot has to eject, and air refueling aircraft. Israeli fighter jets had flown 862 miles to Greece. The distance from Israel to Iran's uranium enrichment facility at Natanz was coincidentally 860 miles. You couldn't miss the message the Israelis were sending.[10]

There would be no military strikes on Iran's nuclear program, either by the United States or by Israel, but there were other setbacks to Iran's program. As Mike Hayden observed in his memoirs, someone was killing scientists associated with Iran's nuclear program.[11] Someone was also using a cyber weapon to cause Iran's centrifuges to crash.[12] Although the Iranians were eventually able to replace their losses, our counter-proliferation efforts, enabled by some truly outstanding clandestine collection, had achieved the limited objectives Presidents Bush and Obama had established: they bought time for sanctions that would bring Iran to the negotiating table to work, and they prevented an Israeli strike on Iran.

In February 2013, the Obama administration initiated secret talks with Iran to constrain its nuclear program. A final deal, the Joint Comprehensive Plan of Action, or JCPOA, was reached in July 2015. In return for a gradual lifting of sanctions, 98 percent of Iran's stockpile of enriched uranium was removed, along with two-thirds of its centrifuges. The deal also eliminated other pathways to a bomb, including the capacity to produce weapons-grade plutonium. It was a good if less-than-perfect deal. It constrained Iran from developing nuclear weapons for at least a decade, and Iran's "breakout time"—the amount of time it would need to enrich enough uranium to weapons grade to produce one nuclear weapon—was extended from two to three months to more than a year.[13] Pushing Iran back further from that line was clearly in America's interest.

The JCPOA did not, however, place any restrictions on Iran's missile program and was silent on Iran's malign activities throughout the Middle East. I will have a lot more to say about Iran's malign activities in the next chapter. In May 2018, President Trump pulled the United States out of the JCPOA and intensified sanctions on Iran. Iran responded by enriching uranium to 60 percent, and has indicated it may start enriching to 90 percent, bringing it within days or a few weeks of having enough weapons-grade material for a nuclear weapon. (The time required for Iran to deploy an operational weapon, once its leadership made the decision to do so, would likely remain much longer, though. A reliable weapons design, warhead, and delivery system are also needed.)

In the years since I left government, however, Iran has continued to suffer setbacks to its nuclear program. In July 2020 and April 2021, explosions rocked Iran's nuclear enrichment facility at Natanz, destroying advanced centrifuges, setting back centrifuge production and causing other damage to the facility. Another explosion in July 2020 severely damaged an Iranian missile production facility in Tehran, and in November 2020, Iran's top nuclear weapons scientist, Mohsen Fakhrizadeh, was killed in a vehicle ambush in Damavand. The effort to prevent or at least delay Iran from getting the bomb continues.

NORTH KOREA'S NUCLEAR WEAPONS AND MISSILES

After Iran, North Korea was our next-highest counter-proliferation priority. But it was a much harder target. The regime had already developed a nuclear weapons capability and had begun testing it by the time I had reentered government in 2007, and it conducted additional nuclear tests at its Punggye-ri test site in 2009 and 2013. By 2013, the North Koreans had achieved a significant nuclear yield, in the range of 7 to 16 kilotons of TNT. (For reference, the atomic bomb dropped on Hiroshima was roughly equivalent to 15 kilotons.) The North Koreans conducted two more tests in 2016, further increasing the yield of their weapon. And in 2017, they tested what appeared to be a thermonuclear weapon, with a yield up to 250 kilotons. A recent Rand study estimates that North Korea could have as many as two hundred nuclear weapons in the near future.

Given North Korea's success in developing nuclear weapons, we primarily focused our counter-proliferation efforts on its delivery means. According to the same Rand study, North Korea could have dozens of intercontinental ballistic missiles capable of reaching the United States by 2027.[14] We thus had a compelling reason to do everything we could to set back their development. We pursued a number of counter-proliferation approaches, including engaging countries who had influence on the North Korean regime, but unfortunately we had only limited success against both its nuclear weapons and its missile programs. Our diplomatic efforts over several decades have produced similarly meager results. President Trump's personal diplomacy with Kim Jong Un to denuclearize the Korean Peninsula also ended in failure.

––––––––––

What I learned from our counter-proliferation operations against Iran and North Korea is that while counter proliferation is a critical mission, it is a very, very difficult one. We could delay a state's efforts to acquire nuclear weapons and the means to deliver them, but we couldn't prevent a state from eventually getting them if that's what its leaders were determined to do. Some operations failed completely.

Counter-proliferation operations require exceptional intelligence and access to be operationally feasible. A state's nuclear weapons program is the hardest of "hard targets"—strategic capabilities that a state will do its utmost to protect. Operational successes in counter proliferation, moreover, are almost always ephemeral; with time, a state can discover and fix a problem in the reliability of its arsenal or rebuild a capability if it is found to be damaged beyond repair. All these challenges aside, the mission is too important to not give it our best shot.

Although it's not a counter-proliferation issue, it's worth mentioning North Korea's cyberattack on Sony before I wrap up this brief discussion of North Korea's nuclear weapons and missile programs and our efforts to delay them, because it raises some important issues. In late November 2014, North Korea conducted a massive cyberattack on Sony Pictures Entertainment that destroyed two-thirds of Sony servers and wiped clean several thousand computers. The North Koreans also stole and exposed highly sensitive corporate data and embarrassing personal emails from the company's top executives. The North Koreans had built a cyber force of several thousand operators and had conducted several cyberattacks in South Korea prior to attacking Sony. The motive for the attack was punishment for Sony's impending release of *The Interview*—a comedy whose plot revolves around two hapless individuals sent into North Korea by the CIA to assassinate Kim Jong Un, the North's leader. Kim, needless to say, is not portrayed positively in the film.

The IC was able to attribute the attack to North Korea within a few weeks. Our challenge was how to respond. We quickly discovered that we didn't have cyber options that would be effective against North Korea. Other military options that we did have didn't seem appropriate to the situation. It also wasn't clear to President Obama and others in the administration whether North Korea's destructive attack was a cybercrime or a military strike. The attack ended up being described as a "national security event."

This was more a policy choice than an accurate portrayal of what had happened. There was no doubt that a foreign state had attacked and destroyed the property of a U.S. company on U.S. soil. If the

North Koreans had employed physical violence instead of cyber violence, there would have been no ambiguity. In the end, the administration opted to impose sanctions.[15] I was frustrated, but there weren't any better options immediately available. We would need to fix that. Presidents always want more options.

OPERATIONS IN COLOMBIA AND MEXICO

Terrorism and the proliferation of WMD weren't the only bad things we had to counter during my eight years in the Bush and Obama administrations. I was also engaged in helping Colombia defeat its Marxist insurgency and helping Mexico battle its drug cartels. Our assistance to Colombia would prove very successful; our efforts in Mexico, while tactically successful, made much less of a difference strategically.

I made my first trip to Colombia as assistant secretary of defense for special operations, low-intensity conflict, and interdependent capabilities in late June 2008. I had last been to Colombia as a Special Forces officer in 1981. A lot had changed. In the early 1980s, my primary concern was a Colombian terrorist group, M-19. I had been sent to Colombia to collect the intelligence our special operators would need if Americans were taken hostage in the Andean nation. The Colombians were also combating a Marxist insurgency, but other Special Forces teams were responsible for helping the Colombian armed forces against the FARC (Revolutionary Armed Forces of Colombia) and ELN (National Liberation Army), Colombia's two main insurgent groups.[16]

During the late 1980s and the 1990s, the U.S. government's focus had shifted to combating Colombia's drug cartels. Our special operators had played an important role in taking down Pablo Escobar, the most notorious of Colombia's drug lords, but Colombia's cocaine continued to flow into the United States. And by the final years of the Clinton administration, the FARC had reached the gates of Bogotá. The United States responded with Plan Colombia, a large, multiyear security assistance program that combined Special Forces trainers and advisers and helicopters and other equipment the Colombian armed forces needed to push the FARC back and eventually defeat the group.

During the Clinton administration, Plan Colombia was focused primarily on counter-narcotics operations. After the Bush administration took office, it was expanded to counterinsurgency. By 2005, the United States had provided $4.5 billion in security assistance to Colombia.[17]

With the election of Álvaro Uribe as Colombia's president in 2002, Plan Colombia was kicked into high gear. Uribe significantly expanded the Colombian armed forces and created new units to combat the insurgency. His strategy had two phases: first, to push back the FARC fronts that were encircling Bogotá, and then to go after the FARC's base areas deep in Colombia's interior. By 2008, the strategy was well into its second phase.

I went to Colombia in June 2008 for three reasons, one urgent and the other two longer term. The longer-term reasons had to do with our operational support for Colombia in its war against the FARC. We had set up an intelligence fusion center in our embassy and were flying ISR missions using special operations aircraft to help the Colombians find and fix the FARC's senior leaders. We also provided the Colombians with precision-guided munitions. One of FARC's top leaders, Raúl Reyes, had been killed in a strike just across the border at a camp in Ecuador at the beginning of March. Colombian special forces had recovered a treasure trove of intelligence after the strike. I had reviewed it in Washington and wanted to discuss its implications with Colombia's military leadership in greater detail.

I also wanted to see with my own eyes Colombia's operations against the FARC in the forward areas. Under President Uribe, the armed forces had been very successful in pushing the FARC back into remote jungle areas deep in Colombia's interior. I flew on a Colombian Air Force plane to a special forces camp in Guaviare, a FARC stronghold. I listened to an operations order for an upcoming operation in Spanish and went on a patrol with the Colombians. It brought back memories of my days in the Special Forces in Latin America.

The primary purpose of my visit, though, was to review plans for a clandestine hostage rescue operation that would be attempted the following week. Three Northrop Grumman employees, Marc Gonsalves, Thomas Howes, and Keith Stansell, had been held hostage by the FARC for five years. Also held by the FARC were Ingrid Betancourt, a former presidential candidate, and eleven Colombian soldiers and national policemen. A Colombian special reconnaissance team had recently spotted the hostages on the Apaporis River in Guaviare, not far from the special forces camp I had just visited.

An elaborate deception was central to the plan to rescue the hostages. Colombian special forces soldiers would pose as NGO aid workers and fly to Guaviare in an NGO-painted helicopter to move the hostages to another FARC camp. A clandestine penetration of the FARC had arranged the transfer, and the FARC's local commander in Guaviare, who went by the nom de guerre Cesar, had agreed to the transfer of hostages. I asked about a quick reaction force in case the deception plan failed and was told that a large force would be positioned within fifteen minutes of the helicopter landing zone that was going to be used in the deception operation. All good, I thought.

On July 2, Cesar and another FARC member boarded the helicopter with the fifteen hostages and were quickly subdued. The Colombian special forces soldiers then told the hostages, *"Somos el Ejército Nacional"* (We are the Colombian Army). *"Están en libertad"* (You are free). The hostages had been rescued without a shot being fired. It was a flawless operation that bolstered morale in Colombia and, more important, brought three Americans home.

I returned to Colombia at least once every two years to follow up on Plan Colombia's progress. I visited several forward bases in Colombia's interior that the armed forces and National Police maintained, including those at Tolemaida and Larandia. During one visit, I saw Kevin Higgins, a former fellow officer in the 3rd Battalion, 7th Special Forces Group in the early 1980s. Kevin was now advising Colombia's National Police commandos, the *Junglas,* as a State Department contractor. It was a small world. I would see the same special operators and CIA officers in multiple areas of conflict over the course of my career.

In June 2009, Colombia's vice-minister of defense, Juan Carlos Pinzón, established a service-level command that brought together all of Colombia's special operations units (air, ground, and maritime) under one structure, the Joint Special Operations Command, or *Comando Conjunto de Operaciones Especiales.* The command was given responsibility for targeting the top thirty-one of the FARC's leadership. I worked very closely with Juan Carlos, who would soon be promoted to minister of defense. We also became good friends. As a result of Pinzón's reforms, Colombia's campaign to eliminate the FARC's leadership, with our support, became even more effective. In September 2010, Mono Jojoy, the FARC's top military commander, was killed. In November 2011, the FARC's top leader, Alfonso Cano, was killed.

In 2012, Pinzón asked me to help him develop a strategy to finish off the FARC. We met in Miami for three days to develop a plan. Pinzón brought General Alberto José Mejía, the commander of Colombia's Joint Special Operations Command, and the chief of National Police Intelligence, who, because he was still serving as this book was being written, shall remain nameless here.

Together, we sketched out a plan to establish nine joint task forces to take the fight to the remaining FARC members deep in Colombia's interior and border regions and to its remaining leadership hiding in Venezuela. The police intelligence chief sat across from me in the hotel bar and moved in close, "nose to nose and knee to knee," as they are accustomed to in Latin America, and said several times, "I'm going to f—— the FARC!" I admired his conviction. Pinzón, the police intel chief, and General Mejía are great Colombian patriots who played key roles in bringing Colombia's long war with the FARC to an end. In 2016, a peace deal was signed, and most of the FARC laid down their arms and reintegrated into Colombian society. Approximately two thousand dissident FARC members would later resume insurgent operations against the Colombian government. This was down from the twenty thousand or so that were waging a guerrilla war when President Uribe took office. Our effort in Colombia is a great example of the indirect approach and small-footprint counterinsurgency. Unfortunately, with the election of a leftist government in 2022, Colombia may now be in danger of losing the war it had won.

———

Closer to home, in December 2008, I made the first of several trips to Mexico City and other areas in Mexico. The violence in Mexico perpetrated by the drug cartels had become not just a major counternarcotics problem but a major national security issue for the United States. There were concerns among top Bush administration officials that Mexico could become a failed state.[18] With the demise of Colombia's Medellín and Cali Cartels, Mexico's drug-trafficking organizations (DTOs) had taken over the cocaine trade, and by 2007 they controlled 90 percent of the cocaine entering the United States. Mexico's president, Felipe Calderón, requested assistance from the Bush administration. Mexico's police were overwhelmed by the cartels, who possessed heavy weapons, so Calderón brought in his Army and Navy (mainly the Navy's Marines) to fight the DTOs. I went to Mexico City to consult with U.S. embassy and Mexican officials about special operations and intelligence assistance we could quietly provide to Calderón's government.

We had already been providing limited special operations training to the Mexican Marines for a few years. Colonel Chris Sorenson, the special operations commander for Northern Command, which oversees DOD's security relations with Mexico and Canada in addition to being responsible for homeland defense, had been very successful in expanding our SOF relationship with Mexico. We quickly set up an intelligence fusion center in our embassy modeled after the one we had in Bogotá and expanded our intelligence and special operations relationships with Mexico's Army and Navy. The Marines were particularly effective in going after drug cartel leaders.

Between 2008 and 2012, I would meet regularly with Mexico's secretaries of the Army and Navy and the heads of its intelligence service, CISEN. I would also meet with the commander of the Marines, a real warrior, the commander of the Army's special forces, and the director of the Federal Police. During one of my visits, I watched the Army's top counterterrorism force, trained by U.S. Special Forces, perform a simulated takedown of a drug kingpin. I was also treated to a lavish banquet, with music by a mariachi band.

The violence from the drug wars was horrific, resulting in more than sixty thousand dead between 2006 and 2012. We had great success in decapitating most of the cartels, but this failed to stem the carnage, because the cartels fought each other as well as Mexican forces and terrorized the local population.

In December 2009, Mexico's Marines killed Arturo Beltrán Leyva, the head of the cartel named after him. Mexican forces also captured or killed the Guillén brothers, who headed the Gulf Cartel. The Gulf Cartel had employed a corrupt group of former Mexican special operators, called Los Zetas, as their enforcers. When the Zetas saw that the Gulf Cartel had been weakened, they moved in and created their own cartel. They were Mexico's most violent DTO.

In 2012, the Marines killed the Zetas' leader Heriberto Lazcano and a year later captured his successor, Miguel Treviño. In 2014, the Navy captured Joaquín "El Chapo" Guzmán, the leader of the Sinaloa Cartel. He unfortunately was able to escape from prison in a tunnel that had been dug for him but was captured again two years later and was extradited to the United States, where he was put on trial and convicted. The drug war went on, however.

Leadership decapitation by itself is not an effective counterterrorism strategy, and this applies doubly to counter-narcotics operations. It can disrupt a group's operations temporarily, but that's about it. My main takeaway from my experience in counter-narcotics operations is that it's very hard if not impossible to translate tactical gains into lasting strategic success. Achieving strategic success in counter-narcotics operations, I learned, is even harder than it is in counter-proliferation operations. As long as there is demand for narcotics, the cartels will find ways to get them into the United States. New technologies, such as small, commercially available unmanned aerial vehicles only make our interdiction problem worse. We can disrupt the drug cartels and bring some of their leaders to justice, but we haven't been able to dismantle and defeat them and prevent their reconstitution or replacement by another cartel. The cartels are even more resilient than the global jihadists.

THE BATTLE FOR THE MIDDLE EAST

IRAN'S MALIGN INFLUENCE

Stopping Iran from getting the bomb, or at least substantially delaying when it would get it, was just one of the challenges we faced from the Islamic Republic. We were also engaged with Iran in a "Battle for the Middle East," a region-wide convulsion and conflict that stemmed from two causes: Iranian malign influence and the Arab Spring. The Iranians have been engaged in a covert war and battle for hegemony in the Middle East with Saudi Arabia since the founding of the Islamic Republic in 1979. Tehran has supported armed groups in both Saudi Arabia and Bahrain. A key target for Iran in Saudi Arabia is its Shi'a-dominated and oil-rich Eastern Province.

In August 2012, Iran conducted an offensive cyberattack on Saudi Aramco (the Saudi Arabian Oil Company) using a "wiper" virus called Shamoon that destroyed thirty-five thousand, or three-quarters, of the company's computers. The attack set the company back to the 1970s for a period and led to months of disruption at Saudi Aramco's head-quarters. Fortunately, the systems controlling oil production had been on a separate network and continued to operate. The Iranians also conducted offensive cyber operations against the United States in 2012, targeting nearly four dozen major American banks and other businesses with "distributed denial of service," or DDoS, attacks, causing temporary disruption.

Masters at asymmetric and proxy war, the Iranians supported Shi'a extremist groups in Iraq, Lebanese Hezbollah in Lebanon, Bashar al-Assad in Syria, and the Houthis in Yemen. The Saudis referred to this as Iran's "four capitals" strategy—Baghdad, Damascus, Beirut, and Sana'a. Qassem Soleimani, the head of the Islamic Revolutionary Guard Corps' Quds Force and the general behind this strategy, was widely regarded as the second most powerful man in Iran after Supreme Leader Ayatollah Khamenei. Soleimani's aim was to drive the United States out of the greater Middle East, topple the Saudi monarchy, and establish Iranian hegemony in the region.[1] (Soleimani was killed in a U.S. drone strike at Baghdad's airport on January 3, 2020—small recompense for the American blood he had on his hands. The Iranians have vowed to avenge him, but so far, other than some missile strikes against U.S. forces in Iraq, they haven't. They have long memories, however, so we shouldn't let our guard down.)

The Iranian regime has also regularly threatened to close the Strait of Hormuz through which a third of the world's oil supply transits. CENTCOM accordingly has developed contingency plans to reopen the shipping lanes, should that prove necessary. The Islamic Revolutionary Guard Corps Navy also regularly harasses our naval vessels in the Gulf.

With the exception of al-Qa'ida, Iran has been responsible for the deaths of more Americans during the past four decades than any other actor. Tehran sponsored the 1983 Beirut embassy and Marine barracks bombings by Lebanese Hezbollah that killed 258 Americans. The Iranians sponsored Hezbollah's kidnapping and murder of several Americans, including the CIA station chief Bill Buckley. In 1996, operatives from Iranian-sponsored Saudi Hezbollah blew up Khobar Towers at an Air Force base in Saudi Arabia, killing 19 Americans. Iran provided training in guerrilla warfare and terrorism to Shi'a extremist groups in Iraq and supplied them with "explosively formed projectiles"—advanced improvised explosive devices that could cut through our heaviest armor—which led to the deaths of at least 600 Americans between 2003 and 2011. After 2013, Iran also supported the Taliban in Afghanistan, which killed and wounded still more Americans. The Iranian regime has also held Americans illegally in prison in Iran, one of whom, Robert Levinson, was a former FBI special agent. Levinson's family recently reported that he had died in captivity.

Iran's most brazen plot against the United States, however, occurred not in the Middle East but right in our nation's capital in September 2011. Iran's target was Cafe Milano, a bustling Italian restaurant in Georgetown. Iran plotted to bomb the restaurant to kill the Saudi ambassador to the United States, Adel al-Jubeir. A friend of mine and a first-rate strategic thinker, Adel was a very effective ambassador.

A Drug Enforcement Administration informant reported that he had been asked by Manssor Arbabsiar, an Iranian American, to assist in blowing up a target for the Iranian government. Arbabsiar's cousin, we learned, was a general in Iran's elite Quds Force. Iran offered the informant, whom it believed was connected to Mexico's most violent drug cartel, the Zetas, $1.5 million to help assassinate Adel. If the operation was successful, there would be more. Iran's next target, the informant was told, would likely be the Israeli embassy in Washington, followed perhaps by additional Saudi targets in South America. To show they were serious, the Iranians made a $100,000 down payment to Arbabsiar. Needless to say, I followed all of this intelligence closely.

In August 2011, Arbabsiar traveled back to Iran to meet with Gholam Shakuri and other Quds Force senior leaders to review the plan. In early September, Arbabsiar called the informant from Iran and asked if the "building is getting painted." The plot was a go. The tenth anniversary of the 9/11 attacks was drawing near, a perfect time for a major attack on the United States.

DEA came up with a plan to lure Arbabsiar back to the United States, which we had approved at a small group meeting of the NSC's Deputies Committee. The informant told Arbabsiar that the Zetas were holding him as collateral in Mexico while the assassination was carried out to ensure they would get paid. When Arbabsiar arrived in Mexico to meet with the informant, he was turned away at the airport and forced to return to Europe, from where he had flown. He transited through Kennedy Airport in New York and was arrested by the FBI as he landed. Arbabsiar quickly told all to FBI interrogators. He identified the other senior Quds Force official he had met with from a photo lineup and, at the FBI's direction, placed a phone call to Shakuri using the code word they'd agreed upon. "The Chevrolet is ready, it's ready to be done. I should continue, right?" "Yes, yes, yes," replied Shakuri, "just do it quickly." Iran's intent to have a bomb detonated in a packed Georgetown restaurant was unmistakable.

Fortunately, good intelligence had foiled the plot.[2] Iran's leaders were deterred from attempting additional lethal attacks against the United States, no doubt aware that this could trigger unacceptable consequences, but they weren't deterred from continuing to challenge the United States in the Middle East. They still engage in cyberattacks against the United States and could decide that a covert lethal attack is worth the risk. We need to remain vigilant and be prepared to respond accordingly.

The Arbabsiar operation reinforced why it was so important for us to stop Iran from getting the bomb. If Iran's leaders were willing to sponsor a mass-casualty terror attack in our nation's capital when their country didn't have nuclear weapons, what will they be willing to do after they have acquired them?

AL-QA'IDA SPRING

The Arab Spring revolution that began in Tunisia in mid-December 2010 quickly spread to Egypt and the rest of the Middle East. It was the most significant upheaval in the Middle East since the collapse of the Ottoman Empire after World War I. Arab Spring's largest political effects occurred in Tunisia, Egypt, Libya, Syria, and Yemen. The autocrats who had ruled these countries for decades were toppled in all but Syria, and in Syria, it was a near-run thing.[3]

By early February 2011, mass protests had broken out across the Arab world.[4] Our allies in the region wondered who would be the next to fall and whether the United States would stand by them. Crown Prince Mohammed Bin Zayed of the U.A.E. warned Secretary Gates that Egypt would become a Sunni version of Iran. He added that U.S. actions in Egypt reminded him of the days of Jimmy Carter during the fall of the shah.[5]

President Obama felt blindsided by the Arab Spring. The IC had warned for years about the powerful pressures at work in the Arab world and that the status quo couldn't last. Political, demographic, economic, and societal trends all portended trouble for authoritarian regimes in the region. But the IC failed to provide tactical warning that the crisis was about to unfold, and it failed to warn about the magnitude it would assume.

To be fair, predicting political and social revolutions is one of the most difficult intelligence problems. It is not clear, moreover, that if the IC had precisely predicted the events and scope of the Arab Spring, our policy response would have been any different. As the crisis evolved, the IC's collection ramped up and partially compensated for any shortfalls in analysis. We were able to consistently provide excellent tactical intelligence on pending developments to the White House. Our analysis quickly caught up and got ahead of events as well.

Where the IC missed the mark was not understanding how the new social media tools could greatly accelerate the process of revolutionary change once the fuse had been lit. The IC also failed to sufficiently mine the wealth of social media information to get ahead of events, and it had not been sufficiently in touch with the pulse of the Arab street. Probably the biggest misjudgment on the IC's part, though, was in believing that the Arab Spring would damage al-Qa'ida by undermining the group's narrative that the only path to political change in the Middle East was through violence. The way the Arab Spring played out actually made al-Qa'ida stronger.[6] It weakened the capabilities and will of several Arab states to conduct counterterrorism operations, creating a strategic vacuum that al-Qa'ida and other extremists quickly filled.

Arab Spring turned out to be an "al-Qa'ida spring" as much as an Arab one, particularly in Syria and Yemen.[7] Between 2011 and 2013, I visited several of the countries that were experiencing unrest due to the Arab Spring, but my main focus was the three countries convulsed by war and where al-Qa'ida had its strongest presence—Syria, Yemen, and Libya. Of these, it was the civil war in Syria and our support for the moderate opposition there that commanded most of my attention. The war in Syria would be the most important battle in the Battle for the Middle East.

THE FREE SYRIAN ARMY—A MISSED OPPORTUNITY

The Syrian revolution began in early March 2011 with peaceful protests in Syria's southern city of Dara'a and quickly spread to Damascus and other parts of the country. As protests spread across the country, the Assad regime responded with machine-gun fire, mass arrests, and "disappearances," including of young children. By late May, the

Syrian people had taken up arms. As the commander of one armed opposition group in Syria's north said, "Picking up guns was not what we had in mind when we first took to the streets. But we were being slaughtered like lambs, simply for peacefully protesting. We had to protect our people. We realized the regime was not backing down."

A "Free Syrian Army" led initially by a former Syrian military officer, Colonel Riyad al-Asad, was formed on July 29, 2011. The FSA consisted of defecting officers and soldiers, but mostly carpenters, bricklayers, and other Syrian civilians. Approximately 65 to 70 percent of Syria's twenty-three million people are Sunni Arabs, so not surprisingly Sunnis made up the bulk of the Syrian insurgency.[8]

The Syrian opposition's ranks would swell to 75,000–100,000 within two years.[9] The FSA comprised Syria's moderate opposition. "Moderate" in the context of the Syrian insurgency meant those groups who supported the original ideals of the Syrian protest movement—dignity, justice, freedom, and liberty—and who sought to establish a representative government with a regular rotation of power. Moderate groups were nationalist in orientation and tended to be local in terms of their membership, fighting where they lived.

The Syrian insurgency also included Islamist groups, Salafist groups, and global jihadists. Those groups tended to have larger formations and had a presence in multiple provinces across Syria. Jordan, Saudi Arabia, and the U.A.E. supported the moderate groups. Turkey and Qatar supported both moderates and Islamists. None of the five supported the global jihadists.

As I watched the insurgency expand, Assad looked increasingly vulnerable. His security forces were suffering major defections, and the situation in Syria reminded me of the early days of the Afghan resistance. The number of raids and ambushes by insurgent forces doubled between January and April 2012. Nearly a thousand security force personnel had been killed in Free Syrian Army–linked attacks by June. By March 2012, sixty thousand soldiers had defected from Assad's Army. Many had joined the insurgency.

I believed we had a compelling strategic interest in supporting the Syrian opposition. In my view, and in the view of others in the administration at the time, like Deputy Secretary of State Bill Burns, we missed a big strategic opportunity in not supporting the Syrian resistance earlier and in not acting more aggressively when we finally did support it.[10] We had several of our enemies—the Iranians, Lebanese Hezbollah, and later the Russians—converging in Syria. Helping the opposition depose the dictator Assad would deal a major blow to all of them.

Saudi Arabia, Qatar, and Turkey were providing arms and ammunition to the resistance in Syria while we sat on the sidelines. Jordan and the U.A.E. were also providing support of various kinds. Going in more forcefully in the early years of the insurgency would have given us much greater leverage with our allies on Syria, particularly the Turks, Qataris, and Saudis, who often worked at cross-purposes with each other and with us, and would have strengthened the hand of the moderates against the Islamists and global jihadists. It would have also made our counterterrorism problem in Syria more manageable and could have largely prevented the humanitarian catastrophe that befell Syria.[11] But instead, we ceded the strategic initiative and escalation dominance to the Iranians and Russians.

Iran's Quds Force would send nearly a thousand advisers to Syria to keep the Assad regime from falling. The Quds Force mobilized large militias from Shi'a populations in the region to bolster Assad's fragile armed forces. Several thousand Lebanese Hezbollah troops, the Quds Force's primary proxy force, were also sent to Syria to combat the insurgency. Removing Assad would have dealt a strategic blow to both.

As the conflict dragged on, Russia would weaponize refugee flows to intimidate European governments and provide direct combat support to the Assad regime. Russia's intervention in Syria's civil war was an opportunity to deliver a blow to Putin as well. But, again, we demurred.

We could defeat 125,000 Soviet troops in Afghanistan in the 1980s but were intimidated by the introduction of 2,500 Russian troops in Syria thirty years later. It was heartbreaking to watch as Russia, supported by Iran, shifted the balance in Assad's favor.

———

President Obama didn't become interested in supporting the Syrian opposition until late 2012. He was concerned about getting involved, even indirectly, in another Middle Eastern conflict.

President Obama had called for Assad's departure early after the Syrian revolution had begun, but as Bill Burns later wrote, "we combined maximalist aims with minimal means"—never a good recipe for success in foreign policy. We promised too much, declaring that "Assad must go" and setting "red lines," but applied the tools available to us "too grudgingly and incrementally."[12] I couldn't agree more with Bill's judgment.

Contrary to what a few former Obama administration officials have written, the Syrian insurgency had many of the factors required for success.[13] It had a large population base that supported the insurgency and tens of thousands of Syrians who were determined to fight and had already joined the rebellion. The insurgency had strategic sanctuaries in countries bordering Syria: Turkey and Jordan. It had the support of several external sponsors. In addition to Turkey and Jordan, Saudi Arabia, Qatar, and the United Arab Emirates were all providing lethal and nonlethal support to the Syrian resistance. Several of our European allies were also engaged in providing various levels of support.

Conceptually, we had three broad options in Syria. A large-scale, conventional force invasion would provide the surest means of removing Assad, but it would also result in significant American casualties, because our forces would be targeted by Iran, Lebanese Hezbollah, al-Qa'ida, and ISIS, and it would involve us directly in another major Middle East war. It would have been strategic folly to invade and occupy Syria with a large conventional force. And even if we had wanted to, we didn't have enough forces to do so without jeopardizing our interests elsewhere. Syria, moreover, hadn't attacked us. The threat it posed was to its own people.

Our second option would be to combine an air campaign with support for the moderate opposition, as we had done in Afghanistan in 2001. This might not have been the option we wanted to start with, but it had plenty to recommend it. As I will discuss later in this chapter, we used American and coalition airpower to topple Qaddafi and support the Libyan opposition, and we could have done the same in Syria. A third option was to support Syria's moderate opposition with arms, ammunition, training, intelligence, and strategic and operational advice. This was the most feasible option politically, but it would take longer to be successful than the second option. It was the course of action we should have pursued in the summer of 2011.

A major strategic risk with supporting the Syrian insurgency was the presence of global jihadist groups in their ranks. We didn't want weapons, particularly advanced weapons, to fall into the jihadists' hands. This would require careful vetting and monitoring of insurgent groups. We would also need to wage a counterterrorism campaign against the global jihadist groups in Syria, something we began only in late 2014 with our strike on al-Qa'ida's Khorasan Group, and in 2015 with our war against ISIS. We should have targeted both groups more aggressively much earlier. The moderates would have been strengthened had we done so.

In July 2012, all of President Obama's top advisers recommended providing lethal assistance to the Free Syrian Army. Among those supporting it were Secretary Clinton, Secretary Panetta, and CIA Director Dave Petraeus. I strongly supported the provision of lethal assistance in the NSC's Deputies Committee meetings. President Obama, though, wasn't ready to approve lethal support (arms and ammunition) to the moderate opposition. He did approve nonlethal support (vehicles, communications equipment, food, and medical supplies), but that was it.

As Bill Burns would later write, "the unspoken predicate" behind providing lethal assistance was the "legendary success" we had had with our covert support for the Afghan resistance during the 1980s. The only problem with this analogy was that while some senior administration officials viewed our secret war during the 1980s through the lens of driving the Soviets out of Afghanistan and helping to end the Cold War, others, including the president, viewed it more through the prism of Afghanistan's subsequent civil war, the Taliban's takeover, and al-Qa'ida's sanctuary there that, in their view, had led to the 9/11 attacks.[14]

In early 2013, as the situation grew worse in Syria, President Obama finally authorized lethal support.[15] I was very pleased with his decision and was determined to make the expanded program a success. Immediately after the president's decision, I traveled to Jordan, Turkey, Saudi Arabia, and Qatar to meet with Free Syrian Army commanders and fighters and our foreign partners to get a sense of the prospects for the resistance. It was my first of several trips to the region between 2013 and 2015.

As I met with FSA commanders and fighters, I thought back to my Special Forces training nearly four decades earlier on how to conduct a meeting with a guerrilla chief and how to train and motivate resistance fighters and the meetings I'd had with Afghan resistance command-ers in the 1980s. I also thought back to my CIA experience in helping the Afghan resistance defeat the Red Army against all odds during the 1980s. We should have begun providing lethal assistance in Syria two years earlier, but I felt there was still time to transform the war in the opposition's favor. We hadn't adopted a war-winning strategy in our secret war in Afghanistan until the conflict was entering its fifth year. My challenges this time were almost completely in Washington. We weren't providing the opposition with the support they needed to prevail against the Assad regime and its allies. It was a pale reflection of what we had provided to the Afghan resistance.

During my visit to Turkey, I met with Salim Idriss, the new chief of the FSA's Supreme Military Council.[16] The meeting was a classic engagement with a G (guerrilla) chief. Accompanying me were the senior CIA officer in country and a senior Special Forces officer who had been detailed to the CIA to help the FSA with high command and resistance strategy. A former senior military officer with the Assad regime, Idriss was engaging, and we talked long into the night, par-ticularly about an operation he was currently conducting in Latakia, the stronghold of the Alawites. Idriss and the FSA had organized the resistance into five fronts: North, centered on Aleppo; West, centered on Idlib; East, centered on Deir ez-Zour; Central, centered on Homs; and South, centered on Dara'a. The FSA command structure further extended down to military councils in each of Syria's fourteen prov-inces and then to the armed opposition groups that made up the FSA. It seemed like a step in the right direction that could help counter the gains the Islamist groups had been making at the FSA's expense. Idriss complained about supply interruptions that the FSA was experienc-ing from its eastern European suppliers. He added that even when the supplies were flowing, the FSA wasn't receiving nearly enough weapons and ammunition. I assured him I would work to resolve both issues. I wanted the FSA to win.

In Jordan, I met with King Abdullah to discuss Syria strategy and with Faisal Shobaki, the chief of Jordan's General Intelligence

Directorate. I had been meeting with the king regularly since 2007, on issues ranging from al-Qa'ida to Afghanistan, where Jordan had a special forces unit deployed. The king is a former commander of Jordan's special forces, so we bonded easily and talked about strategy for hours. On this visit, the king was thinking about ways to stabilize Syria, including sending a Jordanian Army force into Syria's south and east. It was a bold idea, but one that was beyond Jordan's means to sustain. Shobaki became a good friend. Even though I was the head of defense intelligence, Shobaki considered me CIA, his main partner, and thus "family."

In Saudi Arabia, I met with my old friend Prince Bandar Bin Sultan. Now the king's national security adviser, Bandar had been the Saudi ambassador to the United States during the 1980s and a great partner of ours during our secret war in Afghanistan. We reminisced over dinner and cigars about the old days and spent hours talking about Syria strategy. It felt as if the band had gotten back together again. My CIA colleagues struggled to write everything down. They later told me they had produced eleven intelligence reports from just one meeting I had with Bandar.

I came away encouraged by what I saw in the FSA's training camps and my discussions with the FSA's commanders and the regional intelligence chiefs who were supporting the Syrian opposition, but I knew we had our work cut out for us. The past two years had seen an expanding but increasingly Islamist insurgency, which would make our support more problematic.

In late 2012, with U.S. leadership still largely absent, the Syrian resistance had split into Islamist and moderate factions. Three large groups, Liwa al-Islam (later called Jaish al-Islam) in the greater Damascus area, Suqor al-Sham in Idlib, and Liwa al-Tawhid in Aleppo, formed the twenty-two-group Syrian Islamic Liberation Front in September 2012. The SILF, still aligned with the FSA if Islamist in orientation, now comprised about 50 percent of the insurgency. In December, Ahrar al-Sham, another large Islamist group, formed a non-FSA group called the Syrian Islamist Front that comprised about 25 percent of the insurgency, further weakening the moderate FSA.[17]

To make matters worse, the Iranians and Russians, concerned about the deteriorating situation in Syria, were escalating at the same time we were. It brought back memories of 1985, when we and the Soviets both escalated the Soviet-Afghan War at the same time. The Syrian regime had been steadily losing ground to the opposition, and regime morale was plummeting. Assad was also having trouble getting new recruits to make up for the large number of defections from his military, and the Russians were growing nervous about Assad's staying power. Iran came to Assad's rescue with a large influx of Hezbollah fighters and substantial matériel support.[18] Quds Force officers began organizing Shi'a militias, importing large numbers of fighters from outside Syria, and Assad's fortunes slowly began to turn.

The situation got even worse several months later when we failed to strike the Assad regime after it used sarin gas to kill nearly fifteen hundred civilians, a third of them children, in East Damascus in August 2013. After that, FSA fighters moved in large numbers to the Islamist groups. The Syrian Islamist Front then dealt a deathblow to the Supreme Military Council, seizing its logistics headquarters near the Bab al-Hawa border crossing between Turkey and Syria.

The Military and Regional Operations Centers we had established to support the FSA in Jordan and Turkey partially filled the vacuum left by the SMC's demise, but U.S. credibility and the moderate opposition had suffered very damaging blows. In late 2013 and early 2014, a number of the vetted armed opposition groups in the FSA merged into larger groups. The Syrian Revolutionary Front under Jamal Maarouf had fourteen groups under its command. Jaish al-Mujahideen consolidated another eight groups. Twelve additional fighting groups were united under Harakat Hazm. On yet another trip to the region, I met with commanders and fighters from Harakat and listened in as they gave their operations brief for upcoming actions in Syria. Harakat had been the first opposition group to receive the advanced U.S. TOW anti-tank missile system that was being supplied to the resistance, and its shooters had been very effective with it, destroying scores of regime combat vehicles.

New weapons like the TOW and short-range remotely piloted aircraft that could be fitted with a small amount of explosives had improved the moderate opposition's ability to conduct standoff attacks. Providing surface-to-air missiles to the resistance to better enable it to defend itself and civilian population centers was still precluded by U.S. policy, however, though our foreign partners did supply a few

Chinese-made SAMs to the resistance, resulting in a couple of aircraft shoot-downs in 2016.

A southern front was established in February 2014, bringing fifty-four FSA fighting groups under its control. All told, eighty-eight vetted moderate fighting groups were again semi-unified under larger commands. The southern front conducted offensives against regime forces in Dara'a and Quneitra in the spring of 2014. This latest consolidation of the moderate opposition unfortunately unraveled under extremist pressure at the end of 2014, when Jabhat al-Nusra (al-Qa'ida's affiliate in Syria) attacked Harakat Hazm and the SRF and drove them from the battlefield, taking all of their supplies. We should have supported the moderate groups against the extremists, but we didn't. Yet another strategic mistake.

An effort by Central Command to stand up a separate resistance force to go after ISIS in Syria was an unmitigated disaster. The Syrian opposition didn't want to fight ISIS unless provoked by the group. They wanted to fight the Assad regime. Thus, the CENTCOM force ended up with very few recruits. The plan had been poorly conceived from the start, and the program was eventually terminated after hundreds of millions of dollars had been expended with little to show for it.

In 2015, the Russians entered the war on Assad's side and further turned the tide in the regime's favor. By then, we had largely given up. We weren't in it to win it. The Iranians and Russians were.

———

Several policy choices significantly hampered our support to the anti-Assad resistance. The first of course was that we began providing lethal support too late. In Afghanistan in the 1980s, we had arms flowing to the resistance ten days after the Soviets invaded. In Syria, it had taken more than twenty months before we decided to provide lethal support. By then, the Islamists and global jihadists had gained considerable strength.

We also overly restricted the supply of weapons and ammunition, requiring that each member of an armed opposition group receive training before he could be supplied. This was again in sharp contrast to what we had done in Afghanistan. From 1985 onward, we provided more ordnance in one month to the Afghan resistance than we provided to the Syrian resistance in twenty months. We were definitely not employing all means available in Syria.

President Obama should have ordered a military strike on the Syrian regime after its poison gas attack in East Damascus. A U.S. air strike targeting Assad's military capabilities would not only have punished the Syrian dictator for his reprehensible actions and better deterred his future use of chemical weapons (which he used again, despite assurances that he wouldn't); it would have been a big psychological boost to the resistance and would have provided the opportunity to really shift the military balance in the opposition's favor. Instead, we succumbed to Russian diplomacy and let Assad off the hook.

A military strike in response to Assad's chemical weapons use would have also opened the policy door to a combined military-CIA, Title 10–Title 50 campaign, much like the one we conducted in Afghanistan to overthrow the Taliban in 2001. With a limited number of U.S. advisers to support the opposition, we could have aided them with airpower and supplied more advanced weapons like man-portable surface-to-air missiles. That would have grounded Assad's Air Force, and it would have given us and the opposition escalation dominance. Assad wouldn't have been able to survive it. We could have won our proxy war in Syria, but we failed to seize the moment. With the opposition on the offense and eventually in power, our terrorism problem in Syria from ISIS and al-Qa'ida would have become far more manageable, too. ISIS's invasion of Iraq from Syria might never have taken place, nor would a six-year war to defeat the group have likely been required. Our failure in Syria was as big a strategic "underreach" as our war in Iraq was a strategic "overreach."

After I had retired from government service, I argued in an op-ed for a "Syria first" strategy in our war with ISIS. Syria was where the global jihadist threat to the U.S. homeland was emanating from, not Iraq. Unfortunately, we pursued an Iraq first strategy. Syria, not Iraq, was the primary front in the Battle for the Middle East. I argued that we needed to increase our support for the moderate Syrian opposition before it was too late, and for a campaign in Syria along the lines of what we had done in Afghanistan in 2001 (a combination of military and CIA, using both Title 10 and Title 50 authorities). I also warned that our strategy against ISIS in Syria and Iraq was not succeeding or at least not succeeding fast enough. We were playing a long game in Syria and Iraq when a more rapid and disruptive strategy was needed. I argued that with ISIS's sanctuary in Syria, time was not on our side. ISIS wasn't just a regional threat. It had become the leader of the global jihadist movement. It would conduct more attacks in the West if it was not disrupted.[19]

Two years later in another op-ed, I urged the Trump administration not to give up on the Syrian opposition. Like the Obama administration after I had retired, they didn't heed my advice.[20] In the summer of 2017, the administration cut off all support for the anti-Assad Syrian opposition. Both administrations had looked to the Russians for help in ending Syria's civil war. Putin was interested in ending it, but only on his terms—after he had won. We had lost the most important battle in the Battle for the Middle East.

THE HOUTHI TAKEOVER OF YEMEN—A CASE OF STRATEGIC MYOPIA

Syria was not the only war we lost in the Battle for the Middle East. In late September 2014, the Hadi government in Yemen was driven out of Sana'a by the Houthis, a minority group from Yemen's far north who had received covert assistance from Iran's Quds Force.[21] With the overthrow of the Hadi government, we lost a key counterterrorism partner in our war with al-Qa'ida in the Arabian Peninsula, and Iran gained another victory toward its goal of achieving hegemony in the Middle East. Between 2009 and 2014, we had invested hundreds of millions of dollars to build up Yemen's armed forces and its intelligence service, particularly the National Security Bureau, our key CT partner. I had made multiple trips there, traveling to Sana'a, Ma'rib, Aden, and al-Anad Air Base in Yemen's south, where a contingent of our special operators was training Yemen's security forces. All the gains from our engagement and investment evaporated as the Houthis took Sana'a.

Iran's Quds Force began providing limited support to the Houthis after 2003. We periodically detected the Quds Force's presence in

Yemen from 2010 onward. Abdel Reza Shahlai, a Quds Force brigadier general, made several trips in and out of Yemen, occasionally supplying the Houthis with small arms. We did our best to capture Shahlai on his trips to Yemen, but had not succeeded. Shahlai was wanted by the United States for his role in facilitating the attempted bombing of Cafe Milano in Washington, D.C., in 2011, as well as for his role in enabling Iranian Shi'a proxy forces to kill American soldiers in Iraq.[22]

But it wasn't the Iranians who decisively shifted the strategic balance in Yemen. It was Yemen's former president, Ali Abdullah Saleh. Forced to resign after the Arab Spring protests and cede power to his vice president, Abd Rabbu Mansur Hadi, Saleh, who had ruled Yemen for thirty-three years, had remained in the country and retained dominant influence over Yemen's armed forces. As the Houthis advanced on Sana'a, Saleh aligned himself with his former enemy, and successfully persuaded the bulk of Yemen's security forces not to oppose the invasion.

As former senior CIA analyst Bruce Riedel has observed, even by the standards of Middle East politics, it was a remarkable case of treachery and a hypocritical reversal of alliances.[23] In addition to turning on his former vice president, Saleh had turned on Islah, Yemen's Muslim Brotherhood party and his former ally. Islah had helped Saleh prevail in the civil war with the south in 1994. Islah general Ali Mohsen al-Ahmar, the powerful commander of the First Armored Brigade, had waged Saleh's six campaigns against the Houthis.[24] As the Houthis advanced on Sana'a, Saleh undermined Ali Mohsen, allowing the Houthis to run him out of Yemen as Hadi's defenses collapsed. "Wily Ali" had outfoxed us all.[25]

In addition to secretly partnering with Saleh, their former enemy, the Houthis were duplicitous in other ways. They had participated in the "National Dialogue Conference" during 2013–2014 and had reached agreement on elections and power sharing with the other major parties in Yemen. As we would painfully learn from our dealings with the Taliban in 2021, insurgent groups can't be counted on to negotiate in good faith. In any event, when the strategic opportunity that Saleh offered became evident, they plunged all in.

As the Houthis advanced toward Sana'a, Hadi requested ISR and strike support from the United States. I participated in several meetings of the NSC's Deputies Committee on Hadi's request and the

Houthi threat to Sana'a. Most were focused on how to get our embassy personnel out of Sana'a. We agreed to provide some limited ISR support but would not agree to Hadi's request for U.S. strikes on Houthi formations. It was a big mistake.

Hadi had supported us against our enemy AQAP, but we didn't support him against his. We suffered from a bad case of strategic myopia when it came to our interests in Yemen and what it took to protect them. That was another major reason why Yemen's government fell to the Houthis.

The Houthis took the capital, and we entered into talks with them to evacuate the remaining American personnel. Hadi was placed under house arrest but escaped to Aden in late February. The Houthis continued their advance south and took Aden in early April 2015 but not before Hadi had escaped to Riyadh.

I made a final trip to the Middle East in late March 2015. One stop was Riyadh just as the Saudi high command was making its decision to launch air strikes and lead a coalition that included the U.A.E. and other Arab states against Houthi-occupied Yemen. The Saudis asked for limited U.S. support, mostly air refueling for their strike aircraft, and intelligence. They also wanted to ensure a continuous supply of munitions. The Saudis were confident the war would be over quickly. They were wrong. The war went on for years. Yemen turned into a humanitarian disaster even worse than Syria's. Iran substantially increased its military assistance to the Houthis, enabling them to strike targets in Saudi Arabia and the U.A.E. with ballistic missiles and unmanned aerial vehicles and shoot-down some of our drones, complicating our counterterrorism operations. This all could have been avoided had we more forcefully backed the Hadi government.

LEADING FROM BEHIND IN LIBYA

The third Battle for the Middle East was in Libya. It was the least consequential strategically, and it, too, did not end well. On February 17, 2011, Libyans rose up to demand Muammar Qaddafi's ouster. Groups opposed to his government declared a "day of rage" and quickly seized Benghazi in eastern Libya. Libyan Army and police forces either stood by or joined the cause. Libya was split in two, with Qaddafi controlling

Tripoli and the area west of the capital, and the opposition controlling Benghazi and the territory east.

Qaddafi had no intention of giving up without a fight, however. The regime used its airpower to attack the opposition, triggering calls by Senator John McCain and others for the United States to impose a no-fly zone on Libya. Military units loyal to the regime pushed eastward to reclaim territory. By March 15, there was a real fear among NSC principals that Qaddafi's forces were about to move on Benghazi. They were approaching Ajdabiya, and nothing stood in their way. Qaddafi, meanwhile, was talking about a bloodbath, encouraging his troops to take no quarter.

President Obama convened an NSC meeting on March 15 to discuss how the United States should respond. I attended with Secretary Gates. The president was not happy with the initial military options he had been given. Admiral Mullen, our JCS chairman, warned that imposing a no-fly zone would likely have little effect on the movement of Qaddafi's forces. It was clear, moreover, that a UN Security Council resolution would be needed to authorize the use of force to halt the movement of Qaddafi's army and protect Benghazi's civilian population from genocide. Our ambassador to the UN, Susan Rice, quickly obtained one.

Things came to a head in a second NSC meeting on March 17 that I again attended with Secretary Gates. Gates strongly believed that attacking a third Muslim country within a decade to bring about regime change would be a mistake, no matter how odious the regime. Gates made the point that in the early twenty-first century crises didn't come and go as they had during the Cold War. They came and stayed. Vice President Biden, Chief of Staff Bill Daley, Tom Donilon, Denis McDonough, and John Brennan all agreed with him. Secretary Clinton, Ambassador Rice, and the NSC staffer Samantha Power favored U.S. military intervention, arguing that the United States had a "responsibility to protect" civilian populations from genocide. Our British and French allies were also strongly in favor of military intervention in Libya.

President Obama decided that we couldn't stand idly by in the face of a potential humanitarian disaster and ordered a limited military intervention. The United States would take the lead in destroying

Libya's air defenses and then hand over the air campaign to NATO. No U.S. ground forces would be committed to the conflict.[26] This approach would soon become known as "leading from behind."

The coalition air campaign in Libya began on March 19, with the United States providing the majority of air strikes during the war's initial phase.[27] U.S. Navy ships launched 112 Tomahawk cruise missiles at Libya's air defense and command-and-control sites. The Royal Navy launched 12 more. Three U.S. B-2 stealth bombers flew lengthy round-trip missions from their base in Missouri to strike Libyan airfields, dropping forty-five precision-guided weapons. Two days later, two B-1 bombers flying from South Dakota struck other targets, ranging from ammunition depots and command-and-control sites to Libyan combat aircraft parked on the ground. In all, U.S. bombers struck about 150 fixed targets. U.S. fighters based in Europe also participated in the first phase of the air campaign. By March 22, Libya's air defenses had largely been disabled.

U.S. and coalition airpower then turned to relieving the pressure that Qaddafi's ground forces were exerting on the Libyan opposition in the east. Beginning on March 20, coalition strike packages hit Qaddafi's forces as they closed on Benghazi, causing shock and disarray. They also struck Libya's supply lines and reinforcements coming from Sirte, Qaddafi's hometown. Qaddafi's forces abandoned their advance on Benghazi and pulled back to Ajdabiya. Coalition airpower continued to pound Qaddafi's forces, and on March 26, Libyan regime forces were forced to retreat farther west.[28]

On March 31, the United States ceased flying air combat missions and transferred the operation to NATO.[29] As a consequence, the intensity of the air campaign dropped off significantly. Between March 19 and 31, U.S. combat aircraft had dropped fewer than five hundred precision-guided munitions.[30] By comparison, between early November and early December in our war against the Taliban in Afghanistan in 2001, U.S. bombers had delivered approximately ten times the number of PGMs.

My role in the operation to topple Qaddafi was very limited. I would be called alongside Director Panetta to testify before the congressional Intelligence Committees about our plans to support the Libyan opposition. We had been restricted by the president from providing arms and ammunition but could offer operational advice and logistical movements for Libya's opposition forces.[31] Given our minimal effort, I wasn't disappointed that I wasn't involved more. I was plenty busy as it was with the operation to kill Usama Bin Ladin, overseeing the surge in Afghanistan, and trying to delay Iran's pursuit of nuclear weapons.

The cessation of U.S. air strikes and the limits that had been placed on our support to the Libyan opposition had unnecessarily prolonged the conflict and the suffering of the Libyan people. Toppling Qaddafi took seven months. We had toppled the Taliban in two. As the opposition advanced on Tripoli from the east and the west, regime forces defected. Tripoli fell on August 22, and Qaddafi fled to Sirte. On October 20, coalition aircraft struck a convoy Qaddafi was traveling in. Qaddafi survived the strike and leaped into a nearby drainpipe, where he attempted to hide. Rebel fighters quickly converged on him and shot the Libyan dictator in the head. That ended this phase of the Libyan war.

I flew into Tripoli a week after Qaddafi was killed, the first senior American official to visit. The mood in Libya's capital was jubilant, and it affected my own mood. I thought Libya would have a bright future. I followed that visit with another two months later with Deputy CIA Director Michael Morell. Morell and I explained to Libya's new prime minister that al-Qa'ida had set its sights on Libya and that it was urgent that he build a new intelligence service that could deal with the problem. The prime minister pushed back and said he was only leading an interim government and that "it would take time to figure out how to build a new service in the right way."[32] The prime minister was rightly concerned that Libyans didn't want to risk repeating the abuses that Qaddafi's service had inflicted on the political opposition. Time, however, was not something Libya would have a lot of.

I would make several more trips to Libya's capital in 2012 and 2013 to work with its new government in an effort to stabilize the country after Qaddafi's fall. Each time I went, it seemed as if I met with different Libyan leaders in a rotational transitional government. There was a lot of rotating but not much governing.

We had successfully, if too gradually, deposed Qaddafi with a light-footprint approach. We and our European allies took an even more hands-off approach to stabilizing Libya after Qaddafi's fall. It didn't work. Libya descended into warring factions, with the government soon controlling only parts of Tripoli. A large-footprint approach to stabilization was clearly a nonstarter. Whether we could have been more successful with a more robust light-footprint strategy remains an issue of debate. I believe we could have, but the way we had contracted out our support for the Libyan opposition to Qatar and others, and reduced what little presence we had in eastern Libya, doomed us to failure. The Libyan model unfortunately diverged from the more successful approach we had pursued in Afghanistan in late 2001 in more ways than one.[33]

Our failure to stabilize Libya would come back to haunt us in Benghazi in September 2012. In the months prior, we had observed Islamist extremists gathering in Darnah in eastern Libya. Soon, extremists had taken over large parts of Benghazi. In July, CIA produced a paper that was titled "Libya: Al Qa'ida Establishing Sanctuary." In a closed hearing with the Senate Armed Services Committee, I had warned about the danger from Islamic extremists gathering in eastern Libya, but was challenged on that by Senator McCain. Libya had just had democratic elections, and he and a few other SASC members were very upbeat about the country's prospects.[34]

On September 11, 2012, the State Department's Temporary Mission Facility and our CIA base in Benghazi came under attack from Islamic extremists. Our ambassador to Libya, Chris Stevens, and another State Department officer, Sean Smith, died from suffocation from the fire the militants had started while sacking the TMF. Later that night, two CIA officers, Glen Doherty and Tyrone Woods, were killed by mortar fire while they were defending the CIA base after it too had come under attack.[35] We redirected a Predator that had been flying over Darnah that evening, but by the time it reached Benghazi, the assault on the TMF was over. We also alerted our Stuttgart-based Commander's In-Extremis Force, a Special Forces company-sized element, as well as fighter aircraft based in Europe, but neither could get to Benghazi in time.

Shortly after the assault on the TMF had begun, two DOD special operators in Tripoli volunteered to go to Benghazi to help repel the attack on our CIA base. They arrived early the following morning.

The CIA officers and DOD special operators defending CIA's base had fought bravely. Even more lives would have been lost if not for their heroism.

The tragedy at Benghazi and what actually happened that night unfortunately became highly politicized in an increasingly partisan Washington, and our intelligence community was caught in the cross fire.[36] There had been some initial confusion whether the assault on the TMF had been a spontaneous protest or a deliberate terrorist attack. Looking at the raw intelligence, it was clear to me the day after the attack that a representative from al-Qa'ida in the Islamic Maghreb and other extremists had been involved. CIA immediately characterized the attack as an organized military assault, but then expanded its analysis to state that the attack had evolved from a protest outside the TMF, adding that there was evidence of extremist and al-Qa'ida involvement as well. That last part was apparently missed by critics of the administration, who charged that CIA was politicizing intelligence. It wasn't true.[37]

Soon, the facts hardly mattered. My good friend Mike Rogers, chairman of the House Intelligence Committee, conducted a thorough investigation of the Benghazi attack and concluded that there had been no political influence on the intelligence process. He was rebuked by his fellow House Republicans for not being "tougher on Benghazi."[38] I admired Mike for telling it straight.

In June 2014, I helped plan a special operations raid to capture Ahmed Abu Khattala, one of the participants in the Benghazi attack. The clandestine operation was a brilliant example of intelligence and special operations tradecraft, and I was very proud of the Army special operations unit that had conceived and executed it. Khattala was brought to the United States to stand trial and was convicted on terrorism-related charges in 2017. He is serving twenty-two years in prison.

Nine months earlier, I had also overseen a raid by the same force to capture a key al-Qa'ida operative, Abu Anas al-Libi, in Tripoli. Libi was building al-Qa'ida's capabilities in Libya at the time of his capture and had participated in the 1998 bombings of our embassies in Kenya and Tanzania. It felt good to bring both men to justice, but overall our intervention in Libya had largely failed. Leading from behind turned out to be more behind than leading.

The Battle for the Middle East is far from over. In the decades ahead, while proxy war with Iran and state failure in the Arab world will likely remain prominent features of the strategic landscape, they will be supplemented by great power competition as China and Russia seek to make greater inroads in the Middle East at America's expense. The battle for influence will be global, and the Middle East will be a big part of it.

21

CRISIS AND CHANGE
IN DEFENSE INTELLIGENCE

UNDERSECRETARY OF DEFENSE

In September 2010, President Obama nominated me to be undersecretary of defense for intelligence. I had been deeply honored that the president had asked me to stay on in his administration as the assistant secretary of defense for special operations, low-intensity conflict, and interdependent capabilities, and was now even more honored that he had the confidence in my abilities to nominate me to be USD(I). Congress had established the position of USD(I) at Secretary Rumsfeld's urging in 2003. It was a very important post-9/11 reform. Before the creation of USD(I), there was no official within DOD at that level charged with overseeing the vast defense intelligence enterprise. Defense intelligence comprised eight of the sixteen organizations of the U.S. intelligence community and had the lion's share of the IC's budget. The USD(I) exercises authority, direction, and control over the defense intelligence enterprise for the secretary of defense, overseeing the National Security Agency, the Defense Intelligence Agency, the National Reconnaissance Office, the National Geospatial-Intelligence Agency, and the intelligence components of the Air Force, Army, Navy, Marine Corps (and now the Space Force), and the combatant commands. The USD(I) is also the senior official responsible for all of DOD's clandestine operations and programs and oversees several special access programs.

Since 2007, the USD(I) has also been dual hatted as the director of defense intelligence under the director of national intelligence. He works very closely with the DNI on the defense aspects of the National Intelligence Program and is the program executive within DOD for the Military Intelligence Program. He also exercises authority over DOD's Battlespace Awareness Portfolio, which includes intelligence and intelligence-related activities. In all, the USD(I) directly oversees or heavily influences up to $80 billion in annual spending and oversees a military and civilian workforce of around 180,000. The USD(I) is also the top security official within DOD. He oversees the Defense Counterintelligence and Security Agency (formerly the Defense Security Service), which is responsible for protecting our defense industrial secrets.

In April 2010, Director Panetta had briefly considered me for CIA's deputy director after Steve Kappes retired, but chose his deputy director for intelligence, Michael Morell, instead. Panetta made the right choice. Morell was a CIA insider, the right complement for Panetta, and a great analyst and briefer. He also had a good grasp of operations. He turned out to be a great deputy director. We would become and remain close friends.

When Jim Clapper was in the process of being vetted and nominated to be director of national intelligence, Secretary Gates, one of the most important mentors in my life, told me that I had been his backup choice as DNI and that he wanted me to replace Jim as USD(I). He added that one of the reasons he had been willing to let Jim go was that he knew he had me "in the bullpen." I thanked him and told him I hadn't thought about being USD(I). He told me it was the job I needed to do next to fully prepare myself to become CIA director. I was sold.

The Senate Armed Services Committee, unfortunately, wasn't able to hold a hearing for me before the Christmas recess. The SASC staff director told Gates's chief of staff that I'd be confirmed unanimously early in the New Year and that it was fine with the SASC if DOD used the Federal Vacancies Act to put me in the position as acting USD(I) before my confirmation. This was almost never done, because it presumed Senate confirmation. Gates liked the idea, and I became acting USD(I) while also dual hatted as ASD SO/LIC&IC for six weeks. In mid-February, I had my confirmation hearing and was unanimously confirmed by the SASC soon afterward.[1]

During my hearing, I had my wife, Melana, and four of my five daughters sitting behind me. The senators couldn't beat me up too much, I figured, with my daughters present, and I introduced them all as I began my opening statement. More seriously, the hearing was a good civics lesson for all my daughters. My youngest, Kalyna, was only six at the time, so Melana gave her a drawing pad to keep her occupied. She drew a sketch of her dad sitting at a small witness table, with giant-sized likenesses of the SASC chairman, Senator Carl Levin, and the ranking member, Senator John McCain, towering above me on the dais, with their names appended to their towering figures. My wife handed it to McCain's staff director after the hearing. That night Senator McCain called Kalyna at home and told her that he loved her drawing, and that her dad had done great. He later sent her an autographed picture. I thought it might have been the best covert action I had unwittingly ever conducted.

After I became USD(I), Secretary Gates asked for a memo outlining how I proposed to take defense intelligence to the next level. After years of waging war with al-Qa'ida, I knew I needed to get defense intelligence ready to meet the challenges of a rising China and an increasingly revanchist Russia. I outlined my priorities: transforming our overhead architecture (the National Reconnaissance Office's constellations of spy satellites) to provide more persistent and integrated collection while building within the NRO the capability to better defend its satellites from attack; working with NSA to stay ahead of the cryptologic challenges that were coming down the road; strengthening DIA's human intelligence capabilities by creating a Defense Clandestine Service; and building up the Air Force's penetrating intelligence, surveillance, and reconnaissance capabilities to counter the growing anti-access/area-denial threat from China.[2] I also wanted to sustain and continue to improve our counterterrorism capabilities, specifically our Predator fleet. Gates liked the memo, as did Leon Panetta when he replaced Gates as secretary in July 2011.

Secretaries Gates and Panetta asked me to keep the counterterrorism portfolio when I moved to USD(I). I also continued to be a member of the NSC's Deputies Committee, keeping my hand in national security policy making. I had to give up most of my oversight of SOF and the strategic capabilities and conventional force transformation portfolio I had overseen as ASD SO/LIC&IC. I still advised the department's leadership informally in these areas, however. In turn, I now had authority, direction, and control over the defense intelligence enterprise.

A typical day in the life for me as USD(I) was not that different from what it was as ASD SO/LIC&IC. I still traveled just as much to war zones and other hot spots around the globe, and added travel to Russia, China, and the nations around their periphery as I tried to posture defense intelligence for renewed great power competition. I worked closely with the chiefs of several intelligence services around the world. I regularly participated in NSC Deputies Committee meetings and in senior leader meetings at DOD. I testified frequently before Congress, often side by side with my good friend Jim Clapper.

Like ASD SO/LIC&IC, it was a great job. I was able to tailor it to my interests and strengths, focusing on operations as well as intelligence. I hadn't set out to become USD(I), but once I had the job, I was determined to make the most of it. A new responsibility for me was to be one of the select few in the U.S. government to receive the President's Daily Brief, or PDB. Panetta had told the PDB staff that he wanted me to see everything he did, so he and I had the highest accesses, seeing intelligence that was restricted to the president and only a handful of his most senior advisers. I took my PDB responsibilities very seriously and devoted an hour a day to reading all the intelligence. I also regularly provided comments back to the analysts who had written pieces for that day's PDB, since timely and substantive feedback is critical to keeping analysts focused on policy makers' needs. I also had the authority to task PDB "memos," or additional questions for the IC's analysts, which I frequently did.

After I was confirmed, Secretary Gates presided at another memorable swearing-in ceremony for me, with Director Panetta, Deputy Director Morell, and lots of the CIA officers I was working secretly with on the Bin Ladin operation in attendance. I'm sure eyebrows were raised when the ceremony and reception had to be cut short, and several of us had to depart for the White House for another secret meeting with the president on the pending operation.

After the Bin Ladin operation, and as we drove core al-Qa'ida closer and closer to operational defeat, I began to devote more time to the challenges a rising China and revanchist Russia would pose, and how defense intelligence needed to be transformed for renewed great power competition. As I discussed in the previous chapter, our support for the Syrian opposition also took up a lot of my time, but preparing defense intelligence for a new cold war loomed large in my calculus. My time as USD(I) would also present challenges of a different sort, ranging from assessing and responding to the damage caused by Edward Snowden, to dealing with a failure in top leadership at DIA.

THE SNOWDEN LEAKS

In early June 2013, the U.S. intelligence community started hemorrhaging secrets. First, the U.K.'s *Guardian* newspaper reported that NSA was collecting the phone records of millions of Verizon customers daily. This was a reference to the now-declassified telephony metadata program, which had been authorized by Section 215 of the Patriot Act. Under this program, the telephone companies, operating under a broad court order, provided NSA with metadata on international calls made to and from the United States—the phone numbers involved and the duration of the call, but no information on the content (what was actually said) or the identities of the callers.

The Washington Post followed the next day with a story that revealed that the United States was intercepting the email communications of people overseas as it passed through the United States. This program, which had been authorized by Section 702 of the Foreign Intelligence Surveillance Act, focused on foreign-to-foreign communications that, because of the nature of the internet, were routed through the United States.

NSA's director, Keith Alexander, had already briefed me on the source of these leaks: Edward Snowden, an IT contractor who had been working at NSA's Hawaii facility. Snowden had fled to Hong Kong on May 20, carrying a bag of laptops with hundreds of thousands, perhaps millions, of compartmented intelligence documents with him.[3] He subsequently fled to Russia, where he was granted asylum and, more recently, citizenship. In addition to divulging to the media gravely damaging secrets about how the U.S. intelligence community operates, I believe, as do many of my IC colleagues, that Snowden provided U.S. secrets to the Chinese and Russians.[4]

Keith told me that Snowden had been able to steal this large quantity of highly classified information because NSA had not completed its installation of auditing and monitoring tools, which flag when users with access to its system download an unusually large quantity of intelligence documents or documents that are outside their normal duties and work behavior.[5] NSA had installed these capabilities at its headquarters and at other NSA cryptologic centers, but hadn't done so yet at NSA Hawaii. In the interest of internally sharing knowledge among its workforce about the agency's capabilities, moreover, NSA had made too much compartmented information available to a very wide group of users.

The potential damage was binned into three categories: files we knew Snowden had stolen; files he might have stolen; and those he might have looked at. The potential damage ranged from hundreds of thousands of files to several million. The worst case was too awful to contemplate, not just in the volume of information Snowden might have taken, but in the grave damage it would cause to the national security of the United States if Snowden gave it to our adversaries. Included in the huge number of classified documents Snowden had stolen was the IC's Congressional Budget Justification Book, the IC's annual report to Congress that describes the full extent of our intelligence programs and capabilities—how they worked and the results they produced—to justify our funding requests for the coming year. The CBJB covered, for example, how we protected our forces from insurgent attacks, how we assessed the intentions of our adversaries, and how we monitored the proliferation of weapons of mass destruction in North Korea and Iran.[6] I participated in several NSC Deputies and Principals Committee meetings on the damage Snowden had done to U.S. national security and the steps we would take to mitigate that damage. I also briefed the Congressional Intelligence and Armed Services Committees on the damage, both known and potential.

To deal with the fallout from Snowden, President Obama established a national commission to provide recommendations for reform of the IC as a result of Snowden's act of betrayal.[7] I met with the commission during its deliberations. Our DNI, Jim Clapper, had worried that the Snowden leaks would lead to unrealistic restrictions being imposed on our ability to collect signals intelligence. Clapper jokingly referred to it as a desire for "immaculate collection."[8]

In their final report, which was issued in December 2013, the commissioners made forty-six recommendations, the most important of which was that NSA no longer hold the U.S. telecom metadata itself and that it obtain a court order anytime it wanted to query the data. Previously, NSA could make queries based on a general court order. Equally important was the commission's recommendation that senior policy makers review any collection that carries significant political, economic, or foreign policy risks. President Obama accepted both of these recommendations and many others. He rejected 15 percent of the recommendations and wanted to study more carefully another 15 percent before deciding one way or the other.[9] We had several NSC meetings to discuss the Review Group's recommendations, particularly those the president had wanted to study further.

One recommendation that the president didn't accept deserves special mention. The commission recommended that our policy and practice of having a senior military officer "dual hatted" as both the director of NSA and the commander of Cyber Command be ended. The commissioners also favored making NSA's director a civilian. These two actions, the commissioners believed, would increase public trust in NSA.

At an NSC meeting with the president in early 2014 on the NSA-CYBERCOM issue, Secretary Chuck Hagel delegated the meeting to me as USD(I), so I represented DOD, along with our JCS chairman, General Marty Dempsey. Keith Alexander also attended to offer his personal views on a potential NSA-CYBERCOM split. All of the president's top advisers supported the Review Group's recommendation, including Director Clapper and D/CIA John Brennan. There were only three of us who argued against it: Marty, Keith, and me.

I argued that ending the "dual hat" relationship would be a good idea down the road, because the time would come when NSA and CYBERCOM would need to be separated due to their different and somewhat conflicting missions. Having the ability to appoint a career civilian as NSA director would also be a plus, because the civilian workforce was where the real expertise at NSA resided, and we couldn't appoint a civilian to head NSA as long as the director of the NSA was dual hatted as a combatant commander. But I argued that CYBERCOM's capabilities were still too immature to separate the two organizations at this point.[10] Surprisingly, the president went against the recommendation of the vast majority of his senior advisers and supported Marty, Keith, and me.

TURMOIL AT THE TOP

Jim Clapper and I made a number of changes in the leadership of our defense intelligence agencies in 2014 and 2015, with the top leadership of DIA, NSA, and NGA all turning over.[11] By law, the secretary of defense nominates or appoints the directors of our defense intelligence agencies with the concurrence of the DNI. The secretary of defense delegated authority, direction, and control of the Defense Intelligence Enterprise to me, so the individuals that I selected, with Jim's concurrence, were whom the secretary would appoint. Jim and I always sought the concurrence of the chairman of the Joint Chiefs of Staff prior to making these nominations as well.

All of these leadership transitions went smoothly except for one: DIA's. Lieutenant General Mike Flynn had had a very rocky first year and a half at the helm of the agency, a 16,500-person organization that was going through a significant transition in strategic direction at the time. Mike had had a distinguished career up to that point and had been our unanimous pick for DIA's director in 2012. He had spent five years in combat in Iraq and Afghanistan and had played a major role in developing the "find, fix, finish, exploit, and analyze" targeting cycle that had produced great success against al-Qa'ida in Iraq and Shi'a extremist groups.

Mike hadn't led a large global intelligence organization before, however. He also hadn't had much experience with a large career civilian workforce, and nearly three-fourths of DIA's workforce was made up of civilian intelligence professionals. Mike had also shown little interest in the major reforms his predecessor, Ron Burgess, had initiated, such as the Defense Clandestine Service, delegating that to David Shedd, his deputy director, and others. The DCS was a major reform of mine, aimed at strengthening DIA's ability to collect clandestine HUMINT, which would become increasingly important in the new era of great power competition with China and Russia that we were now entering. DIA had also recently experienced a major operational failure overseas that had caught the attention of our congressional oversight committees, and Mike hadn't been engaged in fixing that problem either.

Mike had clashed repeatedly with Shedd, a CIA officer on detail to DIA, and several other DIA senior leaders, lecturing and hectoring his senior staff. His primary interest was in tinkering with DIA's organization. Organizational change without the requisite capabilities is like moving deck chairs on the *Titanic*. Mike wanted to "centerize" DIA—combine analysis and collection into regional and functional centers—much as John Brennan would later do at CIA. Centerizing DIA might be a good idea down the road, but not before the agency had built the new collection and analytical capabilities it would need. Mike hadn't kept DIA's workforce informed of these changes and threatened to fire several of his senior staff when they questioned his decisions. When Mike briefed me on his proposed changes, I strongly advised against them. DIA needed to focus on building new capabilities, not rearranging its organizational chart and reporting lines, I told him. To my astonishment, Mike made the changes anyway. I only learned about it when I got a memo that he had just issued from a senior DIA officer. I called Mike in the next day and asked him to explain why he had done it, despite my clear direction to the contrary. I told him to immediately rescind the change, which he did.

These were serious issues, but not enough yet to force me to remove Mike as DIA's director. From there, unfortunately, Mike's mismanagement and insubordination only got worse. What brought Jim Clapper and me reluctantly to the conclusion that Mike needed to go was the deteriorating leadership climate at DIA, as reflected in our annual climate surveys and from interviews with all of the key leaders at the organization. The situation at DIA was bad and getting worse with each passing month, and it was affecting workforce morale. Jim and I finally decided, after consulting with Secretary Hagel (who became secretary after Panetta left in early 2013) and General Dempsey, that the best course of action was to tell Mike that he wouldn't be extended for a third year as director, but would finish out his full second year and retire as a three-star. We called Mike into my office in late 2013 to inform him of our decision. Mike asked if he was being fired, and we assured him that he wasn't. He just wouldn't get a third year at DIA.[12]

Mike initially accepted our decision, but grew angrier as time went on, particularly after he retired from military service. In April 2014, four months before he was scheduled to retire, he tried to get himself extended for another year, after our first nominee to replace him as DIA director got held up in an IG investigation (from which she ultimately was cleared). JC Campbell, the Army's vice-chief of staff, immediately called me and asked if Clapper and I approved of Mike's extension, and I told JC that we did not. Mike called me that evening to rant. Clapper met with Mike the next day and told him that if he didn't apologize to me immediately, he would be fired on the spot. Mike complied and said he had been "out of line."

After he retired, Mike claimed that he had been "fired" for warning Congress that America was less safe in 2014 than it had been in 2012, particularly where the threat from global jihadists was concerned.[13] Nothing could be further from the truth. Mike, Jim, and I had very similar views on the growing threat landscape, with the exception of Russia, which Mike considered far less of a threat than Jim and I did. The decision to remove Mike after two years was based solely on the poor command climate that developed at DIA under his leadership and the need for a fresh start. Jim and I had taken the decision only with great reluctance and had tried to implement it with as much care and compassion as we could. In February 2015, Lieutenant General Vince Stewart, the first Marine and first African American to become DIA's director, assumed command. Doug Wise, another career CIA officer, succeeded Shedd as DIA's deputy director.

I was then shocked, as were all of my former IC colleagues, to see Mike sitting next to Vladimir Putin in December 2015 at a Russia Today anniversary gala in Moscow. I was even more appalled to see Mike lead chants of "lock her up," referring to Hillary Clinton, at the 2016 Republican National Convention. As Jim Clapper wrote in his memoirs, it wasn't the Mike we thought we knew.[14] And things only got worse from there. In December 2020, Flynn called for the U.S. military to seize voting machines in several states and "rerun" the presidential election in favor of Donald Trump.

In 2014, Admiral Mike Rogers succeeded Keith Alexander at NSA and CYBERCOM, and Robert Cardillo succeeded Tish Long as director of NGA. Keith and Tish had both completed very successful tours as directors and had had distinguished careers in intelligence. Thankfully, these changes of leadership were far less dramatic than DIA's had been.

22

THE RETURN OF
GREAT POWER COMPETITION

GREAT POWER SIGNALING

Three events in early 2007 signaled that we had entered a period of renewed great power rivalry. Two of the events were provocative military actions by China and Russia; the third was a fire-breathing speech by Vladimir Putin. The events made clear that we were dealing with not only a rising China but a far more assertive one. It was also clear that we were dealing with a revanchist Russia, particularly as long as Putin is in charge.

On January 11, 2007, the Chinese launched a direct-ascent anti-satellite (ASAT) weapon to destroy one of their weather satellites in low earth orbit. The multistage, solid fuel missile, called the SC-19, was a variation of China's long-range DF-21 surface-to-surface missile. The SC-19 had been modified to include an infrared imager to close in on its target, and a kinetic kill vehicle to destroy it. The KKV struck the weather satellite orbiting about 540 miles above the earth at nearly eighteen thousand miles per hour, shattering it into thousands of pieces of space debris. China's ASAT test was the largest single space debris event in history, constituting nearly a third of all the debris the U.S. military tracks in space. The debris from the Chinese ASAT test will remain in low earth orbit for decades, and perhaps centuries, posing a risk to other satellites and space vehicles operating in that orbital regime.[1] More significantly, a new era of space as a contested war-fighting domain had begun.

The second and third events that signaled a return to great power competition emanated from Russia. The first was a speech Putin gave at the Munich Security Conference in early February. Every winter, top security officials gather in Munich to discuss the issues of the day. Putin's speech at the conference wasn't the only indicator of renewed Russian belligerence, however. The Ukrainian president Viktor Yushchenko's badly disfigured face was another reminder. The leader of Ukraine's 2004 "Orange Revolution," Yushchenko had barely survived after he had been poisoned—most likely at Russian instigation—at a dinner in Kyiv in early September 2004.[2]

When it was his turn to speak, Putin launched into a diatribe against the United States. He claimed that the United States had used its uncontested military power to create and exploit a "unipolar" world and that because of U.S. dominance the world had become more destabilized and was seeing "more wars and regional conflicts." Putin said that the "almost unconstrained hyper-use of force" by the United States and its disdain for the basic principles of international law had stimulated an arms race as insecure countries turned to weapons for security, including weapons of mass destruction. Putin asked why the United States was creating frontline bases with up to five thousand troops on Russia's borders; why NATO was expanding aggressively toward a nonthreatening Russia; and why a missile defense system was being deployed in Poland, close to the Russian border. He concluded by saying that Russia, "with 1,000 years of history," hardly needed advice on how to act on the international scene.

When it came time for his remarks the next day, Secretary Gates joked that "as an old Cold Warrior" he found that Putin's remarks had "*almost* filled him with nostalgia for a less complex time." He then dismissed Putin's diatribe by saying that "one Cold War was quite enough."[3] As an old cold warrior myself, I was proud of my boss.

A few months later, the Russians launched a cyberattack against Estonia after the government in Tallinn removed a six-foot statue of a Soviet soldier that had long stood in the capital. A massive botnet attack overwhelmed nearly every website in the tiny country. ATMs went down, and government services ground to a halt. The attack went on for days. The malicious botnet traffic seemed to be emanating from servers and internet providers that belonged to the Russian Business Network, a den of online criminal activity based in St. Petersburg. As

Estonia's defense minister would say, "This was the first time that a botnet threatened the national security of an entire nation."[4]

Putin's diatribe was a blast from the past—Cold War redux. China's satellite shoot-down and Russia's cyberwar, on the other hand, foreshadowed the importance these two domains would have in great power competition and future warfare. But all three warned of increased tensions ahead as we entered a new era of strategic competition with China and Russia.

I had been focused on the dangers a more powerful China would pose since the early 1990s, including the high likelihood of future war in space. China's ASAT test was a surprise to many, but it wasn't to me. I had not focused much on Russia, however, since the end of the Cold War. It would be Russia, though, that would demand more of my attention during my final years in government.

From 2007 onward, I spent an increasing amount of time ensuring that we would have the capabilities we would need—a new stealth long-range bomber; penetrating intelligence, surveillance, and reconnaissance aircraft; long-range missiles; a larger submarine fleet; robotic combat systems; and space warfare and cyber warfare capabilities—to deter a rising China and a revanchist Russia.[5] After I became the undersecretary of defense for intelligence, I began transforming defense intelligence for this new era of great power competition, and I spent increasingly more time assuring our allies on China's and Russia's periphery, building up their capabilities, and overseeing sensitive joint operations with some of them. My views on the threats posed by a rising China and a revanchist Russia had also evolved considerably. I increasingly saw economic and technological competition with China and covert and overt aggression from Russia as our main challenges, and I spent a lot of time thinking about how we and our allies should respond to these new threats. It was clear we were entering a new cold war. I will have more to say about how we can win it in the next chapter.

MEETINGS IN MOSCOW

In late May 2011, I traveled to Moscow for discussions with the chief of the GRU, General Aleksandr Shlyakhturov, and other senior Russian defense and intelligence officials. My predecessor as undersecretary of defense for intelligence, Jim Clapper, had hosted Shlyakhturov's predecessor, General Valentin Korabelnikov, in Washington, and the GRU was reciprocating by hosting me in Moscow.[6]

The Russians didn't make my travel to Moscow easy. They refused to clear the Air Force Gulfstream aircraft that I normally traveled in, so my team and I had to fly commercial. After we landed, we were forced to wait for about two and a half hours in an airport lounge until we were allowed to depart for our hotel, supposedly because the "prime minister" of Transnistria was arriving, and the airport was being locked down. Transnistria, a Russian-occupied part of Moldova, was one of Russia's "frozen" conflicts. We were being frozen in place at the airport. There was probably a message in that.

On my United Airlines flight from Washington, I thought about my initial desire to serve in Moscow as a CIA officer and the secret war we had fought against the Russians in Afghanistan. This would be my first visit to Moscow and Russia, and I was a bit apprehensive about how I'd be treated. I knew I'd be an intelligence target for the Russians, so before I landed in Moscow I disassembled my cell phone and gave the parts to my security detail to store in an electronically shielded bag. I didn't want to bring home any unwanted "friends."

My host in Moscow was Steve, a longtime Russia hand. He had me over for dinner my first night in Moscow, and we chatted about his tour and what was going on back home. During my visit, I thought about the CIA officers who had served in Moscow over the years, men and women who developed the innovative tradecraft needed to operate in the most hostile operating environment there is. Most of all, I thought about the Soviet and Russian agents who provided critical information to CIA and U.S. policy makers at enormous risks to themselves.

Our day with the GRU began with a meeting between Shlyakhturov and me. The GRU was undergoing some major reforms, and Shlyakhturov discussed them a bit during our private meeting. He wouldn't say much, however, about reforms the GRU was making in the *spetsnaz*, or special forces, area, despite my probes. I told him that the *spetsnaz* had acquitted themselves well in Afghanistan. It was clear that the Soviet-Afghan War during the 1980s was not something he wished to discuss. Perhaps the memories were too painful.

After our meeting, Shlyakhturov gave us a tour of the GRU's new headquarters. We then spent the rest of the day exchanging views with the GRU's analysts on al-Qa'ida, Afghanistan, North Korea, Iran, and other areas of common interest. The Russians seemed particularly interested in stopping the flow of heroin that was making its way from Afghanistan through central Asia and into Russia. As we ended our day with the GRU, I gave a short speech in which I thanked "our Russian friends" for hosting us. One of the Russians, perhaps recalling my history in waging a secret war against the Red Army in Afghanistan that killed tens of thousands of Soviet soldiers, retorted by saying, "Mr. Vickers just called us his friends." I pretended not to notice his sarcastic tone.

That evening, General Shlyakhturov hosted a nice dinner for me at one of Moscow's fanciest restaurants, the Yar, in the Sovietskiy Hotel. I used my limited Russian with him as much as I could. Fortunately, my wife, who speaks fluent Russian, filled in when I got stuck. Shlyakhturov opened up over dinner and drinks, despite the loud music and a strange live show that involved a woman in an aquarium. He talked about his daughters and grandchildren, and how his daughters chided him for being out of touch with the times. No doubt my daughters would say the same thing about me. I ended up liking him and concluded that he was a soldier who had served his country just as I had served mine.

My meeting on counterterrorism cooperation with Alexander Bortnikov, the chief of the Federal Security Service, or FSB, was mostly a waste of time. To be honest, there wasn't any CT cooperation for us to discuss. One interesting aspect of my meeting, however, was the presence of Aleksandr "Sasha" Zhomov, a longtime counterintelligence professional and the FSB's top America specialist. (Steve had informed me that Zhomov might attend our meeting with Bortnikov). During the 1980s, Zhomov had supervised the surveillance teams who watched American diplomats twenty-four hours a day. He later ran double-agent operations against us.[7] Like me, he had been in his early thirties then. Much older now, he was as determined as ever to catch Russian spies working for the United States. I watched him warily as the conversation about counterterrorism cooperation blathered on.

The only Russian intelligence service I didn't meet with during my trip to Moscow was the SVR, its overseas spying arm. Perhaps it was because the service was still reeling from the recent arrest of eleven of its deep cover, "illegal" officers in the United States.[8] I had been briefed on the operation ten months earlier by Cindy, CIA's chief of counterintelligence. A CIA source in Moscow had identified the illegals, and the FBI took it from there. The Russian operation was something right out of the TV series *The Americans*—except for the fact the Cold War had ended two decades earlier.[9]

My meetings with Russia's deputy defense minister and deputy chief of the General Staff were little more than haranguing sessions. They berated our team about U.S. missile defenses and the threat they posed to Russia. I replied that physics were physics and numbers were numbers. Our anti-missile missiles were too few, too slow, and too poorly positioned to be any threat to Russia's strategic nuclear deterrent. I didn't make any headway at all.

I wish I could say my visit to Moscow made a small contribution to improved relations between our two countries. But it didn't. For most of my visit, an angry, belligerent Russia was on full display. And beginning in 2012, our relations would get worse—much worse.

XI'S AND PUTIN'S INTENSIFICATION

The reelection of Vladimir Putin to Russia's presidency on May 7, 2012, and the election of Xi Jinping, first as general secretary of the Chinese Communist Party and chairman of the Central Military Commission, on November 15, 2012, and then as China's president on March 14, 2013, substantially intensified the great power competition that had been under way for half a decade. The two men had come to power—or back to power in Putin's case—through very different processes: Xi was essentially anointed; Putin's return triggered huge protests, and he was only installed after the Kremlin rigged the election in his favor.[10]

Both men brought with them visions of an illiberal world order in which China and Russia would have a much greater share of world power, and both quickly became far more aggressive internationally.[11] Both leaders also moved rapidly to consolidate their political power. Within five years, the CCP granted Xi one-man rule for life. Putin's Russia followed suit a few years later.

Between 2012 and 2015, I devoted more and more time to intelligence about China and Russia. I had analysts in several times for deep dives on particular topics. CIA concluded that we were facing stronger, more assertive leaders than we had since the Cold War and noted that Putin was increasingly restricting his inner circle to former members of the intelligence and security services and the military, who were referred to as *siloviki*, or "strongmen."

I also met regularly with senior CIA officers overseeing clandestine collection and FBI officials overseeing counterintelligence investigations to get updates on important developments. In one instance, I arranged a meeting with a senior U.S. military officer for a CIA asset who had been exfiltrated from Russia and resettled in the United States. The asset had provided volumes of unique intelligence, so I was pleased to help CIA with its request. Unfortunately, I can't say more about it.

Overall, our collection and analysis on China and Russia was outstanding. Some of it was even breathtaking. Our growing challenges with the great powers weren't from a lack of good intelligence. They were strategy and policy related.

Under Xi, China began several new efforts, most notably in space, to strengthen China's military capabilities. Xi also significantly expanded Chinese military planning beyond its traditional focus on Taiwan, envisioning conflicts with Vietnam and Japan, among others. Between 2000 and 2014, China's defense budget had increased nearly 500 percent in real terms. Chinese military strategy was aimed at "winning local wars under 'informationized' conditions." Its principal aim was to deter or prevent us, principally with its anti-access/area-denial capabilities, from defending our allies and interests along the East Asian littoral.[12]

By 2014, China had thousands of ballistic and cruise missiles capable of projecting power out to Guam and the Second Island Chain. China had modernized its nuclear forces with mobile, solid fuel, intercontinental ballistic missiles equipped with multiple, independently targeted, reentry vehicle warheads, and had developed a new Jin-class fleet ballistic missile submarine and a new submarine-launched ballistic missile. Chinese nuclear strategy remained focused on "counter-value" targets—striking U.S. population centers with multimegaton warheads to ensure strategic deterrence. China also dramatically increased its space capabilities and had fielded a very large cyber force. It was meanwhile making great progress in artificial intelligence, quantum technologies, and synthetic biology.

Xi militarized the South China Sea with a string of constructed island bases by dredging sand over coral reefs to create new Chinese islands eight hundred miles from the mainland, de facto extending its sovereignty claims over the large body of water. Xi also increased tensions with Japan in the East China Sea.

China had steadily and successfully pursued an asymmetric strategy to counter American strengths, and as a result our strategic position along the East Asian littoral had deteriorated markedly over the past two decades. It was a problem that we needed to fix urgently.

———

To fuel its economic growth and military modernization, China's intelligence services were working overtime to steal our military, industrial, and technological secrets. In February 2013, the IC published a National Intelligence Estimate on China's intellectual property theft and its economic impact. The NIE concluded that China was conducting "a massive, sustained cyber-espionage campaign that threatened the economic competitiveness of the United States." It added that China was "aggressively seeking to penetrate the computer systems of America's businesses to gain access to data that could be used for economic gain." The IC estimated that several tens of billions of dollars of intellectual property were being stolen annually from the United States. As a CIA officer during the Cold War, I periodically observed the Soviet Union's attempts to clandestinely acquire advanced Western technology. I remember thinking that if the Soviets had to go to all this trouble to illicitly acquire advanced technology, they'd never be able to compete with us economically. China's success in economic espionage, made possible by cyber operations, has made me rethink my views on the benefits of intellectual property theft to economic growth.

In February 2013, the U.S. cybersecurity firm Mandiant released a report describing an online threat it called "Advanced Persistent Threat 1," or APT1. "Advanced persistent threat" is a term used to describe nation-state adversaries engaged in offensive cyber operations. Within a few years, more than forty APTs would be identified, many of them emanating from China. APT1 was in reality the Second Bureau of the People's Liberation Army General Staff's Third Department (3PLA), the PLA's equivalent of NSA. APT1 came from a 3PLA element known as Unit 61398. Unit 61398 conducted economic espionage on an industrial scale. It commanded a vast global cyber infrastructure, with nearly a thousand servers around the world, including more than a hundred in the United States. It had penetrated more than 140 American businesses across twenty industry sectors and stole hundreds of terabytes of data from these companies. In May 2014, the Justice Department indicted five members of Unit 61398 for intellectual property theft. The indicted PLA officers were in China, and thus the charges were largely symbolic, but they did have a deterrent effect on Chinese cyber behavior for a while.

In June 2014, a second U.S. cybersecurity firm, CrowdStrike, published a report on another cyber economic espionage threat from China, APT2. APT2 was in reality Unit 61486 of 3PLA. APT2 targeted U.S. defense and aerospace companies, and it had stolen Boeing's detailed designs for its C-17 transport aircraft. The IP theft had enabled China to develop, build, and deploy a copy of the C-17 in a third of the time it had taken the United States to do so. The Chinese also stole massive computer data relating to the Air Force's advanced fighters, the F-22 and F-35, enabling the PLA to understand and copy the designs of our newest combat aircraft. The Chinese also stole designs from our land- and sea-based missile defense systems, our helicopters, and our naval surface combatants. They were hoovering up everything they could get their hands on.[13]

For its part, Russia had been embarked on a defense modernization and buildup since the 2008 Russo-Georgia War. We knew from multiple intelligence sources that Putin sought to improve Russia's international power position by selectively modernizing Russia's military in areas that provided maximum strategic leverage to the Russian state, and the Russian Navy was making great advances in undersea warfare—an area of strategic advantage for the United States and one that I followed very closely as USD(I).

In 2013, the Russians commissioned two new submarines, the *Dol-gorukiy,* a nuclear-powered, fleet ballistic missile submarine that could deliver Russia's new submarine-launched ballistic missile (the Bulava) and the *Severodvinsk,* a nuclear-powered cruise missile submarine that could fire the Kalibr land-attack cruise missile, among other weapons. Both submarines employ very advanced quieting technology, on par with our newest submarines. These advances in stealth could potentially enable Russian subs to show up off our shores undetected and launch decapitating missile strikes targeting our national leadership. We accordingly monitored Russian submarine development and deployments very closely.

There were also Russian special weapons programs capable of inflicting immense damage on the U.S. homeland and the global economy that we closely monitored as well. The Russians viewed these weapons as "great equalizers" in the event of a war with the United States. The programs had their origins in the late Cold War and had been sustained even during the dire years of the 1990s, when the Russian economy was on its deathbed.

We also closely followed increasing evidence of new thinking about the character of war within the Russian high command. In January 2013, Russia's chief of the General Staff, General Valery Gerasimov, gave a talk in Moscow at the Academy of Military Science in which he argued that there had been a blurring of the lines between peace and war. Subversion, disinformation, and sabotage would prepare the ground in modern conflict for eventual kinetic operations, and the role of these "non-military means" in achieving strategic goals had now exceeded in many cases the power of traditional military force in effectiveness. Gerasimov argued that information had become the critical element in warfare. It was provocative thinking, but, as I learned long ago, Russian doctrine and the capabilities needed to implement that doctrine are often very different things.[14]

RUSSIA'S COVERT AND OVERT WAR IN UKRAINE

"Slava Ukraini!" (Glory to Ukraine), I said as I greeted Valentyn Naly-vaichenko, the chief of Ukraine's Security Service, or SBU. Naly-

vaichenko smiled and responded with *"Heroyam Slava,"* "Glory to the Heroes." Our exchange of greetings was a reference to Ukraine's freedom fighters, the most recent of whom were the heroes of the Maidan Revolution, the students and other protesters who had swept the pro-Russian regime of Viktor Yanukovych from power in February 2014.[15]

Nalyvaichenko was my primary interlocutor in the Ukrainian government.[16] He had just begun a major reform of the SBU and wasn't sure whom he could trust in the organization. The security service had been a close partner of the Russian FSB under the Yanukovych regime, and he was concerned that it had been thoroughly penetrated by the Russians. He was right. He had his work cut out for him.

The SBU was in charge of Ukraine's "Anti-Terrorist Operation" in the Donbas, in easternmost Ukraine, to contest Russia's covert intervention there. Russia had earlier seized and annexed Crimea from Ukraine. The IC had closely monitored the buildup of Russian forces around Crimea, but our Russia analysts didn't think that the Russians would invade and certainly hadn't considered the possibility that Putin would quickly move to annex it.

I traveled to Ukraine only a few days after the Russians had shot down a civilian airliner, Malaysia Airlines Flight 17, on July 17, 2014, killing all 298 passengers and crew onboard. MH-17 had been en route from Amsterdam to Kuala Lumpur when Russian soldiers in eastern Ukraine operating an SA-11 "Buk" surface-to-air missile system mistook the civilian airliner for a military aircraft. The SA-11 had been driven into eastern Ukraine from Russia and returned to Russia shortly after the shoot-down. Using our satellites, intercepts, and social media monitoring tools, we were able to attribute the attack to Russia within hours.[17]

That didn't stop the Russians from denying the shoot-down had been carried out by their forces, however. It was the start of a new approach to covert action by the Russians—what some have described as "implausible deniability." Covert action planners normally try to hide who is behind a covert action through a variety of means, aiming at a minimum for "plausible deniability" that their government sponsored the action. The Russians increasingly didn't seem to care if their denial of their covert involvement was plausible. They'd still deny it even when their denials were patently absurd. We believed that they wanted some of their covert operations to be easily discoverable to show that Russia could act with impunity.

After the MH-17 shoot-down, Russia's propaganda machine sprang into high gear. Russia Today, the Russian government-sponsored TV network in America, claimed preposterously that the U.S. intelligence community had cleared Russia of wrongdoing. RT then reported that Ukraine had shot down the plane, using a laughably fake photograph as "evidence."

In addition to Nalyvaichenko, I met with Yuriy Pavlov, the chief of military intelligence, or HUR, and Viktor Hvozd, the chief of foreign intelligence, the SVR, or FISU, as we called it. I also met with the chief of the General Staff, General Viktor Muzhenko, and Ukraine's minister of defense, Valery Heletey. On subsequent visits, I also met with Heletey's successor, Stepan Poltorak. Each gave me urgent requests for arms and other assistance, which I passed on to the NSC.

As I concluded my first visit to Ukraine, I realized that Putin might have the upper hand for now, but he had done something no Ukrainian politician had been able to do: he ignited Ukrainian nationalism. Ukraine was now a vastly different and vehemently anti-Russian country.

In March 2014, demonstrations by pro-Russian groups broke out in the Donetsk and Luhansk oblasts in eastern Ukraine, collectively known as the Donbas. The demonstrations quickly escalated into armed conflict. Russian weapons and "volunteers" poured into eastern Ukraine. Russian intelligence officers had been operating there for several months, preparing the environment for possible insurrection. One we followed closely went by the nom de guerre of Igor Strelkov. His real name was Igor Girkin.[18]

The separatists in Donetsk and Luhansk were mostly a bunch of street thugs, leavened by Russian professional soldiers. Our NATO commander, General Phil Breedlove, a friend of mine, said in April 2014 that "what is happening in eastern Ukraine is a military operation that is well planned and organized and we assess that it is being carried out at the direction of Russia." People's Republics of Donetsk and Luhansk were quickly established by the supposed Ukrainian separatists. On April 17, Putin told an interviewer that the territories of Kharkiv, Luhansk, Donetsk, Kherson, Mykolaiv, and Odessa were all part of *Novorossiya,* or "New Russia," laying the political foundation for his 2022 invasion of Ukraine.

Putin's proxy war in the Donbas wasn't exactly the most covert of covert operations. In Rostov-on-Don on Ukraine's eastern border, some thirty to forty thousand troops were being mobilized for action. Russia's "secret war" was about to become even less of a secret. Through satellite imagery and social media monitoring, we watched as Russian regular Army forces and heavy weaponry infiltrated into eastern Ukraine. Russian Army soldiers would pose with their armored personnel carriers and antiaircraft weapons near clearly recognizable Ukrainian landmarks. Heavy weapons sent in from Russia were visible all throughout eastern Ukraine. Yet Putin claimed the continuous flows of arms and soldiers were only humanitarian aid convoys.

Ukrainian forces went on the counteroffensive right away. In early July, they captured the cities of Sloviansk and, a few weeks later, Kramatorsk. Separatist forces in Donetsk were driven back to Horlivka, Debaltseve, and Donetsk city. The Ukrainians, however, lost several helicopters in the operation, including one piloted by First Lieutenant Nadiya Savchenko. Savchenko was captured and transported to Russia, where she was detained, tortured, and put on trial for the supposed "murder" of two Russian journalists while piloting her helicopter during the Sloviansk operation. She would be exchanged two years later for two GRU officers, Yevgeny Yerofeyev and Alexander Alexandrov, whom the SBU had captured in May 2015. The Russian Ministry of Defense said that the GRU officers were "former military who were not on active duty" when they were captured in Ukraine.

To counter the Ukrainian threat to Russia's mostly irregular forces in eastern Ukraine, the Russian military shifted to conventional operations as part of its hybrid warfare strategy. A flood of heavy weapons poured into eastern Ukraine from Russia in August. We monitored it all with our overhead systems and other intelligence capabilities. But we didn't do anywhere near enough to help the Ukrainians counter Russian aggression.

After Ukrainian forces had taken the city of Ilovaisk in mid-August, the Russians counterattacked with superior forces and trapped the

Ukrainians inside the city. The Ukrainians were allowed safe passage out, but the separatists and Russian regular forces quickly reneged on the deal. The surviving Ukrainian forces were caught in the open and destroyed by Russian artillery, some of it coming from across the Russian border. In January and February 2015, Ukrainian forces suffered another major defeat at Debaltseve.[19]

I had made several more trips to Ukraine between July 2014 and February 2015, and it was heartbreaking to observe the turn of events. The Obama administration's primary response to the Ukraine crisis was to impose sanctions on Russian officials, banks, and defense and energy entities. These sanctions, unfortunately, weren't sufficient to pressure Putin to end his covert and overt occupation of eastern Ukraine. The administration did take steps, including the multibillion-dollar European Reassurance Initiative, to bolster the defenses of frontline NATO states. The administration also provided significant economic support to Ukraine.

Our military support, however, was unfortunately limited to nonlethal equipment—rations, blankets, trucks, communications gear, night vision goggles, body armor, helmets, and so on. We also provided military training and advice on defense reform. What the Ukrainians needed most was weapons: specifically, Javelin anti-tank weapons that could destroy Russian armor. The Ukrainians also needed intelligence support and counter-battery radars that could pinpoint the location of Russian artillery so the Ukrainians could return lethal fire. We provided some counter-mortar radars, but they weren't effective against longer-range artillery. It was long-range artillery that was killing Ukrainian soldiers.

I argued strenuously for the Javelin and other lethal support, as did General Dempsey and Assistant Secretary of State for European Affairs Toria Nuland. My former colleagues Michèle Flournoy and Admiral Jim Stavridis, both now retired, also supported lethal assistance, as did several former U.S. ambassadors to Ukraine. The president wouldn't sign off on more than nonlethal support, however, preferring to keep "off-ramps" open for Putin in case he wanted to come back in from the cold. (He didn't.) The Trump administration eventually provided Javelins to the Ukrainians, but, bizarrely, required that they be kept hundreds of miles from the front and prohibited them from being used in combat.

Unfortunately, Putin saw President Obama's restraint as a sign of weakness and a green light for further aggressive behavior. A year and a half after he invaded and annexed Crimea and started his covert and overt war in eastern Ukraine, he intervened militarily in Syria, providing air support, *spetsnaz,* and combat advisers to the Assad regime. Less than a year after that, he would intervene in the U.S. presidential election to elect Donald Trump. President Obama believed that no matter what we did in Ukraine, the Russians would win in the end. That may have been true, but we would certainly have been much better off if we had made Putin pay a much higher price. We had ceded escalation dominance to the Russians without putting up a fight. Not surprisingly, seven years later, Putin would try to take all of Ukraine. Russia's military failures in 2022 and Ukraine's successful resistance certainly would suggest that we were way too cautious in 2014–2015. I will have more to say about Russia's 2022 invasion in the next chapter.

BEIJING PLUS THIRTY

In January 2015, I made my first visit to Beijing in nearly three decades. Accompanying me on my trip were Dave Helvey, DOD's top China policy expert, and Todd Lowery, my executive director. Much had changed. China was now an economic powerhouse, and I could see abundant evidence of this as we drove into the city from the airport— from the cars and trucks on the high-speed highway that had replaced the bicycles I used to see, to the factories and new construction. And Beijing was by no means the center of China's economic power.

I was eager to see what the new China was like. I had been focusing on China's rise as the next big security challenge for the United States since the early 1990s but hadn't visited. I had been in Hong Kong with Melana for the British "handover" to China in 1997, but that had been it since my meetings in Beijing during the 1980s.

The host for my visit was Admiral Sun Jianguo, one of the five deputies on the PLA General Staff and its head of intelligence and foreign affairs. Admiral Sun was a career submariner with an impressive naval background. A few months earlier, I had hosted him in Washington.[20]

During his visit to the Pentagon, we talked about North Korea and its continued development of nuclear weapons. We agreed that it was in both our countries' interests to have a nuclear-free Korean Peninsula, but that was about as far as the Chinese government would go. China wanted the Koreas to remain divided and didn't want to do anything that would destabilize North Korea or threaten the regime's continued rule.

I sought to engage Sun on undersea warfare, but he wanted to stick to U.S.-China relations and the risks of war. I told Admiral Sun that the United States and China had been allies during the late Cold War and had accomplished much together, referring to our secret partnership in defeating the Red Army in Afghanistan. He acknowledged as much, but quickly added that today China had very good relations with Russia, "much better ones than China enjoyed with the United States."

We then had a very frank one-on-one discussion in which I told him that China had to cease its cyber operations against the United States. He responded by saying that if we pushed China to war, China would fight, even though the Chinese knew they would lose. He repeated it a few times and said he wanted to make sure that I understood. I bent forward closer to him, looked him in the eye, and told him that I understood. I added that he was right that China would lose, but more important, a war between us would serve neither side's interests.

On a lighter note, during his visit to Washington, I had Admiral Sun and his delegation to lunch at Morton's of Chicago in downtown Washington, D.C., thinking that the Chinese would consider it a special treat. Several of them complained, however, about the oversized steaks they were served. Not quite as bad as my CIA experience taking an Islamic fundamentalist brigadier to see *Godspell,* but a puzzle nonetheless.

———————

During my trip to Beijing, I visited a special forces unit and was given a demonstration of its close-quarter battle capabilities. I told the commander that when I was a young Special Forces soldier, I had dreamed about fighting with the Chinese in a war against the Soviets. He laughed. As I was departing, he presented me with a crossbow, the unit's symbol for its stealth approach to warfare.

I also visited a joint intelligence site we had run with the Chinese since the late 1970s. I was given a tour and briefed on how the mission and location for the site had changed since the end of the Cold War.[21] The staff at the site had kept a log of all the important U.S. visitors they had had. I was added to the roster. Looking at the list, I saw a lot of familiar names.

I met with General Fan Changlong, the vice-chairman of the Central Military Commission, the highest-ranking military official in China after Xi Jinping. The CMC vice-chairman only rarely met with his U.S. counterparts, so it was a sign that the Chinese took my visit very seriously. We discussed the importance of cooperation between our two militaries to avoid an accident at sea or in the air. We also discussed many of the same topics that I had covered with Admiral Sun.

Finally, I was hosted at China's National Defense University for a dinner conversation with several of its leading strategists. They wanted to pick my brain on everything from cyberwar to nuclear deterrence. Several of them also summarized the major research projects they had under way and asked questions that they thought would further their research. It was a friendly but tough group. It was clear they believed China was in a strategic competition with the U.S. whether we accepted it or not. And it was one they were confident they would win.

23

WINNING THE NEW COLD WAR

THE NEW COLD WAR: CAUSES, CHARACTERISTICS, AND STRATEGIC AIMS

America is in a new cold war that pits the United States and its allies against China and Russia and their allies.[1] The New Cold War has three main causes: a failure to fully integrate China and Russia into the American-led international order, significant changes in the balance of power, and China's and Russia's perception that America is in terminal decline. China's and Russia's authoritarian governments are the major reasons behind the first cause, suppressing any dissent at home and becoming more aggressive abroad. China's economic and military might has grown substantially over the previous decades, which has led to a large shift in the international balance of power, while Putin's Russia has benefited from high energy prices that have allowed it to partially modernize its military and become more assertive internationally. The perception that America is in terminal decline was reinforced by the 2008 financial crisis, U.S. withdrawal from the Middle East and Afghanistan, and the seeming ineffectiveness of democratic governance.[2]

The New Cold War will be very different from the decades-long struggle between the West and the Soviet Empire. It will be waged under different political, economic, and technological conditions, and it could carry an even greater risk of turning into a hot war. Like the Soviet-American Cold War, the New Cold War will have an ideological dimension, but it will take place in a very different information environment. The central competition in the New Cold War will be economic and technological, pitting authoritarian capitalism against democratic capitalism. We will face a competitor in China that will almost certainly have a larger economy than ours, the only question is how much larger. The primary "arms" race in the New Cold War will be in emerging technologies—in artificial intelligence, quantum computing, biotechnology, and so on—and not in nuclear weapons and missiles. Space will be a far more important battleground than it was during the Soviet-American Cold War.

China's grand strategic aim in the New Cold War is to supplant the United States at the top of the international system. Russia's aim is to weaken us so that its influence can increase commensurate with its ambitions. The tacit alliance between China and Russia poses a threat to the Eurasian landmass and world that we haven't faced since the early Cold War. China's Belt and Road Initiative—a network of rail and road corridors across Eurasia and sea routes in the Indo-Pacific and beyond—seeks economic hegemony on a scale that is also unprecedented.[3] Our aim should be to win the New Cold War while keeping it cold. Winning means keeping America preeminent and securing a world that advances our interests and values.

America will need an effective grand strategy if it is to prevail in the New Cold War. We haven't had a truly successful one since the end of the first Cold War. In the pages that follow, I offer what I believe is just such a strategy. A successful grand strategy, in my mind, must contain five essential elements: rebuilding our national ambition, unity, and resilience; posturing ourselves to prevail in the race for economic and technological supremacy; winning the intelligence and covert action wars; strengthening regional and global deterrence and, if required, defeating aggression; and transforming our alliances and national security institutions for our new era of great power competition.

As we learned from our experience in the Soviet-American Cold War, getting the big ideas right at the outset significantly increases one's prospects for strategic success. Then, as the competition evolves, strategists can adapt ways and means to changing circumstances and national security policies. It is imperative that our national leadership get us and our allies on the right path at the dawn of the New Cold War, just as an earlier generation of Americans did during the early years of the Soviet-American Cold War. It is in some sense 1947 all over again. This decade could well prove decisive, and the side that prevails will likely determine what kind of world we live in for the remainder of the twenty-first century.

CORE COMPETITIONS IN THE NEW COLD WAR

The New Cold War will likely be characterized by several "core competitions" among states and societies, in intelligence, and in the military realm. As I discussed in an earlier chapter, I developed the "core competitions" concept nearly three decades ago to describe the major trends and asymmetries that would shape warfare against a more powerful China during the 2020s and beyond. I extend it here to include core competitions at the societal or grand strategic level and to those that will likely take place in the realm of intelligence. The concept can help strategists and operators focus on what their core competitions are and how they can posture their side to win them.

At the grand strategic level, there will be a democracy-autocracy competition that will pit authoritarian capitalism against democratic capitalism. Like the Soviet-American Cold War, the New Cold War will fundamentally be a contest of systems. The outcome of the democracy-autocracy competition will depend on the economic, technological, and military power that can be generated by the two opposing sides. Achieving supremacy in comprehensive national power will depend in turn on the two sides' ability to sustain broad popular support, recover from setbacks, and export their model internationally. It is by no means clear that the United States and its democratic allies are currently postured to prevail in this competition.

Also at the grand strategic level, there will be critical competitions in several emerging technologies—in automation and artificial intelligence, 5G and 6G communications, quantum computing and other quantum technologies, additive manufacturing, biotechnology, and nuclear fusion and other clean, renewable energy technologies, to name just the most important ones. The competition in disruptive technologies is the central one of the New Cold War, and its outcome will determine relative wealth and power. At present, the United States has the advantage, but China is catching up fast in several areas and has the lead in some.

A third competition at the grand strategic level is the one that will take place in the strategic information sphere. There will be a competition between fake and real, between what is true and what is not true. The outcome of the "fake-real" competition will play a large role in determining who wins not only the political competitions but also the economic, technological, and military ones. Here, the advantage currently lies with Russia and China.

The intelligence world will have several competitions of its own. One of the big ones will be a "reveal-conceal" competition in which intelligence services seek to reveal the activities of their adversaries while concealing their own. Attribution-non-attribution of covert attack will be a subset of the reveal-conceal competition. There will likely be a strategic competition between code making and code breaking based on quantum computing and other new technologies, and new persistent surveillance technologies in space will make it much harder for a great power to conceal its activities in peacetime.

At the operational level, ubiquitous technical surveillance technologies, which combine technical surveillance, including "digital dust" and DNA surveillance, with artificial intelligence, will make clandestine operations more challenging to conduct. Big data, ubiquitous transparency, and artificial intelligence will also make covert action more challenging. It is clear that the reveal side of the competition will get much stronger, but there will still very likely be ways to conceal operations through deception, "blackouts," and so forth.

In the military realm, there will be four core competitions. The first will pit anti-access (A2) and area-denial (AD) capabilities against global power projection. Regional denial will extend to global denial, though, at present, the United States dominates in global power projection. China can be expected to close the gap in the not-too-distant future. China will present the greatest "A2/AD" challenge, but A2/AD capabilities will also be present to a lesser extent in Russia and Iran. China and Russia can also be expected to export these capabilities to their future allies and partners.

A second military competition is the one between "hiders" and "finders." Due to advances in surveillance of all kinds, the ability to "find" has dramatically increased and will continue to do so. Targeting has gotten down to the individual level. Presently, the United States enjoys a great advantage in global surveillance, though China has made impressive gains in its region and, to a lesser extent, globally. As with the reveal-conceal competition, however, there will still be opportunities to hide, particularly once the shooting starts and sensors get destroyed. One warfare area where the hiders will still have the advantage is undersea, and the United States maintains a sizable advantage in this area, though Russia has made gains in submarine stealth.

The third military competition will be one between offense and defense across domains and capabilities. Long-range strike systems will compete with air and missile defenses, and long-range strike systems that employ advanced stealth, electronic warfare, speed, or numbers will continue to overwhelm defenses. That will place a premium on going first. Cyber and information warfare offense will compete with cyber and information warfare defense, bio-offense will compete with bio-defense, and space offense will compete with space defense. In most cases, the offense will have the advantage.

Cyber warfare could become far more powerful, benefiting from advances in AI and quantum computing, for example, and will almost certainly be the most usable form of warfare. Space superiority will be to twenty-first-century conflict what air superiority was to twentieth-century conflict. In space warfare, in particular, there will be a big premium on going first. War in space is far more likely in this new era of great power competition than it was during the Cold War.

Remote warfare (long-range aircraft and missiles, unmanned systems, cyber, and space) will increasingly dominate personal, close-in warfare. New forms of war will also become more prominent. Cognitive warfare will target an adversary's mind and sense of reality, identity warfare will be used to target key individuals through a variety of means, algorithmic warfare will pit computer programs against each other, and pre-positional and supply chain warfare will be used to get inside an enemy's systems before conflict.

A fourth military competition will be one between humans and machines and between performance-enhanced humans and natural humans. There will also be a competition between intelligent machines. Performance-enhanced humans may well dominate ordinary humans, but increasingly intelligent machines and autonomous systems will dominate over even the most performance-enhanced or machine-enabled human. Automation and artificial intelligence will increasingly play larger and larger roles in every warfare domain. It is also possible a few decades from now that AI-enabled intelligence, planning, decision making, and command and control could become the "killer app" in warfare, directing and controlling everything else.

More generally, societal war—covert and overt war against societies—will increasingly supplant war against an opponent's armed forces. Great power conventional war will likely be rare unless a belligerent can find a way to make its gains stick and avoid the risk of escalation to the strategic level—nuclear and otherwise. Great power war, if it does occur, however, will likely be protracted, placing a premium on mobilization capacity.

Strategic warfare—attacks on homelands—will become more likely in any great power war, as more non-nuclear options— destructive cyberattacks, conventional, long-range precision strikes, attacks on critical economic infrastructure such as fiber-optic cables, bio-sabotage, and so on—become increasingly available. Strategic nuclear deterrence—avoiding an all-out nuclear exchange—is likely to hold for the foreseeable future, however.

Covert and indirect war—activities below conventional war—thus will likely be the dominant form of conflict among great powers, just as it was during the Soviet-American Cold War. Adversaries will seek to employ a variety of means, ranging from information influence operations to strategic sabotage and proxy war to weaken their opponents and achieve strategic gains. The line between peace and war will become increasingly blurred.

REBUILDING NATIONAL AMBITION, UNITY, AND RESILIENCE

As George Kennan, the father of the U.S. Cold War strategy of containment, wrote in his "Long Telegram" in 1946, "Much depends on the health and vigor of our own society." America won the Cold War because it was a more competitive, dynamic, and resilient society than the Soviet Union. The New Cold War will similarly be a contest of systems. A recent Rand study identified seven societal characteristics that lead to national competitive success: national ambition and will, a unified national identity, shared opportunity, an active state, effective institutions, a learning and adapting society, and competitive diversity and pluralism. The study suggests that while the United States continues to possess many of these characteristics, multiple trends are working to weaken U.S. advantages.[4] More and more Americans do not see our country as an exceptional nation and do not believe America should strive to remain the leading power in the world. Our politics are far more polarized than they have been in my lifetime, and, as former Trump administration NSC staffer Fiona Hill has recently written, polarization has become a national security threat.[5] Americans' sense of a common national purpose has been badly eroded, and identity politics has increasingly supplanted traditional politics. Alternative facts now compete with actual facts. My friend Mike Hayden has written a must-read book called *The Assault on Intelligence: American National Security in an Age of Lies* in which he points out that it is not just our system of intelligence that is under assault; all of our fact-based institutions are—the media, our system of justice and the rule of law, law enforcement, and science.[6]

Rebuilding national ambition and unity is a task for our political leaders, and it is our core national security imperative. We need to reincorporate civics into our elementary and secondary school programs and develop a curriculum that inspires young Americans, teaching them what has made America exceptional and about the many heroes who made it so, while being honest about where we have failed to live up to our ideals.[7] To help build an even stronger American identity, we should embrace a national service program that would provide education and other benefits in return for service in the military, in the federal government, in federally sponsored volunteer organizations, and in disadvantaged public schools.

It is imperative that we clean up our information environment and harden our democracy against foreign influence and alternative facts. Democracy as we know it won't survive if we don't. Protecting our democracy against political violence and insurrection is equally critical. The oath that every national security official takes to support and defend the Constitution of the United States against all enemies, foreign and domestic, took on new meaning for me after the attack on our Capitol on January 6, 2021. I had just finished reading a book on how political violence had brought down the Roman Republic, and it looks eerily as if we could be heading down the same path.[8] We must defeat the threat from domestic extremists, just as we defeated the foreign extremists who threatened our liberty, and rid our politics of violence.

We must also take action to rebuild our national unity on the economic front. Economic opportunity and the American dream are slipping beyond the reach of far too many Americans, even those with college educations. American workers have seen again and again jobs lost to globalization and automation. Of the two, automation is by far the greater long-term threat to a broad-based prosperity in America. Larger and larger numbers of Americans may become not just unemployed but unemployable. To be sure, globalization and automation have had very positive effects on the U.S. economy, and the positive effects have far outweighed the negative ones from a macro point of view. But the benefits have been unevenly distributed, and we have to figure out how to make globalization and automation work better for all Americans.

Automation will only intensify in the coming decades. Continued rapid advances in technology will threaten the existence of a vast swath of jobs up and down the socioeconomic ladder, from high-tech manufacturing to highly skilled white-collar services.[9] Technological change is likely to occur more rapidly than economies can adapt to it, creating dislocation and political instability. The ability to adapt to technology disruption will be a key determinant of whether China or the United States wins the New Cold War.[10]

Given the high likelihood of rapid job obsolescence in the decades ahead and the increasing substitution of capital for labor, we will need to ensure that we have a highly skilled and educated workforce that is capable of quickly mastering new skills. We will need to get serious about lifetime learning and retraining, and place as much emphasis on continuous adult education as we have on primary, secondary, and college education. Adults in the future may have to reinvent themselves several times during their working lives. We will also need to take steps to reduce income inequality and our growing national insolvency. This will require redistributing some wealth and providing basic income while fully embracing automation and putting our fiscal house back in order.

Most important, we must significantly increase government spending on R&D to stimulate innovation in, and American leadership of, critical emerging technologies while protecting our technological secrets. We should take a lesson from the Eisenhower administration. During the 1950s, we started building our interstate highway system. It was a great boon for the economy and for our national security. It helped unify the country and distribute our capabilities. We need to do something similar today, more widely distributing our national capabilities in terms of access to broadband communications, quality education, and high-tech jobs. Doing this will significantly bolster economic opportunity and strengthen national unity and national security.

One look at the CEOs who lead many of our most successful high-tech companies should also make it abundantly clear that we need highly skilled immigrants, particularly those with advanced degrees in science and technology. Immigration is a critical source of American advantage. We also need immigrants who are willing to do the jobs that Americans aren't willing to do. Our task is to attract and assimilate.

PREVAILING IN ECONOMIC AND TECHNOLOGICAL COMPETITION

As President Biden's national security adviser, Jake Sullivan, has rightly noted, U.S. foreign policy makers now face a world in which power is increasingly measured in economic terms. The relative strength of our economy, as much as anything else, will determine the United States' success or failure in geopolitics.[11] The outcome of our economic and technological competition with China will largely determine who the leading power in the international system will be in future decades and how much power the winner will have over the others. Winning it should be our top national security priority, and we need to get started now.

We face two major challenges in our economic and technological competition with China. The first is the potential size of China's economy relative to that of the United States. By 2012, China had already reached 60 percent of U.S. GDP on an exchange-rate basis (though it was still substantially poorer than the United States on a per capita GDP basis). Sometime in the 2030s, China is projected to surpass the U.S. economy in size. Within three decades, China's economy could be twice the size of America's, giving it important scale advantages, analogous to what the United States enjoyed in the twentieth century.[12] Throughout the previous century, America never faced a strategic rival that had more than 50 percent of U.S. GDP. The Soviet Union and Nazi Germany had at most 50 percent of U.S. GDP, and Japan's economy was 15 percent the size of ours. One of the many things that makes the New Cold War new is that the "economic escalation dominance" that the United States enjoyed throughout the twentieth century will no longer be there.[13]

To compete effectively, it is imperative that we get our fiscal house in order. Since the start of the COVID-19 pandemic, there has been a dramatic increase in federal spending, and this came on top of fifty years of chronic deficits. Our national debt is now greater than our GDP. The Congressional Budget Office forecasts that unless major reforms are made to entitlement programs (Social Security, Medicare, and Medicaid), these programs and debt servicing will consume 82 percent of the federal budget by mid-century. By 2040, unless something is done, interest on the national debt will likely eclipse all federal discretionary spending, defense and nondefense.[14] Restoring our fiscal health will require major reforms (for example, raising the retirement age for Social Security), reductions in federal spending, shrinking the size of government, and revenue increases. Deferring the day of reckoning much longer will only make it worse.

The second major challenge we face is the battle for supremacy in key emerging technologies. U.S. trade relations with China are a problem, but strategically we are more engaged in an investment war with China than we are in a trade war. Given the economic size advantages China could have, if we're going to prevail, we're going to need to out-invent it.[15] Conversely, if China were to out-invent us, our strategic position would deteriorate substantially.

With his "Made in China 2025" initiative, Xi announced plans to "catch up and surpass" (*ganchao*) the U.S. economy in several key areas within little more than a decade: information technology (with a special emphasis on semiconductors and 5G communications), robotics, electric vehicles and other green technologies, aerospace, ocean engineering, rail transportation, power, new materials, medical devices, and agricultural machinery. Xi wants to not just surpass the U.S. economy but substantially reduce China's dependence on it. (The United States, for its part, needs to reduce its supply chain vulnerability from

China in a number of areas ranging from semiconductors to rare-earth and other critical minerals. U.S. national security concerns must also be considered in any new trade agreements.[16])

China has some important scale advantages in the technological arena as well. Its practice of "civil-military fusion" enables the Chinese government to assert considerable state control over its private sector companies, mandating compulsory data sharing and other areas of "cooperation." China, though, may suffer from too much government involvement in research and development, stifling innovation, while the United States, compared with the late 1950s and early 1960s, suffers from too little.

Xi has set a goal of making China dominant in artificial intelligence, quantum technologies, and biotechnology. AI and biotechnology will likely be the building blocks for an economic transformation on a scale not seen since the Industrial Revolution. AI and autonomous systems, and possibly quantum technologies, will almost certainly have a revolutionary impact on the conduct of war as well. Advances in biotechnology will greatly improve human health and agriculture, but these same technologies could also be used covertly to impose costs on an adversary (ranging from inducing a pandemic to sabotaging food production).[17]

Artificial intelligence is generally described as three levels of capability: artificial narrow intelligence, or ANI; artificial general intelligence, or AGI; and artificial superintelligence, or ASI. ANI's performance is generally bounded by the domain in which it operates, for example, self-driving vehicles. AGI has a general level of performance that is equivalent to humans. ASI has performance that is well beyond the cognitive capacity of all humans who have ever existed.[18]

All of the enablers for rapid advances in ANI are already present—successful deep learning and machine learning algorithms, large data sets, natural language processing, and advanced microelectronic processors that can handle the large data sets. The amount of data in the digital universe is increasing at an exponential rate, doubling every two years. More powerful, AI-customized processors are on the horizon.

Over time, advancements in ANI will likely make unmanned systems superior in tactical performance to manned systems. Areas of warfare where speed of action is critical—electronic warfare and cyber operations, for example—will benefit immensely from advances in AI. Advances in ANI will also greatly enable information influence operations. In war, AI could be used as "fog of war" machines, creating decisive uncertainty about the quality of information that precision warfare increasingly demands. AI will also greatly enable population control measures by authoritarian regimes—for example, China's growing "surveillance state." There will likely be national security implications well beyond these four.[19]

Chinese military thinkers increasingly talk about the "intelligentization" of warfare, applying AI's machine speed and processing power to military planning, operational command, and decision support. In the Chinese view, a new "cognitive domain," enabled by AI, will come to dominate the other warfare domains—air, land, sea, space, and cyber/electromagnetic. The boundary between peace and war will become increasingly blurred. Human-on-human warfare will be replaced by machine-on-human and machine-on-machine warfare. "Super soldiers" will be created by integrating humans with machines through brain-machine interfaces, external skeletal systems, wearable devices, and devices implanted into human bodies. Intelligent control will become the center of gravity in future warfare.[20] At the Nineteenth Party Congress in October 2017, Xi Jinping urged the PLA to accelerate the development of military intelligentization.

China has important advantages in the AI competition—better access to large data sets through "civil-military fusion" and a large and growing technical workforce that can innovate rapidly. Kai-Fu Lee, a U.S.-educated Taiwanese computer scientist based in Beijing, argues that if the AI competition turns out to be more about engineering capacity than about new scientific breakthroughs, China will have a big advantage over the United States.[21]

The United States has advantages in AI research and in the hardware that powers AI applications. Advances in microelectronics will enable technological revolutions in communications and in AI. Maintaining U.S. commercial leadership in microelectronics is a national security imperative. Microelectronics manufacturing has largely moved overseas, but the United States retains global leadership in design, machine tools, capital equipment, and custom ASICs—application-specific integrated circuits. The United States needs to "onshore" microelectronics fabrication and packaging to reduce its supply chain vulnerability. We also need to restore our technological leadership in precision microelectronics manufacturing. Taiwan Semiconductor Manufacturing Company, for instance, is now the world leader, with the ability to manufacture chips at a three-nanometer scale; we are currently able to manufacture at the six-nanometer scale. (The CHIPS and Science Act, signed into law in August 2022, is supposed to address these shortfalls in microelectronics manufacturing.)

The United States needs to invest in large, labeled training data sets for defense and intelligence mission applications. This is currently a key area of advantage for China in AI. It is also critical to national security that the United States maintain its lead in autonomous systems. Coupled with AI, autonomous systems have the potential to significantly shift strategic balances in the United States' favor. In addition to investments in autonomous systems across domains, we need to invest in enabling technologies like sensors and batteries.

Leadership in global telecommunications will confer significant national security advantages. Unfortunately, the United States has fallen seriously behind in this area. Investments are needed in radio access networks and core networks to accommodate the significant change in radio technologies, wireless architectures, the use of new radio frequency bands, and the incorporation of cloud and edge computing that 5G and 6G will bring.

In biotechnology, the United States maintains the lead in research, but China has made impressive strides in growing its bio-economy. China's biotechnology industry also benefits from civil-military fusion, as do its other strategic industries. The U.S. government's investment in the biotechnology area should be increased and focused on genomics, synthetic biology, precision medicine, pandemic situational awareness, and the design and production of biomedical countermeasures. Synthetic biology—the ability to create new biological parts, devices, and systems, or redesign organisms already found in nature—is particularly important. It could be more transformative than AI. The United States should embrace biomanufacturing and realign global supply chains to its advantage.

Three additional areas the United States needs to exploit further are energy, minerals, and agriculture. China is dependent on imports for both food and energy. The United States is the world's energy superpower, but it fails to sufficiently use that power. In the wake of Russia's invasion of Ukraine, we should dramatically increase production and seek to displace Russia in European energy markets to eliminate its ability to coerce our allies, and facilitate a more rapid shift to natural gas and clean, renewable energy, including next-generation nuclear power and fusion. Fusion power seems to always be thirty years away, but within the next twenty to thirty years, commercially viable fusion power has a very good chance of becoming a reality. The United States is also the world's agriculture superpower, and advances in biotechnology will only accentuate America's advantage. We'd be foolish not to exploit our growing power in this area as well and should seek to displace Russia in global wheat markets. The United States and its allies, moreover, have the potential to significantly reduce our dependence on Chinese and Russian minerals, including rare earths. Our economic well-being will depend on how well we respond to this challenge.

The strategic technological competition that we are engaged in with China is somewhat analogous to the competition we were in with the Soviet Union during the late 1950s and the 1960s. The challenge then was the development of intercontinental ballistic missiles and space capabilities. Today, it's a much broader set of technologies that will have a much greater impact on the international balance of power. During the 1950s, we pursued a very effective grand strategy that included establishing the Defense Advanced Research Projects Agency and NASA. While we should robustly fund DARPA and its biomedical equivalent, BARDA, and our National Quantum Initiative—passed by Congress in 2018—we will need additional national security instruments and new partnerships with private sector companies to prevail in our technological competition with China. More fully leveraging our venture capital and start-up ecosystem—a key area of U.S. economic and technological advantage—for national security purposes will also be essential.

We will need significantly more government spending on research and development, in technologies that hold the promise of fundamental breakthroughs and in emerging technologies that will reshape industries. The private sector, driven by returns on investment, cannot be expected to provide the capital for fundamental breakthroughs, given the uncertainty of success and the difficulty of capturing the returns in a time frame that will satisfy investors. The U.S. government can, however, if competing with China for global technological leadership is seen as a national priority. By the mid-1960s, the peak of the technological "arms race" that was begun under President Eisenhower, we were spending 2 percent of GDP on federally funded research and development, and spending on R&D accounted for 17 percent of all discretionary federal outlays. Today, we are spending around 0.6 percent of GDP on R&D.[22] The United States must also do a better job of commercializing government-developed technology. Too much of advanced technology—at DARPA, for example—is being left on the cutting room floor.

Finally, the United States must focus more of its intelligence collection and analysis resources on key emerging technologies. We must have an accurate picture of how we're doing in this competition and what we need to do to stay ahead. We did this very well during the Cold War and must do it again under very different conditions. The United States must also do a better job of protecting our key secrets in emerging technologies. Protecting our technological secrets is far more challenging in a globalized world than it was during the Cold War. China is also far more capable at exploiting U.S. technology than the Soviet Union ever was. A number of measures have recently been put in place to further restrict Chinese investment in the United States in key emerging technologies, and to protect critical emerging technologies that lie outside the traditional defense sphere. This is a good start.

CYBERCOM should be assigned the mission of assisting the Department of Homeland Security and the FBI in protecting critical U.S. technology from cyber theft. The FBI will also need additional resources to counter illicit technology transfer more broadly. Our high-technology businesses will also have to develop new supply chains outside China to reduce the impact of Chinese appropriation of U.S. technology. Naming and shaming and indicting a few PLA officers who will never be extradited is not sufficient.

WINNING THE INTELLIGENCE AND COVERT ACTION WARS

Intelligence will be as central to strategic success in the new national security era as it was during the Cold War and the wars with al-Qa'ida and ISIS. I have already described in previous chapters the actions

I took as USD(I) to transform defense intelligence for this new era, and the need for intelligence transformation has only grown since I left office. More resources will need to be found for intelligence to enable the change required and provide sufficient coverage of emerging challenges.[23]

During the Cold War, the CIA developed denied-area tradecraft often referred to as "Moscow Rules" to communicate and meet with agents behind the Iron Curtain. The CIA must now develop "Beijing Rules" that will enable its officers to continue to collect vital human intelligence in the face of ubiquitous technical surveillance. Simply put, ubiquitous technical surveillance (UTS), digital dust, and big data pose existential threats to clandestine human intelligence operations. We must solve the UTS problem and prevail in the reveal-conceal competition.

We will also need to devote more resources to cyber intelligence, space intelligence, and biological intelligence, and we will need to significantly increase our domestic intelligence capabilities by providing more resources and manpower to the FBI. The FBI's job jar has expanded significantly since 9/11 as a result of growing intelligence threats to our technological secrets and threats from domestic insurrectionists and international terrorists.

A whole host of new technologies will transform the conduct of intelligence, ranging from AI to quantum. We must exploit them for intelligence purposes before our adversaries do. We will need to more fully exploit open-source intelligence for all sorts of purposes while improving our ability to steal secrets. We will need more operational intelligence for covert action and vulnerability assessments of our adversaries.

Covert action will be central to U.S. national security, more than it has been since the end of the Cold War. Covert action capabilities, infrastructure, and methods, however, will need to be adapted to new strategic priorities and operational realities. Covert action can be used for defensive and offensive purposes and for a wide range of effects, from counterterrorism to countering the proliferation of weapons of mass destruction and advanced conventional weapons, political and psychological action, support for an insurgency or resistance movement, counterinsurgency, and counter-narcotics. We must not be reluctant to use the third option, including in new ways, particularly those enabled by new technologies. Our adversaries will try to undermine us through covert action, including through advanced technical means. We must fight back and prevail in this competition.

Russia had extraordinary success with its covert influence operations during the 2016 U.S. presidential election cycle.[24] It is hard to disagree with my friend Jim Clapper's assessment that the Russians swung the election to Trump. The Russians may not have changed any votes after they had been cast, but they probably influenced minds with their large covert social media presence. What we do know is that Trump openly asked for Russian support—"Russia, if you're listening"—and that he received it.[25]

Russia's attack on the 2016 presidential election was the 9/11 of politics. As long as segments of the U.S. population remain susceptible to information influence operations, Russia will continue to have ample strategic opportunities to weaken the will and power of the United States. Russia used America's strengths—our openness and our technological innovations—against us. Russia also tried to swing the 2020 election to Trump, exacerbate sociopolitical divisions within the United States, and undermine Americans' confidence in the electoral process, but, fortunately, it didn't succeed this time.[26] Let's hope that we learn from what happened in 2016 and prevent it from ever happening again.

Russia already employs automated bots and other information technologies to amplify its covert messaging. The technology for deceptive information influence operations unfortunately is advancing more rapidly than the technologies needed to counter it, a trend that will work in Russia's and China's favor. A good example of this is what is referred to as "deep fakes" technology. Deep fakes are digitally manipulated audio or video material that is designed to be as realistic as possible. Researchers at Stanford and the University of Washington have used AI and lip-synching technology to generate a deep fake video of Barack Obama saying sentences he never actually uttered. It doesn't take much imagination to see how this technology could be used for manipulative purposes. Deep fakes are hard to detect, and any detection algorithm will not likely work for long. They are another example of "algorithmic warfare," where the offense has a big advantage over the defense. We fail to recognize the increasing power of covert influence operations at our peril.

As with our competition with China in key emerging technologies, intelligence will play a central role in our information influence competitions with Russia and other malign actors. We must make it a top priority for the IC and direct significant collection and analytical resources to the problem. As Michael Morell and Amy Zegart note, our first intelligence failure of the information influence age was not detecting Russia's weaponization of social media in the United States for at least two years.[27] This failure to see what Russia was doing cost President Obama valuable time and took away many of his options.

We will need to enlist the help of the private sector to combat information influence operations. More regulation, particularly with regard to a platform's responsibility for false content, will be required. And, as the experience of some of our European partners, particularly Estonia, has shown, a public education program is also critical.

Deterring and countering Russian covert influence operations isn't just about ensuring that we remain able to have free and fair elections without foreign influence, as important as that is. Covert information influence operations are an attack on our political cohesion and national will. It is a secret war with profound strategic consequences, and it is a war that we must win.

Countering covert information influence operations should be a key mission for both CYBERCOM and the U.S. intelligence community. The IC needs to develop capabilities to detect what are likely to be increasingly difficult to detect covert influence operations, and CYBERCOM needs to be able to counter them by active defense—striking back at the source. The FBI has its hands full enough with combating cybercrime. Covert action of our own will be an important tool in changing Russia's behavior in this area. As Bob Gates has recently written, we need to go on the offense in the information influence arena and give Putin a "taste of his own medicine."[28]

Russia, moreover, may also be attacking the United States with more than information operations. Since 2016, U.S. diplomats and intelligence personnel posted in or traveling to Havana, Cuba, and other countries around the world, including Russia, have been subjected to mysterious illnesses that have resulted in serious, permanent brain injury in some cases. A December 2020 National Academy of Sciences report concluded that the most likely cause of these injuries was directed, pulsed radio-frequency energy. The study also noted that previous research on this type of injury had been carried out in the Soviet Union.[29] A subsequent report by the Office of the Director of National Intelligence largely affirmed these findings.[30]

The CIA reviewed all of its intelligence and thoroughly examined each case, which had reached into the thousands, and found no evidence of foreign power involvement. The agency found that it could attribute all but two dozen cases to preexisting health conditions and natural phenomena. It is continuing to work on the twenty-four cases for which there is no plausible explanation.

U.S. intelligence must continue to collect against this target. New intelligence can fundamentally change analytical lines. If the Russians are using radio frequency or other weapons to covertly target and incapacitate even a few of our personnel, it would represent a major and unacceptable escalation in our intelligence war, and we would be compelled to respond in a manner that will deter any future use of such weapons.

Finally, it may be time to consolidate some of our intelligence agencies. My former boss Bob Gates has suggested that we "rewind the clock" and abolish the Office of the Director of National Intelligence and return to the director of central intelligence/director of the CIA model that existed between 1947 and 2005, with one deputy focused on the IC and one on helping to run CIA. Proponents of the DNI reforms argue that the CIA director had a conflict of interest between running CIA and being the top official overseeing the IC. Critics argue that CIA remains our central agency, and it is reasonable to organize the IC around it. The Office of the DNI, critics also note, lacks the organizational capabilities needed for effective oversight. The DNI has also proven to be very personality dependent, performing well under Jim Clapper's leadership, but less so under others. Structurally, I find Gates's argument compelling, but for a host of reasons it may not be possible to go back in time. The NRO and major parts of NGA could be reintegrated with CIA and manned jointly by CIA and the military. Parts of DIA could be transferred to CIA and the rest consolidated with the Combatant Command Joint Intelligence Operations Centers. CIA itself could benefit from some "rewinding of the clock" and internal consolidation. Strong consideration should be given to disbanding the Directorate of Digital Innovation and devolving its components back to their prior organizations. Several regional and functional mission centers could also be consolidated, and the global authorities of the core deputy directors restored. It's at least worth a look in the next round of IC reform.

STRENGTHENING DETERRENCE AND DEFEATING AGGRESSION

We face two broad military challenges with respect to China: a contest for military supremacy in East Asia and a potential contest for military supremacy globally. Our military position has eroded substantially over the past two decades along the East Asian littoral. China's growing anti-access/area-denial capabilities have effectively "demassed" the U.S. military in the western Pacific. Our forward air bases and aircraft carriers and other surface ships within the Second Island Chain have become increasingly vulnerable to Chinese precision strike capabilities. Beyond the East Asian littoral, we must prevent China from breaking out militarily to become a global power and prevent it from achieving strategic superiority over the United States.[31] China is already a global economic power, but in the military realm, once China's military ventures beyond two thousand miles from the mainland, the United States dominates. We should do our best to keep it that way.

We also must ensure that China cannot knock out our space assets and battle networks in a first strike. We cannot project rapid, effective power without our space assets. As I noted earlier, space superiority is to twenty-first-century conflict what air superiority was to twentieth-century conflict. We must also defend our networks to ensure effective command and control of our forces and population against what the Chinese describe as "system destruction warfare."

Conflict with China, it must be added, is by no means inevitable, despite what Graham Allison refers to as the "Thucydides Trap," which occurs when a rising power challenges the current dominant power. The result historically has almost always been great power war.[32] Thucydides was brilliant in his analysis of the Peloponnesian War between Athens and Sparta, and wrote a book, as he hoped, "for the ages," but he couldn't have envisioned how nuclear weapons would change war when he wrote his history. Nuclear weapons kept the Cold

War cold, and they almost assuredly will have a similar strategic effect on the U.S.-China competition.

The military challenges we face from Russia stem from its use of hybrid warfare on its periphery and its growing capability to inflict unacceptable destruction on the United States and the U.S. economy. Russia's goal is to win a local war through subversion and, if it can't do that, to win quickly before the United States can respond and then deter a U.S. counteroffensive with the threat of strategic strikes on the U.S. homeland, employing what they call an "escalate to de-escalate" strategy.

Russia's invasion of Ukraine in February 2022 shows that it will also move well beyond hybrid warfare when it believes it's in its interest to do so. The Biden administration responded reasonably well to Russian aggression during the first year of the war, but was overly deterred by fears of Russian escalation. The administration failed to use all means available, it responded too slowly, and it ceded escalation dominance to Putin.

The United States should have supplied Ukraine with all the aircraft, cannon and long-range missile artillery, air defense, armored vehicles, ammunition, training, and intelligence it needed. The administration should have made it clear to Putin that any escalation on his part—attacking Ukraine's supply lines in NATO states or using weapons of mass destruction in Ukraine—would be met with U.S. and NATO entry into the conflict. U.S. airpower would make short work of Russian forces in Ukraine. The United States should have also pushed harder to sanction all Russian energy exports sooner; it is insane to be fighting your enemy and funding his war machine at the same time. The United States should also have done more to undermine Putin's grip on power and his hold on Belarus through overt and covert means. (Before the war began, I wrote an op-ed in *The Washington Post* suggesting how the Biden administration could deter Russian aggression against Ukraine, and should deterrence fail, how the U.S. and its allies could defeat it. This and my CIA history in waging war against the Red Army in Afghanistan must have been sufficient cause for the Russian foreign ministry to place me on its sanctions list alongside currently serving, high-ranking U.S. national security officials.)

Putin made a major strategic blunder in invading Ukraine. As 2022 drew to a close, the Russian army in Ukraine appeared to be on the verge of collapse. Let's hope the West exploits this and Ukraine emerges victorious in 2023. The United States—the arsenal of democracy—and the West should have no trouble besting Russia in arms production. The United States and its allies possess the means, moreover, to severely damage the Russian economy. What has been lacking so far is only the will to do it. Our best China strategy in the near term is a defeated and weakened Russia. It is likewise our best Europe strategy. The only way Ukraine can lose is if the West gives up.

———

To meet the longer-term challenges posed by China and Russia, and to strengthen regional and global deterrence, we need to do several things. First, we need to buy back "mass" by increasing the number of survivable, forward-stationed, or forward-deployed systems and global, rapid-reinforcing systems. Second, we need to invest heavily in our cyber and space capabilities, both offensive and defensive. Strengthening our survivable and immediately responsive forces and hardening our space and cyber defenses will complicate China's and Russia's strategic calculus and convince them that they can't win an intense, short-duration war before the United States can respond. It would have the effect of turning China's anti-access/area-denial strategy against the PLA. It's long past time that we went symmetric on China's successful asymmetric strategy.

As a first step, we need to significantly increase our procurement of ground-, sea-, and air-launched missiles that can be fired from standoff range.[33] This would include, now that we're out of the Intermediate-Range Nuclear Forces Treaty, mobile, intermediate-range, ground-based missiles; submarine-launched missiles; and air-launched missiles for our bomber force. Due to their shorter development cycles, they can be available sooner, and we should procure lots of them as a near-term gap filler.

Over the mid-term, we need to go all in on unmanned systems, stealthy long-range air forces, and long-range missiles, to include hypersonic weapons, undersea warfare capabilities, and space and cyber capabilities. Over the longer term, we need to prioritize defense research and development in autonomy, artificial intelligence, quantum computing, nuclear fusion, and other emerging technologies.

On the air side, we are currently projected to buy up to a hundred B-21 stealth bombers, and there are calls for more. The B-21 and other aircraft with equivalent stealth can penetrate China's and Russia's most advanced air defenses and deliver far less expensive, direct-attack munitions, which is important in any protracted campaign. Bombers can also generate more electrical power than fighters, which will be important as we move into an era of directed energy weapons.

It is time to shift to a global-range Air Force, with a mix of penetrating and standoff bombers and long-range, penetrating intelligence, surveillance, and reconnaissance aircraft. We should consider doubling our buy of B-21s and configure some of the fleet as fighters and electronic warfare aircraft. Air-to-air combat has moved past the dogfight stage: long-range sensors and weapons determine the outcome in air-to-air combat these days. Fast missiles have supplanted fast fighters. Bombers have more than four times the range of fighters, and China has exploited our overreliance on short-range airpower to its advantage. Over time, our fighter force could be significantly reduced in size. The B-21 fleet should also be augmented by a fleet of unmanned aerial vehicles to further maximize combat power. One B-21 could control multiple strike and air dominance UAVs.

We should also exploit the ability of penetrating UAVs to overwhelm an adversary's defenses with swarms. The AI technologies to do so are at hand. The fiscal and manufacturing challenge will be how to produce enough of them to make a difference operationally. If swarm UAVs can be made cheap enough while still being effective, they can even be attritable, expected to be lost in combat.[34] We should also accelerate and expand our conventional prompt global strike capabilities—intercontinental and intermediate-range missiles that can deliver many independently targetable warheads. The combination of missiles with global reach and penetrating strike and surveillance aircraft would represent a very powerful global conventional deterrent.

To better locate mobile targets, we should procure several hundred multipurpose, stealthy, long-range (air refuelable), surveillance-strike UAVs. Such a force would give us the ability to achieve widely distributed effects while being highly survivable. As we learned in counterterrorism operations, our problem is not finishing the enemy; it's finding him. This is likewise true for a wide range of targets in a great power war, from mobile missiles to mobile air defense systems. If a target can be found, it can be killed. The type of UAV I'm thinking of can be procured for an affordable cost—under that of a fifth-generation fighter. These UAVs would have four times the combat endurance of a fighter and can be made much stealthier. They would also be much cheaper than a bomber. Penetrating bombers still have an important role in deterrence and great power war, but in terms of numbers of aircraft we should shift our emphasis to armed reconnaissance. Persistence matters and numbers matter.

Finally, we will need to expand our tanker fleet and provide our refueling aircraft with the sensors and weapons necessary to defend themselves from Chinese missiles. It is also past time to begin procuring unmanned tankers. As I discussed in an earlier chapter, we also need to develop stealthy, long-range aircraft to clandestinely insert SOF into denied areas.

Undersea warfare is a key area of American global advantage that we must preserve and maximize.[35] Our current plans are to field an attack submarine force of sixty-six submarines, but even sixty-six will not provide us with sufficient capacity, particularly if we have to fight both China and Russia at the same time. Buying a lot more submarines, at $3–$4 billion or more a copy, will be unaffordable. The most cost-effective approach is similar to what I just proposed for our air forces: go all in on lower-cost, long-endurance unmanned undersea vehicles and couple that with a large fleet of unmanned maritime patrol aircraft.

The technology exists to build very long endurance, stealthy autonomous UUVs that can be armed with acoustic sensors and torpedoes. We could buy several tens of them for the cost of one submarine. A large UUV fleet would greatly extend the coverage area and combat power of our submarine fleet. We should also go all in on what is called seabed warfare. Remote-controlled missile pods on the seafloor and other systems would further complicate China's strategic calculus.

We should also consider upping and speeding up the procurement of Columbia-class fleet ballistic missile submarines so that several of them can be converted to conventional guided-missile submarines, attack submarines, and seabed warfare platforms. To pay for a larger undersea fleet, we should reduce the size of our surface fleet, including our aircraft carriers. Land-based, global airpower has significantly reduced the need for them.

Finally, we need to make a number of investments in the space and cyber domains to ensure we can win those critical battles. Achieving space and cyber superiority is critical to operations in other domains, and operations in other domains are critical to achieving space superiority—neutralizing ground-based space capabilities, for example. We need to be able to protect our systems and neutralize our enemy's, and we need to be able to rapidly reconstitute a portion of our capabilities if some are destroyed.

Cyber operations and information security are critical to our nation's defense in peace and war. Cyber conflict will be a continuous feature of our national security landscape going forward. The Biden administration should fully embrace the recommendations of the Cyberspace Solarium Commission to deny our adversaries the benefits of cyberattack on the United States and our allies, and to impose costs that will deter them from attempting such attacks in the first place, strengthening both our defensive and our offensive capabilities and our will to use them.[36]

Among the many things we need to do in the cyber realm is to strengthen our defenses against catastrophic countervalue attacks on our critical infrastructure.[37] This is primarily the responsibility of the private sector and the Department of Homeland Security, but NSA and CYBERCOM have important roles to play as well. Additional offensive cyber options also need to be developed to strengthen our strategic cyber deterrent. During the early 1970s, we realized that our presidents needed to have a range of nuclear options available in a crisis. The same is true with respect to cyber. A particular challenge in the cyber realm is the constantly changing configuration of cyber defenses. Precise, current intelligence and pre-positioned options are critical.

Space superiority, as I've said earlier, will be critical. We must not lose a space war. We will need to develop the new Space Force into a war-fighting service and Space Command into a war-fighting command. We will need to exploit the "high ground" of cislunar space. Lagrange points in cislunar space will become key terrain, and space will almost certainly also become a domain for future economic as well as military competition. If history is any guide, the flag will follow trade. We must be ready.

The air, missile, undersea, space, and cyber force we build to better deter China and Russia will be fungible globally, providing the United States with a global denial and conventional deterrent that only needs to be augmented with a few additional capabilities tailored for other regions and potential conflicts. To better deter Russia in the Baltics, for example, we will need robotic combat vehicles reinforced by land-based, long-range precision fires.

Special operations forces will remain essential to our national security. They will be a key instrument in countering Chinese and Russian influence and in strengthening the resistance capabilities of key allies and partners, such as Taiwan and the Baltic states. They will also provide a small but potent ground force in anti-access/area denial and other low-footprint contingencies, and collect valuable intelligence in peace and war. Sustaining our Predator fleet is also essential. It will be our nation's primary intelligence and precision strike asset in counterterrorism operations.

For other contingencies, we will need to maintain general-purpose ground forces of a reasonable size, though we will no longer need to maintain the capabilities for forcible entry amphibious operations and protracted stability operations. We will still need capabilities to insert large formations from the sea, but not against adversaries with anti-access/area-denial capabilities. It's a losing game, and we shouldn't play it any longer.

Finally, we'll need to bolster our industrial capacity to help countries like Ukraine defeat aggression. Indirect conflict and proxy war between the U.S. and Russia and China are far more likely than direct conflict. Great power conflict, should it occur, is also likely to be protracted, which could give the side with the greatest industrial might a decisive advantage as the conflict goes on. We were the arsenal of democracy in World War II, and we can become so again. We cede this source of advantage at our peril.

TRANSFORMING ALLIANCES AND INSTITUTIONS

America's alliances and partner relationships are a great strength of ours. We have them, and China and Russia do not. Our alliances and partnerships will need to be refashioned for new purposes, however.

To increase our odds of prevailing in economic and technological competition with China, we should leverage our strategic alliances and partnerships with Europe, Japan, India, and others to create additional economic and technological mass. The United States and its major allies currently constitute 50 percent of the world's economy and are the leaders in advanced technology, but that share is likely to decrease as China's share increases. We made a start in this area with the stillborn Trans-Pacific Partnership and need to revisit the idea. We must develop a counterweight to the likely size of China's economy and its Belt and Road Initiative. Similarly, we should also leverage our allies and key partners in our information security competition (cyber and covert influence) with Russia and China. They face the same threats.

Our allies and partners will need to maintain forces for common defense, but their capabilities should likewise be transformed to better meet the demands of the new national security era. In the western Pacific, we should work with Japan and our other allies and partners, as my former think tank colleague Andy Krepinevich has suggested, to create an "archipelagic defense, developing a large number of hardened, island bases that can evade and withstand China's growing strike capabilities."[38] In Taiwan and in the Baltic states, we need to build "porcupine" defenses to significantly raise the cost to China and Russia, should they invade our allies' and partners' territory.

We will also need to rethink burden sharing. The United States provides extended nuclear deterrence to Japan and Germany. The Germans and Japanese are both world leaders in robotics. It would seem reasonable for them to make focused investments in autonomous systems—robotic combat vehicles in Germany's case and unmanned undersea vehicles in Japan's. As noted above, they face the same threats.

We will also need to rethink our national security system and preparedness to deal with the new threats we face. In the 1990s, President Clinton established the National Economic Council to better develop and implement economic policy across the government. The time has come to establish a National Emerging Technologies Council to help ensure U.S. leadership in this critical area. The NETC would focus on policies and programs that will ensure our economic competitiveness in an increasingly technological age. It should also focus on the links between technological supremacy and economic and national security, something that is missing today.

We are also in desperate need of a National Information Security Council to develop and coordinate policy against foreign cyber and information influence threats. We must be able to counter both. Currently, our focus has been on cyber threats to the nation, and even these efforts have been insufficient to protect our security. Since an NISC would primarily be concerned with foreign threats to our information security, unlike the NETC, it would most likely belong under the NSC. The key point is to have the NSC develop greater expertise and depth to focus on this core threat to our security.

Similarly, if the COVID-19 crisis has taught us anything, it's the need for a Strategic Health Reserve, and perhaps a Strategic Health Council in the White House. We created the Strategic Petroleum Reserve after the oil shocks of the 1970s. It's time to do the same thing for our strategic health security. We need to be ready when the next pandemic comes. The way we have responded to this one has been woefully inadequate. New technologies, such as mRNA, can substantially increase our readiness, as can better health surveillance infrastructure and hospital surge capacity.

TOWARD A NEW GRAND STRATEGY

Winning the New Cold War starts with understanding the new strategic landscape—the nature of our adversaries, the core threats they will pose, their vulnerabilities, our own vulnerabilities, and our existing and potential sources of enduring advantage. From that diagnostic net assessment, we can formulate a grand strategy to compete effectively. The first challenge is getting the diagnosis right. Then we have to do something about it. As I hope I've shown, competing successfully in this new era will require far more than military strength. Our military and intelligence power, moreover, must be transformed to reflect new realities, as must our alliances and national security institutions.

But it all begins at home, and succeeding at home is how we'll win.

PART V

REFLECTIONS

___

24

INTELLIGENCE, SPECIAL OPERATIONS, AND STRATEGY

LESSONS LEARNED AND RELEARNED

A memoir wouldn't be complete without reflecting a bit at the end. As I conclude, I want to offer a few thoughts on the practice of intelligence, special operations, and strategy—what we got right, what we got wrong, how things changed over the course of my career, what mattered most in the end, what I learned along the way, and what I had to relearn, sometimes painfully. I also want to offer a few thoughts on strategic leadership, why and how I made the decisions I did, and what enabled me to succeed.

INTELLIGENCE AND COVERT ACTION

Intelligence is a major source of American advantage in national security policy making and war fighting. Intelligence and covert action were central to our victory in the Cold War, and both have been central to American national security since the 9/11 attacks. Operationally, CIA had many successes as well as some notable failures during the Cold War. The greatest success of them all, according to my former boss Robert Gates, was our secret war in Afghanistan.[1] With the billions of dollars in covert assistance that the United States and its partners provided, the Afghan resistance was eventually able to force the Soviet Army to withdraw. Covert action against Soviet client states in Angola and Nicaragua also forced them to seek a political solution to end the conflicts.

Elsewhere in the Third World, CIA worked quietly and successfully with governments friendly to the United States to combat subversion by the Soviets or their surrogates. We waged a war of ideas and covertly supported dissidents in the Soviet Union and Eastern Europe, most notably in Poland. We began the Cold War by helping non-Communist governments to prevail in Western Europe, most notably in Italy. We secretly acquired a wide array of Soviet military equipment for the U.S. military to dissect and study. We stole Soviet weapons manuals, recruited scientists and engineers who told us about weapons research and development, and developed agents who revealed much about Warsaw Pact war plans and military capabilities. We developed and emplaced astonishingly advanced technical devices that yielded much information on the Soviet military and its operations. The Clandestine Service's record of accomplishment in the last half of the Cold War had no equal, and it far surpassed that of its Soviet opponents.[2]

On the negative side, we were never able to recruit a spy who could give us unique information from inside the Kremlin, though we did have a significant number of Soviet and East European clandestine sources who provided outstanding reporting on everything from Soviet weapons technology to Soviet plans and intentions.[3] We were duped by double agents in Cuba and East Germany and were penetrated with devastating effect by the KGB and its CIA and FBI moles Aldrich Ames and Robert Hanssen.[4] We also had several covert action failures during the early Cold War, including at the Bay of Pigs in Cuba.

The IC's performance against the full range of intelligence targets in the years since the 9/11 attacks was also very good. We have prevented another 9/11 attack, and we closely monitored military developments in China, Russia, Iran, and North Korea. We recruited and sustained a number of important human penetrations against our adversaries. Stealing our adversaries' secrets remains a critical mission for the IC. NSA enjoyed a "golden age" of SIGINT collection for much of the period after the 9/11 attacks. The Predator revolutionized counterterrorism operations, providing persistent surveillance and the ability to strike our adversaries with great precision in areas where we had no other option. We had some great covert action successes, some notable failures, and several programs that produced useful if unspectacular results.

CIA's analysis on al-Qa'ida and ISIS, on Iran and North Korea, on the wars in Afghanistan and Iraq, and on China and Russia was for the most part excellent. Our analysts weren't always right, but they were right the majority of the time. As I've noted, we wouldn't have had anywhere near the success we had in counterterrorism operations without the outstanding intelligence that the agency's analysts produced. They also called it as they saw it on the wars in Afghanistan and Iraq, even when our policy makers or senior war fighters didn't like the conclusions they reached.

Where our analysts most missed the mark, of course, was in their assessment that Saddam Hussein had weapons of mass destruction and active WMD programs. CIA had also failed to correctly assess the strategic consequences of the Arab Spring and the boost global jihadist groups would get from it. It also failed to anticipate Vladimir Putin's aggressive actions between 2014 and 2016. We had significantly reduced collection on Russian conventional forces after the end of the Cold War and had to play catch-up after the Russians invaded Georgia and then Ukraine. Our intelligence gaps on Russia were an unfortunate downside of focusing so much of our intelligence resources on counterterrorism after 9/11. And while CIA did correctly predict Russia's 2022 invasion of Ukraine, it missed the mark in its overestimation of Russian military capabilities and its underestimation of Ukraine's military prowess.

The biggest improvement in our intelligence capabilities after 9/11 came not from reorganizing within and across agencies but from developing new capabilities within our agencies and reallocating resources within them. This was most evident in Bob Mueller's transformation of the FBI, where he changed what had been largely a law enforcement organization into one with significant national security capabilities, but there were also important capabilities and capacity developed in CIA, NSA, and our other intelligence agencies.[5] The real test of any organizational change is whether you perform your mission—for example, in CIA's case, collecting intelligence, analyzing it, and conducting covert action—better as a result. The majority of redesigns have not delivered on their promise.

A word about congressional oversight. It is an essential part of America's system of intelligence. Very little intelligence information can be disclosed to the public, so our elected representatives become critically important in providing oversight in our republican system of government. I made it my practice to be as forthcoming as I possibly could with our congressional Intelligence Committees, something I learned from Bob Gates, believing that it was much better to have Congress as a partner than as an adversary. From what I was told on several occasions, the committees appreciated my willingness to share our secrets with them and to tell it to them straight.[6]

———————

Covert action deserves a bit more discussion given the central role it played in our victory during the Cold War and the important role it has played in U.S. national security policy since the 9/11 attacks. While the specifics and even the existence of many covert action programs cannot be discussed here, a few general principles and observations about how and why we employ covert action can be.[7]

Covert action is employed for defensive and offensive purposes, using both nonlethal and lethal means, and it is used to build the capacity of allied intelligence services, conduct political and psychological action (covert influence), support insurgents and counterinsurgents, and conduct counterterrorism, counter-proliferation, and counter-narcotics operations.[8] The scope of a covert action program can be global or focused on one country. The primary reason the United States maintains covert action as a key part of its national security tool kit is that our presidents want options between diplomacy and military force. It is a core mission for CIA. As Director Casey liked to say, "You can't change the world with collection and analysis."

Every president since Harry Truman has employed covert action as a key foreign policy instrument, and there have been hundreds of programs since CIA was established in 1947. Since the mid-1970s, all covert action programs have required a presidential "finding" in writing that a program is necessary to protect U.S. national security interests. They are also subject to close congressional oversight.[9]

Beyond presidents' wanting a "third option" between diplomacy and military force, there are two additional foreign policy reasons why the United States employs covert action as a key tool in its national security arsenal. The first is that our foreign allies and partners often prefer to keep their operational relationship with the United States covert and within intelligence channels to minimize their strategic risk. Similarly, American presidents prudently want to limit the strategic risk that an operation poses to the United States. Covert action carries significantly less risk of escalating to a military conflict than more overt options do.[10]

The best example of this is the Afghanistan program in the 1980s. Through covert action, we were able to defeat the Red Army in Afghanistan without triggering a big escalation by the Soviets. The Soviets almost certainly would have responded more forcefully against the United States and our partners had we supported the mujahedin overtly.

When we employ covert action, we should always endeavor to employ it in pursuit of a clear strategic objective and ensure that it is integrated with broader policy.[11] We should "play to win," not just play, even when we have limited objectives.[12] In other words, we should use all means available, employ the right ways and means, and seek to achieve escalation dominance. Some covert action operations depend heavily on precise tactical intelligence while others do not. The Afghanistan program in the 1980s and our operation to overthrow the Taliban in 2001 required very good intelligence, but not exquisite intelligence in most cases, to enable operations. Information influence operations also depend on very good intelligence, but usually not precise tactical intelligence to be effective. In counterterrorism and counter-proliferation operations, on the other hand, the requirement for precise intelligence is far greater.

Some of our most successful covert actions have actually been the least covert. It's the action part, after all, that really matters. Programs that have a likelihood of resulting in a major foreign policy success are usually scaled up significantly, with secrecy traded off for increased strategic effectiveness. The Afghanistan program in the 1980s is the best but by no means the only example of this. The overthrow of the Taliban regime in 2001 is another example, combining covert action with the overt use of military force. For the reasons noted above, however, it is imperative that even very large and successful programs and even those with overt supporting elements remain covert. Their strategic viability and success could easily be jeopardized if they aren't kept secret to some degree.

Covert action is an area where CIA plays a significant policy role. Some senior officials on both the intelligence and the policy side believe that intelligence chiefs should never offer policy advice, lest it cast doubt on the objectivity of the intelligence they present. I understand this view, but don't share it. The CIA director's role in covert action is analogous to those of the secretary of defense and the chairman of the Joint Chiefs of Staff when it comes to the use of military force. While the president ultimately decides whether to employ covert action and military force, the CIA director, secretary, and chairman of the Joint Chiefs don't just present options to the president and the NSC; they are asked for their policy recommendations on whether these options should be employed. They are the experts, and presidents want to know what they think—whether we should conduct a covert action or a military operation, not just how we'd do it, and what its consequences are likely to be. More broadly, I am also of the view that our presidents are best served when they hear from the DNI and D/CIA on policy choices, including those that do not involve covert action.[13]

Finally, covert action must be consistent with American values. The test I use is that if the American people were to learn about a covert action, they should understand why their government employed it and find it consistent with American national security interests and values.[14] Put another way, if a majority of the American people were likely to conclude that a covert action program, if revealed, is inconsistent with American interests and values, the program shouldn't be initiated in the first place.[15]

SPECIAL OPERATIONS

Since the 10th Special Forces Group was established in 1952, there have been three periods of major expansion for U.S. special operations forces: the 1960s under President Kennedy, the 1980s under President Reagan, and the first decade of the twenty-first century under President George W. Bush. When I joined the Special Forces in 1974, we had three active Special Forces Groups, down from seven during the Vietnam War. We also had two Navy SEAL Teams, which had been established in early 1962. In 1974, the Army reactivated two Ranger Battalions. In the late 1970s, a new Army special operations unit was established for special missions.

In the early 1980s, a new parallel SEAL unit was also established, along with a new Army Special Operations Intelligence unit and the 160th Special Operations Aviation Regiment. Four Underwater Demolition Teams were converted to SEAL Teams. Two more active Special Forces Groups were added, along with a third Ranger Battalion and a Ranger regimental headquarters. To oversee SOF, Congress, overriding fierce opposition from the Pentagon, established the Special Operations Command and an assistant secretary of defense for special operations and low-intensity conflict.

To meet the demands of the wars in Afghanistan and Iraq and the war with al-Qa'ida, a third major expansion of SOF was initiated in the first decade of the twenty-first century—an expansion I played a major role in leading. The Marine Corps Special Operations Command was established, and existing SOF units were increased by 33 percent. On the air side, a second active Air Force Special Operations Wing was established. As a result of this growth in the size and diversity of the force and in assigned missions, the United States fielded the most robust special operations force in the world. The SOF expansion we undertook in the past two decades will continue to pay dividends in the new era of great power competition.

Between 2001 and 2010, SOF's manpower doubled, its budget tripled, and its operational tempo increased by a factor of more than four. Several of SOF's innovations, moreover, were of strategic importance: the new and more powerful form of unconventional warfare SOF and CIA pioneered that combined covert action, special operations, and conventional precision airpower in 2001; the sustained counterterrorism campaigns in Iraq and Afghanistan between 2003 and 2014; and the use of tribal engagement for counterinsurgency purposes in Afghanistan between 2008 and 2014. The raid on UBL's Abbottabad compound was a masterpiece of special operations planning and execution. SOF has had much to be proud of, and I am proud to have been a part of it.

There are a couple of important points to make about SOF growth, however. The first is that while these expansions were all necessary, SOF cannot be mass-produced; the quality of the force is more important than its size. We took great pains to ensure that we maintained quality during our large expansion in the first decade of the century and the early 2010s by fully resourcing our schoolhouses and strengthening and expanding our training. We ensured that some of our best operatives were sent as instructors and that the training cadre was fully manned. We also expanded the SOF curriculum to ensure that we were producing the best special operator possible. We hadn't done this during the big buildup of SOF during the Vietnam era, and SOF quality suffered as a result.

A second point is that even with a large expansion in special operations force structure, SOF will still be dependent on conventional force support for most of its operations. We would never have enough special operations helicopters or ISR assets to meet our needs. A third point is that even with a major expansion, some aspects of SOF's current and future readiness will still suffer. Proficiency in important contingency foreign languages—Russian, Chinese, Korean, and Persian Farsi, for example—was hard to maintain while Special Forces were making near-constant deployments to Iraq and Afghanistan. The skills required for operations in denied areas also atrophied, and our expansion didn't meet all of SOF's future needs. We had to prioritize the capabilities we needed for our current wars and didn't have the resources to procure all of the costly new capabilities we would need to clandestinely infiltrate and operate in denied areas. A final point is that even with a major expansion, we still overused SOF, perhaps necessarily so, but with increasingly bad effects within SOF as the wars went on. The wars took a toll on our operators and their families. While continuous deployments greatly increased the combat proficiency of the force, they also caused some of our professionalism to fray at times.

The missions assigned to special operators have also grown or changed substantially over the past several decades. During the 1950s, the principal mission of Special Forces was preparing to conduct unconventional warfare in Eastern Europe in the event of war. A second mission was counterinsurgency, principally in Southeast Asia. During the 1960s, counterinsurgency became the primary focus for special operations forces. Special reconnaissance was also added as an important mission, particularly for operations in Laos, Cambodia, and occasionally in North Vietnam. With the end of the Vietnam War, unconventional warfare, special reconnaissance, and direct action became the primary missions for SOF. Counterterrorism was also added to SOF's mission set in the 1970s.

During the 1991 Gulf War, special reconnaissance was the primary mission for SOF. During the 1980s and 1990s, SOF also built stronger ties with conventional forces, a lesson learned from mistakes special operators had made in Vietnam. These relationships paid dividends in the 1990s during the "invasion" of Haiti and would pay even bigger dividends in Afghanistan and Iraq. Counter proliferation of weapons of mass destruction was also added to the SOF mission set during the 1990s, and SOF developed new capabilities to address this threat. SOF also focused on counter-narcotics operations in Colombia and acquired new skills after it was assigned a "man hunting" mission to go after war criminals in Bosnia. SOF's original mission, unconventional warfare, had almost dropped off the SOF mission set in the 1990s before it came roaring back in the CIA- and SOF-led campaign to topple the Taliban in 2001. Some senior SOF leaders believed that unconventional warfare was no longer a viable mission, given the end of the Cold War, and moved to refocus our Special Forces on other missions. Thank heavens they didn't completely eliminate unconventional warfare. It is one of the missions, like strategic counterterrorism and counter proliferation of weapons of mass destruction, that truly distinguishes SOF from other forces.

After the 9/11 attacks, in addition to the return of unconventional warfare, SOF counterterrorism operations were transformed from episodic operations to sustained campaigns. This, as I observed earlier, was a major innovation. Counterinsurgency and foreign internal defense also became primary SOF missions between 2002 and 2014. SOF contributed to our counterinsurgency campaigns by conducting counterterrorism operations, leading partner forces on raids, conducting tribal engagement, and building the capacity of our foreign SOF partners. After 9/11, a secondary mission for SOF, support for special activities, also became a bit more prominent.

When not engaged in combat operations, SOF also performed an important "global scouts" role for our combatant commanders. Special operators provided strategic access to key areas and established and built relationships that might be needed in the future. Given the nature of the intelligence war, SOF also focused on collecting intelligence outside war zones more than it had before 9/11. Finally, following Russia's invasion of Ukraine in 2014, parts of SOF became more focused on countering the unconventional warfare and hybrid warfare of our enemies. After Jim Mattis became secretary of defense, SOF refocused on how it could contribute to great power competition and conflict.

There were a few special operations organizational reforms that I thought about while in office that I either elected not to pursue at the time or ran out of time to get done before I moved on. The first idea was to create a three-star, joint operational command for special or unconventional warfare, much like the one we have for joint special operations. SOF in war zones is almost always placed under a conventional force commander at the three- or four-star level. When we are engaged in an irregular war, our strategic and operational commanders ought to have significant experience in irregular warfare.

A new joint special warfare command would provide the greatest focus on unconventional warfare and counterinsurgency. A few senior SOF leaders have embraced the idea in recent years that there are really two core missions for SOF: special warfare, which encompasses unconventional warfare and counterinsurgency (people's war); and surgical strike (counterterrorism, counter proliferation, and direct action). Over the past four decades, the latter has received much higher priority than the former in terms of resources and command positions. That's essentially the idea behind the new command.

Admiral Olson and I decided not to pursue it, however, due to manpower shortages. We needed all of our SOF operators in operational units, not on yet another headquarters staff. We opted instead to create a two-star task force under the Army's existing Special Forces Command, but this isn't an ideal solution from either a rank or a joint warfare perspective. It was a step in the right direction, though. Navy Special Warfare and Marine Corps Special Operations also need two-star, deployable operational commands.

I also think we should revisit the idea of making SOCOM a supported combatant command for special operations, following CIA's successful global model for counterterrorism. The alternative is to select more SOF officers for regional combatant command positions when the primary challenge in a theater is irregular war. The downside with that approach, however, is that you don't get the benefits of a true global strategy when the war extends beyond a single theater.

The final SOF organizational reform that Admiral Olson and I briefly considered but ran out of time before we could seriously think about implementing was to combine Naval Special Warfare and Marine Corps Special Operations into a three-star Maritime Special Operations Command. This would provide a service three-star for SOF within the Department of the Navy. At present, only the Army and Air Force have three-star SOF component commands; the Navy and Marine Corps have two-star commands.

COUNTERTERRORISM STRATEGY

On September 11, 2021, our war with al-Qa'ida reached the two-decade point. Our primary objective of preventing another 9/11-scale attack has been achieved—at least for now. We also achieved President Obama's goal of disrupting, dismantling, and defeating core al-Qa'ida in the Afghanistan-Pakistan border region. We have also had considerable success against core al-Qa'ida's most dangerous affiliate, al-Qa'ida in the Arabian Peninsula, and al-Qa'ida in Syria, core AQ's next most dangerous affiliate. Against core al-Qa'ida we used all means available and achieved escalation dominance. We didn't always against AQAP and al-Qa'ida in Syria and against ISIS in Iraq and Syria, but fortunately prevailed nonetheless. Almost all of al-Qa'ida's pre-9/11 leadership has been killed or captured. ISIS has been operationally defeated in Iraq and Syria, its caliphate has been eliminated, and most of its top leaders have been killed or captured.

Al-Qa'ida and ISIS failed to achieve their primary aims during the first two decades of war. Al-Qa'ida was unable to conduct follow-on catastrophic and economically crippling attacks against the United States and the West. It failed to catalyze a general uprising in the Islamic world, and it failed to overthrow any of what it considered apostate regimes in the Middle East and South Asia. ISIS proved incapable of successfully defending the caliphate it had established.

Our most effective counterterrorism strategy has been one that has combined four elements: (1) hardened defenses; (2) intelligence-driven operations; (3) aggressive and sustained offensive campaigns to deny AQ and ISIS any sanctuary; and (4) a global network of partners to restrict the reach of global jihadist groups. Each was implemented to varying degrees after the 9/11 attacks and has been adapted as changing operational circumstances warranted.

Hardening our defenses has made us much safer. In commercial aviation, we immediately took steps to prevent travel by known terrorists or potential terrorists, implement improved screening at airports, and lock and harden cockpit doors. After we discovered and disrupted the 2006 plot to blow up multiple commercial airliners over the Atlantic Ocean, we restricted items that can be brought on board aircraft. The FBI's transformation after 9/11 significantly strengthened our ability to prevent attacks on the American homeland.

Since the Beirut bombings in the early 1980s, we have taken measures—the so-called Inman reforms—to harden and, in several cases, relocate our embassies. We have also put in place hardened defenses at critical installations and events around the United States. As with civil aviation, these measures have paid off in terms of increased security. Our hardening of our defenses overseas has allowed us to maintain a presence in some dangerous environments.

Our long war with al-Qa'ida and ISIS has primarily been an intelligence war. Intelligence from multiple sources—human penetrations, detainee debriefings, signals intelligence of all sorts, full-motion video imagery, and liaison reporting—has been the motor that has driven U.S. counterterrorism operations. Precise intelligence placed al-Qa'ida's senior leaders, operatives, and safe haven providers "on the X" for targeting by Predator and raids by special operations forces. Intelligence gathered by the United States and its partners also made al-Qa'ida, its allies, and its offshoots vulnerable to capture operations. Aggressive foreign and domestic intelligence operations disrupted numerous plots, and intelligence gained from sensitive site exploitation, interrogation, and post-strike monitoring produced a targeting cycle that turned single operations into counterterrorism campaigns.

After 9/11, the United States shifted from a reactive to a proactive counterterrorism strategy. The instruments employed by the

United States in its counterterrorism campaigns varied by region and adversary. A sustained offensive campaign that combined persistent surveillance, precision strike, and high operational tempo was the primary means we used to disrupt, dismantle, and defeat core al-Qa'ida in the Afghanistan-Pakistan border region. The same approach was applied against al-Qa'ida's affiliates in Yemen and Syria, though for several years it was applied with far less intensity and therefore less effectiveness.

The Predator has been the signature weapon of our counterterrorism campaigns against al-Qa'ida. It represented a revolution in counterterrorism capabilities. The effectiveness of the Predator was dramatically increased by policy changes approved by President Bush in 2008, and continued by President Obama, and by the transfer of twenty-two Predator orbits to the strategic CT mission between 2007 and 2012. Continued innovation in Predator tactics and sensor advances have further contributed to U.S. counterterrorism success through the Trump and into the Biden administrations. It is a capability we give up at our peril.

In Iraq and Afghanistan, special operations raids were the United States' counterterrorism instrument of choice. Against the Taliban in 2001 and ISIS between 2015 and 2019, local forces supported by U.S. advisers and airpower were our primary operational instrument. U.S. success in its wars with al-Qa'ida and ISIS also relied heavily on a "global counterterrorism network" that the United States built and led, largely through the provision of intelligence. In many cases, the United States also provided operational advice and financial support to its foreign partners. Joint capture operations with foreign intelligence, military, and police forces were a central instrument in CT operations in urban areas to disrupt plots and capture jihadist operatives.

———

Despite our many counterterrorism successes, our war with al-Qa'ida and ISIS and other global jihadists is almost certainly far from over. There are several reasons why the war has lasted so long and why it will likely continue for the foreseeable future.

The first is that while al-Qa'ida failed to catalyze a general uprising across the Islamic world, it was successful in creating a global jihadist insurgency through its creation of several regional affiliates. ISIS had similar success in branching out beyond its core base in Syria and Iraq. Insurgencies confined to one country often last for several decades. Defeating a global jihadist insurgency will likely take at least as long.

The war with al-Qa'ida and ISIS is a war of attrition. Operational successes do not cumulate in a global counterterrorism war anywhere near as fast as they do in conventional wars. Wars of religion tend to be more protracted than wars fought for other reasons. The ideology that produced al-Qa'ida and ISIS retains its power, and the causes that motivated these groups to wage war against the United States and the West remain.

There are still numerous ungoverned areas in the Middle East, South Asia, and Africa where al-Qa'ida and ISIS can find safe haven, and there is little prospect that this vast territory will come under the control of local government forces anytime soon. U.S. counterterrorism pressure is the only thing that prevents al-Qa'ida and ISIS from reconstituting in several areas.[16]

New technologies such as readily available commercial encryption have made global jihadists harder to find; social media tools have made it easier for them to spread their ideology; and new forms of standoff attack, such as explosive-laden, commercially available, remotely piloted aircraft, have increased their ability to strike targets. From a global jihadist perspective, moreover, the war is cheap. Al-Qa'ida ran its global war on a core budget of only tens of millions of dollars per year. The 9/11 attacks cost the group only $500,000 to execute. Al-Qa'ida unfortunately was able to employ a very effective cost-imposing, asymmetric strategy against us.

CHANGES IN WARFARE, CHANGES IN STRATEGY

Over the course of my more than four-decade career, warfare changed significantly across the spectrum of conflict. Changes in warfare require a commensurate change in strategy. In some cases, it was the United States that brought about the change, forcing its adversaries to adapt. In other cases, it was our adversaries who did.[17]

During the late 1970s and the 1980s, our new military strategy of deep attack (known in the NATO context as "follow-on forces attack") and the new capabilities that enabled it changed the conventional balance of power in Europe. The new strategy combined ballistic missiles and stealth aircraft that could penetrate an enemy's air defenses; sensors that could see deep into an enemy's rear, day or night and in any weather; precision-guided munitions that could provide one shot, one kill against enemy targets; and battle networks that could connect these capabilities into a system of systems. The new U.S. approach caused the Soviet high command to worry that its strategy, which relied on firepower and superior numbers to achieve rapid operational breakthroughs, had been rendered obsolete. It is a prime example of how a shift to new ways and means can alter a military balance in your favor.

From a Soviet perspective, moreover, the military balance would only grow more unfavorable with each passing decade. This realization was a major reason why senior Soviet military officers, including hard-liner Marshal Nikolai Ogarkov, the chief of the Soviet General Staff, supported Gorbachev in his efforts to reform the Soviet economy. Had the Cold War continued, it was highly unlikely that the Soviets would have been able to counter the new U.S. strategy, given the rapid decline of the Soviet economy and, more important, the Soviet Union's increasing technological obsolescence. What the Soviet military most likely would have done is what the Russian Federation's military would later do itself—rely even more on nuclear weapons to make up for a growing weakness in conventional warfare.

The new U.S. approach to conventional warfare would prove even more successful after the Cold War. The United States easily defeated Iraqi forces in 1991 and 2003, and Serb forces in 1995 and 1999. I readily acknowledged the power of this new way of war, but warned of its coming obsolescence. As I had predicted, China adopted a military strategy based on anti-access/area-denial capabilities that largely rendered obsolete the U.S. way of conventional war in the East Asian littoral. To rebuild our conventional deterrent, I helped lead a major effort to rethink our approach to conventional war, and successfully advocated for investment in new capabilities to implement the new strategy. There is more to be done, however.

There were new developments and shifts in strategic warfare as well. For the first two decades of the nuclear age, the United States and the Soviet Union employed "countervalue" strategies, targeting the other side's population. During the 1960s, both sides switched to "counterforce" strategies, targeting the other side's nuclear weapons, its nuclear infrastructure, and command and control. China has maintained a countervalue strategy since its development of nuclear weapons and the means to deliver them.

Although I can't get into the specific details, Russia developed new countervalue capabilities that could inflict grave damage on U.S. population centers and on the U.S. and global economy. Cyber capabilities and strategies developed by both Russia and China have also been designed to be used in a countervalue context. U.S. counterforce strategy remained sensible for nuclear deterrence, but it seemed less so when it was applied to strategic cyber deterrence. I struggled in vain to get CYBERCOM planners to develop concepts and capabilities for cyber deterrence. The planners argued that the United States had far more to lose in any strategic cyber exchange than our adversaries. I countered that unilateral restraint was not a good deterrence strategy. Our planners were still working on a strategy for effective cyber deterrence when I retired. Presidents need a range of options, from very precise, limited cyber counterforce strikes, to countervalue options to deter our adversaries. I hope we're getting on with it.

Space had also become a contested domain after 2007 as China and Russia developed strategies and capabilities to deny U.S. forces the military use of space. Here, too, I faced an uphill battle in getting DOD to take space warfare seriously. Fortunately, I had far greater success with the NRO.

There were also major changes in irregular warfare beginning in the 1980s. As the Soviet-Afghan War demonstrated, resistance movements armed with sophisticated weapons became increasingly capable of defeating occupying armies and overthrowing regimes. The big change in terrorism was the shift in the 1990s to religious terrorism, a focus on inflicting catastrophic losses on the United States and the West, and a dramatic expansion in the political aims of the global jihadists to overthrowing the current world order. Al-Qa'ida and its global jihadist allies have used all means available to them, and for a period they achieved escalation dominance.

In Afghanistan in 2001, the United States perfected a new, more lethal form of unconventional warfare by supporting the opposition to the Taliban with conventional airpower. The result was the rapid overthrow of the Taliban regime, something unconventional warfare had not been able to accomplish previously in that brief a time frame. As it had in conventional war, precision airpower came to dominate counterterrorism operations, in this case with Predator armed reconnaissance aircraft. With this innovation, we denied al-Qa'ida sanctuary in Pakistan, Yemen, Syria, Libya, and other areas.

As insurgents in Iraq and Afghanistan increasingly relied on terrorist tactics, our primary operational challenge in these wars became counterterrorism rather than traditional counterinsurgency. Across the Middle East and South Asia, the United States learned how difficult it is to stabilize countries after regime change. A lack of strategic patience for long-duration counterinsurgency, moreover, remained America's Achilles' heel. In Ukraine, Russia combined subversion and unconventional warfare with conventional military operations into what we called hybrid warfare, posing a serious challenge for American strategy.

THE SEARCH FOR AN EFFECTIVE GRAND STRATEGY

As Bob Gates has written, the last really successful grand strategy the United States had was the one we pursued against the Soviet Union between 1946 and 1991. Since the end of the Cold War, we have been far less successful strategically for a variety of reasons, and this shortfall has been across the board, from the wars we have been engaged in, to great power competition.[18]

Our late Cold War strategy evolved considerably over time as President Reagan expanded his strategic objectives for our secret war in Afghanistan at the beginning of his second term and as the Soviet Union entered into its death spiral between 1988 and 1991. The strategy combined an opening to and alliance with China, the aggressive use of covert action to roll back Soviet and Soviet-client gains in the Third World and preserve opposition movements in Poland and the Soviet bloc, a new military strategy supported by new capabilities and a large defense and intelligence buildup, the threat of a strategic breakout through the Strategic Defense Initiative, restrictions on technology transfer, and arms control agreements and very effective personal diplomacy by Reagan, George Shultz, George H. W. Bush, and Jim Baker with Mikhail Gorbachev and Eduard Shevardnadze. Gorbachev of course was absolutely essential to the strategy's ultimate success, but it is also true that the United States, across five administrations and considerable domestic turmoil, developed and implemented a winning strategy.

Why have we failed to develop effective strategies for strategic competition with China? As Kurt Campbell, a China hand with prior service in DOD, the State Department, and now President Biden's NSC, has observed, the United States has always had an outsized sense of its ability to determine China's course. Until Nixon and Kissinger's opening to China, Chinese realities always upset American expectations, from George Marshall's failed attempt to broker a peace between the Nationalists and the Communists, to the Korean War, when the Truman administration thought it could dissuade Mao from sending his troops across the Yalu River, to the Vietnam War, when the Johnson administration hoped that China would restrict its support for the North Vietnamese.[19]

We had had a very productive alliance with China against the Soviet Union from the late 1970s to the end of the Cold War, but after the Cold War ended, the United States' and China's interests diverged. Some of our greatest Cold War statesmen had a hard time accepting this reality.

After the Cold War, the United States engaged China while trying to hedge militarily against its rise. American presidents from Nixon to Obama believed that the United States could tame China by engaging it. Deepening commercial, diplomatic, and cultural ties would transform China's internal development and external behavior. The Chinese favored engagement as well, but for different reasons—to use it to build up China's strength. Looking back from today, it is increasingly clear that successive administrations had placed too much faith in our power to shape China's trajectory. Free trade and foreign direct investment had not tamed China, nor had America's evident military superiority during the 1990s.[20]

A similar mistake was made with respect to Russia. We largely ignored the signs of growing Russian hostility toward the United States during the first decade of the twenty-first century and didn't want to abandon our policy of "resetting" relations with Russia during the Obama administration. We repeatedly failed to deter Putin from pursuing an increasingly aggressive foreign policy. After President Trump took office, our policy toward Russia became one of appeasement. When the administration wasn't appeasing, it worked at cross-purposes. The inevitable result was that Russia was not deterred.

GOOD STRATEGY, BAD STRATEGY

I'd like to offer a few general observations about strategy before I conclude with my thoughts on strategic leadership. As Clausewitz observed, strategy is hard. Bad strategy is unfortunately far more common than good strategy. There are several reasons for this. Establishing unrealistic goals is a frequent cause of bad strategy. Our aim to transform the Middle East through regime change and democracy in Iraq is a prime example of a big overreach in feasible strategic ends. Misalignment between ends and means and the use of inappropriate ways are additional causes of bad strategy. As Bill Burns and others have observed, we had a big mismatch between our ends and our means in our policy and strategy toward the Assad regime in Syria. Relying on Pakistan to prevent al-Qa'ida from attacking the American homeland between 2005 and 2008 is an example of an inappropriate way to achieve a feasible strategic objective. Fortunately, President Bush adopted a far more effective strategy in 2008.

A second set of reasons for bad strategy has to do with a strategy's focus and scope. Focusing on the "main objective" is critically important, but unfortunately it is a principle that is all too often ignored. Invading Iraq before our war with al-Qa'ida was won is one example of not keeping the main thing the main thing. Wanting to assign strategic priority to our counterinsurgency campaign in Afghanistan over our war with al-Qa'ida is another.

"Not making a problem big enough," as President Eisenhower observed, can be another cause for failure. Our failure to remove Assad while combating the global jihadist threat in Syria is one example. Our failure to prevent the Houthis from overthrowing the Hadi government is another, and our failure to deter Putin's increasing aggression in Ukraine, in Syria, and against the United States is a third. Not thinking big enough can be every bit a cause of strategic underperformance as thinking too big is for strategic overreach. An example of strategic success from setting a more ambitious goal is President Reagan's decision to drive the Soviets out of Afghanistan "by all means available." Before Reagan's decision, the Soviet-Afghan War had been stalemated.

There is a tension between building and conserving power and using it. Good strategy creates power; bad strategy reduces or wastes it. The hard part is knowing when to conserve and when to use power. Do too little and you miss opportunities. Do too much and you expose yourself to significant additional strategic risk. That's why strategy is an art. Good strategy is made by good strategists. Who the people are making strategy matters enormously.

Good strategy often involves getting your enemy to play your game. An example of this is the defeat of the Taliban and al-Qa'ida in Afghanistan in 2001 using indigenous forces supported by CIA and SOF advisers and U.S. airpower. Another example is using our Predator aircraft to deny al-Qa'ida any sanctuary. A third example is our use of forward submarine operations during the late Cold War to hold Soviet fleet ballistic missile submarines at risk, thereby strengthening strategic and conventional deterrence. Understanding precisely the competition or war you're in and where your areas of advantage lie is key to good strategy.

A lesson I learned in the Cold War is that offense is often the best defense. This applies to the Predator and undersea warfare examples above, as well as to several other cases. There was a big debate, for example, during the late 1970s and the 1980s about whether we should pursue a purely defensive conventional military strategy in Europe or an offensive defense. The former would emphasize capabilities like close air support, the latter, deep strike systems. Those who advocated for the former were concerned about being too "provocative" toward the Soviets, noting that NATO was a defensive alliance. Advocates of this approach, however, conflated political aims with military means. Fortunately, we pursued an offensive defense, and that choice turned out to be decisive, rendering Soviet conventional military strategy obsolete. It also deterred war better than the alternative would have.

The installation of nuclear-armed Pershing II missiles in Europe in the 1980s greatly unnerved the Soviet leadership. From its firing positions in Europe, the Pershing II could reach Moscow in minutes. The Soviets at great expense had built a special underground train system to evacuate their leaders from the Kremlin in the event of an impending nuclear strike. Pershing II's short flight time put the Soviet leaders' ability to evacuate at significant risk. A few years after the Pershing II's deployment, the Soviets agreed to a landmark nuclear arms control treaty on intermediate nuclear forces that eliminated Soviet SS-20s that threatened all of Europe in return for the United States' withdrawing its Pershing IIs. It made the European continent much safer in the final years of the Cold War.

Another lesson I learned from the Vietnam and Iraq wars, on the one hand, and the Soviet-Afghan War, on the other, is that a strategist should avoid exposing his side to unnecessary risk while taking advantage whenever one's opponent does. It is much better to be the puncher than the punching bag. We missed an opportunity to be the puncher in Syria. We didn't miss it in Afghanistan during the 1980s. Convincing your adversary that you have escalation dominance, I learned from my Afghan experience, is also good strategy.

Integrated and comprehensive strategy usually leads to better strategy. Single-element strategies, such as sanctions or arms control agreements, rarely lead to strategic success. We were more effective with integrated strategy during the late Cold War when we pursued warmer relations and arms control agreements with Gorbachev while we continued to escalate our covert efforts to defeat his army in Afghanistan than we were with Iran between 2013 and 2015, when our sole focus was on securing a nuclear agreement. This goal unfortunately came at the expense of deterring Iran's increasingly malign influence in the Middle East.

Paradoxically, sometimes you can even win by losing. Egyptian President Anwar Sadat's decision to launch the 1973 Middle East war is a good example of this. Sadat secured a good peace out of a well-fought but lost war. President Obama thought we couldn't win in Ukraine, and therefore decided not to provide the Ukrainians with lethal military assistance. What we got in return was even more aggression by Putin.

Finally, strategy, good or bad, is fundamentally subservient to politics, both in the United States and abroad. Lack of political support can derail strategy, as in the case of our failure to strike Syria after Assad killed fifteen hundred of his own people with a chemical weapons strike in 2013. Bad politics can also undo previous successes, as we saw in Iraq and Yemen in 2014. In our own country, the anti–"forever war" politics embraced by both major political parties led to our completely unnecessary defeat in Afghanistan.

SUCCESS IS NEVER FINAL

It is important to remember that strategy is competitive and that your adversary is always trying to defeat you through one means or another. Success, unfortunately, is never final—a painful lesson I learned after we won a historic victory with our secret war in Afghanistan, only to have al-Qa'ida plan its 9/11 attacks from its sanctuary in Afghanistan a decade later. Even the most successful strategies must be followed up with new strategies as conditions change. Similarly, our very successful strategy against al-Qa'ida and the Taliban in 2001 only worked for so long. Our strategy had to be fundamentally rethought and redesigned after both groups found safe haven in Pakistan and reconstituted.

At the level of grand strategy, the right strategy can result in sustained success. Containment proved to be a very successful strategy for the United States during the Cold War, though as John Lewis Gaddis has noted, U.S. grand strategy is better understood as *strategies* of containment rather than a single overarching strategy. It goes without saying, moreover, that some U.S. strategies during the Cold War were far more successful than others.

Bipartisanship and continuity in strategy have played important roles in sustaining good strategy. The Afghanistan program was started by President Carter and expanded to victory under President Reagan. Carter also began the defense buildup and initiated the "offset strategy" in Europe that would change the conventional balance in our favor. Both of these were also expanded by Reagan. President George W. Bush began the new counterterrorism strategy to deny core al-Qa'ida its sanctuary in the Afghanistan-Pakistan border region, and President Obama expanded it and sustained it until it achieved our strategic goals.

Strategic failure from time to time is unfortunately inevitable, either from overreach or from underreach. Every administration since Truman has experienced it in one way or the other. The Reagan administration badly overreached and erred with Iran-contra, and the George W. Bush administration overreached with the invasion of Iraq. The Clinton administration underreached in failing to deal with the growing threat from al-Qa'ida, and the Obama administration underreached in its approach to Syria, Yemen, and Russia between 2012 and 2016. Each administration had its share of great strategic successes: Reagan in Afghanistan and elsewhere in the "Third World War" and in Cold War strategy; Clinton in the Balkans campaigns; Bush in Afghanistan in 2001 and against core al-Qa'ida in 2008; and Obama against core al-Qa'ida between 2009 and 2012 and in Afghanistan between 2010 and 2015. On balance, America has had more successes than failures, and the successes have been far more consequential.

The key is to learn from one's mistakes and adapt and move on. Fortunes can change rapidly. The Soviets were seemingly on a roll in the 1970s, only to see the United States increasingly seize the strategic initiative during the 1980s and win the Cold War by the decade's end. The Iraq war and the subsequent war with ISIS were won and lost several times. Our war with al-Qa'ida has had similar shifts in strategic initiative.

STRATEGIC LEADERSHIP

Over the course of my career, I served from the entry level as a Special Forces soldier to the senior national level as the undersecretary of defense for intelligence. Along the way, I developed a number of core ideas about leadership and career development. They are listed here as ten core principles that worked for me. Some are, not surprisingly, very closely related.

My first core principle was to take only jobs that I really liked and where I thought I could make a real difference. And then to make the most of it—to take bold action, and not just warm the seat.

This approach won't work for everyone and it certainly can have its career pitfalls, but it worked for me, and I am happy with the choices I made. I was guided by this principle when I made my decision to stay in the Special Forces after becoming a second lieutenant, with my decision to seek the Afghanistan Covert Action Program job, and with my decision to return to government as an assistant secretary overseeing SOF and all of DOD's operational capabilities and my subsequent decision to become USD(I). Each turned out to be the right move. I had been blessed to be able to do what I loved in my twenties and thirties, and to do what I still loved in subsequent decades.

My second principle, as I noted in the chapters on my formative experience in the Special Forces, is my belief in the importance of expert and referent power. Expert power is possessing the strategic, tactical, and technical skills necessary to lead. Referent power is having one's ability to lead recognized by others, independent of one's position. These two approaches are by no means the only way to lead, but they guided me from the beginning of my career. It's why I went into the Special Forces and why I decided to stay in the Special Forces until I felt I was ready to join CIA. I believe my adherence to this principle enabled me to win the confidence of subordinates and superiors alike. It enabled me to do what I did as a CT unit commander, as a CIA operations officer in the invasion of Grenada and in the secret war in Afghanistan, and in the senior jobs I later held at the Pentagon. I kept it as a core principle throughout my career.

A third principle is one I followed long before I knew what to call it. Late in my career, I heard former Goldman Sachs CEO and U.S. Treasury secretary Hank Paulson explain that "job enlargement" had been a key to his success. In each of the key jobs he held throughout his career, Paulson said, he had sought to take on more responsibilities. As I thought about what he had said, it seemed to also apply to me. In each of my key jobs, from Special Forces soldier to commander of a Counterterrorism Intelligence Unit, to Afghanistan Covert Action Program officer at CIA, to assistant secretary of defense for special operations, low-intensity conflict, and interdependent capabilities, to USD(I), I sought to enlarge the scope of my responsibilities as much as possible and benefited from these big "stretch" assignments in terms of my career trajectory. I was lucky I didn't make too many bureaucratic enemies along the way, but the strategy consistently paid off.

You can't apply my third principle without having bosses who believe in you. My fourth principle is the importance of mentors. It goes without saying that several of them provided me with unprecedented responsibilities. I benefited in the Special Forces from Gene

Russell, at CIA from Bill Rooney, Gust Avrakotos, and Bert Dunn, in the Office of Net Assessment from Andy Marshall, and in the Pentagon from Bob Gates. I learned something from Secretary Gates nearly every time I interacted with him. In my mind, he is America's greatest living statesman.

I came to believe that having the right boss and the right constellation of a few bosses is all-important for strategic success. A critical insight I learned fairly early on is the absolute importance of having a few key individuals in the right positions. That makes all the difference between success and failure, particularly when it comes to world-changing events and major changes in strategic direction. I was blessed at CIA with Gust, Bert, John McMahon, Bob Gates, and Bill Casey. That constellation and Charlie Wilson made all the difference. At the Pentagon, I was blessed with Bob Gates and Eric Edelman and Michèle Flournoy and then with Leon Panetta and with Jim Clapper when he was DNI. Throughout my career, having the right partners like Eric Olson, Bill McRaven, Mike Hayden, Michael Morell, and many others I unfortunately can't name here also contributed immensely to my success. I was lucky again and again.

A fifth principle is to develop deep expertise in an important area and then broaden to develop expertise in other important areas. I spent the operational half of my career in the Special Forces and CIA but then broadened and gained expertise in nuclear, cyber, and space strategy and capabilities, future warfare, and conventional force transformation. Eliot Cohen, who tutored me in strategy, was another important mentor. All this paid off when Eric Edelman told me he was creating a new senior job for me that would have oversight of all of DOD's operational capabilities. The expertise I developed in other intelligence disciplines and capabilities beyond human intelligence and covert action was also a great benefit after I became USD(I).

A sixth principle is the importance of building and rebuilding intellectual capital. I sought to build intellectual capital throughout my career in each job I held, but I also benefited immensely as I rose to senior national security policy and leadership positions from my time at the Wharton School and my PhD studies at Johns Hopkins SAIS. My decision to retire at the end of April 2015 was also motivated by a need to rebuild my intellectual capital and have some time to think before taking on a new adventure. I realized that my public service was most likely over, but if I were asked to return, I wanted to be ready. Writing this book has been part of that rebuilding effort, as have my new experiences in the private sector.

A seventh principle derives from the need for at least some senior national security policy makers to have deep operational expertise. I believe I was more effective in NSC meetings and with the top leadership at the Pentagon, the CIA, and the IC because of the operational expertise I had developed over the years. It is not enough to be smart. You have to be intimately familiar with the immense operational tool kit at your disposal, and what will work in a given situation and what will not. This only comes, in my view, from deep operational experience, expertise in a wide range of areas, and a deep understanding of strategy and history.

An eighth principle is the importance of recognizing when you need to modify your long-held views and adapt your thinking to new realities. I did this in every decade of my career, from the 1970s to the 2010s. In the 1980s, I came to the conclusion that Afghanistan and the Middle East were where the action was, after coming into CIA thinking I'd focus on the Soviet bloc or on Latin America. In the 1990s, I thought that an emerging revolution in war and the rise of China were the next big challenges for America, and I focused on them. I shifted gears again in the years after 9/11 to focus on the war with al-Qa'ida and other operations. After 2015, I significantly changed my views on what will matter in our strategic competition with China and Russia.

A ninth principle is the importance of strategic vision and leadership, identifying what really matters and then ensuring that the most important things get done. I followed this principle throughout my career, but it became especially important after I rose to the national and enterprise level of leadership.

My final principle is to leave things better than you found them, and to make a difference. I hope I did.

25

THE LONG GOODBYE

FAREWELLS: DEFENSE, CIA, THE PRESIDENT, AND CONGRESS

After serving for nearly eight years as a national security policy maker and intelligence community leader across both Republican and Democratic administrations, I decided it was time to hang up my spurs, at least for a while. I had accomplished far more than I thought I would when I reentered government service in 2007, largely because I had stayed for eight years rather than the two I originally thought, and had served in two big jobs instead of one.

It had been a hard eight years, especially for my family, with long hours, missed vacations, and near-constant travel. It was time to go. As part of my farewell speech, I made a joke that I knew I had been given a sign when I imagined finding my wife, Melana, listening to the Eagles' "Hotel California" over and over. ("You can check out anytime you like but you can never leave.")

Secretary of Defense Ash Carter—the fourth secretary under whom I'd served during the past eight years—graciously hosted a retirement ceremony for me on my last day in office. Our chairman of the JCS, General Marty Dempsey, attended, as did Admiral Sandy Winnefeld, our vice-chairman. Both were good friends of mine. My dear friend and close colleague DNI Jim Clapper attended and presented me with the National Intelligence Distinguished Service Medal. D/CIA John Brennan came, along with a bus full of about sixty senior CIA officers I'd served with.

Ash, Marty, Jim, and John all made very gracious remarks. Several senior White House officials also attended. My close friends Michael Morell, Admiral Eric Olson, and Admiral Bill McRaven, who were all retired, also came. It meant a lot.

Bill gave a great speech at the reception Melana had arranged afterward at the Fort Myer Officers' Club, recounting what I had done for our special operations forces, and my daughters ate it up. After retirement, Bill had become the chancellor of the University of Texas system. In 2014, he had given a blockbuster commencement speech at the university—where our daughter Sophie had just completed her junior year—about the importance of the little things in life, starting with making your bed.[1] Our two youngest ones, Oksana and Kalyna, hadn't quite mastered that critical life lesson yet—another reason I needed more time with my family.

The highlight of my retirement ceremony was a personal letter President Obama had written to me. It was read out loud at the ceremony:

I want to personally thank you for your more than four decades of service to our nation: as a Special Forces non-commissioned officer and officer, CIA operations officer, national security policy maker and Intelligence Community leader. Your storied career has become legend in the national security community: from your leading role in the 1980s as the principal strategist for the program that defeated the Red Army in Afghanistan and accelerated the end of the Cold War, to your leadership in devising the strategy that would disrupt, dismantle and defeat core al-Qa'ida in the Pakistan border region, and your key role in planning for the operation that brought justice to Usama Bin Ladin. Finally, you have led Defense Intelligence through a comprehensive, mission-focused transformation—aligning capabilities for 21st-century challenges and driving integration between the National and Military Intelligence Programs. For 42 years, you have had a knack for being precisely where our nation has needed you most. Our nation owes you a great debt for your service. I wish you all the best in whatever adventure comes next. I'm certain you will find a way to continue to lead and contribute. Thank you for your professionalism, dedication and stalwart love of our nation.

Ten days earlier, Senator Richard Burr, the Republican chairman of the Senate's Select Committee on Intelligence, had read a statement into the *Congressional Record* recognizing my service. A flag was also flown over the U.S. Capitol in my honor. Senator Burr recognized my roles in driving the Soviets out of Afghanistan as a CIA officer in the 1980s and in the operation that brought justice to Usama Bin Ladin. He also noted that my service as a senior national security policy official had spanned the administrations of George W. Bush and Barack Obama. He said that I had helped shape U.S. national security policy for three decades and the nation was safer as a result. I greatly appreciated the special recognition.

The Pentagon ceremony, the letter from President Obama, and the recognition of my service by the SSCI had been an incredible send-off. But my farewell wasn't quite over yet.

Many at CIA who wanted to attend my retirement ceremony at the Pentagon weren't able to, so CIA hosted its own retirement ceremony for me in its Atrium in late May. What was especially meaningful about CIA's goodbye was that it had been organized by the career workforce. As I walked to the Atrium, I passed by CIA's small internal museum, with memorabilia from the Cold War to the raid that killed Usama Bin Ladin. On the wall at the museum's entrance is an inscription that sums up the agency's operational mission: "CIA does what others cannot do and goes where others cannot go." It gives me goose bumps every time I walk by it.

There was a big reception waiting for me in the Atrium as former colleagues from all components of the agency came to say their goodbyes. I was really touched and didn't want to leave. Before the reception, a few senior colleagues I had worked especially closely with over the years hosted a lunch for me in CIA's Executive Dining Room. That meant a lot as well.

Finally, after the formal events were over, I was asked to come to CIA's Counterterrorism Center for one last visit to see "Jane," a colleague who has played an absolutely central role in our war with al-Qa'ida. We reviewed a few of the counterterrorism operations we had collaborated on recently and chatted about what we had accomplished and what there was still left to do. America is very fortunate that she has dedicated her life to serving her country. I really miss working with her.

RECEIVING THE NATIONAL SECURITY MEDAL AND DONOVAN AWARD

In late June, President Obama presented me with the National Security Medal, our nation's highest award in the field of intelligence. Melana and four of my five daughters were able to attend the ceremony in the Oval Office. Susan Rice, the president's national security adviser, and several other senior White House staff joined us as an aide read the extensive citation. The president pinned the medal on my chest, and then graciously spent time talking with Melana and each of my girls and posed for several photos. I was profoundly grateful.

Meeting with the president in the Oval Office was an unforgettable experience for my girls, and they treasured every moment. A few years earlier, when Denis McDonough, the president's chief of staff and my friend, learned that our daughter Oksana had the same birthday as the president, he arranged for an autographed photo and a personal note from the president to be sent to her on her birthday.

It had been the honor of a lifetime to serve under President Obama for six years. It had also been a great honor to serve under President George W. Bush between 2007 and 2009. In all, I had served under six presidents during the course of my career.

Two years later, I received the William J. Donovan Award, named after the founder of World War II's Office of Strategic Services, on the seventy-fifth anniversary of the OSS's founding. The OSS had been the predecessor of both the CIA and the Special Forces, and Donovan was a personal hero of mine, so receiving the prestigious award was especially meaningful. Previous recipients included three U.S. presidents, Dwight Eisenhower, Ronald Reagan, and George H. W. Bush. Bob Gates, Leon Panetta, Eric Olson, and Bill McRaven are also among the select few who have received the award. Margaret Thatcher had also received it, a fact I mentioned in my acceptance remarks, noting that my right thumb wants to manipulate the toggle switch on a Blowpipe surface-to-air missile launcher every time I think of her.

The OSS Society had made an over-the-top but lovely film about my career, which was shown at the black-tie dinner. Bob Gates, Jim Clapper, Bill McRaven, and Jim Mattis, at the time our secretary of defense, all gave tributes. My dear friend Eric Olson presented the award. Melana, all five of my girls, my brother and his wife, my in-laws, and a soon-to-be son-in-law attended with me, along with Todd Lowery and several other close friends. My old boss from my CIA days, Bert Dunn, attended, as did Claudette Avrakotos, Gust's widow, which made the event even more special. It was another unforgettable experience.

As I completed my long goodbye, I had just one regret: I wished that I could begin my Special Forces, CIA, and DOD career all over again. Like John le Carré's fictional master spy George Smiley, I've concluded that a major purpose of my life might have been to help end the times in which I lived.[2] Writing my memoirs, though, has also made me realize that I'm not ready to give up the fight. I don't know what the future holds, but I want to continue to contribute to America's security in any way I can. I hope this book will be part of that contribution.

ACKNOWLEDGMENTS

I incurred a number of debts in writing this book, and, more important, in living the life that led to it. My father and mother, the late Alfred and Betty Vickers, did not live to see most of the events in this book. I thank them for believing in me, even when they had their doubts about the path I had embarked upon. Before their deaths in 1980 and 1994, they could not have been prouder of what I had accomplished, though they knew few of the details of what had actually transpired. I hope that if they had been able to know the full story, they would have been even prouder.

I wish to also thank the late Dr. Anthony DeRiggi for planting the initial seed that started me on this journey, then–Staff Sergeant Jim Maniatis for showing me that I could enlist directly into the Special Forces if I had what it takes, and Dr. Patricia Dice at the University of Alabama for helping me complete my B.A. in the shortest amount of time.

To my many colleagues in special operations, CIA, DOD, the intelligence community, the State Department, and the National Security Council, and to the many international partners I worked with over the years, you made whatever I was able to accomplish possible. There are far too many of you to list, but suffice it to say, my debts include those who mentored me in special operations and intelligence and, in later years, in strategy. In the later years of my career, the example set by great special operators like Eric Olson, Bill McRaven, Stan McChrystal, and many others reaffirmed for me why I wanted to become a special operator in the first place. The same is true for my CIA brothers and sisters who go where no one else can go and do what no one else can do. America is truly blessed that men and women of such caliber continue to answer our nation's call to duty. It was the honor of a lifetime to serve alongside all of you in such noble endeavors. It is with great sadness that I note that many of you did not live to see this book published. You are gone, but you are certainly not forgotten. I hope I got your story right.

I have a special debt to the heroic members of the Afghan resistance. You defeated an evil empire against all odds and changed the world for the better. I can only hope that the Afghan people will someday receive the blessings of liberty that have long been denied them.

I'd like to thank a few leaders and mentors who believed in me at various stages of my career: Colonel Eugene Russell (U.S. Army, retired); the late Bill Rooney, the late Gust Avrakotos, the late Bert Dunn, and the late Andrew Marshall; Eliot Cohen; Eric Edelman and Michèle Flournoy; Jim Clapper; and Robert Gates and Leon Panetta. Colonel Russell gave me my first big command. Bill gave me my first major operational responsibility in CIA while I was still just a trainee. Gust and Bert selected me for and supported me in the job of a lifetime. Andy Marshall taught me much about strategy and net assessment and encouraged me to think imaginatively and rigorously about future warfare and the future of American power. Eliot Cohen provided me with an unparalleled graduate education in strategic studies that laid the foundation for my service in senior national security positions. I could not wish for better bosses and colleagues than Eric and Michèle, and I likewise could not wish for a better DNI or intelligence partner and friend than Jim Clapper. Secretary Gates was my continuity across national security eras and a constant example in wise, decisive, and principled leadership. I am hard pressed to think of a statesman who has served America as long or as ably during the past several decades. Like Secretary Gates, Secretary Panetta taught me much about decisive leadership at the highest levels of government. He also taught me about the politics of national security, the pulse of America, and what it means to be a true patriot.

As I reflect back upon my career, I still stand in awe of President Reagan and former director of central intelligence Bill Casey for believing that it was possible to drive the Soviets out of Afghanistan, dismantle the Soviet Empire, and bring the Cold War to an end—and for supporting the efforts that turned that vision into a reality. It is still hard to believe that it really happened the way it did. As my former boss Bob Gates has written, "It was a glorious crusade."

I am likewise profoundly grateful to President George W. Bush and President Barack Obama for giving me the opportunity to return to government service, contribute to the dismantling of al-Qa'ida, deliver justice to Usama Bin Ladin, expand our special operations forces, and transform our intelligence and defense capabilities for a new era of great power competition. It was the greatest privilege to serve in your administrations.

Several close friends and former colleagues read the draft manuscript to help ensure its completeness and factual accuracy. I wish to thank Jonathan Bank, Jim Clapper, Eliot Cohen, Chris Darby, Robert Gates, Todd Lowery, Jim Mattis, Stan McChrystal, Bill McRaven, Michael Morell, Eric Olson, Phil Reilly, and Jim Thomas for their very helpful comments. You made the book much better than it otherwise would have been. Any errors of fact or judgment that remain are mine alone.

I wish to thank the Defense Office of Prepublication and Security Review, and in particular, Kelly McHale, for shepherding the manuscript, despite the travails of the COVID-19 pandemic, through the required U.S. government–wide, prepublication security review. The review was thoroughly professional and eminently fair. Thank you, Kelly and the entire DOPSR team, for your lead role in clearing the manuscript for public release.

I also wish to thank the professionals at CIA's Prepublication Classification Review Board for their review of the entire manuscript. Thank you for helping to make this book possible.

I wish to thank my agent, Eric Lupfer, and my editors at Knopf, Andrew Miller and Todd Portnowitz. Your belief in this project, your patience during this book's long gestation, and your skill in editing it turned it into a book that is as good as I can make it. It was my hope from the beginning that this book would be more than a memoir, that it would be instructive to future generations of Americans. To the extent I succeeded in this aim, I owe the credit to Eric, Andrew, and Todd.

Finally, I wish to thank my wife, Melana, for her unwavering love and support. A professional intelligence officer in her own right, Melana patiently but persistently encouraged me to finish the book, read and reread every page of the manuscript, and offered many helpful edits and suggestions for how to tell my story better. She was my first and best editor. No man could wish for a better wife and partner in all things.

Last but not least are my wonderful daughters, Alexandra, Natasha, Sophia, Oksana, and Kalyna. I thank them for their steadfast love and support and hope they are proud of their dad. I could not be prouder of them.

NOTES

PROLOGUE

1. For Clapper's recollection of this trip, see James R. Clapper, *Facts and Fears: Hard Truths from a Life in Intelligence*, with Trey Brown (New York: Viking, 2018), 119–20. Clapper became the director of national intelligence in 2010, and I succeeded him as USD(I).

2. Bruce Riedel, *What We Won: America's Secret War in Afghanistan, 1979–89* (Washington, DC: Brookings Institution Press, 2014), ix.

3. I used as a model my former boss's first memoir, Robert M. Gates, *From the Shadows: The Ultimate Insider's Story of Five Presidents and How They Won the Cold War* (New York: Simon & Schuster, 1996), which covers Gates's career as a CIA officer and member of the National Security Council staff. A subsequent memoir, *Duty: Memoirs of a Secretary at War* (New York: Alfred A. Knopf, 2014), covers his years as secretary of defense.

CHAPTER ONE GREEN BERET

1. Henry Kamm, "C.I.A. Role in Laos: Advising an Army," *New York Times*, March 12, 1971.

2. Like most men of his era, my father made his living by practicing a trade. He had been co-owner of a successful funeral business in Chicago and had owned an airplane and boat. He was also a very skilled carpenter who'd come to Los Angeles from Chicago with his Italian-born parents in the early 1950s to build and then sell or rent small apartment complexes and single-family homes. For a few years, he also built movie sets for Twentieth Century–Fox. My mother worked the graveyard shift as an admitting clerk at Kaiser Foundation Hospital, subsisting on four hours of sleep so she could be awake when I came home from school. After she earned her GED, she eventually became an assistant hospital administrator in charge of several departments, providing income stability for our family after a trucking business my father had started went bust, wiping out all our family's savings.

3. Today, prospective Green Berets are required to complete a nineteen-day Special Forces Assessment and Selection Course before attending the Special Forces Qualification Course. It better prepares SF candidates for the physical demands of SFQC, but it does not assess their ability to make critical decisions as rigorously as the SFSB did.

4. SFQC is a much longer course these days. It now includes a course in survival, evasion, resistance, and escape (SERE) and training in one of several foreign languages, depending on which group a soldier is being assigned to. Officer training is also now integrated with enlisted training. In my day, officer training was separate, and we received advanced SERE and language training after we completed SFQC and joined an SF Group.

CHAPTER TWO SPECIAL FORCES OPERATOR AND COMMANDER

1. The 10th Group commander during my final year at Fort Devens, Colonel Othar Shalikashvili, was an émigré (a native Georgian). Several other émigrés held command and other senior positions in the Group.

2. Colonel Francis Kelly, *U.S. Army Special Forces, 1961–1971* (Washington, DC: Department of the Army, 1973), 93–95.

3. Given the high terrorist threat in Europe during the 1970s, SF Berlin, or "Detachment A," as it was known, was tasked with providing a counterterrorism force for hostage rescue operations. Elements from Det A participated in the failed mission to rescue American hostages in Iran in April 1980. In addition to its stay-behind mission, Det A also had a task (an impossible one, as it turned out) that required a few of its teams to escape from Berlin in the event of conflict with the Soviets and conduct special operations in East Germany. See James Stejskal, *Special Forces Berlin: Clandestine Cold War Operations of the US Army's Elite, 1956–1990* (Havertown, PA: Casemate, 2017).

4. For additional details on Special Forces and special atomic demolition munitions, see ibid., 55–59; and Colonel Tom Davis, *The Most Fun I Ever Had with My Clothes On: A March from Private to Colonel: A Memoir* (Sylva, NC: Old Mountain Press, 2014).

5. A second military free-fall technique is high altitude, high opening, or HAHO, in which jumpers open their chutes at very high altitudes, allowing them to traverse much greater ground distances and fly across a border under canopy undetected. Using HAHO, a jumper is under canopy and breathing oxygen for hours instead of minutes and employs navigation aids.

6. U.S. special operators attempted to rescue the American hostages being held in Iran in April 1980, but they had to abort the mission before they reached Tehran. Eight special operators died when a rescue force helicopter crashed into a C-130 transport at a desert landing site as the force was leaving Iran. The assault force commander aborted the mission after losing three of the mission's eight helicopters due to mechanical problems and a blinding sandstorm. Planning for a second rescue attempt began almost immediately, and the new unit's recruiters interviewed officers

and NCOs from all of the Special Forces Groups for possible inclusion in the operation. The task force that attempted the original rescue attempt had been hastily assembled from disparate units from across the military services. This was judged to be one of the causes behind the mission's failure. As a result, the Joint Special Operations Command was created in 1981 to better prepare special operators for these and other missions.

7. Troops in special mission units are commanded by majors or lieutenant commanders.

CHAPTER THREE GOING TO WAR WITH CIA

1. The CT Program also included a few new hires headed for the Directorate of Intelligence (now called the Directorate of Analysis) and the Directorate of Science and Technology. Today, each directorate has its own version of the CT Program.

2. The CT program had previously included a six-week covert action and counter-intelligence course following special operations training, but it was discontinued beginning with my class.

3. For additional details, see Martha D. Peterson, *The Widow Spy: My CIA Journey from the Jungles of Laos to Prison in Moscow* (Wilmington, NC: Red Canary Press, 2012).

4. Described in Gates, *From the Shadows*, 177.

5. For a discussion of the proposed covert action program in Suriname, see George P. Shultz, *Turmoil and Triumph: My Years as Secretary of State* (New York: Charles Scribner's Sons, 1993), 292–97. A brief reference to potential action in Suriname is also in Gates, *From the Shadows*, 256. Use of force options in Suriname are briefly discussed in Duane R. Clarridge, *A Spy for All Seasons: My Life in the CIA* (New York: Scribner, 1997), 248.

6. Gates, *From the Shadows*, 143.

7. Clarridge, *Spy for All Seasons*, 250–56.

8. National Security Decision Directive 110A, "Response to Caribbean Governments' Request to Restore Democracy in Grenada," White House, Oct. 23, 1983.

9. Clarridge, *Spy for All Seasons*, 255.

10. For unclassified official histories of the planning and execution of the invasion, see Ronald H. Cole, *Operation Urgent Fury: The Planning and Execution of Joint Operations in Grenada, 12 October to 3 November 1983* (Washington, DC: Office of the Joint Chiefs of Staff, Joint History Office, 1997); and *Operation Urgent Fury: The Invasion of Grenada, October 1983*, U.S. Army Center for Military History, CMH Pub 70-114-1.

CHAPTER FOUR COUNTERTERRORISM OPERATIONS, OPERATIONAL CERTIFICATION

1. Mohtashamipur died at age seventy-four in 2021.

2. Syria was also complicit in the so-called Mountain War. Druze militia, supported by Syria, regularly shelled the Marines. The battleship *New Jersey*, with sixteen-inch guns firing shells that weighed as much as a Volkswagen, provided fire support for

the Marines. Shi'a militia in South Beirut also regularly fired on Marine positions. See Col. Timothy Geraghty, USMC (Ret.), *Peacekeepers at War: Beirut 1983—the Marine Commander Tells His Story* (Washington, DC: Potomac Books, 2009.)

3. See Fred Burton and Samuel M. Katz, *Beirut Rules: The Murder of a CIA Station Chief and Hezbollah's War Against America* (New York: Berkley, 2018), 333–42.

4. The SOTC was dropped from the CT program after the Cold War ended. Recently, CIA's Deputy Director for Operations announced plans to add a shorter version of the course back into the training program for operations officers.

5. The DDO eliminated home basing for operations officers several years ago. The decision received increasingly critical reviews, however, noting the time required to develop the expertise needed for operations against China, Russia, or in the Arab world, and home basing was recently reinstated.

6. With the breakup of IAD into separate organizations, Glerum's plan was stillborn. It was later implemented to some extent, however, by the Special Activities Center and its predecessor organizations by having paramilitary operations officers attend the Ops Course and serve a few tours as regular case officers. Post-9/11, a few paramilitary operations officers have risen to the top ranks in the clandestine service.

CHAPTER FIVE **THE GREAT COMMISSION**

1. Director of Central Intelligence, "Use of Toxins and Other Lethal Chemicals in Southeast Asia and Afghanistan," Special National Intelligence Estimate, Volume 1—Key Judgments, SNIE 11/50/37-82JX, Feb. 2, 1982, approved for public release 2010. See also Memorandum to Holders, "Use of Toxins and Other Lethal Chemicals in Southeast Asia and Afghanistan," SNIE 11/50/37-82, approved for public release 2008.

2. For additional details on the rise of the Afghanistan Communist Party and the Saur Revolution, see Peter Tomsen, *The Wars of Afghanistan: Messianic Terrorism, Tribal Conflicts, and the Failures of Great Powers* (New York: PublicAffairs, 2011), 87–178. A career diplomat, Tomsen served as special envoy to the Afghan resistance during the George H. W. Bush administration.

3. The full scope of Soviet intelligence activity in Afghanistan before and after the 1979 invasion would not become known to us until the KGB archivist Vasili Mitrokhin defected in 1992. See Vasili Mitrokhin, "The KGB in Afghanistan," Working Paper 40, Cold War International History Project, Woodrow Wilson International Center for Scholars, July 2002/2009. See also Christopher Andrew and Vasili Mitrokhin, *The World Was Going Our Way: The KGB and the Battle for the Third World* (New York: Basic Books, 2005), 386–402.

4. Consisting of sparsely populated and isolated settlements tucked in the steep valleys of the towering Hindu Kush range, Nuristan, on which Rudyard Kipling's "The Man Who Would Be King" is based, is one of the most remote provinces in Afghanistan. The Hazaras, Afghanistan's third-largest ethnic group after the Pashtuns and Tajiks,

are Shi'a, and are looked down upon by the majority Sunni population. Their name comes from "Hazar," or "one thousand," which is thought to have originated from one of Genghis Khan's military formations.

5. Vladimir Kuzichkin, *Inside the KGB: My Life in Soviet Espionage* (New York: Pantheon Books, 1990), 315.

6. For additional details on the Soviet invasion, see Gregory Feifer, *The Great Gamble: The Soviet War in Afghanistan* (New York: HarperCollins, 2009), 9–84; and Rodric Braithwaite, *Afgantsy: The Russians in Afghanistan, 1979–89* (Oxford: Oxford University Press, 2011), 58–117. For the official Russian General Staff account, see Russian General Staff, *The Soviet-Afghan War: How a Superpower Fought and Lost*, trans. and ed. Lester W. Grau and Michael A. Gress (Lawrence: University Press of Kansas, 2002), 15–18.

7. The Soviets had used deception to ensure that their invasion would have the element of surprise and would largely be unopposed by Afghan forces. Amin had requested Soviet forces to help pacify the north, and so the motorized rifle divisions entered without incident. Soviet generals coordinated the entry of Soviet forces with senior Afghan officials while concealing their ultimate purpose.

8. KGB snipers attempted to kill Amin on a Kabul road, but the sudden acceleration of his car foiled the plot. An earlier attempt by Amin's KGB cook to poison him also failed, though it seriously injured his nephew and secret police chief.

9. U.S. intelligence had observed the mobilization and increased readiness of Soviet forces in central Asia and the unusually high alert status of Soviet airborne forces, but had assessed that the Soviets were unlikely to intervene in Afghanistan on a large scale. Gates, *From the Shadows*, 131–34. See also Douglas MacEachin, "Predicting the Soviet Invasion of Afghanistan: The Intelligence Community's Record," Central Intelligence Agency, Center for the Study of Intelligence.

10. Feifer, *Great Gamble*, 83.

11. Overall, there were some five hundred Soviet fighters, fighter-bombers, and helicopters deployed in Afghanistan at any given time.

12. The 40th Army's ground order of battle in 1980 consisted of three motorized rifle divisions, one airborne division, two separate motorized rifle brigades, one air assault brigade, and three separate regiments.

13. Russian General Staff, *Soviet-Afghan War*, 44.

14. In addition to conducting hit-and-run raids against Soviet and Afghan forces in the Panjshir during the offensive, Massoud was able to conduct operations outside it, including a raid that destroyed several MiG-21 fighters on the ground at Bagram Air Base.

15. We also paid attention to another Wardak, Rahim, a former colonel in the Afghan Army, who was affiliated with the National Islamic Front. He would become a defense minister in the new Afghan government after the fall of the Taliban.

16. See "The Soviet Invasion of Afghanistan: Five Years After," Central Intelligence Agency, May 1985, approved for public release 1999. The Soviets generally had the same assessment of insurgent strength. See Russian General Staff, *Soviet-Afghan War*, 24.

17. Gates, *From the Shadows,* 147; Charles G. Cogan, "Partners in Time: The CIA and Afghanistan Since 1979," *World Policy Journal* 10, no. 2 (Summer 1993): 79.

18. Riedel, *What We Won,* 102.

19. Gates, *From the Shadows,* 146.

20. More than a few in CIA suspected that Charlie was getting a commission on the deal, though we never found any evidence of that. One of my early tasks was overseeing the training program for Pakistani instructors and the Afghan resistance on the new weapon. We deployed the first Oerlikons into Afghanistan in the summer of 1985.

21. Howard Phillips Hart, *A Life for a Life: A Memoir: My Career in Espionage Working for the Central Intelligence Agency* (Morrisville, NC: Lulu Publishing Services, 2015).

22. For additional details on CIA's relationship with Pakistan during the Soviet-Afghan War, see Riedel, *What We Won,* 56–73.

23. For Prince Turki's view of the Afghanistan program, see Prince Turki Al-Faisal Al-Saud, *The Afghanistan File* (Cowes, Isle of Wight: Arabian Publishing, 2021).

24. For additional details on the relationship with the Saudis during the Soviet-Afghan War, see Riedel, *What We Won,* 74–80.

25. When he wasn't increasing our budget, he could usually be found in the company of beautiful women. His largely female staff was known as "Charlie's Angels," and they were as formidable as the TV show's protagonists.

26. Gates, *From the Shadows,* 319–21.

CHAPTER SIX DEVELOPING A WAR-WINNING STRATEGY

1. George Crile, *Charlie Wilson's War* (New York: Grove Press, 2003). The movie of the same name was released in 2007.

2. The program in turn also made important contributions to U.S. intelligence on Soviet weapons. "SOVMAT"—the clandestine procurement of Soviet war matériel for our military's use—was an important worldwide tasking for CIA. It enabled our military to develop countermeasures, and the war in Afghanistan was our most productive source of this matériel. We turned over Hind helicopters, an Su-22 fighter-bomber, and a lot of other war matériel to DOD.

3. Additional betrayals by another CIA officer, Edward Lee Howard, and by FBI special agent Robert Hanssen compromised other operations and assets. Ames was a counterintelligence disaster for CIA of the highest magnitude. The Soviets, it should be noted, suffered equally grave losses during the spy wars of the 1970s and 1980s. And in contrast to our traitors, who were mostly troubled souls, the Soviets had been betrayed by their elites, those who benefited the most from the system. It seemed to me that the spy war was telling us something much larger about the U.S.-Soviet competition during the final decade of the Cold War.

4. Riedel, *What We Won,* 48–49.

5. A "hunter-killer" surface-to-air missile team with two to three gunners per team might conduct two offensive engagements per month. Additional SAMs would also

be expended in defensive operations. I planned on fielding twenty to forty SAM teams.

6. Gates, *From the Shadows*, 310–11.

7. To further expand its training throughput, ISI also trained some mujahedin as instructors in guerrilla warfare weaponry and tactics—a "train the trainer" approach—to provide additional training to resistance fighting groups in their operational base areas inside Afghanistan.

8. Iman had come up through the SSG and had attended the Special Forces Officer Course at Fort Bragg, North Carolina. Khawaja had served in the Pakistani Air Force's Special Service Wing before joining ISI. During the 1990s, Iman would serve as a key adviser to Mullah Omar, the leader of the Taliban. After I had returned to government service as an assistant secretary of defense, Colonel Iman reached out to me in 2008 through a former CIA colleague to ask if I was interested in meeting to discuss how the United States might reconcile with the Taliban. After consulting with my interagency colleagues, I declined. Both he and Khawaja were killed by militants in Pakistan's border region in 2010 and 2011.

CHAPTER SEVEN CRITICAL DECISIONS: MARCH 1985 TO JANUARY 1986

1. Achieving escalation dominance is by no means always feasible. The most obvious case is in the strategic nuclear realm where the best that can be achieved is deterrence through mutually assured destruction. That's not to say that nuclear superpowers don't strive for escalation dominance, but thus far they've accepted that they can't achieve it. Simply possessing superior capabilities, moreover, is not always sufficient for escalation dominance. A nuclear-armed power, for example, can lose to a non-nuclear one, as we did in Vietnam and more recently in Afghanistan. The key is *usable* escalatory capability. Escalation dominance of course also cuts both ways. As I noted earlier, Iran and Hezbollah had it against us in Lebanon between 1983 and 1985.

2. Cited in Kirsten Lundberg, "Politics of a Covert Action: The US, the Mujahideen, and the Stinger Missile," John F. Kennedy School of Government Case Study Program, Harvard University, 1999, 21.

3. National Security Decision Directive 166, "U.S. Policy, Programs, and Strategy in Afghanistan," White House, March 27, 1985, Top Secret Veil, declassified in full on Sept. 8, 2008.

4. Lundberg, "Politics of a Covert Action," 23–27.

5. Casey was by no means alone in his pessimistic view of the Afghan resistance's prospects. Deputy Director McMahon reportedly told Casey that "it is unlikely that the Soviet Army would allow itself to be defeated." Chuck Cogan, the chief of the NE Division in CIA, said that "not until 1985 did it appear possible that the Soviet Union could be forced to withdraw." Republican Senator Malcolm Wallop of Wyoming, a staunch supporter of anti-Communist rebels around the world, stated in early 1985, "I don't know anyone who believes that we will overthrow the Soviet-supported

regime in Afghanistan." See James M. Scott, *Deciding to Intervene: The Reagan Doctrine and American Foreign Policy* (Durham, NC: Duke University Press, 1996), 48.

6. Gates, *From the Shadows*, 199. For a biography of Casey, see Joseph E. Persico, *Casey: The Lives and Secrets of William J. Casey, from the OSS to the CIA* (New York: Penguin Books, 1990).

7. The kits included plastic explosives, detonating cord, blasting caps, electronic and fire-initiated firing systems, and time pencils for delayed detonation.

8. In our search for a more effective round for the 12.7 mm machine gun, I also explored restarting the manufacturing line of a tungsten carbide-tipped, .50-caliber round one of our allies used to produce. CIA tests had shown that the round could penetrate the Hind's armor. The costs of restarting the line and resizing the round to 12.7 mm, slightly larger in diameter than a .50 caliber, were prohibitive, however, so we decided not to pursue this option.

9. For a discussion of the U.S.-China intelligence relationship and China's role as a supplier to the Afghanistan Covert Action Program, see Gates, *From the Shadows*, 122–23, 174–75, 348–49. See also Jack Devine, *Good Hunting: An American Spymaster's Story*, with Vernon Loeb (New York: Sarah Crichton Books, 2014), 36–40; and Riedel, *What We Won*, 63, 107.

10. William J. Daugherty, *Executive Secrets: Covert Action and the Presidency* (Lexington: University Press of Kentucky, 2004), 93.

11. Years later, I reminded Gates of this episode and told him how much I admired the bureaucratic courage he had shown. As before, he just shrugged and smiled. There was one final wrinkle to the MON. DDCI McMahon thought that it might be useful "political insurance" if the Joint Chiefs took a look at our weapons mix, given the massive increases in program funding. McMahon's request was assigned to the Special Warfare Center at Fort Bragg for action, and the answer came back ninety days later. The Joint Chiefs agreed that our weapons mix was sound, and had no recommendations to alter it.

12. For U.S. and British support for the Blowpipe's introduction into Afghanistan, see Riedel, *What We Won*, 63.

13. Milt Bearden and James Risen, *The Main Enemy: The Inside Story of the CIA's Final Showdown with the KGB* (New York: Random House, 2003), 245.

14. Shultz, *Turmoil and Triumph*, 652.

CHAPTER EIGHT **DRIVING THE SOVIETS OUT**

1. CIA, "The Soviet Invasion of Afghanistan."

2. CIA's analysts noted that if the situation were to deteriorate drastically in Afghanistan, the Soviets could expand their forces by as many as 50,000 men, but even then they would not have enough troops to maintain control in much of the countryside as long as the insurgents had access to strong external support and open borders. It was pretty clear that at least ten times that number would be required, and numbers

that large were out of the question. Soviet war planning prioritized NATO as the central front in a global, multi-theater war with the United States, with China as the second front, and Southwest Asia as a distant third. This put an upper limit on Soviet escalation options in Afghanistan.

3. William E. Odom, *The Collapse of the Soviet Military* (New Haven, CT: Yale University Press, 1998), 249.

4. Riedel, *What We Won*, 37–39.

5. Mitrokhin, "KGB in Afghanistan."

6. Michael R. Fenzel, *No Miracles: The Failure of Soviet Decision-Making in the Afghan War* (Stanford, CA: Stanford University Press, 2017), 97.

7. For a summary of Mullah Malang's ambush in September 1984, see Ali Ahmad Jalali and Lester W. Grau, eds., *Afghan Guerrilla Warfare* (St. Paul: MBI, 2001), 43–48.

8. Ibid., 97–99, 63–65.

9. Mohammad Yousaf and Mark Adkin, *Afghanistan: The Bear Trap: The Defeat of a Super-power* (Havertown, PA: Casemate, 1992), 151, 157.

10. Yousaf was passed over for promotion and retired from the army in 1987 when it was discovered that ISI had been supporting limited cross-border attacks by the mujahedin into Soviet Uzbekistan. He then progressively went off the deep end in his animus toward CIA and the West. In 1988, following a massive explosion that destroyed ten thousand tons of program-supplied weapons and ammunition at the ISI's Ojhri arms depot in Rawalpindi, Yousaf argued that with the Soviet withdrawal under way, the United States no longer supported the Afghan resistance, and that the explosion at Ojhri had been a joint CIA-KGB operation. Two years later, he authored an article in a Pakistan daily in which he argued that the United States was implementing a "deliberate and well-thought-out covert plan" to deny victory to the fundamentalists and prevent them from establishing an Islamic state in Afghanistan. Yousaf's ultimate goal was an Islamic bloc consisting of Pakistan, Afghanistan, Iran, Turkey, and the Islamic Soviet Republics aligned with China that would stand against America, what was left of the Soviet Union, and India. It was chilling to read.

11. Right after the Soviet withdrawal, ISI would encourage the mujahedin to again shift to conventional war and conduct a direct frontal assault on Jalalabad. It was another disaster, leaving three thousand resistance fighters dead and providing a much-needed psychological boost to the beleaguered Afghan government. ISI also tried to install Hekmatyar in Kabul through failed coup attempts after the Soviets withdrew. Massoud saved the day in October 1990 by calling a *shura* of resistance commanders from all over Afghanistan and getting them to adopt an "out-in" military strategy, focusing on simultaneous operations against district capitals before trying to take provincial capitals and provincial capitals before trying to take Kabul. The Taliban would follow a similar strategy in 2021.

12. See Alan J. Kupperman, "The Stinger Missile and U.S. Intervention in Afghanistan," *Political Science Quarterly* 114, no. 2 (1999): 219–63. See also Fenzel, *No Miracles*, 6, 100–101.

13. Fenzel, *No Miracles*, 93.

14. Kupperman, "Stinger Missile and U.S. Intervention in Afghanistan," 239–40.

1. That one of the rockets had struck that particular spot was a stroke of luck, but the mujahedin were shelling Kabul and other targets around Afghanistan daily. They had acquired plenty of practice with direct lay aiming methods (taking a direct bearing to the target and adjusting the elevation and direction of the launcher), and the laws of probability suggested they were bound to get lucky sooner or later. Plus, CIA had been supplying the mujahedin with satellite-imagery-derived target folders that enhanced the accuracy of the shelling attacks.

2. Bearden and Risen, *Main Enemy*, 227–31. See also Crile, *Charlie Wilson's War*, 424–26.

3. For details of the shoot-down, see Bearden and Risen, *Main Enemy*, 242–52; and Yousaf and Adkin, *Bear Trap*, 174–78. A second team, also from Hekmatyar's party, had been deployed to the Kabul area at the same time as Ghaffar's team had been deployed to Jalalabad, but it did not have success, firing three missiles at Soviet fighters and fighter-bombers that were out of range. That team received refresher training in Pakistan and scored two shoot-downs on its next deployment.

4. Devine, *Good Hunting*, 93.

5. A quarter century later I was invited to CIA headquarters with several of my former colleagues from the 1980s for the unveiling of a painting CIA's Historical Office had commissioned about the Jalalabad shoot-downs. Titled *First Sting*, it hangs today in one of the main-floor corridors of CIA's headquarters building, along with paintings of other famous operations conducted by the agency. I also have a print copy (signed by Charlie Wilson and me) prominently displayed in my home office.

6. Gates delved into the operational details of the program, receiving regular updates and traveling to Pakistan to see the program in action firsthand. (Gates, *From the Shadows*, 429.) A quarter century later, when Gates was secretary of defense and I was assistant secretary of defense for special operations, low-intensity conflict, and interdependent capabilities and undersecretary of defense for intelligence, Gates and I would reminisce about the program, its success in driving the Soviets out of Afghanistan, and the briefings he had received, including more than a few from me.

7. For more on McMahon, see "An Interview with Former DDCI John N. McMahon," *Studies in Intelligence*, Central Intelligence Agency, approved for public release June 28, 2010. McMahon had had a distinguished career in CIA, serving in all of its directorates and leading two of them (the DDO and DDI) before becoming deputy director of central intelligence in 1982. He had managed the U-2 program and had prevailed in ensuring CIA's leadership of the nation's overhead (space) reconnaissance program when others at CIA, including Director McCone, were in favor of giving it to the Air Force. As the deputy director for intelligence, he forged one of the most significant reforms in the analytical directorate's history by moving the DI from a functional organization (separate political, economic, military, and leadership analytical offices) to a geographically oriented one where functional analysts were integrated into single organizations.

8. Gates, *From the Shadows*, 400–403. Gates makes a strong if circumstantial case that

Casey did not know about the diversion of funds from the Iran operation to the contras, citing sworn testimony from National Security Adviser John Poindexter and other sources.

9. "The War in Afghanistan: Taking Stock," Central Intelligence Agency, Feb. 1987, sanitized copy approved for public release, Sept. 13, 2011.

10. Yousaf and Adkin, *Bear Trap*, 186.

11. Braithwaite, *Afgantsy*, 203.

12. It should be remembered that when we decided to pursue the Blowpipe and improved SA-7s at the beginning of 1985, the Stinger wasn't an option. Had the Stinger not been approved by President Reagan and President Zia, we would have worked to make both systems an even greater success. It should also not be lost that Prime Minister Thatcher and Deng Xiaoping made very gutsy decisions in the first half of 1985 to authorize the deployment of the improved SA-7 and Blowpipe into Afghanistan.

13. Russian General Staff, *Soviet-Afghan War*, 65–69.

14. Ibid., 44.

15. Braithwaite, *Afgantsy*, 174.

16. Alexander Alexiev, *Inside the Soviet Army in Afghanistan* (Santa Monica, CA: Rand, 1988), vi.

17. Central Intelligence Agency, "USSR: Domestic Fallout from the Afghan War," Feb. 1988, approved for public release April 26, 2013.

18. Bearden and Risen, *Main Enemy*, 358–59.

19. In 1993, I attended a ceremony in CIA's auditorium (called "the Bubble" due to its geodesic shape) to honor Charlie Wilson for his critical support of the Afghanistan Covert Action Program. Most of my former program colleagues were there—Bert, Gust, and many others. Frank Anderson, then chief of NE Division, presented the award, making Charlie an "Honored Colleague" of the division.

20. Anthony Arnold, *The Fateful Pebble: Afghanistan's Role in the Fall of the Soviet Empire* (Novato, CA: Presidio Press, 1993), vii.

21. Riedel, *What We Won*, ix.

22. Ibid., 56–73.

23. Zia died, along with General Akhtar, eight other Pakistani generals, and U.S. ambassador to Pakistan Arnie Raphel in a mysterious plane crash shortly after taking off from Bahawalpur in August 1988. A crate of mangoes had been placed aboard just before takeoff, and suspicions immediately arose that a bomb had been inside the crate. Zia certainly had more than a few enemies, ranging from the KGB and KHAD, the Afghan secret police, to the PLO and other Pakistani generals. An investigation showed, however, that the most likely cause of the crash was mechanical failure.

24. Gates, *From the Shadows*, 327, 331.

25. For a good discussion of the role of the Arab volunteers and their ties to the Haqqanis, see Riedel, *What We Won*, 80–89.

26. Gates, *From the Shadows*, 560.

CHAPTER TEN BUILDING NEW INTELLECTUAL CAPITAL

1. Some of the material in this section has been recounted previously in Crile, *Charlie Wilson's War,* 428–36.

2. For those interested in the details of my dissertation, see Michael G. Vickers, "The Structure of Military Revolutions" (Johns Hopkins University, 2010). During my dissertation defense, Frank Fukuyama, famous for, among other things, his very provocative 1989 article declaring the "end of history," and the chair of my committee, thought that my structural theory wasn't predictive enough. Fortunately, the others came to my aid, arguing that providing a good explanatory framework for four thousand years of history was more than enough for one dissertation.

3. For a biography of Marshall, see Andrew Krepinevich and Barry Watts, *The Last Warrior: Andrew Marshall and the Shaping of Modern American Defense Strategy* (New York: Basic Books, 2015).

CHAPTER ELEVEN NO SANCTUARY

1. A number of the ideas that I had developed working for Andy Marshall—the growing threat posed by China's anti-access/area-denial strategy and the need to transform the Air Force and Navy to strengthen our deterrent in East Asia, for example—were reflected in the report, which I had played a large role in drafting. (For additional information, see "The Quadrennial Defense Review," Department of Defense, 2001.)

2. Riedel, *What We Won,* 83–89.

3. George Tenet, *At the Center of the Storm: My Years at the CIA,* with Bill Harlow (New York: HarperCollins, 2007), 102–3.

4. Michael Morell, *The Great War of Our Time: The CIA's Fight Against Terrorism from Al Qa'ida to ISIS,* with Bill Harlow (New York: Twelve, 2015), 13–20.

5. Tenet, *At the Center of the Storm,* 112–14.

6. Tenet, *At the Center of the Storm,* 111, 127. See also Henry A. Crumpton, *The Art of Intelligence: Lessons from a Life in the CIA's Clandestine Service* (New York: Penguin Press, 2012), 148–55; and Alec Bierbauer and Mark Cooter, *Never Mind, We'll Do It Ourselves: The Inside Story of How a Team of Renegades Broke Rules, Shattered Barriers, and Launched a Drone Warfare Revolution* (New York: Skyhorse, 2021).

7. For a discussion of the first Northern Alliance Liaison Team mission inside Afghanistan before the war, see Crumpton, *Art of Intelligence,* 127–32.

8. See Gary Schroen, *First In: An Insider's Account of How the CIA Spearheaded the War on Terror in Afghanistan* (New York: Ballantine Books, 2005), 3–8.

9. Tenet, *At the Center of the Storm,* 208.

10. For additional discussion of the Counterterrorism Center's decision to arm the Predator, see Crumpton, *Art of Intelligence,* 156–60.

11. Tenet, *At the Center of the Storm,* 175–78. Turning Pakistan away from its support of the

Taliban was critical. On September 13, Deputy Secretary of State Richard Armitage met with Pakistan's ISI chief and told him that Pakistan was either with us or against us. Armitage demanded that Pakistan apprehend al-Qa'ida operatives at the border, grant the United States blanket overflight and landing rights for all necessary military and intelligence operations, provide territorial access to American and allied intelligence agencies, and cut off all fuel shipments to the Taliban. Within hours, President Musharraf had agreed to all of Armitage's ultimatums.

12. Tenet, *At the Center of the Storm,* 207–8. CIA's Counterterrorism Center ran the war on the CIA side. Cofer Black, a charismatic career Africa hand who had been chief of station in Khartoum when the infamous terrorist Carlos the Jackal was captured, was CTC's director. Hank Crumpton, another career African hand, was chief of special operations for CTC. CTC has been the epicenter of U.S. counterterrorism operations since 9/11. It was renamed the Counterterrorism Mission Center in 2015.

13. Donald Rumsfeld, *Known and Unknown: A Memoir* (New York: Sentinel, 2011), 368–78.

14. Wolfowitz was the principal proponent of this view and had proposed it to President Bush. Fortunately, the president rejected it.

15. Schroen, *First In,* 15–24, 169.

16. Crumpton, *Art of Intelligence,* 190–97.

17. Robert Grenier, *88 Days to Kandahar: A CIA Diary* (New York: Simon & Schuster, 2015). See also Duane Evans, *Foxtrot in Kandahar: A Memoir of a CIA Officer in Afghanistan and the Inception of America's Longest War* (El Dorado Hills, CA: Savas Beatie, 2017); and Gary Berntsen and Ralph Pezzullo, *Jawbreaker: The Attack on Bin Laden and Al-Qaeda: A Personal Account by the CIA's Key Field Commander* (New York: Crown, 2005).

18. For a detailed accounting of Army special operations, see Charles Briscoe et al., *Weapon of Choice: U.S. Army Special Operations Forces in Afghanistan* (Fort Leavenworth, KS: Combat Studies Institute, 2003).

19. For an excellent account of ODA 595's mission, see Doug Stanton, *Horse Soldiers: The Extraordinary Story of a Band of U.S. Soldiers Who Road to Victory in Afghanistan* (New York: Scribner, 2009).

20. Rumsfeld, *Known and Unknown,* 391; Tenet, *At the Center of the Storm,* 214.

21. Tenet, *At the Center of the Storm,* 216–17.

22. Walter Perry and David Kassing, *Toppling the Taliban: Air-Ground Operations in Afghanistan, October 2001–June 2002* (Santa Monica, CA: Rand, 2015). See also Anthony Schinella, *Bombs Without Boots: The Limits of Airpower* (Washington, DC: Brookings, 2019), 97–163.

23. Tenet, *At the Center of the Storm,* 240; Crumpton, *Art of Intelligence,* 253. See also Aki Peritz and Eric Rosenbach, *Find, Fix, Finish: Inside the Counterterrorism Campaigns That Killed Bin Laden and Devastated Al-Qaeda* (New York: PublicAffairs, 2012), 38–42. Peritz is a former CIA counterterrorism analyst.

24. Tenet, *At the Center of the Storm,* 219–20, 224–25.

25. Ibid., 225.

26. Morell, *Great War of Our Time,* 75–76.

CHAPTER TWELVE DISRUPT, DISMANTLE, DEFEAT

1. I argued that we were engaged in an intelligence, covert action, and special operations war. Denying al-Qa'ida any sanctuary was critical. Two states were of particular importance: Pakistan, with its nuclear weapons; and Saudi Arabia, with its oil
wealth and custody of two of Islam's three holiest sites. They must be denied to the
jihadists. I also argued that we were in a war with perhaps 100,000 global jihadists and
their allies out of a global Muslim population of 1.5 billion. UBL's aim was to make
the conflict an inter-civilizational war. Our aim should be to prevent him from doing
so, and to separate the 100,000 global jihadists from the rest of the Islamic world to
the greatest extent feasible.

2. Other al-Qa'ida or al-Qa'ida-affiliated leaders planned or conducted other attacks.
The Indonesian-born Riduan Bin Isomuddin, known to his extremist colleagues as
"Hambali," and the leader of Jemaah Islamiyah, helped plan the October 2002 Bali
bombing that killed more than two hundred people. Hambali also facilitated financ-
ing for the August 2003 bombing of the Marriott Hotel in Jakarta. Abd al-Rahim
al-Nashiri, who helped lead the attack on the USS *Cole,* conducted a successful attack
on the French tanker MV *Limburg* off Yemen in October 2002.

3. KSM's nephew Ramzi Yousef was the principal behind the 1993 World Trade Center bombing that killed 6 and injured more than a thousand. Yousef said he had
hoped to kill 250,000 people. The plot had been hatched and training in explosives
had been provided at the Khaldan terrorist training camp run by Abu Zubaydah
on the Afghanistan-Pakistan border. In January 1995, Yousef had also been involved
with KSM in a failed plot in Manila to blow up twelve passenger airliners over the
Pacific. Yousef was captured in a joint Pakistan-U.S. raid in Islamabad later in 1995.
He was extradited and tried in the United States and is serving a sentence of life plus
240 years at the supermax prison in Colorado.

4. Before his capture, Zubaydah had facilitated the clandestine movement of jihadis to
and from al-Qa'ida's training camps. He provided volumes of information to CIA,
and his interrogation, among other things, led to the capture of Ramzi Bin al-Shibh,
who had intended to be one of the 9/11 hijackers, but had failed to get a U.S. visa.
Bin al-Shibh's capture, in turn, led to the capture of another senior al-Qa'ida leader,
Khalid Bin Attash. Bin Attash would provide important intelligence that would help
lead us eventually to Usama Bin Ladin. Intelligence obtained from Zubaydah also
led to the capture of Abd al-Rahim al-Nashiri, the leader of the attack on the USS
Cole. Tenet, *At the Center of the Storm,* 242–43. See also Grenier, *88 Days to Kandahar,*
328–33; and Jose Rodriguez, *Hard Measures: How Aggressive CIA Actions After 9/11 Saved
American Lives,* with Bill Harlow (New York: Simon & Schuster, 2012), 82–84.

5. KSM confessed that he had personally decapitated *Wall Street Journal* reporter Daniel Pearl in Karachi in early 2002. His interrogation also led to another major capture,
"Hambali," in Bangkok. Hambali, who had sworn allegiance to UBL in the 1990s,
confirmed that a cell of the al-Qa'ida affiliate Jemaah Islamiyah was being groomed
for a future aviation attack on the West Coast of the United States. (Rodriguez, *Hard
Measures,* 85–97. See also Peritz and Rosenbach, *Find, Fix, Finish,* 57–70.) KSM and

other high-value al-Qa'ida detainees remain at Guantánamo Bay, awaiting trial by military commission.

6. Grenier, *88 Days to Kandahar,* 386. See also Peritz and Rosenbach, *Find, Fix, Finish,* 51–56. Al-Qa'ida was a multinational terrorist organization with global presence. UBL was a Saudi. Bin Ladin's successor, Ayman al-Zawahiri, killed in a U.S. drone strike in late July 2022, was an Egyptian. A significant portion of its senior leadership was also Egyptian, but other top leaders were Libyan, Pakistani, Syrian, Saudi, Yemeni, Somali, Sudanese, Mauritanian, Algerian, Jordanian, Palestinian, Qatari, Bahraini, and Indonesian. Al-Qa'ida's operative ranks included all these plus Turks, Moroccans, Lebanese, Iraqis, Kurds, Nigerians, Russians, Chechens, Uzbeks, Tajiks, Uighurs, and Malaysians, along with a number who hailed from Western countries, including the U.K. and the United States.

7. See George W. Bush, *Decision Points* (New York: Crown, 2010), 168–71.

8. While Pakistan was the primary refuge for al-Qa'ida after the group was ejected from Afghanistan, several AQ senior leaders and their families found limited sanctuary in Iran. Iran also became a facilitation hub for al-Qa'ida operatives transiting from the FATA to Iraq and Turkey. In 2005, Saif al-Adel, a former Egyptian Army special forces colonel and one of al-Qa'ida's top military commanders "detained" in Iran, prepared a new strategy for UBL. Consisting of seven stages, the strategy bolstered the view of al-Qa'ida's senior leaders that they would prevail in the long run. For additional details, see Bruce Hoffman, *Inside Terrorism,* 3rd ed. (New York: Columbia University Press, 2017), 326–27.

9. Imtiaz Gul, *The Most Dangerous Place: Pakistan's Lawless Frontier* (New York: Viking, 2009).

10. Leon Panetta, *Worthy Fights: A Memoir of Leadership in War and Peace,* with Jim Newton (New York: Penguin Press, 2014), 241.

11. Morell, *Great War of Our Time,* 118.

12. For a fuller treatment, see Aki Peritz, *Disruption: Inside the Largest Counterterrorism Investigation in History* ([Lincoln, NE]: Potomac Books, 2021).

13. Morell, *Great War of Our Time,* 128–29. See also Rodriguez, *Hard Measures,* 4–10; and Peritz and Rosenbach, *Find, Fix, Finish,* 138–48.

14. Morell, *Great War of Our Time,* 129–30. See also National Intelligence Council, Office of the Director of National Intelligence, "The Terrorist Threat to the US Homeland," unclassified key judgments, July 2007.

15. Bill Roggio, *FDD's Long War Journal,* www.longwarjournal.org.

16. Tenet, *At the Center of the Storm,* 240. See also Peritz and Rosenbach, *Find, Fix, Finish,* 150–54.

17. Morell, *Great War of Our Time,* 130.

18. For a summary of my memo, see Rumsfeld, *Known and Unknown,* 696–97.

19. The president's full national security team—Vice President Cheney, National Security Adviser Steve Hadley, Secretaries Rice and Rumsfeld, JCS chairman General Pete Pace, Director of National Intelligence John Negroponte, whom I knew from my Special Forces days when he was ambassador to Honduras, and CIA director Mike Hayden—was already there when we arrived. General John Abizaid, our

CENTCOM commander, and General George Casey, our commander in Iraq, joined by secure video teleconference.

20. Kagan and I were the principal debaters, because we offered recommendations that were polar opposites. For additional details, see Timothy Andrews Sayle et al., eds, *The Last Card: Inside George W. Bush's Decision to Surge in Iraq* (Ithaca, NY: Cornell University Press, 2019), 6–64, 69, 347.

21. During the 2006 QDR, I had three different jobs: I was a senior adviser to the main QDR, which was led by my old friend Jim Thomas; I led a "Red Team" of retired four-star generals that provided separate recommendations directly to the secretary and deputy secretary of defense; and I helped draft the Downing Report, which provided recommendations on SOF to the secretary. The Red Team and the Downing Report (named after the former SOCOM commander General Wayne Downing) were a way to go around and above the bureaucracy. Our recommendations became the QDR's decisions.

22. I believed we would also need to develop long-range, stealthy, special operations aircraft to clandestinely infiltrate SOF in anti-access/area-denial environments. Future SOF will also need penetrating (stealthy), persistent ISR.

23. See Morell, *Great War of Our Time*, 130, for a brief discussion of President Bush's decision to shift to a new CT strategy in the Afghanistan-Pakistan border region.

24. My Joint Staff counterpart was General James "Hoss" Cartwright, the vice-chairman of the Joint Chiefs of Staff.

25. Michael Hayden, *Playing to the Edge: American Intelligence in the Age of Terror* (New York: Penguin Press, 2016), 346. See also Morell, *Great War of Our Time*, 130.

26. There was only one issue that was hotly debated. The deputies had decided fairly early that neither CIA nor DOD would be in overall command of the operation. Each would conduct its operations under its own authorities, and these operations would be coordinated at the operational command level between CIA and DOD. If there was a dispute, the issue would be raised to the Deputies Small Group. General Cartwright wanted the CIA representative at Bagram Air Base in Afghanistan to have chief of station command authority for the Pakistan border region, cutting out the CIA chiefs in Afghanistan and Pakistan. CIA's deputy director, Steve Kappes, vehemently objected. It was not the way CIA ran its overseas operations. Plus, the senior operational commander on the CIA side, the director of the Counterterrorism Center, was at headquarters. I sided with CIA on this issue, and the agency's view prevailed.

27. In early July 2007, a violent confrontation broke out at Lal Masjid, the "Red Mosque," in Islamabad. The mosque was a hotbed of extremism, and the militants barricaded inside had taken multiple hostages. The Pakistani Army laid siege, and when negotiations broke down, Musharraf ordered the Special Service Group, in which he had served for several years earlier in his career, to storm the complex. More than ninety militants died in the operation, along with ten SSG commandos, including the commander of the elite Karrar Company. Following the raid, al-Qa'ida declared war against Pakistan.

28. Large, sustained demonstrations by Pakistan's lawyers provided the initial spark that

led to Musharraf's removal from power. Far more important, though, Musharraf had lost support in the army's senior ranks due to his retention of the chief of Army Staff position while serving as Pakistan's president.

29. Bush, *Decision Points*, 217–18.

30. Panetta, *Worthy Fights*, 242.

31. Hayden, *Playing to the Edge*, 337–39.

32. General Stanley McChrystal, *My Share of the Task: A Memoir* (New York: Penguin Books, 2013), 153–55.

33. Peritz and Rosenbach, *Find, Fix, Finish*, 154–58.

34. Bush, *Decision Points*, 217–18. See also Hayden, *Playing to the Edge*, 335–36; and Roggio, *FDD's Long War Journal*.

35. Hayden, *Playing to the Edge*, 336–37.

36. Roggio, *FDD's Long War Journal*.

37. A twenty-four-year-old Afghan national and U.S. citizen who had lived in the United States since he was ten, Najibullah Zazi, had traveled to Pakistan in 2008 and was provided with training in improvised homemade explosives. In 2009, his al-Qa'ida masters, including the operations chief, Saleh al-Somali, directed him to bomb the New York City subway system. The IC and FBI were fortunately able to track Zazi and maintain constant surveillance on him as he made his way to New York from his Aurora, Colorado, home. We had also obtained the recipe he was using for his bomb, so we could track his purchases. On September 22, Zazi was arrested before he could carry out his plot. Saleh al-Somali was killed in the Predator strike in December. On May 1, 2010, another attack was attempted against New York by Faisal Shahzad, a thirty-one-year-old naturalized U.S. citizen born in Pakistan and the son of a Pakistani air vice-marshal. He had been trained by the Pakistan Taliban in Waziristan and provided with $12,000 to carry out his mission. Shahzad had driven a Nissan Pathfinder to Times Square, where he left it packed with improvised explosives. Fortunately, a T-shirt vendor became concerned and called over a mounted NYPD officer. NYPD's bomb squad rushed to the scene and found the bomb had not been properly assembled. Shahzad was arrested at New York's Kennedy Airport as he tried to flee the country. See Panetta, *Worthy Fights*, 247–48, 267. See also Peritz and Rosenbach, *Find, Fix, and Finish*, 167–85.

38. Hayden, *Playing to the Edge*, 336. Pakistan's military leaders felt a campaign of U.S. raids into Pakistan would make their populace question what it had an army for. Predator contributed something they didn't have; raids didn't, even though our capabilities were vastly superior to theirs.

39. Bush, *Decision Points*, 217–18.

40. Peritz and Rosenbach, *Find, Fix, Finish*, 1–2.

41. Panetta, *Worthy Fights*, 260–69.

42. Peritz and Rosenbach, *Find, Fix, Finish*, 164.

43. Panetta, *Worthy Fights*, 291. See also Roggio, *FDD's Long War Journal*.

44. During my four years as ASD SO/LIC&IC, the Air Force more than tripled the number of Predator orbits, or "combat air patrols," it could sustain to support the wars in Iraq and Afghanistan and the war with al-Qa'ida. Increasing Predator orbits

and improving the capabilities of Predator had been one of my top priorities. We stopped at sixty-five orbits in 2011, but had a capacity to surge to eighty-five. Trained crews were our principal limiting factor.

45. Peritz and Rosenbach, *Find, Fix, Finish,* 160–64.

46. Roggio, *FDD's Long War Journal.*

47. Peritz and Rosenbach, *Find, Fix, Finish,* 210.

48. Roggio, *FDD's Long War Journal.*

49. Office of the Director of National Intelligence, "Summary of Information Regarding U.S. Counterterrorism Strikes Outside Areas of Active Hostilities," 2016.

50. For a good argument on the necessity, precision, and effectiveness of U.S. drone strikes, see Daniel Byman, "Why Drones Work: The Case for Washington's Weapon of Choice," *Foreign Affairs,* May 1, 2013. See also Michael Hayden, "To Keep America Safe, Embrace Drone Warfare," *New York Times,* Feb. 19, 2016. To get a sense of the meticulous procedures involved in drone strikes outside areas of active hostilities, see also Hayden, *Playing to the Edge,* 331–33; and John Brennan, *Undaunted: My Fight Against America's Enemies, at Home and Abroad* (New York: Celadon Books, 2020), 209–15.

51. Hayden, *Playing to the Edge,* 337–39.

52. For a summary of the Biden administration's new policy on drone strikes, see Charlie Savage, "White House Tightens Rules on Counterterrorism Drone Strikes," *New York Times,* Oct. 7, 2022. I did plan for this so-called over-the-horizon contingency, though I hoped it would never come to pass. One of my final acts as the undersecretary of defense for intelligence was to ensure that we would still have the means to strike the Afghanistan-Pakistan border region if we withdrew all our troops and lost our air bases in Afghanistan. Working with the Air Force's "Big Safari" program, we developed a version of the Predator B/MQ-9 with a big wing, doubling the aircraft's range and persistence. It is now in service and performing well.

CHAPTER THIRTEEN **THE WAR BEYOND THE CORE**

1. Tenet, *At the Center of the Storm,* 244.

2. Peritz and Rosenbach, *Find, Fix, Finish,* 189–94.

3. Ibid., 195.

4. Clapper, *Facts and Fears,* 123–24. See also Panetta, *Worthy Fights,* 241.

5. Clapper, *Facts and Fears,* 127; Panetta, *Worthy Fights,* 257–60.

6. An al-Qa'ida attack on a Western housing compound in Riyadh in May 2003 had killed thirty-five people, including ten Americans, and wounded more than two hundred. The Saudis began to take action, capturing or killing many of the senior al-Qa'ida operatives involved in the plot. They also began to clamp down on al-Qa'ida's finances and engaged their clerical establishment to issue fatwas that condemned extremist violence.

7. Tenet, *At the Center of the Storm,* 248–50.

8. Panetta, *Worthy Fights,* 243–44.

9. Morell, *Great War of Our Time*, 309.

10. Ibid., 137–38.

11. Panetta, *Worthy Fights*, 385–87.

12. See Charlie Savage, *Power Wars: Inside Obama's Post-9/11 Presidency* (New York: Little, Brown, 2015), 227–54. For the OLC opinion on Awlaki, see U.S. Department of Justice Office of Legal Counsel, "Memorandum for the Attorney General Re: Applicability of Federal Criminal Laws and the Constitution to Contemplated Lethal Operations Against Shaykh Anwar al-Aulaqi," Washington, DC, July 16, 2010.

13. Panetta, *Worthy Fights*, 385–87.

14. Morell, *Great War of Our Time*, 309.

15. The Obama administration would eventually disclose the number of strikes we took and the limited number of noncombatant casualties they caused. This didn't end the controversy about civilian casualties.

16. Morell, *Great War of Our Time*, xi–xii.

17. McChrystal, *My Share of the Task*, 249–50.

18. Morell, *Great War of Our Time*, 271.

19. Admiral William McRaven, *Sea Stories: My Life in Special Operations* (New York: Grand Central Publishing, 2019), 217–39.

20. McChrystal, *My Share of the Task*, 270–71.

21. McRaven, *Sea Stories*, 241–57.

22. Several Somali Americans had traveled to Somalia to join al-Shabaab's jihad as foot soldiers. Two U.S. citizens, Omar Hammami and Jehad Serwan Mostafa, rose to senior positions in al-Shabaab. Hammami broke with the group in 2013 over a disagreement about strategy, criticizing its leaders for their lack of interest in sponsoring attacks outside East Africa. He was assassinated shortly thereafter by al-Shabaab.

CHAPTER 14 HVT 1

1. Panetta, *Worthy Fights*, 289. We would learn after UBL had been killed that he lived in several places before settling down in Abbottabad in August 2005. Amal, UBL's youngest wife, testified that she had been reunited with the al-Qa'ida leader in Peshawar in mid-2002. Late in 2002, they traveled to the Shangla district of Swat. Khalid Sheikh Mohammed, the mastermind of the 9/11 attacks, visited them there and stayed for about two weeks. Three days after KSM was captured in Rawalpindi in March 2003, UBL and Amal left Swat. They then moved to Naseem Town, a suburb of Haripur, and stayed there until relocating to Abbottabad in August 2005. Steve Coll, *Directorate S: The C.I.A. and America's Secret Wars in Afghanistan and Pakistan* (New York: Penguin Press, 2018), 547–51.

2. McChrystal, *My Share of the Task*, 265–66.

3. Morell, *Great War of Our Time*, 145.

4. Panetta, *Worthy Fights*, 291.

5. Morell, *Great War of Our Time*, 145.

6. Bill Harlow, ed., *Rebuttal: The CIA Responds to the Senate Intelligence Committee's Study of*

Its Detention and Interrogation Program (Annapolis, MD: Naval Institute Press, 2015), 162–64.

7. Ibid.

8. Morell, *Great War of Our Time*, 146.

9. Panetta, *Worthy Fights*, 293. CIA had first learned Abu Ahmed's partial true name from a detainee, but that detainee claimed that Abu Ahmed had died in Afghanistan in 2001. CIA later discovered through signals intelligence, a clandestine source, and other detainees in CIA custody that this detainee had confused Abu Ahmed with his deceased brother. CIA was then able to use Abu Ahmed's partial true name to acquire additional information about him.

10. Harlow, *Rebuttal*, 163.

11. Panetta, *Worthy Fights*, 294.

12. Gates, *Duty*, 589.

13. Panetta, *Worthy Fights*, 294–96; Morell, *Great War of Our Time*, 147–48.

14. Panetta himself acknowledged that he had considered removing CTC's Pakistan-Afghanistan Department chief. It was good that he didn't, as the PAD chief was one of CIA's best operations officers and was critical to the CT fight. Panetta, *Worthy Fights*, 297.

15. Ibid.

16. Morell, *Great War of Our Time*, 152.

17. Panetta, *Worthy Fights*, 292–93.

18. Morell, *Great War of Our Time*, 153–55. See also Panetta, *Worthy Fights*, 299–300.

19. Morell, *Great War of Our Time*, 153. A political crisis with Pakistan during the first months of 2011 complicated our planning. On January 27, Ray Davis, a security officer assigned to the American consulate in Lahore, had been accosted at a jammed intersection by two armed men on a motorcycle. Davis shot them both and called the consulate. A crowd surrounded him and prevented him from leaving the scene, however. To make matters worse, a car from the consulate rushing to the scene to rescue Davis struck and killed a pedestrian. Davis was taken into custody and held for almost two months in prison even though he was in Pakistan on a diplomatic passport and visa. The Pakistani public, egged on by extremist groups, demanded that Davis be executed. The United States demanded his immediate release, citing his diplomatic immunity. On March 16, the matter was settled in a Pakistani court. The families of the deceased agreed to accept $2.4 million in compensation. Davis was released into American custody and immediately flown out of the country. See Panetta, *Worthy Fights*, 304–8; and Morell, *Great War of Our Time*, 171–72.

20. McRaven, *Sea Stories*, 271–74.

CHAPTER FIFTEEN **NEPTUNE'S SPEAR**

1. Panetta, *Worthy Fights*, 308–9. See also McRaven, *Sea Stories*, 287.

2. I had asked Morell if he could read in the undersecretary for policy, Michèle Flournoy, my former boss, as we began the series of NSC meetings. I also asked him

to read in Admiral Olson, our SOCOM commander, who was Bill McRaven's boss. He agreed to both.

3. Morell, *Great War of Our Time*, 150–51.

4. Ibid., 153–55, 157; Panetta, *Worthy Fights*, 299–300; McRaven, *Sea Stories*, 271–72.

5. McRaven, *Sea Stories*, 280–83, 288.

6. Ibid., 288.

7. Elisabeth Bumiller, "Soldier, Thinker, Hunter, Spy: Drawing a Bead on Al Qaeda," *New York Times*, Sept. 3, 2011.

8. Panetta, *Worthy Fights*, 309. Secretary Gates had initially favored the B-2 option, as had the president and most of the NSC's principals. Gates acknowledged that a special operations raid was the only option that would provide proof that we got UBL in addition to bringing back a potential intelligence windfall. He said he had high confidence in the ability of McRaven's Special Operations Task Force to carry out the mission, though based on his experience with the Iran rescue attempt, he was also worried that many unexpected things could go wrong, particularly with helicopters. He was also concerned that a successful raid would be a humiliation of the worst kind for the Pakistani Army. Gates, *Duty*, 539–40.

9. Gates, *Duty*, 311–12.

10. McRaven, *Sea Stories*, 294–95.

11. Ibid., 297, 312.

12. Morell, *Great War of Our Time*, 158–59. See also Panetta, *Worthy Fights*, 312.

13. McRaven, *Sea Stories*, 296–300.

14. Ibid., 302–3.

15. Gates, *Duty*, 541–42.

16. McRaven, *Sea Stories*, 303–6.

17. Ibid., 323.

18. Ibid., 306.

19. Gates, *Duty*, 542.

20. Quoted in Savage, *Power Wars*, 257.

21. Morell, *Great War of Our Time*, 150.

22. McRaven, *Sea Stories*, 306–8.

23. Morell, *Great War of Our Time*, 159–61.

24. Panetta, *Worthy Fights*, 314.

25. Gates, *Duty*, 543.

26. Panetta, *Worthy Fights*, 319–20.

27. McRaven, *Sea Stories*, 308.

28. Also by Bill's side was Chris Faris, his command sergeant major, a veteran Army special operator, and an outstanding leader. Chris had been in almost continuous combat since he was twenty. He would follow Bill to SOCOM when Bill succeeded Eric Olson months later.

29. A small Air Force element was also in Bill's JOC to help with the intelligence, surveillance, and reconnaissance aspects of the mission. McRaven, *Sea Stories*, 309–13.

30. Craig Whitlock, "Defense Department's Vickers Is a National Security Star—Again," *Washington Post*, April 29, 2011, A1. The reporter had been working on the

story since September, and I had no idea what it would say or when it would come out. I had declined to be interviewed for it because I had just been nominated to be USD(I) when the reporter called, and I didn't want to make any news before my confirmation. Given my responsibilities, I generally avoided the press, or didn't say much on the few occasions when I agreed to be interviewed. I was pleasantly surprised, if more than a bit embarrassed about its timing, how well the story turned out. Four and a half months later, there would be a similar front-page story in *The New York Times.*

31. Panetta, *Worthy Fights,* 321; Morell, *Great War of Our Time,* 165–68.

32. McRaven, *Sea Stories,* 315–17.

33. Robert O'Neill, *The Operator: Firing the Shots That Killed Osama Bin Laden and My Years as a SEAL Warrior* (New York: Scribner, 2017), 308–9.

34. McRaven, *Sea Stories,* 317–26. See also O'Neill, *Operator,* 306–11.

35. O'Neill, *Operator,* 311.

36. Panetta, *Worthy Fights,* 327.

37. For a summary of a few illustrative letters from UBL between 2006 and 2011, see Combating Terrorism Center at West Point, "Letters from Abbottabad," May 2012, 1–3. For a more thorough analysis, see Nelly Lahoud, *The Bin Laden Papers: How the Abbottabad Raid Revealed the Truth About Al-Qaeda, Its Leader, and His Family* (New Haven, CT: Yale University Press, 2022). For the life and death of UBL, see Peter Bergen, *The Rise and Fall of Osama Bin Laden* (New York: Simon & Schuster, 2021).

CHAPTER SIXTEEN AF-PAK

1. After U.S. forces had gotten trapped in an insurgency and sectarian civil war of increasing intensity in Iraq, it became popular in some circles of the U.S. foreign policy establishment to call the war in Afghanistan our "good war" and a "war of necessity," since we had been attacked from there on 9/11. The Iraq war was a "bad war," a "war of choice."

2. Antonio Giustozzi, *The Taliban at War, 2001–2018* (Oxford: Oxford University Press, 2019), 28–32, 35–36, 62. Al-Qa'ida was particularly important to the Haqqanis' reconstitution during the early years of the Afghan war. Its commanders ran training camps for the group and led operations. Foreign fighters, particularly Pakistani militants, were also critical, making up a significant percentage of the group's initial fighting strength. The Miram Shah Shura (Council) was established to command operations inside Afghanistan on April 14, 2003. The Haqqanis nominally aligned themselves with the traditional Taliban later in 2003 after the Quetta Shura was established.

3. Carlotta Gall, *The Wrong Enemy: America in Afghanistan, 2001–2014* (Boston: Houghton Mifflin Harcourt, 2014), 67.

4. The founding members of the Quetta Shura, besides Omar, were Mullah Abdul Ghani Baradar, the Taliban's former deputy minister of defense; Mullah Dadullah, a top military commander; and Mawlavi Akhtar Mohammad Mansur, the former

minister of civil aviation. The group's operations were confined to Kandahar and Helmand in 2003, but they expanded into Uruzgan, Zabul, Ghazni, Paktia, and Paktika by the end of 2004. Giustozzi, *Taliban at War,* 32–35, 43–46, 53–60.

5. Gates, *Duty,* 198. The first significant encounter with a revitalized Taliban for U.S. forces came in Konar Province in eastern Afghanistan on June 28, 2005. Four Navy SEALs on a special reconnaissance mission were ambushed in a well-organized attack by local insurgents, and a helicopter carrying a quick reaction force was shot down. Three of the four SEALs on the ground were killed in the battle with insurgents, and all sixteen special operators—eight SEALs and eight special operations aviators—on the rescue aircraft perished as well. The SEAL leading the ground patrol, Lieutenant Michael Murphy, was posthumously awarded the Medal of Honor.

6. Mullah Dadullah, often called Dadullah Lang or Dadullah the Lame, because he had had one of his legs amputated, was the Taliban's senior military commander until his death by an air strike in Helmand in May 2007. He had commanded as many as two thousand fighters in the south. (See McChrystal, *My Share of the Task,* 264–65.) Dadullah had also not been shy about revealing the Taliban's ties to al-Qa'ida. In 2006, he told an interviewer in Pakistan, "We like the al-Qa'ida organization. We have close ties and constant contacts." (See Coll, *Directorate S,* 255.) In 2005, four *loy mahazes* (large fronts) were established in 2005 under Dadullah, Baradar, and two other military commanders to keep pace with the expanding Taliban insurgency.

7. Giustozzi, *Taliban at War,* 44–45, 53–54, 62–63, 71–76.

8. Gates, *Duty,* 199. During the Soviet-Afghan War, the mujahedin had refrained from suicide attacks. Afghanistan's warrior culture emphasized individual bravery, but, where possible, living to fight another day. The Taliban, however, embraced suicide bombing, or "martyrdom" operations, in January 2006. Where there had been only eight suicide bombings, all in Kabul, between December 2001 and December 2004, in 2006, suicide bombers struck two or three times a week across Afghanistan. The Taliban's recruiters and trainers preferred boys who were seriously ill or mentally challenged or had a reason for revenge. Suicide vests worn by those who suffered from mental impairment were remotely detonated. The Taliban paid the families of recruits between $2,000 and $10,000 for an attack. The Taliban's use of improvised explosive devices continued to rise as the war went on. (See Coll, *Directorate S,* 254–56, 260–64.)

9. The Taliban had largely failed to expand their insurgency into eastern Afghanistan during the first several years of the war, and as a result, in 2005, a rival power center emerged, the Peshawar Shura, whose reach extended from Nangarhar to Nuristan. The *shura* later extended its reach across northern Afghanistan, bringing significant numbers of non-Pashtun fighters (Tajiks, Uzbeks, and so on) into its ranks. Like the Haqqanis, the Peshawar Shura relied extensively on foreign fighters, most of whom were Pakistanis, but Arabs, Chechens, and central Asians were also included in the *shura*'s ranks. The *shura* also had ties with al-Qa'ida.

10. Giustozzi, *Taliban at War,* 2.

11. Prolific fundraisers in Gulf Arab countries, the Haqqanis were financially indepen-

dent of the Quetta Shura. Throughout the Afghan war, the Haqqanis also received financial support from AQ, unique among Taliban groups. From 2012 onward, moreover, the Haqqanis had ties with and received support from Iran's Islamic Revolutionary Guard Corps.

12. That said, we did find some additional troops to send to Afghanistan in 2007 and 2008. U.S. troop levels in Afghanistan doubled to twenty thousand in 2004, but remained there through 2006. In 2007, President Bush approved an increase of five thousand more troops, and in 2008 he approved six thousand more. It was what the president called his "silent surge." By comparison, nearly thirty thousand additional troops had been sent to Iraq in 2007 as part of the Iraq surge. (Gates, *Duty*, 199.) The administration's spending on Afghan security forces, particularly for NDS, would also increase substantially, greater in 2007 than in the previous five years combined.

13. Bush, *Decision Points*, 218. In the late summer of 2008, our new commander in Afghanistan, General Dave McKiernan, told Secretary Gates that he needed three additional combat brigades plus a combat aviation brigade, because helicopters were essential to conduct operations in the vast territory of Afghanistan—twenty thousand more troops in all. McKiernan told Gates that if we could take care of the safe havens in Pakistan, he could secure Afghanistan in six months. Unfortunately, eliminating the Pakistan safe havens was a problem that we were never able to solve across the Bush, Obama, and Trump administrations.

14. Gates, *Duty*, 222. Gates was growing increasingly worried that our foreign military presence could reach the point where Afghans would begin to see us as "occupiers" rather than allies. Gates and I both knew from personal experience that the Soviets had paid a very high price for their occupation, and they had failed to defeat the Afghan resistance even though they had at the height of their buildup 125,000 troops in country, four times more than we had in early 2008.

15. Bush, *Decision Points*, 222; Gates, *Duty*, 223.

16. Bureaucratic politics played a role in where the seventeen thousand troops were headed. Of the seventeen thousand additional troops, eight thousand were Marines. The Marines had been lobbying for a regional command of their own in Afghanistan. U.S. and coalition forces in Afghanistan were divided among five regional commands: RC-Central, around Kabul, RC-East, RC-South, RC-West, and RC-North, each led by a general officer. The United States had RC-East, the Canadians, Dutch, and British rotated command of RC-South, the Italians had RC-West, the Germans had RC-North, and the French had RC-Central. In November 2010, the United States would assume command of RC-South as well. General Conway, the commandant of the Marine Corps, asked for and got a new regional command, RC-Southwest, in Helmand Province, that would be led by a Marine general. Command at the top was divided into two parts: the NATO-led International Security Assistance Force mission, with its regional commands, and Operation Enduring Freedom, a separate U.S. command retained after ISAF was established in 2006 to conduct counterterrorism operations. ISAF reported to the NATO commander; OEF reported to CENTCOM. The complicated arrangement was certainly far from unity of command, a key principle of war.

17. For a summary of the Obama administration's initial force decisions on Afghanistan, see Gates, *Duty*, 337–44.

18. McChrystal, *My Share of the Task*, 285.

19. Gates, *Duty*, 344–46.

20. Ibid., 353–56, 359. See also McChrystal, *My Share of the Task*, 330–33.

21. More intelligence, surveillance, and reconnaissance assets were also essential. Fortunately, Secretary Gates had gone around the Pentagon bureaucracy in the fall of 2007 and established an "ISR Task Force." Soon, scores of new armed ISR platforms, from Predators and Reapers to a new, manned MC-12 Liberty aircraft, a variant of the civilian Beechcraft King Air, were flowing to Iraq and Afghanistan.

22. See also McChrystal, *My Share of the Task*, 357.

23. For Secretary Gates's perspective on the Obama administration's Afghanistan strategic review, see Gates, *Duty*, 335–85.

24. At the beginning of the Obama administration, we also had serious concerns about the Pakistan Army's continued will to combat the growing insurgency inside Pakistan. The Tehrik-e-Taliban Pakistan, or TTP, had taken over Swat, an idyllic region in northwest Pakistan, in March 2009 under the command of Maulana Fazlullah, the TTP's leader in the area, destroying more than four hundred schools and imposing Sharia law on the local populace. At first, the Army did nothing. The NSC principals, particularly Secretary Clinton, wondered whether the Pakistan Army had lost the will to fight. After the insurgents took Buner, and looked as if they had a straight run to Islamabad, however, the Army launched a counteroffensive in late April and, by mid-June, had retaken both Buner and Swat. The Special Service Group had played an outsized role in the operation. In October 2009, ten militants wearing Army uniforms staged a commando attack on the Army's General Headquarters in Rawalpindi, taking forty-two people hostage, including several senior military officers. The militants nearly reached General Kayani's office before being stopped. SSG commandos rescued the hostages, though nine commandos were killed in the operation. I visited Kayani in his office a few weeks later and was surprised at how close the militants had managed to get to it. Pakistan's security lapses were serious concerns, but the real problem was its strategic distancing from the United States.

25. Kayani had brought with him a slide of a blown-up building in Lahore. It had been the regional office of ISI. He argued that ISI couldn't possibly be supporting extremist violence if it was the victim of it itself. But ISI was supporting extremists—extremists who were killing Americans. He assured us that ISI was not a rogue agency and that it was aligned with Army policy—all true, but it would have been better for us if ISI had been a rogue agency and not an arm of official state policy.

26. In 2013, the Pakistan Army finally conducted operations in the Tirah Valley in Khyber Agency, a long-standing al-Qa'ida stronghold, and in the Shawal Valley in North Waziristan, another AQ stronghold. This caused some displacement of AQ. In June 2014, the Pakistanis launched a major ground offensive in North Waziristan, which they had resisted since the 2006 peace agreement. What finally provoked it was an attack by Islamic Movement of Uzbekistan militants on Jinnah International Airport in Karachi. The Army's resolve to go after militants in North Waziristan stiffened

further after the Pakistan Taliban murdered scores of children at an Army school in Peshawar. I had traveled to Islamabad just prior to the offensive to discuss it with General Raheel Sharif, Kayani's successor as chief of Army Staff. I again offered U.S. support, but as usual the Pakistanis declined. Some thirty thousand troops were involved, and by its end Pakistan claimed to have killed thirty-five hundred militants. The Haqqanis and other militants favored by Pakistan were safely relocated before the offensive.

27. Coll, *Directorate S*, 425–27, 434, 439–40, 459–62, 501–3.

28. Gates, *Duty*, 477.

29. Pakistan had made important contributions to the war with al-Qa'ida, helping us capture AQ senior leaders from 2001 to 2010 and giving us permission to conduct essentially unilateral Predator strikes in the FATA from 2008 onward. We also had a robust special operations partnership with Pakistan between 2008 and 2010. Admiral Olson called it our "From the East" strategy, but the Pakistanis never bought fully in. Almost all SOF cooperation ceased in 2010.

CHAPTER SEVENTEEN **SURGE, DRAWDOWN, TRANSITION, DEFEAT**

1. McChrystal, *My Share of the Task*, 362–68. Unrealistically, Marjah was seen as a test for the new counterinsurgency strategy the president had approved. Both proponents and opponents of the COIN strategy found evidence in the operation to support their case. Proponents of the Afghan surge were hoping for quick results, based on our experience in Iraq. But Afghanistan wasn't Iraq. In Iraq, the insurgency had largely devolved into sectarian conflict between Sunni and Shi'a. The Anbar Awakening had seriously weakened al-Qa'ida in Iraq before the surge, as had the task force's relentless counterterrorism campaign. Iraq was an urban country, and Baghdad was the center of gravity. Ethnic cleansing by both Sunni and Shi'a in Baghdad's neighborhoods before the surge had made it easier to reduce the violence with the surge of forces President Bush had sent in. Afghanistan was rural. In Afghanistan, the surge of forces would have to be distributed across several provinces to achieve effects. There was no single center of gravity in Afghanistan other than Kabul, and it wasn't being seriously contested by the Taliban, save for the occasional suicide bombing and small group attack. The Taliban insurgency also benefited immensely from its sanctuary in Pakistan, a condition that had not been present to anywhere near that degree in Iraq.

2. Mullah Mansur replaced Baradar as the deputy to Mullah Omar. There had been another big change in the makeup of the Quetta Shura the year before as well. Mullah Abdul Qayum Zakir took over as head of the Taliban's Military Commission, succeeding Dadullah Lang. Zakir had strong ties to ISI and had clashed with Baradar. No doubt that played a role in ISI's decision that the Taliban would be better off without Baradar, at least for several years.

3. McChrystal, *My Share of the Task*, 377–83.

4. Gates, *Duty*, 485–86, 492.

5. McChrystal, *My Share of the Task*, 387–88. See also Gates, *Duty*, 487–92.

6. The conference was first established in 2003 by General John Abizaid, the CENTCOM commander. It brought together CIA, DOD, CENTCOM, and the Special Operations Task Force. See McChrystal, *My Share of the Task*, 116–17.

7. Gates, *Duty*, 490.

8. During one of my visits to Afghanistan during the surge, I met with Brigadier General H. R. McMaster, the head of Petraeus's anticorruption task force and a great warrior and intellectual. McMaster briefed me on his task force and said, "If we don't eliminate corruption, we can't win in Afghanistan." I said, "If that's the case, we should pack our bags and go home now. We will never eliminate corruption in Afghanistan. We can't eliminate it in the United States." Don't get me wrong, corruption was a very serious problem in Afghanistan, and we needed to combat it as best we could. But we were never going to eliminate it.

9. After I became the undersecretary of defense for intelligence, part of my job was to "darken the sky" over Afghanistan, providing a surge of manned and unmanned ISR aircraft to enable these operations, along with tethered aerostats around our forward operating bases to provide protection. We also placed special sensors on some of our manned ISR aircraft to detect IEDs. The results were very positive, and a lot of troops' lives were saved.

10. The CIA had started doing "district assessments" of the war in 2007 to measure our progress against the insurgency. It was a very valuable product, though our commanders in Afghanistan often didn't agree with its findings, which were more negative than our commanders perceived the situation to be. I was a strong supporter of these assessments and told CIA analysts to call it as they saw it. The assessments measured control of each of Afghanistan's more than four hundred districts, those under Afghan government or Taliban control, those that were under local control, and those that were being contested.

11. See Linda Robinson, *One Hundred Victories: Special Ops and the Future of American Warfare* (New York: PublicAffairs, 2013), 14–16.

12. For Gant's story, see Ann Scott Tyson, *American Spartan: The Promise, the Mission, and the Betrayal of Special Forces Major Jim Gant* (New York: William Morrow, 2014).

13. President Karzai was always courteous and thoughtful when I met with him, despite his growing alienation from the United States after Richard Holbrooke had overtly but unsuccessfully worked to prevent his reelection in 2009. Karzai never understood why we couldn't solve our Pakistan problem, how a country that could send a man to the moon couldn't bend a middle power and ally to its will. Karzai eventually concluded that we didn't want to for some reason. He was also increasingly frustrated by the number of civilian casualties the war had been inflicting on Afghanistan until Stan McChrystal tightened control of ISAF military operations.

14. Gates, *Duty*, 559.

15. Robinson, *One Hundred Victories*, 21–37.

16. Atmar had been on the Communist side during the Soviet-Afghan War and had been

badly wounded in battle near Jalalabad. As a result, he walked with a cane. Other Afghan leaders who had been on the mujahedin side, such as Bismullah Khan, teased Atmar that they and I had given him that limp. Atmar was an Afghan nationalist who was fiercely dedicated to freeing his country from the scourge of the Taliban.

17. Giustozzi, *Taliban at War*, 120.
18. Robinson, *One Hundred Victories*, 250–51.
19. Gall, *Wrong Enemy*, 275.
20. Robinson, *One Hundred Victories*, 19, 242–43, 250, 252–53.
21. Panetta, *Worthy Fights*, 357–58. See also O'Neill, *Operator*, 323.
22. "U.S. Watchdog Details Collapse of Afghan Security Forces," *Washington Post*, May 18, 2022.
23. The rapid collapse of Afghan security forces shouldn't have come as a surprise. We saw other forces in which we had invested heavily collapse suddenly in both Iraq and Yemen in 2014. It was clear between April and August 2021 that a similar process of psychological defeat was playing out in Afghanistan. We watched it, but did nothing to prevent it.

CHAPTER EIGHTEEN **IRAQ: HIDDEN SURGE TO ISIS**

1. See Robert Baer, *See No Evil: The True Story of a Ground Soldier in the CIA's War on Terrorism* (New York: Crown, 2002).
2. When I was on a visit to Erbil in Iraqi Kurdistan after I returned to government service, Masoud Barzani, the president of the Kurdistan Region, told me that I would love it there. "Kurdistan is just like Afghanistan," Barzani said. "We have mountains, our men wear baggy pants, and we love to fight." Barzani was right. I found Iraqi Kurdistan to be a different world from the rest of Iraq. The Kurds, moreover, were our most reliable partners. Years later, the war with ISIS would largely be waged from and on Kurdish territory.
3. See Nada Bakos, *The Targeter: My Life in the CIA, Hunting Terrorists and Challenging the White House*, with Davin Coburn (New York: Little, Brown, 2019), 129–30.
4. The IC had assessed in a National Intelligence Estimate that Iraq had continued its weapons of mass destruction programs in defiance of UN resolutions. The NIE assessed that Saddam had active chemical and biological weapons programs, and was reconstituting his nuclear weapons programs, which were constrained only by a lack of fissile material. Iraq also had produced missiles with ranges far in excess of UN limits. The IC was wrong about everything except the range of some of Saddam's missiles. The IC had underestimated how close Saddam had been to a nuclear weapons capability before the Persian Gulf War of 1990–1991. Our intelligence professionals didn't want to be wrong again, and they had failed to properly vet and evaluate their sources. After the intelligence failure, the IC provided "confidence levels" with all of its analytical judgments, a major improvement in tradecraft. It was as significant in my mind as the reform that Bob Gates had initiated as DDI in the

early 1980s when he insisted that logic trails and full sourcing be clearly identified in analytical products.

5. To DIA's credit, after it learned that its source was a fabricator, it recalled the original reporting. The Germans also had a source, known as "Curveball," who had also fabricated information about Saddam's WMD programs. He later admitted that he had lied because he wanted Iraq to be free from Saddam.

6. Many CIA analysts, it should be noted, had believed that overthrowing Saddam would open Pandora's box. CIA also got it right in assessing that there was no credible information linking Saddam's regime to al-Qa'ida and the 9/11 attacks. See Morell, *Great War of Our Time*, 86–91, 96–99; and National Intelligence Council, Office of the Director of National Intelligence, "Prospects for Iraq's Stability: A Challenging Road Ahead," unclassified key judgments, Jan. 2007.

7. For more details on the process leading up to the surge and its operational success in quelling the violence in Iraq, see Peter Mansoor, *Surge: My Journey with General David Petraeus and the Remaking of the Iraq War* (New Haven, CT: Yale University Press, 2013). An NSC review in the fall of 2006 focused on three different options: accelerating the training of Iraqi security forces; pulling all U.S. military forces out of Baghdad and letting the sectarian fires burn themselves out, with U.S. forces continuing to target AQI; and conducting a "fully-resourced counterinsurgency campaign" to secure the Iraqi people. The risk with the second option was that the death toll among Iraqis would have been grim. The risk with the third option was that U.S. casualties would likely have increased significantly. Casey and Abizaid favored transferring security responsibility as soon as possible; Petraeus favored the fully resourced COIN approach. Secretary Gates recommended that Petraeus replace Casey in Iraq, and that Casey become the Army's new chief of staff. President Bush agreed. See Gates, *Duty*, 42–48.

8. For a brief description of Shahwani and the Special Tactics Unit, see Hayden, *Playing to the Edge*, 200–203.

9. McChrystal, *My Share of the Task*, 252–53.

10. Ibid., 92–93, 105–7, 109, 117–19, 137–39, 148–49, 155–58, 161–65, 177–79, 180, 199–203, 213, 222.

11. McRaven, *Sea Stories*, 180–99.

12. McChrystal, *My Share of the Task*, 188–236. For CIA's role in the hunt for Zarqawi, see Bakos, *Targeter*, 203–85.

13. Hayden, *Playing to the Edge*, 19–23.

14. Ledgett's quotation is from Catherine Herridge, "Inside the Government's Secret NSA Program to Target Terrorists," Fox News, May 17, 2016.

15. McChrystal, *My Share of the Task*, 145, 160–61, 175–76, 181–88, 237, 240–42, 247, 255.

16. Mansoor, *Surge*, 120–47. See also Carter Malkasian, *Illusions of Victory: The Anbar Awakening and the Rise of the Islamic State* (New York: Oxford University Press, 2017), 1–15, 117–59.

17. McChrystal, *My Share of the Task*, 256–58.

18. Mansoor, *Surge*, 242–44.

19. In late October 2008, I also oversaw a cross-border raid into Syria to kill Abu Ghad-

iya, al-Qa'ida's top facilitator in the region. We had received human intelligence that Ghadiya would be moving to his compound near Abu Kamal, just fifteen kilometers from the Syria-Iraq border, and until this point he had been very hard to track, and even harder to fix in an area where he could be killed or captured. Colonel Mark Erwin, the commander of an elite special operations unit in Iraq, had been tasked to come up with a plan. A small force of operators would fly in two Black Hawk helicopters right to the target. They would be supported by two special operations helicopter gunships to provide fire support if needed. We decided to do the operation under CIA authorities to provide an element of deniability. We waited for nearly three months for a targeting opportunity to present itself. At 1630 hours on October 26, the strike force lifted off. The raid had to be conducted in daylight, something we preferred not to do, but events had forced our hand. Within minutes the fight was over. Ghadiya and all of his men had been killed; women and children in the compound were unharmed. Total time of the mission was seventeen minutes. See McRaven, *Sea Stories,* 200–213.

20. William McCants, *The ISIS Apocalypse: The History, Strategy, and Doomsday Vision of the Islamic State* (New York: St. Martin's Press, 2015), 42.

21. Abu Bakr had been captured in early 2004 in Fallujah by U.S. forces and was placed in detention at Camp Bucca. He was released after ten months because there wasn't evidence to prove that he had joined the insurgency. Camp Bucca, with its twenty-four thousand detainees, was a terrorism "academy," bringing together jihadists with former members of Saddam's military and security services. A year after he was released, Abu Bakr joined AQI.

22. McCants, *ISIS Apocalypse,* 15, 42, 45, 73–105.

23. Malkasian, *Illusions of Victory,* 168–73.

24. Clapper, *Facts and Fears,* 263–64. See also Susan Rice, *Tough Love: My Story of the Things Worth Fighting For* (New York: Simon & Schuster, 2019), 418.

25. ISIS would never have been able to conquer northern Iraq if we had acted sooner against the group in Syria. The group also might not have been able to carry out attacks outside Syria if we had struck them sooner. In October 2015, an ISIS affiliate in Egypt blew up a Russian airliner, killing 224. An attack in Paris in November killed 130 and wounded 300. In June 2016, a lone wolf who had pledged his allegiance to ISIS killed nearly 50 people at an Orlando nightclub.

26. For a discussion of U.S. military strategy against ISIS during the final years of the Obama administration, see Ash Carter, *Inside the Five-Sided Box: Lessons from a Lifetime of Leadership in the Pentagon* (New York: Dutton, 2019), 226–57; Dana Pittard and Wes Bryant, *Hunting the Caliphate: American's War on ISIS and the Dawn of the Strike Cell* (New York: Post Hill Press, 2019); and Derek Chollet, *The Long Game: How Obama Defied Washington and Redefined America's Role in the World* (New York: PublicAffairs, 2016), 147–57.

27. President Trump declared ISIS defeated in December 2018 and announced his intention to withdraw the two thousand U.S. forces, mostly special operators, from Syria. Fortunately, he was persuaded to change his mind, at least partially, leaving five hundred troops in Syria.

CHAPTER NINETEEN COUNTER PROLIFERATION, COUNTER NARCO-INSURGENCY

1. Hayden, *Playing to the Edge*, 290.
2. Thermonuclear weapons, or "hydrogen bombs," require additional nuclear materials and more complex warhead designs. They are also substantially more difficult to produce.
3. National Intelligence Council, Office of the Director of National Intelligence, "Iran: Nuclear Intentions and Capabilities," unclassified key judgments, Nov. 2007.
4. Hayden, *Playing to the Edge*, 295.
5. Ibid., 294.
6. Ibid., 302.
7. Gates, *Duty*, 193.
8. Hayden, *Playing to the Edge*, 300.
9. Before my first meeting with Dagan, someone on his staff told him that I would be wearing a tie to the meeting, something that one almost never does in Israel. Dagan showed up looking clearly uncomfortable, wearing a too-short tie that appeared to be choking him. He looked at my open collar and gave a "what the f——?" look at his aide, who was about to close the door for our one-on-one meeting. He quickly yanked off his tie, and our meeting went much better after that.
10. Gates, *Duty*, 192.
11. Hayden, *Playing to the Edge*, 302–3, 307.
12. Ibid., 307.
13. For additional details, see William J. Burns, *The Back Channel: A Memoir of American Diplomacy and the Case for Its Renewal* (New York: Random House, 2019), 337–87.
14. See, for example, Bruce Bennett et al., "Countering the Risk of North Korean Nuclear Weapons," Rand, April 2021.
15. John Carlin, *Dawn of the Code War: America's Battle Against Russia, China, and the Rising Global Cyber Threat*, with Garrett Graff (New York: PublicAffairs, 2018), 307–41.
16. For a good overview of the history of the Colombian insurgency and the government's efforts to combat it, see Lionel Beehner and Liam Collins, "Welcome to the Jungle: Counterinsurgency Lessons from Colombia," Modern War Institute, West Point, May 2019.
17. Mark Moyar, Hector Pagan, and Wil Griego, "Persistent Engagement in Colombia," Joint Special Operations University, July 2014, 15–19, 25–38, 40–41.
18. See, for example, Condoleezza Rice, *No Higher Honor: A Memoir of My Years in Washington* (New York: Crown, 2011), 565–66.

CHAPTER TWENTY THE BATTLE FOR THE MIDDLE EAST

1. For more on Soleimani, see Seth Jones, *Three Dangerous Men: Russia, China, Iran, and the Rise of Irregular Warfare* (New York: W. W. Norton, 2021), 79–126. There are three schools of thought as to why the Iranians pursue such an aggressive foreign policy. The first is that Iran's leaders seek hegemony over the Middle East. This was the

best, but only a partial explanation. An alternative view is that Iran is focused on assisting oppressed Shi'a populations in the Middle East. The problem with this theory is Iran's support for Hamas and the Taliban, Sunni extremists who are no friends of Shi'a. A third explanation for Iran's aggressive behavior is that its leaders were pursuing a strategy of "forward defense." Iran's leaders often told the Iranian people that it was better to fight the United States in Iraq and elsewhere than to have to fight it in Iran.

2. Carlin, *Dawn of the Code War*, 211–31.

3. Ironically, the Arab monarchies proved to be more resilient to the effects of the political and social upheaval sweeping the Middle East than Arab states ruled by non-royals. Perhaps it was because the legitimacy of the Arab monarchies rested on a different foundation. A more likely explanation is that the monarchies had more capable intelligence and security services. Another reason is that several Arab monarchies had the resources to provide their populations with material comforts and education opportunities.

4. One area that remained largely immune from the Arab Spring was the West Bank. To help advance Israeli-Palestinian peace, I met several times with senior intelligence and security officials of the Palestinian Authority in Ramallah between 2008 and 2014. The PA's intelligence and security services had played a large role in bringing stability to the West Bank after the Second Intifada and had earned the deep respect of Israeli security officials. Senior Israeli security officials told me that because of their excellent partnership with the PA the conditions required for Israeli-Palestinian peace and a two-state solution were at hand from a security point of view. Unfortunately, a steady drift to the right in Israeli politics and the inability of PA political leaders to deliver made peace as elusive as ever. The intelligence and security professionals had done their job; politicians on both sides had not. Tragedy unfortunately is a constant companion in the Middle East.

5. Gates, *Duty*, 507.

6. Morell, *Great War of Our Time*, 178–80.

7. Ibid., 178, 186–87.

8. Assad's ruling Alawites, a branch of Shi'a Islam, constitute less than 10 percent of Syria's population.

9. For a good overview of the Free Syrian Army and the Syrian insurgency through early 2016, see Charles Lister, "The Free Syrian Army: A Decentralized Insurgent Brand," Brookings, Nov. 2016.

10. Burns, *Back Channel*, 322–28.

11. More than 500,000 Syrians would die in the country's civil war, most of them civilians. Thirteen million more—approximately two-thirds of Syria's prewar population— would be driven from their homes. Half of them fled across Syria's borders, placing great economic burdens on neighboring states and destabilizing the region.

12. Burns, *Back Channel*, 323, 335–36.

13. See, for example, Ben Rhodes, *The World as It Is: A Memoir of the Obama White House* (New York: Random House, 2018), 197–98. See also Rice, *Tough Love*, 367–68; and

Philip Gordon, *Losing the Long Game: The False Promise of Regime Change in the Middle East* (New York: St. Martin's Press, 2020), 203–42.

14. Burns, *Back Channel,* 327–28. For Secretary Clinton's recounting of the proposal to provide arms to the Syrian resistance during July 2012, see Hillary Rodham Clinton, *Hard Choices* (New York: Simon & Schuster, 2014), 461–64.

15. Panetta, *Worthy Fights,* 449–50.

16. While in Turkey, I also met with Hakan Fidan, the chief of Turkey's National Intelligence Organization. Fidan and I would see each other regularly and become good friends. While we talked mostly about Syria and al-Qa'ida, he would also convey Turkey's concern about Fethullah Gulen, a former political partner of President Erdogan's now living in the United States. Erdogan believed that Gulen had a large underground following in Turkey, and was plotting to overthrow him. There wasn't much I could do but listen to Fidan on this. After a failed military coup against him in July 2016 that Erdogan claimed had been instigated by Gulen, he jailed nearly 80,000 suspected Gulen supporters. A government purge resulted in another 160,000 losing their jobs. Those detained or fired included soldiers, judges, and teachers. If Gulen's clandestine network in Turkey had been that strong, U.S. intelligence had missed it. Gulen had followers, to be sure, but nothing on that scale.

17. Lister, "Free Syrian Army," 4–8.

18. Burns, *Back Channel,* 326.

19. Michael G. Vickers, "Former Obama Terrorism Advisor: Change Your Strategy, Mr. President," *Politico,* Nov. 20, 2015. I wasn't the only former senior Obama administration official criticizing our policy in Syria. Similar critiques were made by Fred Hof, previously the State Department's senior adviser on Syria, and Robert Ford, our former ambassador in Damascus.

20. Michael G. Vickers, "The Trump Administration Should Not Give Up on Removing Assad in Syria," *Washington Post,* July 23, 2017.

21. The Houthis are Zaydi Shi'a, a minority sect that split off during the ninth century from the main branch of "Twelver" Islam (belief in twelve Imams) practiced in Iran and elsewhere in the Shi'ite Muslim world. The Houthis became radicalized after the U.S. invasion of Iraq in 2003. They derive their contemporary name from its leaders, Hussein al-Houthi, whom Yemeni forces killed in the first of six short wars that Saleh's government waged with the Houthis between 2004 and 2010, and Abdul Malik al-Houthi, Hussein's brother and the movement's current leader.

22. According to media reports, the United States tried to kill Shahlai with a drone strike in Sana'a in January 2020 but missed him. For additional detail on Iran's support for the Houthis, see Nader Uskowi, *Temperature Rising: Iran's Revolutionary Guards and Wars in the Middle East* (Lanham, MD: Rowman & Littlefield, 2019), 115–28.

23. Yemen is noted for the curved daggers, or *jambiya,* that many Yemeni men wear openly and prominently in their belts. Saleh had given me one during my first visit to Yemen in 2008. I thought about that dagger as Saleh's treachery unfolded.

24. The Houthis had also fought a limited border skirmish with the Saudis in 2009–2010.

25. Saleh would make one betrayal too many, however. After he offered to turn on the

Houthis and ally with the Saudis in Yemen's civil war, the Houthis executed him in December 2017.

26. Gates, *Duty,* 518–19.

27. For the first two weeks of the war, General Carter Ham, the commander of U.S. Africa Command, was the overall commander of the operation. Admiral Sam Lock-lear, the commander of U.S. Naval Forces in Europe, was the Joint Task Force, or operational, commander. See Christopher Chivvis, *Toppling Qaddafi: Libya and the Limits of Liberal Intervention* (New York: Cambridge University Press, 2014), 87–88.

28. Schinella, *Bombs Without Boots,* 249–56. Schinella was the national intelligence officer for military issues on the National Intelligence Council and a friend. He died tragically in 2020.

29. For additional details on the NATO campaign, see Admiral James Stavridis, *The Accidental Admiral: A Sailor Takes Command at NATO* (Annapolis, MD: Naval Institute Press, 2014), 50–65. Stavridis is a brilliant strategic thinker and a longtime friend of mine.

30. Chivvis, *Toppling Qaddafi,* 89.

31. Morell, *Great War of Our Time,* 191. The U.K., France, Italy, Qatar, and the U.A.E. also inserted small groups of special operations forces into Libya to conduct special reconnaissance of regime positions and increase the capabilities of the opposition. Qatar's role in building up the capabilities of the opposition was particularly important. Qatar sent several thousand tons of weapons and ammunition to rebel groups, mostly to Benghazi and eastern Libya, and provided tens of millions of dollars in aid. See also Morell, *Great War of Our Time,* 154–59; and Schinella, *Bombs Without Boots,* 260–63.

32. Morell, *Great War of Our Time,* 195–96.

33. Schinella, *Bombs Without Boots,* 273–83.

34. Morell, *Great War of Our Time,* 198.

35. Ibid., 205–10.

36. Clapper, *Facts and Fears,* 171–81. See also Morell, *Great War of Our Time,* 212–14.

37. Morell, *Great War of Our Time,* 218–19.

38. Ibid., 216.

CHAPTER TWENTY-ONE **CRISIS AND CHANGE IN DEFENSE INTELLIGENCE**

1. I brought Todd Lowery with me to my new office. After a few promotions, he became my executive director, the third in command, and my chief of staff.

2. A key theme of mine was the growing requirement to have to "fight" for intelligence in the event of conflict with China or Russia. I also believed that the tremendous increase in intelligence we would collect in peacetime would pay big dividends in the event we *had* to go to war.

3. Clapper, *Facts and Fears,* 214.

4. Morell, *Great War of Our Time,* 284–85.

5. I later learned as NSA's investigation progressed that Snowden had tricked his col-

leagues into giving him their passwords so he could log on from their workstations. Snowden had also used his system administrator credentials to steal the very difficult qualification test required for acceptance into NSA's Tailored Access Operations unit, or TAO, the agency's elite group of offensive cyber specialists. He was offered a position in TAO, but fortunately he turned it down, claiming that he made more money as an IT contractor. (Morell, *Great War of Our Time,* 287–88; Clapper, *Facts and Fears,* 228–29.) Rick Ledgett, an outstanding officer who would later become NSA's deputy director, led the damage assessment and provided me with regular updates.

6. Clapper, *Facts and Fears,* 240.

7. Called the Review Group on Intelligence and Communications Technologies, it included among its members three distinguished law professors, Dick Clarke, who'd served as counterterrorism and cyber adviser in the Clinton and George W. Bush administrations, and Michael Morell, who had just retired from CIA following thirty-three years of service.

8. Clapper, *Facts and Fears,* 269.

9. Morell, *Great War of Our Time,* 290–92. See also Report and Recommendations of the President's Review Group on Intelligence and Communications Technologies, "Liberty and Security in a Changing World," Dec. 2013.

10. Three years later, I changed my mind when Jim Clapper and I met with the Trump administration's secretary of defense and my old friend, Jim Mattis, to offer some advice on intelligence. We both argued that CYBERCOM, while still developing the capabilities it needed to fully execute the missions it had been assigned, had become the dominant concern of its commander, and NSA had suffered as a result. Besides having an NSA director who would focus solely on NSA, separating the two organizations would allow an NSA civilian to be appointed as the agency's director, and Jim and I had one in mind, NSA's former deputy director Chris Inglis. Jim and I also believed that CYBERCOM, which was established as a sub-unified command to STRATCOM, needed to become an independent combatant command. The speed of cyber operations demanded it. We called the combined concept "elevate and separate"—elevating CYBERCOM and separating it from NSA. The former has been accomplished, but the latter hasn't been.

11. The leadership of the NRO had turned over in 2012 when Jim and I made Betty Sapp the NRO's new boss. As we expected, Betty turned out to be a fantastic director, completing a seven-year tenure and putting the NRO on a great path through the mid-2030s.

12. For Director Clapper's perspective, see Clapper, *Facts and Fears,* 330–32, 341. Flynn and Shedd were supposed to retire at roughly the same time, but Shedd's retirement got delayed six months after our initial nominee for Mike's replacement, the Army lieutenant general Mary Legere, unfortunately had to withdraw from being considered due to an IG investigation into a major acquisition program she had been involved with. Mary was eventually completely cleared, but it was too late for her to become DIA director.

13. Lieutenant General Michael Flynn and Michael Ledeen, *The Field of Fight: How We*

Can Win the Global War Against Radical Islam and Its Allies (New York: St. Martin's Press, 2016), 4.

14. Clapper, *Facts and Fears*, 341.

CHAPTER TWENTY-TWO **THE RETURN OF GREAT POWER COMPETITION**

1. See Senate Armed Services Committee, "Worldwide Threat Hearing," Feb. 27, 2007. See also Craig Covault, "Chinese Test Anti-satellite Weapon," *Aviation Week and Space Technology*, Jan. 17, 2007; and Craig Covault, "China's ASAT Test Will Intensify U.S.-China Faceoff in Space," *Aviation Week and Space Technology*, Jan. 21, 2007. A year later, we conducted a satellite shoot-down of our own, though it wasn't a counter-space demonstration. We were alerted in early January that a U.S. satellite was falling out of orbit. There was less than a 10 percent chance that the deorbiting satellite would hit a populated area, but because the satellite was fueled by hydrazine, a toxic propellant that posed a serious health risk to humans, we developed options to shoot it down. Two SM-3 missiles were launched from the USS *Lake Erie* as the satellite tumbled to earth. The satellite's highly toxic propellant tank was destroyed on impact, and the debris from the satellite landed in the ocean.

2. Medical specialists had found extremely high concentrations of tetrachlorodiben-zodioxin in Yushchenko's blood. The dioxin was so pure, the specialists added, that it could only have been made in a laboratory.

3. Gates, *Duty*, 155–56.

4. Carlin, *Dawn of the Code War*, 135. The attack raised difficult questions. Estonia was a member of NATO. Could the Estonians invoke "Article 5," declaring themselves under attack, and rally Europe and the United States to their defense? How should the alliance respond to a cyberattack? Russia's cyberattack went unanswered, though Estonia got serious about cyber defense and became a leader in this area.

5. After the 2006 Quadrennial Defense Review, the Air Force had begun a new stealth bomber program, which Secretary Gates decided to revisit at the beginning of the Obama administration. The bomber's cost had gotten prohibitive, approaching a billion dollars per plane, but its advanced stealth was essential to penetrating the most capable air defenses. Once again, I found myself on the opposite side of an argument from our vice-chairman, General "Hoss" Cartwright. Cartwright expected that any war with China would be limited in duration and believed that our ability to hold a few Chinese targets at risk with conventional missile strikes and cyber capabilities would be sufficient. I believed that for conventional deterrence as well as for war-fighting purposes, we needed to present the Chinese with multiple dilemmas, and long-range penetrating aircraft with state-of-the-art stealth was an important part of the mix. Initially, Ash Carter, our undersecretary of defense for acquisition, technology, and logistics, sided with Hoss, and the anti-bomber side won the first round. OSD Policy was tasked with leading a long-range strike systems study to examine the need for a new bomber. Eventually, Carter came over to our side, as

did Cartwright. Secretary Gates approved a new bomber program, one with half the payload and half the cost, but with all of the stealth. In undersea warfare, we started a program (the Virginia payload module) to increase the missile-launching capacity of our Virginia-class submarines to partially offset the shortfall in strike capability that would occur when our four Ohio-class guided missile submarines are retired. On the cyber side of things, we established U.S. Cyber Command in June 2009. It was assigned three missions: defending DOD's networks from attack, supporting our combatant commanders with cyber operations, and defending the United States against destructive cyberattacks that went beyond criminal activity. Over the next several years, we built a cyber force that comprised 133 Cyber Mission Teams with personnel from all four military services.

6. Korabelnikov had headed the GRU for twelve years. He had reportedly been in charge of the operation in 1996 that killed the Chechen rebel leader Dzhokhar Dudayev. Shlyakhturov, a courtly man who had specialized in technical intelligence, had been Korabelnikov's deputy. He was only a few months away from retiring when we met.

7. Bearden and Risen, *Main Enemy,* 202–3, 297–307, 432–34, 446–48, 534.

8. An "illegal" is a Russian term for an intelligence officer serving abroad who assumed a false identity in the target nation and did not have any overt association with Russia. Some had posed as immigrants from Canada; others had stolen the identities of American children who had died decades earlier.

9. The FBI arrested four couples in New York, New Jersey, and Virginia, along with two single officers. Two of the illegals were undercover as real estate agents, one worked for a travel agency, another for a telecommunications firm. Yet another was a teacher, one wrote columns for a Spanish-language newspaper, and still another was in the tax advice business. The ten illegals were swapped for four Russians who were being held in prison in Russia, among whom was former GRU officer Sergei Skripal, whom the GRU would try to assassinate (and his daughter as well) with a chemical nerve agent in the U.K. in 2018. Another Russian illegal was arrested in Cyprus but skipped bail and escaped. A twelfth illegal working for Microsoft was arrested in Seattle and was deported back to Russia.

10. Putin called the protesters mere "pieces on the chessboard" and claimed that they were being directed by an "unseen hand"—including his old nemesis, the CIA. Russian state media portrayed Putin as the only leader who could stand up to the United States. As an aide to Putin put it in October 2014, Russians understand that "if there is no Putin, there is no Russia." Stephen Kotkin, "The Resistible Rise of Vladimir Putin," *Foreign Affairs,* March/April 2015.

11. For a good overview of Xi Jinping's strategy, see Elizabeth Economy, *The Third Revolution: Xi Jinping and the New Chinese State* (New York: Oxford University Press, 2018). For a good overview of the challenges for U.S. strategy posed by China and Russia, see Eliot Cohen, *The Big Stick: The Limits of Soft Power and the Necessity of Military Force* (New York: Basic Books, 2016), 99–125, 151–56.

12. Chinese strategy aimed at sea and air control over the "First Island Chain," which

extended from Japan through the Philippines down to Malaysian Borneo. China also sought to hold at risk U.S. and allied forces in the "Second Island Chain," which included Guam—seventeen hundred miles from the Chinese mainland.

13. Carlin, *Dawn of the Code War*, 242–50, 265–77.

14. Russia formally updated its military doctrine in late 2014. The new doctrine designated NATO as the main geopolitical threat to Russia, with the main operational threat coming from U.S. conventional global strike capabilities. The new military doctrine also asserted that an even bigger threat to Russia came from information warfare and political subversion. It said that Russian youth were particularly vulnerable to foreign-financed subversion and that extensive exploitation of popular protests and the use of special operations forces were core elements of modern warfare.

15. The 2014 Ukraine crisis had begun in November 2013 when Ukraine's pro-Russia president, Viktor Yanukovych, abruptly backed out of an association agreement with the European Union—a deal strongly opposed by Vladimir Putin. Political protests against Yanukovych's decision followed immediately, and after the protesters were attacked by government forces, their number grew into the hundreds of thousands. The protests became known as the "Maidan Revolution," or "Euromaidan," named after Maidan Nezalezhnosti, or Independence Square. On February 18, 2014, the police tried demolishing the barricades, but the protesters held their ground and advanced toward the Rada building (Ukraine's parliament), demanding the restoration of Ukraine's 2004 constitution. Five days of deadly clashes followed, with snipers from Yanukovych's Berkut special police murdering more than a hundred protesters before Yanukovych fled to Russia. In July 2014, I observed the makeshift memorials of photos and flowers that had been placed on the sidewalks to commemorate the fallen heroes. It was extraordinarily moving.

16. Nalyvaichenko had attended the KGB's Academy as the Soviet Union was breaking up, but then decided after graduating that he didn't want a career in the security services. He had been SBU chief under Viktor Yushchenko after the Orange Revolution, but left office when Yanukovych was elected in 2010. He had been reappointed as the SBU's director after Maidan.

17. Clapper, *Facts and Fears*, 266–67.

18. Ukraine's SBU had also provided signals intelligence intercepts linking Putin's presidential adviser Sergei Glazyev with efforts to finance and supply weapons to the supposed Ukrainian separatists. Glazyev had written a propaganda tract in which he asserted that a cabal of neoliberals had deliberately destroyed Russia in the 1990s. He was a "Eurasianist" who believed that Russian power was meant to dominate a "great space" from the Atlantic to the Pacific Ocean. The official Foreign Policy Concept of the Russian Federation in 2013 embraced Eurasianism and argued that in the future "law would give way to a contest of civilizations." See Timothy Snyder, *The Road to Unfreedom: Russia, Europe, America* (New York: Tim Duggan Books, 2018), 97–99.

19. After early 2015, the conflict in eastern Ukraine largely became frozen. Combat continued, however. By 2020, the war in the Donbas would take more than thirteen

thousand lives. In December 2015, the Russians also conducted a major cyberattack, shutting down electrical power in Ivano-Frankivsk oblast for several hours.

20. I had previously met with one of my Chinese intelligence counterparts, Major General Yang Hui, China's chief of military intelligence, or 2PLA, during a May 2012 visit by China's defense minister to the Pentagon. Yang was a rising star in the PLA who spoke fluent Russian and had earned a PhD in Russian literature with a dissertation on Anton Chekhov. He was extremely impressive and we hit it off. I told Yang about my visits to China in the 1980s, and he insisted that I return soon. Yang unfortunately was moved to a big job in the Chinese operational command opposite Taiwan soon after our meeting in Washington, so my trip to China was delayed a couple years.

21. See Gates, *From the Shadows*, 123, for the establishment of the joint technical intelligence relationship with China.

CHAPTER TWENTY-THREE WINNING THE NEW COLD WAR

1. As our preeminent Cold War historian John Lewis Gaddis has recently written in *Foreign Affairs* with Hal Brands, "It's no longer debatable that the United States and China ... are entering their own new cold war." Gaddis and Brands add, "Xi Jinping has declared it, and a rare bipartisan consensus in the United States has accepted the challenge." (Hal Brands and John Lewis Gaddis, "The New Cold War: America, China, and the Echoes of History," *Foreign Affairs*, Nov.–Dec. 2021, 10.) Some in the U.S. national security establishment, however, are still reluctant to use the term, preferring instead to describe the great power rivalry as "strategic competition."

2. For a good discussion, see Hal Brands, *The Twilight Struggle: What the Cold War Teaches Us About Great-Power Rivalry Today* (New Haven, CT: Yale University Press, 2022).

3. China could pursue two paths to global leadership. The first, which has been the consensus position, is that China will first seek preeminence in East Asia and then turn globally. An alternative view is that China will go global first, heading west and relying principally on its economic power and Belt and Road Initiative, rather than east and its growing military power. Until recently, it appeared to me that the second route was actually China's preferred path, but Xi's bellicose rhetoric regarding Taiwan recently has called that into question.

4. Michael J. Mazarr, *The Societal Foundations of National Competitiveness* (Santa Monica, CA: Rand, 2022).

5. Fiona Hill, "The Kremlin's Strange Victory: How Putin Exploits American Dysfunction and Fuels American Decline," *Foreign Affairs*, Nov.–Dec. 2021, 46.

6. Michael Hayden, *The Assault on Intelligence: American National Security in an Age of Lies* (New York: Penguin Press, 2018).

7. See Eliot Cohen, "History, Critical and Patriotic," *Education Next* (Spring 2020).

8. Edward J. Watts, *Mortal Republic: How Rome Fell into Tyranny* (New York: Basic Books, 2018).

9. See, for example, Martin Ford, *Rise of the Robots: Technology and the Threat of a Jobless Future* (New York: Basic Books, 2015).

10. See, for example, National Intelligence Council, Office of the Director of National Intelligence, "Global Trends 2040: A More Contested World," March 2021.

11. Jennifer Harris and Jake Sullivan, "America Needs a New Economic Philosophy, Foreign Policy Experts Can Help: The United States Cannot Get Grand Strategy Right if It Gets Economic Policy Wrong," *Foreign Policy*, Feb. 7, 2020.

12. For the importance of economic strength in great power competition, see Paul Kennedy, *The Rise and Fall of the Great Powers: Economic Change and Military Conflict from 1500 to 2000* (New York: Random House, 1987).

13. Assuming labor remains a central input to economic growth, China, with four times the population of the United States, has a long-term advantage as its economy develops. Most likely, however, automation will lead to sharp declines in the value of labor relative to capital in the decades ahead, and automation and capital intensity work to the advantage of the United States. That, plus China's unfavorable long-term demographics, have caused China's leaders to increasingly place their bets on winning the automation competition.

14. Molly Dahl et al., "The 2020 Long-Term Budget Outlook," Congressional Budget Office, Sept. 2020.

15. Jonathan Gruber and Simon Johnson, "To Counter China, Out-Invent It," *Foreign Affairs*, Sept. 12, 2019.

16. Aaron Friedberg, "Rethinking the Economic Dimension of U.S. China Strategy," American Academy of Strategic Education, Aug. 2017.

17. New biotechnologies like CRISPR (clustered regularly interspaced short palindromic repeats—short pieces of DNA that can be edited and manipulated) and "synthetic" biology could significantly augment human performance and create new means for economic warfare and for targeting specific population groups or even individuals with genetically engineered weapons. They have other national security implications as well.

18. The transition from ANI to AGI is generally thought to be harder and to take longer than the transition from AGI to ASI. Some AI futurists predict the advent of AGI within two to three decades, but even if this is too optimistic, advances in ANI will have major economic and national security implications. Once the AGI level is reached, moreover, the front-runner in the competition could achieve an insurmountable and decisive strategic advantage. For an overview, see Nick Bostrom, *Superintelligence: Paths, Dangers, Strategies* (Oxford: Oxford University Press, 2014); and Kai-Fu Lee, *AI Superpowers: China, Silicon Valley, and the New World Order* (Boston: Houghton Mifflin Harcourt, 2018).

19. In 2018, Congress established the National Security Commission on Artificial Intelligence. In September 2019, I was asked to meet with the commission to offer my thoughts on national security and AI and what kind of competitive strategy the United States should adopt. I offered my thoughts on asymmetries in the competition with China, how to preserve and extend our current advantages, U.S. vulnerabilities, and where DOD and the IC should focus their efforts. The commission

recommended creating a National Technology Competitiveness Council, analogous to the National Security Council we established in 1947 to better wage the Cold War. It recommended boosting spending on AI R&D to $32 billion annually by 2026 and spending $35 billion to onshore manufacturing of advanced microchips. The commission recognized that AI will revolutionize warfare, intelligence, and strategic competition. It recommended that DOD spend $8 billion annually on AI science and technology and that the IC monitor foreign AI developments as a priority mission. The commission also recommended that to boost our human capital, we invest in STEM education, establish a U.S. Digital Service Academy, and create a National Digital Reserve Corps. For additional details, see National Security Commission on Artificial Intelligence, "Final Report," March 2021.

20. Yang Wenzhe, "How to Win Intelligentized Warfare," *Jiefangjun Bao*, Oct. 22, 2019.

21. Lee, *AI Superpowers*, 83.

22. Gruber and Johnson, "To Counter China, Out-Invent It." See also Jonathan Gruber and Simon Johnson, *Jump-Starting America: How Breakthrough Science Can Revive Economic Growth and the American Dream* (New York: PublicAffairs, 2019); and Christopher Darby and Sarah Sewall, "The Innovation Wars: America's Eroding Technological Advantage," *Foreign Affairs*, March/April 2021.

23. We will also need a new series of net assessments to measure how well we're doing in this new era, and where new strategic opportunities lie. Top priority should be given to assessing our economic and technological competition and global influence competition. Deeper dives will also be needed in several critical technologies, ranging from AI to quantum technologies and synthetic biology. We will also need net assessments in space, cyber, global strike, and undersea warfare.

24. According to Jim Clapper's memoirs, the most classified version of the Intelligence Community Assessment on Russian interference in the 2016 presidential election showed unambiguously that Putin had ordered the multifaceted campaign to influence the U.S. election and elect Trump, who the Russians believed would serve their strategic goals. The ICA documented Russia's cyber intrusions and described its pervasive propaganda efforts. It provided historical context to show just how much of an unprecedented escalation in directness, level of activity, and scope of effort Russia's 2015–2016 covert influence campaign represented. Russia had done all this at minimal cost, some $30 million. And it had no incentive to stop these covert influence campaigns against our democracy. Unfortunately, the ICA fell on deaf ears, at least where the incoming Trump administration was concerned. For the unclassified version of the ICA, see Office of the Director of National Intelligence, "Background to 'Assessing Russian Activities and Intentions in Recent US Elections': The Analytic Process and Cyber Incident Attribution," Jan. 6, 2017. See also Clapper, *Facts and Fears*, 362, 366–67, 373–76.

25. Clapper, *Facts and Fears*, 375, 395–96. For additional information on Russian interference in the 2016 presidential election, see the five-volume report produced by the Senate Select Committee on Intelligence. Trump's body language when he met with Putin in Helsinki suggested a man under the Russian leader's influence if not his control.

26. National Intelligence Council, Office of the Director of National Intelligence, "Intelligence Community Assessment: Foreign Threats to the 2020 US Presidential Election," March 10, 2021.

27. Amy Zegart and Michael Morell, "Spies, Lies, and Algorithms," *Foreign Affairs*, May/June 2019.

28. Robert M. Gates, *Exercise of Power: American Failures, Successes, and a New Path Forward in the Post–Cold War World* (New York: Alfred A. Knopf, 2020), 290.

29. National Academy of Sciences, Engineering, and Medicine, "An Assessment of Illness in U.S. Government Employees and Their Families at Overseas Embassies," 2020.

30. Office of the Director of National Intelligence, Executive Summary of the IC Experts' Panel on Anomalous Health Incidents, Feb. 2022.

31. The worst-case scenario would be a China that could effectively "disarm" the United States. As long as the United States maintains a credible strategic deterrent, China's (or Russia's) ability to impose its will on the United States will not pose an existential threat, but there are no guarantees that this will always be the case. The most obvious way a disarming strike, or the threat of one, could occur would be a breakthrough in missile defenses that would create an impenetrable shield, much like President Reagan's long-term vision for the Strategic Defense Initiative in the 1980s. It is also not beyond the realm of possibility that a disarming strike could come from AI and quantum-enabled cyber capabilities that could disable nuclear command-and-control systems.

32. Graham Allison, *Destined for War: Can America and China Escape Thucydides's Trap?* (Boston: Houghton Mifflin Harcourt, 2017).

33. For a discussion of how procuring additional weapons could bolster U.S. defenses in the western Pacific, see David Ochmanek et al., *U.S. Military Capabilities and Forces for a Dangerous World* (Santa Monica, CA: Rand, 2017).

34. The major challenge we will have to overcome to make a large-scale shift to unmanned warfare is cultural—what it means to be a warrior.

35. The most likely option for a Chinese global breakout would be to exploit Russian advanced submarine technology and procure a large number of autonomous undersea systems to win command of the sea through quantitative superiority and perhaps technological superiority. Undersea warfare is a key source of American advantage that we must maintain. If the Chinese were able to shift the balance in undersea warfare, it would have a major impact on the global balance of power. A complementary strategy would be for China to use its growing economic power and political influence to bolster the anti-access/area-denial defenses of its partners in key regions.

36. Cyberspace Solarium Commission, Final Report, March 2020.

37. We also need to develop countermeasures to Russia's other ways of attacking our economy. I can't say more than that here, but fortunately some steps are already being taken to address this problem. More can be done, however.

38. Andrew Krepinevich, "How to Deter China: The Case of Archipelagic Defense," *Foreign Affairs*, March/April 2015.

CHAPTER TWENTY-FOUR INTELLIGENCE, SPECIAL OPERATIONS, AND STRATEGY

1. See Gates, *From the Shadows,* 565.
2. Ibid., 560–61.
3. CIA and the IC were even more successful in technical collection. CIA's Directorate of Science and Technology pioneered reconnaissance aircraft, including the U-2 and A-12/SR-71, and imaging satellites that allowed us to see behind the Iron Curtain. During the 1980s, all-weather, day/night radar imaging satellites were added to our overhead constellation, further contributing to our ability to monitor Soviet military activity 24/7. As a result, there were virtually no Soviet military surprises during the last half of the Cold War of broad strategic importance. The detailed knowledge the IC developed about Soviet forces after the mid-1960s from its technical collection systems made it virtually impossible for the Soviets to deceive us. NSA's record in SIGINT collection was equally exemplary. Gates, *From the Shadows,* 562.
4. Ibid., 565. The IC's analytical performance was also quite good, and much better than many have alleged. CIA accurately described the growing economic, political, and social weaknesses of the Soviet Union and its worsening systemic crisis. CIA's analysts pointed out the futility of tinkering with the Soviet system. They noted that Gorbachev was undermining its foundations without offering a new system to replace the old one, and by 1988–1989 they warned of a deepening crisis, the potential for a rightist coup, and the possible collapse of the entire system. On the negative side, the IC's analysts underestimated the growth of Soviet strategic forces during the late 1960s and early 1970s, and then overestimated Soviet growth in strategic systems during the 1980s. In the economic area, CIA's statistics and models overestimated the size of the Soviet economy, and therefore CIA underestimated the magnitude of the burden that Soviet military expenditures were imposing on the Soviet economy. CIA also understated Soviet involvement in international terrorism. (563–65.) Recruiting and handling spies against hard targets, as the term implies, is very hard. Getting analysis right all of the time is impossible.
5. John Brennan "centerized" CIA during his tenure as director, establishing geographic and functional mission centers that combined personnel from all CIA's directorates. This reduced the authority of the directorate heads, particularly operations and analysis, significantly. Mike Pompeo and Bill Burns have made tweaks to Brennan's plan, adding and subtracting mission centers, but have left his basic design in place. (Burns recently established a China Mission Center, breaking it out from the East Asia Pacific Center, and a center that is partially focused on strategic technologies and technological competition with China.) NSA also underwent a major reorganization under Mike Rogers. The results of all this change have been mixed at best.
6. During my time as USD(I), Jim Clapper and I always made it a practice to testify together on intelligence budgets, giving Congress a complete picture of our intelligence capabilities and how they were integrated. I also sought to consider the IC's need for additional capabilities and capacity when doing intelligence, cyber, space, and special operations force planning for DOD. Likewise, when looking at our national intelligence collection systems, I always sought to advocate for DOD's war-

fighting needs when they went beyond the IC's requirements. DOD's relationship with CIA and the director of national intelligence is a "hidden hand" that makes our IC far more effective. DOD, of course, comprises the majority of the IC, but more than that, DOD, CIA, and the IC develop new systems together, we share costs, we conduct joint operations, and we jointly manage some important intelligence programs. Pooling our collection and analytical resources has also led to several intelligence breakthroughs against hard targets.

7. For a good, though dated, discussion on the philosophy of covert action, see Richard Bissel Jr., *Reflections of a Cold Warrior: From Yalta to the Bay of Pigs,* with Jonathan Lewis and Frances Pudlo (New Haven, CT: Yale University Press, 1996), 205–24. Bissel was the CIA's deputy director for plans (later changed to the Directorate of Operations) from 1959 to 1962.

8. CIA and DOD maintain a division of labor and authorities in paramilitary operations and unconventional warfare that has served our nation well. CIA primarily conducts paramilitary covert action during peacetime, and DOD conducts unconventional warfare in wartime. Some have periodically recommended transferring responsibility for paramilitary covert action from CIA to DOD. Recommendations along these lines were made after the Bay of Pigs by the CIA's inspector general, and after al-Qa'ida's attacks on the World Trade Center and the Pentagon by the 9/11 Commission. Fortunately, our presidents and Congress have consistently rejected these recommendations.

9. Daugherty, *Executive Secrets,* 12–22, 39–40, 71–89, 91–111.

10. For a good discussion of this, see Austin Carson, *Secret Wars: Covert Conflict in International Politics* (Princeton, NJ: Princeton University Press, 2018).

11. An example where covert action wasn't properly integrated with or supported by broader U.S. foreign policy is Afghanistan after the Soviet withdrawal. Covert action had done its job, but U.S. policy failed to consolidate our success after 1989–1992. That's one of many reasons why we descended from Cold War triumph to the 9/11 attacks.

12. Presidents on occasion resort to covert action to rescue a failing policy. This obviously reduces the likelihood of success substantially. They often want to be seen by Congress and the political opposition as doing something, even when the likelihood of success is very low.

13. Given the DNI's and D/CIA's role in intelligence, and the need to tell it straight to our national security policy makers, however, it is essential to not mix policy recommendations with the presentation of intelligence. This is a challenge that our intelligence chiefs have that our DOD leaders do not. The best way to avoid the perils of mixing intelligence and policy and the risk that entails to the perceived objectivity of intelligence is for a D/CIA and DNI to generally refrain from offering policy advice until the president or national security adviser asks for it.

14. The dilemma here, of course, is that as with any policy choice, people and policy makers will have varying views. Values may also change over time. What might have been viewed as necessary and therefore acceptable immediately after 9/11, for example, may no longer be viewed that way in later years. That's why it's so important

to thoroughly consult with Congress on covert action and adapt as circumstances change.

15. There is a David-versus-Goliath test that is worth considering when contemplating a covert action. Put simply, it is generally better to be seen as David, or on the side of David, than Goliath. A case in point here is the broad, bipartisan support our secret war in Afghanistan enjoyed in Congress compared with the controversy surrounding our support for the Nicaraguan resistance. In Afghanistan, we were seen as David. In Nicaragua, we were seen as Goliath. It's not a showstopper, but it occurs regularly enough that it is worth reflecting upon before embarking on a covert action against a much less formidable adversary.

16. The wars with al-Qa'ida and ISIS saw several shifts in momentum during their first two decades. Between 1998 and 2001, al-Qa'ida had the upper hand due to its sanctuary in Afghanistan and its successful attacks in East Africa, Yemen, and the United States. Between 2001 and 2003, the strategic initiative shifted to the United States and its allies after the Taliban regime was toppled and several al-Qa'ida senior leaders and operatives were captured in Pakistan's settled areas and other locations. Between 2003 and 2008, the momentum shifted back to al-Qa'ida after we invaded and occupied Iraq. Al-Qa'ida reconstituted in the Federally Administered Tribal Areas, and it added several affiliates in Iraq, the Arabian Peninsula, North Africa, and Somalia. Between 2008 and 2013, the momentum shifted back to the United States and its allies after we commenced our new counterterrorism campaign in the Afghanistan-Pakistan border region. We all but defeated al-Qa'ida in Iraq, killed Usama Bin Ladin, and engaged AQAP in Yemen. Between 2013 and 2016, momentum shifted back to the global jihadists as ISIS established its caliphate and global jihadists conducted a number of attacks against the United States and the West. Finally, between 2017 and 2020, momentum shifted back to the United States and its allies as ISIS's caliphate was eliminated and global jihadist leaders were killed in Syria, Yemen, Pakistan, and Afghanistan. We haven't likely seen the last shift in momentum in this war, however, particularly given our withdrawal from Afghanistan.

17. Transformational change in military capabilities, as I noted in my PhD dissertation, can stem from disruptive advances in technology, new operational concepts and organizational arrangements, and/or a dramatic expansion in key resources. It can occur in peacetime or wartime, and I personally experienced both in my career. In war, I oversaw the transformation of the Afghanistan Covert Action Program during the 1980s and our counterterrorism campaigns against al-Qa'ida beginning in 2007. Since the early 1990s, I have also been helping the Department of Defense prepare for the challenges a revolution in military affairs and a more powerful China would pose.

18. Gates, *Exercise of Power,* 11.

19. Kurt Campbell and Ely Ratner, "The China Reckoning: How Beijing Defied American Expectations," *Foreign Affairs,* March/April 2018.

20. For an excellent analysis of how many American policy makers got China wrong, see Aaron Friedberg, *Getting China Wrong* (Cambridge, U.K.: Polity Press, 2022). The University of Chicago political scientist John Mearsheimer has recently argued that

the failure to recognize China as a future strategic competitor to the United States and contain its rise after the end of the Cold War was a major strategic blunder. (See John Mearsheimer, "The Inevitable Rivalry: America, China, and the Tragedy of Great Power Politics," *Foreign Affairs,* Nov.–Dec. 2021, 48–58.) It is very difficult to see how such a containment policy could have been politically feasible, however. In 1992, Undersecretary of Defense for Policy Paul Wolfowitz proposed in the draft Defense Planning Guidance that a core aim of the United States after the end of the Cold War should be to prevent the rise of another major competitor. At one level, perhaps, it was a nice goal to have, but it was totally unachievable. Preventing China's rise was not something the United States could do.

CHAPTER TWENTY-FIVE **THE LONG GOODBYE**

1. Admiral William McRaven, *Make Your Bed: Little Things That Can Change Your Life and Maybe the World* (New York: Grand Central Publishing, 2017).

2. John le Carré, *The Secret Pilgrim* (New York: Alfred A. Knopf, 1990), 12.

INDEX

Page numbers in *italics* indicate maps and illustrations. Page numbers followed by "n" and number indicate note and note number. Page numbers followed by "nn" indicate multiple notes on the page.

ILLUSTRATION CREDITS

MAPS
107 Library of Congress, Geography and Map Division
219 Library of Congress, Geography and Map Division
244 Council on Foreign Relations

INSERT
All photos are courtesy of the author, except where noted.

Gust Avrakotos: *Charlie Wilson's War*
In Cairo, 1984: *Charlie Wilson's War*
William J. Casey: Central Intelligence Agency
Charlie Wilson: Congressional Pictorial Directory
Ahmad Shah Massoud: Wikimedia Commons, photograph by Hamid Mohammadi
Christopher Denham: Courtesy of Universal Studios Licensing LLC
Anwar al-Awlaki: Wikimedia Commons
Usama Bin Ladin's compound in Abbottabad, Pakistan: Wikimedia Commons,
    Sajjad Ali Qureshi
Admiral William McRaven: United States Navy

A NOTE ABOUT THE AUTHOR

Michael G. Vickers has served multiple roles in the Defense Department and Intelligence Community, most recently as undersecretary of defense for intelligence under President Barack Obama. He also served under President George W. Bush and President Barack Obama as the assistant secretary of defense for special operations, low-intensity conflict, and interdependent capabilities, where he had policy oversight of all of U.S. military capabilities, from nuclear weapons to special operations forces. During the Cold War, he served as an operations officer in the CIA and as both a commissioned and a noncommissioned officer in the Army's Special Forces. He lives near Washington, D.C.

A NOTE ON THE TYPE

This book was set in Janson, a typeface long thought to have been made by the Dutchman Anton Janson, who was a practicing typefounder in Leipzig during the years 1668–1687. However, it has been conclusively demonstrated that these types are actually the work of Nicholas Kis (1650–1702), a Hungarian, who most probably learned his trade from the master Dutch typefounder Dirk Voskens. The type is an excellent example of the influential and sturdy Dutch types that prevailed in England up to the time William Caslon (1692–1766) developed his own incomparable designs from them.

COMPOSED BY NORTH MARKET STREET GRAPHICS, LANCASTER, PENNSYLVANIA

PRINTED AND BOUND BY BERRYVILLE GRAPHICS, BERRYVILLE, VIRGINA

DESIGNED BY MAGGIE HINDERS